History of Rumford, Oxford County, Maine, from its first settlement in 1779, to the present time

William Berry Lapham 1828-1894

RUMFORD UPPER FALL.

HISTORY OF RUMFORD

OXFORD COUNTY, MAINE

FROM ITS FIRST SETTLEMENT IN 1779

TO

THE PRESENT TIME

BY WILLIAM B. LAPHAM.

*"Should auld acquaintance be forgot
And days of auld lang syne?"*

AUGUSTA:
PRESS OF THE MAINE FARMER.
1890.

DEDICATION.

TO THE NATIVE NON-RESIDENTS AND TO THE RESIDENTS
OF THIS TOWN WHO HAVE
AIDED AND ENCOURAGED IN THE CONSUMMATION OF THIS WORK,
AND THEREBY ASSISTED IN SAVING FROM OBLIVION
SOME OF THE
RECORDS AND REMINESCENCES OF THEIR ANCESTORS;
TO THE MEMORY OF THE PIONEER SETTLERS OF

New Pennacook and Rumford,

WHO LEFT TO THEIR CHILDREN THIS GOODLY HERITAGE,
AND FINALLY,
TO THE SONS AND DAUGHTERS OF GOOD OLD RUMFORD,
WHEREVER THEY ARE,
THIS VOLUME IS RESPECTFULLY INSCRIBED AND DEDICATED,
BY THEIR FRIEND AND SERVANT,

THE AUTHOR.

Augusta, Maine, January 1, 1890.

PREFACE.

"What sum will it be necessary to pledge to induce you to compile a history of the town of Rumford?"

The above question was asked me by Mr. John M. Adams of Portland, so long ago that the circumstance had entirely passed from my mind until recalled by Mr. Adams in the spring of 1888, coupled with the remark that he was ready to guarantee the sum named, and that I could enter upon the work as soon as convenient. The task therefore was not a self-imposed one, and was entered upon with considerable reluctance. While I had had some acquaintance with certain representative men of the town in bygone years, with a large proportion of the people I was unacquainted, never having spent much time in Rumford, and having for nearly a generation resided out of the county. Without the hearty co-operation of the people of a town, it is difficult even for a resident, to gather the materials for such town's history, and for a non-resident it is much more difficult. This co-operation, I feared I might not have, and in some degree, such has been the case. But I was pledged to the work and went immediately about it, and the result, such as it is, will be found in the following pages. While some have not shown that degree of interest in the work which was desirable, and which, if felt and had been given expression in deeds, would have added materially to its interest and value, yet there have been honorable exceptions. My obligations are due to the municipal officers of 1888, for permission given to make abstracts from the town records at my own home. Without such permission the work could not have proceeded and must have been abandoned. To the town clerk, Mr. James S. Morse, I am indebted for other favors which have ever been cheerfully granted. Winfield S. Howe of Hanover, has responded to calls for copies of records with commendable alacrity. Mr. Merrit N. Lufkin has shown a deep interest in the work from its inception, and has done all he could to help it along.   His words of encouragement have not been the least of his contributions. Henry W. Park of Mexico, and Henry M. Colby, have cheerfully supplied me with material for an outline sketch of Blazing Star Lodge of Masons.   Dr. John F. Pratt of Chelsea, Mass., has laid me under renewed obligation by furnishing copies of original documents in the archives of Massachusetts.   But to no one am I more indebted than to Mr. Chaplin Virgin, whose good intentions crystallized into deeds, and who has greatly assisted me in gathering material for every department of the work.   Years hence, when all who have had to do with the publication of this book, and all those mentioned therein who now survive, shall have passed away, the descendants of Rumford people who peruse this and the following pages, will hold in grateful remembrance the names of those who aided in gathering up and passing down to them some account of the lives and deeds of their ancestors, who cleared and cultivated Rumford lands.   And to those natives of Rumford residing elsewhere, who have shown their interest in the work by contributing eleven-twelfths of the sum pledged to insure its writing, I feel under just as deep obligation as though I had solicited the task, and had received a compensation commensurate with its performance.

WM. B. LAPHAM.

ABSTRACT OF CHAPTERS.

ILLUSTRATIONS.

INDEX TO PERSONAL NOTICES.

PATRONS.

The following persons became patrons of this work by the payment of the sums set against their respective names :

John M. Adams, Portland	$50 00
Charles H. Kimball, New York	50 00
Wm. W. Kimball, Chicago	50 00
Charles Walker, Lewiston	50 00
Wm. Wirt Virgin, Portland	20 00
James M. Kimball, Portland	20 00
Henry F. Blanchard, Augusta	10 00
Wm. W. Bolster, Auburn	10 00
John A. Rolfe, Boston	10 00
Charles A. Kimball, Rumford	10 00
Waldo Pettingill, Rumford	10 00
Chaplin Virgin, Rumford	5 00
Augustus H. Adams, Haverhill, Mass	10 00

SUBSCRIBER'S NAMES.

RUMFORD SUBSCRIBERS.

C. B. Abbot	2	T. H. Burgess	1
Chandler Abbot	1	A. P. Beattie	1
Charles H. Abbot	1	S. S. Blodgett	1
Samuel V. Abbot	1	Mrs. Ella S. Brown	1
Edwin Abbot	1	Mrs. Hannah Childs	1
Henry M. Abbot	1	T. D. Colby	2
Amos S. Austin	1	Henry M. Colby	1
Hiram F. Abbot	1	Royal A. Clement	1
J. H. Barker	1	Mrs. Ella E. Dolley	1
R. H. Bixby	1	F. S. Delano	1
A. L. Bixby	1	R. C. Dolloff	1
Wm. M. Blanchard	1	Cotton Elliot	1
J. A. Bartlett	1	G. F. Elliot	1

C. M. Elliot	1	Wm. Martin	1
Wm. Elliot	1	Jas. S. Morse	3
C. P. Eaton	1	Fred A. Porter	1
Mrs Mary W. Farrar	1	Waldo Pettingill	2
Mrs. Hannah Farnum	1	Benj. P. Putnam	1
D. G. Farnum	1	F. P. Putnam	1
Wm. H. Farnum	1	Wm. Phinney	1
Livingston Glover	1	James F. Putnam	1
Lewis L. Glover	1	D. F. and J. P. Roberts	1
J. C. Graham	1	Mrs. C. F. Richardson	1
Alvin G. Goddard	1	M. L. Rowe	1
Mrs. Sarah Godwin	1	Mrs. Sally E. Richardson	1
Otis Howe	1	J. C. Small	1
Otis Howe, 2d	1	J. E. Stevens	1
J. H. Howe	1	G. T. Silver	1
Miss Catherine S. Howe	1	W. R. Swain	1
L. T. Howe	1	Charles L. Simpson	1
John Howe	2	D. E. Simpson	1
P. C. Howard	1	Wm. F. Stevens	1
Mrs. Mabel Hardy	1	Y. A. Thurston	1
George Hoyt	1	John Thompson	1
A. J. Knight	1	Miss S. A. Thompson	1
Mrs. Fanny Kennison	1	C. P. Thomas	1
M. F. Knight	1	G. C. Twombly	1
Chas. A. Kimball	1	G. T. Thurston	1
Asa Kimball	1	W. W. Virgin	1
D. L. Kimball	1	Chaplin Virgin	1
Merrit N. Lufkin	1	B. B. Wyman	1
A. B. Lovejoy	1	J. H. Wardwell	1
John Martin	1	W. A. Wyman	1
C. K. Martin	1	Mrs. Luna Walker	1
S. L. Moody	1	Miss Cynthia Walker	2
J. H. Martin	1		

OTHER SUBSCRIBERS.

Adams, John M., Portland	2
Adams, A. H., Haverhill, Mass	1
Bolster, William W., Auburn	1
Brown, John M., Portland	1
Blanchard, H. F., Augusta	2
Bisbee, George D., Buckfield	1
Chisholm, Hugh J., Portland	2
Cushman, Samuel D., Dexter	1
Dwinel Lester, Bangor	2
Elliot, J. F., Hyde Park, Mass	2
Farnum, William F., Lawrence, Mass	1
Gallison, Jefferson C., Franklin, Mass	1
Haines, John, Waltham, Mass	1
Kimball, Charles H., New York	4
Kimball, William W., Chicago	1
Lufkin, Randall, Concord, N. H.	1
Library, Maine State, Augusta	1
Library, M. & M., Lewiston	1
Library, Portland Public, Portland	1
Library, Lithgow, Augusta	1
Library, Maine Historical, Portland	2
McClurg, A. C. & Co., Chicago	1
Putnam, G. P. Sons, New York	1
Peabody, Frank D., Lancaster, N. H.	1

ERRATA.

No doubt errors will be found in this book of which the compiler has no knowledge, and after the work is completed, he does not care to know. A few errors which might be misleading are here corrected, while mere typographical mistakes where the meaning is obvious, are not.

Page 64, line 19 from bottom, for Jackson Graham, read Joshua.
" 86, line 6 from bottom, for George K. Martin, read Jonathan K.
" 117, line 15 from bottom, for Glenis, read Glines.
" 188, second paragraph, for Simeon, read Simon.
" 289, top line, for father, read brother.
" 361, bottom line, for 1782, read 1882.

History of Rumford.

CHAPTER I.

THE town of Rumford is situated in north latitude forty-four degrees and thirty minutes, and in longitude west from Greenwich, seventy degrees and forty minutes. The lines as described above, cross each other near the center of the town.

It is situated near the center of the county of Oxford, is about twenty miles north-north-west from Paris, the shire town of the county, and about seventy miles from Portland, the nearest seaport.

Its adjoining towns at the present time (1890) are Andover, Roxbury, Mexico, Peru, Franklin Plantation, Milton Plantation, Hanover, Bethel and Newry.

The town was run out seven miles and forty rods square. Its easterly and westerly lines were run eighteen and one-half degrees west of north, and its northerly and southerly lines seventy-one and one-half degrees east of north. On account of the variation of the magnetic needle, these points do not exactly correspond with the lines at the present time. A small allowance must be made in tracing the old lines.

The Androscoggin river flows through the town from west to east. The Ellis river enters the town from Andover, and, flowing southerly, empties into the Androscoggin river near Rumford Point. Swift river forms the dividing line between Rumford and Mexico.

White Cap and Black Mountain are situated in the north part of the town, and Glass Face between Rumford Point and the Center. Hemmingway mountain is in the extreme south part of the town, and there are several other minor mountains in town which have no specific names. Three of these are below the Center, and north of the road leading from the Center to East Rumford.

Concord river, in ordinary low water, is nothing more than a

brook.   It rises in Woodstock and Milton Plantation, and flows
northwardly into the Androscoggin at the bend of the river near
the junction of the Rumford and Paris with the South river roads.
It forms the water power for Abbot's Mills, and in spring and fall
carries a large body of water.   The South river road crosses it near
where it *debouches* into the great Androscoggin.   Split brook flows
into the Androscoggin at Rumford Center, and furnished the power
for early mills.   Several small brooks flow into Ellis river, some
from the easterly and some from the westerly side.   Some of these
have supplied the power for small mills.   Pleasure brook flows
from White Cap and empties into Ellis river, and below this is
Meadow brook flowing into the same.   There are also brooks rising
in the vicinity of Black Mountain and flowing into Swift river.

The town of Rumford is much broken into hills and mountains.
Along the borders of the principal rivers are belts of interval more
or less broad, very fertile and productive.   There are also some
good upland farms, and the hill-sides furnish excellent pasturage.
The north-eastern part of the town is of but little value for purposes
of husbandry.

The inhabitants of Rumford are engaged mostly in agriculture.
There are no large manufacturing establishments in town, although
the great falls afford an unlimited water power.   There are a few
small stores in different parts of the town which supply the local
demands, but no important centers of trade or business.   The
farmers generally are thrifty and prosperous.   There are small
lumber mills in the north part of the town, at the Center, on Concord river, and at the Falls, sufficient to supply the local demand.

The soil of Rumford is generally granitic.   The intervals are
composed of alluvium, and their richness is frequently renewed by
spring freshets.   The uplands are a gravelly loam, and are more or
less fertile according to the amount of vegetable matter they contain.

The geology of Rumford is much the same as that of other towns
in central and northern Oxford county.   The mountains are mostly
made up of coarse granite or gneiss, and cobble knolls and ridges
show evidence of ancient glacial action.   Dr. Jackson, in the report of his geological survey of Maine, made in 1837, speaks of
good granite at Holmes' brook and Peavy's mountain in Rumford,
and also of granite and limestone at the Falls; also of limestone at
the Point.   He also speaks of finding mica, slate, feldspar, sahlite,

lead ore and plumbago in this town. He also describes the Paint Mine referred to elsewhere by Rev. Daniel Gould. Dr. Jackson says:

"The locality in question is upon the estate of Mr. Samuel Lufkin. It is on a hill-side, where a mineral spring, issuing from the rocks, has deposited a conical heap of the red ochreous red oxide of iron, amid a clump of trees. The paint is capable of being wrought advantageously for the manufacture of red ochre, since the quantity is large, and it is constantly forming by gradual deposition from the water of the spring. It may be rendered of a very bright red, simply by the process of roasting it, and then it may be rendered fine by levigation with water, or by sifting. I found a bed of bog iron ore collected in the lowlands around, whose length was four hundred and fifty feet, breadth ninety feet, and depth two feet, enough to supply a small blast furnace for ten years, and to yield about two thousand tons of iron. It will yield fifty per centum of iron and will smelt easily, making good cast iron."

Dr. Jackson adds: "Rumford is a picturesque spot, surrounded by rugged granite mountains, among which the beautiful Androscoggin winds its devious way." Speaking of the Great Falls he says: "Rumford Falls are produced by the bounding waters of the great Androscoggin, as they sportively leap over abrupt and craggy ledges of granite rocks, and dash their spray high in the air. There are at present three or four waterfalls where anciently there must have been others of greater magnitude, for deep holes are seen worn high up the rocky banks where the waters never ran in modern times. On a point just below the falls, there is a bed of granular limestone. It is coarse and of the crystaline variety of carbonate of lime, containing scattered green crystals of actynolite and pargasite, in small grains and fibres. Some of the beds are of ten feet in thickness. I should estimate the quantity of lime that may be made here at one hundred thousands casks, and it is easy to quarry and burn. In order to bring it to land, it will be needful to make an inclined plane of timber, like those used in saw mills, and the machinery of the saw mill immediately above, will drag the rock to the bank where it is to be burned."

The flora of Rumford presents no peculiarities. White pine was quite abundant here when the first settlers came. There was also abundance of spruce, hemlock and fir. Of the hard woods, yellow birch, beech and the rock maple were the principal varieties. Elms were found on the rivers, cedars in the swamps, and an occasional bass-wood in the forest. Poplar and white birch have come up in some localities as a second growth. The native plants are the same as those found in most other localities in this latitude, and the exotics, many of them in the shape of weeds, are as numerous and troublesome as elsewhere. The "Wake Robin," both white and purple, is seen on the margin of woodland streams in early spring, the purple Rhodora in the lowlands and blue and white violets on the sunny slopes, and these are followed by the long train of native flowering plants which bloom in their season.

The black bear was found here by the early settlers, and has infested the mountainous region to the northward, ever since. He frequently raids the sheep-pastures, and corn planted on new land, back from the settlements, sometimes suffers more or less from his ravages. Coons were common when the township was first settled, but have mostly disappeared. Sables were successfully hunted for their skins, and loupcerviers were often seen in the forest. The deer and moose were no strangers to the early settlers, and supplied the larder with excellent food. The smaller animals were the wily fox, the timid mink, the prickly hedgehog, the odoriferous skunk, the hibernating woodchuck, and several varieties of the agile squirrel family. The early settlers were sometimes startled in the night-time, by the blood-curdling cry of the American panther, called by them, the "Indian Devil," but no encounters with them, by Rumford pioneers, are on record. One of them once followed a Paris man, who had been to New Pennacook after seed potatoes, to his home on the bank of the Little Androscoggin. He entered his house, and had just time to close the door and bar it, when the infuriated and disappointed animal came against it. But the door was stoutly made and resisted his attacks, and after hanging around awhile, he uttered a fearful cry and plunged into the forest. This man had stopped at an old camp near North Woodstock, intending to spend the night there, but, after it became dark, he was startled by the cry of a panther not far away, and knowing that the old shanty would afford no protection, he shouldered his bag and started for home by the narrow path through the woods. The animal followed him but seemed in no haste to seize him, evidently supposing him to be his own, and that he could take him when he pleased. Macomber, for that was his name, when the animal came quite near, threw down his bag of potatoes which stopped him a few moments, and afterwards threw off his coat for the same purpose, and with the same effect. After satisfying his curiosity, the mammoth cat on each occasion, set up his fearful scream and followed on. Macomber's escape was marvelous, and the incident was talked over at the firesides of the settlers for many a day and year.

CHAPTER II.

BRIEF SKETCH OF THE PARENT TOWN.

THE parent town of Rumford, beautifully situated on the banks of the Merrimac, was Concord, in the State of New Hampshire, and from that town came many of the early settlers. A brief sketch of early Concord, is therefore essential to a clear comprehension of the causes that led to the settlement of Rumford. The long controversy between the Masonian Proprietors of New Hampshire and the Government of the Massachusetts Bay, respecting the division line between the two Provinces, is recorded in history, and an epitome of this controversy is briefly as follows: The terms of the Massachusetts charter, granted in the year one thousand six hundred and twenty-eight, and confirmed in one thousand six hundred and ninety-one, established the northern boundary of the Province, three miles north of the Merrimac river, and each and every part of it, obviously meaning, three miles beyond the river. It was then supposed that the general course of that river was from west to east, while, as a matter of fact now well known, at a point about thirty miles from the sea, it makes almost a right angle and from that point stretches almost due north. There was no mistake as to the meaning and intent of the grant in fixing this northern boundary, but when Massachusetts wished to find a pretext for taking possession of a large proportion of the grants to Gorges and Mason, a new interpretation was given to the language describing the boundary, and instead of a line three miles across the river at its mouth, a point was taken three miles north of its headwaters, and from that a line easterly to the sea. If this interpretation had been sustained, nearly the whole territory of New Hampshire would have gone to Massachusetts. The Masonian proprietors stoutly resisted

this encroachment, and in the settled towns on the disputed territory, there was constant trouble. Governor Belcher in a letter to
the Lords of Trade in London, said: "the borderers on the lines,
(if your Lordships will allow me so vulgar an expression), live like
toads under a harrow, being run into jails, on the one side and the
other, as often as they please to quarrel, such is the sad condition
of his Majesty's subjects that live near the lines. They pull down
one another's houses, often wound each other, and I fear it will end
in bloodshed, unless his Majesty, in his goodness, gives some
effectual order to have the bounds fixt." While this controversy
was going on, the Massachusetts Bay government was annually
making grants within the limits of the contested territory until no
less than thirty-seven townships were granted.

Petitions for a grant from the territory on the Merrimac known
as Pennacook were presented to the Massachusetts General Court,
as early as one thousand six hundred and fifty-nine, and periodic-
ally from that time to one thousand seven hundred and twenty-five.
The petitions were mostly from Haverhill, Andover, Ipswich,
Methuen and Salem. On the seventeenth day of January, one
thousand seven hundred and twenty-six, the general Court decided,
"that it will be for the interest and advantage of this Province that
part of the lands petitioned for be assigned to the petitioners for a
township, and to contain seven miles square." The usual conditions were inserted in the grant. The township was surveyed in
May of this year. Meetings of the proprietors were often held,
sometimes in Andover and sometimes in Ipswich. The proprietors
took active measures for carrying their purpose into effect. The
first settler, Ebenezer Eastman, was located within the plantation
in one thousand seven hundred and twenty-seven.

While these proprietors were thus vigorously bringing forward
their plantation under the auspices of the government of the Massachusetts Bay, the government of New Hampshire, on May twentieth, one thousand seven hundred and twenty seven, made a grant
to Jonathan Wiggin and one hundred and six others, of a tract of
land covering the greater part of the grant just made by Massachusetts, and including also parts of the present towns of Pembroke and
Hopkinton. The settlers of Pennacook were not at first molested
by the New Hampshire grantees, and the plantation grew and prospered. The first settled minister was Rev. Timothy Walker of
Woburn, who was the great grandfather of Hon. Timothy Walker,

late of Rumford. Among the other early settlers, were Virgins, Elliots, Abbots, Farnums, Colbys, Martins, Hutchins, Wheelers, Rolfes and Halls, all of whom have decendants among the settlers of Rumford. In February, one thousand seven hundred and thirty-three, by an act of the Great and General Court of the Massachusetts Bay, the plantation of Pennacook was incorporated into a town by the name of Rumford. The origin of the name is in doubt, but it is generally supposed that the town was named for a place in England, from which some of the early settlers or their ancestors came.

Meanwhile the contest between the two Provinces concerning the disputed boundary was sharply carried on, and after commissioners appointed for that purpose, had failed to come to a decision, the matter was referred directly to King George the second, whose royal decision promulgated on the 5th of March, 1740, was far better for New Hampshire than ever the Masonian proprietors claimed. It established a curved line, "following the course of the river Merrimac at the distance of three miles on the north side, beginning at the Atlantic ocean and ending at Pawtucket Falls (now Lowell), thence due west to His Majesty's other governments." This is the present line between the two States. By this decision, all the grants made north of this line by Massachusetts, were rendered null and void. Nearly forty towns were involved in the issue ; some of the grantees made terms with the Masonian proprietors, and remained upon their lands, while others abandoned them. The territory granted by New Hampshire in the year one thousand seven hundred and twenty-seven, to Wiggin and others, was nine miles square, and by the same authority, it was incorporated into a town by the name of Bow. As already stated, this grant embraced a large part of the town of Rumford, and soon after the boundary question was settled in favor of the New Hampshire claimants, legal steps were taken to test the rights of the rival claimants to the soil. A test case was made "by the proprietors of the common and undivided lands lying and being in the town of Bow," in an action commenced November fourteenth, one thousand seven hundred and fifty, against Deacon John Merrill. Many other suits were afterwards instituted, but the one against Merrill involved the principle on which all the cases were finally adjusted. The town of Rumford (Concord) voted to pay the cost in this case, and to meet these expenses, the proprietors from time to time, ordered the sale of so much of the common and undivided lands as should be necessary for that purpose. In the autumn of one thousand seven hundred and fifty-three Rev. Timothy Walker sailed for England, and presented "to the King's most Excellent Council," a petition drawn up by himself in which the claims of Rumford were concisely set forth. Mr. Walker went in the capacity of agent of the proprietors of the town. A grant of one hundred pounds sterling was made by the General Court of Massachusetts, to defray Mr. Walker's expenses. Not much was accomplished by this visit to England, and it became necessary for Mr. Walker to go again. Meanwhile, the government of New Hampshire took up the quarrel in behalf of Bow, and advanced one hundred pounds to defray expenses. Judgment had been rendered against the proprietors of Rumford in the courts of the Province, and at length, after long and anxious delay, December twenty-third, one thousand seven hundred and sixty-two, Mr. Walker announced from London, that at the Court of Saint James, before King and Council, the judgment against the proprietors of Rumford had been reversed, and that the appellants were restored to what they had lost by means of the judgments rendered against them. Yet notwithstanding this favorable decision, the controversy had become so complicated, and involved so much interest and feeling, that it was not until the year one thousand seven hundred and seventy two, that the difficulty was finally settled. The troubles of the proprietors with regard to the validity of their titles to their homes, were now at an end. They had established their right to the soil, but instead of living under the jurisdiction of Massachusetts, as they at first supposed was the case, they were declared to be in New Hampshire. On the twenty-fifth day of May, one thousand seven hundred and sixty-five, an act was passed by the New Hampshire Legislature, "setting off a part of the town of Bow, together with some lands adjoining thereto with the inhabitants thereon," investing them with "such priviledges and immunities as towns in this Province have and do enjoy." To this new town was given the name of Concord, said to have been named in commemoration of the adjustment of their perplexing and protracted difficulties. The bounds of Concord vary considerably from those of its predecessor, Rumford, the change resulting in two gores, long known as "Bow Gores," but which were finally annexed to Concord. As a compensation for their trouble and great expense in settling their status in Concord, the first set of proprietors petitioned the General Court for a grant of eastern lands, the particulars of which are set forth in their petition which begins the next chapter.

CHAPTER III.

PAPERS RELATING TO THE GRANT.—PETITION OF COL. TIMOTHY WALKER AND ASSOCIATES.

To His Excellency, THOS. HUTCHINSON, ESQ., *Capt. General and Governor of the Province of the Mass. Bay:*

To the Honorable His Majesty's Council and House of Representatives of said Province in General Court assembled, Jan. ye 26, 1774. The petition of Timothy Walker Jr., on behalf of himself and associates, hereby, sheweth that they and their associates in the year 1725 for a valuable consideration, purchased a Township of a little more than seven miles square, of this goverment at a place then called Pennicook, afterward Rumford on Merrimac river. That not at all doubting the authority of this goverment to make the said grant the Grantees not with standing the extreme difficulty and cost of effecting a settlement, so far up in the Indian country at that time, yet so vigorously applied themselves *thereto that in the year 1733* consequent upon ye report of a comittee sent by them to view the same, the General Court of this Province declared that the Grantees had to full satisfaction fulfilled the terms of their grant, and incorporated them by the name of Rumford, that by the determination of the boundary line between this Province and that of New Hampshire, by his late Majesty in the year 1740, the said township fell near four miles to the northward of the dividing line. That about the year 1749 a society under a grant from the Province of New Hampshire began to molest us in our possessions and sued us in several actions of ejectment and always recovered against us in the courts of New Hampshire. In this distressed state of our affairs we applied to the government to enable us to lay our case before his Majesty by way of appeal that of several grants from the government amounting in the whole to about the original purchase consideration together with simple interest for the same, and also by much larger sums raised amongst ourselves we have been enabled to prosecute two appeals to His Majesty and although in each we obtained a reversal of the judgment that stood against us here, yet the Royal order extending in express terms no further than the lands sued for, the advantages fell far short of the expense and our adversaries went on troubling us with new suits. Thus exhausted and seeing no end of our troubles we have been reduced to the necesssity of repurchasing our township of our adversaries at a rate far exceeding its value, in its nude state.   That we have been at a considerable expense in taking a view of a tract of land on Amoroscoggin River on the easterly side of Sudbury Township (so called) which we apprehend would answer for a Township. We, therefore, pray that your Excellency and Honors would be pleased so far to pity our hard case, as to make us a grant of a Township at said place to lie on each side of Amoroscoggin River of equal extent, with that formally granted us by this Province on such reasonable terms as you shall think proper, and your Petition. ers shall as in duty bound ever pray.

(signed)   TIMOTHY WALKER, JR.
In behalf of himself and associates.

THE PETITION GRANTED.

In House of Representatives, Feb. 3, 1774.

Whereas, It hath been represented to this court, by Timothy Walker Jr., in behalf of himself and associates that in the year 1725, they purchased of this Province a Township of land of seven miles square which by the running of the line between this Province and New Hampshire in the year 1740, was cut off to that Government, by which means the Original Purchasers have been vexed with many expensive law-suits, and at last were obliged to purchase the same lands of claimers under New Hampshire, having enquired into the matter, this court find that the facts set forth in said petition are true.   And that the cost of defending their title at the Court of Great Britain have exceeded the grants made to them by this Government, to enable them to carry on the prosecution there.

Therefore, Resolved that there be granted to the original proprietors of the Township granted by this Province by the name of New Pennycook, their heirs or assigns who were sufferers by said township falling into New Hampshire, a township of seven miles square to be laid out in regular form on both sides of Amoscoggin River, and easterly of and adjoining to Fullerstown (so-called), otherwise Sudbury Canada laid out to Josiah Richardson Esq. and others, Provided the grantees within six years, settle thirty families in said township, and lay out one full share to the first settled minister, one full share for the ministry, and one full share for the school, and one full share for Harvard College : and provided the petitioners within one year, return a plan thereof taken thereof by a surveyor and chainman under oath, into the Secretary's Office, to be accepted and confirmed by the General Court

And in order that justice may be done to the sufferers, it is further

Resolved, That Mr. Webster and Colonel Gerrish with such as the Hon. Board shall join, be a Committee to repair to the said township of Pennycook who shall there enquire into and make out a list of the sufferers, and that they return a list for confirmation to the General Assembly, and that said committee give suitable notice of the Time of their meeting by publishing an advertisement in the *Essex Gazette* and one of the Portsmouth Newspapers, three weeks successively, two months before the time of their meeting; that any person claiming right to the grant aforesaid, may appear and lay in their claim.

Sent up for concurrence,

T. CUSHING, *Speaker.*

In Council Feb. 3d, 1774; Read and concurred in, and Samuel Phillips, Esq., is joined in the affair.

JNO. COTTON, *Dept. Secretary.*

Consented to, T. HUTCHINSON.

ASSIGNMENT OF RIGHTS OR SHARES.

The committee appointed by the Great and General Court at their session in Boston, Feb., 1774, (upon the petition of T. Walker, Jr., and his associates) to enquire into the sufferings and make out and return a list of said sufferers, having notified, met and heard said sufferers, as directed by said Court, Report the following list of names to whom Rights are to be assigned, viz. :

Timo. Walker, Jr., of Concord, N. H.	Three Rights.
Geo. Abbott of Concord, N. H.	Two "
Thos. Stickney of Concord, N. H.	Three "
John Chandler of Concord, N. H.	Three "
Wm. Coffin of Concord, N. H.	One "
Ebenezer Hall of Concord, N. H.	One "
Jona. Merrill of Concord, N. H.	One "
Amos Abbott of Concord, N. H.	Two "
Edward Abbott of Concord, N. H.	Two "
Ephraim Farnum, Jr., of Concord, N. H.	One "
Benj. Farnum of Concord, N. H.	Two "
Joseph Farnum of Concord, N. H.	One "
Timo. Bradley of Concord, N. H.	One "
Rev. Timo. Walker of Concord, N. H.	Two "
Joseph Eastman of Concord, N. H.	One "
Aaron Stephens of Concord, N H.	Two "
Moses Hall of Concord, N. H.	One "
Philip Kimball of Concord, N. H.	One "
Ebenez. Eastman of Concord, N. H.	One "
David Hall of Concord, N. H.	One "
Philip Eastman of Concord, N. H.	Two "
James Walker of Concord, N. H.	One "
Chas. Walker of Concord, N. H.	One "
Richard Hazeltine of Concord, N. H.	One "
Paul Walker of Concord, N. H.	One "
Jeremiah Bradley of Concord, N. H.	One "
Hannah Osgood of Concord, N. H.	Two "
Asa Kimball of Concord, N. H.	One "
Moses Eastman of Concord, N. H.	One "
John Bradley of Concord, N. H.	One "
Jona. Stickney of Concord, N. H.	One "
Reuben Kimball of Concord, N. H.	One "
Benj. Abbott of Concord, N. H.	One "

Joshua Abbott of Concord, N. H	One	Right.
Abiel Chandler of Concord, N. H	Five	Rights.
Timothy Walker Tertius of Concord, N. H	One	"
Nath'l Eastman of Concord, N. H	Two	"
The Heirs of Ebenez. Virgin of Concord, N. H	Three	"
Peter Green of Concord, N. H	One	"
Ephraim Carter of Concord, N. H	One	"
Heirs of Jeremiah Dresser of Concord, N. H	One	"
Nath'l Rolfe of Concord, N. H,	One	"
John Chase of Concord, N. H	One	"
Benj. Thompson of Concord, N. H	Six	"
Paul Rolfe of Concord, N. H.	Five	"
Ebenez. Harden Goss of Concord, N. H	Four	"
Nathan Abbott of Concord, N. H	One	"
Gustavus Adolphus Goss of Concord, N. H	One	"
Amos Eastman of Hollis, N. H	One	"
Abraham Kimball of Bradford	One and three-quarters	"
Timo. Walker of Conway	One and three-quarters	"
Ebenez. Hall of Sanford	One	"
Jeremiah Eastman of Sanford	One	"
Dr. Chas. Chauncey of Boston	One	"
The Heirs of Rev. Sam. Phillips of Andover	One and one-half	"
Stephen Farrington of Fryeburg,	One	"
The Heirs of Abner Fowler of Coos	One	"
Elijah Durgin of Hopkinton	One	"
Caleb Smart of Hopkinton	One	"
Jona. Straw of Hopkinton	One	"
Benj. Gale of Haverhill	One	"
Cutting Marsh of Haverhill	One-quarter	"
Nath'l Marsh of Haverhill	One-quarter	"
James McHurd of Haverhill	One-half	"
Robt. Davis of Concord, N. H	Three-quarters	"
Anna Stevens of Concord, N. H	——	"
Henry Lovejoy of Concord, N. H	One-quarter	"
Phineas Kimball of Concord, N. H	One-quarter	"
Henry Rennals of Boxford	One-quarter	"
Sam'l and Wm. Dana of Groton	One-half	"
Dudley Coleman of Newbury	One-half	"

N. B. Hon. Joseph Gerrish, Esq., (one of said Committee) was present at said meeting and consented to the foregoing report.

Haverhill, Nov. 18, 1774.

(signed.)   SAM. PHILLIPS, } *Committee.*
                             JONA. WEBSTER, }

PETITION FOR RE-CONFIRMATION.

To the Honorable General Court of the State of the Massachusetts Bay, convened at Boston, April 7, 1779.

The Petition of Timothy Walker, Jr., on behalf of himself and associates, humbly sheweth, that in February, 1774, your petitioners obtained of the General Court a grant of a township of the contents seven miles square on Ammenoscoggin river, by way of compensation for the trouble and expense they and their ancestors had been at in endeavoring to defend and finally repurchasing a Township formerly purchased by them of this province at a place called Pennycook, on Merimack River, on certain conditions, some of which were the following: that your petitioners returned into the Secretary's office here, a plan of the granted premises taken by a surveyor and chainman under oath, within a year from the grant, as also a list of the sufferers who were to be benefitted thereby, certified by a committee appointed by the said court, to enquire into and ascertain the same, which conditions your petitioners punctually complied with, within the limited time, but by the great confusion this metropolis was very soon after thrown into, the said papers are lost, and the surveyor who drew and returned the plan is dead; whereupon your petitioners have been at the trouble and expense of procuring a new survey and plan of the premises which, together with a list of the grantees certified by a major part of the committee appointed to that service (who still survive). Your Petitioners pray you will please to accept this instead of that formerly returned but lost. And whereas the term allowed for settlement will expire next February, and the cares and efforts of your petitioners have been so entirely absorbed in the general Defence of the country during the present Distressing War, as to render them incapable of taking the least advance in towards completing the same, they therefore pray that the said period may be extended to such future day as your honors shall please to appoint; and also that you would appoint some suitable person to warn a meeting of said Grantees at such a place, and in such a manner as you may judge legal, in order to adjust accounts of past expenses, and to transact any matter or thing necessary to forward the settlement of the said Township, and also to order where and how future meetings of the said Grantees shall be warned, and your petitioners shall as in duty bound, ever pray.

TIMOTHY WALKER, JR.

RE-CONFIRMATION OF THE GRANT.

In the House of Representatives, Apr. 13, 1779.

Upon the Petition of T. Walker Jr. in behalf of himself and associates, praying that this Court would accept of a second plan and list of sufferers instead of the first that was returned into the Secretary's Office agreeable to the conditions in the original grant of a Township of land to the said Timo. Walker Jr. and others upon Amoscoggin River in Feb. 1774 which plan and list of sufferers are since lost; also praying that a longer time may be allowed for settlement and that some suitable person may be appointed to warn a meeting of the Grantees &c.

Resolved, That the prayer of the Petition be granted and that the plan of a Township taken by Wm. Chamberlain's survey under oath bounded as followeth, namely, beginning at a tree upon Sudbury Canada line, &c., &c.

Be and hereby is accepted in lieu of a Plan returned into the Secretary's Office by said Walker agreeable to the grant of said Township, and it is further

Resolved, That the said list of sufferers as agreed upon by Joseph Gerrish, Sam. Phillips and Jona. Webster, Esqs., the committee appointed by the General Court Feb. 1774, to enquire into the sufferings of Pennacook Grantees and make out and return a list of such sufferers, Be and hereby is accepted instead of the first list returned into the Secretary's Office and since lost. And be it further resolved that the time limited to said Grantees for settling thirty families within said Township, be extended to the term of five years longer. And it is further resolved that the Rev. Timo. Walker be and hereby is empowered and directed to call a meeting of said Proprietors to be held in the town of Haverhill in the County of Essex, at such time as he shall think proper for publishing the same with the business with which they are to meet in Willis' newspaper three weeks, successively ending at least one week before said meeting and posting the same at the several public houses or taverns in the town of Concord, in the state of New Hampshire, one month before said meeting. Also when met to agree upon and determine the manner of warning and place of holding future meetings in any town within this State, or if more convenient in any town within the State of New Hampshire.

Sent up for concurrence,

JOHN PICKERING, *Speaker.*

In Council, April 13, 1779. Read and concurred,

JOHN AVERY, *D. Sec'y.*

Consented to,

(signed)

JER. POWELL,
W. SEVER,
A. WARD,
T. CUSHING,
B. WHITE,
B. AUSTIN,
TIMO. DENNISON,
J. STONE,
H. GARDNER,
JNO. PITTS,
O. WENDALL,
SAM. NILES,
E. BROOKS,
N. CUSHING,
A.(?) FULLER.

CHAPTER IV.

THE PROPRIETARY.—CALL FOR THE FIRST MEETING.

Whereas, The Honorable General Court of the State of Massachusetts Bay, has authorized the subscriber to warn a meeting of the Proprietors of a new Township on Amoscoggin River, granted by a former General Court of the said (then) Province, to Timothy Walker, Jr. and Associates by way of compensation for the loss of Pennycook; said Proprietors are hereby notified and warned to assemble and meet at the Dwelling House of Capt. Daniel Bradley in Haverhill, on the last Wednesday in May next, at three o'clock in the afternoon, for the following purposes, viz :

To choose a Moderator and Clerk.

Also to determine whether they will order a division of any part or the whole of said Township into severalty, and if so,

To choose and instruct a committee chosen for that service how, and how far to proceed.

Also to conclude what shall be done with respect to clearing roads, either in said township or from it to any other place they shall judge proper.

Also to see if the proprietors will build a mill or mills in their township, and if so,

To choose a committee to agree with some suitable person to undertake the same, and for encouragement, to give them such a sum of money or grant of land as they shall think reasonable ; also,

To direct the manner of warning and place of holding future meetings of said Proprietors ; also,

To raise such a sum of money as they shall think necessary ; also,

To choose a collector to gather in the same ; and finally,

To choose a committee to adjust all accounts of said Proprietary, with orders to receive from the collector sufficient money to enable them to pay the just debts of the Proprietary ; and also,

To carry into execution whatever may be resolved upon, with respect to the above mentioned articles.

Boston, April 14, 1779.   Timothy Walker.

THE FIRST MEETING.

Essex ss.   *State of Massachusetts Bay.*

At a legal meeting of the Proprietors of a New Township on Ammoscoggin River, granted to Timothy Walker, Jr., and Associates, by the Great and General Court of the State of Massachusetts

Bay, held at the house of Capt. Daniel Bradley, innholder in Haverhill in said County, May 26, 1779, voted,

That Lieut. Timothy Bradley be Moderator.

That Timothy Walker, Jr., be Clerk.

That there be laid out to each right, one hundred acres of land.

That there be a road cleared through said township.

That forty-five pounds lawful money be raised upon each right to defray the expenses of said Proprietary.

That Mr. David Hall, Colonel Thomas Stickney and Capt. Reuben Kimball be assessors to assess the above tax of forty-five pounds upon each right.

That Timothy Walker, Jr., Esq., be collector to collect the above tax.

That this meeting be adjourned to the first Wednesday in August next, then to meet at the dwelling house of Capt. Aaron Kinsman, in Concord in the State of New Hampshire, at one o'clock in the afternoon.

A true copy of the proceedings of the above meeting.

Attest :   TIMOTHY WALKER, JR.,
                                            Proprietors' Clerk.

OTHER MEETINGS.

August 4, 1779.   Met according to adjournment, and the Moderator being present declared the meeting to be open. Voted,

That a committee be appointed to repair to the township lately granted to Timothy Walker, Jr. and associates, and make a division of one hundred acres of land to each full right, and that Colonel Thomas Stickney, Ensign Jonathan Eastman and Ebenezer Harnden Goss, Esq., Ephraim Colby and Amos Abbot, Jr., be said committee.

That each of the above committtee have for their service, six shillings per day, making the money as good as it was in April, 1775, during the time they shall be employed in the service of the Proprietary.

That the clerk be desired to purchase a book for the use of said Proprietary.

That fifteen pounds lawful money be assessed upon each right, in addition to the forty-five pounds raised in May last, and that Col. Thomas Stickney, Mr. David Hall, and Capt. Reuben Kimball be assessors to assess the above sum, and that Timothy Walker, Jr., Esq., be a collector to collect said sum of fifteen pounds ; and that the tax for both the said sums of forty-five pounds and fifteen pounds, be made by the assessors in one list.

That the committee appointed to make the above division of land, be directed to employ suitable persons, if they think proper, to cut and clear a road passable for horses through the above town, and down Amoscoggin River to a place called Bog Brook.

That Captain Reuben Kimball, Lieut. John Chandler and Mr. David Hall be a committee chosen, appointed and fully empowered to examine all charges that have arisen and that shall hereafter arise in bringing forward the settlement of said Township, and to allow as in their judgment shall be just and equal, and also to draw money out of the Treasury for defraying said charges.

That the clerk be directed and fully empowered, upon the request of one-sixteenth of the owners of said township, to call future meetings of said proprietors, by advertising the same in one of the Boston newspapers.

That this meeting be adjourned to the first Wednesday in December next, then to meet at the house of Capt. Aaron Kinsman, innholder in Concord, at one o'clock in the afternoon, then and there to receive the report of the Committee appointed to make a division of land in said township, and if said committee shall have completed said division, for the proprietors to draw their respective lots.

Wednesday, Dec. 1, 1779. The meeting met and adjourned to Dec. 3d.

Dec. 3, 1779. The moderator being present, declared the meeting to be open. Voted,

That Mr. Jonathan Kies be allowed to pitch four interval lots and the four upland lots which are joined with them.

That the committee on claims be directed to allow thirty for one, in order to make the money good.

That Ebenezer Harnden Goss, Esq., be allowed to pitch one interval lot and the upland lot which is joined with it.

That fifteen pounds be raised upon each full right.

That the same assessors be appointed to assess and the same collector to collect that were appointed to assess and collect the last rate.

That the return and plan of the committee appointed to lay out a division of one hundred acres of land to each right be accepted, and that a highway be reserved four rods broad through each of the upland lots, and that a highway two rods broad be reserved through the interval lots, as shall best accommodate the public."

The report of the committee stated first, that they had laid out twenty-seven interval lots on the westerly side of Ellis River, lot number one beginning at a maple tree on the bank of the river, where the town line crossed it, and farther described by metes and bounds. Upon this lot other lots were run out and numbered accordingly. They then run out and numbered eleven interval lots on the easterly side of Ellis River. Forty lots were then run out and described on the south side of the Great River, the first beginning at a maple tree on the bank of the river where the town line crosses it, and next twenty-seven interval lots were run out, on the north side of the Great River.

2

Eighteen upland or house lots were then laid out on the westerly
side of Ellis River, twenty-seven on the east side, thirty-five on the
north side of the Great River, and thirty-one on the south side.
The report was signed by Thomas Stickney, Jonathan Eastman,
Ephraim Colby and Ebenezer H. Goss.

DRAWING OF THE LOTS.

The drawing of the lots in accordance with the survey and plan
just accepted, was next in order, and resulted as follows:

George Abbot, interval lot No. 17 and house lot No. 10, South of Great
River.
George Abbott, interval lot No. 18 and house lot No. 24. North of Great
River.
Amos Abbot, interval lot No. 27, West side Ellis River; house lot No.
18, East side Ellis River.
Amos Abbot, interval lot No. 16, West side Ellis River; house lot No.
15, East side Ellis River.
Edward Abbot, interval lot No. 6 and house lot No. 5, North of Great
River.
Edward Abbot, interval lot No. 1 and house lot No. 1, East side Ellis
River.
Benj. Abbot, interval lot No. 4 and house lot No. 4, North side Great
River.
Joshua Abbot, interval lot No. 9 and house lot No. 9, North side Great
River.
Nathaniel Abbot, interval lot No. 19 and house lot No. 26, North side
Great River.
Timothy Bradley, interval lot No. 7 and house lot No. 8, East side Ellis
River.
Jeremiah Bradley, interval lot No. 27 and house lot No. 22, South side
Great River.
John Bradley, interval lot No. 11 and house lot No. 20, East side Ellis
River.
William Coffin, interval lot No. 7 and house lot No. 7, West of Ellis
River.
Lt. John Chandler, interval lot No. 21 and house lot No. 23, North of
Great River.
Lt. John Chandler, interval lot No. 19 and house lot No. 11, South of
Great River.
Capt. John Chandler, interval lot No. 4 and house lot No. 4, West of
Ellis River.
Capt. Abiel Chandler, interval lot No. 34 and house lot No. 32, South of
Great River.
Capt. Abiel Chandler, interval lot No. 27 and house lot No. 31, North of
Great River.
Capt. Abial Chandler, interval lot No. 11 and house lot No. 11, North of
Great River.
Capt. Abial Chandler, interval lot No. 26 and house lot No. 18, West of
Ellis River.
Capt. Abial Chandler, interval lot No. 20 and house lot No. 14, West of
Ellis River.
Ephraim Carter, interval lot No. 15 and house lot No. 11, West of Ellis
River.

John Chase, interval lot No. 14, West of Ellis River, and house lot No. 11, East of Ellis River.

Dr. Chas. Chauncey, interval lot No. 24 and house lot No. 28, North of Great River.

Jeremiah Dresser's Heirs, interval lot No. 1 and house lot No. 18, South of Great River.

Elijah Durgin, interval lot No. 22 and house lot No. 13, South of Great River.

Joseph Eastman, interval lot No. 5 and house lot No. 5, East of Ellis River.

Ebenezer Eastman, interval lot No. 7 and house lot No. 7, North of Great River.

Philip Eastman, interval lot No. 2, South of Great River, and house lot No. 20, East of Ellis River.

Philip Eastman, interval lot No. 25 and house lot No. 15, South of Great River.

Moses Eastman, interval lot No. 30 and house lot No. 25, South of Great River.

Nathaniel Eastman, interval lot No. 15 and house lot No. 19, North of Great River.

Nathaniel Eastman, interval lot No. 33 and house lot No. 31, South of Great River.

Amos Eastman, interval lot No. 23, West of Ellis River, and house lot No. 12, East of Ellis River.

Jeremiah Eastman, interval lot No. 15, South of Great River, and house lot No. 16, North of Great River.

Ephraim Farnum, interval lot No. 18 and house lot No. 13, West of Ellis River.

Benj. Farnum, interval lot No. 10 and house lot No. 5, South of Great River.

Benj. Farnum, interval lot No. 39 and house lot No. 29, South of Great River.

Joseph Farnum, interval lot No. 12 and house lot No. 12, North of Great River.

Stephen Farrington, interval lot No. 6 and house lot No. 2, South of Great River.

Abner Fowler Heirs, interval lot No. 9, West of Ellis River, and house lot No. 3, East of Ellis River.

Peter Green, interval lot No. 5 and house lot No. 6, North of Great River.

Ebenezer H. Goss, interval lot No. 25 and house lot No. 30, North of Great River.

Ebenezer H. Goss, interval lot No. 14 and house lot No. 9, South of Great River.

Ebenezer H. Goss, interval lot No. 5 and house lot No. 5, West of Ellis River.

Gustavus A. Goss, interval lot No. 7 and house lot No. 3, South of Great River.

Benj. Gale, interval lot No. 3 and house lot No. 4, East of Ellis River.

Ebenezer Hall, interval lot No. 38 and house lot No. 30, South of Great River.

Moses Hall, interval lot No. 20 and house lot No. 12, South of Great River.

David Hall, interval lot No. 16 and house lot No. 20, North of Great River.

Richard Hazletine, interval lot No. 23 and house lot No. 17, South of Great River.

Ebenezer Hall, Jr., interval lot No. 21 and house lot No. 21, South of Great River.

Philip Kimball, interval lot No. 24 and house lot No. 17, West of Ellis River.

Reuben Kimball, interval lot No. 9 and house lot No. 13, East of Ellis River.

Asa Kimball, interval lot No. 11 and house lot No. 6, South of Great River.

Abraham Kimball, interval lot No. 35 and house lot No. 34, South of Great River.

Jonathan Merrill, interval lot No. 36 and house lot No. 35, South of Great River.

Hannah Osgood, interval lot No. 19, West of Ellis River, and house lot No. 18, North of Great River.

Hannah Osgood, interval lot No. 20 and house lot No. 22, North of Great River.

Rev. Sam'l Phillips' Heirs, interval lot No. 23 and house lot No. 27, North of Great River.

Nathaniel Rolfe, interval lot No. 2 and house lot No. 2, North of Great River.

Paul Rolfe, interval lot No. 22 and house lot No. 25, North of Great River.

Paul Rolfe, interval lot No. 37 and house lot No. 33, South of Great River.

Paul Rolfe. interval lot No. 2 and house lot No. 2, East of Ellis River.

Paul Rolfe, interval lot No. 10 and house lot No. 9, West of Ellis River.

Paul Rolfe, interval lot No. 12 and house lot No. 7, South of Great River.

Thomas Stickney, interval lot No. 40 and house lot No. 28, South of Great River.

Thomas Stickney, interval lot No. 6 and house lot No. 6, East of Ellis River.

Thomas Stickney, interval lot No. 17 and house lot No. 22, North of Great River.

Aaron Stevens, interval lot No. 32 and house lot No. 27, South of Great River.

Aaron Stevens, interval lot No. 3 and house lot No. 3, North of Great River.

Jonathan Stickney, interval lot No. 2 and house lot No. 2, West of Ellis River.

Caleb Smart. interval lot No. 31 and house lot No. 26, South of Great River.

Jonathan Straw, interval lot No. 6 and house lot No. 6, West of Ellis River.

Benj. Thompson, Esq., interval lot No. 10 and house lot No. 14, East of Ellis River.

Benj. Thompson, Esq., interval lot No. 18 and house lot No. 20, South of Great River.

Benj Thompson, Esq., interval lot No. 26 and house lot No. 29, North of Great River.

Benj. Thompson. Esq., interval lot No. 26 and house lot No. 14, South of Great River.

Benj. Thompson, Esq., interval lot No. 22 and house lot No. 16, West of Ellis River.

Benjamin Thompson, Esq., interval lot No. 4, South of Great River, and house lot No. 13, North of Great River.

Ebenezer Virgin Heirs, interval lot No. 21 and house lot No. 18, South of Great River.

Ebenezer Virgin Heirs. interval lot No. 3, South side Great River. and house lot No. 16, East of Ellis River.

Rev. Timothy Walker. interval lot No. 1 and house lot No. 1, North of Great River.

Rev. Timothy Walker, interval lot No. 8 and house lot No. 8, West of Ellis River.

Capt. Timothy Walker, interval lot No, 8 and house lot No. 9, East of Ellis River.

Timothy Walker, Jr., interval lot No. 5 and house lot No. 1, South side of Great River.

Timothy Walker, Jr., interval lot No. 11, West of Ellis River, and house lot No. 7, East of Ellis River.

Timothy Walker, Jr., interval lot No. 28, and house lot No. 23, South of Great River.

James Walker, interval lot No. 12, West of Ellis River, and house lot No. 10, East side of Ellis River.

Charles Walker. interval lot No. 21 and house lot No. 15, West of Ellis River.

Paul Walker, interval lot No. 9 and house lot No. 19, South of Great River.

Timothy Walker, 3d, interval lot No. 17 and house lot No. 12, West of Ellis River.

Capt. Timothy Walker, et als., interval lot No. 1 and house lot No. 1, West of Ellis River. Three-fourths of the above right to Walker, and one-fourth to Rev. Samuel Phillips' Heirs.

Abraham Kimball, et als.. interval lot No. 13 and house lot No. 10, West of Ellis River. Three-fourths to Kimball, one-fourth to Phillips' Heirs.

James McHurd, et als., interval lot No. 8 and house lot No. 4, South of Great River. McHurd one-half, Nathaniel Nash one-fourth and Cutting Marsh one-fourth.

Robt. Davis, et als.. interval lot No. 16, South of Great River, and house lot No. 17, North of Great River. Davis three-fourths, and Anna Stevens one-fourth.

Henry Lovejoy, et als.. interval lot No. 29 and house lot No. 24, South of Great River. Lovejoy one-fourth, Phineas Kimball one-fourth, Samuel Runnels one-half.

Sam'l and Wm. Dana and Dudley Colman, interval lot No. 3 and house lot No. 3, West of Ellis River. Danas one-half, and Coleman one-half.

Minister, interval lot No. 13 and house lot No. 14, North of Great River.

Parsonage, interval lot No. 14 and house lot No. 15, North of Great River.

College, interval lot No. 25, West of Ellis River, and house lot No. 16, East of Ellis River.

School, interval lot No. 10 and house lot No. 10, North of Great River.

At an adjourned meeting Feb. 2, 1780, it was voted that one hundred dollars be raised upon each full right to defray the charges of the Proprietary.

A committee was chosen, consisting of Timothy Walker, Jr., Thomas Stickney and David Hall, to make sale of delinquent proprietors who had not paid their assessments.

At an adjourned meeting April 3, 1780, John Chandler, Thomas Stickney and Timothy Walker were made a committee to confer with person or persons with regard to building a saw and grist mill in the New Township, and report at the next meeting.

At an adjourned meeting July 3, 1780, Mr. John Stevens was added to the committee on mills.

At an adjourned meeting August 28, 1780, John Stevens was

chosen chairman, in place of Thomas Stickney, who asked to be excused from serving. It was voted "that five Spanish milled dollars be raised upon each full right, to defray the expense of laying out and clearing roads in said Township now called New Penny-cook.* Jonathan Eastman, Ebenezer H. Goss and Ephraim Colby were made a committee to lay out and clear the roads, and that each be paid one Spanish milled dollar per day."

At an adjourned meeting Sept. 8, 1780, it was voted to give Lieut. John Chandler four hundred hard dollars and one hundred acres of land, provided he, within fifteen months, build and keep in good repair forever, one good saw mill and one good grist mill upon Concord River (so called), in said township of New Pennacook, and that four hard dollars be raised upon each full right to defray the expense of building mills above mentioned. Timothy Walker, Jr., Ebenezer H. Goss and John Stevens were made a committee to look after the building of the mills.

At an adjourned meeting Dec. 4, 1780, Capt. Joel Dodge was given leave to "pitch" one hundred acres in the common land in New Pennacook, provided he settle upon the premises within one year.

At an adjourned meeting Aug. 6, 1781, it was voted that a cart road be cleared up Ellis River on the west side "as far as David Sessions' house lot." Ebenezer H. Goss, John Chandler, Phineas Kimball and David Sessions were made a committee for clearing out the road. At this meeting, Jonathan Keyes, Phineas Kimball and David Sessions† were chosen a committee, in behalf of the Proprietary, to prosecute any person or persons who should trespass upon the common lands in said township.

After this meeting, the proprietors met several times and adjourned without transacting any business, probably due to the fact that the handful of settlers in New Pennacook had been frightened away by the Indian raid into Bethel, and did not return until the war of the Revolution was practically closed and all danger from hostile Indians had passed.

At an adjourned meeting holden January 6, 1783, measures were taken to collect taxes of delinquents, by advertising the same, and selling all lots upon which taxes should not be paid within a specified time.

* This is the first appearance of this name for the "New Town."
† These men were presumably residents of the township, but three days before this vote was passed, the hostile Indians had raided Bethel, and the New Pennacook settlers had fled to New Gloucester.

At a meeting May 19, 1783, Timothy Walker, John Stevens and Jonathan Eastman were made a committee to try and induce persons to settle in New Pennacook. At a meeting July 28 following, Mr. John Stevens was requested to petition the General Court for an extension of time for the settlement of thirty families within their township. It was also voted that John Stevens, Jonathan Eastman and Phineas Kimball be a committee to proceed to New Pennacook and lay out one hundred and thirty-four lots of one hundred acres each, "as soon as may be," and five shillings per day were voted as the compensation of each. It was "voted that provided thirty persons shall appear to make actual settlement upon said township of New Pennacook in one year, each of them shall be allowed to pitch one lot out of the division now ordered to be laid out."

At a meeting December 1, 1783, it was voted that sixteen shillings be raised upon each right. Jonathan Keyes was allowed three pounds and four shillings for extra services.

The next meeting at which any business was performed was holden May 17, 1784. It was then voted that the following persons be allowed to pitch each a one hundred acre lot gratis, and a one hundred acre lot for a second division upon their respective rights, they and each of them clearing and sowing to grain five acres of land this year, in said township, and making actual settlement upon the premises within one year from the date last mentioned, viz :

That Jacob Eastman have for settlement the one hundred acre lot number eighty-two, north of Great River, and also that he be allowed to pitch the hundred acre lot number one hundred and four on the west side of Ellis River, for a second division, on the right of Nathaniel Eastman.

That Ebenezer H. Goss, Esq., have for settlement the hundred acre lot number two on the north side of the Great River, and to pitch the hundred acre lot number three on the north side of Great River, for a second division on the original right of Charles Chauncey.

That Philip Abbot have for settlement the one hundred acre lot number seven, north of Great River, and be allowed to pitch the one hundred acre lot number eight, on the north side of Great River, for a second division, on the right of Ebenezer Hall, Senior.

That Lieut. John Chandler have for settlement the hundred acre lot number eighty-three on the north side of the Great River, and be allowed to pitch number sixty-four on the same side of said river, for a second division, to the right of Capt. John Chandler.

That Daniel Stickney have for settlement number seventeen north of Great River, and be allowed to pitch number eighteen on the same side of said river, for a second division of the right of Jonathan Stickney.

At a meeting August 2, 1784, it was voted that James Scales, James Scales, Jr., and Oliver Scales, be allowed to pitch respectively, lots ninety-two, ninety-three and ninety-eight, on the north side of the Great River, provided they make actual settlement in New Pennacook within one year. Jonathan Eastman and Phineas Kimball were made a committee to make necessary roads to accommodate the settlers in New Pennacook. It was also voted that land of delinquents be advertised for sale, as soon as possible, in some one of the Boston papers.

A meeting was held at the inn of Benj. Hannaford in Concord, January 1, 1785, at which the committee on roads in New Pennacook presented their accounts, amounting to fifty-eight pounds and nine shillings, which were allowed.

At an adjourned meeting May 16, Mr. John Stevens was appointed a committee to petition the General Court for another extension of time.

At an adjourned meeting August 6, 1785, a tax of six shillings per right, was levied. At the same meeting, Benjamin Farnum and Philip Abbot were appointed a committee on roads in New Pennacook. At a meeting August 22, Mr. Stevens reported that the proprietors had been granted an extension of two years in which to comply with the terms of their grant.

A meeting was held January 2, 1786, at which a committee on new settlers was appointed, and authorized to pay six pounds to each actual settler in New Pennacook, in one year. Eight dollars were assessed upon each right.

At a meeting in April, the Clerk was directed to procure a plan of New Pennacook, as soon as possible.

No further business was transacted by the Proprietary until January 1, 1787, when the committee appointed in 1783, to lay out one hundred and thirty-four lots of one hundred acres each in New Pennacook, made a return of their survey, which was accepted, and the clerk directed to record the same. The return showed a survey of one hundred and four lots, with a reservation of a four rod road through each lot.

At a meeting May 15, 1787, a committee was chosen to inspect the mills in New Pennacook, consisting of Eleazer Twitchell,* Francis Keyes and Philip Abbot. Jonathan Keyes, the first settler in the township, died Nov. 9, 1786, and at this meeting his widow, Sarah Keyes, was permitted to pitch a one hundred acre lot as a settler.

At a meeting July 30, 1787, Stephen Farnum and Philip Abbot were chosen a committee to clear a horse road from the lower end of New Pennacook to Butterfield† (so called).

At a meeting Dec. 26, 1787, John York ‡ and Jesse Duston ‡ were added to the committee to inspect the mills.

No further business was transacted until a meeting held February 23, 1789, when Stephen Farnum, Philip Abbot and Francis Keyes were instructed to clear out a road from the mouth of Ellis River to New Andover (so called). The committee to inspect the mills submitted the following report:

"NEW PENNACOOK, Oct. 4, 1788.

We, the subscribers, being chosen as a committee by the proprietors of said New Pennacook, for to view Lieut. Chandler's mills in said New Pennacook, and do report, and our report is the said mills are finished and are fit for the Proprietors' use."

JOHN YORK,
PHILIP ABBOT,
FRANCIS KEYES, } *Committee.*
JESSE DUSTON,
ELEAZER TWITCHELL,

At a meeting Feb. 15, 1790, the road to New Andover not having been built, a new committee was appointed to build a road "from the river Amoscoggin to New Andover," consisting of Stephen Farnum, Philip Abbot and Francis Keyes. At the same meeting, Philip Abbot and Francis Keyes were chosen a committee to make and present a list of those who had completed a settlement in the township, also to report the number of the hundred acre lots they had pitched upon. At an adjourned meeting January 17, 1791, Henry Rolfe was added to the committee. This committee did not report until March 10, 1792, when they submitted the following:

---

* He was of Sudbury Canada (Bethel).
† Sumner and Hartford were once called Butterfield.
‡ Both Sudbury Canada men.

NORTH SIDE OF THE RIVER.

Philip Abbot	No. 7	Moses Kimball	No. 3
Jacob Abbot	" 73	Stephen Putnam	" 22
Jacob Eastman	" 82	Henry Rolfe	" 2
Osgood Eaton	" 18	Josiah Segar	" 84
Jacob Farnum	" 4	John Stevens	" 72
Samuel Goodwin	" 17	John Stevens	" 77
Robert Hinkson	" 67	John Stevens	" 92
James Harper	" 98	John Stevens	" 97
Sarah Keyes	" 90	Daniel Knight	" 20
Francis Keyes	" 78	James McAllister	" 64
Nathaniel Knight	" 21		

SOUTH SIDE OF THE RIVER.

David Abbot	No. 20	Edmund Page	No. 22
Benj. Elliot	" 5	Joel Stone	" 1
Benj. Farnum	" 11	Moses Stone	" 2
David Farnum	" 10	Benj. Sweat, Jr.	" 4

The report was accepted, with the exception of James McAllister and Daniel Knight, who were rejected as actual settlers.

The committee on location of lots having previously made a return of their survey comprising one hundred and four lots each of one hundred acres, it was voted at this meeting to draw these lots, which resulted as follows :

George Abbot	No. 3,	North of Great River.	
George Abbot	" 58,	"	"
Amos Abbot	" 56,	"	"
Amos Abbot	" 49,	"	"
Edward Abbot	" 68,	"	"
Edward Abbot	" 29,	"	"
Benj. Abbot	" 40,	"	"
Joshua Abbot	" 14,	"	"
Nathaniel Abbot	" 76,	"	"
Timothy Bradley	" 12,	South of Great River.	
Jeremiah Bradley	" 8,	"	"
John Bradley	" 11,	North of Great River.	
William Coffin	" 101,	"	"
John Chandler	" 26,	South of Great River.	
John Chandler	" 50,	North of Great River.	
John Chandler	" 20,	South of Great River.	
Abial Chandler	" 19,	North of Great River.	
Abial Chandler	" 65,	"	"
Abial Chandler	" 87,	"	"
Abial Chandler	" 85,	"	"
Abial Chandler	" 80,	"	"
Ephraim Carter	" 70,	"	"
John Chase	" 71,	"	"
Charles Chauncey	" 62,	"	"
Jeremiah Dresser	" 51	"	"

Joseph Eastman....................No. 55, North of Great River.
Ebenezer Eastman.................. " 23, " "
Philip Eastman.................... " 34, " "
Philip Eastman.................... " 79, " "
Moses Eastman.................... " 13, " "
Nathaniel Eastman................ " 10, " "
Nathaniel Eastman............ .... " 104, North side of Great River.
Amos Eastman.................... " 57, " "
Jeremiah Eastman................. " 29, " "
Ephraim Farnum.................. " 103, " "
Benj. Farnum .... " 13, " "
Benj. Farnum .... " 6, South side of Great River.
Joseph Farnum........... .... " 22, " "
Stephen Farrington............... " 52, North side of Great River.
Abner Fowler .... " 46, " "
Peter Green .... " 16, South side of Great River.
Ebenezer H. Goss .... " 41, North side of Great River.
Ebenezer H. Goss .... " 24, " "
Ebenezer H. Goss .... " 14, " "
Ebenezer H. Goss .... " 94, " "
Ebenezer II. Goss .... " 13, " "
Benj. Gale....................... " 27, South side of Great River.
Ebenezer Hall................... " 8, North side of Great River.
Moses Hall...................... " 15, " "
David Hall....................... " 25, " "
Richard Hazeltine .... " 96, " "
Ebenezer Hall, Jr................ " 43, " "
Philip Kimball................... " 42, " "
Reuben Kimball.................. " 6, " "
Asa Kimball...................... " 75, " "
Abraham Kimball .... " 30, South side of Great River.
Jonathan Merrill....... .... " 16, North side of Great River.
Hannah Osgood.................. " 9, " "
Samuel Phillips.................. " 60, " "
Nathaniel Rolfe .... " 32, " "
Paul Rolfe .... " 61, " "
Paul Rolfe .... " 48, " "
Paul Rolfe .... " 63, " "
Paul Rolfe .... " 19, South side of Great River.
Paul Rolfe .... " 33, North side of Great River.
Thomas Stickney................. " 12, " "
Thomas Stickney................. " 25, South side of Great River.
Thomas Stickney................. " 1, North side of Great River.
Aaron Stevens................... " 30, " "
Aaron Stevens................... " 51, " "
Jonathan Stickney................ " 7, South side of Great River.
Caleb Smart... .... " 74, North side of Great River.
Johathan Straw .... " 89, " "
Benj. Thompson.................. " 17, South side of Great River.
Benj. Thompson.................. " 59, North side of Great River.
Benj. Thompson.................. " 28, South side of Great River.
Benj. Thompson.................. " 9, " "
Benj. Thompson.................. " 18, " "
Benj. Thompson.................. " 15, " "
Ebenezer Virgin .... " 95, " "
Ebenezer Virgin .... " 27, " "
Ebenezer Virgin....... .... " 26, " "
Timothy Walker................ ... " 44, " "
Timothy Walker.................. " 5, " "
Timothy Walker.................. " 86, " "
Timothy Walker....... .... " 81, " "

Timothy Walker....... ....No. 66, South side of Great River.
James Walker...................... " 37,   "   "
Charles Walker.................... " 69,   "   "
Timothy Walker, 3d............ ... " 28,   "   "
Capt. Timothy Walker............. " 47,   "   "
Paul Walker,..................... " 99,   "   "
Capt. Timothy Walker, et als .... " 100,   "   "
Abraham Kimball, et als........... " 102,   "   "
James McHurd, et als............. " 24, South side of Great River.
Robert Davis, et als.............. " 91, North side of Great River.
Henry Lovejoy, et als............. " 45,   "   "
Sam'l and Wm. Dana, et al. .... " 83,   "   "
Minister....................... " 35,   "   "
Ministry.................. .... " 36,   "   "
School .... " 39,   "   "
Harvard College.................. " 38,   "   "

At a meeting Jan. 7, 1793, Dea. David Hall was chosen treasurer, in place of John Stevens, deceased. Henry Martin, Timothy Walker and Stephen Farnum were appointed a committee to settle all accounts with Mrs. Sarah, widow of John Stevens.

The next meeting at which business was transacted was holden Jan. 27, 1794. It was then voted that fifteen pounds be expended on the roads in New Pennacook, the current year, and David Farnum, Edmund Page and Jacob Abbot were made a committee to expend the money.

The next meeting of the Proprietary, and the first one held in New Pennacook, was held at the house of Aaron Moor, Sept. 8, 1794. Francis Keyes was moderator. Fifteen additional pounds were raised to be expended on the roads, and Phillip Abbot, Stephen Farnum and Richard Dolloff were made a committee to lay out the money.

Several adjourned meetings were then holden at the Inn of Benj. Hannaford in Concord, but no business transacted.

PETITION CONCERNING TAXES.

This year, the Inhabitants of the Plantation, through a committee, made the following statement concerning a tax that had been laid upon them by order of the General Court at Boston:

To the Honorable Senate and House of Representatives of this Commonwealth, in General Court assembled:

The petition of the subscribers of a plantation called New Pennicook, in the County of York or Cumberland, humbly sheweth:

That whereas your honors have seen fit to lay a tax on said plan tation of ten pounds and odd, we as a plantation met to consult upon the same, but we found ourselves so few in numbers (only twenty-two families and eight single men, which abscond in the winter season), therefore we found ourselves unable to pay said tax. Furthermore, we labor under many difficulties: We are upward of seventy miles from Portland, which is our best place of market; the distance is nothing compared with the roughness of the roads between us and the first inhabitants; most of it is through State's land, exceedingly uneven and miry, through which we have to transport our salt and other necessaries on horseback in summer, and in winter to go on snow shoes and haul them by hand. We, having no representation, have undertaken to represent ourselves in some measure, and we presume if your Honors had right information of our small abilities, you would not think of taxing so small a Plantation. For we have never yet been able to advance one shilling to hire a day's preaching nor a minute's schooling for the benefit of our children. For the above reason and a number of others not named, your Petitioners Pray your Honors to exempt us from this tax, also from further Taxes for a few years, and your Petitioners as in duty bound, will ever Pray.

Newpennicook, Dec. 25th, 1794.

(Signed)   BENJ. SWEET,   ⎫ *Committee Chosen*
             JOSHUA GRAHAM,   ⎬   *by said*
             FRANCIS KEYES.   ⎭   *Plantation.*

Many meetings were held and adjourned in Concord without the transaction of any business. At a meeting held at the Inn of David George in Concord, Dec. 6, 1802, the committee to settle with the estate of John Stevens, late treasurer of the Proprietary, reported that the whole amount received by John Stevens, treasurer, in paper and silver money, amounted to eleven thousand, two hundred and forty pounds, which sum had been paid out on orders on file, and it was voted that Mrs. Stevens be discharged from all liability on account of the same.

Adjourned meetings were held from time to time at the house of David George in Concord until Aug. 3, 1807, but to adjourn was the only business transacted. This meeting was then dissolved, and was the last meeting of the Proprietary held in Concord.

On June 11, 1807, the members of the Proprietary resident in New Pennacook, which had now become Rumford, petitioned to Timothy Carter of Bethel, for a warrant for a meeting to be held at the dwelling house of Francis Keyes, on Monday the 31st day of August, following. The petition for the meeting was signed by

Francis Keyes, Benj. Farnum, David Farnum, Kimball Martin, Philip Abbot, and by Timothy and Charles Walker by their Attorney. At this meeting Joshua Graham was chosen Moderator, and Francis Keyes Clerk. It was voted to make a third division of land in the township, and David Farnum, Francis Keyes and Philip Abbot were made a committee for this purpose. The same committee were authorized to settle all outstanding accounts against the Proprietary. It was voted to ratify and confirm the proceedings of all preceding meetings. The committee were directed, in laying out new lots, to equalize them by making some larger and others smaller, according to the quality of the land.

At a meeting Sept. 1, 1808, John Thompson, Esq., and David Abbot were added to the committee on laying out the third division of lots. At a meeting Oct. 25, 1808, the Proprietary met, and voted to accept the plans and survey of the committee. The committee reported that they had surveyed and lotted out all remaining undivided land in Rumford, except three small pieces which they proceeded to describe.

It was voted that this committee pitch the four public lots in the third division.

It was voted to give lot numbered one hundred and twelve to Timothy Walker, Esq., in consideration of losses by drawing poor lots in previous divisions. For the same reason, it was voted to give lot numbered one hundred and eleven to Lt. Joseph Walker, lot numbered seventy-two to Gustavus A. Goss, and parts of lots eighteen and nineteen to William Simpson. A committee was chosen to receive proposals for five reserved lots.

At a meeting Jan. 2, 1809, the committee appointed to pitch the four public lots in the third division of lots, reported to Harvard College, number forty-seven ; minister, twenty-two ; ministry, fifty ; and to schools, number sixty-five. Certain lots were also described and confirmed as mill rights, being the same granted to John Chandler for building a saw and grist mill on Concord River. On the twenty-third of January, a meeting was held at the house of Simon Virgin. Lot number twenty-seven of the third division was here sold at auction, and bid off by Simon Virgin at sixty dollars. Other common lots were sold, the purchasers being David Farnum, Francis Keyes, Philip Abbot, John Thompson and Abel Wheeler. Simon

Virgin was allowed the sum of eight dollars and sixty cents for the expenses of this meeting, though the items are not recorded.

Several meetings were held in the year 1810, Mr. Joshua Felt serving as moderator, but no business was transacted; the same was true of meetings held in 1811, 1812, 1813 and 1814. Then occurred a hiatus of three years.

A meeting was called at the house of Francis Keyes, Nov. 29, 1817, by virtue of a warrant issued by Peter C. Virgin, Esq. Kimball Martin was chosen moderator, and Francis Keyes clerk. The business transacted was unimportant, and after adjourning from time to time until April 24, 1819, the meetings again lapsed.

The next meeting was held at the office of Peter C. Virgin, Jan. 26, 1828. Daniel Martin was chosen moderator, and Francis Keyes clerk. Francis Keyes, Kimball Martin and Stephen G. Stevens were made a committee to ascertain the common and undivided lands within the town, and they were allowed to employ one chainman and one man to spot the lines. The same committee was empowered to dispose of the common lands at private sale.

At an adjourned meeting, Dec. 15, 1828, the committee on sale of the common lands, reported progress, and that they had sold several lots to parties, and at prices specified. Dec. 29, another meeting was held, and Peter C. Virgin was allowed ten dollars for granting the warrant and warning the meeting. The committee on sale of the common lands made a further report.

At a meeting Dec. 14, 1829, it was voted to sell at auction all the remaining common lands belonging to the town. Accordingly, common lots numbered three, four, five and six, were duly sold, and bid off, the first three by Francis Keyes, and the fourth by Moses F. Kimball.

From this time the organization was kept up, and meetings occasionally held at the dwelling houses of the proprietors, until the year 1847. Josiah Keyes was the last proprietors' clerk, and his last record was for an adjourned meeting, which was probably never held.

At a meeting Sept. 2, 1833, it was voted to choose Josiah Keyes clerk, to finish the records of the Proprietary from minutes left by his late father, Francis Keyes, formerly clerk of the Proprietary, who died leaving the records unfinished.

The warrant for the last meeting was called on the petition of Timothy Walker, John Thompson, Hezekiah Hutchins, Jr., Daniel Martin and Kimball Martin, and the object as stated was to confirm the doings of previous meetings, and the doings of committees appointed at such meetings.

The first meeting of the Proprietary was holden in Haverhill, May 26, 1779, and the last in Rumford, Oct. 18, 1846, the meetings covering a period of sixty-seven years. But few of the original proprietors settled in Rumford, and but very few of the early settlers were living at the time the meetings of the Proprietary closed.

CHAPTER V.

JANUARY 3, 1800. Timothy Walker of Concord, to Daniel
Knight of New Pennacook, one whole right of which Ebenezer Hall was the original grantee, except twenty acres already sold.

April 15, 1792. John Chandler of Concord, to Aaron Moor of
New Pennacook, one hundred acres with saw and grist mill thereon,
being the same land granted him by the proprietors.

July 12, 1779. John Chandler of Concord, to Samuel Runnels
of Boxford, one whole right in New Pennacook, "the same inherited
from my honored father, the original grantee."

January 30, 1792. John Stevens of Concord, to John Stevens
Partridge of same, first division of a right in New Pennacook,
granted to Aaron Stevens, one hundred acres number twenty-seven,
and interval lot number twenty-two, south of Great River.

March 16, 1792. John Stevens of Concord, to William Manley
of same, number seventy-seven north of Great River, one hundred
acres.

March 16, 1792. John Stevens of Concord, to Benjamin Lufkin
of New Pennacook, numbers eleven and six, south side of river,
original grant of Asa Kimball.

December 25, 1780. John Stevens of Concord, to Henry Martin
of same, one whole right of land in New Pennacook.

May 2, 1794. Thomas and Molly Capen of New Pennacook, to
Francis Keyes of same, part of the right of Dea. George Abbot,
number fourteen and ten, south of river.

June 20, 1794. Francis Keyes of New Pennacook, to John Martin of same, number seventy-eight, second division, north of river.

October 5, 1788. John Stevens (merchant) of Concord, to Thos.
Capen of New Pennacook, first division lots number seventeen and
ten, original right of Dea. George Abbot.

July 3, 1797.   Sarah, relict of John Stevens, to Stephen Putnam of Temple, N. H., number one south of river, one hundred acres.

Wiggin Taylor of New Pennacook, to Stephen Putnam of same, one whole right of land in New Pennacook, interval lot eighteen and upland twenty-four, drawn to right of Dea. George Abbot.

Nathaniel Rolfe, Jr., of Concord, to Stephen Putnam of New Pennacook, one whole right, being the original right of Rev. Timothy Walker, numbers eight and eight, west side of Ellis River.

Sarah Stevens of Concord, to Jeremiah Pecker of same, one hundred acres, number seventy-two, in New Pennacook, original right of John Stevens.

May 22, 1797.   Same to William Virgin (joiner) of same, eighty acres, more or less, number twenty-one, north side of river, granted originally to Thomas Stickney.

Nathan Abbot of Concord, to Jacob Abbot of same, one whole settler's right or share in New Pennacook, granted originally to Nathaniel Abbot.

December 19, 1800.   Nathan Abbot to Henry Martin, twenty acres lot number five, and eighty acres of same, east side of Ellis River, right of Jonathan Eastman.

February 15, 1802.   Nathan Abbot to Richard Dolloff of Rumford, one hundred acres, north of river, number ninety-two.

June 4, 1802.   Same to Ebenezer Fogg of same, lot number twenty, east side of river, right of Philip Eastman.

March 6, 1781.   Reuben Kimball of Concord, to Samuel Runnels of Boxford, Mass., one whole right, of which grantor was the original grantee.

Sept. 26, 1799.   Moses Kimball and Phebe Kimball of New Pennacook, to William Virgin, Jr., of Concord, lot number three, north of river.

October 22, 1794.   Philip Abbot of New Pennacook, to Stephen Putnam of same, one half the house lot number thirty-four, south of the Great River.

March 29, 1804.   David Abbot of Rumford, to Cotton Elliot of same, number twenty in the second division.

March 7, 1804.   Nathaniel Sanborn of Rumford, to Cotton Elliot of same, part of lot number thirty-two, second division.

October 17, 1793. Samuel Runnels of Boxford, Mass., to Joshua Graham of Concord, N. H., one whole right in New Pennacook, of which Samuel Runnels, Phineas Kimball and Henry Lovejoy were the original grantees, lying south of the Great River.

February 8, 1794. Benj. Rolfe of Concord, to Stephen Putnam of New Pennacook, right of Paul Rolfe, south side of river.

May 31, 1803. Benj. Rolfe of Rumford, to Phineas Wood of same, one whole share in the common lands, original right of Paul Rolfe, south side of river.

January 3, 1777. Dr. Ebenezer H. Goss of Concord, to Jonathan Keyes of Shrewsbury, Mass., two whole rights in New Pennacook, of which he (Goss) was the original grantee.

March 16, 1789. Ebenezer H. Goss of Concord, to Joshua Atherton of Amherst, Mass., two full rights in New Pennacook, the same drawn to Moses Eastman and Edward Abbot.

October 2, 1795. Same to James C. Harper of New Pennacook, one whole right purchased of John Stevens, lying on Ellis River.

June 18, 1801. Jacob Farnum to Nathan Brown, both of Rumford, second division lot number four, north of river.

May 7, 1794. Thomas Capen of New Pennacook, to Francis Keyes of same, numbers fourteen and ten, south of river, right of George Abbot.

June 5, 1794. Francis Keyes to John Martin, number seventy-eight in second division, north of river.

October 16, 1799. Ebenezer Keyes of Gardner, Mass., to Francis Keyes of New Pennacook, land bequeathed by their father, Jonathan Keyes, in severalty and undivided.

October 26, 1799. Sarah Keyes (Tailoress) to Francis Keyes, number ninety, second division, north of river.

October 26, 1799. Same to same, in consideration of love to her son, etc., all her personal effects, goods and chattels.

August 6, 1786. Jonathan Eastman of Fryeburg, to Francis Keyes of New Pennacook, whole right in New Pennacook, being the same of which he (Eastman) was the original grantee.

February 3, 1777. Dr. Ebenezer Harnden Goss of Concord, to Jonathan Keyes of Shrewsbury, Mass., two full shares or settler's rights in New Pennacook.

December 1, 1779.   Robert Davis and widow Anna Stevens, both of Concord, to Jonathan Keyes of New Pennacook, one whole right in New Pennacook, of which "we were the original grantees."

Danforth Keyes of Western, to Benj. Green of Marblehead, a right of land in New Pennacook; "said lot was drawn in my own name."

June 21, 1796.   Jeremiah Richardson of Gilmanton, N. H., bought of Samuel Goodwin of Warner, N. H., one hundred acres of land in New Pennacook, on the north side of the river that runs through the town.

August 21, 1793.   Edward Dow of Concord, to David Abbot of New Pennacook, the whole of the first division laid out to the right of Ebenezer Eastman.

September 20, 1794.   Benjamin Lufkin of same, to same, the original right of Asa Kimball.

April 11, 1795.   Paul Rolfe of Concord, to same, south of river, interval lot number twelve and house lot number seven, of which said Rolfe was the original grantee.

June 11, 1806.   Enoch Adams of Andover, to Moses Varnum of same, one-half right number one, east side of river, with rest part of said right.

July 13, 1795.   Paul Rolfe of Concord, to Ephraim Colby of same, number nineteen south of Great River, in second division. (Colby sold this lot to Joshua Graham, Sept. 1, 1801.)

March 25, 1805.   Joshua Felt of Rumford, to Gustavus A. Goss of same, ten acres of lot three, south of Great River.

October 7, 1799.   James C. Harper to Benj. Lufkin, two hundred acres in second division, numbers ninety-three and ninety-eight.

March 1, 1790.   Timothy Walker of Concord, to Henry Rolfe of same, one full right, lots number twenty-five and thirty, north of Great River, granted to Dr. Ebenezer H. Goss.

April 17, 1797.   Sarah Stevens of Concord, to Abel Wheeler of same, the original right of Hannah Osgood, number two, north side of Great River; also interval lot laid out to Thomas Stickney.

November 29, 1784.   Aaron Stevens of Loudon, N. H., to John Stevens of Concord, two whole rights in New Pennacook.

November 16, 1780. Jonathan Eastman of Concord, to John Stevens of same, the original right of Benjamin Abbot.

June 20, 1803. Sarah Stevens of Concord, to Benjamin Wood Stevens of same, minor, land in Rumford.

August 23, 1806. John Virgin of Concord, to William Knowles of same, eighty acre lot east side of Ellis River, drawn to right of heirs of Ebenezer Virgin.

August 23, 1806. William Virgin of Rumford, joiner, to John Whittemore of same, eighty acres north of Great River, granted to Thomas Stickney.

September 19, 1804. Benj. Morse of Rumford, cordwainer, to John Virgin of Concord, eighty acres east of Ellis River, drawn to heirs of Ebenezer Virgin.

March 11, 1807. Nathan Hunting of Rumford, to Enoch Adams and Abel Wheeler of same, mortgage deed of saw mill on his farm and one acre of land.

CHAPTER VI.

INCORPORATION.

THE town of Rumford was incorporated the one hundred and twenty-third town in Maine, by an act of the General Court, approved February twenty-first, one thousand eight hundred. The petitioners refer to "many inconveniences and disadvantages," but they do not specify what they were. It will be noticed that the petitioners asked to have the town called CHINA, and no reason appears in the report of the committee or in the act of incorporation for not complying with the request. There was no town in Maine called by this name, until eighteen years after, so the question of duplication could not have been raised. But this case is not an isolated one. The petitioners for the incorporation of Woodstock asked to have it called *Sparta*, and those for Newfield wanted it Washington, but no heed was paid to these requests and no reason assigned for not granting them. As the plantation name of Rumford followed that of the Indian name of the parent town, when New Pennacook was to be enacted into a town, it was quite natural that the first corporate name of old Pennacook should be selected for its Maine namesake.

THE PETITION.

To the Honourable the Senate and the Honourable the House of Representatives In General Court Assembled at Boston In the Commonwealth of Massachusetts

The Petition of the Inhabitants of a Plantation called New Pennycook lying in the County of Cumberland Humbly Sheweth That said Inhabitants labour under many Inconveniences and Disadvantages for want of Incorporation Therefore we the subscribers being a committee appointed to Petition your Honours for Incorporation —humbly pray your honours to Incorporate said Plantation according to the bounds and points of compass hereafter mentioned in this Petition—Beginning with a Hemlock Tree standing upon Bethel line then running North 18 & 1-2 Degs West crossing Amherscogin River seven miles and forty rods to a Spruce Tree then turning and running North 71 & 1-2 Degs East seven miles and forty rods to a Beech Tree then turning and running 18 & 1-2 Degs East crossing Amberscogin River again seven miles and forty rods to a nother Beech Tree then turning and running South 71 & 1-2 Degs West seven miles and forty rods to the bounds first mentioned—The plan of said Plantation being drawn and sent with this Petition

We the subscribers humbly Pray your Honours to Incorporate said Plantation by the name of *China* otherwise relieve your Petitioners as you in your wisdom shall think fit—and your humble Petitioners in Duty bound shall ever Pray

(Signed)

FRANCIS KEYES	*Committee appointed*
JOSHUA GRAHAM	*to Petition for*
PHILIP ABBOT	*Incorporation*

New Penny cook Jan 22nd 1799

ACT OF INCORPORATION.

Commonwealth of Massachusetts.   In the year of our Lord one thousand eight hundred.

An Act to incorporate the Plantation heretofore called New Pennycook, in the County of Cumberland. into a town by the name of Rumford.

Section 1.   Be it enacted by the Senate and House of Representatives in General Court assembled, and by the authority of the same, that the Plantation heretofore known by the name of New Pennycook, in the County of Cumberland, and as described in the following bounds, together with the inhabitants thereon, be and hereby are incorporated into a town by the name of Rumford :

"Beginning at a hemlock tree standing on the line of the town of Bethel, thence running north eighteen degrees and one-half west, crossing the river Ameriscoggin, seven miles and forty rods to a spruce tree ; thence turning and running north seventy-one and one-half degrees east, seven miles and forty rods to a beech tree ; then turning and running south eighteen and one-half degrees east, crossing Ameriscoggin river again, seven miles and forty rods to another beech tree ; then turning and running south seventy and one-half degrees west, seven miles and forty rods, to the bound first mentioned."

And the said town is hereby vested with all the powers, privileges and immunities which other towns do or may enjoy by the Constitution of this Commonwealth.

Section 2.   And be it further enacted that Job Eastman, Esquire, be and hereby is authorized to issue his warrant directed to some suitable inhabitant of said town, requiring him to notify and warn the inhabitants thereof to meet at such time and place as he shall appoint, to choose all such officers as towns are by law required to choose, in the month of March or April, annually.

In the House of Representatives, Feb. 18, 1800.
This bill having had three several readings, passed to be enacted.

ED. H. ROBBINS, *Speaker.*

In Senate, Feb. 21, 1800.
This bill having had two several readings, passed to be enacted.

SAMUEL PHILLIPS, *President.*

Feb. 21, 1800.   By the Lieut.-Governor approved.

MOSES GILL.

A true copy.   Attest: JOHN AVERY, *Secretary of State.*

CHAPTER VII.

BENJAMIN THOMPSON.—COUNT RUMFORD.

IT has been said that this town was named in honor of Count
Rumford, and this may or may not be the fact. Concord,
N. H., the parent town of Rumford, Maine, was originally called
Pennacook. When incorporated, it was called Rumford, supposed
to be from Rumford in England, from which some of the early settlers or their ancestors came. Finally, when the difficulties with the
adjoining town of Bow had been settled, the name was changed to
Concord. When the eastern land grant was made to citizens of
Concord, the territory was called New Pennacook, doubtless in commemoration of the early name of Concord. When the inhabitants
of New Pennacook asked to be incorporated as a town, they asked
to have their town called China; but for some reason not explained
and not easy now to ascertain, the word China was left out and the
word Rumford inserted in its place. In one thousand eight hundred, when this town was incorporated, Count Rumford was still
living and had been famous for many years, and it may be that the
committee of the legislature to whom the petition for the incorporation of New Pennacook was referred, adopted the name in his
honor; but it is more than probable that it was so named to com-
memorate the second name of the parent town. It may be remarked
in this connection, that when Benjamin Thompson received his
Order from the Elector of Bavaria, he chose for it the name of
Rumford, in honor of the New Hampsire town where he had lived,
and where his family still continued to reside. But whether this
town was named for the parent town, or the man, makes no material difference. Count Rumford was allied by marriage to several
of the grantees of New Pennacook and to some of the early settlers
here, and a brief sketch of his public career is not out of place in
this connection.

Benjamin Thompson was the son of Benj. and Ruth (Simonds)
Thompson, and was born in the village of New Bridge, now North

Woburn, Mass., March twenty-six, seventeen hundred and fifty-three. He was descended from James Thompson, who came to this country in sixteen hundred and thirty, and became one of the early settlers in ancient Woburn. The unpretentious house is still standing, where Count Rumford first saw the light, and in a fairly good state of preservation. When Benjamin was only a year and a half old, his father died, and two years later his mother became the wife of Josiah Pierce, Jr. Mr. Pierce was a farmer, but young Thompson, as he grew up, did not take to farming, and his step-father is reported to have said that Benjamin preferred anything to work. At the age of eleven he was sent to school at Medford, and at thirteen he was apprenticed to a merchant at Salem. He failed as a clerk as he had at farming, and busied himself most of the time with tools and implements. He was fond of music, played the violin, was clever at drawing, and was especially enthusiastic in experimental philosophy. At the age of sixteen he returned to his home in Woburn. A second time he was sent to a store, this time in Boston, but he did not long remain. He then commenced the study of medicine and attended scientific lectures at Harvard, walking to and from the college with a young man named Baldwin, who was afterwards a Colonel in the patriot army, and who originated and named the famous Baldwin apple.

Young Thompson early engaged in teaching school, and in this capacity he was employed in Bradford, Wilmington, and in Concord, then a Massachusetts town in Essex county and called Rumford. He is described at this time as possessing a fine manly figure, nearly six feet in height, handsome features, auburn hair and bright blue eyes. At Rumford he had the influence, friendship and pastoral aid of Rev. Timothy Walker, the first settled minister there, and a native of Woburn. It was here, also, that he formed the acquaintance of Mrs. Sarah, widow of Colonel Benjamin Rolfe, and daughter of Rev. Timothy Walker, who became his wife in 1772. Thompson was still a minor, and his wife was fourteen years his senior.

This marriage secured to him quite a large property, relieved him of the necessity of teaching, and brought him into new and important social relations. He became acquainted with Governor Winthrop of New Hampshire, who discovering the young man's ability, took him into close friendship, and introduced him to Governor Gage at Boston, which, in the excitement of popular discontent in the Colonies, caused him to be an object of patriotic suspicion, and in the near future caused him no little embarassment. Public opinion was at this time quite intolerant of coquetry with royal governors, and to the "Sons of Liberty" in Concord, it was enough to concentrate suspicion of disloyalty upon him, that he was in favor with the Governor. For this and other reasons, he was accused of being unfriendly to the cause of liberty, and was summoned before a committee to answer to the charge. He was acquitted, but public opinion was not satisfied, and his house having been mobbed, he fled to Woburn, fifty miles away. But suspicion still followed him, and here he was again arrested, tried by a committee and again acquitted. From Woburn he went to Charlestown, where he is known to have applied to Washington for a commission in the patriot army, which was refused him on account of the interference of officers of the New Hampshire militia. Finding that his countrymen were bound to consider him disloyal, he became disgusted, and in the bitterness of his spirit he cried out: "My enemies are indefatigable in their efforts to distress me, and I find to my sorrow that they are but too successful."

Two months later he left Woburn, where he had been in hiding, never to return. Taken by his step-brother to the shore of Narraganset Bay, he was taken on board a British frigate and taken to Boston. On the evacuation of Boston in 1776, Thompson, still only twenty-three years of age, was sent to England with the news. In England he was received with great favor. He was taken into the office of the Secretary of State and made Secretary for the Province of Georgia. He also resumed his favorite studies, and at intervals of leisure he wrote and published the results of his investigations and experiments in the Transactions of the Royal Society, of which he was elected a fellow in 1778. This was a high honor for one of his age. He was afterwards appointed to a Colonelcy in the dragoons, a regiment of refugees raised in New York. He sailed for New York, but adverse winds drove the ship southward to the Carolinas, and before he assumed command Cornwallis had surrendered and the war was virtually over. He was in command, however, for a short time, of a detached company of cavalry in South Carolina, and is said to have had a brush with the celebrated Marion and to have routed him. Thompson had been proscribed in New Hampshire by the Alienation Act of 1778, and by an act of 1781, his property was confiscated. At the close of the war, there-

fore, it was impossible for such as he to live in this country, and he
resolved to go to the Continent and offer his services to the Austrian
Government in their threatened war against the Turks.   He went
to Strasburg, where the Prince Maximilian, afterwards Elector of
Bavaria was in camp, and his fine appearance made a favorable impression.   He became the guest of the Prince, and so favorably
impressed him that he gave him a letter to his uncle, the Elector,
and advised him to visit him, which he did.   This incident determined his destiny.   He was cordially welcomed at Munich, and was
there introduced into the Austrian Court.   The Turkish war cloud
had dissipated, but he was invited by the Elector to enter his service in a joint military and civil capacity, which place he accepted.
He was still a Colonel in the British army, and he immediately visited England with the view of asking permission to enter the service
of the Elector.   This was readily granted, and on taking leave of
England he received the order of Knighthood at the hands of the
King.

When Thompson returned to Munich he was thirty-one years of
age.   His reception was little less than royal.   A palatial residence
was set apart for him, a military staff was provided, and a corps of
servants.   Thompson at once set about informing himself concerning the social conditions of the Electorate.   He mastered its resour-
ces and learned its weaknesses.   He received from the Elector a
commission to introduce a new system of order and discipline into
the army, in which he was eminently successful.   Under the new
order of things, the soldier was converted into a citizen, was better
fed, better clothed and better paid.   Military gardens were established, and the soldiers became proficient in horticulture.   Army
workshops were also founded, in which all supplies needed by the
army were manufactured.   Munich at this time abounded in mendi-
cants, and in no place had begging been more successfully reduced
to a science.   Thompson resolved to abate the nuisance, and on
New Year's day, which had become the beggar's great day, he
caused every mendicant to be arrested; all who could work were
consigned to comfortable quarters and supplied with work.   The
grateful citizens contributed money and hospitals were built for
those who could not work, and the thing was accomplished.   This
was in the year seventeen hundred and ninety.

Sir Benjamin also established a military academy for the education of promising youth of all classes.   He took measures to im-

prove the breeds of horses and cattle in Bavaria, by the establishment of a large stock farm under able jurisdiction. He redeemed a tract of waste land near the city, nearly six miles in circumference, and upon a portion of it was his stock farm established. This is still known as "The English Garden." Honors were now heaped upon him. His fame had spread over Europe. King George the Third had already Knighted him. The King of Poland conferred on him the Knighthood of the order of St. Stanislaus. He was commissioned by the Elector, Major General of Cavalry, and appointed Counsellor of State and Head of the War Department. In seventeen hundred ninety-one, he was invested with the rank of a Count of the Holy Roman Empire, and he chose as the title of this new dignity the name of the little New Hampshire town where he had left his wife and infant daughter fifteen years before, and where they still lived, though his wife died there the following year.

The active mind of Count Rumford was not content with carrying out the details of the reforms above described, but engaged in other important investigations which covered a wide range. He engaged in meterological experiments, and studied carefully the properties of gunpowder. Among other pursuits, he devoted much time to the subject of furnishing nutritive and economical food to the poorer classes. He is said to have first utilized the use of the potato as a food. He published rules for the construction of public kitchens, investigated the nutritive properties of various kinds of food, and tabulated and published the results with scientific precision. Preeminent among his investigations is a series of experiments into the properties of heat, which annihilated all antecedent theories, and makes him the undisputed discoverer of that grand law of the correlation and equivalence of physical forces.

A dangerous illness at this time obliged him to suspend work, and he obtained permission to travel, visiting most of the countries on the continent. In seventeen hundred ninety-five, he revisited England. While there he called attention to the measures he had so successfully carried out in Germany, and many of them were adopted. At this time he contributed five thousand dollars to the American Academy of Science and Art, for the purpose of supplying a "Rumford Medal." He likewise gave a fund to the Royal Society of London, "for the purpose of encouraging such practical experiments in the generation and management of heat and light, as tend directly and powerfully to increase the enjoyments and com-

forts of life, especially in the lower and more numerous classes of
society." The first award of the "Rumford Medal" made by the
Royal Society, was to Count Rumford himself,—a fitting and graceful tribute for his own important discoveries in that direction.

Count Rumford never saw his wife after he first left America, and
she died sixteen years after the separation. In seventeen hundred
ninety-two, his only child, Sarah, whom he had left a child, afterwards known as Countess of Rumford, visited him in Munich,
where she was received at the Court and pensioned. She was born
in the Rolfe Mansion at Concord, October 18, 1774. She remained
abroad a large portion of the time after her mother's death, until
1845, when she returned to Concord and soon after died, bequeath-
ing her large property to relatives and various charitable and benev-
olent institutions.

Count Rumford's health again failing, and desiring to again visit
England, the Elector kindly made him Minister Plenipotentiary to
the Court of Saint James. Soon after this his thoughts were turned
toward his native land, and he wrote to the friend of his youth, Col.
Baldwin, asking him to procure for him some "little quiet retreat,
not far from his old home." He had correspondence with the
American minister with regard to the removal of his disabilities,
which elicited from the President of the United States a cordial
acknowledgement of the Count's illustrious labors for the good of
mankind, and an offer of patronage should he return. But nothing
came of it. The Count was soon engaged in other enterprises such
as the founding of the Royal Institution ; he also became entangled
in matrimonial affairs, which postponed the desired return and prevented it. In eighteen hundred and three he left England for the
last time. He went to Paris, where he was introduced to Bonaparte,
then Consul, and then proceeded to Munich, where he received a
magnificent reception. He returned to Paris, where he became fas-
cinated with a French lady, the widow of Lavoisier, the celebrated
chemist, whom he married. The marriage was not a happy one,
and in eighteen hundred fourteen, at Auteuil, which is included
within the walls of Paris, he died, and was buried in the local cemetery, where a simple monument marks his last resting place.

The fame of Count Rumford is lasting, and his career was most
remarkable. What might have been had he remained in America
and been loyal to the popular cause, it is difficult to tell. That he
was inclined to loyalty, there is not the least doubt, but he was

proud spirited, and the snspicion that was cast upon him and the treatment he received, drove him to desperation. It is not strange that he sought the British camp, nor that he went to England, but that he should return with a commission to fight his countrymen, is a dark stain upon his otherwise glorious record. He was a philanthropist in the highest sense of the word, his efforts being directed to the amelioration of the condition of the masses of the people. It is a matter of regret that he did not return to this country after having firmly established the monument of his genius, and spent a useful and honored old age among his kindred, instead of being ensnared by the charms and embittered by the disappointments of his second marriage. The poor of the world will ever love and bless his memory, and his life, after he left this country, is an eloquent tribute to the power of enthusiastic fidelity to a noble purpose.

CHAPTER VIII.

THE FIRST SETTLERS.

IT is agreed on all hands that Jonathan Keyes was the first person to settle within the limits of this town. He was born in Shrewsbury, Mass., Jan. 21, 1728, and was the son of Dea. Jonathan and Patience (Morse) Keyes. He married Sarah, daughter of Ebenezer Taylor, January 23, 1752. He purchased land in Sudbury Canada, now Bethel, in 1772, and again in 1774. He spent some years in Bethel before he came to Rumford, but just how many the records do not show. A deed recorded with the Cumberland records, recites that March 14, 1777, Jonathan Keyes of Sudbury Canada, sold to Samuel Ingalls of Fryeburg, four hundred acres, or four lots of land, situated and being on the south side of Androscoggin river, in a place called Sudbury Canada. The deed further states that upon one of the lots Mr. Keyes had made considerable improvement, had built a house, a barn for grain and another for English hay. January third preceding, Mr. Keyes had purchased of Dr. Ebenezer Harnden Goss, two full rights in the township of New Pennacook. That Mr. Keyes moved his family to Bethel, is not probable. Two of his sons, Ebenezer and Francis, were there with him, and it is stated on good authority that Mr. Keyes returned to Shrewsbury one fall, and left his two sons in care of his camp, and that for some reason not mentioned, he did not return until spring. Ebenezer was about fourteen years of age and Francis nine, and they remained in this then remote region all through the long and inclement winter with no companionship save that of the Indians. Ebenezer Keyes afterward settled in Jay, and has descendants in Franklin county. Jonathan Keyes died November 7, 1786; his wife died November 14, 1799.

In the absence of record evidence, it is often difficult after the lapse of a century, to know who was the first settler in any given town, and precisely when a settlement was made. Tradition cannot be relied upon. That Jonathan Keyes was the first white man to make his home in Rumford, and move his family here, has never been disputed. Hunters may have previously camped here, but they came not to make them a home. Among papers left by the late Francis Keyes of Rumford, is one which gives some account of the early settlement of the town. This paper is in the handwriting of Mr. Keyes, and as he was an actor and eye-witness of what he describes, it is entitled to the utmost confidence. Mr. Keyes wrote as follows :

"This town was granted February 3d, 1774, to Timothy Walker, Jr., and associates ; the condition of the grant was to put on thirty families within six years. The records having been lost, the grant was renewed April 13, 1979, and the time lengthened for completing the settlement five years from that time. The first proprietors' meeting was held at the house of Capt. Daniel Bradley in Haverhill, Mass., with leave to adjourn and hold future meetings in any town in this State, and if more convenient, in any town in New Hampshire. Said meeting was adjourned to Concord, N. H., and with one adjournment all subsequent meetings were held there until Aug. 31, 1807, when they were held in Rumford. In the Fall of 1776, the proprietors sent a committee to this town, consisting of Colonel Thomas Stickney, Ensign Jonathan Eastman, Dr. Ebenezer Harnden Goss and Ephraim Colby, to make a division of one hundred acres to each right. In 1777, my father, Jonathan Keyes of Shrewsbury, purchased four rights of land in this town, and on the tenth of March, 1777, set out with myself and my mother and came to New Gloucester. From there my father and I come to this town in the August following, and began a settlement where I now live, the first settlement made in this town. After bringing the farm forward so far as to support a small family, my father moved my mother in on the 29th day of October, 1779. In 1781, three other persons began making settlements in this town, and on the third of August of that year, a small scouting party of Indians from Canada, with one who before that time lived in these parts, commenced plundering in Sunday River Plantation and Sudbury Canada, and took some prisoners and killed two men in Peabody's Patent. Not considering it safe to continue here, we moved off on the sixth of the same month, and did not return until the Spring of 1783, and began our settlement anew. July 28, 1783, it was voted to lay out one hundred and thirty-four one hundred acre lots, and give thirty of the first settlers their pick out of the whole of them. In the Spring

4

of 1784, Philip Abbot, Jacob Eastman and Daniel Stickney had begun actual settlement. May 6, 1784, John Stevens of Concord, was chosen to petition for a longer time for settling said town, and obtained an extension of two years. Jan'y 2, 1786, John Stevens, Jonathan Eastman and Timothy Walker were appointed a committee to induce settlers to come into town, and were instructed to offer a bounty of six pounds to each actual settler within one year."

The early route to Sudbury Canada and New Pennacook, was by way of the Saco river to Fryeburg, and then by the Indian trail across through Lovell and Waterford. Standish was then the rallying point to settlers going to Fryeburg and beyond. Before 1781, when the family fled for safety to New Gloucester, a road had been opened between that town and Paris, rendering this route to the older settlements more feasible and expeditious. While the family was left in the border settlement, Mr. Keyes was preparing a home for them in this wilderness, and in 1783, after the Indian troubles in Maine had forever passed away, he returned to his clearing, and his was doubtless the only family that up to this time had ever lived within the limits of the town.* In June, 1788, Samuel Titcomb of Wells, the old surveyor, wrote to Leonard Jarvis that "a road had lately been cleared out from Butterfield to New Pennacook, Sudbury Canada, &c., which leads through a part of numbers I and II, and another road through parts of numbers III and IV, to Sudbury Canada, &c. In the settlements of Sudbury Canada and New Pennacook, supplies from navigation would be received by this route. The Amoscoggin river abounds in salmon and shad, and has good mill sites."

In just what order subsequent settlers came, there are no means of knowing, nor does it matter much. We know that Aaron Moor and Benjamin Lufkin were soon here, and that after 1784, settlers came in quite rapidly. In 1792, nine years after Mr. Keyes returned, a committee of the proprietors of the township appointed for the purpose, reported the following as the actual settlers in the town: On the north side of the Great River—Philip Abbot, Jacob Abbot, Jacob Eastman, Osgood Eaton, Jacob Farnum, Samuel Goodwin, Robert Hinkson, James Harper, Sarah Keyes, Francis Keyes, Nathaniel Knight, Moses Kimball, Stephen Putnam, Henry

---

* In his statement Mr. Keyes says "three other persons had begun making settlements," but in a statement entered on the town Clerk's records of Rumford, he states positively that to the time of the Indian raid into Bethel, no family except his father's had settled in the township.

Rolfe, Josiah Segar and John Stevens. James McAllister and Daniel Knight had commenced clearings, but were not recognized by the committee as actual settlers. On the south side of the river were David Abbot, Benjamin Elliot, Benjamin Farnum, David Farnum, Edmund Page, Joel Stone, Moses Stone and Benjamin Sweat, Jr. The lots they severally occupied will be found in the abstract of the proprietors' records. A few settlers had not taken up lots, and so their names do not appear in the above list. The death of the pioneer, Jonathan Keyes, was perhaps the first in the plantation. There is no record of a previous one. The first marriage was probably that of Stephen Putnam. This was Stephen Putnam, Jr., but the junior was not added to his name until his father came a few years later. Stephen Putnam, Jr., was married to Sally Elliot, by Rev. John Strickland, Dec. 25, 1789. It is said that Stephen Putnam, Jr., brought the first set of blacksmith's tools into town and shod the first horse. His wife spun and wove the first web of cloth in town. He died July 4, 1853, and his wife survived him six years. Like many of the early settlers, they lived to see "the wilderness bud and blossom as the rose," as the result of their privations and hardships.

DIRECT TAX OF 1798.

In one thousand seven hundred and ninety-eight, a direct tax was laid upon the real estate of the country by the General Government. The tax in Pennacook, now Rumford, was assessed October first of that year. Elijah Livermore of Livermore, was the principal assessor, and his assistants were Nathaniel Perley, William Livermore and Stephen Putnam, the latter known in Pennacook as Stephen Putnam, Jr. Twenty-seven houses were taxed in Pennacook, and thirty-seven resident owners of land. The non-resident lands were also taxed. This list of tax-payers has an historical value, as it shows approximately, at least, the number of households at this period. The population was probably made up of twenty-seven families, and ten single men who had bought lots and were making clearings. It will be noticed that Timothy Walker of Concord, and John Stevens' heirs, also of Concord, were large owners of the non-resident lands of the town :

Names.	No. acres.	Value.	Names.	No. acres.	Value.
Philip Abbot	500	$800	Francis Keyes	1300	$1450
David Abbot	200	500	Benj. Lufkin	200	540
Jacob Abbot	420	720	John Martin	580	735
Osgood Eaton	100	400	James McAlister	100	200
Benj. Elliot	180	480	Edmund Page	100	200
Jacob Farnum	200	480	Stephen Putnam	700	603
David Farnum	400	600	Stephen Putnam, Jr.,	230	375
Benj. Farnum	400	550	Benj. Rolfe	487	600
Joshua Graham	400	544	Henry Rolfe	300	385
Gustavus A. Goss	100	500	Jeremiah Richardson,	100	320
Samuel Goss	100	350	Joshua Ripley	300	250
William Godwin	200	420	Samuel Stevens	100	100
Robert Hinkson	100	350	Benj. Sweat	100	311
Abram Howe	100	170	Nathaniel Sanborn	100	250
Samuel Hinkson	100	85	John Taylor	200	355
Phineas Howe	120	320	Ebenezer Virgin	100	260
James Harper	300	480	John Whittemore	300	250
Moses Kimball	100	255	Abel Wheeler	300	340
Daniel Knight	480	535			

NON-RESIDENT.

Names.	No. acres.	Value.	Names.	No. acres.	Value.
Jeremiah Andrews	600	500	Ezekiel Merrill	100	85
Enoch Adams	300	250	Henry Martin	480	350
Joshua Atherton	300	250	John Martin	100	85
Increase Dolly	100	260	Capt. Marsh	300	250
Richard Dolloff	200	500	Wm. R. Partridge	100	123
John Chandler	300	250	Heirs of John Stevens	5260	4370
Ephraim Farnum	300	250			
Benj. Farnum	300	250	Eleazer Twitchell	300	250
Moses Gale	300	250	Col. Timo'y Walker,	6700	5625

In 1801, returns were made by the town of Rumford to the Massachusetts Secretary of State, of which the following is an abstract: Males over twenty-one years of age, 56; grist mills, 2; saw mills, 2; barns, 35; tillage land, 311 acres; bushels wheat grown, 70; bushels rye, 20; bushels oats, 333; bushels corn, 283; bushels beans, 37; acres English upland mowing, 244; acres pasturage, 198; number of cows, 109; number of horses, 41; number of oxen, 70; number of steers, 117; number of swine, 38.

The statistics in this chapter show the growth and development of the town to the close of the century, and for eighteen years after Mr. Keyes returned from New Gloucester, and the actual settlement may be said to have begun. The plantation of New Pennacook was organized October 20, 1795. A petition signed by Aaron Moor, Francis Keyes, Benjamin Elliot, Benjamin Sweat and Edmund Page, was presented to Isaac Parsons, Esq., asking for a warrant for that purpose, and the meeting was held at the house of

Joshua Graham. The call provided for the election of clerk, assessors, and all other necessary plantation officers. The records of this and subsequent plantation meetings are probably not in existence, and it was only by mere chance that the warrant with the return of Francis Keyes thereon, was preserved. It is known that Francis Keyes was elected plantation clerk, and this is all we do know of the proceedings. After a plantation life of four years, the inhabitants began to think of incorporation as a town, and their action and that of the General Court thereon, have been given in a preceding chapter.

CHAPTER IX.

BRIEF SKETCH OF OXFORD COUNTY.

WHEN Jonathan Keyes came to New Pennacook to select him a lot for a homestead, the wilderness of western Maine had been invaded at many points. General Jonathan Frye begun the settlement of Fryeburg in 1762. Like Rumford, most of the first settlers were from Concord, New Hampshire. Capt. Henry Young Brown of Haverhill, settled Brownfield a year later. Lovell was settled in 1779, Hiram in 1774, Porter in 1781, Waterford in 1775. These were Saco River towns. On the Androscoggin, Turner was settled about 1772, Livermore a little later; Bethel in 1774, and Norway in 1781. Ezekiel Merrill, the first Andover settler, came from Andover, Massachusetts, in 1786, and was the sole occupant of that region, save straggling Indians, for over two years. Paris was settled in 1781, Buckfield in 1777, and Jay about the same time as Paris. Sumner and Hartford, the territory of which was originally called Butterfield, were settled soon after 1780. The small party of first settlers in Rumford, therefore, had neighbors not very far distant, but there were no roads connecting the different colonies, and no communication was feasible, except on foot, through the rough paths of the forest. Spotted trees guided the traveller between the different settlements, but when journeying outside he was obliged to depend partly on his own sagacity and partly on the course of the sun and the position of the mountains.

A census of the District of Maine was taken in 1790, but New Pennacook was not then incorporated and made no report. In

1800, the town was incorporated and its population was then two hundred and sixty-two. There were then between fifty and sixty families in the town. Rumford was in the County of Cumberland until 1805, when the County of Oxford was created, made up of towns which had previously been in the counties of Cumberland and York. The act erecting these towns into a county, was as follows:

"That the counties of York and Cumberland shall be divided by a line beginning at a place called the Crooked Ripples on the Androscoggin river, at the southeast corner of the town of Turner, from thence to run westerly on the dividing line between the towns of Turner and Minot, to the most northeasterly corner of the said town of Minot; from thence southwesterly on the lines between the towns of Minot and Hebron; thence northwesterly on the line between Hebron and Otisfield, to the town of Norway; thence westerly and northerly on the line between the towns of Otisfield and Norway, to the southeasterly corner of the town of Waterford; thence westerly on the line between said Waterford and Otisfield to the northeasterly corner of the town of Bridgton; thence westerly on the northerly line of said Bridgton to the northeast corner thereof; thence southerly on the westerly side of said Bridgton to the southeast corner thereof; thence westerly on the north line of the town of Baldwin and Prescott's Grant, to Saco river; thence down the middle of said Saco river to the mouth of the river called the Great Ossipee; thence westerly by a line drawn on the middle of the river last mentioned, to the line of New Hampshire, and the county of York and Cumberland aforesaid: That all that part and parcel of the counties of York and Cumberland situated on the northerly side of the line before described, and extending northerly and westerly so as to comprehend all the territory lying between the State of New Hampshire and the County of Kennebec, and on the northerly side of the line aforesaid, excepting the towns of Wilton, Temple, Avon, and township number three on Sandy river, northerly of Avon, which towns shall be considered as belonging to the County of Kennebec, shall be and the same is erected into an entire and distinct county by the name of Oxford."

The subjoined list embraces the original towns in Oxford County, the date of their incorporation, and the name of their first Representative to the Great and General Court:

Paris ....June 20, 1793.......... Elias Stowell.
Hebron...............March 6, 1792.......... William C. Whitney.
Buckfield ....March 16, 1793......... Enoch Hall.
Turner ....July 7, 1786 .... John Turner.
Livermore............February 28, 1795...... Simeon Waters.
Hartford.............June 13, 1798.......... David Warren.
Sumner .... June 13, 1798.......... Simeon Barrett, Jr.
Norway ....March 9, 1797.......... Luther Farrar.

Fryeburg..............January 11, 1777.......John McMillan.
Brownfield............February 20, 1802......Joseph Howard.
Lovell ....November 15, 1800 .....Philip C. Johnson.
Waterford.............March 2, 1797..........Eber Rice.
Albany ....June 20, 1803..........Asa Cummings.
Bethel.. ....June 10, 1790..........Eliphaz Chapman.
Jay ....February 26, 1795......James Starr, Jr.
Dixfield ....June 21, 1803..........Silas Barnard.
Rumford...............February 21, 1800......William Wheeler.
Gilead................June 23, 1804..........Eliphaz Chapman, Jr.
Newry ....June 15, 1805..........Melvin Stowe.
East Andover..........June 23, 1804......... .Edward L. Poor.

The following are the names with the dates of incorporation, of the towns incorporated since the County of Oxford was formed:

Byron ....January 24, 1833.
Canton................February 5, 1821.   (Taken from Jay).
Denmark...............February 20, 1807.
Greenwood.............February 2, 1816.
Grafton ....March 19, 1852.
Hanover ... .February 14, 1843.   (Taken from Bethel).
Hiram.................February 27, 1814.
Mason.................February 3, 1843.
Mexico................February 13, 1843.
Oxford................February 27, 1829.   (Taken from Hebron).
Peru..................February 5, 1821, (changed from Partridgetown).
Porter................February 20, 1807.
Roxbury ....March 17, 1835.
Stoneham ....January 31, 1834.
Stowe. ....January 28, 1833.
Sweden ....February 26, 1813.
Upton.................February 9, 1860.
Woodstock ....February 7, 1815.
Carthage ....February 20, 1826.
Weld ....February 8, 1816.

Franklin county was erected in 1838, and took from Oxford county the towns of Jay, Carthage and Weld. The town of Berlin, which was formerly an Oxford county town, was absorbed in the town of Philips, and the name of Berlin was dropped. Androscoggin county was erected in 1854, and took the towns of Livermore and Turner. The following statistical table taken from Greenleaf's Survey of the State, shows the comparative standing of Oxford county towns in population, for the years specified:

POPULATION.

Towns.	1790.	1800.	1810.	1820.
Andover	22	175	264	368
Albany	–	69	165	288
Bethel.......................	100	616	975	1,267
Brownfield.............	250	288	388	727
Buckfield	453	1,002	1,251	1,501

Towns.	1790.	1800.	1810.	1820.
Denmark	–	–	436	972
Dixfield	–	–	403	595
Dixfield and Mexico	–	137	–	–
Fryeburg	547	734	1,004	1,057
Gilead	–	88	215	328
Greenwood	–	–	273	392
Hartford and Sumner	189	–	–	–
Hartford	–	243	720	1,113
Hebron, including Oxford	530	981	1,211	1,727
Hiram	192	203	336	972
Jay, including Canton	103	430	1,107	1,614
Livermore	–	863	1,560	2,174
Lovell and Sweden	–	147	365	–
Lovell	–	–	202	430
Mexico	–	–	14	148
Newry	–	92	202	203
Norway	448	609	1,010	1,330
Paris	–	844	1,320	1,894
Peru	–	–	92	343
Porter	–	272	292	487
Rumford	–	262	629	871
Sweden	–	–	–	249
Turner	349	722	1,129	1,726
Waterford	150	535	860	1,035
Woodstock	–	–	236	509
Weld	–	–	318	495

CHAPTER X.

ABSTRACT OF TOWN RECORDS.—1800–1820.

THE town records of Rumford commence with the incorporation in the year eighteen hundred. They have been as well kept and are in as good state of preservation as those of most other towns. The town has been fortunate in preserving them from the ravages of fire, for the records of so many towns have been burned that their destruction by that element has come to be regarded as only a question of time. The details of town meetings, as a rule, make dry and uninteresting reading. The abstract of the doings of town meetings which follow, have been made as brief as possible, and at the same time show the growth and progress of the town. This will be seen in the increased amount of money raised from year to year for various purposes, notably that for schools, and in the efforts to secure good roads and bridges for the accommodation of public travel. The principal town officers since the incorporation are given together in another place, and only a few are given in the abstract. The proceedings of the first meeting only, are given in full :

WARRANT.

CUMBERLAND, SS.

To MR. FRANCIS KEYES *of Rumford, in said County, yeoman,*

GREETING :

In the name of the Commonwealth of Massachusetts, you are hereby required to notify and warn all freeholders and other inhabitants of said town of Rumford, qualified to vote in town meetings as the law directs, to meet at your dwelling house in said Rumford, on Monday the fourteenth day of April next, at eleven o'clock in the forenoon, to act and vote on the following articles, viz :

1st. To choose a moderator to regulate said meeting.
2d. To choose a town clerk.
3d. To choose three or more suitable persons to serve as selectmen the year ensuing.
4th. To choose any or all other town officers which towns are by

law authorized to choose at their annual meeting in March or April.

5th. To vote and agree at what time in the month of March or April their annual meetings shall be held in future.

6th. To vote in what way and manner their meetings shall be warned in future.

And make due return of this warrant and your doings hereon, unto myself, on or before the fourteenth day of April next.

Given under my hand and seal at Norway, in said county, this twenty-fourth day of March, A. D. 1800.

[L. s.] JOB EASTMAN, *Justice of the Peace.*

Rumford, April 1, 1800.

Pursuant to the foregoing warrant, I have notified the inhabitants of said town, qualified as therein expressed, to meet at the time and place and for the purposes within mentioned.

FRANCIS KEYES.

I hereby certify that the above return was made on the back of the warrant that was given out under the act of incorporation, by Job Eastman, Justice of the Peace, and by mistake was omitted to be recorded at the bottom of said warrant, therefore I have annexed it to the margin of said book, against where it ought to have been recorded.

Attest : FRANCIS KEYES, *Town Clerk.*

THE MEETING.

Rumford, April 14, 1800.

Pursuant to the foregoing warrant, the inhabitants of said town being assembled, the meeting was opened and passed the following votes, viz. :

1st. Made choice of Joshua Graham for moderator.

2d. Made choice of Francis Keyes for town clerk, and was sworn in open town meeting by the moderator.

3d. Made choice of Francis Keyes, Philip Abbot and John Martin for selectmen and assessors.

4th. Made choice of David Farnum for town treasurer.

Voted, that the collection of taxes be vendued, and struck off to the lowest bidder, with his getting two bondsmen, and (it) was struck off to Edmund Page at six cents on each dollar for collecting, and (he) was chosen collector accordingly, with Gustavus A. Goss and John Whittemore for bondsmen, and was accepted by the town.

Voted, to conclude the business of this meeting by hand votes.

Made choice of Edmund Page for constable.

Made choice of David Farnum, John Martin, Francis Keyes and Osgood Eaton for surveyors of highways.

Made choice of Benjamin Elliot and Daniel Knight for surveyors of lumber of all sorts.

Made choice of Francis Keyes, Philip Abbot and John Martin for fence viewers.

Made choice of Benjamin Farnum, John Whittemore and Joshua Ripley for tythingmen.

Made choice of Gustavus A. Goss, John Whittemore, John Martin and Daniel Knight for hog-reeves.

Made choice of John Whittemore and Joshua Graham for pound keepers.

Made choice of Francis Keyes, Philip Abbot and John Martin for field drivers.

5th. Voted to hold their annual meeting on the first Monday of April, annually.

6th. Voted, that one warrant should be sufficient for warning a meeting, a copy of which shall be posted up by the constable, at the place where the meeting is to be held.

All the foregoing officers were sworn to the faithful discharge of their several duties, before Gustavus A. Goss, except the town clerk and said Goss.

A true record.

Attest: FRANCIS KEYES, *Town Clerk.*

The next meeting was held at the house of Benjamin Farnum, on the first day of May, 1800, when the following votes were passed:

Made choice of Abel Wheeler for moderator.

Voted, to raise twenty dollars to defray the charges of the town, the ensuing year.

Voted, to raise three hundred dollars to be laid out on the road, at twelve and one-half cents per hour from the first of May until the first of July, and nine hours per day, and from that time to the first of October, nine cents an hour and eight hours a day.

A meeting for the acceptance of town ways laid out by the selectmen, was held at the house of Benjamin Farnum, August thirtieth. The first road accepted was one beginning at Bethel line on the South side of the river, and running down the river eight and a half miles to a point a little below David Farnum's place. Another road was described as beginning at the town line, north side of the Great river, at Swift river below Ebenezer Virgin's place, "to a leaning pine standing on the bank of the river opposite Mr. Graham's." Two other short roads were accepted, one beginning near Philip Abbot's home, and the other near Mr. Richardson's corner.

Another meeting to consider the subject of roads was held September twenty-ninth. It was voted to accept the survey of a road from Abel Wheeler's barn to the West line of Rumford. Also a road from a beech tree below Stickney brook, on the South side of the river, to the East line of the town. Voted to discharge Stephen Putnam from paying the taxes of one thousand seven hundred and ninety-eight, and to give John Taylor the taxes assessed against him, it being the first tax ever assessed in town.

Another meeting was called on November third, of the male inhabitants, twenty-one years of age, having a freehold estate within the town, of the annual income of ten dollars, or any estate to the value of two hundred dollars, and residents of Rumford for one year, to vote for member of Congress for the second Eastern district. Peleg Wadsworth had all the votes thrown, numbering seven. These were all the meetings held during Rumford's first year as a town.

1801. On the sixth day of April, one thousand eight hundred and one, a meeting was called to vote for State officers, with the following results:

Caleb Strong, for Governor, had thirty-two votes, and Elbridge Gerry, five. For Lieutenant Governor, Edward H. Robbins had thirty-two votes, and Samuel Phillips, eleven. For Senators and Councillors, John K. Smith had twenty-six, and Stephen Longfellow thirty-one votes, respectively.

The town business was also transacted on the same day. The town clerk and treasurer were re-elected, and Francis Keyes, Stephen Putnam and Jeremiah Richardson were chosen selectmen. James C. Harper bid off the taxes, and was elected constable. Gustavus A. Goss, Benjamin Sweat and Benjamin Farnum were his bondsmen. Among the new names in the list of officers elected this year, were Richard Dolloff, William Virgin, Daniel Martin, Phineas How and Moses Kimball.

It was voted to raise fifty dollars for town charges, sixty dollars for schools, and three hundred dollars for roads at eighty-three cents per day. A committee consisting of Francis Keyes, Stephen Putnam and Jeremiah Richardson was raised, to divide the town into School Districts.

The selectmen were made a committee "to purchase burying yards."

At an adjourned meeting held July first, the report of the committee dividing the town into five school districts and describing the bounds of each, was accepted. The report also provided that the money arising from the taxes of non-resident owners, should be equally divided among the several districts, according to the number of house-holders in each.

At a meeting holden August eighteenth, the selectmen made a report recommending that guide posts be erected at the following points: One on the main road at the corner leading to Harper's Ferry; one at the corner leading to Paris; one at the corner below Abbot's Mills; the above to be erected on the South side of the river. On the north side of the river, one at the corner of the road near Phineas Howe's; one at the corner near the mouth of Split Brook, so-called, and one at the angle of the road leading from the mouth of Split Brook to East Andover. The selectmen were authorized to erect the above guide posts. At a meeting October third, the town declined to send a delegate to Paris, to a convention called to consider the subject of a new county.

1802. At the election in one thousand eight hundred and two, for Governor, Caleb Strong had twenty-seven votes, and Elbridge Gerry, seven.

At the annual meeting this year the selectmen elected were Francis Keyes, Philip Abbot and John Martin. John Puffer bid off the collection of taxes, and was elected constable. Among the new names in the list of town officers were those of Stephen Putnam, Jr., John Howe, Jacob Abbot, Phineas Wood and Benjamin Rolfe. Seventy dollars were raised for schools, sixty for town charges, and four hundred for roads. No other town meetings were held this year, except for the election of member of Congress.

1803. The meeting for one thousand eight hundred and three was holden at the dwelling house of Silas How, April fourth. Lists of the principal town officers are given in tabular form elsewhere, and will not be repeated here. James Colman Harper again bid off the taxes. The new names among the town officers this year were Kimball Martin, Ephraim Colby, Nathan Silver, Nathaniel F. Higgins, Israel Putnam and Nathan Brown. Eighty dollars each for schools and for town charges were raised, and five hundred for roads. It was voted to erect a meeting house on the north side of the river, as near the center as may be from east to west on the river road. Francis Keyes, Ebenezer Virgin and John Martin were chosen a locating committee. The widow McAlister's tax for the year one thousand eight hundred, was remitted. One hundred dollars were raised toward building the meeting house. It was voted to hold annual meetings hereafter on the second Tuesday of March. At an adjourned meeting, the committee on location of a meeting house reported in favor of a spot half way, or thereabout, between Swift and Ellis rivers and a little below Split Brook. It was voted to build a house forty feet square, twelve foot post, and with a hip roof. Samuel Knight was excused from paying an old tax. The frame of the proposed meeting house was struck off to Francis Keyes at forty dollars. He also bid off the boarding and shingling for forty-six dollars. At an adjourned meeting June sixth, Enoch Adams had a tax remitted, and Enoch Brister was released from certain obligations relative to bidding off school lands. Thirty dollars additional were raised for the meeting house, and the frame erected by Francis Keyes was accepted. At a meeting December fifteenth, Francis Keyes was chosen a committee to attend a convention at Paris, to consider the subject of the erection of a new county.

1804. The annual meeting in eighteen hundred and four, was held at the house of Joshua Graham, March thirteenth. One hundred dollars were raised for schools, fifty for town charges, and six hundred dollars for roads ; also thirty dollars for the church building. The selectmen were directed to lay out a burying ground on the parsonage land, and make report. Among the new names introduced at this meeting were Samuel Stevens, Samuel Simpson, Benjamin Morse and Jacob Farnum. James Harper was collector and constable. The meeting was adjourned to the house of Nathan Hunting. Joshua Graham was elected collector of taxes at this meeting, with Henry Rolfe and Jeremiah Richardson as bondsmen. This meeting was adjourned to the meeting house in Rumford. It was voted to choose two selectmen and assessors, and the meeting accordingly elected Abel Wheeler and Kimball Martin. The boarding and shingling of the meeting house, as done by Francis Keyes, were accepted. At an adjourned meeting in January, the town voted in favor of the erection of a new county, as petitioned for by Levi Hubbard and others.

1805. In eighteen hundred and five, the town meeting was held in the new meeting house. Joshua Graham was chosen collector and constable. The new names on the record of this year were Abraham Howe, Nathan Silver, Kimball Martin, Hezekiah Hutchins, Wm. Godwin, Josiah Hall, John E. Adams and William Wheeler. School committee chosen, Francis Keyes, Joshua Graham and John Whittemore. One hundred and fifty dollars were raised for schools, one hundred for town charges, and eight hundred for roads, one hundred dollars to be laid out in winter at fifty cents per day. Jacob Farnum, John Whittemore and Benjamin Farnum were made a committee on accounts. A road was accepted from Ephraim Colby's to the mouth of Ellis river. Fifty dollars were raised for the purchase of military stores. James Sullivan for Governor, had forty-nine votes, and Caleb Story, fourteen. The town treasurer was authorized to take James C. Harper's note for the balance of taxes collected by him, payable in one year with interest. A road was accepted leading from Ebenezer Virgin's to Samuel Hinkson's; also several other minor roads. It was voted to sell at auction the timber on the easterly side of the brook that falls into Nathan Hunting's mill pond, and the same was struck off to Hunting at one hundred dollars. The town voted in favor of Paris as the shire town and against the pretensions for Fryeburg.

1806. At the meeting in eighteen hundred and six, Francis Keyes was again elected chairman of the Board of Selectmen, but declined to serve. He was re-elected clerk. Joshua Graham was continued as collector. Benjamin Lufkin and Jeremiah Hall were among the new officers. School districts were authorized to choose their own agents. One hundred and sixty dollars were raised for schools and the usual amount for other purposes. Weights and measures for the use of the town were provided this year at a cost of fifty-four dollars. William Wheeler procured a jury box for the use of the town. A meeting was held September fifteenth, and it was voted to build a bridge across Ellis river near the mouth, the job to be set up at auction and completed within one year. Nathan Hunting, Kimball Martin and Daniel Knight were made a committee on location. It was voted that the burying yard be cleared, fenced on three sides with logs, and the fourth with boards. At an adjourned meeting, the bridge committee reported in favor of erecting it at the point where the river was forded, and that the bridge should be supported on three piers. The bridge was built by Richard Estes, and one hundred and seventy dollars paid therefor.

1807. At the meeting in eighteen hundred and seven, Francis Keyes was again elected clerk and chairman of the selectmen. William Wheeler bid off the taxes and was made constable. Ninety dollars were raised for town charges, eight hundred dollars for ways, and one hundred and seventy dollars for schools. John Thompson's name is mentioned this year in the town records. James Sullivan had fifty votes for Governor, Caleb Strong eight, and Levi Lincoln two. A meeting was held April sixth, to consider the question of separation from Massachusetts, and resulted in fifty-seven votes in favor and five opposed. Dorcas Winkley, a pauper, was set up at auction, and her support for one year struck off to Cotton Elliott, at seventeen dollars and seventy-five cents. A committee was appointed to report a readjustment of the school districts in Rumford; at a subsequent meeting this committee made a report which was accepted. Nathan Hunting was authorized to make a door for the meeting house and hang the same; also to make the window frames and sashes and procure and set the glass, for all which he should be paid twenty-five dollars. The bridge built across Ellis river was accepted.

1808. William Wheeler was chosen moderator at the March meeting of one thousand eight hundred and eight, and Jackson Graham, clerk. The highway surveyors this year, were Daniel Martin, Benj. Elliot, Colton Elliot, Daniel Knight, Israel Putnam, Osgood Eaton, Abel Wheeler, Stephen Farnum, John Kimball, Enoch Adams and John Rolfe. Sixty dollars were raised for town charges, two hundred for schools, eight hundred for roads and twenty for support of poor. It was voted that one-third of the money be expended for women's school, and the balance for men's. Simon Virgin was collector this year. Joshua Graham was chosen agent to represent the town at a court of common pleas to be held at Paris. A road was discontinued from the foot of Daniel Knight's Hill to Simon Virgin's house. It was voted to build a town pound within twenty rods of the meeting house. Voted to raise eighteen dollars to pay the minute men.

1809. Joshua Graham was elected clerk in eighteen hundred and nine. Edmund Page was chosen collector. It was voted that the selectmen serve as school committee. Two hundred and fifty dollars were raised for schools, and for other purposes, the same as last year. The survey of a road was reported leading from Ephraim Colby's on the upland, to Jesse Duston's shop. Levi Lincoln had fifty-two votes for Governor, and Christopher Gore had twenty-four. It was voted to give Nathan Adams fifty dollars besides his and his son's taxes, to build a comfortable wheel road from Ellis River, by his house to the west line of the town. Benjamin Simpson, William Simpson, Stephen Hodsdon and Hezekiah Hutchins are mentioned in the record of this year. Nathaniel F. Higgins was allowed for three pails used as camp kettles.

1810 Hezekiah Hutchins was chosen moderator, and for highway surveyors, Simon Virgin, Colman Godwin, Stephen Putnam, Jr., Aaron Stevens, Nathan Silver, Hezekiah Hutchins, Stephen Farnum, John Kimball, Samuel Farnum, John Howe, Benjamin Sweat and Nathaniel Farnum. John Rolfe was chosen collector and constable. One hundred dollars were raised for town charges, two hundred and fifty for schools, one thousand for roads and one hundred for the support of the gospel, and Hezekiah Hutchins, Wm. Wheeler and Joshua Graham were made a committee to hire a minister. The selectmen were authorized to manage with Mrs. Winkley and her children as they should think best. The following stands on the record: "This may certify whom it may concern that the Methodist Episcopal church in the town of Rumford have made choice of Abel Wheeler and Ebenezer Virgin for the time being, to form a committee with the public teacher of said church to give certificates to those who usually attend on the administration of the word in such manner as the law directs."

JOSHUA RANDAL, Preacher.

Wm. Wheeler was chosen agent to look after a road indictment found against the town. It was voted to build a bridge over Concord River, and the job was struck off to Luther Bean for ninety dollars.

It was voted to give Rev. Samuel R. Hall two hundred and fifty dollars, sixty in money and the balance in produce, per year, so long as he should be able to perform his duties in the town as Congregational minister; conditioned that he should relinquish all right to the ministerial lands within the town. It was voted that Mr. Hall might be absent four Sundays in a year, and a church committee was chosen, consisting of Nathan Adams, Peter C. Virgin, Hezekiah Hutchins, Benj. Farnum and Daniel Knight. It was voted to ask the Legislature for permission to dispose of the public lands, and that Francis Keyes, William Wheeler, Daniel Knight, Nathan Adams, Joshua Graham, Hezekiah Hutchins and Peter C. Virgin, be a board of trustees to have charge of the funds arising from such sale. The town was represented in the General Court this year for the first time. William Wheeler was elected, receiving thirty-seven out of forty-eight votes. In Francis Keyes' account for laying a road, he charged "paid William Witt for rum, sixty-seven cents., and paid Esquire Smith for rum, one dollar."

1811. Francis Keyes was again chosen clerk, and John Rolfe constable and collector. Three hundred dollars were raised for schools, eight hundred for roads, one hundred for town charges, and one hundred for preaching. The selectmen were authorized to draw an order on the treasury for the minister tax to the amount of the taxes of those who, in their opinion, will conscientiously pay such taxes, and that the warrant be drawn in favor of a committee chosen by the Methodists. The Concord river bridge was completed and accepted. A list of jurors was accepted, made up as follows: Philip Abbot, Enoch Adams, Nathan Adams, Benj. Elliot, Osgood Eaton, Daniel Farnum, Zebediah Farnum, Jacob Farnum, Benj. Farnum, Joshua Graham, John Howe, Hezekiah Hutchins, Nathan Hunting, Francis Keyes, Daniel Knight, Kimball Martin, Jeremiah Richardson, Edmund Page, William Virgin, Eben Virgin, William Wheeler and Abel Wheeler. And of petit jurors: Henry Abbot, Jeremiah Virgin, Nathan Adams, Jr., Luther Bean, Cotton Elliot, Stephen Farnum, Jeremiah Farnum, John Farnum, Samuel Farnum, Nathaniel Farnum, Increase Dolly, Daniel Greenleaf, William Godwin, Aaron Graham, Samuel Hinkson, Phineas Howe, Ezra Hoyt, Abraham Howe, Robert Hinkson, John Kimball, Joseph Lufkin, Daniel Martin, Stephen Putnam, Jr., Jonathan Stevens, Samuel Putnam, Israel Putnam, Aaron Stevens, Benj. Sweat, Samuel Stevens, Nathan Brown, Simon Virgin, Phineas Wood and Joel Howe.

1812. Colman Goodwin bid off the taxes and was chosen constable. Among the highway surveyors were Samuel Goss, Caleb Eastman, John W. Farnum and John Puffer. For school committee the town made choice of Peter C. Virgin, Joshua Graham, Daniel Knight, William Wheeler, Joseph Wardwell, Nathan Adams, Enoch Adams and Rev. Samuel R. Hall. One year's salary was voted to Rev. Samuel R. Hall. Three hundred dollars were raised for schools, and the usual sums for other purposes. "Voted Isaac W. Clisby, for keeping Samuel Clark forty-two weeks, nineteen dollars and sixty-four cents." A representative to the General Court was again chosen this year, and William Wheeler was elected, receiving fifty-four out of seventy-nine votes cast. It was voted that the pay of the soldiers detached for the service of the United States, be made up to ten dollars per month, from the town treasury. Peter C. Virgin was chosen agent to answer to the indictment found against the road from the meeting house to Swift river bridge; also voted that the same agent answer to the charge against the town for disposing of twenty pounds of gunpowder.

1813. William Wheeler was chosen town clerk, and Colman Godwin, collector. The usual amount of money was raised, including two hundred and fifty dollars for Rev. Samuel R. Hall. The support of Samuel Clark was struck off to Francis Smart at fifty cents per week. Ephraim Carter's name appears on the record. William Phillips had thirty votes for Lieut.-Governor, and William King had fifty-eight. For Governor, Caleb Strong had thirty-six votes, and Joseph B. Farnum, sixty. It was voted to build a house for a town magazine, to stand on the land of Colman Godwin. Voted not to send a representative to the Legislature. John Swain's name appears. Another indictment had been found against a road and Peter C. Virgin was instructed to look after it.

1814. David Kimball bid off the taxes to collect for nothing, and was chosen constable. The school committeemen were Peter C. Virgin, Abel Wheeler and Dr. Benjamin Flint. The support of Samuel Clark while a minor, was struck off to Phineas Wood for what work he could make him do. Just one hundred votes were thrown for Governor this year, of which Caleb Strong had thirty-nine, and Samuel Dexter sixty-one. Colman Godwin was chosen sexton. Voted "that every man shall kill his thistles." A bridge across Ellis river was provided for and the job struck off to Phineas Wood at two hundred dollars. At a meeting in September, Peter C. Virgin was chosen collector of taxes, and Francis Smart, constable. A new road was accepted this year to connect with the new Ellis river bridge. At a meeting holden March 29, 1815, it was voted to give Rev. Daniel Gould a call to settle over the Congregational church, and a committee was chosen to communicate with him.

1815. William Wheeler was made clerk, and Ephraim Powers, collector and constable. Elijah Mansur was one of the highway surveyors. The usual sums were raised for various purposes. Voted it inexpedient to send a representative to the Legislature. At a meeting in November, Joshua Graham was chosen collector and constable. Voted unanimously in favor of separation from Massachusetts.

1816. David Kimball was chosen collector and constable. The highway surveyors were Eben Virgin, Jr., James Godwin, Joshua Graham, David Farnum, Jeremiah Virgin, William Wheeler, John Swain, Aaron Virgin, Kimball Martin, John Dolloff, John Kimball, Elijah Mansur and Aaron Stevens. Surveyors of lumber: Aaron Virgin, Daniel Knight, Nathan Adams, Jr., Ezra Hoyt, John Thompson and Rufus Virgin. Voted that William Virgin, Osgood Eaton, Nathan Brown, Jeremiah Richardson, Robert and Samuel Hinkson, John Swain, Joseph Hall, Caleb Eastman, Moses and Daniel Carlton, with their farms, constitute in part the eighth school district. On the question of separation, the town voted in favor, fifty-four votes; against, eighteen. Peter C. Virgin was elected representative.

1817. Edmund Page agreed to collect the taxes without compensation, and was elected collector and constable. The names of Francis Cushman, Charles Adams, Samuel Bartlett, Samuel Lufkin, Asa Graham and Wade Moor, appear on the records. For Governor, William King had fifty-seven votes, and William Phillips forty-five. Voted to re-fence the burying ground, and have a gate with iron hinges. Phineas Wood agreed to do the job for sixteen dollars. Among the town's poor set up at auction this year were Burry, Melinda and Susanna Colby. The support of Ephraim Colby was also set up and bid off by Hezekiah Hutchins, at two dollars and fifty cents per week, "to be moved as soon as Dr. Joseph Adams says he can be." At the same meeting, a committee was appointed to confer with the town of Bethel, respecting the legal residence of these Colbys.

1818. John E. Adams was chosen collector and constable. Samuel Putnam, Jr., Stephen Putnam, Jr., Merrill Farnum, Otis Howe, Wm. Frost, Joseph H. Wardwell and George Graham, were chosen hog-reeves. Two hundred dollars were raised for schools, and one thousand for roads. It was voted that the law restricting the killing of snipe should be repealed. It was voted to re-district the town for school purposes. Peter C. Virgin was re-elected representative, receiving thirty votes to ten for Daniel Knight.

1819. Peter C. Virgin was elected clerk, and also treasurer. Alvan Bolster's name appears first on the record this year; also Obadiah Kimball, Samuel Rolfe, Solomon Cushman and Osgood E. Virgin. Four hundred dollars were raised for schools. Peter C. Virgin was elected delegate from Rumford to the convention in Portland, to form a constitution for the new State of Maine. William King had eighty-eight votes for Governor. Peter C. Virgin had ninety-one votes for representative to the first Maine Legislature, John Thompson had thirty-one, and Zebediah Farnum had one.

CHAPTER XI.

DIRECT TAX OF 1816.

IN 1816, a direct tax was assessed on the real estate of the country to meet the expenses of the war with England, which had just closed. The total tax was three millions of dollars, and was provided for by act of Congress passed May 5th, 1816. Joseph Howard of Brownfield, was collector for the county, and for the sub-district which included Rumford, the tax was collected by Ebenezer Poor, Esq., of Andover. The proportion of Oxford county was $5,585.31. The list for Rumford which is here given, shows the number and names of real estate owners in town at the time, and also conveys some idea of the financial condition of each; but as personal property was not taxed, it only gives an approximation of each. There were, doubtless, citizens of Rumford at this time who were not possessed of real estate, and consequently their names do not appear.

Names of Taxable Persons.	*Value.*	*Tax.*
Philip Abbot...........................	$1,786	$3 83
Jacob Abbot............................	1,985	4 37
David Abbot............................	794	1 76
Henry Abbot............................	496	1 09
Nathan Adams, Jr......................	2,184	4 80
Charles Adams.........................	292	66
John E. Adams.........................	1,405	3 19

Names of Taxable Persons.	Value.	Tax.
Joel Austin........................	236	58
Nathan Brown......................	595	1 31
Daniel Carr.......................	397	88
Daniel Carlton....................	75	17
Eben Abbot........................	200	44
Nathaniel Abbot...................	248	55
Ephraim Carter....................	595	1 31
Increase Dolly....................	397	97
John Dane.........................	397	87
Richard Dolloff & Son.............	3,384	3 05
Benjamin Elliot & Son	734	1 62
Cotton Elliot.....................	1,176	2 58
Osgood Eaton......................	1,318	2 92
Caleb Eastman.....................	397	87
Francis S. Cushman................	209	46
Benjamin Farnum...................	1,989	4 38
David Farnum......................	1,588	3 50
Jacob Farnum	794	1 75
Stephen Farnum	496	1 09
Jeremiah Farnum...................	794	1 76
John W. Farnum	198	44
Charles Ford......................	149	33
Dr. Benjamin Flint................	297	65
Zebediah Farnum	992	2 18
Samuel Farnum	347	77
Moses Carlton.....................	75	17
Aaron Graham......................	1,221	2 09
George Graham.....................	635	1 39
James Godwin......................	694	1 53
Colman Godwin	430	95
Daniel Greenlief	297	65
Israel or Timothy Glines	357	79
Chandler Glines...................	297	65
Elisha Goddard....................	374	82
Abraham Howe......................	1,240	2 73
Robert Hinkson....................	1,050	2 31
Samuel Hinkson....................	646	1 42
Phinehas Howe.....................	1,837	4 02
John Howe, Jr.....................	596	1 31
Joseph Adams, for the Hutchins place.............	940	2 07
David Hutchins, Jr................	595	1 31
David Hutchins, 3d.	–	–
Jeremiah Hall	834	1 83
Joseph Hall.......................	747	1 65
Ezra Hoyt.........................	153	33
Hezekiah Hutchins.................	149	33
John Howe.	893	1 97
Joel Howe.........................	496	1 09
Eli Howe..........................	397	88
Samuel Lufkin.....................	149	33
Daniel Hodgdon	357	79
Moses Kimball.....................	1,141	2 51
Moses Kimball, Jr.................	466	1 02
Samuel Knight.....................	167	30
Daniel Knight.....................	645	1 40
Francis Keyes.....................	2,779	12
John Kimball......................	1,797	3 96
Daniel Martin	797	1 76
Kimball Martin	1,489	3 30
Benjamin Morse....................	26	06

Names of Taxable Persons.	Value.	Tax.
William Morse	198	44
Elijah Mansur	694	1 53
Wade Moor	200	44
Samuel Bartlett	200	44
Aaron Marean	209	46
Stephen Putnam	972	2 18
Israel Putnam	820	1 80
Samuel Putnam	794	1 76
Edmund Page	1,786	3 93
Stephen Putnam, Jr.	94	21
John and James McAlister	200	44
Jeremiah Richardson	626	1 37
Joshua Ripley	357	79
Henry Rolf	1,489	3 28
Samuel Rolf	146	31
John Rolf	447	99
Nathaniel Rolf	200	44
Nathan Silver	688	1 52
Samuel Stevens	567	1 24
Aaron Stevens	496	1 09
Jonathan Stevens	297	65
Benjamin Simpson	39	09
William Simpson	198	44
Samuel Simpson	595	1 31
Stephen G. Stevens	608	1 38
John Swain	642	1 41
Benjamin Sweat	545	1 20
Francis Smart	198	44
Job Tyler	154	34
Jeremiah Virgin	416	91
Eben Virgin	9 92	2 18
William Virgin	1,136	2 50
Elijah Virgin	893	1 97
Simon Virgin	893	1 97
Peter C. Virgin	99	22
Aaron Virgin	247	53
Ebenezer Virgin	1,090	2 40
Rufus Virgin	245	1 20
Abel Wheeler	992	2 18
William Wheeler	2,250	4 95
Phinehas Wood	1,654	3 64
Joseph Wardwell	992	2 18

CHAPTER XII.

1820. Curtis P. Howe was chosen collector and constable. Three hundred dollars were raised for schools, one thousand for roads. Voted that all the lands belonging to Charles Walker, Esq., of Concord, all of John Bradley of Fryeburg, all of John Chandler of Boscawen, all of Nathaniel and Jacob Eastman, shall be taxed towards building a school house in the first district. William King had eighty-eight votes for Governor, the entire number thrown.

1821. Three hundred and six dollars were raised for schools. Voted that the selectmen be paid for their services, in wheat, corn and rye, and that the school tax be paid in the same produce. The price of wheat was fixed at eight shillings per bushel, corn at one dollar, and rye at seventy-five cents. Fifteen hundred dollars were raised for the repair of roads. Voted that yoked swine be allowed to run at large. Among the new names in the record this year were: John Wheeler, Ephraim Carter, Jeremiah Eaton, Elisha Goddard, Asa Howard, Baxter Lyon, John Estes, 2d, and Henry C. Rolfe. Hezekiah Hutchins was chosen collector and constable. The selectmen were authorized to build a bridge across the mouth of Concord River. For Governor, Albion K. Parris had fifty-three votes, Ezekiel Whitman twenty-nine, and Joshua Wingate twelve. Peter C. Virgin was re-elected representative. Solomon Crockett and Joshua Graham were licensed as retailers of strong liquors out of their stores; also Wm. Wheeler.

1822. Aaron Graham was chosen collector and constable. Three hundred and seven dollars were raised for schools, and one thousand for roads. Voted that hereafter the annual meeting shall be held on the second Monday in March. The support of Mary Hemingway was set up at auction, and bid off by Zebediah Farnum at two shillings per week. Ann Farnum and Charlotte Lamb were also disposed of in the same way; the former was bid off by Samuel

Lufkin at six cents per week, and the latter by Hazediah Silver at two shillings. Voted to build a house for ammunition. Governor Parris had fifty-four votes for re-election, and Ezekiel Whitman forty-seven. For Senator, Samuel Small had ninety-three votes, and Peter C. Virgin seventy-four. The following persons were licensed to sell strong liquors: Joshua Graham, Alvan Bolster, Philip Abbot, Francis Cushman, Solomon Crockett and Benj. Morse. A town pound was built and accepted. It was voted to resist in the suit brought by Bethel for the support of Burry Colby.

1823. Henry C. Rolfe was elected collector and constable. Among the new names in the record are Asaph Brown, Alanson Hinkley, Jonathan S. Millett, Isaac Rolfe, James B. Greenleaf, Leavitt Virgin, Porter Kimball, Jeremiah Hall and Jesse Putnam. Money was raised the same as last year. Jonathan S. Millett was a young physician from Norway, and had just settled in this town. Jonathan Stevens was allowed twenty dollars for the support of his daughter, Sally Stevens of Number 7.

1824. Colman Godwin was elected constable and collector. The number of school committeemen was this year reduced from five to three, and Peter C. Virgin, Joseph Adams and Jonathan S. Millett were elected. Saint Luke Morse was chosen sexton. Money was raised in amount the same as last year. Moses F. Kimball was elected representative.

1825. Three hundred and forty dollars were raised for the support of schools. Gates or bars were allowed on certain roads, among others the one leading from Ephraim Carter's to William Chamberlain's. The support of Belinda Colby and child was set up at auction. Caleb Eastman was allowed twenty dollars for the support of his father, Stilson Eastman. Three hundred dollars were voted for town expenses. Moses F. Kimball, Alvan Bolster and Joshua Graham were licensed as inn-holders. Solomon Crockett, Thomas Crocker, Francis Cushman and Aaron Stevens were licensed as retailers of strong liquors. The town lines were perambulated by the selectmen this year.

1826. Nehemiah Putnam was chosen collector and constable. Voted to choose a committee to examine a place and draw a plan of a bridge across Ellis River; chose Nathan Knapp, Rufus Virgin and Colman Godwin. The bridge was located below Asa Howard's

shop, and the job was bid off by Phineas Wood. At a subsequent
meeting, it was voted to build the bridge on the site of the old one.
Only fifty-three votes were thrown for Governor, all but one for
Enoch Lincoln.

1827. The usual amount of money was raised for various purposes. The selectmen were instructed to place guide boards where
the same should be needed, the price of each not to exceed fifty
cents. Enoch Lincoln had thirty-three votes for Governor, this
being the whole number thrown. It was voted to give the old meeting house to Asa Graham, Henry Martin and their associates for
ever, reserving the right to use the house for the transaction of
town business.

1828. Nathan Abbott was chosen collector and constable.
Among the new names were Simeon Fuller, Simeon Farnum, John
M. Brown, Robert C. Kimball, James Farrington, David Elliott,
Otis C. Bolster, Isaac N. Stanley, Daniel Hall and Timothy J.
Carter. The school committee this year was made up of Peter C.
Virgin, Timothy J. Carter and Curtis P. Howe. Voted to accept
the road leading from William Chamberlain's to George Graham's,
as a "bridle road."

1829. Daniel Martin, Jr., bid off the collection of taxes, and
was chosen constable. Three hundred and fifty dollars were voted
for schools, "including the school fund." It was voted to bind out
the child of Churchill Cobb, and that the selectmen take care of the
family of Joseph Chase. Asa Abbott's family were set up at auction, and their support bid off by various persons. Nehemiah
Putnam was voted twenty-five dollars on account of breaking his
arm from defective road. Samuel E. Smith had ninety-two votes
for Governor, and Jonathan G. Hunton had fifty-nine. For representative to the Legislature, Francis Cushman had seventy-four
votes, Curtis P. Howe thirty-nine, and Alvan Bolster forty-four.
At a sebsequent meeting, Francis Cushman had seventy-nine, Curtis
P. Howe sixty-five, and Alvan Bolster one.

1830. Four hundred dollars were appropriated for schools.
School committee chosen, Peter C. Virgin, Simeon Fuller and Sullivan S. Rawson. Asa Graham was chosen constable and collector.
A lengthy report was made by the committee appointed to redistrict
the town for school purposes, which was accepted. The town lines

were again perambulated. At a meeting in August, Wm. Frost was chosen collector of taxes. A chest was authorized for the selectmen, and a desk for the town clerk, in which to keep the town's books and papers. One hundred and eighty-one votes were thrown at the election meeting this year. Four hundred and fifty dollars were raised to defray the expenses of a lawsuit with the town of Peru.

1831. Moses F. Kimball was chosen town agent. William Frost was chosen collector, and he and David B. Glines constables. Barzilla Streeter Cobb was indentured by the selectmen to Hezikiah Hutchins, Jr.; he was the son of Churchill Cobb. A movement was made this year for the purchase of a town farm. A committee was appointed to settle the accounts of Aaron Virgin, a former town treasurer. The selectmen were instructed to call a meeting of delegates from the towns and plantations in this representative district, for the purpose of making an apportionment for the next ten years. Samuel E. Smith had ninety-six votes for Governor, and Daniel Goodenow seventy-five.

1832. Lyman Rawson was elected one of the selectmen. Fifteen hundred dollars were appropriated for roads, and two hundred and fifty dollars for town expenses. A report was made of the ministerial and school funds belonging to the town, and held by parties in the town, amounting to two thousand four hundred seventy dollars and forty cents. Voted four hundred and nine dollars for schools. Samuel E. Smith had one hundred and four votes for Governor. Eliza Bellows became a pauper and the selectmen were authorized to notify Bridgton, where she probably belonged.

1833. The same amount of money was raised for various town purposes as was raised last year. It was voted to fence the several burying yards in town. New names mentioned are David and Timothy Holt, Josiah Parker, Simon Parlin, Warren Mansur, John Dolloff and William R. Hemmingway. Francis Hemmingway was voted a sum for saving Concord river bridge in 1830 and 1831. Joshua Graham was collector and constable. Otis C. Bolster had seventy-four votes for representative, and Robert P. Dunlap one hundred and eight for Governor. Voted to allow David A. Godwin for caring for Concord river bridge.

1834. Voted to raise the usual sum for schools and for other

town purposes. Joshua Graham was re-elected collector and treasurer. Jane Milliken was among the paupers whose support was
sold at auction. Voted that the act authorizing the division of the
ministerial and school funds be put in force. Robert P. Dunlap
had one hundred and twenty-six votes for Governor, and Peleg
Sprague eighty-four. Alvan Bolster had one hundred and twenty-
eight votes for representative to the Legislature; Otis C. Bolster
had eighty-six. At a meeting September eighth, it was voted to
dismiss Rev. Daniel Gould as minister of the town. A suit between
the town and New Portland was provided for.

1835. The appropriations of money were essentially the same
as last year. Joshua Graham was continued as collector and constable. James McCrillis and Ira Elkins are new names on the
records; also John M. Eustis. For representative, Richard T.
Lurvey had ninety-three votes, and Rowse Bisbee had fifty-seven.
These candidates lived in Woodstock. The ministerial fund of the
town was reported at two thousand six hundred and five dollars,
and the school fund at seven hundred dollars.

1836. Lyman Rawson was chosen town agent, and Simeon
Fuller, Nathan Sheldon and Elijah Walker, school committee.
Joshua Graham again bid off the collectorship and was elected constable. Appropriations were made the same as last year. The
selectmen were authorized to look after the management of the
ferries in town. It was voted that the selectmen receive the ministerial and school funds from the trustees, and assume the duties
of trustees hereafter.

1837. Timothy Walker's name is among the list of minor town
officers this year. Joshua Graham was elected collector and constable. School agents were chosen as follows: Eben Virgin, 2d,
for number one, Stephen G. Stevens for two, William Hill for three,
Josiah Parker for four, John Howe for five, Samuel Lufkin for six,
Asa S. Howard for seven, John Dolloff for eight, Jesse Putnam for
nine, Ebenezer Virgin for ten, Wade Moor for eleven, and Enoch
Stiles for twelve. Voted that the poor for this year be left in care
of the selectmen. This vote was reconsidered, and the whole number of paupers were set up at auction and bid off by Phineas Wood,
at three hundred and fifty dollars. Two thousand dollars were
raised for roads, and five hundred for town charges. Dr. Elijah
Walker's name appears on the records. Joshua T. Hall was elected

agent to go to Augusta and receive the surplus revenue belonging
to the town. Voted to keep said revenue as a fund, and never
spend any part of it. Voted that the treasurer loan said revenue to
persons giving good security, in sums not exceeding one hundred
and not less than twenty-five dollars, interest to be paid in advance.
The total amount of the money received was eighteen hundred seventy dollars and forty-four cents. As the amount received was a
fraction over one dollar and sixty-six cents for each person, the
population of Rumford at this time was about eleven hundred and
twenty-five. The names of the persons who hired the money of the
town in sums varying from twenty-five to eighty-five dollars, were
David Colby, Jacob Abbot, Stephen Farnum, Jr., Asa S. Howard,
Henry Abbot, Jacob Putnam, Colman Godwin, Asa Graham, Chas.
E. Virgin, Osgood Eaton, Daniel G. Abbot, Simeon O. Reynolds,
David F. Adams, Francis Cushman, Generous Ames, Simon Parlin
and Enoch Knapp. At a meeting June 20th, it was voted to dis-
tribute the surplus revenue. At a meeting July eight, it was voted
that the town use a portion of the surplus revenue to pay the pauper
bill due New Vineyard, and the debt of one hundred and fifteen
dollars and fifteen cents due Aaron Stevens. Gorham Parks had
one hundred and twenty-five votes for Governor, and Edward Kent
seventy-seven. Lyman Rawson had one hundred and eighteen votes
for representative to the Legislature, Spencer Drake seventy-nine,
and Joseph Lufkin two.

1838. Chose Joshua Graham collector, constable and town
treasurer. Among the new names on the record were Enoch Perry,
Philip Hoyt, Peter D. Brackett, Benj. W. Stevens, Daniel Hodsdon,
Abel Chapman, Jr., John Thomas, Harmon Eastman, Josiah Keyes,
James Merrill and Luther Trumbull. Voted to divide the surplus
revenue per capita without security, and that it be done in August
next. Six hundred dollars were raised for town charges, and the
usual amount for other purposes. The town's poor, consisting of
Bartlett Hutchins, Burry Colby, Charlotte Virgin, Samuel Morse
and family, Wm. H. Stevens, wife and children, Olive Hinkson.
William Chew and Seth Puffer, were disposed of in various ways.
Wm. R. Hemmingway bid off the contract to fence the town burying grounds. Money was raised this year to make good the amount
of the surplus revenue used by the town. John Fairfield had one
hundred and sixty-eight votes for Governor, and Edward Kent one
hundred and fifteen.

1839. Timothy Walker was chosen constable and collector. For school committee, Albion K. Knapp, Peter C. Virgin and Elliot Richmond. Two thousand dollars were raised for roads, and the usual amount for other purposes. Timothy Walker, Samuel Barker, William Kyle, William W. Farnum, Jeremiah Richardson, Charles E. Virgin, Eliab Richardson, Joseph Lufkin, Otis C. Bolster, Eben Abbot, Enos Abbot and Robert Kimball, were chosen school agents. The support of the poor was bid off by Colman Godwin for four hundred and fifty dollars. Voted to let out the building of the bridge near Abbot's Mills, across Concord river. The selectmen were authorized to settle with R. B. Jennings and Col. Silas Morse for damage received by them at Rumford Falls.

1840. Timothy Walker was re-elected collector and constable. New names in the record were David Knapp, Calvin Howe, Isaac Robinson, Samuel S. Snow, Wm. Ackley, Livermore C. Hall, John Clement, Jr. The town agent was instructed to see that a boat be kept at the mouth of Swift river; also to obtain for the use of the town, a license of the ferry at Rumford Point. At a meeting in July, Jeremiah Martin was chosen collector of taxes. At the meeting for choice of presidential electors, the democrats polled one hundred and forty-three votes, and the whigs one hundred and fourteen.

1841. Samuel B. Bodwell bid off the taxes and was chosen constable. It was voted to send Bartlett Hutchins, son of David Hutchins, to the Insane Hospital, if the selectmen think best. Six hundred dollars were raised for town expenses, four hundred and nine for schools, and two thousand for roads. At an adjourned meeting Colman Godwin was elected collector. It was voted that "some one go to Alna and get William Stevens' children which are there on expense to the town." The support of David King Dolloff was bid off by John Dolloff at two cents per week. Edward Kent had one hundred and twenty-two votes for Governor, and John Fairfield one hundred and forty-two. A bridge was voted across Bog Brook, and Rufus Virgin was appointed to superintend its building. Dr. Thomas Roberts had settled in town.

1842. The following school agents were chosen: Jonathan Virgin for district number one, William Ackley for number two, Peter A. Thompson for number three, David W. Abbot for number four, John Howe for number five, Samuel S. Snow for number six,

Francis Cushman for number seven, Wm. M. Morse for number eight, Henry C. Rolfe for number nine, Enoch Knapp for number ten, John Swain for number eleven, and Asa Green for number twelve. One thousand dollars were raised for defraying town charges. The pauper bills were very light this year. Colman Godwin was chosen collector and constable. The whole number of votes cast for Governor was two hundred and fifty-five. For representative to the Legislature, several ballotings were had without choice. At the third trial, Amos Dwinal had eighty-four votes, Joseph Lufkin fifty-seven, and David Knapp forty-one. At the fourth trial, November fourteenth, Mr. Dwinal received one hundred and three votes, out of one hundred and eighty-nine. Eleven persons received votes. At the seventh trial, on January sixteenth, Amos Dwinal received one hundred and twenty votes out of one hundred and ninety-two. This ended the contest.

1843. Timothy Walker was chosen town agent, a position he had held for several years. Five hundred seventy-seven dollars and sixty cents were raised for schools. Colman Godwin was again elected collector and constable. Charles A. Kimball bid off a portion of the town's poor at four hundred and twenty-three and a half dollars. Several had previously been set up singly and disposed of. Nearly forty persons presented claims against the town for various services. The town voted to oppose a road asked for across the Androscoggin at East Rumford, unless assurance could be given that a bridge should never be asked for. For representative, David Knapp had one hundred and eight votes, and Amos Dwinal one hundred and nine; scattering, five. Action was had to prevent Moody F. Abbot and others from being annexed to Hanover.

1844. James M. Dolloff was chosen collector and constable. The town's poor were disposed of as follows: Mrs. Samuel R. Morse and five children to Moses F. Kimball; David Silver, wife and five children to Theodore Russell; Marion Stevens to John Thomas; Hazen Virgin to Wm. B. Walton; Charlotte Virgin to H. W. Silver; Phebe Virgin to Hezekiah Hutchins; Esther Abbot and child to James H. Farnum; Alphonso Dolloff to Ebenezer Virgin, 2d; Nathaniel S. Warren's family left in charge of the overseers of the poor; Charles Dore to Theodore Russell; E. B. Hutchins to David Hutchins; Lucy Morse to Samuel Morse; Olive Hinkson to

Asa Abbot; Jeremiah Virgin to Ebenezer Virgin, 2d; Benj. Allen and wife to Benj. Allen, Jr.; the sick McAllister girl in Harrison, to the care of the selectmen; subsequently this was reconsidered, and the whole were set up together and bid off by Henry C. Rolfe for three hundred and three dollars.

1845. Dr. James Bullock was chosen collector of taxes and constable. The additions to the poor list this year were Jacob Puffer, wife and children, George F. Moody, and widow Peavy. The usual amounts were raised for town and other purposes. At a meeting holden April seventh, resolutions were passed in favor of temperance, and against licensing any person to sell liquor in town other than for medical and mechanical purposes. This meeting was presided over by Timothy Walker, and it was voted that the selectmen carry out the spirit of the resolutions by prosecuting every person violating the same. It was voted to build a pound near the Center Meeting House. Several disputes with regard to lines were settled this year, and placed on record.

1846. The poor of the town this year were left in charge of the selectmen. Fourteen hundred and fourteen dollars were appropriated for town expenses, and the usual amounts for other purposes. Colman Godwin was again chosen collector of taxes. The claim of Roxbury for the support of Jonathan S. Bunker, deceased, was left to the care of the selectmen. It was voted not to purchase a town farm for the support of the poor. Voted that physicians be employed to examine the case of Esther Abbot, and see whether or not she has been benefitted by her treatment at the Maine Insane Hospital. Several meetings were held to choose a representative to the Legislature, and on the fourth trial Alvin Kimball had ninety-three votes out of one hundred and seventy-six polled. Rufus Virgin had seventy-two. Mr. Kimball was of Mexico.

1847. For school committee, Dr. Zenas W. Bartlett, Rev. Eliphalet S. Hopkins and Wm. W. Virgin. Moses F. Kimball was elected collector and constable. The poor were again left in the hands of the selectmen. It was voted to allow Thomas Carey, Nathaniel S. Warren, William Lang, Livingstone Glover, Peter C. Virgin, 2d, George A. Ray and Elijah Ray, "what school money their children draw, to be expended in schooling their own children." Jonathan Virgin and Joshua Graham were licensed to sell liquor for medicinal and mechanical purposes only. The question of annexing that part of the town lying west of Ellis river to Bethel, came up again this year, and the town voted to oppose it. For Governor, John W. Dana had one hundred and twenty votes, David Bronson ninety-five, and Samuel Fessenden six.

1848. Eliphalet S. Hopkins, Wm. W. Virgin and Henry Abbot were elected school committee. Virgin declined to serve and Alvan B. Godwin was chosen to fill the vacancy. Benj. Morse, Nathan Abbot and Jeremiah Andrews were chosen sextons. Bartholomew Coburn was allowed to draw his school money and pay it out in Andover. John Poland was set on to another district. James M. Dolloff was elected collector and constable. This year, Samuel Fessenden's vote for Governor was thirteen, showing a steady gain for the Free-Soil party. The Free-Soil electors polled fifteen votes.

1849. The usual sums were voted for town purposes. James M. Dolloff bid off the taxes, and was elected collector and constable. The selectmen were authorized to oppose the location of a road prayed for by Hiram Ricker and others. The partition fence between John and Alvan B. Godwin was adjusted. It was voted to open the road from Putnam's Ferry to David W. Abbot's. John Hubbard had one hundred and thirty-five votes for Governor, and Elijah L. Hamlin eighty-seven. The following were chosen highway surveyors, the several districts having been numbered the past year: James M. Dolloff for district number one; Jeremiah Martin, number two; Edward Stevens, number three; Samuel V. Abbot, number four; Charles Carter, number five; Benj. F. Virgin, number six; Merrill Farnum, number seven; Daniel F. Putnam, number eight; David W. Abbot, number nine; Jesse Putnam, number ten; Daniel G. Abbot, number eleven; Joshua T. Hall, number twelve; Stephen Philbrick, number thirteen; Samuel Arnold, number fourteen; Livingston Glover, number fifteen; Oren H. Lufkin, number sixteen; Reuben Farnum, number seventeen; Ira A. Putnam, number eighteen; Samuel H. Wood, number nineteen; Eliphalet E. Lufkin, number twenty; Asa Richardson, number twenty-one; John C. Dearborn, number twenty-two; and Wm. H. Caldwell, number twenty-three.

1850. James M. Dolloff was again chosen collector and constable. Patrick Hoyt was elected clerk. He had already served as such a part of the previous year in place of Zenas W. Bartlett, resigned. The poor were left in charge of the overseers, as had been the custom for some years. It was voted to paint and repair the Center meeting house. Eliphalett S. Hopkins resigned as school committee, May 9th, and Nathan S. Lufkin was appointed to the vacancy.

1851. It was voted to raise three thousand dollars for the repair of highways, and the usual amount for schools. The matter of guide boards was attended to. Several roads were accepted as located by the selectmen, one upon the application of Ira A. Putnam.

1852. Dr. Thomas Roberts was elected clerk, Peter C. Virgin treasurer, Alvan B. Godwin school committee and Lyman Rawson agent. Voted that no agent be appointed to sell spirituous liquors. Barzilla Curtis was chosen collector of taxes. For Governor, John Hubbard had one hundred and thirty-six votes, Anson G. Chandler one hundred, Wm. G. Crosby fifty-nine and Ezekiel Holmes 1. For representative to the Legislature, Timothy Walker had one hundred and thirty-nine and Charles E. Virgin one hundred and forty-six. A committee was chosen to look after the rebuilding of the bridge across Ellis river.

1853. Otis C. Bolster, David Kimball and Charles E. Virgin were chosen selectmen. Charles E. Virgin was chosen collector and constable. The selectmen were instructed to deed to Nathaniel S. Warren "the farm on which he lives, on the payment of fifty dollars." For Governor, Albert Pillsbury had one hundred and fourteen votes, Wm. G. Crosby seventy-five, Anson P. Morrill seventy-four and Ezekiel Holmes nine. Peru sent the representative this year, and the vote in Rumford stood for Lyman Bolster one hundred and fifty-five, to one hundred and fifteen for Stephen Gammon.

1854. Alvan B. Godwin, Hiram Abbot, Jr., Caleb Eastman, George G. Martin, James M. Dolloff and James Bullock were chosen constables, and P. W. Abbott, Burt Kidder, Jeremiah Andrews, Benj. F. Ford and David Elliot, sextons. Six hundred and eighty-seven dollars and fifty cents were voted for schools. Joseph E. Colby bid off the taxes and was chosen collector. For Governor this year the following votes were thrown: for Anson P. Morrill, one hundred and twenty-one; Isaac Reed, twenty-nine; Albion K. Parris one hundred and one, and Shepard Cary, eleven.

1855. The selectmen this year were Joseph E. Colby, Frye H.

Hutchins and John Martin. Asa S. Howard was elected town agent. Four thousand dollars were appropriated for roads, sixteen hundred and fifty for town charges, and what the law required for schools. Dr. James Bullock bid off the taxes and was elected collector and constable. It was voted not to have a liquor agent appointed. William Moody was chosen agent to expend money on the road between Rumford Falls and John Swain's. A suit was pending between Rumford and the town of Industry. Jacob Elliott was appointed liquor agent in June. For Governor, Anson P. Morrill had one hundred fifty-three votes, Samuel Wells one hundred fourteen, and Isaac Reed fourteen.

1856. Patrick Hoyt was chosen town agent. Eight hundred and fifty dollars were raised for the support of primary schools. James Bullock was continued as collector. Four hundred dollars were raised to defray the expenses incurred in the suit of Swain against Rumford. For Governor, Hannibal Hamlin had one hundred and seventy-seven votes and Samuel Wells one hundred and twenty-three. The republican ticket for electors of President and Vice President polled one hundred and seventy-nine votes, and the democratic one hundred and four. The town lines were perambulated this year.

1857. Patrick H. Virgin was elected town agent. Timothy Walker was elected special agent to look after Rumford matters in Augusta. The movement to set off the west end of the town to Hanover was renewed. James Bullock again bid off the taxes. The rebuilding of Ellis River bridge, which had fallen, again came up, and a committee was chosen to look after it. A meeting was called at Rumford Point, at which it was voted to rebuild Ellis River bridge at the site of the old one, and Alvan Bolster was appointed a committee to oversee the work. James Bullock having died, Joseph E. Colby was appointed, July first, tax collector in his stead. For Governor, Lot M. Morrill had one hundred and ninety-four votes and Mannasseh H. Smith had one hundred twenty-seven. January twenty-third, the special agent on Ellis River bridge made a final report of his doings, that the bridge was completed, and was discharged.

1858. Elisha F. Goddard was chosen moderator and Hiram F. Abbot school committee. A committee consisting of Joseph E. Colby, Jeremiah Richardson and David Kimball was chosen "to settle and close up all the unsettled business of the town." Seven hundred dollars were raised in addition to other regular appropriations, to meet the first installment due for money raised to rebuild Ellis River bridge. Thirty-two lots of land were advertized by the collector for non-payment of taxes. The selectmen as a finance committee reported outstanding orders against the town, three thousand and four hundred and five dollars and ninety-nine cents; interest on same, three hundred dollars; orders drawn last two years, four thousand five hundred forty-six dollars and fifty-seven cents, and orders renewed, eight hundred sixteen dollars and fifty-one cents.

1859. Orrin H. Lufkin was chosen moderator, James M. Dolloff treasurer, Charles A. Kimball agent and Elias B. Richardson school committee. It was voted to purchase a farm for the town's poor, and one thousand dollars were raised for support of poor and other town expenses. Joseph E. Colby was chosen collector of taxes. The surveys of several roads were accepted. A movement was made to divert the school fund and expend it for a town farm, but was voted down. The vote in favor of giving the public lands to aid in the construction of a railroad to Aroostook stood three in favor and sixty-one opposed.

1860. Dexter D. W. Abbot, Patrick Hoyt and Jonathan K. Martin were chosen selectmen, and John Elliot school committee. James M. Dolloff was elected collector. Three thousand dollars were raised for roads, eight hundred and twenty-five for schools and fifteen hundred for town expenses, including poor. Paupers were no longer sold at auction, but were cared for by the overseers of the poor. At a meeting March twenty-fourth, William Irish was chosen selectman in place of Dexter D. W. Abbott, resigned. Israel Washburne had two hundred and fifteen votes for governor, and Ephraim K. Smart one hundred and three. For representative, Patrick Hoyt had two hundred and three, and James M. Dolloff, one hundred and eleven. The republican candidates for electors of president had one hundred and seventy-three votes, the democratic sixty-five and the third party twelve. The selectmen were instructed to settle with former collectors and treasurers.

1861. Wm. Irish, Jonathan K. Martin and Frye H. Hutchins were chosen selectmen, and Henry F. Howard, school committee. Five hundred dollars were raised for the support of the poor, and one thousand to defray town charges. James M. Dolloff was elected treasurer. Israel Washburne had one hundred and seventy-three votes for governor, Charles D. Jameson sixty-two and John W. Dana twenty-two. At a meeting December seventh, it was voted to build a bridge across Swift river.

1862. Timothy Walker, Frye H. Hutchins and Henry Abbot, Jr., were chosen selectmen, Dr. Frank G. Russell school committee. Alvan Bolster was chosen collector of taxes. Eight hundred dollars were raised for support of poor. Timothy Walker was appointed agent to hire three thousand dollars to pay the outstanding liabilities of the town. Four thousand dollars were raised for roads. Voted to purchase a farm for the town's poor, and that the selectmen be a committee to receive proposals. It was voted to borrow the school fund with which to purchase a poor farm. The selectmen were directed to hire five hundred dollars to aid soldiers' families. At a meeting July twenty-fourth, it was voted to pay those who would enlist on the quota of the town under the late call for troops, the sum of fifty dollars. Alvan Bolster, collector of taxes, having died, William Frost was elected collector in his stead. At a meeting September tenth, voted to pay soldiers who enlist for nine months, twenty dollars bounty and nine dollars per month. Voted to rebuild Swift River bridge.

1863. William Frost was again elected collector of taxes at two cents on the dollar. The appropriations of money were large this year, growing out of the expenses of the war. The meeting house at Rumford Centre was ordered shingled. It was voted to pay a bounty of one hundred dollars to such persons as should enlist or furnish substitutes for the army under the conscription act. The selectmen were directed to furnish ropes and boats for Putnam's Ferry, and employ some person to tend the ferry. Samuel Cony had two hundred and thirteen votes for governor and Bion Bradbury had seventy-six. At a meeting November twenty-first, it was voted to pay recruits on Rumford's quota a bounty of two hundred and fifty dollars, as soon as mustered into United States service, and to assess and collect the money for this purpose forthwith. At a meeting December third the bounty was increased to three hundred dollars, and five dollars were offered the recruiting committee for each recruit.

1864. Timothy Walker, Henry Abbot and Orlando W. Blanchard were chosen selectmen, and Asa Howard and Hiram F. Abbot school committee. Voted that the town pay William Frost one hundred and twenty-five dollars for collecting the taxes the ensuing year. It was voted to raise four thousand dollars to pay town debt and interest, and the usual amount besides. Voted that the town fence the new burying ground near Rumford Corner. Samuel Cony had two hundred and eight votes for governor, and Joseph Howard sixty-six. The question of allowing soldiers to vote for president wherever they might be, stood two hundred and forty in favor and fifteen opposed. The republican electors polled two hundred and twenty-four votes, and the democratic seventy-seven. Charles A. Kimball and Nathan S. Lufkin were appointed recruiting committee for the next call, and the treasurer was authorized to hire the necessary funds.

1865. William Frost was elected collector and the same compensation allowed as last year. F. P. Putnam was chosen school committee. The appropriations this year amounted to about ten thousand dollars, including four thousand for roads. Timothy Walker was authorized to hire what money should be needed to aid soldiers' families, and "to borrow the school funds in the hands of the treasurer, and such as can be readily collected by him." Samuel Cony had two hundred and nine votes for governor and Joseph Howard forty-nine.

1866. Henry Abbot was chosen collector of taxes, and for selectmen, Wm. Irish, Jonathan K. Martin and George W. Perry. The chairman of the board was made auditor of accounts. Francis A. Bacon, treasurer, having deceased, Calvin Howe was elected to fill the vacancy. A committee was chosen to oppose a road contemplated by way of the Falls. At a meeting in part to see if the town would erect a monument to the memory of deceased soldiers, the article was passed over. For governor, Joshua L. Chamberlain had two hundred and seventeen votes and Eben F. Pillsbury eighty-eight.

1867. George K. Martin, George W. Perry and Prentiss M. Putnam were chosen selectmen. Charles V. Martin bid off the taxes and was elected collector. John N. Irish and Waldo Pettingill were chosen school committee. Twelve hundred dollars were voted for the support of schools. Voted to purchase a town farm. Five thousand dollars were raised for town charges. The act additional to an act for the suppression of the Liquor Traffic, submitted to the voters of the State was approved in Rumford, fifty-three in favor and thirty-nine opposed. At a meeting June twenty-ninth it was voted to discharge the town farm committee and leave the management of the town farm to the overseers of the poor. The matter of a soldiers' monument was again put into the warrant and again passed over in silence.

CHAPTER XIII.

HISTORY OF RUMFORD, 1826.—BY REV. DANIEL GOULD.

IN 1826, Rev. Daniel Gould, then a resident minister in Rumford, was asked by Hon. William D. Williamson, author of the History of Maine, to furnish some data for his work, concerning the town of Rumford, with which Mr. Gould complied. A copy of this, with some additions, was left among his papers, and has been preserved to the present time, though somewhat damaged by fire, and also considerably worn. Mr. Gould wrote as follows:

"The town of Rumford lies on both sides of the Great Androscoggin River, and above and below the Great Falls, in the same. It was a grant made by the General Court of Massachusetts to Timothy Walker, Jr., Esq., of Concord, N. H., and his associates, being eighty-four in number, to compensate for some evils which had arisen to the proprietors of Concord, at the time Concord was under the jurisdiction of Massachusetts Bay, which according to their charter was three miles north of the most northerly branch of Merrimack river, which would have extended at least as far as Wells, or farther, in this State. But the Court of Massachusetts Bay granted Concord and many other towns in New Hampshire, until the line was settled and established by the crown in 1740. Many charters of towns covered each other in part. This created troubles, law suits and great expenses, to prevent which, appeals were made to the crown of England for a redress of grievances. The Rev. Timothy Walker of Rumford, was sent as agent for the Proprietors, and before the difficulty was settled, he crossed the Atlantic three times to the King upon this business.

Bow or Johnson's Grant, below Concord, formed a part of Concord until the line was settled. The proprietors of Concord had been at great expense in getting the line established, and Timothy Walker, Jr., Esq., and his associates, petitioned the General Court of Massachusetts Bay for a township on the Androscoggin River.

The court granted their petition on the fourth of February, 1774, but the next year the revolutionary war commenced, and put everything into confusion. The Massachusetts records, or many of them, were either lost or carried away, and before the proprietors of Rumford had obtained their charter of the town, they were again under the necessity of petitioning for it. It was again granted and ratified by the General Court of Massachusetts, on the third day of April, 1779.

This year the town was surveyed, and a division was made which gave to each proprietor, now increased to one hundred, one hundred acres. A second division was made in the year 1788, of one hundred acres to each proprietor as before. The proprietors became acquainted with their lots in the former division, and finding many of them to be poor, and some of very little value, owing to rocky hills and barren land, they made a third division in 1788. This division gave to each proprietor different quantities of land to compensate for poor lots, so as to make them equal in quantity and quality.

There is yet some undivided land in town, belonging to the proprietors, as well as rocky and barren mountains and barren land, which will never be settled nor improved even for grazing.

In the town are four public rights, laid out by the proprietors, viz: one right for the use and benefit of Harvard College, one for the schools, one for the first settled minister in the town, and one for the ministry or parsonage.

The town was laid out in a square form of seven miles and forty poles on each side, and is bounded as follows: Beginning on Bethel, thence running north 18½ degrees west, by Bethel, Howard's Gore and Newry; thence north 71½ degrees east by Andover and Number VII; thence south 18½ degrees east by Mexico and Peru; thence south 71½ degrees west by Number II to the first mentioned bound.

About one-quarter part of the town is under improvement, and one-quarter part may be allowed for water, barren lands and rocky mountains; the other half of the town remains unimproved.

There are no ponds of any magnitude, nor islands in the river of any consequence.

The town was first settled in 1779. In the autumn of this year, Mr. Jonathan Keyes moved his family here. This was the first family which settled in the place.

Mr. Aaron Moor soon after moved his family here, but his wife, through fear of the Indians, went to Bethel, where a son was born which she called Waid. If she had remained in town, he would have been entitled to a lot of land granted by the proprietors to the first male child born in the place. Sometime after, Mr. Benjamin Lufkin moved into town with his family. She soon after had a son which she named Samuel. A dispute arose between them relative to the first-born in the place, and somehow or other they both lost the right. Both of them are yet living.

The town was incorporated Feb. 21, 1800, by the name of Rumford. It never had an Indian name. Until incorporated, it was called New Pennicook by the proprietors and the first settlers, from the ancient Indian name of Concord in New Hampshire. Concord was named Rumford when incorporated in 1733, by the General Court of Massachusetts. From this year to 1765, it bore this name, and after, a parish of Bow. As it had been called Rumford, the proprietors and inhabitants who chiefly came from Concord to this place when it was first settled, it was called Rumford; and likewise for the peculiar regard the proprietors had for Count Rumford who was a large proprietor and entitled to six rights in the township, and in hopes he would give them his shares for giving his name to it. Hence the town received its name.

The town records commenced on April 14, 1800, the same year it was incorporated. Francis Keyes, Esq., was chosen clerk and first selectman; Mr. Philip Abbot and Mr. John Martin being the other two this year.

Androscoggin River runs through the town from west to east in a pretty straight course. In its windings, there are excellent turns of interval which are rich and very productive. This river is generally rapid through the town, as is its general character from its source in Umbagog lake, till it empties into Merrymeeting Bay where it meets the Kennebec River, and the two empty themselves into the Atlantic Ocean.

There are two or three ripps in this river as it passes through the town. They are rocky and rapid, but in high water, rafts pass over them in safety.

The Great Falls on the river, or as they are sometimes called "Pennycook Falls," are in the easterly part of the town. They are the largest falls in the river. The water at the falls gathers into a very narrow channel when it comes to them, owing to the lofty rocky mountains on both sides of the river which crowd upon it. There are several sharp pitches before the water comes to the great cascade. The water falls here about seventy-five feet in the short distance of two or three rods. The water then falls into a large basin, as it were to refresh itself till it comes to another large fall in the river. After the water is precipitated, it gradually slackens its pace till it gains its usual course at the mouth of Swift River.

In dry weather, when the river is low, at the "narrows," as they are called, at the top of the Great Falls, the water in the river is only a few feet over and, by the help of a plank thrown over, people pass to the opposite side in safety. In high water, in the spring or fall, it presents a majestic and terrifying scene, and shows that it will not be trifled with nor insulted. In falling over rocks, its roaring is heard at a considerable distance. Some of the logs in passing the river, when the water is high, jump out of the water, others pass under water, and some of a good rift strike the rocks and are rift asunder, and many are much broomed and bruised in passing the falls.

In the course of half a mile, the water falls over the rocks about one hundred and forty feet.   It is in contemplation to build a bridge over the head of the Great Falls.

At the head of this fall, Mr. Rufus Virgin and Mr. Nathan Knapp, two ingenious, enterprising and persevering young men, have erected a carding, and a shingle machine, a saw-mill, and a grist-mill carrying two pairs of stones, by the same water.   These mills are well supplied with water at all seasons of the year.   The water is brought from the river in a canal formed partly by drilling the rocks with much labor and expense and partly by plank.   By their labor and industry the town and others are well supplied with flour at all seasons of the year.   It is contemplated to erect other machinery at this place.

There is no bridge built over this river in this town.   A grant has been obtained to erect one at the Point, but no preparations as yet are making to accomplish the object.   But there are three established ferries in the town, namely: one at the Point, one at the Center and one at the lower part of the town.   The one at the Point is most valuable, has the most custom, and the post passes this ferry.

The other rivers in the town are Ellis, Concord and Swift rivers. Ellis river east branch rises in Number VIII and the west branch in Andover Surplus; they unite their waters in Andover, and the river pursues its course through Rumford and empties its waters into the Androscoggin at the Point.   The river is lined with high ragged mountains, especially on the west side.   It, however, affords good turns of interval on both sides of it, and is settled on each bank.   It affords no mill privilege in this place.   It has an expensive bridge near its mouth to be maintained, and is much exposed by freshets and logs.   Concord river rises in Woodstock, passes through Hamlin's Grant, a corner of Bethel and Number II, and empties into the Great River in the southwest part of the town. The westerly branch of the river affords no mill privilege.   The mountains crowd upon it, especially on the westerly side.   In passing on the easterly bank of it, on the "Whale's Back," so called, to Paris, the traveller passes higher than the tall pines which grow on the margin.   Another branch of this river rises from two ponds in Number II, and meets the other branch near the Great River.   Mr. David Abbot's grist and saw mills are erected on this branch of the river.   A fulling mill and a carding machine are erected on this stream, a short distance below Abbot's mills, owned by Mr. Samuel Page of Brunswick.   There is an expensive bridge to maintain over this river near its mouth.   It is exposed to ice, freshets and logs. The stream however is small, and affords water but a part of the season.

Swift river, which divides this town from Mexico, rises in Number VII and VIII.   It is a wild, rapid river and affords much good interval on each side.   The uplands are generally poor and mountainous.   It affords no mill privileges owing to its wildness and rapidity.   Small rains will raise it, and they rush from the mountains and pour their waters into it.   It often falls as rapidly as it rises. A bridge has been erected over it near its mouth, where it flows into the Great river, and where the post travels from the east, but it has been swept away by the freshets, ice and logs : but it has not been rebuilt and it would be very expensive to build one, and uncertain how long it would stand. In the summer season, the river is easily forded by horses, but when it is high, it cannot be passed without ferry boats.

Split brook rises on the north of the town among the mountains. It empties its waters into the Great River at the Center of the town. Graham's mills are erected thereon, near the Great River. Here are a saw and grist-mill carrying two pairs of stones. The stream is small and affords water only a part of the season ; and when the water is high, they are troubled with back water from the Great River ; therefore, these mills are not very profitable to the owners. It is difficult also, to make a dam stand, as the ground is muddy and soft.

The mountains in the town are numerous. The most noted are White Cap, Glass Face and Black mountains. These are the only mountains in town which have names. White Cap is situated in the north-westerly part of the town, and lies between Rumford and Andover. It is naked and bare on the top, and hence its name. On the south side it is very steep, rocky and barren. On the north side, there is an easy ascent to its summit, and is thinly covered with wood. It is about four hundred feet high, and on its summit there are fine and picturesque views of the country and hills in all directions which fascinate the eyes of the beholder. It is remarkable for the great quantities of blueberries which it produces every year. Cartloads of these berries are carried from it every season. When they are ripe, the mountain has many visitors both for pleasure and profit. This is the most remarkable mountain in the town.

Glass Face lies near the center of the town, on the road and near the river, and on the north side of it. It is about three hundred feet high, is rocky and steep in front, and impassible. It is barren on its summit. It may be ascended with ease from the north side. There is still some pine timber on the north side of the mountain. This mountain also affords abundance of blueberries. It is visited by many when the fruit is ripe, and affords pleasure and profit to its visitors at this season of the year.

Black mountain is situated on the north-east part of the town. Indeed, there is a continued range of mountains through the north part of the town from White cap to Black mountain. This is said to be the highest mountain. It is in the neighborhood of black land, and hence its name. As there is no settler contiguous to it, it is but little known.

These mountains as well as others in the town afford lurking places for bears, foxes and other animals, and they often prey upon sheep and poultry ; but there are no rattlesnakes nor other poisonous serpents to be found in this place or vicinity. Indeed the town and the surrounding country abound with rocky and barren mountains and hills which are scattered over the surface of the country.

They are steep and pointed at their summits, like sugar loaves. Generally, on the south side of them, they are steep, rocky and barren; but on the north side, they are covered with wood and timber. On some of the hills, there is good land and fit for tillage and grazing, such as Eaton Hill, Red Hill and some others, and still others not yet improved. In the sags between the mountains, the land is good and fertile. There are no caves in the mountains or hills.

There has not yet been found any iron ore within the town; neither limestone nor clay of any value. There is, however, a large body of paint. It is at the foot of a mountain near the road that leads from the center of the town to Andover. There are three sorts of it, red, yellow and black. It has been used in painting buildings, but it requires considerable preparation before it is used. It needs boiling and grinding, and then it is fit for use. The red when prepared and used, is of a lively color like vermillion. It has been used in painting weather boards and ribbons for barns. It appears durable. The yellow is prepared in the same way and has been used in painting buildings. It resembles spruce yellow in color, but is not as durable. The black is really so, and when it has been analyzed, and the method of preparation known, it may be as durable and handsome as any paint of the like color, and would be very valuable.

The east and west parts of the town are the most settled, owing to crowding of mountains in the center. The Point at the upper part will make a handsome village, and will be the center of business. The road from Andover and the back towns, up and down the river and also to Portland, all center at this place. Much business is done here, and it will be increasing in business and population continually. On both sides of the river in this place, there are some handsome buildings, and they are increasing every year.

The center and lower part of the town, can never make a center for business, owing to the mountains crowding upon them. A road from Andover meets the river road at the Center, but there is no cross road here or at the lower part of the town. The river roads lead to Augusta, Hallowell, Brunswick, &c., but none directly to Portland. The Point has the advantage of all these towns for trade and market. At the Great Falls, though a good place for mills and other machinery, yet it can never make a village, owing to the crowding down of the mountains on each side.

As there are no squatters in the town, every one of them holds the title of his land in fee simple from the original proprietors. The price of lands at the present time is very low, and but few who buy can sell their farms. The wild land is worth from one dollar to three dollars per acre; but all land is valued according to its intrinsic value, whether cultivated or wild.

There are in the town three taverns: Kimball's at the Point, Graham's at the Center and Bolster's at the lower part of the town. They are all emblazoned with the square and compasses of the Free Masons.

There are six stores in town; two on the south side of the Great River, owned by Crockett and Cushman, and three on the north side of it, owned by Stevens, Kimball and Bolster; one at the lower part of the town, north of the Great River, owned by Bolster.

There are roads passing up and down the Great River, one on each side. One at the Point leads from Andover, through the town at the Point, to Portland, and one from the Center to Andover; and one on the west side of Swift River leading to Number VII. There are no other roads leading into the town. The other roads lead to various parts of the town. About twenty miles of the roads in town are county roads. A tax of one thousand dollars is raised annually to mend and repair the roads.

The orchards are yet in their infancy. The first settlers planted themselves on the intervals where the soil is not suitable for orchards, but since the uplands have been reduced to farms, or-charding has been attended to very well. About a dozen orchards begin to be profitable, and have produced some apples and cider for several years past.

There are five paupers who have been provided for more or less for some time past, and have been at some expense to the town; but they have generally supported themselves, and are doing so at the present time.

The number of bushels of wheat raised annually is not easily ascertained, but is supposed to be eighteen hundred. It is a good wheat and grain country. The land produces well, so that the inhabitants are amply supplied with breadstuff, and much is carried away to market.

As to the religious concerns of the town, there is nothing at the present time very encouraging. There are two religious orders, but they are not properly separated into distinct societies. The Congregational and the Methodist, except two or three Baptists, compose the different orders. The Congregational Church was organized August 5, 1803, which now consists of forty-six members, and the Methodists in the town are twenty-five.

There is a meeting house in the center of the town erected several years ago, but it was never finished and it is much fallen into decay. During the summer season the Congregational order worship in it, but during winter, they hold their meetings alternately in the school houses at each end of the town. It is now in contemplation to erect another meeting house at the Center for the use of those who choose to worship God in it. The Methodists have the last season erected a meeting house at the lower part of the town, and expect to finish it the present season. Both orders have met alternately, the present winter, in this house.

The first settled minister in this town was the Rev. Samuel R. Hall, who was ordained Nov. 14, 1811, and died Nov. 4, 1814. His ministry was short but useful. He was a lay preacher, and was orthodox in his persuasion. His successor was the Rev. Daniel Gould, formerly a minister at Bethel. He was preaching in this town during the sickness of Mr. Hall. Soon after his death the church and people gave him a call to settle with them in the gospel ministry. He accepted, and was installed May 31, 1815. The Methodists support their preachers by contribution, and have no settled minister with them. The Congregational order support their minister partly by subscription and partly by a fund arising from the sale of the ministerial lands in town. Mr. Hall was aged when he settled here, and gave up the ministers' right of land for the benefit of the Congregational order. From what has been sold of both rights, the interest amounts to one hundred and forty dollars annually, which is principally the salary for the support of Mr. Gould. The subscriptions have amounted to but little. When the two rights shall be sold the funds will be a handsome sum.

The literature of the town is not great, but we have very good schools, and they are generally well attended. The number of scholars from four to twenty-one years of age is three hundred. The town raises three hundred and seven dollars for the use of schools. There is also a fund of forty dollars for the support of schools, arising from the interest of school lands already sold. When the whole right is sold, the interest will make a handsome sum for the support of schools.

There is only one man in the town who has had a full public education, viz., Rev. Daniel Gould. He has been in this town and in Bethel twenty-eight years, in the work of the gospel ministry. During this time he has paid particular attention to the education of youth and children. He has generally furnished these towns and vicinity with the teachers of their schools. From his unwearied attention and exertion the schools, which, before he came here, were in a miserable condition, are now in flourishing circumstances. He has spent much time in visiting and encouraging the scholars in these and the neighboring towns, and has excited a laudable ambition in parents, youth and children, to promote education and to gain knowledge. He has therefore placed the schools in a respectable situation. He has likewise the satisfaction to see that his labors have been blessed.

A learned ministry is a great blessing to a town or society. Such men are a great stimulus to education, piety and morality. The school laws do not now, as formerly, require the aid of ministers to promote the education of youth and children. Then they were required *ex officio* to attend the schools, to visit and encourage children and youth in their education, and they were remunerated by a freedom from taxation.

It is a fact that unless the direction of youth and children be duly attended to, we shall never secure our civil and religious privileges, and a free government. Ignorance lays the foundation for absolute monarchy, oppression and slavery. Hence the necessity that every citizen in these States should exert himself to promote the education of youth and children, and to use all means to encourage these important objects.

There has not been public spirit enough in the town to establish a social library. Several attempts have been made to effect such a source of useful knowledge. The people seem to have but little taste for reading. It is hoped that this state of things will not last long. Such an institution is extremely valuable in society and affords much knowledge at a cheap rate. There is a small church library in the town, of religious books only. There is also a small female tract society, and it is popular at the present time. It is hoped that it may increase and remain popular.

Peter C. Virgin, Esq., is the only lawyer here. He does much business and is valuable in his profession. He is a man of steady habits, a good citizen and a useful member of society.

In this town there are two physicians, Joseph Adams and Simeon Fuller. They are settled in the eastern and western parts of the town. They are valuable in their profession.

The newspapers taken in this town are forty in number. There are two post offices in town. The first of these was established January 1, 1815, at the point. The other is at the lower part of the town and was established October 10, 1825. The Post riders meet at the Point every week, one of them riding from Portland to the Point, and the other from Hallowell to the same place. Another rides from Andover to the Point.

The number of families in the town is one hundred and fifty-seven. There are one hundred and seventy ratable polls and as many voters in the town. The town is increasing in numbers, and will increase in population till the lands suitable for improvement shall be occupied.

The inhabitants are generally industrious and enterprising. They are mostly employed in farming, in clearing the land, in making farms from the wilderness, and are generally steady in their habits. There are four who are shop joiners and who do cabinet work, and they display much ingenuity in their employment. There are others who are carpenters and blacksmiths. Two of these do most of the business of this kind and are situated at each end of the town. There are also shoe-makers in the place, some of whom are good workmen.

The most eminent men in town, both in ancient and modern times, are William Wheeler, Francis Keyes, John Thompson, Francis Cushman, Moses F. Kimball, Alvan Bolster and Colman Godwin. There are others who have and do take the lead in business in town affairs. There are many valuable men in the town, and as is always the case, there are some not so valuable, and some are poor and idle.

The town was first represented in the General Court in 1811, by William Wheeler; also in 1812. From this year to 1818, the town sent no representative. Peter C. Virgin, Esq., represented the town from 1818 to 1821. This year the representative was Moses F. Kimball, and in 1825, Francis Cushman.

There are several in town who were soldiers in the Revolutionary war. Two only receive pensions. The author of these pages was one of those soldiers. It would seem that if one drew pensions, all should. Those who are the subjects of their country's beneficence have generally not been the best of citizens; but those who have been industrious and frugal are otherwise. When all shared the fatigues, labors and hardships in that war, and received but little pay from their country at that time, but at the present time, the country is able to reward them. Their fellow citizens are enjoying the happy fruit of their labors. It is thought that all those soldiers ought to be treated alike and be equally rewarded.

GENERAL REMARKS.

There are no monuments or ancient relics of the Indians in this town, though it is apparent that they were very numerous in this region in former times. But after Lovel's fight, one hundred years ago; and after the taking of Quebec by General Wolf in 1759, through fear they deserted this part of the country, and there was no danger, at least in this town when it was settled by the English. The first settlers in Bethel during the Revolutionary war, suffered from the Indians, and two of the inhabitants were taken by them and carried to Canada.

Several in this town were engaged in the late war with England. Two died in the army, and one was so badly wounded in the arm that it was amputated. He is yet living and a pensioner. The people in this place were in favor of this war, and exerted themselves in prosecuting it.

HOWARD'S GORE.

By the politeness of Ezra Smith,* Esq., at my request, I am able to give a sketch of Howard's Gore, of which he is an inhabitant. Howard's Gore was purchased of the government of Massachusetts in the year 1792, by Mr. Phineas Howard, from whom it takes its name.† It is in the form of a scalene triangle, and is nearly a right angled triangle. The base is bounded on the northwest on Newry, four miles and one hundred and fifteen poles. The northeast line, being the perpendicular, is bounded on Rumford one mile and one half. The other line or leg of the triangle is bounded on the north line of Bethel, due east and west, being the base of the triangle. It contains twenty-one hundred acres. Three years after he had begun a settlement, Mr. Howard built a grist mill at the outlet of a pleasant pond containing about two hundred and fifty acres, in the centre of the Gore, in an elevated situation among the hills. In this pond are trout. Some iron ore has been discovered in the borders of it, but has not been analyzed. The water from the pond in its winding way to the Androscoggin River, falls about three hundred feet in as many rods, before it reaches the flat ground at the foot of the hill. There are, on its descent, one saw mill, one

*Mr. Smith died Feb. 10, 1846, aged 82 years, and is buried at Rumford Point.

†Howard's Gore and a part of Bethel were united and incorporated as Hanover, Feb. 14, 1843.

fulling mill, three grist mills, one clapboard and one shingle machine, and an ample privilege for many other mills and machinery by using the same water. There are now eleven families and about seventy inhabitants in the plantation, some of whom have attended to orcharding, which produces apples and some cider."

CHAPTER XIV.

THE ANDROSCOGGIN RIVER.

THE Androscoggin is a beautiful river, and the scenery bordering upon it is picturesque and often grand. Persons born and reared upon its banks have an attachment for it which is never weakened in after years, however distant they may wander and whatever may be the lapse of time. Its broad intervals, decorated here and there with drooping elms, rising into table lands with sunny slopes and backed by wooded hills or craggy mountains, make up a succession of vistas which become indellibly stamped upon the memory. Its course, from the northern forests to the sea, is somewhat eccentric, though its general course, like all our Maine rivers, is from north to south. In size and importance it is the third river in the State, and in the amount and quality of its water power it is second to no other. Taking its rise in the great forest belt between Maine and Canada, it leaves Umbagog Lake in the town of Errol, New Hampshire, and passing through that town and other New Hampshire towns of Cambridge, Dummer, Milan, Berlin, Gorham and Shelburne, it enters the State of Maine in the border town of Gilead. Its course from the lake to Gorham is nearly due south, but when fairly outside the White Mountain range, it turns and makes almost a right angle, and when it enters Maine, its course is nearly eastward. Between Milan and Bethel the river falls several hundred feet, the most of it at Berlin Falls.

In the town of Bethel, the river turns to the north until it reaches the south line of Newry, near the mouth of Bear River, when it again changes its course toward the east, forms the dividing line between the lower part of Bethel and Hanover, enters Rumford near the mouth of Ellis River, passes through the town in a general northeasterly direction, making several quite sharp turns, enters

Mexico at the mouth of Swift River, and passes southeasterly through the town and as far as Livermore, and from thence, by a general southerly direction, to Merrymeeting Bay. While the length of Rumford, from Hanover to Mexico, is only a trifle over seven miles, the river in its eccentric course makes a little over eleven miles in passing through the town.

In its course from the lakes to Merrymeeting Bay, the Androscoggin passes through varied scenery. For several miles after leaving the Umbagog, its course is through the wilderness, where it encounters numerous rapids, and in Dummer is the most picturesque fall on the river, known as Pontook Falls. Through Milan and a part of Berlin its current is quite sluggish, but before leaving Berlin, the entire volume of water is forced into a narrow gorge only a few feet wide, and the river is almost lost sight of until it emerges at the foot of the precipice, several hundred feet below. After this there is no important fall for many miles, but there are numerous rapids, and in many places the current is swift and strong. Sometimes the mountains and hills are so near the river that there is only room enough for a narrow road along its banks, and then they recede, leaving broad belts of interval on either side. No more charming views can be had anywhere than along the Androscoggin from Gorham, New Hampshire, to Lewiston. The road follows the high banks, and panoramic vistas of mountain, hill, valley, forest and cultivated fields succeed each other, and the broad stretches of interval, with the graceful elms bordering the river as they burst upon the view at each turn of the road, seem almost like an enchanted land.

Through Rumford, the current of the Androscoggin is alternately sluggish and rapid, until the river approaches the east part of the town, and here is the most important fall on the river, and the largest water power in New England. The height of the fall is one hundred and sixty-two feet and eight inches in a running distance of one mile. There is a succession of falls, and along this mile the water can be used for driving mills, many times over. The width of the river at the head of the fall is only ninety feet, and the bottom and sides of the channel are of solid granite. As regards the mass of its water, the Androscoggin is a variable river, due to the mountainous character of its catchment basin at the upper portion, and the extreme nakedness of much of the mountain surfaces which form its water-shed. It rises very rapidly and as rapidly subsides; runs very high in the spring freshets, and very low in the drouths of summer. Rumford Falls has a modifying influence upon the character of the river below in time of freshet. From the narrowness of its channel and the imperishable character of its sides and bottom at the head of the fall, it dams back the water, causing a great rise above and equalizing the flow below. By this means the manufacturing interests below the falls are in a manner protected from the chances of destructive rises of water.

The principal falls on the Androscoggin below Rumford are at Livermore, Lewiston and Brunswick. The falls at Livermore were early known as Rockomeco; those at Lewiston, Amitgonpoutook, afterward Harris' Falls and then Lewiston Falls. Those at Brunswick were called by the Indians Pejepscook, also written Pejepscot. The river at the head of Rumford Falls is six hundred feet above tide water, and at Bethel, opposite the Hill, six hundred and twenty feet. At the State line, it is six hundred and ninety feet; at the head of Berlin Falls, one thousand and forty-eight feet; at Umbagog Lake, twelve hundred and fifty-six feet, and at the extreme forest source of the river, three thousand feet. The Androscoggin takes its origin and name only from the point of confluence of Magalloway River and Umbagog Lake waters. The length of the Androscoggin proper is one hundred and fifty-seven miles, and from the head of Rumford Falls to tide water is seventy-five miles. At Merry-meeting Bay, between Brunswick and Bath, the Androscoggin mingles its waters with those of the Kennebec, and loses its identity. Several rivers flow into this bay, and hence its name, as stated by some; but this is not strictly true. It was so named because here was the place of meeting of the different tribes of Indians on the Androscoggin and Kennebec and along the sea-coast. The Indian name of this bay was Quabacook.

The Indians applied different names to different portions of the Androscoggin River, and the various names also have a variety of spellings. From Quabacook (Merrymeeting Bay) to Amitgonpon-took (Lewiston Falls), the river was called by the Indians Pejeps-cook also written Pejepscot, and the falls at Brunswick have ever borne this name. Above Lewiston Falls and away to the lake region, the river was called Ammascoggin, often written Amaris-coggin, and now uniformly spelled Androscoggin. These ortho-graphical varieties are due to the fact that the Indians had no written language, and persons who heard them pronounce the names of different objects did not always understand alike, and when writing the word each spelled it as he understood it. It is not probable that our present orthography of the name of this river is correct or represents the Indian pronunciation, but it has come to stay. It has been supposed by some that the river was named in part in honor of one of the early colonial governors of Massachusetts, but Governor Andros was not one whom the people would be likely to honor in this way. The meaning of the word which we call Androscoggin, which Captain John Smith, the early navigator, wrote Aumoughcougen, and which in colonial records is spelled Amascoggin and Amariscoggin, in the Indian language meant the " Fish Spearing River." The early settlers of Bethel and Rumford generally abridged the word, and called the river "Scoggin." From Merrymeeting Bay to the sea, the accumulated waters of the several rivers were known as the Sagadahoc, and the river was so called by the early voyagers, who learned it from the Indians. The first voyagers up the Sagadahoc to Merrymeeting Bay appear not to have discovered the Kennebec, but followed up the Pejepscot (Androscoggin) to Brunswick and perhaps to Lisbon. They described the falls which rendered the river unnavigable, and returned home in ignorance of the existence of the noble and navigable Kennebec.

CHAPTER XV.

THE Indians had villages and places of burial in the town of Bethel, the town next above Rumford, and in the town of Canton below, but there is no evidence going to show that they had either in Rumford. That they were often here and spent more or less time here, there is every reason to believe. Arrow heads and spear heads, gouges, chisels, tomahawks and other rude implements all wrought in stone, were frequently found by the early settlers, and are still occasionally unearthed. It is much to be regretted that the Indian name of the great falls in this town has not been preserved. A fall so important must have had a name, and it seems a little strange that the early settlers did not learn it. Some writers have suggested that Pennycook was the Indian name of the falls, but the idea has no substantial foundation. As has been shown elsewhere, the name Pennacook was transferred from Concord, New Hampshire, with the prefix of "new," and there is no evidence that the name was known in this region until after the township had been granted to Colonel Timothy Walker and associates. Then the name was applied to the township and sometimes to the falls.

When the first settlers came, the Androscoggin abounded with salmon, and there is no doubt that a notable fishing place was at the foot of the falls, but what the aborigines called it, or how they designated the place, will probably never be known. Implements of war and for hunting purposes, as well as those for domestic use, found in the region of the falls by the early settlers, show that this was a favorite haunt of the savages, though their stay here was only at intervals. Their homes, where their families remained and where they cultivated broad areas of maize, and where they buried their dead, were at other points on the river. There were few Indians here, except scattering ones, travelling to and fro after the destruction of the Pequaket and Norridgewock tribes, and with the exception of the raid into Bethel during the war of the revolution, in 1781, there were no acts of hostility committed by Indians in Maine after the fall of Quebec and the conquest of Canada in 1760. Small parties came here occasionally to fish and to hunt, but they were peaceable and friendly, and seemed desirous of being on amicable terms with the early white settlers.

The Indians on the Androscoggin were called "Anasagunticooks," and claimed the territory from the lakes to Merrymeeting Bay. The Rokomekos were a sub-tribe, and had their headquarters at Canton. There is a curious analogy between the name Anasagunticook and the word Amoscoggin, the name by which the river was once called, and it is probable that they have about the same signification. The Androscoggin Indians, as they will hereafter be designated in this work, had several sub-tribes into which they were divided before white men came among them. Those below Lewiston Falls were called Pejepscots. Canton Point appears to have been the headquarters of the Androscoggins, where they are said to have had five hundred acres cleared, which they annually planted to corn. Here were held the councils of the sub-tribes, but a general council place for all the Indians in central and southern Maine was Abagudasset Point on Merrymeeting Bay.

The Androscoggin Indians were more hostile and intractable than any other of the Maine tribes. They took a prominent part in Phillip's war, which broke out in 1675, and made hostile excursions to the settlements along the coast, at Falmouth, Yarmouth, Scarborough, Wells, and at the towns on the lower Kennebec. Mugg was a noted Androscoggin chief, and with one hundred warriors made a raid on Scarborough in 1676. Colonel Church, the famous Indian fighter, made an attack on the Androscoggin Indians in 1690. He captured their fortified place in Brunswick and killed many, but it is uncertain how far up the river he came. They released a number of captives whom the Indians had taken in their raids the year previous. In 1703, Governor Dudley had a conference with the Indians at Casco Bay, and two chiefs, Mesambomett and Wexar, accompanied by two hundred and fifty warriors, represented the Androscoggins on that occasion. About this time, persuaded by the Jesuits, many of the Maine Indians, including a large proportion of the Androscoggins, moved to Canada and settled on the Becancourt and Saint Francois rivers. In the subsequent Indian wars affecting Maine, the headquarters of the Indians

were on the above-named rivers, though the Androscoggins as a tribe
did not leave the lower Androscoggin River until about fifty years
later. During the last Indian war, and about the year 1756, a
small force of men was sent up the Androscoggin in whale boats,
and penetrated as far as Rumford Falls. If there were Indians in
this vicinity at that time, they fled before their invaders, but the
party measured distances and took note of the general character-
istics of the country.

A treaty was made with the Indians at Falmouth, in 1749, and
among the Androscoggins present and who signed the treaty were
Sawwaramet, Ausado, Waaununga, Sauquish, Warcedun and Wa-
wawnunka. Incited by the French, the Saint Francis Indians, as
the amalgamated tribes were called, continued to make raids into
Maine. In 1750, they attacked New Meadows, North Yarmouth
and New Gloucester, burned buildings, destroyed cattle, and killed
or captured quite a number of the inhabitants. At the falls on the
Little Androscoggin in Paris, they came across two hunters. One
of them, named Snow, shot and killed the chief of the Indians, and
was in turn riddled with Indian bullets. Snow's Falls commemo-
rate the incident and the name of the brave but reckless hunter.
In 1759, Major Robert Rogers, with a party of rangers, attacked
and nearly annihilated the Saint Francis Indians, and after this we
hear scarcely anything of Indians in Maine. Scattered families
lived at Fryeburg and in Canton, and there were the Penobscots
and Passamaquoddies in eastern Maine, but their power was broken,
and their tribal relations, except in case of the last two, entirely
destroyed.

The Androscoggin Indians always claimed that they never conveyed to the English any of their territory above Rumford Falls.
The deed of Worombo to Richard Wharton in 1684, says: "All
the land from the falls to Pejepscot, and Merrymeeting Bay to
Kennebec, and toward the wilderness. to be bounded by a southwest and northwesterly line, to extend from the upper part of the
said Androscoggin uppermost falls," etc. If, by uppermost falls,
Rumford Falls are meant, the position taken by the Indians is
correct. At any rate Indians continued to hang about Bethel after
the first settlers came, and Jonathan Keyes left his two sons with
them for a whole winter, when the nearest white settlement was
Fryeburg. It is said that one of these sons, Francis Keyes, learned
something of the Indian language, and became quite proficient in

the use of the bow. It has been said, but with how much truth cannot now be known, that it was a desire to be revenged upon the whites for the occupancy of the soil of Bethel, that incited the raid upon the few settlers of that town in August of 1781. Some of the Indians making this attack, were well known to the settlers, had been fed by them and given places to sleep by their firesides, and up to this time had always appeared friendly. One of them named Tomhegan, led the attack.

Persons now living have been favored with the sight of the last two members of the once powerful tribe of Anasagunticook Indians. Molly Ockett was once a member of the Rokomeko sub-tribe, but she went to Canada and joined the Saint Francis tribe. She came from Canada to Fryeburg, and then to Bethel. She lived with an Indian named Sabattis, who when a boy, is said to have been brought from Canada by Colonel Rogers. She travelled through various towns in Oxford county, a sort of tramp, and was well known to many, three-quarters of a century ago. She was in Andover and was present at the birth of the first child. This child was Susan, daughter of Ezekiel Merrill, who became the wife of Nathan Adams, and a resident of this town. Molly Ockett died in Andover at a great age, and was buried in that town. Another, and the last of the Anasagunticooks, was Metalluc, variously called "Natalluc" and "Metallic." Of his early history little is known. Lieut. Segar, who was captured at the time of the raid into Bethel, often said he saw him with the Saint Francis Indians when he arrived at their settlement in Canada. He is said to have been banished from the tribe for some misdemeanor, and he settled in the Umbagog lake region, probably near the haunts of his earlier years. He lived in this region a long time, and was visited by many people, including Governor Lincoln. He became blind in 1836, and died six or seven years after, in Stewartstown, N. H. He was probably born on the Androscoggin, and at the time of his death is thought to have been more than a hundred years old. Thus has passed away from this region and from this river and its tributaries, a whole people, who are to be hereafter known only in song and in story. The only evidence that remains to us that they ever lived here, is found in the rude implements buried in the soil and turned up by the plow. These speak to us of their domestic employments, of their hunting and fishing excursions, and of their engagements in deadly strife. They are gone, and whether deprived of their inheritance rightfully or not, matters little now. It may be remarked here, that one of the captives taken by the Indians at York, was Joseph Bean or Bane. He was with them several years, and learned their language. After his release his services were in great demand, as an interpreter, at Councils with the Indians. He was a relative of Josiah Bean, an early settler of Bethel, two of whose daughters married and lived in Rumford.

CHAPTER XVI.

HOW THE FIRST SETTLERS LIVED.

IT is impossible for any person without some experience in the same school, to form an adequate conception of the privations and hardships incident to a new settlement in this high northern latitude. The first settlers of Rumford were not accustomed to luxury in the homes they left behind, for they had little wealth, nor were they inured to privations for they had lived where labor and prudence had kept the wolf from the door. They were plain people who were accustomed to getting their living by the labor of their hands, and they were not ashamed of their occupation. But when they made up their minds to leave their old homes in New Hampshire and Massachusetts, homes which their fathers had reared under circumstances very similar to those in which they themselves were to be placed, and come into this eastern wilderness and make homes for themselves and their posterity, they had need of strong hands and stout hearts to carry their purposes into effect. The usual practice at the period when Rumford was settled, was to take the family and the few household goods to the nearest settlement where they could find temporary accommodations, leave the wife and the younger children there, while the father with his older sons went through the woods to the site of the proposed clearing, felled trees and burned them, erected a log house and made other preparations for receiving the family. For the settlers in Bethel, Fryeburg was the rallying point the same as Standish had previously been for Fryeburg. For Rumford, Paris and Dixfield, the usual stopping place was New Gloucester, while for Turner and Livermore, it was North Yarmouth or Freeport.

Jonathan Keyes, the first settler in Rumford, left his family in New Gloucester and fled to that place when the Indians threatened the Androscoggin settlements. Other settlers made this their rallying point until the settlement became large enough to accommodate temporarily, the new comers. The first log houses were of the simplest kind. Straight trees were felled of the right size, and when cut to the right length they were notched at the ends and laid one upon another, and in this way the four walls were laid up. Places were cut out for small windows and a door. The interstices between the logs were filled with clay or mud, which in a short time would harden and render the walls impervious to cold. Rafters were then put up and the roof covered with bark. Various kinds of bark were used for this purpose, but that of the canoe birch was considered the best. The bark of whatever kind had to be peeled when new wood first began to form, usually early in June, when it could easily be taken off. Nails were then expensive, as it was before the days of cut nails, and all had to be hammered out by hand ; the bark was generally placed upon the roof and kept in place by weights of either stone or timber. Oiled paper was used for windows, for there was no glass. The naked earth formed the floor of the cabin, and under constant use, this soon became almost as hard as pavement. The fire was built upon the ground and the smoke found its way out through a hole in the roof. For cooking purpose, two forked sapplings were cut and put up, one on each side of the fire, a cross piece put on and to this were suspended pots and kettles by means of hooks and trammels. All the work was carried on in this one room, and at night the entire family retired to rest here. A similar log building was put up for the little stock which the first settlers brought along with them. It was some years after the first settlers came before the mills on Concord river were completed, and until then there could be no boards for floors or for other building purposes. Some of the more enterprising laid floors of hewn timber, and re-covered the roofs of their houses with long shingles rifted from the clear white pine and shaved by hand, while others lived upon the earthen floors until they could get a supply of sawed boards.

The first chimneys were built partly of stone and partly of wood. The fireplace was made of stone and the chimney up to the chamber floor. Then small pieces of wood laid "cob-house" fashion were used to complete it, and the inside of this, as fast as it was laid, was

·covered with clay mortar. There were no ovens, and bread was baked in a spider before the fire. Hard wood coals were placed under the spider to bake the bottom of the bread, and then the spider was turned up in front of the fire to bake the top. Corn and rye bread were baked in this way, and flour when it could be had, but flour was very scarce. When the Dutch oven came it was a great improvement. The common tin baker followed, and then the brick oven which was regarded as perfection. In the early days, food was not cooked for several days in advance as it now is, but every meal was newly prepared and rarely was anything left over. The food was of the plainest character, but labor and a good appetite gave it a relish which the costliest viands fail to have under different circumstances. The family retired early and were astir with the birds in summer and long before daylight in winter. Sheep were kept as soon as possible, and flax was an essential crop in the system of agriculture of the early settlers. Flax was dressed, carded, spun and woven at home, the product being used for summer clothing for both sexes, for towels and table linen. Wool also was carded, spun and woven by the thrifty housewife and her daughters, and little save homespun clothing was worn in the settlement. Cotton was but little worn in those days and was too expensive for the family of the pioneer settler. Calico, called India cotton, was worth seventy-five cents per yard, and plain cotton cloth fifty cents. They wore better than prints and sheetings do in our day.

The early settlers were neighborly and kind to each other. In case of sickness of the head of a family, all the neighbors turned out and gave his work a lift, and took care that his family did not suffer for fuel. The mode of traveling for some years, was either on foot or on horse-back. Women thought little or nothing of traveling miles through the woods to visit a neighbor, and men often made the journey to Paris, Turner, New Gloucester and even to Portland, on foot. The first settlers went to Bethel Hill to get their corn and rye ground, and when this mill was out of repair, as was frequently the case, they were obliged to go to Paris. There was no miller at Twitchell's mill in Bethel; when a person came to mill he hoisted the gate, ground his grist, deposited the toll for the use of the mill, and taking the balance went his way, and there was no one about to molest nor make him afraid. Hay was hauled in on sleds the same as those used in winter. Carts were not introduced for sometime. The first wagon in town, though rudely constructed, created a sensation. The body rested on the axles and was nearly as large as a modern cart body. The first improvement was a thoroughbrace made of leather, and this was a great advance : steel springs with light and neat body and wheels were a much later production. In those days children were obedient to their parents, and it was considered the proper thing for children to assist their parents until they became of lawful age to act for themselves. All this is now changed, and parents are expected to give their children such a start in life as shall obviate the necessity of hard work ; this is no improvement.

The early settlers were descendants of the Puritans and Pilgrims, and had been taught to respect the Sabbath and its institutions. The masses, as soon as meetings were established, attended them, none but the sick and those having the care of them, ever remaining away from the Sabbath service. Mothers carried their babes in their arms, and the aged were always there, the two extremes thus meeting at the house of worship. The early meetings were held at private houses in winter and in barns or groves in summer. The school-houses were much utilized for Sunday meetings and then the churches came. At meeting, strict attention was paid to the words of the preacher, and sleeping in church was considered a great misdemeanor. The utmost decorum was observed in going to and from church, and nothing was allowed to be said or done either in church or at home that was incompatible with the sacred day and its proper observances. They may have carried their puritanical notions somewhat too far, but certainly not as far as modern practices are carried in the opposite direction. It will be a sorry time, if it ever comes, when the puritan Sabbath shall be abolished or materially modified.

When young men went to work out by the month, eight dollars per month for the six busiest months in the season, was considered good wages, and not more than ten dollars was ever paid for an extra hand. The labor day was a long one, from four o'clock in the morning until dark. Every sick day and every holiday was deducted at the time of settlement. It was stipulated at the beginning that no money should be required. The legal tender in those days was the product of the farm. Girls who went out to service received from fifty to seventy-five cents per week. If their work was spinning wool, the "stint" or day's work was five skeins of warp or six of filling. They would generally do this and gain a little time to work for themselves, but with India cotton at fifty to seventy-five cents a yard, it took several weeks' work to secure a calico dress, though it required much less for a dress then than it does now.

Farming utensils in the days of the early settlers of Rumford, were rude and bungling, and labor saving machines were unknown. Plows were made of wood, covered with strips of iron, had straight handles and were very unwieldy. Hoes, shovels and pitchforks were of iron and three times as heavy as they need to have been. Scythe snaths were nearly straight and the scythe bore little resemblance to the elegant implement of to-day, although it cost many times more. The horse-hoe and rake, the mowing machine and harvester, were all unknown and undreamed of, and even the handy grain cradle had not then come. The sickle was the implement used for cutting the grain, and back-aching work it was. Yet under all these disadvantages, large areas were cultivated and good crops raised. It required long days of hard labor to accomplish this, but the fathers were equal to the emergency. The early settlers were not free from the superstitions peculiar to their day and generation. They observed the signs of the zodiac, and regulated the planting of the seed, the harvesting of their crops, and the killing of domestic animals for food by what the almanac said of the position of the "sign." Many of them believed in hobgoblins, in witches, and demonology generally. Friday with them was an unlucky day in which to engage in any new business or enterprise, and it made some persons exceedingly unhappy to get the first sight of the new moon over their left shoulder. Persons could be found who claimed the power of charming wounds, thereby easing pain and hastening the healing process. In fact there was scarcely any end to their fancies and foibles, and traces of these superstitions are still found in some localities.

But the early settlers of Rumford were grand people in their way. They were heroes and heroines. They did not make war on their kind and subdue cities, but they subdued the howling wilderness and caused it to bud and blossom as the rose. By their hardships and privations, by their energy and perseverance, they paved the way and made it easy, for the peace and plenty which their posterity enjoys. They not only left a goodly heritage in cultivated and productive lands, but that unparalleled patriotism which showed itself in the late war for the perpetuity of the union, and which sent to the front nearly half of the legal voters of the town, was but the elaboration of that spirit which incited the fathers to take up arms in the war for independence; it was a determination to preserve what the fathers achieved, the perpetual union of these States. The fathers have passed away. The Abbots, the Ackleys, the Adamses, the Farnums, the Martins, the Howes, the Virgins, the Colbys, the Lufkins, the Kimballs, the Silvers, the Keyeses, the Rolfes, the Eatons, the Moors, the Dolloffs, the Dolleys, the Bartletts, the Morses, the Richardsons and scores of others who came to this town when it was a wilderness and who aided in making it what it now is, have long since mingled with the soil upon which they trod, and few, very few of their sons or daughters survive. But their memory lives, and let it live, and ever remain green and fragrant, and let their achievements be repeated to their children's children through succeeding generations, and if this volume shall in any degree contribute to that end, its mission will not have been in

CHAPTER XVII.

POST-RIDERS AND POST OFFICES.

IN 1815, the first Post Office in Rumford was established, and until there was a Post Office, mail carriers were, of course, unnecessary. A Post Office was established in South Paris in 1801, and in Norway Village the same year. One had been established in Waterford the year previous, and in Fryeburg in 1798, and for many years these offices supplied all the back towns in the county. There were comparatively few papers printed then, and in Maine no dailies; postage and stationery were expensive, money very scarce, and very few letters were written or received. What a contrast in this regard, between 1800 and 1890! Now a daily mail from Boston is supplied to nearly all the interior towns of the State, and on all the lines of railway two or more mails daily. In Rumford, where seventy-five years ago scarcely half a dozen weekly papers were taken, and a letter was seldom seen, large pouches are now required to convey the numerous papers and periodicals and the scores of letters daily received and sent out by the people. What would a citizen of Rumford say to-day, if he had to go nearly twenty-five miles to the nearest Post Office, but sudh was the case at the beginning of the year one thousand eight hundred and fifteen, and prior to one thousand eight hundred and one, the nearest offices were at Fryeburg and New Gloucester. When the first office at the Point was opened in 1815, the mail was brought through on horseback. The Post-rider came from Portland by way of Baldwin, and after distributing the mails in western Oxford, on Monday, he would come by way of Norway to Paris through Woodstock to Rumford. The mail was supposed to arrive here once a week, but there were many lapses and failures to do so owing to severe storms, the bad condition of the roads, and other, and sometimes trivial, causes. About the year 1812, a carriage was put on the route between Portland and Paris, and in 1820, a four horse coach was needed and put upon the route. After a few years, as offices were established, the route was extended to Andover, and down the river to Dixfield and Peru.

The first Post Office was established at Dixfield in 1817, with John Marble, Jr., as Postmaster; at Andover in 1824, with Sylvanus Poor as Postmaster; at Mexico in 1829, with Isaac Gleason as Postmaster; in Hanover in 1850, with Phineas H. Howe as Postmaster; in Peru in 1833, with Hezekiah Walker as Postmaster; at North Bethel (Bean's Corner) in 1831, with Phineas Frost as Postmaster; in Newry in 1828, with John Kilgore as Postmaster. The first Post Office in this town was near Rumford Point, which was then the principal business center. It continued to be kept here until 1849, when it was moved across the river to Rumford Corner. The following year an office was established called Rumford Point, with Otis C. Bolster as Postmaster. There are now five Post Offices in town, and the date of their establishment, with the names and date of appointment of the earlier Postmasters, are given below :

RUMFORD. Nathan Adams, Jr., Jan. 12, 1815; Stephen G. Stevens, Mar. 23, 1830; Moses F. Kimball, Feb. 24, 1831; Otis C. Bolster, July 23, 1841; Lyman Rawson, July 29, 1845; Edward Stevens, June 9, 1849; Timothy Walker, June 6, 1853; William J. Hayden, Dec. 24, 1856; Peter C. Virgin, May 8, 1861; Eliphalet H. Hutchins, April 5, 1870. Postmasters since appointed: Fred A. Barker, Otis Howe and John H. Wardwell.

RUMFORD POINT. Otis C. Bolster, June 20, 1850; Warren Mansur, Apr. 6, 1855; Charles A. Kimball, Oct. 4, 1862. Postmasters since : Charles W. Kimball, H. Eloise Abbot.

RUMFORD CENTER. Joshua Graham, Aug. 1, 1849; Patrick Hoyt, Apr. 6, 1853; James M. Dolloff, July 31, 1854; Francis A. Bacon, July 6, 1861; Betsey Eaton, Nov. 8, 1866; Henry A. Small, June 17, 1867; Nathan S. Farnham, Mar. 31, 1881. Appointed since : Ronello C. Dolloff.

EAST RUMFORD. William Wheeler, Jan. 31, 1823; Alvan Bolster, Feb. 12, 1825, Dennison S. Marble, Apr. 5, 1857; Clarendon D. Marble, Nov. 16, 1859; Nathan Abbot, Oct. 23, 1860; Phebe S. Mitchell, Dec. 17, 1863; Augustus J. Knight, June 20, 1864; Henry S. Hall, Sept. 21, 1868; Wilson Thomas, Oct. 26, 1868; Charles E. Virgin, Apr. 26, 1871; Charles F. Wheeler, June 3, 1872; Wilson Thomas, July 30, 1873; Ebenezer Virgin, 2d, Jan. 24, 1876; Floretta L. Virgin, Dec. 5, 1877; Daniel F. Putnam, Sept. 11, 1879. Since appointed : Wilson Thomas.

NORTH RUMFORD. Simeon F. Frost, June 5, 1868; Thomas L. Smith, Apr. 22, 1870; Frank E. Hoyt, July 11, 1872.

The first mail-carrier or post-rider to bring the mails into Oxford county was Jacob Howe, a native of Ipswich, Mass. He commenced in 1799, and for two years his route was from Portland to Bridgton. Then he extended it to Norway and Paris, and in 1802, he commenced going weekly rounds, starting from Portland and passing through Gorham, Raymond, Standish, etc., to Bridgton and Waterford, and returning by way of Norway, Paris, Hebron, Poland, New Gloucester and North Yarmouth. Mr. Howe was succeeded by Seba Smith of Bridgton, and he by William, son of General Benjamin Sawin of Waterford. Joshua Pool of Norway was also an early post-rider. James Longley of Waterford, was the first to run a stage direct from Paris to Portland, and return by the same route. He was succeeded by John B. Stowell, and he by Grosvenor G. Waterhouse. When Mr. Waterhouse became proprietor of the route, he run a daily stage from Portland to Paris, where he connected with two tri-weeklies, one for Lancaster, N. H., by way of Bethel, and the other for Rumford, Andover and Dixfield.

The early post-riders went on horseback, having their mail pouch strapped on behind the saddle. They also carried mail matter in their pockets and in their hats, which they kindly distributed along their route. They were not obliged to do this, but it was a great convenience to the scattering settlers in a new country, where the Post Offices were far distant. The post-rider generally carried a tin horn, and a blast from it would warn the householders of his approach so that he would be delayed as little as possible. When people lived off from the route, a little box fastened to a post where their road turned off, became the depository of their letters and papers. The post-rider was well known to every man, woman and child along his route, and his arrival and departure were the chief incidents of the week. When a tri-weekly mail between Portland and Rumford was established, it seemed as though the *ne plus ultra* in mail arrangements had been reached, and the people along the route felt themselves highly favored. The principal drivers at this time were Mr. Waterhouse himself, Oren Hobbs, William Gallison and Addison A. Latham. From Rumford to Dixfield, and also to Andover, extra drivers were employed.

The building of the Atlantic and Saint Lawrence railroad through Oxford county in 1850 and 1851, wrought a great change in staging and mail facilities. Bryant's Pond station on this road was opened in 1851, and since that time a daily stage to Rumford, Andover and Dixfield, has furnished the towns on its route with a daily mail. The old through drivers of stage coaches, Waterhouse, Latham, Hobbs and Gallison, all became conductors on the railroad, and have long since been dead. Some of the drivers on the new route between Bryant's Pond and Rumford and beyond, have been James W. Clark, James Dingley, Stephen Seavey, Edmund M. Hobbs, Joseph Tuttle, John F. Wright, Henry Abbot, Azel Tuttle and John Woodman. The early post-riders from Paris to Rumford and Andover, were hired by the contractors between Portland and Paris, and their names have not come down to us. Among the early carriers down the river was Grosvenor Farwell, who rode on horseback and delivered the mail to the settlers along the route. But all such primitive methods have long since passed away, and are remembered only by a few aged people. In newly settled regions, remote from railroad facilities, the same thing is now going on, and in our extended country it will be a long time ere the log-house and the post-rider will be everywhere numbered with the things of the past.

CHAPTER XVIII.

RUMFORD SURNAMES AND THEIR ORIGIN.

SURNAMES are of comparatively recent origin, and were only adopted when they became necessary to distinguish families as well as individuals. The adoption of Hebrew names, such as David, Moses, Joshua, etc., which followed the spread of Christianity, rendered these names so common that it became necessary to have some other name to distinguish persons, and at first and for some time soubriquets or nicknames were used for this purpose. Surnames began to be used in France in the tenth century, and in England immediately after the Norman conquest, and some say a little before. Surnames are derived from objects in nature, from color, quality, professions or occupations, from the seasons and other subdivisions of time, from arms, costumes, and there are many the origin of which cannot now be given, though there were doubtless good and sufficient reasons at the time of their adoption. The prevailing names in Rumford are the same as those in other towns in the county, though there are a few exceptions. A list of Rumford surnames, with the origin of such as are known, is given below.

ABBOT, the head or chief of an abbey.
ADAMS, same as Adamson; son of Adam.
ACKLEY, from *ack*, oak, and *leigh*, land; oakland.
AUSTIN, a contraction of Augustine; great; renowned.
ANDREWS, son of Andrew.
ARNOLD (German), faithful to his honor.

BISBEE, originally BESBEDGE, derivation not known.
BARTLETT, little Bart.
BLAKE, a corruption of Ap Lake; son of the lake.
BERRY, from Berri, a province in France.
BRAGG, eloquent; also, accomplished; brave.
BOLSTER, an intrenchment; also, a place in Wales.

BAXTER (Anglo-Saxon), *bagster*, a baker.
BUNKER (Gælic), a strong foundation.
BLACK, color.
BROWN, color.
BLANCHARD, or BLANCHER, a bleacher.
BAKER, a trade; a baker.
BARKER, same as Tanner; a tanner.
BURKE, a corruption of Burgs; a fort or castle (Norman).
BOSWORTH (Gælic), *bosch*, a wood, and worth, a place or farm.
BRACKET, a bracket.
BEAN, meaning obvious.
BRYANT, dignity, honor.
BOWKER, a Swedish name.
BUCK, armorial bearings.
BROCK (Saxon), a badger.
BODWELL (Cor. Br.), *bod*, a house; house by the well or spring.

COBURN, a high hill.
CURTIS, courteous.
CUSHMAN.
COBB, meaning obvious; also, a harbor.
CROCKETT (Danish), crooked, bowed or bent.
CHILD, a child.
CARTER, name of a trade.
CHAMBERLAIN, a chamberlain.
CHAPMAN, a trader.
CLEMENT (Latin), mild, gentle.
COLBY, local; a town in Denmark.
CALDWELL, *Colwold;* wood of hazels.
CHEW.
CHASE, obviously, the "chase."
CHANDLER, originally a maker and seller of candles.

DOOR, a door.
DALLOFF, or DOLHOOF.
DELANO (French), *De la Noye.*
DOLLY, same as Doyle: *D'Oily*, a place in France.
DURGIN (Gælic), *duirche*, dark; hence swarthy.
DWINAL.
DOUGLASS (Gælic), the dark, green river.

DUNLEY, from *dun*, a castle, and *leigh*, a pasture.
DAVIS, son of David.
DRAKE (Gælic), a drake.
DUNN, a parish in Scotland.
DEARBORN, well born.
DUSTIN (Welsh), steward of a feast.

ELLIOT (Welsh), *Heliot*, a huntsman.
ELLIS, contracted from Elias.
EATON, *ea*, water, and *ton*, a town.
EASTMAN, an eastern man.
EVANS, the Welsh for John; same as Johns.
ETHRIDGE (Saxon), a range of high hills.
ELKINS, little Eli, or son of Eli.

FARNUM or FARNHAM (Saxon), *fearn*, fern, and *ham*, home.
FLINT, meaning obvious; also, a town in Wales.
FROST, meaning obvious; also (Welsh), a brag.
FULLER, same as clothier.
FRYE (Cornish), a hill or eminence.
FOYE, local.
FINNEY (Gælic), sincere, true.
FOX, an animal; hence crafty, sly.

GRAHAM (Anglo-Saxon), sullen, stern, courageous.
GLENIS, from glyn, a woody place.
GODWIN, same as Goodwin, or Gooden; win by help of God.
GODDARD, God-like.
GREENLEAF, the green leaf.
GOULD, or GOOLD, same as Gold.
GREEN, with reference to color.
GOODNOW, GOODENOUGH and GODENOT, a town in Germany.
GOODWIN, same as Godwin.
GLOVER, a trade.
GOSS (Saxon), a goose.

HANNAFORD, the old way.
HARDING, an encampment.
HOLT, a peaked or pointed hill.
HOPKINS, same as Hobkins; little Hob, or little Robert.
HOWARD, keeper of a hall.

HUTCHINS, child of Hugh.

HUTCHINSON, son of Hutchins.

HODSDON or HODGDON, strong counsel.

HOWE, *hoo*, a hill.

HEMMINGWAY or HEMMENWAY, the right way.

HINKSON, son of Hink.

HALL, a hall, a public room.

HARDY, bold, free, noble.

HOYT.

HOLMAN (German), *Allemand;* a mixture of all men.

HARPER, a harper.

HUGHES, son of Hugh.

HIGGINS, little Hig or Hugh; son of Hugh.

IRISH, a native of Ireland.

JACKSON, son of Jack or John.

JACOBS, son of Jacob.

JORDAN (Hebrew), river of Judgment.

JUDKINS, little Jud, or son of Judd.

KIMBALL, or KEMBLE, same as Campbell.

KEYS or KEYES, an old Roman word for warden.

KIDDER, a dealer in corn.

KNAPP, a lad, boy, servant or workman.

KNIGHT, an officer; a knight.

KYLE (Gælic), *Coill*, a wood; local.

KING, a head or leader; a king.

KENNISON, son of Kennard, which means a leader.

LANE, a plane; level land.

LUFKIN or LOVEKIN, meaning obvious.

LOVEJOY, meaning obvious.

LANG, same as Long.

LITTLE, with regard to size.

LINDSEY, local: a manor in Essex, England.

LITTLEHALE, meaning obvious.

MANSUR or MANSER (Dutch), a male issue.

MARTIN, a chief; a warrior (Gælic).

McALLISTER, son of Allister.

MONROE. *Mont Roe,* a mountain in Ireland.

MOODY, an anchorite or monk.

MOORE (Gælic), great; chief; tall; mighty.

MORSE, a contraction of Morris; a hero.

MORTON, great or big hill.

MERRILL, *Merel*, a town in Savoy.

MOREY or MOER, a marsh or fen.

MANN (German), a master; same as *Herr*.

MARSTON, a fortified town or place.

MITCHELL, a corruption of Michael.

NEEDHAM, a market town in Suffolk, England.

NEWTON or NEWTOWN, meaning obvious.

NELSON, son of Neil or Nel.

PAINE, a rustic.

PAGE, a page.

PEABODY or PABODIE, the mountain man.

PERRY, a strong place.

PORTER, a porter.

PUTNAM (Dutch) house by the well.

PUFFER, same as Blower.

PARKER, keeper of a park.

PARLIN.

POLAND, name of a country.

PHILBROOK, from *philos*, lover, and brook.

PETTINGILL, a small woody glen.

RAWSON, corruption of Ravenson.

REYNOLDS, sincere.

RICHARDSON, son of Richard.

RICHMOND, eloquent.

RIPLEY, a market town in Yorkshire.

RUSSELL, red-haired.

ROLFE, same as Ralph, a counsellor or help.

ROY, meaning obvious.

ROWE or ROE (Gælic), red-haired, or a river that overflows.

ROBERTS, son of Robert.

SILVER, meaning obvious.

SHAW, a lawn, or an open space in the woods.

SMITH, *smithan*, to smite or strike.

SNOW, *snoo*, cunning, crafty.

STEARNS or STERNE, harsh, severe, crafty.

STEVENS, son of Stephen; (Greek) *Stephanos*.

STILES or STYLES, "At the style," "Atstyle," and then "Styles."

SWAINE, a swan; a youthful herdsman.

SEGAR, *segur* (German), victorious; powerful.

SMALL, with reference to size.

SHORT, refers to height.

SHELDON (Cor. British), local, spring in the valley.

SPOFFORD, from spoor, a projection, and ford.

STOCKBRIDGE, local.

SWIFT, with regard to motion.

TAYLOR, tailor; a trade.

THOMAS, a twin; called in Greek *Didymus*.

THOMPSON, son of Thomas.

THURSTON, the hill where *Thor* was worshiped.

TORREY, a conical hill.

TYLER, a tiler or tyler.

TWOMBLY.

TRASK.

TRUMBULL, same as *Turnball*, signifying strength.

VIRGIN (Latin), *virgo*, a virgin.

WHIDDEN, Wheaden; local; name of a village.

WAKEFIELD, a market town in Yorkshire.

WINKLEY or WINKLEN, derivation not known.

WASHBURNE, from Wash and burn, a brook.

WILLARD, strength of character.

WALKER, a fuller.

WALTON, *wold*, a wood, and ton, a town.

WARREN, *Varenna*, a town in Normandy, whence they came.

WEBSTER, a weaver.

WHITMAN, weighty; ponderous.

WITHINGTON, *Witherington*, the dry hill.

WARDWELL, a good warden or keeper.

WHITTEMORE, same as Whitmore; white, relating to color, and *more*, tall, mighty (Gaelic).

WOOD, meaning obvious.

WHEELER, a maker of wheels; wheelwright.

WRIGHT, an artificer.

WYMAN (Dutch), a hunter.

YORK, a city in England.

YOUNG, with reference to age.

CHAPTER XIX.

THE TEMPERANCE MOVEMENT.

FOR many years after Rumford was settled intoxicating liquors were sold at the taverns and at the stores, and there was scarcely anybody who did not use them in their families. It formed a part of the stock of all traders, and was considered as important to have on hand as other articles of household consumption. It was retailed on the premises and sold in any desired quantity to be carried away. The laborer in the field and shop felt the need of its exhilarating influence; it flowed freely at raisings, felling bees, huskings and trainings; if a neighbor called on a neighbor, it was considered discourteous not to offer him something to drink; it was considered indispensable on funeral occasions; parents drank with their children and the minister with his flock; in fact, its use was universal, and no one, so far as we can see at this day, seemed to see any impending evil in this indulgence. This seems very strange to us now, with the flood of light that has been thrown upon the subject since that time; but they did not have the benefit of modern scientific investigation, and seem also to have been morally blind upon the whole subject.

The result of the unrestricted sale and use of intoxicating liquors after a time began to be seen and felt. Drunkards began to multiply, poverty followed in its train, and the records show that entire families were thrown upon the town, the cause of which could be easily traced to over-indulgence in strong drink. During the ministry of Rev. Daniel Gould, although he did not hesitate to indulge in a social glass when he called upon his parishioners, intemperance became fearfully common in the church, and many members were disciplined for this vice. Not only were male members dealt with for drunkenness and profanity, but occasionally a female was suspended for the same causes, and still there was no organized effort to stay the evil for many years. It continued to be dispensed at the taverns, of which there were several in this town, and at each of the several stores. The men who engaged in the business were the most popular men in town. They were honored with town office, with office in the militia, and were sent as representatives to the Maine Legislature. They were men whose characters were above reproach in all other respects, and it was considered no sin to keep and dispense that for which there was a universal demand.

A movement for the suppression of intemperance was begun in Massachusetts as early as 1812, but it made slow progress. As the result of years of agitation, the American Temperance Society was organized in 1826, and subordinate societies soon began to be organized in the several New England States. In 1829, thirteen of these societies were in Maine. The first one was organized in Prospect in 1827. There was one organized at Livermore in 1828, one at Bethel in 1829, and one in Paris in 1832. In 1834 there were societies in Dixfield, Sumner, Bethel and Andover, but none in Rumford. In 1833, the Maine State Temperance Society was organized in Augusta, with Governor Samuel E. Smith as President. At this meeting reports were made from various towns in this county, but none from Rumford. Buckfield reported, "opposition to temperance reform by political demagogues, followed by their supporters, half drunk." Andover reported, "opposition by the intemperate," and Sweden, "opposition is composed of all classes, but two rival candidates for office have more influence than all others." Later, Rumford may have had a temperance society, under the auspices of the State Society, but if it had, its records are lost, and during those years there is nothing to show that the people here took any active interest in the cause, or made any effort to help it on. Interested in it they must have been from varying reasons, but things appear to have drifted on in much their own way. In 1833, a union temperence society had been organized at Paris, composed largely of lawyers, and Peter C. Virgin was a member. At a meeting this year, committees were appointed in each town to solicit memberships, and the committee for Rumford was Henry Martin. The records are not in existence, and the results attained cannot be stated.

The Washingtonian movement, which began in a small way in the city of Baltimore, reached Oxford county in 1842, and found strong sympathy in Rumford. There was a general awakening here, and many signed the pledge and kept it. David Knapp, who in this and adjoining towns. Inebriates not only reformed themselves, but used every effort to bring others into the organization. It was during this reform that the character of the celebrations on the fourth of July was changed, and temperance advocacy and reform took the place of drunken revelry.

At a town meeting in Rumford, during the latter days of the Washingtonian movement, the following resolutions were offered and passed, practically unanimously, thus showing the advanced position of the people of the town upon the subject of temperance at this time:

"*Resolved*, That we do most earnestly plead with our fellow citizens to quit a business which must be uncomfortable to themselves if they ever reflect on the subject, as being partakers in the crimes and melancholy deaths so frequently occurring under the influence of intoxicating drinks sold by them, and only to get money.

"*Resolved*, That we, the citizens of Rumford, have in lawful town meeting assembled, in behalf of the wives, children and friends of those whose deaths have been caused by rum, and in behalf of our wives, sons and daughters, enter our most solemn protest against liquor selling as a beverage, as an immorality that ought no longer to continue.

"*Resolved*, That the licensing board of this town are hereby instructed to license two persons to sell ardent spirits for medicinal and mechanical purposes only, who shall give bonds for the faithful discharge of their trust; the said venders shall keep an account of their sales, with the names of all purchasers and purposes for which it was bought."

The Washingtonian movement accomplished a great amount of permanent good, but all such movements have their decline and fall as well as their inception and growth. There was wanting in it that concert of action to give it permanency. But Rumford had become a temperance town, and ready to take part in the organizations which have succeeded each other since the great Washingtonian movement died out. The Sons of Temperance, Temperance Watchmen and Good Templars have each served to keep the temperance ball in motion, and each has been productive of great good. The temperance cause, like all great moral movements, requires constant and untiring effort. It requires "line upon line and

precept upon precept," and is worthy the efforts of the greatest
minds. Every new organization brings to the front a new class of
workers, and so the good work goes steadily on. Rumford has not
only endorsed moral means for the recovery of the fallen, but on
each occasion, when the question of prohibition has been submitted
to the people, it has given the principle a hearty support. Among
the persons who were quite early interested in temperance work,
besides the ministers, were Samuel S. Snow and Dea. Henry
Martin.

Rumford Division of the Sons of Temperance was organized at
East Rumford in 1850. William Frost was Patriarch and Ajalon
Godwin, Secretary. The report of the Secretary for July, 1850,
gives thirty-three members. In April, 1851, its membership had
increased to seventy, and in July to eighty-two. At the meeting of
the Grand Lodge in Norway in 1852, Cyrus Small, David Knapp
and William Frost were initiated and became members of the Grand
Lodge. Alvan Bolster was initiated the year previous. In
December, 1852, one hundred members of Rumford Division were
reported, and in July, 1853, one hundred and ten. This was the
largest number reported, and from this time there was a gradual
decline. Alvan Bolster was Grand Worthy Associate of the Grand
Lodge in 1856, and Grand Worthy Patriarch in 1857. In earlier
times in Rumford he had been a retail liquor seller, but he took hold
of the temperance movement with a good deal of energy, and continued active in the cause to the close of his life. He had seen the
evil effects of dram drinking and of the traffic in ardent spirits, and
was prepared to advocate and work for any kind of suasion that
would reform the drinker and put a stop to the traffic.

After Rumford Division had gone down and out, Anchor Division
of the Sons of Temperance was chartered July 14, 1860. Its first
return was made in October of that year. It then had fifteen members. Kimball Martin was Master, and Albert Leavitt, Secretary.
In December it reported eighteen members, with Frank G. Russell
as Patriarch and Mark T. Adams Secretary. Their numbers gradually increased, and in March, 1864, seventy-three were reported,
which was the maximum number. Many of its members, including
Dr. Frank G. Russell, went into the army, some of them never to
return. In September, 1867, its membership was reduced to ten,
and in May, 1868, its charter was declared forfeited. All such
organizations are ephemeral, but these two Divisions of the Sons,

covering a period of some fifteen years, did a great amount of good. Their secret meetings made them attractive, and the ritualistic work when properly rendered, was very impressive and calculated to create a lasting impression. They were educators in the work of temperance and reform, and many who quit the inebriating cup in order to become members, returned to it no more.

CHAPTER XX.

FREEMASONRY.

FREEMASONRY was planted in Rumford in 1819, and in a fertile soil. The movement had a good backing, and the early members were leading citizens in this and the surrounding towns. The nearest lodge had been at Livermore, and several of the charter members of Blazing Star Lodge had been made masons there. The next nearest one and the oldest in the county was Oxford Lodge at Norway. Blazing Star Lodge, therefore, had a large jurisdiction, including, in addition to the town of Rumford, the towns of Mexico, Dixfield, Andover, Newry, Bethel, Woodstock and Greenwood, besides several plantations. The early records are lost, and a consecutive history of the lodge from year to year is quite impossible. The lodge prospered for several years. Its meetings were well attended, and there were constant accessions to its numbers from among the best men within its jurisdiction. But the great anti-masonic movement affected the fraternity here as it did nearly everywhere else. The interest became dormant and in many cases died out. The principles of the order were cherished in the hearts of true masons, but there were no outward demonstrations. This condition of things lasted for several years. There were no meetings, and the valuable early records were either lost or destroyed. Then came a revival; the scattered brethren were called together and the lodge was reorganized. Since that time there has been a steady growth, though slow at times, and Blazing Star Lodge has had its share of prosperity. The jurisdiction of this lodge has been much diminished by the establishment of lodges at Dixfield, Turner, Woodstock and Bethel.

Blazing Star Lodge of Free and Accepted Masons was instituted under the jurisdiction of the Grand Lodge of Massachusetts, March 11, 1819. The charter members appear to have been Joseph K. White, William Wheeler, Joseph Lufkin, Ingalls Bragg, Farnum Abbot, Henry Farwell, Winthrop Knight, Jonah Hall, Tillson Hall, Obediah Kimball and Abel Wheeler. The first communication is said to have been held at the residence of William Wheeler, who was much interested in the establishment of the lodge. The meetings of the lodge were held in Rumford until 1861. In August of that year, a petition for the removal of the lodge to Mexico was approved by the District Deputy Grand Master, and this was carried into effect before the Annual Communication of the Grand Lodge in 1862. The reasons urged for its removal were, that Mexico was more nearly in the centre of the jurisdiction, and that the place of meeting in Rumford was inconvenient and unsafe. The meetings were held in Mexico until 1870, when arrangements were made for a new lodge at Dixfield and the return of Blazing Star Lodge to Rumford Centre. This was carried into effect during the year, and there was rejoicing in Rumford that their old masonic home had been restored.

In 1829, the lodge had twenty-seven members; in 1830, twenty-six members. There had been one death during the year. The same report as to number of members was made in 1831. In 1832 the following officers were elected: Master, Joseph H. Wardwell; Senior Warden, Samuel Lufkin; Junior Warden, Benjamin Poor; Treasurer, Moses F. Kimball; Secretary, Hezekiah Hutchins, Jr.; Senior Deacon, James N. Brickett; Junior Deacon, Amos Andrews; Francis Cushman, Senior Steward; Thomas Bragg, Junior Steward; Curtis P. Howe, Tyler. The following are the members at this time: Francis Swan, Aaron Graham, David H. Farnum, Moses Abbot, Alvan Bolster, Farnum Abbot, Joseph Adams, Moses Merrill, David Kimball, Joseph Lufkin, Joshua Graham, James V. Poor, Jonathan Powers, John Lufkin, Colman Godwin, Abel Wheeler, Cotton Elliot and Stephen G. Stevens. There was no work in the lodge from 1829 to 1833, and from 1833 to and including 1848 no report was made to the Grand Lodge, and Blazing Star had no representation at the annual meetings. During all these years, the District Deputy Grand Master of the Second Masonic District, to which Blazing Star Lodge belonged, made no report. It was a dark period for the ancient order, and many prophesied that it would never revive again. In 1849, the following were elected officers of Blazing Star Lodge: Master, Nathaniel B. Crockett; Senior Warden, Colman Godwin; Junior Warden, Caleb Besse, Jr.; Secretary, Hezekiah Hutchins, Jr.; Treasurer, George G. Bragg; Senior Deacon, James N. Brickett; Junior Deacon, Benjamin W. Tingley; Senior Steward, Alvan Bolster; Junior Steward, David Kimball; Tyler, Farnum Abbot. The whole number of members reported, twenty-two; number initiated during the year, six.

The next report to the Grand Lodge was made in 1853. The whole number of members reported was fifteen; two had deceased during the year. Benjamin W. Tingley was Master; William Frost, Senior Warden; James N. Brickett, Junior Warden; Alvan Bolster, Treasurer, and Caleb Besse, Jr., Secretary. The master was Rev. Benjamin W. Tingley of Dixfield, an enthusiastic mason, and there was a marked revival of interest through his influence. He was re-elected in 1854, with most of the other officers. After 1853, reports to the Grand Lodge were regularly made.

Where the lodge had met in all the years previous to the removal to Mexico, cannot now be stated. At first, meetings were held in private houses at East Rumford and at the Center. For five years prior to 1853, meetings were held at Benjamin Barden's hotel at Rumford Corner. In 1853, meetings were interdicted by the District Deputy Grand Master, because there was no safe and suitable place for holding them. Meetings were held at the house of James H. Farnum, and afterward removed to the house of James M. Dolloff, who kept a tavern at Rumford Center.

On account of the loss of the early records, a list of all the chief officers cannot be given, but the following, the early ones taken from the statements of early members, and the later from the records, constitutes a list as nearly correct as it is possible to make it at this time.

The following persons had served as Masters prior to 1844: Joseph White, Joseph Lufkin, Alvan Bolster, Francis Swan, Joseph H. Wardwell, Benjamin Poor and Hezekiah Hutchins. The Secretaries serving the same period were Abel Wheeler, Curtis P. Howe and Hezekiah Hutchins; and the Treasurers, Jonathan Holman, Abel Wheeler, Moses Merrill, Aaron Graham, Colman Godwin, Amos Andrews and Moses F. Kimball. After the revival in 1844, officers were quite regularly elected, and the records fairly well kept up to 1850, since which time there is no break in the records.

The following lists show the names of the Masters, Secretaries and Treasurers for the years given.

1844.   Hezekiah Hutchins, Joshua Graham, Moses Merrill.

1845.   Hezekiah Hutchins, Joshua Graham, Moses F. Kimball.

1846.   Dennis Gillett, Joshua Graham, Hezekiah Hutchins.

1847.   Dennis Gillett, William Frost, Hezekiah Hutchins.

1848.   Erastus Hilborn, James Russ, Farnum Abbot.

1849.   Nathaniel B. Crockett, James Russ, Erastus Hilborn.

1850.   Nathaniel B. Crockett, George G. Bragg, Hezekiah Hutchins.

1851.   Benjamin W. Tingley, Colman Godwin, Alden Chase.

1854.   Benjamin W. Tingley, Alvan Bolster, David C. Farnum.

1854.   William Frost, David Kimball, James N. Brickett.

1855.   William Frost, David Kimball, James N. Brickett.

1856.   Ivy A. Putnam, David Kimball, James M. Dolloff.

1857.   Ivy A. Putnam, David Kimball, James M. Dolloff.

1858.   William Frost, David Kimball, James M. Dolloff.

1859.   Ivy A. Putnam, David Kimball, James M. Dolloff.

1860.   Ivy A. Putnam, Mark T. Adams, Dura Bradford.

1861.   Stephen E. Griffith, Isaac Randall, Alvan Bolster.

1862.   Dura Bradford, Alvan Bolster, Henry O. Stanley.

1863.   Dura Bradford, John Larrabee, Simeon C. Gleason.

1864.   Dura Bradford, John Larrabee, Simeon C. Gleason.

1865.   Dura Bradford, John Larrabee, Joshua T. Hall.

1866.   Dura Bradford, John Larrabee, David O. Gleason.

1867.   Carleton T. Gleason, John Larrabee, Joseph H. Gleason.

1868.   Carleton T. Gleason, John Larrabee, Joshua T. Hall.

1869.   Carleton T. Gleason, John Larrabae, Benj. W. Stockwell.

1870.   Carleton T. Gleason, John Larrabee.

1871.   Waldo Pettingill, John Larrabee, Nathan S. Farnum.

1872.   Waldo Pettingill, William Frost.

The following is a list of those who became members of Blazing Star Lodge, though how many were raised by this lodge cannot be stated on account of the loss of the records. This list does not include the charter members, whose names have already been given :

1819.   Aaron Stevens, John Lufkin, Moses Kimball, Dr. Benj. Flint, John Kimball, Stephen G. Stevens, Samuel Rolfe, David

Kimball, Freeborn G. Bartlett, Cotton Elliot, Colman Godwin, Ephraim Marble, Jonathan Holman, David H. Farnum, Silas Barnard, Alvan Bolster, Dr. Joseph Adams, Joseph Holland, Jr., Francis Cushman, Isaac Gleason, Moses Kimball, Jr., Joseph Yeaton, Gideon Ellis, Jonathan Powers and Phineas Howard.

1820. Abraham Howe, Moses Abbot, Enoch Abbot, Enos Bragg, James L. Bragg, Nathan Knapp, Curtis P. Howe, Elliot Spear, Moses Merrill and Asa Austin.

1821–3. Elijah Spear, Hezekiah Hutchins, Joseph H. Wardwell, John Stockbridge.

1829. James N. Brickett.

1844. James Russ, Alvah Hobbs, Erastus Hilborn, Wm. Frost.

1845. Jonathan Blake, Charles A. Kimball, Daniel H. Crockett, Joseph Sanborn, Dennis Gillett, Francis Swan, Aaron Graham, Amos Andrews, Eben Webster, Francis M. Kimball, Joshua Graham, Joshua Graham, Jr., Benjamin Poor, James V. Poor, Hosea B. Bisbee, Caleb Besse, Jr., Sylvanus Learned, John S. Cates, Algernon L. Cole.

1846. Nathaniel B. Crockett, Walter N. Barton, Hiram T. Cummings.

1847. James F. Abbot, Benjamin Garland, William Howe, Rev. Mathias Taylor.

1848. George G. Bragg, Aaron J. Abbot.

1849. Edward A. Boyd, Benj. W. Tingley, W. B. Boyd, Rev. John Jones, Horatio G. Russ, Benjamin Brown, J. L. Frazier, John R. Briggs.

1850. Alden Chase, Samuel R. Chapman, Job Pratt, Solomon Cushman, Edmund Estes.

Persons joined since 1850 and prior to 1874: Dr. Thomas Roberts, Rodney M. Farnum, Ivy A. Putnam, James M. Dolloff, Hiram Bartlett, Elbridge G. Dunn, Solomon Cushman, Orrin H. Lufkin, George R. Randall, Levi Hayes, Frank Dresser, Joseph Holman, Hannibal K. Andrews, Simeon C. Gleason, Paschal M. Brackett, Lincoln Dresser, Mark T. Adams, Phineas Taber, Dura Bradford, William W. Bragg, Charles P. Edmonds, Christopher C. Richardson, Nathan S. Farnum, Henry B. Walton, Elisha Winter, William W. Davis, Silas Barnard, Isaac Randall, Stephen E. Griffith, J. A. Livingston Randall, William W. Bolster, John M. Eustis, Isaac Randall, 2d, John Harper, Daniel S. Tracy, Henry O. Stanley, Peter Trask, Henry W. Park, John Larrabee, Harrison S.

Walker, George M. Park, Elias B. Richardson, John M. Pollock, Arthur McQuillan, William Fairgraves, Edwin R. Knight, Daniel Hall, Benj. W. Stockwell, Orestes E. Randall, Joshua T. Hall, Dewit Clinton Chase, John O. Kidder, Isaac G. Virgin, W. Scott Mitchell, Calvin M. Rose, Livingston Glover, Charles H. Fuller, W. Harrison Child, Benj. Thomas, Joseph H. Gleason, Charles F. Wheeler, Asa A. West, Isaiah L. Newman, Oliver P. Gammon, Robert E. Martin, David McCarty, Carlton T. Gleason, Joseph L. Chapman, Geo. D. Bisbee, Benj. Edmunds, Ezra McIntire, David O. Gleason, Harvey A. Reed, William J. Wheeler, Edwin R. Abbot, Lyman J. Ripley, W. Wallace Bartlett, William W. Mitchell, John B. Reed, John S. Deane, Benj. Jackson, Joseph C. Holman, Joseph Hirst, Noah W. Jordan, Patrick H. Hoyt, Lesmore D. Kidder, William H. Fuller, Waldo Pettingill, Daniel E. Durgin, John D. Storer, William H. Wiley, James S. Wright, John F. Holman, Eben N. Harper, Chauncey C. Richardson, John H. Ellis, John F. Stanley, Chas. H. Severy, Harrison Storer, Edward H. Wheeler, Francis S. Blossom, Hiram F. West, George Hayes, Virgil Andrews, George S. Walker, Henry A. Small, Loren Glover, Nathan S. Bishop, Daniel G. Frost, S. Thaxter Putnam, Prentiss M. Putnam, William F. Putnam, Charles G. Hall, H. N. Robinson, Edwin W. Abbot, Frank Stanley, William C. Marble, Eliphalet H. Hutchins, Lewis A. Thomas, Hiram M. Cox, William P. Brackett, Henry Marble, Benj. P. Putnam, H. H. Cole, George W. Roberts, Florus H. Bartlett, Winfield S. Howe, Ronello M. Dolloff, William D. Abbot, John Howe, William F. Stevens, Jonathan K. Martin, Llewellyn G. Martin, William H. Farnum, Charles K. Fox, Lewis W. Child, John W. Martin, Elisha F. Goddard, John W. Bennett, Bradley C. Frost, Jesse B. Howe, Galen Howe, Edgar H. Powers, Lorenzo D. Russell, Elisha A. Childs, J. H. Spofford, John H. Howe, George E. Merrill, Henry M. Colby, Edwin G. Spofford, William M. Blanchard, Virgil E. Fuller, Fred F. Bartlett, Asa K. Frost.

CHAPTER XXI.

ROLFE'S ROCK.

AT the head of Rumford Falls, or just over the head of the pitch, near the centre of the river, is a spur of the ledge which is more or less exposed according to the height of the water. In time of freshet it is liable to be completely hidden beneath the surface, but a portion of the rock can generally be seen. The ledge on each side has been worn away, and as this rock stands near the head of the first fall, it is, of course, unapproachable. The river is not very broad here, as the mountains on each side press upon and contract it, and around Rolfe's Rock a mist rises from the seething waters below. The rock, or the part usually above the surface, is not large, some four or six feet across, but the view from it, provided one could reach it, must be grand beyond the power of description. There was once an involuntary visitor to this rock, one who reached it unexpectedly, and who remained upon it much longer than he desired. This visitor gave his name to it, and the story of his adventure is one of thrilling interest.

Among the early settlers in Rumford, was Capt. Benjamin Rolfe, originally from Concord, N. H. He was a man of great energy and push, of remarkable strength of mind and body; just the qualities to constitute the successful pioneer settler where a home is to be hewn out in the wilderness, and the land is to be subdued and made habitable for civilized man. Mr. Rolfe settled not far above the Falls, and his brother, Henry Rolfe, was on the other side. There was a blacksmith shop, and the nearest one, on the opposite side of the river in 1808, and sometime in the spring of that year, Mr. Rolfe had occasion to cross over to have his horse shod and a broken chain repaired. For the purpose of crossing the river with teams, the early settlers had a large boat constructed of timber and plank, which was set over by means of a stern oar—the process known as sculling. It was a busy season of the year, and Mr. Rolfe wished to occupy as few of the working hours as possible in attending to the business across the river, and so did not go over until toward night. The person having charge of the boat not being present, he set himself across. Now Mr. Rolfe, notwithstanding his good sense and other sterling qualities, had a weakness which was but too common with the early settlers of Rumford and other newly settled towns. He indulged in intoxicating liquors, and sometimes quite freely. On this occasion, while the smithy was doing his work, he went to Wheeler's store, and meeting some of his townspeople there, he indulged in a social glass or two, and did not get ready to recross the river until sometime after dark. The evening was unusually dark, it being both cloudy and foggy. His intellect may also have been a trifle befogged by the potations he had imbibed with his friends. Be this as it may, he found it difficult to keep the right course, and while he plied the oar the current was imperceptibly carrying him toward the great falls.

Near Mr. Rolfe's residence, or near the south side of the landing for the boat, a brawling brook came tumbling over rocks on its way to the river, and hearing the sound of troubled waters, he concluded that he was near his place of destination. But he was soon undeceived. The roaring which he heard was the great cataract, and before he had time to realize his awful situation, the draught of the falls took the boat as though it had been an egg shell and dashed it against the rock in the middle of the river. The concussion threw Mr. Rolfe with his chain upon the rock, and then the boat swung round and was carried over the falls. The horse was also thrown out or jumped out as the boat swung round toward the south bank, and landed near a large rock, but was in such a position that he could not move. The next day he was extricated and proved to be not materially injured.

Mr. Rolfe sat down upon his rock, and his thoughts could not have been of the pleasantest character. He well knew that the roaring of the waters would prevent his voice being heard by his friends, and there was no way but to spend the time until daylight where he was. What added to his discomfort was the rain, which continued through the night, and drenched to the skin, in utter darkness, and deafened by the ceaseless thunderings of the maddened waters, he remained in his perilous situation from ten o'clock in the evening until ten o'clock the next morning, twelve long and dreadful hours. He was constantly tortured by the thought that his friends might not be able to relieve him, even in daylight, and this added greatly to the horrors of his situation.

In the morning his absence became known to the little neighborhood and search began to be made. The ferry boat was missing, but crossing the river in a small boat, it was ascertained at what hour he started on the homeward trip. There was now little doubt that he had been carried over the falls, and preparations were being made to look for his dead body below, when some one* happened to cast his eye along the head of the falls, and saw the outlines of a human being enveloped in mist and standing upon the rock in the midst of the river. The swollen waters nearly covered the rock, so that the lone occupant had little more than standing room.

The whole neighborhood soon gathered at the falls, and some were there from up river, as the news of the probable fate of their respected townsman had rapidly spread. At first they were nearly paralyzed with astonishment, but soon began to devise means for his relief. They first procured a boat, and with bed-cords on each side of the river, let it down to him; but no sooner had it come into the draft of the falls than it rushed by and was dashed in pieces. They then obtained a light board canoe and let it down the river part of the way, and drew it back to try the force of the water, but this was likewise dashed in pieces and destroyed as soon as it entered the swift water on the precipice. They, however, got a rope to him by attaching it to a log which floated down until it struck the rock; he put it around him and under his arms and made it fast, then took the chain which he had carried over the river to get mended, and which had been landed with him upon the rock, and was placing it over one shoulder and under the other arm, to bring it to the shore with him. By reason of the roaring of the water his friends could not converse with him, but they made signs to him to leave the chain where he was, because he would be too heavily loaded to bring it with him, and he left it. When all was prepared and the rope well manned, Mr. Rolfe coolly and calmly stepped into the water, and the men on the shore ran up stream and brought him safely to the bank, to the inexpressible joy of all his friends there present, and especially of his family. No sooner had he safely landed than he asked for a chew of tobacco, saying "he had lodged at a very poor tavern where they had neither rum nor tobacco." But he trembled and turned pale when he talked of the perilous situation he had been in, and the danger of losing his life while on the

*Some say that Jacob Abbot was the first one to spy Mr. Rolfe perched on the rock; but Henry C. Rolfe, now living aged over ninety, recently informed the writer that he himself was the first to see his uncle Benjamin on the rock.

rock and in getting to the shore. After this, his friends and helpers being now about forty in number, retired to their homes, and he into the bosom of his family again, rejoicing in his safe deliverance from imminent danger.

Mr. Rolfe was living in 1826, though at that time he is spoken of by Rev. Mr. Gould as old and infirm, and he died soon after. But his rock remains to perpetuate his memory, and generations to come as they gaze upon it, surrounded by the seething waters, will marvel at his almost miraculous escape from impending death. Had the boat reached the falls a few feet, or perhaps inches, either way from what it did, there had been no *Rolfe's* rock, and no longer any Benjamin Rolfe.

CHAPTER XXII.

CHURCH HISTORY.—THE CONGREGATIONALISTS.

THE Congregational Church of Rumford had a small beginning in eighteen hundred and three, but it increased rapidly in numbers and influence and soon became the leading church and society in the town. Its early records were well kept, more especially during the pastorate of Rev. Daniel Gould, but since that time there have been many omissions. Previous to the organization of the church, there were a few members of what was then called the standing order in town, persons who had been members of the churches where they had previously lived. There had been occasional preaching in town by itinerants and missionaries of this form of faith, and among those who came and preached and baptized the children, were Rev. Joshua Crosby, Rev. Jotham Sewall, and Rev. Daniel Gould who had been settled over the church in Bethel. The latter was here in April, one thousand eight hundred and one, for he records the fact that on the fifteenth day of that month he baptized a child for Nathan Adams by the name of Harriet. On the fifteenth of June following, he baptized a child for Silas Howe by the name of Hannah. On the following day he baptized four children for Benjamin Farnum, by the names of Polly, Merrill, Azubah and Sally. Two years after, July thirty-first, he baptized a child for John Howe by the name of Calvin.

The following document records the beginning of the church organization:

"Joshua Graham, Benjamin Farnum, Hezekiah Hutchins, Sarah Farnum, Betsey Whittemore and Polly Hinkson, having passed examination, and giving satisfaction that they were proper subjects of gospel ordinances, and giving satisfaction to each other, they were by our assistance embodied into a Congregational Church of Christ, and as such they are acknowledged and declared."

JOSHUA CROSBY,   } *Missionaries.*
JOTHAM SEWALL, }

RUMFORD, August 5, 1803.

At this meeting Joshua Graham was chosen moderator and clerk.

At a meeting holden at the house of Abel Wheeler in September following, Sally Hutchins and Olive Hinkson were admitted into the church. Olive Hinkson, before admission, was baptized by Rev. Mr. Strong.

At a meeting held at the house of Hezekiah Hutchins in April, eighteen hundred and four, Polly Elliot was examined and then baptized by Rev. Mr. Chadwick. August nineteenth, Nathaniel F. Higgins was examined, baptized by Rev. Jotham Sewall, and adadmitted into the church. September sixteenth following, John Whittemore was admitted and his children were baptized by Rev. Vincent Gould.

Meetings were held nearly every month at dwelling houses, for the church had no other place of worship and no pastor. In August eighteen hundred and six, a child was baptized for John Whittemore, and was named John. January fourth, eighteen hundred and seven, a letter of dismission was given to Betsey Whittemore, who was about to move from the town. The first discipline of a member is recorded this year, when one is suspended "for taking an order from Joshua Graham and denying it." Rev. Alvan Sanderson, Rev. David Smith, and Rev. Noah Cressey preached in town and baptized children in eighteen hundred and eleven. August third of this year, the church voted unanimously to extend an invitation to Rev. Samuel R. Hall, who had preached more or less for them, to become their pastor. He was ordained November fourteenth following. On the seventeenth, Benjamin Elliot, Elias Bartlett, David Hutchins, Caleb Eastman, Molly Sweat, Hannah Hutchins and widow Silver, were baptized and taken into the church. August second of the following year, Nathan Adams, Isaac W. Cleasby, Molly, wife of Israel Glines, and Mary, wife of Joseph Hinkson, were admitted to the church. October twenty-first, Asa Howard of Howard's Gore, and wife Lydia, were admitted to the church and their children baptized. Dr. Elisha Howe was among those admitted in July, eighteen hundred thirteen. In December of this year, there were admitted Hannah, wife of Joshua Graham, Dolly, wife of Benjamin Morse, Dorothy, wife of Increase Dolly, John Bunker, Abel Wheeler, Cotton Elliot, Ephraim Carter, Mary Cleasby, Gratia Elliot, Hannah Carter, Susanna Hoyt, and Eliza Adams. In January following, Aaron Moor, Thomas Carter and Cyrus and Sarah Putnam.

In the month of February, eighteen hundred and fourteen, Rev. Mr. Hall was taken seriously sick, and the church through a committee invited Rev. Daniel Gould, who had been dismissed from the Bethel church, to supply the pulpit temporarily. November fourteenth Mr. Hall died. Hezekiah Hutchins had previously been chosen deacon and also clerk of the church. March fifteenth the church invited Mr. Gould to become their pastor, in which invitation the town at its annual meeting, concurred, as it also had done in case of Mr. Hall. Mr. Gould accepted the invitation April fifteenth, and was duly installed May third. The officiating clergymen were Rev. John Strickland and Rev. Nathaniel Porter, D. D. At a meeting June twenty-fourth following, Benjamin Farnum and Joshua Graham were chosen deacons. At this meeting, it was voted that no children should be baptized unless one or both their parents were members of some church, and in good standing.

July sixteenth, eighteen hundred and sixteen, Jeremiah Glines was admitted by letter from the church in Concord, N. H. The pastor was chosen librarian to receive and loan out to members the books given to the church. At a meeting a month later, Mrs. Sarah Dane and the widow Sutton were admitted by letters from the church at Concord. About this time the church began to have serious trouble with some of its members. One man violated the eighth commandment and was accused of prevarication to cover it; he confessed and was allowed to remain. Others were guilty of the "foul sin of intemperance," and this vice, so prevalent at this time with all classes, made no end of trouble. Deacon Joshua Graham resigned his office as such, and the same was accepted. Many old members at this time waxed cold, and were visited by committees of the church. Some were severely dealt with, the extreme penalty, that of excommunication, in some cases being enforced. October first, eighteen hundred twenty, the pastor and Deacons Hutchins and Farnum were chosen delegates to go to North Yarmouth and assist in the installation of Rev. Noah Cressey. Two years after, February tenth, the same delegates were sent to Bethel to assist in the installation of Rev. Charles Frost. June second of this year, the church voted to invite James Godwin, Eben Virgin and Henry Martin to assist and take lead of singing in public worship. June twentieth, eighteen hundred and twenty-five, John Dane and wife were dismissed to the church in Fayette. Saturday, June thirtieth, eighteen hundred twenty-seven, was set apart and observed as a day of fasting and prayer "for the outpouring of the Holy Spirit," etc. Elizabeth Ray, wife of Elijah Ray, was admitted to the church by letter from the church of Watertown, Mass. Near the close of this year the church purged itself by turning out several members who had been guilty of very grave offences.

October twenty-ninth, eighteen hundred and twenty-eight, "the meeting house at the Centre was solemnly dedicated to the worship of God." Colman Godwin was chosen deacon, but declined, and thereupon Daniel Hall was chosen, and accepted. During the latter part of eighteen hundred and twenty-seven, and the year following, there was a remarkable revival in the town of Rumford, during which fifty-six members were added to the Congregational church. In two communications to the *Christian Mirror*, Mr. Gould gave a very interesting account of this reformation and its outgrowth, the building of "a new and elegant church edifice at Rumford Centre." He has left on record "that the whole gracious work of the revival was carried on with great solemnity, regularity and order, and was not attended with that blind zeal and enthusiasm which often attend revivals." "It is surprising," he continues, "what a great change it has made in the town, among the citizens at large, within the compass of a year. Public opinion has changed for the better, a spirit of love, kindness and benevolence prevails among the inhabitants, and few, if any, are opposers of the work."

November tenth, eighteen hundred twenty-eight, the church joined the Oxford County Conference. April third of the following year, Henry Martin accepted the office of deacon. At the same meeting, it was voted that Sunday meetings should be held alternately at the Centre and at the Point. October twenty-eight, fourteen members were added to the church. July seventh, eighteen hundred and thirty-one, by request, Alice K. Parker was dismissed to "Dr. Beecher's church in Boston City." June second, eighteen hundred and thirty-three, Miss Abi Trumbull was admitted by letter from the church in Lowell, Mass. August twenty-fourth of the following year, at a meeting of the church, "voted that Sally Farnum, Aaron Virgin, William Delano, Abigail Delano and widow Polly Virgin, be no longer considered under the watch care of this church, they having, without liberty, "left their communion and gone to the Methodists." September thirteenth, two leading members of the church were directed to make public acknowledgment for bad behavior in the singer's gallery, in each naming a different tune, and then disputing about it before the congregation. Mr. Gould having become enfeebled by age, N. W. Sheldon was made associate pastor.

As is usual in such cases, a reaction followed the great revival before spoken of, and there were but few accessions to the church for some years. There was also trouble between the senior pastor, Mr. Gould, and Asa Graham, which was a disturbing element in the church and retarded its progress. Otis C. Bolster and Samuel S. Snow were admitted to the church in eighteen hundred and forty. Mrs. Jeremiah Wheeler was dismissed to the church in Concord. Mrs. Dolly Bolster had previously been admitted to the church.

A council was convened at the house of Peter C. Virgin, Esq., at Rumford Centre, October fourteenth, eighteen hundred and forty, for the purpose of installing Rev. Eliphalet S. Hopkins over the church in Rumford. Rev. Charles Frost was chosen moderator, and William V. Jordan, scribe. Rev. Anson Hubbard of Andover, Rev. William V. Jordan of Dixfield, Rev. Charles Frost of Bethel, Rev. Henry Richardson of Gilead, and Rev. Thomas T. Stone of Machias, were present and participated. "The services were performed in their assigned order."

December twenty-fourth, eighteen hundred and forty-two, Rev. E. S. Hopkins and wife were admitted to the church by letter from the church in New Portland. A better condition of things seems to have followed the installation of Rev. Mr. Hopkins, and additions to the church were more numerous. Among those who joined were Peter Thompson, Ajalon Godwin, Sarah and Melinda Elliot, David Holt, William Morse, Francis Cushman and wife, Timothy Holt and wife, Joseph Holt and wife, Mrs. Mary S. Snow, Nathan W. Elliot, John S. Colby, Henry Abbot, Wm. H. Furness. Many others were admitted during this and the following year. The Millerite craze probably had something to do with it, as this excitement awakened a temporary interest in all the churches in the town and vicinity. Mrs. Mary E. Dearborn was admitted by letter from the church in Pembroke, N. H. May first, eighteen hundred and fifty-two, voted to recommend Samuel S. Snow and wife to the church in Saccarappa. February twenty-seventh, eighteen hundred and fifty-three, the pastor asked for a dismissal, and the same was referred to an ecclesiastical council consisting of Rev. Mark Gould, Rev. John H. M. Leland, Rev. David Garland and several lay delegates. The council granted his request, but expressed sincere regret thereat. He had been a faithful and conscientious pastor, and the severing of the relations between him and the church was deeply regretted by both.

After the dismissal of Mr. Hopkins, the church was supplied during the spring and summer, and near the close of the year extended a call to Rev. Josiah Goodhue Merrill, who had been supplying somewhat for the year past. Mr. Merrill came in January, eighteen hundred and fifty-four, but the church records give no account of his installation. Some difficulty between Mr. Merrill and one of his parishioners occurred, and March twenty-seventh, eighteen hundred and fifty-seven, a committee was chosen "for the purpose of settling it." This committee recommended that the trouble be dropped, and be agitated no more in religious meetings. Miss Phebe N. Merrill was admitted to the church this year, and Henry Martin chosen clerk. He made but few records. Chauncey Holt was admitted to the church August third, and died three days after. Charlotte K., wife of William Elliot, was admitted in eighteen hundred and fifty-nine. In eighteen hundred and fifty-four, the following were admitted: John E. Elliot, Josiah K. Elliot, Lucretia Elliot and Benjamin Elliot. No account is given in the record of Mr. Merrill's dismissal, but it is stated that Rev. Josiah G. Merrill, Harriet Merrill and Miss Phebe M. Merrill were given letters of dismissal July twelve, eighteen hundred and fifty-eight. It was probably a year later. The letter was not used, at least so far as it related to Miss Phebe M. Merrill, for in eighteen hundred and sixty, July twenty, she was dismissed by letter to the church in Salem, Mass.

The next pastor was Rev. John Elliot. There is no account of his installation on the church record, but he moved to Rumford Point from Auburn, November thirtieth, eighteen hundred and fifty-nine, and became acting pastor. He held the pastoral relation over the church until his death, which occurred very suddenly, March fifth, eighteen hundred and seventy-nine. During Mr. Elliot's pastorate he kept the church records, but few entries are made except the marriages, deaths and communion services.

Since the death of Mr. Elliot, the church has had no settled minister. The summer following, the pulpit was supplied by Samuel V. Barnaby, student of Amherst college, and during the summer of eighteen hundred and eighty, Mr. Barnaby again supplied. Rev.

Joseph Garland was the next supply, followed by Albert Donnell of the Bangor Theological Seminary. August twenty-first eighteen hundred and eighty-one. a communion service was held and preaching by Rev. David Garland of Bethel. who exchanged with Mr. Donnell. The following persons were admitted to the church on that day: Cordelia Ray. Jenette J. Peabody. Marie D. and Emma A. Elliot, and Arabella M. Elliot. These were the first additions for eleven years, and the largest number received by profession during any year since the revival of one thousand eight hundred and forty-three. During the summer of eighteen hundred and eighty-two there was preaching by J. A. Jones. a student in Middlebury College. August twenty-sixth. Martha Elliot. Henrietta W. Smith and Maria Ray were baptized and united with the church. Mr. Jones continued to supply for the two following summers. The next supply was by W. J. Cole of Andover Theological Seminary. and during the summer of eighteen hundred and eighty-eight. Thomas McBriar of Boston. from the Bangor Theological Seminary. supplied the pulpit. During all these years. the church has been closed in winter.

LIST OF MEMBERS.

The following is a list of the persons who became members of the Congregational church from its organization in eighteen hundred and three: Joshua Graham. Benj. Farnum. Hezekiah Hutchins. Sarah Farnum. Betsey Whittemore. Polly Hinkson. Sally Hutchins, Olive Hinkson, Polly Elliot, Nathaniel F. Higgins. John Whittemore. Dolly Rolfe. Robert Hinkson. Isabel Knapp. Sally Bunker. Jacob Abbot. Stilson Eastman. Mehitable Eastman. Abigail Elliot. Benjamin Elliot. Elias Bartlett. David Hutchins. Caleb Eastman. Hannah Hutchins. Sally Silver. Nathan Adams. Isaac Walker Cleasby. Molly Glines. Mary Hinkson. Asa Howard. Lydia Howard. Hannah Hall. Dr. Elisha Howe. widow Mary Knight. Chloe Farnum, Sarah Hall. Mary Virgin. Aaron Virgin, Comfort Eastman. Hannah Graham, Dolly Morse. Dorothy Dolly, John Bunker. Abel Wheeler. Cotton Elliot. Ephraim Carter. Mary Cleasby. Gratia Elliot. Lois Elliot. Susanna Hoyt. Eliza Adams. Patty Hemmenway. Daniel Gould. Eunice Gould. John Dane. Sarah Dane. Sally Morse. James H. Withington, Betsey Abbot. Phebe Sutton. Mary Adams. Sarah Virgin, Mary Greenleaf, Betty Farnum. Jeremiah Glines. Mrs. Gurgins, Jeremiah Virgin. Jane Virgin, Moses Gould. John

Wheeler, Sarah Virgin, Mary Rolfe, Elizabeth Woods, Lucinda M. S. Smith, Elizabeth Ray, Colman Godwin, Keziah Godwin, Henry Martin, Sarah Martin, John Thompson, Jane Thompson, Susan Adams, Sarah Brown, Maria Smith, Charlotte Adams, Francis Hemmenway, Rebecca Hemmenway, Phebe Dolly, Jeremiah Wheeler, Colman Hemmenway, David Elliot, Polly Elliot, Wm. Delano, Abigail A. Delano, Mary Martin, James Godwin, John Godwin, Clarissa Godwin, Lucinda Godwin, St. Luke Morse, Asa Graham. Wm. Frost, Wm. Bowen, James Silver, Azubah Abbot, Alice K. Parker, Judith Morse, Daniel Martin, Betsey Martin, Benj. Morse, Peter C. Virgin, Aaron Graham, Geneva Graham, George Graham, Hannah Graham, Samuel Farnum, Luther Trumbull, Lydia Knapp, Daniel Hall, Dolly Hall, Francis Keyes, Sally Virgin, Abigail Godwin, Milla Farnum, Hazen F. Abbot, Hannah Abbot, Polly Putnam, Louisa Farnum, Sarah Crockett, Edmund Abbot, George J. Farnum, John Farnum, Jr., Simeon F. Frost, Susan Farnum, Achsa Chamberlain, Mary A. Rolfe, Judith Rolfe, Sally B. Graham, Sarah P. Elliot, Maria C. L. Virgin, Catherine Virgin, Ruth Cleasby, Mahala F. Godwin, Chloe Holt, Virtue Howard, Betsey H. Harris, Dolly Frost, Abi Trumbull, Mary Abbot, Dolly Bolster, David Colby, Judith Colby, Susan Sheldon, Samuel S. Snow, Otis C. Bolster, Eliphalet S. Hopkins, Mary Anna Hopkins, Peter Thompson, Ajalon Godwin, Sarah S. Elliot, Malinda S. Elliot, David Holt, Wm. Morse, Francis Cushman, Lydia Cushman, Timothy Holt, Nancy Holt, Joseph Colby, Mary V. Colby, Mary S. Snow, Nathan W. Elliot, John S. Colby, Timothy D. Colby, Henry Abbot, Wm. H. Furness, Elizabeth A. Howe, Dolly M. Abbot, Hannah W. Martin, Lydia M. Carter, Wm. Moody, Mrs. Moody, Julian Smith, Sarah A Martin, Jacob Elliot, Betsey Elliot, Sophia Stevens, Mary S. Dearborn, Elizabeth Thompson, Deborah Hutchins, Josiah G. Merrill, Harriet Merrill, Phebe M. Merrill, Josiah K. Elliot, John E. Elliot, Lucetta Abbot, Benjamin Elliot, Nahum P. Moody, Melville Silver, Melinda Moody, Bradbury Richardson, Euthalia W. Roberts, Lucinda G. Howe, Betsey Glines.

The following are the names of persons belonging to the church in August, eighteen hundred and eighty-one. Those marked with a star have since died: Sarah Martin, Hannah F. Abbot, Melinda S. Caldwell, Peter Thompson,* Henry Abbot, Nathan W. Elliot, Timothy Colby, Lydia Carter Elliot, Jane Martin Colby, Hannah W. M. Colby, Loammi B. Peabody,* William Moody,* Lucretia

Abbot, J. Emery Elliot, Josiah K. Elliot, Charlotte K. Elliot,* Arabella B. Elliot, Lucinda G. Elliot, Isabel Martin, Harriet C. Ray, Jenette J. Peabody, Marie D. Elliot,* Emma A. Elliot, Arabella M. Elliot, Martha Elliot, Henrietta W. Smith, Mary M. Ray, Emma S. Atkinson, John F. Elliot, Edwin P. Smith, Charles D. Elliot, Edmund H. Elliot, John J. Elliot, Matthew H. Elliot, Robert T. Howard,* Charlotte M. Elliot, Isabella Elliot, Georgiana B. Abbot, Dorothy D. Howard, Emma B. Pitcher, Pearl M. Elliot, Marshall A. Howard.

The church edifice at Rumford Point, built at an expense of three thousand dollars, was formally dedicated March eighth, eighteen hundred and sixty-five. The following is the order of exercises :

i. Voluntary by the choir.

ii. Hymn read by Rev. N. W. Sheldon.

iii. Reading of scriptures, Rev. J. B. Wheelwright.

iv. Prayer, Rev. Mr. Southworth.

v. Anthem by the choir.

vi. Sermon by Rev. U. Balkam.

vii. Anthem.

viii. Dedicatory prayer by Rev. John Elliot.

ix. Remarks by Rev. David Garland.

x. Anthem.

xi. Prayer and benediction by Rev. Mr. True of the Methodist church.

THE METHODISTS.

A Methodist class was the first religious society organized in town, and this denomination has had a strong following ever since, second to none but the Congregational order, which has always had the lead. Early in the year 1798, Rev. Nicholas Snethen, then stationed in Portland, visited Oxford county and preached in Rumford. This pioneer of Methodism was of Welsh descent, and was born on Long Island, N. Y., Nov. 15, 1769. He became converted to the new faith in 1791, and entered the itineracy in 1794 from Brooklyn. He was ordained deacon in 1796, and the following year was appointed to the Maine circuit with J. Finnegan. Among the other early preachers were Rev. John Adams and Rev. Joshua Randal. Rumford circuit was formerly a part of Bethel circuit, set off with other towns in 1832, and Rev. Job Pratt was appointed preacher in charge. He died in 1833, and was succeeded by Rev. E. Hotchkiss.

John Martin, one of the early settlers, was a local Methodist preacher. He died in 1805, and his is the earliest inscription in the Rumford Center cemetery. At the general conference held in Lynn, Mass., in 1800, Rumford was made a separate charge. The first class was organized at East Rumford, and a church and parsonage were built here in 1825, and this became the headquarters of the circuit. Subsequently a class was formed at Rumford Center. By the decrease of members from their moving from town, the society became weakened, and the meeting house having become dilapidated, it was sold in 1865, and the Methodists united with others in the erection of a union church edifice. The parsonage at East Rumford was also sold, and another purchased at the Center in 1876. The church at Rumford Center was built in 1865, and is furnished with a bell and organ.

An extensive revival prevailed in Rumford in 1843, and the Methodist church especially received large accessions. This revival was largely due to the preaching of William Miller and his followers, who predicted the end of the world and the winding up of all sublunary things during the year 1843. There was a general awakening in religious matters, and all denominations were more or less affected and their numbers increased. Several persons have commenced their ministerial labors in Rumford, and some of them were born in the town. Notably among these were the sons of Benjamin Lufkin, namely, Joseph, Moses and Benjamin. Charles Virgin, son of Ebenezer and Mehitable (Stickney) Virgin, also became a Methodist preacher, and was quite noted in his day. His first station was at Livermore in 1809. He also had settlements in Conway and Grantham, N. H., in New Bedford, Mass., also in Portland in 1818, in Bath in 1819, in Phipsburg in 1820 and in Hallowell in 1821. Later, in 1865, Patrick H. Hoyt, a native of New Hampshire, for some years a trader at the Center, became a preacher, and continued in the work until he died in Monmouth in 1873. In 1886, the Methodist church in Rumford numbered eighty-eight members, and numbered one hundred and seventy scholars in the Sabbath school. Rev. G. B. Hannaford, is the present efficient and popular pastor.

The original class numbered fourteen, but no record has been preserved, and it is impossible after ninety years to give their names. The number doubtless included some of the Martins, Virgins and Wheelers.

The following list embraces the names of the Methodist preachers who have supplied the Rumford circuit:

1802, Daniel Jones; 1803, Daniel Stimpson; 1804, Allen H. Cobb; 1805, Dan Perry; 1806, Clement Parker; 1807, Allen H. Cobb; 1808, Jonathan Chauncey; 1809, Joshua Randall; 1810, William Hinman; 1811, Ebenezer Blake; 1812, Daniel Fillmore; 1813, Benjamin Jones; 1814, John F. Adams; 1815, Joshua Randall; 1816, John Paine; 1817, John Lewis; 1818, James Jaques; 1819, James Jaques; 1820, Job Pratt; 1821, Elijah Speed; 1822, Joshua Randall; 1823, John Shaw; 1824, True Page; 1825, Daniel Wentworth; 1826, Ebenezer F. Newell and James Smith; 1827, Ebenezer F. Newell and Oren Bent; 1828, Pascal P. Merrill and Caleb Fuller; 1829, Caleb Fuller and Isaac Downing; 1830, Wm. Farrington and Ansel Gerrish; 1831, Wm. Farrington, Oren Bent and Mark Trafton; 1832, Job Pratt, died in Rumford February 22, 1833; 1833, Edmund Hotchkiss; 1834, Jesse Stone; 1835, Campmeeting John Allen; 1836, Dan Perry; 1837, Henry W. Latham; 1838, R. C. Bailey; 1839, Huse Dow; 1840, Huse Dow and Joseph Snell; 1841-42, D. F. Quimby; 1842, Charles Mason was with Mr. Quimby; 1843, Henry True; 1844, Jonathan Fairbanks; 1845-46, E. Gammon; 1847, Samuel P. Blake; 1848-49, John Jones; 1850, N. A. Soule; 1851-52, Seth B. Chase; 1853, Joseph Hastings; 1854, Joseph Gerry; 1855-56, Nathan Andrews; 1857-58, George Briggs; 1859-60, Joseph Moore; 1861-62, Luther B. Knight; 1863, George Briggs; 1864, T. J. True; 1865-66-67, Patrick Hoyt; 1868-69, Francis Grosvenor; 1870, Benj. Foster; 1871-72, Richard Vivian; 1873, Alvan Hatch; 1874-75, George Briggs; 1876, George Burbank; 1877-78-79, G. B. Hannaford; 1880, Sylvester D. Brown; 1881-82, Thomas Hillman; 1883-84, N. D. Centre; 1885-86, Luther P. French; 1887-88, G. B. Hannaford.

UNIVERSALISTS.

The two leading religious societies in town have always been the Congregational and the Methodist, but quite early there were those here who believed in the doctrine of Universalism, and in later years the number has increased. They have always been among the most respectable and influential residents of the town. In evidence of this it is only necessary to mention such names as Timothy Walker, Moses F. Kimball, Joseph H. Wardwell, Hezekiah Hutchins, Jr., David Hutchins, John Martin, Jeremiah Martin, Calvin Howe, Jeremiah Wardwell, Rufus Virgin, Charles A. Kimball and Frank G. Russell. In the neighboring town of Hanover were the following persons who united with the Universalists of Rumford in the support of preaching: Joel Howe, Eli Howe, Reuben B. Foster, Eben Abbot, Joseph Staples, Albion K. Knapp, and Gardiner G. Hoyt. The families of all these persons, both in Rumford and Hanover, are much scattered, but whether at home or abroad, they generally adhere to the faith of their fathers.

There has never been any regularly settled Universalist minister in Rumford, but preachers of other towns have often supplied here. One of the churches at Rumford Point is owned by the Universalists, and some twenty-five years ago a place of worship for this denomination was erected at Rumford Corner, a large part of the expense of which was incurred by Hon. Timothy Walker. The Universalists have never occupied it much, and it is for the most part used by the Methodists. Mr. Walker was much interested in the cause, and often attended the meetings at Bryant's Pond. This was especially so when Rev. Zenas Thompson and Rev. Absalom G. Gaines officiated there, both of whom were great favorites of Mr. Walker. Among the Universalist ministers who have preached in Rumford have been : Rev. Benj. B. Murray, Rev. George Bates, Rev. Zenas Thompson, Rev. Benj. W. Tingley, Rev. Absalom G. Gaines, Rev. Ezekiel W. Coffin, Rev. Wm. R. French, Rev. John L. Stevens and Rev. Timothy J. Tenney.

CHAPTER XXIII.

SAMUEL READ HALL, the first Congregational minister in Rumford, was born in Sutton, Mass., January 21, 1755. He was the son of Stephen and Mary (Taft) Read Hall, and a descendant of John Hall of Medford, Mass., in 1675, and in Cambridge in 1652, and who was born in England in 1627. When a young man Samuel R. Hall went to Croyden, Vt., and then to Guildhall, where he resided several years. The people here were destitute of preaching, and Mr. Hall exhorted, conducted prayer meetings, and finally decided to go into the ministry. Just what time he arrived in Rumford does not appear, but probably about the year 1807. A vote was passed in town meeting in 1811, to extend a call to Rev. Samuel R. Hall to become the minister of the town at a salary of two hundred and fifty dollars, sixty to be paid in money and the balance in produce. Mr. Hall's wife was Elizabeth, daughter of Hezekiah Hall, and she died in Guildhall, Vt., June 14, 1806. Mr. Hall died in Rumford in 1814. Most of his family remained in Vermont. His son, Samuel Read Hall, Jr., came to Rumford and was teaching school in town in 1816. He became a famous teacher and introduced many improved methods of imparting instruction, one of which was the use of the black-board, which was used for the first time in an American school, in a district school in Rumford taught by Mr. Hall in 1816. This fact is stated in the Hall Genealogy, and the writer of this volume also heard it from the lips of Abel Wheeler of Rumford, who was a teacher in this town contemporaneous with Mr. Hall. The children of Rev. Samuel R. Hall were:

   I.   *Hannah*, b. Dec. 7, 1776, m. Micah Amy.
  II.   *Betsey*, b. Sept. 10, 1778, m. John Whitten.
 III.   *Lucy*, b. March 12, 1780, m. Caleb Amy.
 IV.   *Samuel*, b. April 23, 1782, m. Hannah Swinnerton.
  V.   *Read*, b. Dec. 12, 1784, d. Dec. 8, 1787.
 VI.   *Chloe*, b. May 11, 1786, m. Asa Swinnerton.

VII.   *Hezekiah*, b. March 16, 1787, m. Mary Hawes.
VIII. *Sarah*, b. Feb. 24, 1789, drowned by falling into a spring while in
       a fit, July 15, 1853.
IX.   *Josiah Brewer*, b. June 14, 1790, m. Roxanna Basset.
X.   *Theodocia*, b. Oct. 9, 1793, d. Feb. 13, 1795.
XI.   *Samuel Read*, b. Oct. 27, 1795, m. Mary Dascomb.

REV. DANIEL GOULD.

Rev. Daniel Gould, the second Congregational minister in Rumford, was born in Topsfield, Mass., Dec. 8, 1753. He was the son of Daniel and Lucy (Tarbox) Gould, and the fifth in descent from Zaccheus Gould, who was born in England about 1589, came to this country in 1638 and settled in Topsfield. He graduated at Harvard College and before entering college, and while a student at Dummer Academy he served a term in the Continental army. Returning, he studied Theology with Rev. Mr. Moody of Byefield. He was admitted to the church in Topsfield, Dec. 7, 1783. He came to Bethel and preached as a candidate in 1798–9, and was installed as the first settled minister in Bethel in October, 1799. He remained here until 1815, when, having received a call, he became the pastor of the church in Rumford and moved here. He was installed as such May 31, 1815. While in Bethel he opened a school for young men in his own house, and several who have since become conspicuous, fitted for college under his instruction. He did the same in Rumford after he became pastor of the church here. He brought the first chaise into Bethel, and was himself a conspicuous figure in his cocked hat, black silk gown and breeches which was the ministerial dress of that day.

He was very social in his habits and popular with all classes. His fund of anecdotes was inexhaustible. He wrote his sermons, and when reading them held the manuscript near his eyes. In his will he left a small sum to Bethel Academy, on the condition that the institution should take his name, which was agreed to by the trustees. His college text-books and several other volumes from his library were presented to the Academy and are preserved there. An oil portrait, said to be a correct likeness, has also been presented to the Academy by Miss Mary Hurd of Topsfield, a niece of Mr. Gould. Mr. Gould married for his first wife, Dec. 24, 1782, Mary, eldest daughter of George Booth of Hillsborough, N. H. She died October 1, 1785. They had one daughter Molly, born

September 28, 1785, and died the December following. December 25, 1788, he married Mrs. Eunice Perley, daughter of Stephen Foster of Andover, Mass., and relict of Jeremiah Perley of Topsfield. She came with him to Maine and died in this town. She had no children. For a third wife Mr. Gould married Mrs. Anna Poor, widow of Capt. Abner Rawson of Paris, who survived Mr. Gould many years, residing in her native town of Andover, Me. She was the second wife of Capt. Rawson, and step-mother of Lyman Rawson, the well-known Rumford attorney. Mr. Gould departed this life very suddenly, while sitting at the table at dinner, May 21, 1842, aged eighty-eight years. The writer of this volume has in his possession one of Mr. Gould's manuscript sermons, said to be the first one ever preached by him. It is written in a very plain, round hand on a page about three by five inches. Mr. Gould was a man of excellent character, and is still referred to with respect and reverence by the elderly people of Rumford, though he has been dead nearly half a century. His second wife died Aug. 21, 1830, and was buried at Rumford Center.

REV. JOHN ELLIOT.

Rev. John Elliot was the son of Andrew and Sally (Melvin) Elliot, and was born in West Nottingham (now Mason, N. H.) October 5, 1801. At the age of three years he came with his father's family to Newcastle, Me. He attended the academies at Lincoln, Gorham and Farmington, hoping to be able to enter Bowdoin College two years in advance, but failing health prevented. He was appointed by the American Board, teacher and catechist to the Indian Missions in New York and left for the Seneca Mission June 6, 1827. He afterwards went to the Tuscarora Mission, near Lewiston, N. Y. At this place, he studied theology with Rev. T. S. Harris, was licensed May 2, 1829, ordained as an evangelist June 28, 1831, and was settled by the Congregational Church at Tuscarora. The failing health of his wife compelled him to give up his mission, and he spent two years at the theological school at Beman, N. Y. He was installed at Youngstown and remained eight years.

Seriously troubled with a bronchial affection, he returned to Maine in 1844, and spent a year at the old homestead in Newcastle. From 1845 to 1848, he supplied at Durham. He then moved to Auburn,

where he remained eight years.   He supplied at West Auburn and
Turner, and on the thirtieth day of November, 1859, he removed to
Rumford Point, was installed pastor and remained here until his
death, which occurred March 15, 1879.   A contemporary minister
in a neighboring town says :   "The death of a son ten years of age
probably did more than anything else to weaken the once firm tab-
ernacle of his strength, and to slacken the tension of the silken,
unseen cords of his mental structure, and hasten his exit from a
state of sighs and tears."

Mr. Elliot married, Nov. 19, 1827, Mary Ward of Wheatfield,
N. J., who died in Durham, Me., Nov. 17, 1847, leaving one
daughter.   For a second wife he married, March 27, 1849, Mrs.
Arabella Newell.   She was the daughter of Edward Berry of Lisbon, granddaughter of Josiah Berry of Lisbon, and great-grand-
daughter of George Berry whose wife was Sarah Stickney of
Falmouth.   Mrs. Arabella Elliot was born in Lisbon, Dec. 25. 1821,
married Stillman Newell, Sept. 3, 1844, who died March 27, 1847,
leaving one son, S. E. Newell, who was born July 4, 1847.   The
children of Rev. John and Arabella Elliot were :

I.   *John F.*, b. Auburn, April 15, 1850.
II.   *Arabella May*, b. May 1, 1852.
III.   *C. D. Elliot*, b. July 2. 1855.
IV.   *Marie Danforth*, b. Rumford, July 16, 1859.
V.   *Robert L. B.*, b. April 20, 1865.

REV. JOSIAH G. MERRILL.

Rev. Josiah Goodhue Merrill was the son of Enoch and Mary
(Ambrose) Merrill and was born in Conway, N. H., Sept. 4, 1787.
He was the seventh in descent from Nathaniel Merrill, who came
from England to Newbury, Mass.   Three of the sons of Enoch
Merrill were Congregational ministers, viz. Josiah G., Stephen and
Henry A.   The latter was settled several years at Norway.   Josiah
G. Merrill was educated at Fryeburg Academy and was ordained at
Otisfield Sept. 4, 1814, and dismissed Nov. 23, 1830.   He subse-
quently had settlements at Elliot, Cape Elizabeth, Washington,
Windsor, Bremen, Eastport, Washburne, Fort Fairfield, Presque
Isle, West Brooksville, North Augusta and came to Rumford in
January, 1854, and remained until 1858.   He was of more than
ordinary mental and bodily vigor and wherever he went he com-

mended himself to the people both as preacher and pastor. He was an industrious worker and accomplished much for the cause which he early espoused and to which he devoted the best years of his long life. He died in Lynn, Mass., Aug. 18, 1872, aged about eighty-five years. He was not installed to the pastorate of the church here, but was simply hired to officiate as acting pastor from year to year. His children were:

I. *Harriet Newell,* b. Sept. 28, 1815.
II. *Caroline Payson,* b. Apr. 17, 1817.
III. *Josiah,* b. Jan. 31, 1819, clergyman, r. Troy, N. H.
IV. *Henry Martyn,* b. Feb. 9, 1821.
V. *Augusta Ilsley,* b. Aug. 3, 1822.
VI. *James Ambrose,* b. Nov. 19, 1824.
VII. *Hannah Elizabeth,* b. Nov. 21, 1826.
VIII. *Edward Payson,* b. Aug. 10, 1828.
IX. *Phebe Moody,* b. Apr. 15, 1830, r. Boston.
The above born in Otisfield.
X. *Helen Wenburg,* b. Cape Elizabeth, Jan. 31, 1833.
XI. *Charles Freeman,* b. Cape Elizabeth, Oct. 10, 1833.
Only two of the above family are now living.

REV. JOSEPH LUFKIN.

Rev. Joseph Lufkin, son of Benjamin Lufkin, was born in Concord, N. H., August 19, 1786, and the following year the family moved to New Pennacook. He was ordained a deacon of the Methodist Church by Rev. Francis Asbury in 1815, and became a member of the New England Conference. He had stations at Lunenburg, Vermont, at Livermore, Maine, and at other places. He finally settled on farm near Rumford Center, and became a local preacher and farmer. He was often called upon to attend funerals and to perform the marriage ceremony; he tied more nuptial knots than any other person who ever lived in town. He was a devoted Freemason, a public lecturer, an advocate of temperance, and in every way a valuable citizen. He departed this life January 16, 1872, retaining fully his mental faculties until the end came. His family record may be found elsewhere.

CHAPTER XXIV.

THE LEGAL PROFESSION—PETER C. VIRGIN.

HON. PETER CHANDLER VIRGIN was the first, and for many years, the only lawyer in Rumford. He was born in Concord, N. H., June 23, 1783, and was grandson of Ebenezer Virgin, the emigrant, one of the founders of Concord, and whose heirs were among the grantees of Rumford. Peter C. Virgin attended school and fitted for college at Phillips Exeter Academy, was for a year or more a student at Harvard College, studied law in the office of Esquire Varnun of Haverhill, Mass., and also with Hon. Judah Dana of Fryeburg, and when admitted to the bar, came to this town to practice. He soon had a large and lucrative practice. He was representative to the legislature of Massachusetts and Maine, member of the convention to form a constitution for the State of Maine, County attorney for several terms, town clerk and agent of Rumford for many years, Postmaster at Rumford Corner and also held other places of trust and responsibility. He was highly respected in town and county. He was a gentleman of the old school, courteous and kind to all. For some years before his death he was the senior member of the Oxford bar. His family record may be found elsewhere. He died April 7, 1871, aged eighty-seven and three-fourths years, and his remains repose in the cemetery at Rumford Point.

LYMAN RAWSON.

Hon. Lyman Rawson, son of Captain Abner and Abigail (Fuller) Rawson of Paris, was born in Paris May 6, 1799. He graduated from Waterville College, now Colby University, in 1827, studied law in the office of Judge Stephen Emery, and when admitted to the Oxford bar, settled at Rumford Point where he continued to practice many years, until his death. He also dealt in real estate and cattle, and engaged more or less in agriculture. He was more or less in political life, was an uncompromising democrat, and a leader in that party. He served several terms in the Maine Legislature, and

Hon. Peter C. Virgin.

also as Judge of Probate for Oxford County. He married May 20, 1832, Jerusha Holmes of Oxford. He died Aug. 22, 1874, and his remains are interred at Rumford Point.

TIMOTHY J. CARTER.

Hon. Timothy Jarvis Carter was the son of Dr. Timothy Carter of Bethel, and was born in that town Aug. 18, 1800. He settled in Rumford, but remained here only a few years and then moved to Paris. While a resident of this town he married Sept. 11, 1828, Arabella, daughter of Samuel and Polla (Freeland) Rawson of Paris. He served as Secretery of the Maine Senate in 1833, and the same year was appointed State's attorney for Oxford County. He was elected to the XXV Congress of the United States and died in Washington, D. C., March 14, 1838. High tributes of respect were paid him by Hon. George Evans of the House and Hon. John Ruggles of the Senate. He was able, popular and successful, but was cut down at an early age and in the midst of a useful career.

WILLIAM K. KIMBALL.

William King Kimball, son of Moses F. and Mary (Bean) Kimball, was born in Rumford June 7, 1820. He attended the academies at Bridgton and Bethel, studied the legal profession at Harvard Law School, and commenced practice in Dixfield. In 1844, he moved to Paris Hill where he subsequently resided. He was twice elected County attorney and served ten years as clerk of the courts. He also served four years as United States Marshal for Maine. In the late war, when the twelfth Maine Regiment was organized, Mr. Kimball was appointed Lieutenant Colonel. He was afterwards promoted to Colonel, and at the close of the war he was mustered out as Brevet-Brigadier General. He was an efficient and popular officer, and retired to private life with the respect and esteem of all those who had served under or with him. He married July 29, 1842, Frances Freeland, daughter of Samuel Rawson of Paris, by whom he had five children. One of his sons, Wm. W. Kimball, is an officer in the United States Navy. Mr. Kimball's death and attendant circumstances, at his home in Paris, in 1875, caused the deepest regret.

WILLIAM WIRT VIRGIN.

Hon. William Wirt Virgin, son of Hon. Peter Chandler Virgin, was born in Rumford, September 18, 1823. He fitted for college at Bridgton Academy and at Gould's Academy in Bethel, and graduated from Bowdoin College with the class of 1844. He studied law in the office of his father, and on being admitted to practice, he settled in Norway Village. He soon took high rank in his profession, both as an attorney and advocate, and for many years he had a part in the management of the leading cases tried in Oxford county. He served one term as County Attorney, was a member of the State Senate and President of that body. He was twice appointed Reporter of Decisions of the Supreme Judicial Court, and in 1872 resigned that position to accept the office of Associate justice upon the bench of the same court, which he still retains. His reports are models of clearness and perspicuity, and his two volumes of Digests of Maine Reports are among the best ever published. He is regarded as among the ablest of the judges upon the bench.

When the war of the Rebellion broke out, Judge Virgin was one of the major-generals of the Maine militia. He was at once placed upon active duty in the recruiting service, and aided in organizing several of the early regiments that went to the front. In the summer of 1862 he resigned his position, and was appointed Colonel of the Twenty-Third Maine Volunteers, one of the regiments enlisted for nine months' service. He was mustered out with the regiment in June, 1863. His family record is elsewhere.

HENRY F. BLANCHARD.

Henry F. Blanchard, son of Benjamin H. and Mary P. (Berry) Blanchard, was born in Rumford, April 26, 1838. When quite young the family moved to Boston, and his early education was received in the public schools of that city. He then came to Kent's Hill and fitted for college. He entered the college at eighteen years of age, but did not take the college course. He taught school winters from the time he was sixteen until he was nineteen years of age, when he entered the law office of McCunn and Moncrief of New York City. He also studied in the office of Hon. F. E. Hoppin of Providence, R. I. He was admitted to the bar while a student in the office of Wm. W. Bolster in Dixfield, opened an office at Rumford Point in 1859, and practiced there until the break-

ing out of the war of the Rebellion. He enlisted and served nearly three years and a half. In 1872, he settled in Augusta, and became a member of the firm of Weeks and Blanchard, Attorneys at Law and Claim Agents, in which business he is still engaged. His military and family record may be found in their appropriate places.

ORLANDO W. BLANCHARD.

Orlando W. Blanchard, son of David S. and Mehitable (Taylor) Blanchard, was born in Rumford, October 7, 1836. He attended the common schools and one or two terms at the Maine Wesleyan Seminary. He read law in the office of Henry F. Blanchard at Rumford Point, and was admitted to practice at the October term of the Supreme Judicial Court held in Paris in 1861. He opened an office at Rumford Point and practised there the brief years of his professional life. He married first, Miss Thirza A. Holt, and second, Catherine, daughter of Charles A. Kimball of Rumford. He died March 2, 1872.

CHAPTER XXV.

THE MEDICAL PROFESSION.

RUMFORD has never been overburdened with physicians, and some of those who settled here did not long remain. Among the earlier practitioners here, were Dr. Elisha Howe and Dr. Benjamin Flint; among those whose practice covered a period of many years, were Dr. Joseph Adams and Dr. Thomas Roberts. Both were highly respected citizens and both labored hard and laid down the burden of life while residents of Rumford. Concerning Doctors Howe and Flint, but little has been learned, and they appear to have left the town after a few years' residence. Dr. Victor M. Abbot was a son of Levi Abbot of this town, and practiced more or less within its borders, but he died much lamented and in middle life in the neighboring town of Mexico.

DR. HIRAM F. ABBOT.

Dr. Hiram F. Abbot, son of Hiram and Mary (Huston) Abbot, born June 2, 1835, studied medicine with Dr. Thomas Roberts and graduated from the Maine Medical School in 1864. He served for about a year in the Regimental Band of the Second Maine Volunteers. He married Mary J., daughter of Warren Mansur, and settled in practice at Rumford Point. He enjoys a good practice, and is deservedly popular. He occupies the mansion house erected and long occupied by Porter Kimball, Esq.

DR. ZENAS W. BARTLETT.

Dr. Zenas W. Bartlett, son of Elhanan and Joanna (Willis) Bartlett, was born in that part of Bethel now incorporated as Hanover, August 10, 1818. He worked upon his father's farm until nearly of age, attended the Academy at Bethel Hill, studied medicine with Dr. Thomas Roberts, graduated at the Maine Medical School in 1840, and commenced practice at the Centre. He was energetic, persevering, and soon became a skillful physician with a large practice. After a few years he moved to Dixfield, where he had a broader field and a still larger practice. He rode through all the towns in Eastern Oxford, and had a large business in East and North Franklin. He gave himself little rest, and literally wore himself out in the practice of his profession, though slight blood-poisoning occasioned by an autopsy, may have hastened the event. He died September 9, 1870. His son, Zenas W. Bartlett, Jr., born January 7, 1848, a graduate of the Maine Medical School in 1870, died in Dixfield, September 29, 1885.

DR. JONATHAN S. MILLETT.

Dr. Jonathan S. Millett, son of John and Martha (Sawyer) Millett of Norway, and born in Norway, October 6, 1794, studied medicine with Dr. Jacob Tewksbury of Oxford, graduated from the Dartmouth (N. H.) Medical College, and commenced practice in Rumford. He remained here only a few years, when he returned to Norway, where he continued in practice until the time of his death, which occurred May 5, 1866. He was skillful in the treatment of chronic diseases, and often effected cures where other physicians had tried and failed. While in Rumford he was appointed Surgeon's Mate in the Maine Militia, but his professional career belongs rather to the history of Norway than Rumford.

DANA BOARDMAN PUTNAM.

Dana Boardman Putnam, son of Jacob and Betsey (Parker) Putnam, born in Rumford, September 19, 1825, fitted for college and graduated from Bowdoin College in the class of 1852. He taught school in Ipswich for one term, then went South and was professor of languages in the Southern Military Institute in Fredonia, Alabama. He studied medicine and took his degree from the Medical College of Georgia, located in Augusta, in 1854, and also took a degree from the Jefferson Medical College in Philadelphia in 1855. He began practice in Lagrange, Georgia, and continued there until 1868, when he came to Boston. He was a contributor to the press, and at the time of his death was collecting materials for a history of the Putnam family in the United States. He held official positions in Masonic and other kindred associations, and was a member of the New England Historical and Genealogical Society. In 1855, he married Huldah J., daughter of Richard Manley of Alabama, and had two sons and three daughters. He died of pneumonia in Boston, February 11, 1881.

DR. THOMAS ROBERTS.

Dr. Thomas Roberts, son of Joshua and Sally (Powers) Roberts, was born in that part of Bethel now the town of Hanover, November 22, 1805. He received what advantages the town schools afforded, attended a few terms at the Academy, studied medicine with Dr. Jonathan S. Millett of Norway, graduated at the Maine Medical School, and after practicing a short time at North Norway he came to Rumford and settled at the Point. He had a large practice here, and as a physician had the confidence of the people of this and the adjoining towns. He did not attempt the higher branches of his profession, but as a family physician in the treatment of ordinary ailments, he had excellent success and was very popular. He was kind and sympathetic, and gave his best services to rich and poor alike. He married Harriet, daughter of Darius and Abigail (Merrill) Wilkins of Norway. They had five children, but all are dead. Dr. Roberts died June 8, 1876.

DR. FRANK G. RUSSELL.

Dr. Frank G. Russell graduated from the Dartmouth Medical College and came to this town from New Hampshire. He settled at Rumford Corner. He was active, energetic, skillful in his profession, and possessed the elements of popularity in a remarkable degree. At the breaking out of the war of the rebellion he enlisted and was commissioned First Lieutenant in the Twentieth Maine Regiment. He never had a strong constitution, and his nervous energy was not balanced by physical strength. He could not stand the hardships incident to active service in the field, and early in 1863 he resigned and came home. He died soon after.

DR. FREEMAN E. SMALL.

Dr. Freeman Evans Small, son of Henry A. and Mary Small, born in Stoneham, Maine, July 24, 1854, graduated from the Maine Medical School in the class of 1879, and commenced practice at Rumford Centre. He married, in October, 1879, Miss Mary E. Hoyt. After practice in Rumford a few years, where he met with good success, he removed to Portland, where he is now engaged in the practice of his profession.

CHAPTER XXVI.

RUMFORD FALLS.

LOWER FALL.

THE chief physical feature of the town of Rumford, one that stands pre-eminent above all others, is the great water-fall, or the succession of falls on the Androscoggin river, known as Rumford Falls. These falls were well known to the Aborigines, though the name by which they were called among the Indians has not come down to us, and this is much to be regretted. Some writers have stated that they were called Pennacook Falls, but there is no evidence that they were ever so called until the plantation was named New Pennacook. Tradition states that this location abounded in salmon when the early settlers came and before the river was dammed at Brunswick, and for the authority of this, there is something more than tradition. It was one of the numerous carrying places on the river, and beaten paths were found along the banks and around the falls by the first English visitors in this region. There is no doubt that the fall was much greater in former times than it now is, the constant friction of the water wearing away the granite of which the bottom and sides are formed, and thereby gradually though slowly lowering the bed of the river.

Aside from the pituresqueness, and in times of high water, the grandeur of these falls which render them an object of great interest to the lover of nature in her wilder moods, they possess a pecuniary value of great importance to the town and to all this region of country. For the purpose of propelling machinery, they are unrivalled by any water fall in New England, and if utilized to their fullest capacity, would furnish employment for hundreds of operatives of both sexes. This great increase of population would make a market for the products of the farm, and would bring hundreds of thousands of dollars worth of taxable property into the town. There is no reason why a Manchester, a Lowell or a Lewiston should not spring up around Rumford Falls at no distant day. When the development of this vast water power is assured, railway facilities will not be wanting, either by the extension of the Buckfield road from Canton, or by a branch road to connect with the Grand Trunk line at Bryant's Pond. As a preliminary to the undertaking, the entire falls with a large tract of adjoining lands, amounting to nine hundred acres, have been purchased by Hugh J. Chisholm and Charles D. Brown, two enterprising business men of Portland, and a careful survey has been made to ascertain fully the capacity of the falls for driving machinery. The result is more than satisfactory, and shows that in previous surveys, which have been much less elaborate, the available power has been considerably underrated.

In round numbers, the head of Rumford Falls is five hundred and eighty-four feet above the sea level, and the foot of the falls four hundred and twenty-two feet. This shows the fall, in a distance of one mile, to be one hundred and sixty-two feet. The Androscoggin is a variable rather than a constant river, as regards the mass of its waters at different seasons of the year. This is due, as stated in another chapter, to the excessively mountainous character of the

MILLS.--RUMFORD FALLS.

upper portion of its catchment basin, together with the bareness of
the mountains which form no small portion of its water shed. This
is its character more especially above Rumford Falls. When these
are reached its character is materially altered. The channel where
the waters begin to pitch over the precipice, is only about a hundred
feet wide, and operating like gates, the waters are held back in time
of freshet, occasioning a great rise above the falls, but equalizing
its flow below them. A dam at the head of the falls, which would
not be very expensive, would tend still further to overcome the in-
constancy of the river, by keeping the waters back, though such a
course might be a damage to low intervale lands bordering upon it.
The water power here consists of the entire flow of the Androscoggin river, and in the mile which is the extent of the falls, the same
water could be used many times over before it reaches still water.
The volume of water is of course less than at Lewiston, and allowing
it to be one-fourth less, which is a liberal allowance, or seventy-one
thousand cubic feet per minute, the whole fall, even in a dry time,
would represent in round numbers twenty-two thousand horse power
sufficient to run eight hundred and seventy thousand spindles. In
time of higher water the power would be proportionately increased,
but even in low water this power represents a business of vast magnitude.

There are at the present time four water falls, but anciently there
must have been several others, for deep holes or basins are worn in
the rocky banks far above present high water mark. There are two
principal falls and two minor, while in other places the water runs
swiftly but is not broken. Two of the falls are about ten feet, one
is about twenty feet, and the other, which is the upper fall, is seventy feet perpendicular. This last is the one that will attract most
attention, for here the torrent of water pouring down with the noise
of thunder and dashing itself into foam as it chafes the rocky walls,
produces an effect of wonderful grandeur. Persons come long distances to witness these falls, and are well repaid for their time and
trouble. Mr. Gould refers to the enterprise of Rufus Virgin and
Nathan Knapp in utilizing a portion of this great power, but a few
years later Mr. Knapp lost his life by going over the falls, and what
was done at that time and all that has since been done, is but an
insignificant fraction of its capacities. With a dam such as the new
survey proposes, the power would be materially increased, and would
be about equal to the combined power on the Merrimac at Manchester, Lowell and Lawrence, or about thirty thousand horse power.

CHAPTER XXVII.

SOLDIERS OF THE REVOLUTION. A considerable number of the early settlers of Rumford had served more or less in the patriot army in the war for independence. They had served practically without compensation, for the depreciated currency in which they were paid was worth but little more than the paper it was printed on, and in a short time it became utterly worthless. But there was no fault-finding among the discharged soldiers; they did not enter the service for pay, but for freedom from British thralldom, and this they had nobly achieved. Eastern lands were abundant and could be had for the settling, so at the close of the war and for several years after, there was a steady emigration from the old Bay State to the District of Maine. The towns of Oxford county, including Rumford, were largely settled by this class of citizens, and the best of citizens they generally were. The second settled minister in Rumford, Rev. Daniel Gould, left school to serve a term of enlistment, returned and graduated, studied for the ministry and then came to Maine. In 1840, there were five survivors of the Revolutionary war then residing in this town. Their names, ages and places of residence were as follows:

Philip Abbot, 83; with Henry Abbot.
Samuel Ackley, 76; with Samuel Ackley.
Richard Dolloff, 85; with John Dolloff.
Joseph Wardwell, 80; with Aaron Graham.
Daniel Gould, 86; with Daniel Gould.

Benjamin Lufkin, formerly of Rumford, then of Roxbury, aged 78, was living with Rufus K. Bunker. Others who had served in this war and came to Rumford, were Amos Howard, Daniel Knight, Stephen Putnam, Benjamin Sweat, Joshua Ripley, Aaron Moor, Josiah Segar, Silas Howe, Benjamin Sweat, Jr., and very likely others whose names have not been found. Some of them had served two or more enlistments, amounting to several years, some had enlisted and served a full term of three years, while others who were quite aged when the war broke out, had served in the brief Rhode Island campaign or acted as home guards.

The early settlers of Rumford were required to do a certain amount of military duty, both before and after the separation from Massachusetts, and the May trainings and fall musters are well remembered by middle aged people as among the enjoyments of their youthful days. Independent companies were sometimes organized and dressed in uniform, but the militia wore their cartridge box and knapsack over such clothing as they happened to have. Officers were chosen by the companies and commissioned by the Governor of the State, and the competition for these offices was generally sharp and sometimes bitter. The office of captain was beyond the reach of a poor man, for that officer, when elected, was expected to dispense the ardent with a liberal hand, and the election often turned upon the ability and disposition of the aspirant to do so. The company books of records of the Rumford militia are probably not in existence, but if they are their whereabouts are unknown to the writer. May trainings were held in different parts of the town, and regimental musters were held, in later years at least, at Rumford Corner. There was also a company of light infantry in Rumford. The following list embraces the names of Rumford officers, in both militia and light infantry, for a period of about twelve years, and are taken from the books in the Adjutant General's office in Augusta. The dates given are those when commissioned :

Moses Kimball, Adjutant, June 7, 1817.
William Wheeler, Colonel, August 8, 1818.
Colman Godwin, Captain, August 31, 1819.
Benjamin Flint, Surgeon's Mate, April 15, 1819.
Ebenezer Abbot, Ensign, August 31, 1819.
David H. Farnum, Lieutenant, August 31, 1819.
Jonathan Millett, Surgeon's Mate, December 15, 1820.
Alvin Bolster, Ensign, May 8, 1821.
Solomon Cushman, Captain, May 8, 1821.
Joseph H. Wardwell, Lieutenant, May 8, 1821.
Peter C. Virgin, Division Quartermaster, March 21, 1821.
Hezekiah Hutchins, Jr., Adjutant, March 19, 1823.

Colman Godwin, Major, July 19, 1823.

David H. Farnum, Captain, November 1, 1823.

Joel Howe, Lieutenant, November 1, 1823.

Henry C. Rolfe, Ensign, May 4, 1824.

Henry Martin, Ensign, May 14, 1825.

Asa Graham, Ensign, August 31, 1825.

Simeon Fuller, Surgeon's Mate, September 8, 1825.

Colman Godwin, Colonel, August 10, 1825.

Simeon Fuller, Surgeon's Mate, September 8, 1825.

Joel Howe, Captain, May 14, 1825.

Henry Rolfe, Captain, May 14, 1825.

Alvin Bolster, Captain, August 31, 1825.

Nathan Abbot, Ensign, July 6, 1826.

Henry C. Rolfe, Captain, June 24, 1826.

Levi Abbot, Lieutenant, June 24, 1826.

Henry Martin, Lieutenant, July 6, 1826.

Colman Godwin, Brigadier-General, September 8, 1827.

Hezekiah Hutchins, Jr., Aide-de-Camp, November 12, 1827.

Joel Howe, Major, September 29, 1827.

Calvin Howe, Ensign, June 19, 1828.

Joel Howe, Lieutenant-Colonel, June 7, 1828.

Henry Martin, Captain, June 19, 1828.

Joseph H. Wardwell, Captain, June 30, 1828.

Nathan Abbot, Lieutenant, June 19, 1828.

Asa Graham, Lieutenant, June 30, 1828.

Alvin Bolster, Major, June 7, 1828.

Henry Martin, Captain, June 19, 1828.

Uriah H. Virgin, Lieutenant, October 6, 1828.

Jesse Morse, Cornet, October 6, 1828.

Asa Graham, Captain, July 11, 1829.

William Frost, Ensign, July 11, 1829.

Timothy Jarvis Carter, Paymaster, April 19, 1830.

Joel Howe, Colonel, November 27, 1830.

Alvin Bolster, Lieutenant-Colonel, November 27, 1830.

Alvin Bolster, Colonel, ———.

The following were those commissioned during the last four years that the old militia law was in force:

Kimball Martin, Cornet, April 9, 1839.

Albion K. Knapp, Adjutant, February, 18, 1839.

Chas. A. Kimball, Brigade Major, March 25, 1839.

Patrick H. Virgin, Aide-de-Camp, March 29, 1839.

William M. Morse, Captain, May 2, 1839.

Loammi B. Peabody, Ensign, May 2, 1839.

Thomas Roberts, Surgeon's Mate, July 20, 1839.

Anson W. Farnum, Paymaster, August 26, 1839.

Lyman Rawson, Division Advocate, September 23, 1839.

William Andrews, Captain, May 5, 1840.

Enoch Knapp, Captain Cavalry Company, August 1, 1840.

Kimball Martin, Lieutenant, August 1, 1840.

Stephen Farnum, Major-General. October 6, 1840.

Albion K. Knapp, Aide-de-Camp, October 24, 1840.

William Andrews, Major, July 6, 1842.

Livermore R. Hall, Lieutenant, July 6, 1842.

Nathan S. Lufkin, Lieutenant, March 3, 1843.

Nathan S. Lufkin, Captain, March 12, 1843.

Joseph W. Elliot, Lieutenant, May 20, 1843.

Warren M. Adams, Ensign, April 20, 1843.

The law requiring annual musters and frequent training by the Maine Militia, was repealed in 1843. William Andrews was promoted from the ranks to be Captain in 1840. He was subsequently promoted to Major and Lieutenant-Colonel, but was not mustered into the latter office until the law was repealed. Among the Light Infantry captains were Alvan Bolster, Solomon Cushman and Joseph H. Wardwell. Joshua T. Hall was Captain of the militia from 1836 to 1840. He was detailed as Captain to serve in the "Aroostook War," so called, and under him were sixteen of the militia and eight of the Light Infantry, all from Rumford. Stephen H. Abbot and Cyrus Small served as Lieutenants under Captain Hall, and Alvan Bolster was subsequently promoted to the command of a Division, and was commissioned as Major General.

The following is a list of Captain Joshua T. Hall's company of infantry for the protection of the northeastern frontier, which was mustered into service March 6, 1839, and discharged March 29, 1839. John C. Stockbridge was Ensign, and John M. Adams, Orderly Sergeant. The men were from Rumford and adjoining towns:

John C. Stockbridge, John M. Adams, John B. Holman, George

K. Smith, Enoch Stiles, George A. Ray, Moulton Ellis, Jr., John W. Dearborn, Rathous B. Waite, Albert G. Glines, William Andrews, James Andrews, Horatio N. Abbot, Jonathan A. Bartlett, William Bailey, James S. Boynton, Simeon Brackett, George Dolly, Abner H. Elliot, William French, Enos A. Hutchins, Kimball Hall, Asa Hardy, Abiathar C. Jennings, Aaron H. Lufkin, Azel Lovejoy, James Lamb, Silas McKenney, Ezra Noyes, Luther Rich, Alsworth Tainter, John Shackley, Benjamin Stevens, Elbridge Tucker, Stephen Virgin, John Winter, Hiram Young, William P. Frost, Ashur Burns, Rufus S. Royal and John I. Cross.

WAR OF 1812.

When the war of 1812 broke out, the people of Rumford were loyal to the General Government, and bitterly opposed to the narrow and almost insurrectionary policy of the Governor of Massachusetts. The latter had a party in town, but it was comparatively small and insignificant. There was not much that a small, inland town could do to show her loyalty except to vote when occasion offered, and the votes of Rumford during those years were very strongly in favor of the war. Several Rumford people also enlisted in the regular service, as it was called; some died while in the service, one returned minus an arm, and others with health more or less impaired. Among those who entered active service early in the war, were William Simpson, Jeremiah Farnum, Paul Simpson, Daniel Hodsdon, Daniel Carr and Alfred Lufkin. Carr lost an arm, and was a well known character in Rumford for many years after his return from the war.

When the militia was called out to protect the City of Portland against a threatened invasion, there was a generous response from Rumford and the adjoining towns. When the orders came, Nathan Adams mounted on horseback, travelled through Rumford, the lower part of Bethel, Newry, Andover, Peru, Dixfield, Albany, Waterford and Norway, and through several neighboring plantations, notifying the people of the threatened attack upon the principal seaport town of the district, and very soon a large and efficient company, under command of Captain William Wheeler of Rumford, was ready to march. This was in the autumn of 1814, and this company was in service at Portland from September twenty-fifth to November ninth. They were in the regiment of Lieutenant-Colonel

William Ryerson. The fears of the attack on Portland were either groundless, or the enemy, learning the preparations made to receive them, thought it the part of prudence to keep at a proper distance. There was no fighting, but those who responded to the call and remained in line of duty until ordered home, were entitled to just as much credit as though they had met and fought the enemy. Their names are given here in alphabetical order, as copied from the original muster-roll:

William Wheeler, Captain.
Asa Burbank, Lieutanant.
Ingalls Bragg, Ensign.
Henry Floyd, Ensign.

Sergeants.

Jesse Duston,
Thomas B. Watson,
Winthrop Newton,
Moses Frost,
Isaac Spring.

Corporals.

Samuel Knight,
Hiram Mayberry,
Benjamin Farrington,
Daniel Crane.

Musicians.

Ebenezer Virgin,
Joseph Killgore.

Privates.

Abbot, Ebenezer
Abbot, Farnum
Abbot, Enos, Jr.
Abbot, Moses
Abbot, Nathaniel
Adams, Nathan
Allen, Joseph
Bell, William
Burnham, Jedediah
Burnham, Ira
Burnham, Bohemia
Barker, Nathaniel
Bothwell, James
Burbank, Stephen

Bartlett, Freeborn
Bailey, Joseph
Boston, William
Crane, John
Chattey, John
Coolbroth, Ebenezer
Chadbourne, Humphrey H.
Coburn, Moses
Dolloff, David
Durgin, Leavitt
Eames, Samuel
Estes, George
Eastman, Haynes
Farnum, Merrill

Farnum, Samuel

Farrington, Philander

Frost, John

Foster, Asa

Foster, Nathan

Glines, Timothy

Glines, David

Graham, George

Godfrey, Joseph

Goddard, David

Howe, Otis

Hodsdon, Daniel

Howe, John

Hewey, John

Howard, John

Hannaford, Solomon

Hayes, John

Henley, John

Jewell, Enoch

Lowell, Moses

Lewis, Noah

Locke, Thomas

Moore, Humphrey

Merrifield, Richard

Moulton, S.

Newton, Lambert

Newton, Holsworth

Nutter, Charles

Osgood, Asa

Putnam, Jacob

Putnam, Stephen

Putnam, Samuel

Putnam, Jesse

Poor, Edward L.

Prince, Benjamin F.

Pearl, Benjamin

Pearl, Dimond

Prince, William

Philbrook, Simpson

Rolfe, Samuel

Rolfe, Nathaniel

Ripley, Joseph

Randall, Ezra

Simpson, Paul R.

Smart, Ira

Stevens, Enoch

Simpson, William

Smith, Peter

Stanley, Elisha

Snow, Joshua

Truett, George

Tripp, Nathaniel

Virgin, John

Varney, Andrew

White, Aaron

Warren, Gilbert

In 1825, the roll of the Rumford company of militia was as follows:

Captain, Joel Howe.
Lieutenant, Henry Martin.
Ensign, Nathan Abbot.

Sergeants.

Calvin Howe,
Daniel Martin,
Daniel Hall.

Corporals.

Eben Glines,
William W. Farnum.

Privates.

Aaron Virgin,
Abial Farnam,
David Abbot, 2d,
David Atkins,
Samuel Bartlett,
William Burke,
Joseph Berry,
Alexis Burnham,
Benjamin Brown,
Sylvester Eaton.
Timothy J. Carter,
Simeon Farnum,
Timothy Glines,
Eben T. Goddard,
John C. Hall,
Asa S. Howard,
Zebediah Hardy,
John Hinkson,
Daniel Hinkson,
John Howe, Jr.,
Isaac Rolfe,
Allen Segar,
Paul Simpson,
Leander Thompson,
Rufus Virgin,
Phineas Wood,
Osgood E. Virgin,

Jeremiah Wardwell,
Shadrac York,
Jeremiah Farnum,
Daniel Holden,
Otis Howe,
Joseph Hutchins,
Alanson Hinckley,
Joshua Hall,
Alexander P. Kimball,
John Lufkin,
Samuel R. Morse,
Sylvester Newton,
Nathan Newton,
True M. Osgood,
Loammi Peabody,
John E. Rolfe,
Joseph Richardson,
Jeremiah Richardson,
Daniel Silver,
George W. Sherborn,
Josiah Parker,
Nathan Silver,
Nathan Knapp,
John Richards,
Waid Moor,
John Mansur,

CHAPTER XXVIII.

WAR OF THE REBELLION.

WHEN the war of the rebellion broke out in 1861, no town in Maine that did not have a company of organized militia, responded more promptly than did the town of Rumford. In response to the first call for seventy-five thousand men to serve for three months, Oxford county was called upon for one company. The only company of organized militia in Oxford county at that time was in Norway, and the Norway Light Infantry formed the nucleus of a company for the First Maine Regiment, which was organized in May and started for Washington on the first day of June. Several Rumford men offered their services in this regiment, but such was the rush for places, that only one actual resident of Rumford was accepted. Several natives of this town, then residing elsewhere, were in the First Maine Regiment. In the Fifth Maine Regiment, which was mustered into the United States service June 24, 1861, were a number of men from this town, there being seven in one company. After this there were Rumford men in nearly every Maine regiment raised down to the close of the war. There were large squads from this town in the tenth, twelfth, fourteenth, seventeenth, twentieth, twenty-third, twenty-ninth and thirty-first Maine Regiments of Infantry, and also in the Seventh Maine Battery of Light Artillery. Following is a list of the names of one hundred and twenty-seven men who served on the quotas of Rumford during the War of the Rebellion, and all but a very small number were residents of the town when they entered the service. It is believed that no other town in the county furnished a larger number of native born citizens, in proportion to its population, than Rumford, and none had more men killed in action or died from wounds. Rumford soldiers had a part in all the great battles of the Army of the Potomac, and in the engagements on the lower Mississippi. Their record is every way honorable, and such as to reflect honor upon themselves and credit to their families and townsmen. Some of their dead repose in the National cemeteries, some were buried where they fell, and in a few instances their remains were brought home and interred by loving hands in the soil of their native town. Rumford has erected no monument to perpetuate their heroic deeds, but their sacrifices in behalf of home and country are not forgotten, and their memory is enshrined in loving and faithful hearts.

Those who were killed in action or who died from wounds are given a conspicious place here, in order that they may be easily referred to, but those who died from disease contracted in the service, in the line of duty, are equally worthy.

FRANKLIN BEAN,
SILAS CURTIS,
HENRY O. EATON,
AJALON GODWIN,
CHARLES A. KNAPP,
CINCINNATUS KEYES,

SAMUEL E. LUFKIN,
RICHMOND M. LAPHAM,
JERRY W. MARTIN,
IRVING G. MARTIN,
ROBERT MAGILL,
ISAAC P. WING.

The following soldiers died of disease before the expiration of their terms of service, and of disease contracted in the service.

WILLIAM ANDREWS,
DAVID W. ABBOT,
WILLIAM J. BAKER,
BARZILLA S. COBB,
JOSEPH E. COLBY,
RUFUS R. DUNN,
OSGOOD EATON,
GEORGE F. FOYE,
SAMUEL GOODWIN,

CHARLES H. HARDY,
HERMAN JACOBS,
HENRY JORDAN, Jr.
ALBERT LEAVITT,
CHARLES H. LUNT,
WILLIAM P. LANG,
NAHUM P. MOODY,
JAMES MULLEN,
BENJAMIN P. THOMAS.

The following list embraces all the names of Rumford Soldiers found on the books of the Adjutant General and is believed to be a correct list of the men who went into the army from this town:

HIRAM F. ABBOT was mustered into the Second Maine Regimental Band, August 30, 1861, and served until the band was discharged by order of the Secretary of War.

JOHN AUSTIN was mustered into Company G, Ninth Maine Volunteers, September 21, 1861, and was discharged for disability, January 5, 1863.

WILLIAM ANDREWS was mustered into Company E, Tenth Maine Volunteers October, 16, 1861, was discharged with the Regiment, May 8, 1863. He re-enlisted in the Seventh Maine Battery, was mustered December 30, 1863, and died in hospital, August 27, 1864.

DAVID W. ABBOT was mustered into Company H, Fourteenth Maine Volunteers, December 14, 1861, and died January 19, 1862.

JOSEPH H. ABBOT was mustered as First Lieutenant in Company F, of the Twenty-third Maine Regiment, and was discharged for disability in November following.

HAZEN M. ABBOT was mustered into Company F, Twenty-third Maine Regiment, September 29, 1862, and was mustered out with the Regiment July 15, 1863. He was promoted corporal. He died of diphtheria soon after his discharge.

HENRY ABBOT was mustered into Company B, Thirty-second Maine Volunteers, March 10, 1864, was wounded May 31, and December 12 transferred to Company B. Thirty-first Maine Volunteers.

CHARLES W. AKELEY was mustered into the Seventh Maine Battery, December 30, 1863, and was discharged for disability July 17, 1864.

CHELSEA C. ABBOT was mustered into Company D, Sixteenth Maine Volunteers, as corporal, August 29, 1862, and was mustered out as such with the Regiment. He was on the quota of Rumford, though reported as from Dixfield in the records of the Adjutant General.

HENRY F. BLANCHARD was mustered as Corporal into Company G, First Maine Cavalry, October 31, 1861; was promoted to Sergeant and First Sergeant; re-enlisted December 31, 1863, and was promoted to Second Lieutenant; he was discharged for disability, March 18, 1865. He was on staff duty as Assistant Adjutant General of the Cavalry depot in 1864 and part of 1865, and also as Assistant Commissary of Subsistence.

STILLMAN BLANCHARD was mustered into the Second Maine Battery, January 1, 1864. He was severely wounded and discharged. He married Eliza, daughter of John G. Burns of Woodstock, and died soon after of consumption.

WILLIAM I. BLANCHARD served in the 19th Massachusetts Regiment.

The above three were brothers.

EUGENE A. BARKER was mustered into Company C, Twentieth Maine Volunteers, August 29, 1862, and was discharged by virtue of Order number 64, War Department.

FRANK Q. BODWELL is reported as having served in a Massachusetts regiment. He enlisted as bugler in the Seventh Maine Battery, was reduced to the ranks and mustered out with the Battery, June 21, 1865. He was the son of Samuel B. Bodwell.

WILLIAM H. BRACKETT was mustered into Company G, Second Maine Volunteers, May 28, 1861; served two years, and was mustered out with the regiment. He re-enlisted in the Twenty-ninth Maine Volunteers, and was mustered December 16, 1863. He was promoted Corporal and mustered out with the Twenty-ninth. In this regiment he is said to be of Auburn. He was a son of Peter D. and Betsey F. Brackett.

FRANKLIN BEAN was mustered into Company I, Fifth Maine Regiment, June 24, 1861, and was killed in battle, July 2, 1863. He was the son of Luther Bean, and was unmarried.

JOHN H. BEAN was mustered into Company D, Twelfth Maine Volunteers, November 15, 1861, and was discharged for promotion in the Second Louisiana Volunteers. He had been a trader at the Centre.

WILBUR J. BAKER was mustered into Company H, Fourteenth Maine Volunteers, December 14, 1861, and died at Carrollton, La., September 7, 1862.

JOHN BROWN was mustered into Company G, Fifteenth Maine Regiment, January 25, 1864, and was reported absent without leave October 10, 1865.

JOSEPH BROWN was mustered into Company F, Twenty-third Maine Volunteers, September 29, 1862, was promoted wagoner, and mustered out with the regiment, July 15, 1863. This man was from Milton plantation, but reported on Rumford's quota.

CHARLES H. BUCK was mustered into Company B, Third Maine Volunteers, July 17, 1863, and was transferred to the 17th Maine and then to the First Maine Heavy Artillery. He deserted to Canada, but returned and has since been pensioned for wounds.

174 . *HISTORY OF RUMFORD.*

Barzilla S. Cobb was mustered into the Second Maine Battery, December 31, 1863, and died of disease July 30, 1864. He was the son of Churchill Cobb, and grandson of Ebenezer Cobb of Norway.

Silas Curtis was mustered into Company A, Twelfth Maine Regiment, and was discharged for disability. He re-enlisted in Company C, Twentieth Maine Volunteers, and died of wounds, July 27, 1864.

Henry M. Colby was mustered into the Second Maine Regiment Band, August 30, 1861, and was discharged with the band by order of the Secretary of War.

John Casey was mustered into Company E, Fifth Maine Regiment, was promoted Corporal, and returned to the ranks at his own request.

Horace K. Chase was mustered into Company I, Fifth Maine Volunteers, June 24, 1861, and served three years.

Bartholomew Coburn was mustered into Company G, Ninth Maine Regiment, September 21, 1861, and was discharged for disability, January 25, 1863.

Francis E. K. Cushman, son of Francis and Lydia (Keyes) Cushman, was mustered into Company A, Twelfth Maine Regiment, November 21, 1861; was detached as brigade wagoner, and subsequently discharged by order of the War Department.

Royal A. Clement was mustered into Company D, Twelfth Maine Volunteers, November 15, 1861; was wounded September 19, 1864; re-enlisted, was transferred to the Twelfth Maine Battalion, and was discharged July 24, 1866.

Reuben B. Coburn was mustered into Company D, Twelfth Maine Volunteers, November 15, 1861; served out his term, re-enlisted, and was subsequently reported a deserter.

Joseph E. Colby was mustered as First Lieutenant of Company B, Thirty-second Maine Volunteers, March 10, 1864, and died at City Point, Virginia, June 25, 1864, of disease.

Elias N. Delano was mustered into Company C, Twentieth Maine Volunteers, August 29, 1862, and was discharged for disability, February 4, 1863.

Francis S. Delano was mustered into Company C, Twentieth Maine Volunteers, August 29, 1862; was transferred to the Invalid

Corps, April 10, 1863, and was discharged by Order Number 94, War Department.

ALPHONSO DOLLOFF served in Company G, First Maine Regiment. He is reported to have enlisted and been mustered into Company G, Seventh Regiment Maine Volunteers, August 21, 1861, and to have deserted the same day. (Adjutant General's Reports.)

GEORGE DOLLY was mustered into Company H, Eighth Maine Regiment as Sergeant, September 7, 1861 ; was promoted to Second Lieutenant, and afterwards discharged to accept a Captaincy in the First Regiment, South Carolina Volunteers.

AMOS H. DWINEL served three years in a Massachusetts Battery. He was the son of Amos Dwinel.

RUFUS R. DUNN was mustered into Company C, Sixteenth Maine Volunteers, September 16, 1862, and died a prisoner in Richmond, July 21, 1863.

ISAAC R. DOUGLASS was mustered into the Twelfth Maine Volunteers, January 1, 1864. This man enlisted at New Orleans, was transferred to the Twelfth Maine Battalion, and discharged July 18, 1865.

CHARLES ESTES enlisted and was mustered into Company C, Twentieth Maine Regiment, August 29, 1862 ; was promoted Corporal, reduced to ranks, and discharged April 4, 1863. He was a resident of Bethel, but went on the quota of Rumford.

EDWARD F. ELLIOT was mustered into Company F, Tenth Maine Regiment, October 4, 1861, was captured at Culpepper, and afterwards returned to duty.

OSGOOD EATON was mustered into Company A, Twelfth Maine Volunteers, November 21, 1861, and died July 3, 1863.

HENRY O. EATON was mustered into Company B, Thirty-second Maine Volunteers, March 10, 1864, and died of wounds, June 3, 1864.

ARBURY E. EASTMAN was mustered into Company G, Fifteenth Maine Volunteers, and was reported a deserter, February 16, 1862. He re-enlisted in the Seventh Maine Battery, mustered December 30, 1863, and was discharged June 20, 1865.

FARNUM A. ELLIOT was mustered into Company G, First Maine Cavalry. (Record incomplete.)

CHARLES A. EASTMAN was mustered into the Ninth Maine Volunteers, September 24, 1862.

DANIEL G. EASTMAN was mustered as Corporal in Company B, Thirty-second Maine Volunteers, March 10, 1864, and was mustered out by consolidation of the regiment with the Thirty-first Maine, December 12, 1864.

HOLLAND F. EASTMAN was mustered into Company F, Twenty-third Maine Volunteers, September 29, 1862, and was mustered out with the regiment.

CHARLES W. FARNUM was mustered into Company H, Thirteenth Maine Volunteers, December 12, 1861, and was discharged for disability in July following.

WILLIAM H. FARNUM was mustered into Company G, First Maine Cavalry, and was discharged February 26, 1865.

WILLIAM G. FARNUM was mustered into Company B, Thirty-second Maine Volunteers, March 10, 1864, and December 12, 1864, was transferred to Company B, Thirty-first Maine Volunteers; he was mustered out with that regiment, July 15, 1865.

RUFUS V. FARNUM was mustered into the Seventh Maine Battery, December 30, 1863, and was mustered out with the Battery, June 21, 1865.

EDWARD FAUNCE was mustered into Company C, Twentieth Maine Volunteers, August 29, 1862, and was discharged with the regiment June 26, 1865.

GEORGE F. FOYE was mustered into Company B, Thirty-second Maine Volunteers, March 10, 1864, and died in Washington, August 1, 1864.

GEORGE L. FARNUM enlisted in the Eleventh Massachusetts Regiment, and was severely wounded in the battle of the Wilderness, resulting in the loss of the use of one of his hands. He afterwards graduated from Colby University, studied law and practiced in Norway. He died in 1877.

ELISHA F. GODDARD was mustered as Quartermaster Sergeant of the Twelfth Maine Volunteers; was promoted to Second and First Lieutenant, and Captain of Company A; re-enlisted and was transferred to Twelfth Maine Battalion. He resigned in November, 1865.

EPHRAIM F. GODDARD was mustered into Company B, Thirty-second Maine Regiment, March 10, 1864, and was transferred to Company B, Thirty-first Maine, December 12, 1864, and was mustered out with the regiment, July 15, 1865.

AJALON GODWIN was mustered into Company H, Fourteenth Maine Volunteers, as Sergeant, December 14, 1861, was promoted First Sergeant, Second and First Lieutenant, and Captain, and died of wounds received September 19, 1864.

JOEL GOODWIN was mustered in Company F, Twenty-third Maine Volunteers, September 29, 1862, and was mustered out with the regiment. He re-enlisted in the Seventh Maine Battery, was mustered December 30, 1863, and was discharged with the Battery, June 21, 1865.

SAMUEL GOODWIN was mustered into Company F, Twenty-third Maine Regiment, September 29, 1862, and was mustered out with the regiment, July 15, 1863. He re-enlisted in the Seventh Maine Battery, was mustered December 30, 1863, and died at City Point, Va., October 4, 1864.

ALVAN B. GODWIN was mustered as Quartermaster of the Twelfth Maine Volunteers, March 9, 1865.

OSGOOD A. HODGMAN was mustered into Company C, Twentieth Maine Regiment, August 29, 1862, and was transferred to the Invalid Corps.

WILLIAM H. HARPER was mustered into Company I, Fifth Maine Regiment, June 24, 1861; was dropped from the rolls by Order number 162, of War Department, and was subsequently restored and served out his term.

CHAS. J. HARDY was mustered into Company A, Twelfth Maine Volunteers, November 21, 1861, and died at New Orleans, June 2, 1862.

JOEL B. HOWE was mustered into Company D, Twelfth Maine Volunteers, November 15, 1861, and was discharged for disability April 15, 1862.

CHARLES F. HOWE was mustered into Company F, Twenty-third Maine Regiment, September 29, 1862, and was discharged with the regiment, July 15, 1863.

WILLIAM C. HUTCHINSON was mustered into the Seventh Maine

Battery, December 30, 1863, and was discharged for disability June 2, 1864.

George H. Hutchins was mustered into the Seventh Maine Battery, December 30, 1863, and was discharged with the Battery, June 21, 1865.

Herman Jacobs was mustered into Company G, Ninth Maine Volunteers, September 21, 1861, and died November 1 following.

William Jacobs was mustered into Company G, First Maine Cavalry; was wounded October 27, 1863, and was discharged June 20, 1864.

Ezekiel E. Jackson was mustered into Company C, Fourth Maine Volunteers, August 29, 1863, and was discharged for disability, December 7, following.

Henry Jordan, Jr., was mustered on the quota of Rumford, into Company H, Fourteenth Maine Volunteers, March 21, 1864; he died in New Orleans. This man's home was in Woodstock.

Charles A. Knapp was mustered into Company G, Second Maine Regiment, July 10, 1861; he was promoted Corporal, wounded in the battle of Gaine's Mill, transferred to the Twentieth Maine Regiment, July 4, 1862, and was killed in battle, May 28, 1864.

Cincinnatus Keyes was mustered into Company A, Tenth Maine Volunteers, October 4, 1861, was wounded in the battle of Cedar Mountain, and died of his wounds.

Albert Leavitt was mustered into Company C, Twentieth Maine Volunteers, August 29, 1862, and died November 3 following.

Samuel E. Lufkin was mustered into Company I, Fifth Maine Regiment, June 24, 1861, and was killed in battle at Crampton Pass.

Abijah Lapham enlisted in Company B, Thirty-second Maine Volunteers, went to the front with the regiment and was accidentally killed by a comrade at North Anna River, Va.

Charles A. E. Lufkin was mustered as private in Company F, Twenty-third Maine Volunteers, September 29, 1862, and was mustered out with the regiment, July 15, 1863.

Joseph C. Lapham was mustered into Company F, Tenth Maine Regiment, October 4, 1861, was captured at Winchester, Va., and paroled. He served out his time in the Tenth, re-enlisted in the

Seventh Maine Battery, mustered December 30, 1863, and was mustered out with the Battery, June 21, 1865.

RICHMOND M. LAPHAM was mustered into Company I, Fifth Maine Regiment, June 24, 1861; he served out his time of three years, re-enlisted, and was missing after the battle of Spotsylvania, May 10, 1864. After the capture of Richmond, a hospital record was found by which it was learned that he was severely wounded, but no account of his death was given. He doubtless died of his wounds. He was the son of Thomas and Sophronia (Crooker) Lapham, and unmarried.

CHARLES H. LUNT was mustered into Company D, Twelfth Maine Volunteers, November 15, 1861, and died at New Orleans, July 15, 1862.

WILLIAM P. LANG was mustered into Company F, Twenty-third Maine Regiment, September 29, 1862, and was discharged with the regiment, July 15, 1863. He re-enlisted in Company F, Twenty-ninth Maine Volunteers, was mustered November 13, 1863, and died of disease, June 26, 1864.

AYERS LITTLE was mustered into Company K, Twenty-ninth Maine Volunteers, January 5, 1864, and was mustered out with the regiment.

WILLIAM LINSEY was mustered into Company K, Twenty-ninth Maine Volunteers, January 5, 1864; was promoted Corporal and mustered out with the regiment.

WILLIAM LOCKMEYER enlisted at New Orleans into Company A, Twelfth Maine Volunteers, August 31, 1862; was taken prisoner at Cedar Creek, September 19, 1864, and subsequently returned and was transferred to Twelfth Maine Battalion. He was discharged October 10, 1865.

NAHUM P. MOODY, son of Hezekiah and Hannah (Estes) Moody, was mustered into Company C, Twentieth Maine Volunteers, Aug. 29, 1862, and died November 28, 1862. He married Melinda S., daughter of David Elliot.

JERRY W. MARTIN was mustered into Company I, Fifth Maine Volunteers, June 24, 1861, and was killed in battle, May 12, 1864.

IRVING G. MARTIN was mustered into Company K, Tenth Maine Volunteers, October 4, 1861, and died of wounds received in action, January 22, 1863.

FRANKLIN MARTIN was mustered into Company A, Twelfth Maine Regiment, November 21, 1861, served his time and was mustered out December 7, 1864.

WILLIAM MARTIN was mustered into the Seventh Maine Battery, December 30, 1863, and was mustered out with the Battery, June 21, 1865.

JAMES MULLEN enlisted in Company A, Twelfth Maine Volunteers, at New Orleans, January 1, 1864, and was credited to Rumford. He was taken prisoner October 19, 1864, and was subsequently transferred to the Twelfth Maine Battalion. He died in rebel prison, November 11, 1864.

WINFIELD S. MARTIN was mustered into Company F, Twenty-third Maine Regiment, September 29, 1862, and was mustered out with the regiment, July 15, 1863.

WILLIAM H. MOORE was mustered into Company A, Twelfth Maine Volunteers, November 21, 1861, served out his term, re-enlisted, was transferred to the Twelfth Maine Battalion, appointed musician, and was mustered out April 18, 1866.

WILLIAM K. MOORE was mustered into Company A, Twelfth Maine Volunteers, November 21, 1861, was promoted Corporal, served out his term and was mustered out December 7, 1864.

GEORGE T. MANSUR was mustered into Company A, Twelfth Maine Volunteers, November 21, 1861, was promoted to Sergeant, served out his term, and was mustered out of service, December 7, 1864.

ROBERT McGILL was mustered into Company A, Twelfth Maine Volunteers, November 21, 1861, and died of wounds, May 26, 1863.

AINSWORTH W. MOREY was mustered into Company F, Twenty-third Maine Regiment, September 29, 1862, and was mustered out with the regiment, July 15, 1863.

LEVI MOODY was mustered into Company B, Thirty-second Maine Volunteers, March 10, 1864, was transferred to Company B, Thirty-first Maine Volunteers, December 12, 1864, and was discharged May 20, 1865, by order of General Dix.

PATRICK McAUDLEY enlisted on the quota of Rumford, in Company H, Fourteenth Maine Volunteers, June 12, 1862, at New Orleans. He deserted, March 27, 1864.

CHARLES L. NEWTON was mustered into Company A, Twelfth Maine Volunteers, November 21, 1861, and was discharged for disability.

CHARLES W. NELSON was mustered into Company C, Twentieth Maine Volunteers, August 29, 1862, and was discharged by Order Number 94, War Department.

HORACE H. PAINE was mustered into Company A, Twelfth Maine Volunteers, November 21, 1861, and was discharged for disability, August 24, 1863.

OTIS PEVERLY was mustered into Company B, Twelfth Maine Volunteers, was transferred to Company A; re-enlisted, was transferred to the Twelfth Maine Battalion, and was mustered out April 18, 1866.

IRVING B. PARKER was mustered into the Twelfth Maine Regiment, Company D, November 15, 1861, was promoted Corporal, and was mustered out at the expiration of his term of service, December 7, 1864.

LEWIS M. PERRY was mustered into Company D, Twelfth Maine Volunteers, November 15, 1861, and was reported absent without leave, August 15, 1863.

JAMES F. PUTNAM was mustered into Company D, Twentieth Maine Volunteers, August 29, 1862, and was discharged November 24, following.

HENRY A. J. ROLFE was mustered into Company D, Sixteenth Maine Regiment, August 14, 1862, and was discharged in November following.

OSCAR D. ROLFE was mustered into Company D, Twelfth Maine Regiment, November 15, 1861, was promoted Sergeant, served out his time, and was mustered out, December 7, 1864.

FRANK G. RUSSELL was mustered as First Lieutenant in Company C, Twentieth Maine Volunteers, August 29, 1862, and resigned January 10, 1863. He was a physician by profession, and practiced some years in Rumford.

ASA RICHARDSON was mustered into the Seventh Maine Battery, December 30, 1863, and was mustered out with the Battery, June 21, 1865. He has since died.

ISAAC SMALL was mustered into the Second Maine Battery, December 31, 1863, and was mustered out with the Battery, June 16, 1865.

GEORGE E. SMALL was mustered into the United States service in Company I, Fifth Maine Volunteers, June 24, 1861, and was soon after detached and placed on gunboat service.

SEWALL C. SMITH was mustered into Company D, Fifth Maine Regiment, June 24, 1861, was promoted Corporal, re-enlisted and was transferred to the First Maine Veteran Volunteers.

BENJAMIN W. STEVENS was mustered into Company A, Twelfth Maine Volunteers, November 21, 1861; served out his term, re-enlisted, was transferred to the Twelfth Maine Battalion, and was mustered out April 18, 1866.

EDWARD E. STEVENS was mustered as Corporal in Company F, Twenty-third Maine Volunteers, and was mustered out with the Regiment, July 15, 1863.

WILLIAM F. STEVENS was mustered into Company F, Twenty-third Maine Regiment, September 29, 1862, and was mustered out with the Regiment, July 15, 1863.   He was mustered into Company K, Twenty-ninth Maine Volunteers, January 5, 1864.

JONATHAN V. SILVER was mustered into Company A, Twelfth Maine Volunteers, November 21, 1861, served out his term and was mustered out of service, December 7, 1864.

JARVIS M. SEGAR was mustered into Company F, Twenty-third Maine Regiment, September 29, 1862, and was mustered out with the Regiment, July 15, 1863.

JAMES W. THOMAS was mustered into Company C, Twentieth Maine Regiment, August 29, 1862, and was discharged by Order Number 94, War Department.

JOHN F. TWOMBLY was mustered into the Twelfth Maine Regiment, Company A, November 21, 1861; was promoted Corporal, re-enlisted, was transferred to the Twelfth Maine Battalion, promoted Corporal, and was mustered out April 18, 1866.

BENJAMIN P. THOMAS was mustered into Company B, Sixteenth Maine, September 5, 1863, and died of disease November 24, following.

AUGUSTUS TAYLOR was mustered into Company H, Nineteenth Maine Volunteers, February 24, 1864; was transferred to the First

Maine Heavy Artillery, and was reported a deserter from August 9, following.

CHARLES K. VIRGIN was mustered into Company F, Twenty-third Maine Regiment, September 29, 1862, and was mustered out with the Regiment, July 15, 1863.

GEORGE E. VIRGIN was mustered into the United States service in Company F, Twenty-third Maine Volunteers, September 29, 1862, and was mustered out with the Regiment, July 15, 1863. He died suddenly while riding in a sleigh, in Mexico, Maine.

JAMES M. VIRGIN was mustered as a private in Company F, Twenty-third Maine Volunteers, September 29, 1862, and was mustered out at the expiration of his term of service, July 15, 1863.

BENJAMIN F. VIRGIN was mustered for the Ninth Maine Regiment, September 13, 1862; was wounded July 14, 1864, and reported a deserter, November 20, 1864, while absent in Maine. He is said to have re-enlisted under another name in New Hampshire, and to have served to the close of the war.

SAMUEL F. WING was mustered into Company E, Tenth Maine Regiment, August 14, 1862, and was transferred to the Tenth Maine Battalion. He was afterwards in the Twenty-ninth Maine Volunteers.

CHARLES K. WYMAN was mustered into Company A, Twelfth Maine Volunteers, November 15, 1861, served out his term, re-enlisted, was transferred to the Twelfth Maine Battalion, and was mustered out April 18, 1866.

OLIVER H. WARREN was mustered into Company D, Twelfth Maine Volunteers, November 15, 1861, and was discharged at Lowell, Mass., January 2, 1862.

CALEB E. WALKER was mustered into Company F, Twenty-third Maine Volunteers, September 29, 1862, and was mustered out with the Regiment, July 15, 1863. He has since died.

NATHANIEL WARREN was mustered into Company A, Thirtieth Maine Volunteers, December 15, 1863, and was reported a deserter January 4, following.

ISAAC P. WING was mustered into Company E, Thirty-second Maine Volunteers, April 2, 1864, and died of wounds, July 24, 1864.

CHAPTER XXIX.

PARSON GOULD, in his brief history, gives some account of educational matters in Rumford at the time he was settled here. There is no doubt the early settlers felt an interest in public schools, and fully appreciated the importance of educating their children. But there was not much wealth among them and money had to be expended in many directions. The highways of Rumford cost the town immense sums of money, and for many years about as many thousands were expended for roads as hundreds for schools. The plantation and early town schools were kept in private houses, and the terms were short and far between. The pay of the teachers was trifling, and this had to be made in the produce of the farm. When the town was incorporated, annual appropriations began to be made for the support of schools, very small at first, but the amount was gradually increased until it was a respectable sum. A full right in the township had been reserved for the benefit of the common schools in town, and after a time this was sold, the amount accruing forming a permanent school fund of which the income only could be used. This amount added to the amount raised by the town, enabled the districts to have two short terms a year.

Some of the early settlers were educated sufficiently to teach the rudiments of an English education, and became teachers of youth in town. John E. Rolfe was a school teacher, but he did not come with the very first settlers. Abel Wheeler was a veteran teacher, and for many years was known as such in Rumford and all the adjoining towns. His services covered a long period, for the writer attended a part of a term which he taught in Bethel when he was nearly seventy-five years of age. Nancy Rolfe, daughter of Henry Rolfe, taught upwards of thirty terms of school, most of them in Rumford. Samuel R. Hall, Jr., son of the first settled minister, became a famous educator. His first schools were taught in Rumford, and here in this far inland town, he invented the black-board, and it was here used for the first time. He commenced teaching when twenty years of age. At Concord, Vermont, in 1823, he opened and taught the first Normal School ever taught in this country. He was associated with Dr. Hitchcock and other learned men of his time ; aided in the geological survey of Vermont ; taught Normal schools at Concord, at Andover, Mass., and elsewhere ; had charge of the Academy at Plymouth, N. H., for many years ; was a preacher and had several settlements, besides being the author of several text-books, among which were "The Child's Assistant to a Knowledge of the Geography of Vermont," "Lectures on Teaching," "The Grammatical Assistant," "A School History of the United States," and the "Alphabet of Geology." His life was a busy one and his reputation wide-spread. It is a source of gratification to the people of Rumford that he commenced his career in this town, and that he here invented and first used the now indispensable black-board.

Virtue Howard is remembered by all middle aged people in this region, as an enthusiastic teacher of public schools. She was never married, and her active experience in teaching covered a period of more than half a century. She taught school both summer and winter and at all seasons, and her services were ever in great demand. Terms of school were often postponed for her until she could fill her prior engagements. She was greatly beloved by a multitude of pupils, and the clouding of her intellect during the last years of her busy and useful life, was a source of sorrow to all.

David Hutchins was an early Rumford school-master, and always went by the name of "Master Hutchins." Charles A. Kimball taught school when quite a young man, and the first master's school ever attended by the writer was taught by him. It was in Bethel, on what was then called Berry's and since Bird Hill, and was about the year 1834. Henry Howard, a nephew of Virtue, became a very popular teacher in later years, but his career was cut short by death. The school on the east side of Ellis river was once taught by Sidney Perham, afterward member of Congress and Governor of Maine, and the one on the west side in the Howe district, by Alden Chase, for many years Register of Deeds for Oxford county. Both of these teachers are kindly and gratefully remembered by their former Rumford pupils. Both were from the town of Woodstock, and both were highly successful teachers. They adopted in teaching, the motto that "Order is Heaven's first Law," and more orderly and systematic schools were never taught in the county than those under their charge.

Rumford has furnished a multitude of teachers first and last, both male and female. All the young men from this town who have obtained a liberal education, have taught more or less in the public schools as a means of raising money to meet their expenses at the academy or college. Among these may be named John M. Adams, William Wirt Virgin, William K. Kimball, Dana Boardman Putnam, Henry Kimball, Curtis P. Howe, Samuel R. Hall, Henry Howard, and there have been many others. The family of Calvin Howe furnished six teachers of public schools, and the Ellis river families of this name have supplied a score or more. The Lufkins have taught school more or less. The writer has pleasant recollections of Orin H. Lufkin, whose school he attended at Locke's Mills in 1849, and acting upon his advice, commenced the study of English Grammar. Two years later, the pupil taught the same school. Mr. Lufkin was a patient and pains-taking teacher, and an excellent disciplinarian. He has long since passed on and joined the great majority, but his memory is cherished by all his old pupils, and in a special degree by one. His wife and other members of the Godwin family were also teachers. The Farnum and Elliot families have turned out a multitude of school teachers, and the Abbot families perhaps more than any others, because the more numerous. The Kimball families have also furnished excellent teachers.

There is no doubt that the advent of Parson Gould into Rumford gave a great stimulus to the cause of education. Liberally educated himself, a man of sound, practical common sense, he well understood the necessity of the education of the masses under a popular form of government. He virtually took charge of the schools here for many years. He visited them often, encouraged the competent teachers, and unhesitatingly discharged those that were otherwise ; and when he closed his active life work, the schools in this town would compare favorably with the best in the county. He took pupils to his house and instructed them, and aided several young men in their preparatory college course. He desired to found a higher institution of learning in town, and offered to give liberally of his means to aid in starting it. But the project did not meet with much encouragement, and Bethel Hill taking hold of the matter, the school was established there, and "Gould's Academy in Bethel," perpetuates the name of one of its principal founders. Had Mr. Gould's views been promptly seconded, this famous institution of learning which has been patronized by many Rumford scholars, could just as well have been established here.

For the first year, the town of Rumford made no appropriation for public schools. The second year a beginning was made, by raising fifty dollars. This was gradually increased until it reached the sum of about four hundred dollars. In 1875, the sum raised was one thousand dollars, and since then it has been gradually falling off, until in 1887 it was only a trifle over eight hundred dollars. In 1875, the interest on the school fund amounted to $199.15, and amount received from the State on account of special taxes for the support of public schools, $780, making the sum available for school purposes for the year, $1979.15. The establishment of what are known as the mill tax and the bank tax, by the State Legislature, has been of great benefit to the cause of popular education in Maine. In this town, while the number of pupils attending school has been very much diminished in later years, the amount of money for school purposes has been increased, so that even the smaller districts are able to have schools of much greater efficiency and length, than would be the case if all the money for their support had to be raised in town. High schools have often been sustained in each of the three principal villages in town. Among those who have taught high schools here have been Stephen A. Holt of Norway, William Wirt Virgin, Larkin Dunton, Rev. Eliphalet Hopkins, Henry F. Howard, Sullivan R. Hutchins, and William M. Brooks of Oxford.

CHAPTER XXX.

OTHER LAND TRANSFERS IN RUMFORD.

OCTOBER 5, 1803. Sarah Stevens, widow of John Stevens, merchant, of Concord, sold to Nathan Adams in consideration of the sum of $1650, eight lots of land in Rumford, consisting of four 20 acre lots of interval, numbered from one to four on the north side of the Great river, and four 80 acre upland lots numbered the same, and adjoining the interval lots, said lots having been drawn to the rights of Timothy Walker, Nathaniel Rolfe, 2d, Aaron Stevens and Benjamin Abbot.

April 7, 1809. Simeon Virgin to Joshua Graham, lot number 27, third division bounded by land of Edmund Page, Timothy Walker, David Abbot, &c.

January 29, 1803. William Virgin to John Whittemore, both of Rumford, lot number 29, north of Great river, original right of Thomas Stickney.

November 17, 1812. Joseph Wardwell to Rev. Daniel Gould, 10 acres of land in Bethel above Capt. Eleazer Twitchell's land.

October 10, 1812. Rev. Samuel R. Hall to Cotton Elliot, part of lot number 22, second division, "it being all of that lot not already sold to said Elliot and Nathaniel Sanborn."

February 7, 1811. Joseph Wardwell of Turner to Nathaniel F. Higgins of Rumford, land in Turner; consideration $2000.

January 26, 1806. Jacob Abbot to William Wheeler, both of Rumford, lot number 20, and interval lot north of Great river.

January 8, 1805. John Chandler, Jr., of Concord, to William Wheeler of Rumford, lot north of Great river, drawn to the right of John Chandler, Senior.

September 21, 1810. Benjamin Morse of Rumford to John Thompson of Number 11, land in Rumford adjoining said Thompson's land.

February 3, 1805. Moses Varnum of Temple, Me., to John Thompson of Thompsontown Plantation, land in Rumford, owned by him in common and bought of Enoch Adams and Jonathan Stevens, it being lots number one each side of Ellis river.

September 22, 1807. Nathan Adams of Rumford to Moses Merrill of East Andover, two undivided rights in said Andover, it being one sixty-fourth part of said town, and supposed to contain four hundred acres. Also lot number 7 in letter Y; lot number 6 range 2; number 2 on letter B; one-half lot number 2, thirteenth range, and one right on sixty-fourth part of the township, and one-half right held in common with Nathan Swan.

January 15, 1814. Obediah Kimball of Bethel to Aaron Marean of Rumford, blacksmith, one acre of land in Rumford, north of Great river; also another lot on same side, and on the south side of a road leading from East Andover to Paris, and bounded easterly by the road leading to the ferry granted to John E. Adams. (Adams had sold this same land May 28, 1811 to said Kimball and William West.)

April 5, 1814. Moses Kimball of Rumford to Samuel Lufkin of same, part of lot number 27, north of Great river.

John E. Adams of Rumford to Asa Hardy of Concord, N. H., one-half of lot, number one hundred, north of Great river.

October 7, 1799. James C. Harper to Benjamin Lufkin, both of New Pennacook, two 100 acre lots, numbers 98 and 93, second division, north of Ammonscoggin river.

February 9, 1812. David Abbot to Ezra Hoyt of Rumford, the Common share belonging to the original right of Peter Green, number 70, third division. (Same day Hoyt sold the same land to Parker Brown of Bow, N. H.)

April 20, 1805. Paul Rolfe of Concord, N. H., to Phineas Howe of same, interval lot, number 22, north of Great river.

1798——Joshua Graham to Samuel Hinkson, both of New Pennacook, lot number 45, second division situated on Swift river.

March 23, 1801. Samuel Hinkson to Samuel Goss, both of Rumford, lot number 67, north of Great river, with house and barn thereon, land granted him by the proprietors.

September 14, 1811. Stephen Putnam to Stephen Putnam, Jr., number 106, third division, and interval lot, number 18, first division.

August 30, 1806. Ebenezer Fogg to William Simpson, both of Rumford, lot number 20, east side of Ellis river, and number 101 north of Great river.

Nov. 16, 1808. Stephen Hodsdon to William Simpson, both of Rumford, part of lot number 103.

November 12, 1810. Edmund Page of Rumford to Samuel Stevens, lot number 27, second division, north of Great river.

September 30, 1810, Samuel Hinkson, blacksmith, to Samuel Stevens, lot number 45, second division, west of Swift river, reserving crops, blacksmith fixings, etc. (Same premises he bought of Joshua Graham in 1798).

June 20, 1803. Sarah Stevens of Concord, N. H., to Stephen G. Stevens of Salem, Mass., cabinet maker, lot number 20, east side of Ellis river; 80 acre lot, number 17, west of Ellis river; lots number 6, 42 and 23 north of Great river; also all the Common land belonging to the above lots. The last four tracts being equal to four common rights and belonging to the rights of Philip Kimball, George Abbot, Thomas Stickney and Ebenezer Eastman.

September 21, 1815. Francis Keyes to Francis Smart, northerly half of lot number 85, 2d division; the same bought of Joseph Lufkin.

John E. Adams to Moses Kimball, blacksmith, several parcels of land in Rumford, all north of great river; one adjoining land of Cushman and Bolster and containing 13 acres, more or less.

September 7, 1806. Joshua Ripley to Nathan Hunting, undivided share or third division drawn against interval lot number one, west of Ellis river.

April 3, 1791. Eleazer Twitchell of Bethel to Joshua Ripley of New Pennacook, three-fourths of a right of land in New Pennacook, it being interval lot and first upland lot adjoining East Andover, on the west side of Ellis river, drawn to the right of Timothy Walker. (In 1811, Ripley deeded the major part of this land to Eben Poor of East Andover).

March 30, 1813. Richard Dolloff to John Dolloff, lot number 92, north of Great River.

February 5, 1799. Timothy Walker of Concord to Increase Dolly of New Pennacook, lot number 86, north of Great river, of which said Walker was the original grantee.

October 21, 1814. Increase Dolly to Phineas Wood, land last named.

Nov. 3, 1800. Daniel Knight to Philip Abbot, lot number 8, north of Great river, right of Ebenezer Hall.

July 3, 1787. Timothy Walker of Concord to Philip Abbot of

same, two whole rights in New Pennacook, of which Jonathan Merrill and Abraham Kimball were the original grantees. Also April 2, 1796, interval lot belonging to original right of Ebenezer Hall.

March 22, 1821. Daniel Carr to David Abbot, 3d, lot number 16, first division north of Great river, excepting 16 acres, sold to Nathan Hunting, and 16 to Francis Smart.

February 30, 1821. Phineas Frost of Howard's Gore to Asa Howard of Rumford, blacksmith, lot number 21, and interval lot, number 11, east side of Ellis river.

March 15, 1821. Robert Hinkson, Jr., of Rumford, to Jesse Delano of Livermore, lot number 58, north of Great river, bounded west by land of Samuel Putnam.

December 20, 1820. Daniel Hodsdon to Francis Cushman, lot number 103, north of Great river, excepting seven acres sold by Stephen Hodsdon to William Simpson.

June 5, 1817. Gustavus A. Goss of Paris to Benjamin Flint of Rumford, Physician, part of 80 acre lots number 20 and 21, and part of interval lot, number 16, north of the Great river.

October 30, 1817. Charles Ford of Rumford, cordwainer, to Gustavus A. Goss of Paris, part of lot number 6, south of Great river; also part of 80 acre lot, number 3, adjoining.

March 28, 1812. Gustavus A. Goss to Daniel Puffer, lot number 9, second division, north of Great river.

CHAPTER XXXI.

RUMFORD CIVIL OFFICERS.

CLERKS.

Francis Keyes, 1800–1807.
Joshua Graham, 1808–1810.
Francis Keyes, 1811–1812.
William Wheeler, 1813–1818.
Peter C. Virgin, 1819.
William Wheeler, 1820.
Solomon Cushman, 1821.
Aaron Virgin, 1825–1828.
Alvan Bolster, 1829–1832.
Edward Stevens, 1833–1834.
Lyman Rawson, 1835–1836.
Alvan Bolster, 1837–1838.
Charles A. Kimball, 1839–1840.
Otis C. Bolster, 1841.
Albion K. Knapp, 1842–1843.
James H. Farnum, 1844–1845.

David Knapp, 1846.
William Frost, 1847.
Zenas W. Bartlett, 1848.
Patrick Hoyt. 1849–1851.
Thomas Roberts, 1852–1854.
William Frost, 1855–1856.
Dexter D. W. Abbot, 1857.
William Frost, 1858–1859.
M. N. Lufkin, 1860–1861.
William Frost, 1862–1865.
Henry M. Colby, 1866–1871.
William Frost, 1872–1879.
Freeman E. Small, 1880–1885.
Clarence M. Hutchins, 1886.
James S. Morse, 1887——.

TREASURERS.

David Farnum, 1800–1805.
Jacob Farnum, 1806–1808.
Abel Wheeler, 1809–1811.
Nathan Adams, 1812.
Aaron Virgin, 1813–1814.
Abel Wheeler, 1815–1816.
Peter C. Virgin, 1817–1819.
Abel Wheeler, 1820.
Colman Godwin, 1821.
Alvan Bolster, 1822–1823.
Aaron Virgin, 1824–1828.
Francis Cushman, 1829–1830.
Otis C. Bolster, 1831.
Joseph H. Wardwell, 1832–1833.
Porter Kimball, 1834–1835.
Joshua Graham, 1836–1840.

Edward Stevens, 1841.
Charles A. Kimball, 1842–1843.
P. M. Wheeler, 1844–1845.
John Martin, 1846.
Otis C. Bolster, 1847–1851.
Peter C. Virgin, 1852–1857.
James M. Dolloff, 1858–1861.
Francis A. Bacon, 1862–1865.
Calvin Howe, 1866–1870.
Henry M. Colby, 1871.
Calvin Howe, 1872–1874.
Oliver Pettingill, 1875–1876.
Henry Abbot, 1877–1878.
Charles W. Kimball, 1879–1882.
Waldo Pettingill, 1883–1884.
Charles W. Kimball, 1885 ——.

SELECTMEN.

1800. Francis Keyes, Philip Abbot, John Martin.
1801. Francis Keyes, Stephen Putnam, Jeremiah Richardson.
1802. Francis Keyes, Philip Abbot, John Martin.
1803. Francis Keyes, John Martin, Wm. Virgin.
1804. Francis Keyes, Joshua Graham, John Martin, Abel Wheeler, Kimball Martin.
1805. Francis Keyes, Abel Wheeler, Wm. Virgin.
1806. David Farnum, Abel Wheeler, William Virgin.
1807. Francis Keyes, Joshua Graham, Kimball Martin.
1808. Joshua Graham, Wm. Virgin, Kimball Martin.
1809. Philip Abbot, Wm. Wheeler, Abel Wheeler.
1810. Wm. Wheeler, Joshua Graham, Daniel Knight.
1811. Francis Keyes, Wm. Wheeler, Daniel Knight.
1812. Francis Keyes, Abel Wheeler, Osgood Eaton.
1813. Wm. Wheeler, Daniel Knight, Wm. Virgin.
1814. Wm. Wheeler, Abel Wheeler, Peter C. Virgin.
1815. Wm. Wheeler, Peter C. Virgin, Abel Wheeler.
1816. Wm. Wheeler, Daniel Knight, John Thompson.
1817. John Thompson, Abel Wheeler, Aaron Virgin.
1818. Abel Wheeler, Aaron Virgin, Kimball Martin.
1819. Wm. Wheeler, Wm. Virgin, Aaron Virgin.
1820. Wm. Wheeler, Moses F. Kimball, Francis Cushman.
1821. Moses F. Kimball, Francis Cushman, Abel Wheeler.
1822. Moses F. Kimball, Wm. Wheeler, Abel Wheeler.
1823. Wm. Wheeler, Abel Wheeler, John Rolfe.
1824. Moses F. Kimball, Joseph H. Wardwell, John Thompson.
1825. Moses F. Kimball, Alvin Bolster, Curtis P. Howe.
1826. Alvin Bolster, Curtis P. Howe, Rufus Virgin.
1827. Solomon Crockett, Hezekiah Hutchins, Jr., William Virgin.
1828. Solomon Crockett, Hezekiah Hutchins, Jr., Nathan Knapp.
1829. Solomon Crockett, Hezekiah Hutchins, Jr., Nathan Knapp.
1830. Solomon Crockett, Hezekiah Hutchins, Jr., Nathan Knapp.
1831. Moses F. Kimball, Alvin Bolster, Curtis P. Howe.
1832. Moses F. Kimball, Alvin Bolster, Lyman Rawson.
1833. Lyman Rawson, Nathan Knapp, Rufus Virgin.
1834. Lyman Rawson, Moses F. Kimball, Otis C. Bolster.
1835. Lyman Rawson, James H. Farnum, David Kimball.
1836. James H. Farnum, David Kimball, Simeon Fuller.
1837. James H. Farnum, Simeon Fuller, Nathan Abbot.
1838. Moses F. Kimball, John M. Eustis, Nathan Abbot.
1839. John M. Eustis, Alvin Bolster, Simon Parlin.
1840. Simon Parlin, Porter Kimball, Stephen Farnum.
1841. Rufus Virgin, John Rolfe, David Kimball.
1842. James H. Farnum, David Kimball, Samuel Barker.
1843. James H. Farnum, Hezekiah Hutchins, Jr., Timothy Walker.

13

1844.   James H. Farnum, Hezekiah Hutchins, Jr., Timothy Walker.
1845.   Timothy Walker, Alvin Bolster, Amos Dwinel.
1846.   Timothy Walker, Amos Dwinel, Asa S. Howard.
1847.   Timothy Walker, Amos Dwinel, Asa S. Howard.
1848.   Amos Dwinal, John Howe, Rufus Virgin.
1849.   Timothy Walker, Amos Dwinal, Rufus Virgin.
1850.   Timothy Walker, Rufus Virgin, David Blanchard.
1851.   Rufus Virgin, David Blanchard, Joseph E. Colby.
1852.   Otis C. Bolster, David Blanchard, David Kimball.
1853.   Otis C. Bolster, David Kimball, Charles E. Virgin.
1854.   James Bullock, Charles E. Virgin, Frye H. Hutchins.
1855.   Joseph E. Colby, Frye H. Hutchins, John Martin.
1856.   Joseph E. Colby, Frye H. Hutchins, Thomas J. Bisbee.
1857.   Nathan S. Lufkin, Thomas J. Bisbee, Samuel H. Wood.
1858.   Nathan S. Lufkin, Samuel H. Wood, D. D. W. Abbot.
1859.   Joseph E. Colby, D. D. W. Abbot, Patrick Hoyt.
1860.   William Irish, Patrick Hoyt, Jonathan K. Martin.
1861.   William Irish, Jonathan K. Martin, Frye H. Hutchins.
1862.   Timothy Walker, Frye H. Hutchins, Henry Abbot.
1863.   Timothy Walker, Frye H. Hutchins, Henry Abbot.
1864.   Timothy Walker, Henry Abbot, O. W. Blanchard.
1865.   Timothy Walker, O. W. Blanchard, William Irish.
1866.   William Irish, J. K. Martin, George W. Perry.
1867.   J. K. Martin, George W. Perry, P. M. Putnam.
1868.   J. K. Martin, P. M. Putnam, Calvin Howe.
1869.   J. K. Martin, P. M. Putnam, George W. Perry.
1870.   P. M. Putnam, George W. Perry, N. S. Farnum.
1871.   Timothy Walker, N. S. Farnum, Henry Abbott.
1872.   Timothy Walker, Henry Abbot, John Swain.
1873.   Henry Abbot, Waldo Pettengill, Henry M. Colby.
1874.   J. K. Martin, Henry M. Colby, John Howe.
1875.   Waldo Pettengill, John Howe, L. G. Roberts.
1876.   Waldo Pettengill, John Howe, L. G. Roberts.
1877.   Waldo Pettengill, John Hiram Howe, Wilson Thomas.
1878.   John H. Howe, Wilson Thomas, Waldo Pettengill.
1879.   M. N. Lufkin, H. F. Abbott, Fred A. Porter.
1880.   Waldo Pettengill, Fred A. Porter, John Howe.
1881.   Waldo Pettengill, Henry Abbot, John Howe.
1882.   Waldo Pettingill, Fred A. Porter, William H. Farnum.
1883.   Fred A. Porter, William H. Farnum, C. W. Kimball.
1884.   William H. Farnum, M. N. Lufkin, Fred A. Barker.
1885.   Waldo Pettengill, Fred A. Porter, Samuel L. Moody.
1886.   Waldo Pettengill, Fred A. Porter, Samuel L. Moody.
1887.   Waldo Pettengill, Samuel L. Moody, Jere H. Martin.
1888.   F. A. Barker, F. H. Bartlett, Samuel L. Moody.
1889.   F. A. Barker, F. H. Bartlett, John E. Elliot.

CIVIL COMMISSIONS.

The following citizens of Rumford have received commissions from the Governor of the State for the offices named. Many of them received several reappointments, but the dates here given represent the first time appointed. The term Justice of the Peace represents also Justice of the Peace and Quorum:

JUSTICE OF THE PEACE. Joseph Adams, 1824; Nathan Abbot, 1838; Alvan Bolster, 1825; Francis Cushman, 1820; Solomon Crockett, 1828; John M. Eustis, 1839; Wm. Frost, 1834; James H. Farnum, 1839; Colman Godwin, 1826; Eben T. Goddard, 1835; Hezekiah Hutchins, 1827; Curtis P. Howe, 1828; Hezekiah Hutchins, Jr., 1838; Francis Keyes, 1821; Moses F. Kimball, 1822; David Kimball; Lyman Rawson, 1830; Aaron Stevens, 1829; Peter C. Virgin, 1821; Joel C. Virgin, 1835; Jonathan Virgin, 1837; Wm. Wheeler, 1820; Abel Wheeler, 1828; Joseph H. Wardwell, 1832; Timothy Walker, 1838; Isaac Whittemore, 1839; David F. Adams, 1842; Henry Abbot, 1848; Samuel V. Abbot, 1858; Wm. W. Bolster, 1858; Zenas W. Bartlett, 1847; Joseph E. Colby, 1851; James M. Dolloff, 1847; Joseph W. Elliot, 1853; William Elliot, 1858; Joshua Graham, 1848; Alvan B. Godwin, 1849; Ajalon Godwin, 1851; Asa S. Howard, 1842; Joseph T. Hall, 1844; Sullivan R. Hutchins, 1859; Patrick Hoyt, 1857; Charles A. Kimball, 1841; Albion K. Knapp, 1847; David Knapp, 1858; Jacob B. Leach, 1840; Orrin H. Lufkin, 1848; Nathan S. Lufkin, 1855; I. Atwood Putnam, 1855; Thomas Roberts, 1849; Charles H. Silver, 1848.

CORONERS. David H. Farnum, 1829; Colman Godwin, 1821; Hezekiah Hutchins, Jr., 1831; Porter Kimball, 1833; Simon Virgin, 1824; Phineas Wood, 1821; William Frost, 1847; Asa S. Howard, 1842; David H. Adams, 1842; John Martin, 1847; Florus H. Bartlett, 1881.

TRIAL JUSTICES. Peter C. Virgin, 1860; Sullivan R. Hutchins, 1887; Charles A. Kimball, 1887; Marcius Knight, 1883; Henry A. Small, 1887.

DEDIMUS JUSTICE. Lyman Rawson, 1839; Peter C. Virgin, 1820; Moses F. Kimball, 1829; Wm. Wheeler, 1820.

TO SOLEMNIZE MARRIAGES. Joseph Lufkin, 1821; Daniel Gould, 1821; Geo. L. Burbank, 1876; Patrick Hoyt. 1866; Richard Vivian. 1872; Luther Walcott, 1862.

JUSTICE OF COURT OF SESSIONS. Peter C. Virgin, 1830; William Wheeler. 1820.

COUNTY ATTORNEY. Peter C. Virgin, 1838, 1841.

Those who held commissions as Justice of the Peace before the Separation from Massachusetts, were, Peter C. Virgin, Benjamin Rolfe, William Wheeler, Francis Keyes, Moses F. Kimball and Joseph Adams.

CHAPTER XXXII.

EARLY ROADS.

FOR more than a dozen years after the settlement of this town, there was no road between here and Portland, by the way of Paris. A settlement on Paris Hill was begun about the time that the first settler came to Rumford, and a few years later, a road had been laid out and built between Paris and Portland, by way of Poland and New Gloucester, but Paris was for some time its northern terminus. There was a path through the woods to Rumford. It followed up the little Androscoggin river to Bryant's Pond, then struck off to North Woodstock, and for several miles was along a peculiar ridge of land, very early, and to the present time, called the "Whale's Back." Persons frequently passed through the wilderness between the settlements on the Androscoggin and the Jackson settlement, as Paris Hill was then called, on foot and sometimes on horseback. The distance was not far from twenty miles, and there was no intervening habitation or clearing. In winter, the journey was generally made on snow-shoes.

In 1795, the inhabitants of New Pennacook petitioned the Court of General Sessions, which held its terms in Portland, for the location of a road from the southeast corner of Paris, by way of a place called "Stony Brook," and "Biscoe's Falls." to the northwest corner of Paris, and from thence through township number 3 to the south line of New Pennacook. The prayer was granted, and the following persons were appointed to locate the road: Nathaniel C. Allen, Isaac Parsons, Ichabod Bonney, John Greenwood and Peleg Chandler. The following are some of the points named in the minutes of the survey: "Beginning at a hemlock tree in the easterly line of Paris standing in the center of the County road to be located and laying two rods on each side of the corner; thence to a point opposite Solomon Shaw's house; thence to a point opposite Abner Shaw's barn; thence to a point opposite Benjamin Hammond's barn; thence to the center of a county road formerly laid out to the center lot in Paris; thence on said road 155 rods to the end thereof;

thence to the bridge over Swift brook; thence to the north end of the bridge over Fall brook; thence to a stake and stones on the easterly bank of the little Amariscoggin river at Biscoe's Falls; thence across said river to a spruce tree, &c., &c., to the northwest corner of Paris; thence through number 3 to the southerly end of a ridge called ' Whale's back;' thence on said ridge to the northerly end thereof near a brook, and thence to a Norway Pine tree standing in the southerly line of New Pennacook." The Commissioners were eleven days in locating this road and the entire expense, including seven days labor by Lemuel Jackson, Jr., and six by Nicholas Chesley, was $99.00. The road here described, and which was opened within a year or two, did not follow the old spotted line and path through Number 3, now Woodstock, but passed over the high lands of that town, where the Bryants soon after began a settlement, and intersected the old foot-path at North Woodstock. In 1802, on petition of Francis Keyes of Rumford, and also parties in Bethel and Paris, the Court of Sessions appointed Michael Little of Lewiston, a committee to repair the road between Paris and Rumford, through Number 3. Mr. Little owned lands in Number 3, now Woodstock, which accounts for his appointment.

One of the earliest roads built in Rumford, was on the south side of the Great Androscoggin river, to connect with a road to Peru and Jay. The town of Jay then included the present town of Canton. There is no record of the location of this road by order of the Court of Sessions, and it was probably laid out and built by the settlers. It was built prior to 1788, for Samuel Titcomb of Wells wrote a letter that year, in which he stated that a road had lately been cleared out from Butterfield to New Pennacook and Sudbury, Canada. Butterfield Plantation then included the present towns of Sumner and Hartford, but just where the road here described entered the Pennacook road, the oldest inhabitant does not know. Between 1784 and 1802, several down river roads were located to connect with the "Pennacook road" as it is invariably called in the records of the Court of Sessions. In 1802, a road was located by Isaac Parsons, Jedediah Cobb, Abijah Buck, John Greenwood, Peter Chandler and John Thompson, a committee appointed by the Court of Sessions, from Isaac Bonney's well in the town of Sumner to the Pennacook road in Jay. Most of the committee were of New Gloucester, but Abijah Buck was of Buckfield, and John Thompson who was the Surveyor of the party, was of Rumford.

The road from Paris to New Pennacook is the only one on record as having been laid out by order of the Court of Sessions to accommodate the settlers of this town. In 1805, the county of Oxford was organized, and county roads in Rumford were thereafter located by the County Commissioners. The Paris and New Pennacook road was only located to the Southerly line of Rumford, where it doubtless connected with a system of roads located and built by the town. It is much to the credit of the early settlers here, that they located and cleared out their own highways, constructed their own bridges, and had no help from the county of Cumberland.

CHAPTER XXXIII.

DEATHS IN RUMFORD.

THE following deaths of Rumford people are from the records of the Congregational Church, and down to eighteen hundred and fifty-two, and in the handwriting of Rev. Eliphalet S. Hopkins.

1840.

Aug. 17, Mrs. Dolly Bolster; Sept. 9, Asa Farnum; Oct. 9, Mrs. Asa Howard; Mrs. Aaron Stevens; Abiel Stevens; Nov. 9, Mr. Wakefield; Asa Howard; Dec. 28, Nathan Adams; Oct., two children of David Abbott; Cyrus Small's child; Mrs. Chew; Mrs. Ackley; Mrs. Robert Hinkson; Mr. Richardson; S. Hall; Mrs. Hoyt; Mrs. Kyle; Mrs. Richard Caldwell; child of Otis Howe; Mrs. Robinson; Mr. Chapman.

1841.

Oct. 6, Mrs. Treadwell; Mrs. Burgess and sister; Nov. 2, Eldad Howard; Nov. 29, Dr. Simeon Fuller.

1842.

January 18, Mrs. Greenleaf; Feb. 6, child of Otis C. Bolster; old Mrs. Ackley; Apr. 6, child of Gardiner Hoyt; May 14, Mrs. Otis Howe; children of John Graham, Wheeler Farnum, Melancthon Wheeler; Eben Virgin; July 1, Mr. F. Putnam, Mrs. Osgood Eaton; Mr. Rice Morse; children of Jeremiah Wardwell and Isaac

Hall; Sept. 10, child of Anson Farnum; Sept. 2, Thatcher Goddard; Oct. 15, Almira Green.

1843.

Mrs. Joshua Graham; Sarah Virgin; Miss Harris; June, Mrs.
Thomas; child of J. Kennison; Aug., Mrs. J. Thompson, Greenleaf Stevens; Nov. 17, Henrietta L. Bolster; Mrs. Morse; Dec. 9,
child of Francis Cushman; Dec. 28, Francis Cushman.

1844.

Apr. 3, Mrs. Trumbull; Apr. 9, Mrs. Richardson; May 27,
child of Timothy Holt; child of Hazen Keach; Aug. 8, child of
Esther Wood; Aug. 17, Nancy Kimball; child of Wheeler Farnum;
Nov., wife of Wheeler Farnum; Dec. 1, child of Hiram Abbot.

1845.

March, Nancy Howe; Solomon Martin; April, Samuel Lufkin;
Mrs. Kimball Martin; Phineas Wood; Calista Green; Sept. 9,
Cornford Cushman; Jeremiah Virgin; child of A. K. Knapp; Oct.
24, Richard Dolloff, aged 91; Mr. Israel Putnam; child of E.
Hinkson; Nov. 14, Charles Adams; child of Cyrus Elliot.

1846.

Ezra Smith, Esq.; March 24, child of Joseph Moody; May 1,
child of Gardiner Hoyt; June 9, Moses Wardwell; Mrs. Knight;
child of Mr. Parker and one of Mr. McCrillis; Sept. 16, M.
Wheeler; Sept. 25, Mrs. Howord; Nov. 16, child of Carter Elliot;
Dec. 8, Mrs. Carr; children of Aaron Elliot; Nathan Abbot; Mr.
Richardson; Mr. Wood and Monroe Morse.

1847.

May 9, Mrs. Brown; Sept., Mrs. Lane; child of Dr. Bartlett;
Oct. 18, child of Loammi B. Peabody; Dec., Angelia Elliot.

1848.

Phineas Howe; son of Jeremiah Farnum; child of Wheeler
Farnum; Mrs. Isaac Whittemore; May 2, Mrs. Cyrus Small;
child of Mr. Richardson; May 6, Daniel Glines; child of William
Martin; July 4, Marshall Hinkson; George Hinkson and Charles
Wood were drowned, near Rumford Point; Aug. 2, child of O. H.
Lufkin.

1849.

March 1, Mrs. Josiah Keyes; March 2, Joseph H. Wardwell; March 5, Capt. Joseph Wardwell, father of the last named; Feb. 24, Charles Virgin; March 3, Miriam Stevens; Apr. 27, Mrs. J. Abbot; May 4, Benj. Morse; May 14, child of Cotton Elliot; June 21, Mrs. Cyrus Small; July 2, Mrs. Holt; Mrs. Deacon Hutchins: children of Mr. Elkins, Warren Adams.

1850.

Child of Charles Virgin; child of Mr. Jones; child of James M. Dolloff; March, Mr. Nathan Silver; Apr., child of Benj. Putnam; child of Osgood Eaton; child of H. Richardson; Mr. Benj. Farnum, aged 82; Mrs. Chandler Abbot; Nov. 25, Samuel Putnam; H. Virgin; John Hinkson; wife of Dr. Small.

1851.

May, son of Jacob Abbot; June, Porter Kimball; July, Mrs. John Howe; Van Rensalier Abbot, at sea; Aug., Mrs. Ackley; Mr. Kimball Martin; Oct. 22, Mrs. Ray; Sept., Mary Lane; Salome Howe.

1852.

Feb. 13, Mary E. Dearborn; child of Manley Farnum; June 11, Jane Moody; Aug. 24, Colman Godwin; Mr. Abel Wheeler; Mrs. Richard Dolloff, aged 87.

The following deaths are recorded in the handwriting of Rev. John Elliot:

Feb. 1859, David Holt, aged 86; March following Mrs. David Holt, aged 88; Feb., Elizabeth Wood; April 27, Marcia Smith, aged 87; May 16, Mr. Poland; March 20, 1861, Dolly Morse, aged 86; April 5, Dolly Farnum; April 8, David Abbot; Apr. 11, Mrs. Susannah Hoyt, aged 86; June 15, Daniel Martin, aged 89 years, 11 months, one of the first settlers; Jane Martin, aged 16½ years; July 6, Mary A. Colby; March 3, 1862, Betsey, wife of Deacon Jacob Elliot, aged 68; Dec. 10, the embalmed remains of Nahum Perkins Moody who died in the army, were brought to Rumford for interment. He died in East Baltimore Nov. 28. He was the only son of Hezikiah Moody of Bethel; Dec. 15, Deacon Daniel Hall at East Rumford; Dec. 20, at East Rumford, Mrs.

Sarah Farnum, aged 93 ; she was one of the five original members of the Congregational church ; May 26, 1863, Dolly Frost ; Aug. 6, of diphtheria, Sarah Augusta Elliot ; June 27, 1864, Lieut. Joseph E. Colby, died at City Point, Va., and his remains were brought to Rumford for interment ; July 29, Judith Colby, aged 72 ; Sept. 21, of diphtheria, Sarah C. Bartlett, aged 19 ; Jan. 19, 1865, widow Hannah Carter, a member of the church for more than fifty years ; July 28, Lyman Martin ; Feb. 9, Sally Morse, in consequence of her clothes taking fire, aged 84 ; Jan. 7, 1866, Aaron Graham ; May 28, 1867, Mary Trumbull ; July 21, Sally Hall ; Oct. 3, David Elliot ; Jan. 13, 1869, Dea. Jacob Elliot, aged 84 years ; August 27, Polly Elliot ; Oct. 6, Gratia, Widow of Cotton Elliot, aged 85 years ; Oct. 24, Mrs. Enoch Knapp ; Feb. 23, 1870, Miss Mary H. Rawson ; Oct. 20, Hazen F. Abbot ; Nov. 9, Mary Howard ; April 8, 1871 ; Peter C. Virgin, Esq., the first lawyer in Rumford, aged 88 years ; Sept. 6, Timothy Holt ; April 8, 1872, Mary Ann, wife of Henry Abbot ; Oct. 2, David Colby, aged 83 ; Nov. 15, Deacon Henry Martin, aged 74 ; May 12, 1873, William Moody, aged 74 ; Oct 13, Phebe Jackson ; Nov. 29, Keziah Goddard in 81st year ; May 13, 1875, Mrs. Euthalia W. Goddard, aged 31 ; Sept. 9, Aaron Graham, aged $87\frac{1}{2}$ years ; Feb. 19, 1876, Miss Virtue Howard, daughter of Asa Howard, and a well known teacher of youth ; she taught seventy-five different terms of school ; March 3, R. L. B. Elliot, youngest son of the pastor ; Dec. 29, Isaac Walker Cleasby, aged 89 years ; July 7, 1878, Mrs. Sarah S. Howe died ; her death was caused by the upsetting of her carriage while on her way to church ; Oct. 11, Mr. Bradbury Richardson of Milton Plantation, aged 83 ; Jan. 21, 1879, Mrs. Sally B. Peabody, aged 66 ; Aug. 29, Mrs. Julia Smith ; March 15, Rev. John Elliot, acting pastor of the church, aged 78 years, 5 months and 10 days ; a faithful minister of the Gospel of Christ ; Feb. 8, 1880, Nancy, widow of Timothy Holt, aged 71.

CHAPTER XXXIV.

Enumeration of 1850.

THE first census of the United States was taken in 1790. Since that time they have been taken for each decade, but the enumeration for 1850 was the first in which a copy of the lists of the names was deposited in the archives of the State. The following enumeration is copied from the volume in the Maine State Library, and is doubtless approximately correct. Some of the early settlers then lingered on the shores of time and their names and ages are herein given, but most of them had passed to their eternal rest. The reader of the preceding pages has not failed to notice that several of the names quite common in town in its early years, had become extinct in 1850, while additional names are by no means numerous. The Abbots, Farnums, Martins and Virgins held their own quite well when this enumeration was made, but many other families still represented, had greatly fallen off in numbers:

Abbott, Stephen	48	Abbott, Spencer	11
Lucy	54	DeWitt C	7
Charles H., carpenter	24		
Maria H.	21	Abbott, John, N. H	70
Mansur, John, Mass	38	Andrew B	38
Susan M	37	Peniel H	24
		David S	5
Abbott, Enos	56	Hannah S	3
Polly	44	Lucy B	1
Hezekiah H	25	Nancy W., N. H	46
Abbott. Hiram, N. H	44	Andrews, Joseph R	37
Mary, Maine	45	Mary S	27
Hannah H., Mass	16	David E	9
Hiram F.. Mass	15	Joseph H	8
William W., Mass	13	Charles A	5
Lucy A., Mass	11	George A	2
Edwin F., Maine	6		
		Abbott, David, N. H	52
Abbott, David, 2d	51	Azubah, Mass	45
Anna H	50	William H., Teamster	28
Galen, blacksmith	25	Charles B., Teamster	23
Calvin M	23		
Alanson M	21	Andrews, Jeremiah. N. H	64
David G	18	Ann, Mass	62
Granville	16	William. Carpenter	29

Andrews, Julia A............ 22

Ackley, William............ 58
    Deborah 56
    Hosea.................. 20
    Ezra 18
    Esther 14

Abbott, Gideon C., Maine...... 40
    Civilia 37
    Charles L 16
    Josiah K 14
    Emily S 11
    Elias B 9
    Civilia 6
    Olive A 3
    Rossila............... 1
Keyes, Josiah, House Carpenter 50

Abbott, Samuel V............ 34
    Mary W 29
    Walter S.............. 5
    Margaret T 3

Ackley, George H............ 21
    Almira 21
    Eugene 1

Ackley, Samuel Jr........... 55
    Eliza.................. 52
    Daniel 20
    Elizabeth 19
    Caleb 17
    Harriet 6
Ackley, Samuel, Mass 88

Adams, Warren M............ 31
    Adriann 24
    Charles H 1

Abbott, David W............ 40
    Experience, Mass....... 79
    Betsey Baxter.......... 55
    Parris A 27

Abbott, Chandler............ 42
    Charity 38
    Shalva F 16
    Cynthia J 14
    Chelsea C 12
    Charles L 10

Allen, Benjamin............. 45
    Sally.................. 37
    Lucy S................ 8
    Sarah L............... 2
Thomas, Sally, Mass 69

Abbott, Henry, N. H. 76
    Susan 86
    Asa 33

Adams, Adam W, Innholder ... 32
    Ann M................ 27
    Alvan E 3
    Lewis E 1

Abbott, Daniel G........... 34
    Cynthia W 28
    Sarah V............... 3
    Louisa E 2
Brackett, Mary E 7

Abbott, Nathan............. 42
    Betsey 44
    Phineas W 24
    Milton 14

Abbott, Henry Jr 26
    Rosilla W 23
    Hora E................ 1

Abbott, Stephen H 39
    Sarah J 34
    Francis M............. 14
    Adeline L............. 12
    Augustus W 6
    Ellen E 9-12

Abbott, Benjamin E 36
    Mahala F 31
    Julia E............... 7
    Loretta L 5
    Delia H............... 1

Abbott, Jacob.............. 46
    Prudence 44
    George 23
    Seth 21
    Alvan................ 19
    Zilpha 18
    Susan 6
    Henry 5

Arnold, Samuel M............ 39
    Mary W..... 37
    Sherebiah M........... 13
    Samuel B............. 11
    Mary E 9
    Eunice R.............. 7
    Charlott C 5
    Joseph A 3
    Martha M.............. 2

Arnold, Sherebiah, Mass....... 72
    Hannah, Mass.......... 68

Abbott, Hazen F., N. H........ 49
    Hannah 48
    Hannah G............. 18
    Lucetta A............. 15
    Hazen M.............. 13

Brister, Enoch, Mass 80
   Sarah 60
   Thurin V 11
Taylor, Obed 35
   Jerusha 35
   Augustus D............ 7

Bolster, Otis C., Merchant..... 48
   Maria C. L 36
   Melinda E............. 12
   Freeland K........... 9
   William H............ 6
   Dolly M............... 4

Barden, Benj., Innholder, Mass., 41
   Christiana, Mass........ 40
   Ezra P., Clerk, Mass.... 16
   Joseph F.............. 10

Bullock, Jas., Physician, Mass., 59
   Mary A., Mass 47
Fuller, Mary A.............. 13

Bryant, Jairus S.............. 26
   Lucina 24
   Addison W............ 9-12

Barker, Samuel, Mass 67
   Rachel, Vt 56
   Samuel 27
   Betsey 30
   Hazen 22
   Lucretia 29
   Juliette 11
Keyes. Cincinatus 11
   George D 1

Bartlett, Jonathan A 32
   Harriet A 32
   Rosabella R............ 8
   Clarissa L. S............ 6
   Flora S....... 4
   Bernaretta H............ 2

Bartlett, Joseph W 30
   Sarah J 56
   Sarah J 18

Beard, Amasa, Vt 29
   Charlotte 22
   Child 1

Bisbee, Thomas J............. 38
   Sylvia 35
   Mary A 7

Bolster, Alvan............... 55
   Cynthia, N. H.......... 48
   Martha V 21
   May J 19
   Cynthia M 16

Bolster, Sarah W. V........... 13
   Alvan A 8
Hinkson, Olive, Mass......... 83
Lovejoy, Charles 15

Blanchard, David, N. H 42
   Mehitable 41
   William M 20
   Maria R............... 19
   Lucien M.............. 18
   Martha A 16
   Orlando W 14
   Mary E 12

Bolster, William W............ 27
   Martha H 25
   Clara M 7-12

Baker, Otis.................. 42
   Melinda 48
   Adeline 17
   Nathan S.............. 15
   Wilber J 12

Colby, Timothy D, N. H 27
   Hannah W 26
   Louisa A..............7-12

Colby, Joseph E., N. H........ 30
   Mary J. F., N. H........ 30
   Henry M.............. 11
   Timothy E 7
   Sarah M 4

Cushman, Isaac D., Merchant.. 24
   Eliza H 19

Cushman, Lydia.............. 47
   Georgiana F............ 14
   Frances E. K..... 13

Clements, Lawson, Tailor, Vt., 26
   Abigail................ 29

Carter, Ephraim, N. H 68
   Hannah, N. H........... 63
   Amos, Millwright 32
   Charles H.............. 24

Cole, Albion, Miller 29
   Susan B............... 20

Carter, James M 35
   Martha A.............. 32
   Mary A................ 4
   Amasa F.............. 2

Curtis, Bailey............... 78
   Abigail P 76
   Bailey Jr.............. 42

Eastman, Polly.............. 38
    Maria E............... 17
    Sarah A............... 16
    Granville 14
    Holland.............. 12
    Jane 10
    Amanda 6
    Almena 3
    ————— 8-12

Eaton, Osgood 45
    Betsey 34
    Abigail G 16
    Laura F............... 13
    Henry O.............. 6
    Cyrus Q.............. 5
Bent, John.... 12
Eaton, Mehitable........... 52
    Bethia, N. H........... 75

Elliott, Cyrus.............. 40
    Betsey R.............. 37
    Caroline V............ 12

Elliot, Cotton, N. H......... 72
    Gracia, Mass........... 66

Elliot, Thomas C........... 42
    Philena, N. H.......... 43
    Sophia 17
    Leonard D............. 14
    Edward 12
    Franklin 7
    Aaron 3

Elliott, Jacob, N. H......... 66
    Betsey, N. H 56
    Josiah R., N. H......... 24
    John E.. N. H.......... 22
    Matthew G., N. H....... 17

Elliot, William, N. H 33
    Charlotte H........... 15

Elliott, David 53
    Polly, N. H 56
    Benjamin W........... 16
    Juliette 7

Elliott, Nathan W.......... 31
    Lydia M.............. 27
    Hannah M............4-12

Elliot, Joseph, Millman, N. H.. 33
    Phebe H............. 32
    Timothy W............ 7
    Charles E...... 2
    Benjamin, N. H......... 61
    Alfred, N. H........... 16

Ford, Benjamin F.,.......... 32

Lord, Mary P 32
    Seth 3

Farnum, Reuben, N. H....... 49
    Susan, N. H........... 75
    Charles 20

Farnum, Anson W........... 43
    Susan, Mass........... 40
    Martha C............. 18
    Daniel G............. 16
    Nathan W............ 14
    Angeline 11
    Margaret M........... 5
    Anson E............. 9-12

Farnum, Simon K 37
    Mary J............... 28
    Charles W............. 8
    Mary J 6
    Sarah M.............. 5
    Luella 3
    ————— 6-12

Farnum, Merrill............ 55
    Louisa 46
    Sarah L.............. 17
    Freelinghuysen 10

Farnum, Benjamin, N. H...... 82
    Sally, N. H........... 80

Farnum, Manly............. 25
    Elizabeth, N. H........ 22
    Alma L., Mass........ 3
    Mary, Mass 1

Farnum, William W......... 45
    Betsey, G., N. H....... 39
    David W............. 17
    Dorcas A............. 8
    William G 4
    James E............. 1
Moody, Levi 24

Farnum, John C............ 30
    Mary R.............. 26
    Walter H............. 1
Nutting, Gustavus........... 14

Farnum, Jeremiah, N. H...... 65
    Sally, N. H 62
    Emily H 33
    Walter H............. 28

Farnum, James H 43
    Clarissa 43
    Juliett H............. 18
    Charles W. 16
    Martha H............. 13
    Maria G.............. 10

Farnum, Dana F.............. 8
    Abby L.................. 4
Carey, John B.............. 11

Farnum, Stephen, House Car-
    penter 41
    Sarah 43
    William V. F........... 19
    Nancy L. V.......... 17
    Francis J............... 13
    Solon S................ 11

Flint, John.................. 57
    Joanna................. 55
    John M................. 20
    Jonathan 18

Farnum, Daniel.............. 50
    Mary W., N. H......... 40
    Lucy A 16
    William H.............. 14
    Edward H............... 12
    Rufus V................ 8
    Victoria S............. 4
    Betsey, Mass........... 84

Fuller, Mary, N. H........... 77

Frost, William, Shoemaker..... 51
    Dorotha.... 54
    Moses S................ 17
    Daniel G............... 13
    Clark B................ 11

Farnum, George J., House Car-
    penter 37
    Hannah F............... 27
    Mary J................. 16
    George L............... 6
    Nancy J................ 4

Farnum, Rodney M., N. H..... 38
    Elizabeth E., N. H...... 37
    Jane E., N. H.......... 14
    Mary S................. 4
    John E................. 2
Glines, David B., N. H 46
    Catherine B............ 41
    Augusta M.............. 17
    Harriet E.............. 16
    Catherine G.... 14
    David G..... 11

Goddard, Elisha, Mass......... 67
    Catherine, Mass........ 67
    Mary A................. 36
    Elisha F............... 13
    Mary K................. 11
    Eben T................. 9

Goddard, Ephraim F., Mass.... 34

Goddard, Mary S 36
    George T............... 5
    Catherine B 2

Graham, George W........... 36
    Irene 34
    Martha A............... 13
    Frances E.............. 12
    Lorette S.............. 5
    Aaron F................ 3

Graham, Aaron, N. H......... 63
    Geneva 60
    Lucina A............... 18

Graham, John C............. 26
    Susan M................ 21
    Charles H..........8-12

Goud, Robert................ 41
    Eliza, N. H............ 42
    Cyrus K................ 19
    Phebe E................ 13
    Robert F............... 11
    James C................ 7
    Charles A.............. 4

Glover, Livingston........... 33
    Abagail 32
    Oreann L............... 9
    Ann A...... 8
    Susannah 6
    Salome T............... 4
    Lucius A............... 1

Graham, Joshua, Merchant.... 46
    Sarah 33
    Nancy B................ 18
    Philadelphia 16
    Caroline C............. 13
    Albert L............... 13
    Ruth................... 10
    Lowell M............... 4
    Zachary T.............. 3

Glines, Chandler, N. H 72
    Betsey, N. H..... 72
    Albert G., N. H........ 47
    Mary S. W 29

Godwin, Colman, N. H........ 68
    Keziah, N. H........... 58
    Julia O................ 29
    Alvan B................ 25
    Cynthia 22
    Mary W................. 13
Bean, Erastus P............. 18

Godwin, John................ 54
    Clarissa 55
    Ajalon 26

Peavy, Martha, Mass 87

Howe, Calvin 48
   Thirsa 44
   Frances A 21
   Mark T 19
   Lucretia T 17
   Julia H 15
   Clara E 13
   Emma 12
   Mary J 10
   Alden C 9
   Nancy 7
   Alethea 6
   Catherine S 5
   Susan K 2
   Rosilla 1

Howe, Otis Jr 31
   Sarah S 24
   Martha A 3
   Diana M 1

Howe. Otis. Mass 56
   Betsey B., N. H 47
   Amos A.,House Carpenter 29
   Salome A 26
   Nancy K 24
   Julia A 22
   Sarah E 17
   John H 20
   Charles F 15
   Edward K 12
   Mary E 4

Hall, Kimball. N. H 46
   Delia G 42
   John K 17
   Phebe L 14
   Abigail D 12
   Nancy M 7
   Mary L 3
   Betsey C 1

Hopkins, Eliphalet S., Con. Cler-
   gyman 38
   Mary A., Mass 38
   Joseph I 9
   Charles T 6
   Frederick W. 4
   Mary E 2

   Hodgdon, Daniel 48
   Mary R 37
   Ann M 12
   Samuel R 9

Howard. Thomas J 48
   Olive 40
   Humphrey B 23
   Elias 17

Howard, Huldah B 15
   Orinthia 13
   Thomas J. Jr 12
   Charles K 10
   John R 8
   Rodney F 6
   Sylvanus P 4
   Olive 6-12

Hemminway, Francis, Cooper,
   Mass 73
   Rebecca, N. B 72

Howard, Asa S 43
   Betsey S 34
   Henry F 13
   Mary W 11
   Asa 9
   Charles W 7
   Abby M 1
   Virtue 38

Hinkson, Aldana 30
   Gracia A 30
   Loring K 4
   Elizabeth M 3
   Charles F 1

Hall, Daniel, N. H 58
   Sally. Mass 59
   Henry S 17

Hoyt, Jesse, N. H 55
   Abigail,   " 55
   Sylvanus. N. H 28
   Andrew J.,   " 26
   Abigail,   " 24
   Nial,   " 20
   Patrick,   " 22
   Mary E. 17
   Loretta A 14
   Lucebia 11

Hall, Jeremiah, N. H. 68
   Betsey 58
   Jeremiah 21

Howe, George W 38
   Deborah, N. H 76

Hall, Joseph, N. H 68
   Judith,   " 66

Hall, Joshua T 44
   Charlotte M 36
   Eugene M 10

Hinkson, John 47
   Sarah 45
   Chestina W 10

Hardy, Zebediah, N. H........ 60
    Sarah, N. H.............. 56
    Asa 33
    Charles H.............. 20
    Martha J............... 17
Ackley, Charles 3

Holt, Alonzo, N. H.......... 41
    Abigail 39
    John N................. 8
    Emily P................ 6
    James.... 5
    —— 10-12
Holt, Timothy, N. H........ 48
    Nancy, N. H........... 45
    Robert S., N. H........ 22
    Chauncey 20
    David 17
    Hannah N............... 13
    Chloe 10
    George L............... 6
    John W................. 4
    —— 7-12
    David, N. H............ 76
    Chloe, N. H............ 79

Howe, John, Mass............ 58
    Nancy 49
    Rufus 21
    Horace................. 19
    John 16
    Lucinda................ 13
    Nancy E 5

Hutchins, Joseph............ 42
    Mary 36
    Joel 18
    Nancy 16
    Asa 11

Hutchins, Benjamin F 32
    Deborah 32
    Eliphalet H............ 9
    Hezekiah E............. 4
    —— 7-12
Mulligan, Mary A., N. Y...... 11
Hutchins, Hezekiah, N. H.. ... 79

Hutchins, Frye H., Innholder.. 40
    Abigail, N. H.......... 34
    Alice J................ 13
    George H 8
    David, N. H............ 81
    Betsey, N. H........... 68
Abbott, Moses B.............. 48
Hutchins, Elijah B............ 23

Jones, John, Meth. Clergyman. 31
    Mary 29
    Susan M............... 6
    George D.............. 3

Jackson, Benjamin, Tailor..... 36
    Sarah, N. H. 34
    Dolly M 14
    Napoleon B............. 13
    Ezekiel E., N. H....... 12
    Silvester S. 9
    Benjamin Jr............ 6
    —— 1
Kimball, Robert, Mass........ 55
    Virtue 47
    Lucinda B.............. 29
    Adam W 17
    Dana L................. 7
Richardson, Columbus......... 14

Kimball, David............... 59
    Lucy, Mass............. 57
    Amanda, C.............. 30
    Columbia 25
    Juliette W............. 24
    William W.............. 22
    David W................ 20
    Virgil 18
    Lucy A 16
    Elizabeth W............ 14

Kimball, Porter, Blacksmith,
    Mass................ 56
    Nancy 50
    Charles H., Teacher..... 21
Small, Henry K.............. 2

Kimball, Moses F............. 60
    Mary 58
    Arabella C............. 20

Kimball, Asa................. 26
    Geneva G............... 28
    Frederick C............ 3
Knight, Winslow............. 18

Kimball, Charles A........... 33
    Elizabeth 34
    Charles W.............. 11
    Adelaide 8
    Caroline W............. 4
Ackley, Cynthia.............. 14

Kyle, William, Vt........... 67
    Susan 60
Knapp, David................. 40
    Clarissa 37
    David S................ 11
    Mary A. G 9
    James H. F...... 7
    Laura F................ 4

Knapp, Enoch................. 39
    Eliza.................. 34
    Helen E................ 13
    Caroline M............. 11

14

Knapp, Charles A............ 8
    Orissa P.............. 2

Kidder, Burt, Mass........... 28
    Harriet C., Mass........ 25

Kenniston, James...... 46
    Fanny 45
    Lois 21
    Diantha 18
    Lovina 12
    Norris 10
    Arvilla 6
Lovejoy, Abial, Mass........ 66
    Lucretia, Mass......... 57
    Martha T........... 25
    Cecelia P............ 22
    Henry A 19

Lufkin, Alfred............ 32
    Dorcas 30
    Charles A E... 6
    Flora R. I............. 4
    George E. A......... 2

Lufkin, Pamela............ 60
    Addison............ 22
    Nathaniel 20
    Horatio 17

Lufkin, Eliphalet E., N. H.... 37
    Mary R 30
    Laura A............ 7
    Emery E............ 6
    Henry H............ 5
    Mary A........... 3
    Elisha R............ 1

Lufkin, Jacob............ 60
    Eleanor, N. H.......... 56
    Samuel 13
Kidder, Jeremiah, Mass....... 34

Lufkin, Joseph, N. H......... 64
    Loruhama........... 58
    Merrit N........... 22
    Mary A........... 19

Lufkin, Oren H............ 27
    Fidelia 26
Lovejoy, Jacob............ 12

Lufkin, Nathan S............ 26
    Elizabeth A........... 24
    Clara E........... 4
    Horace R........... 1

Lang, William, N. H........ 59
    William P., N. H........ 30
    Melinda H., N. H........ 18
    Mercy C., N. H........ 16

Dearborn, Comfort, N. H...... 81

Lovejoy, Christopher......... 38
    Betsey 38
    Lucestia 10
    Alvan B............ 8
    Lyman.... 6
    Harriet 4
    —— 1
    Mehitable, Mass........ 65

Martin, Henry............ 51
    Sarah, N. H..... ... 50
    John H 24
    Sarah A.... 21
    Lydia A........... 19
    Lyman R........... 17
    Jeremiah W........... 12
    Richard E........... 10
    Maria C. L........... 4

Morse, Elijah............ 45
    Lovina S........... 39
    William G........... 20
    Stedman D........... 17
    Sarah F........... 13
    Elias A........... 3

McCrillis, James, N. H........ 56
    Sally, N. H........... 50
    George........... 22
    Noah 17
    Lydia 15
    Ascenath........... 14
    Phebe K........... 12
    Arvilla........... 10
    Lyman R........... 3

Martin, Jeremiah........... 50
    Nancy, N. H........... 49
    Jonathan K........... 21
    Frances E........... 19
    Nancy 17
Willard, Julia........... 10

Martin, William G........... 36
    Louisa L........... 37
    Clinton W.............8-12

Martin, David G......... 33
    Sarah G........... 34
    Daniel, N. H........ 77

Morton, Alfred, Harness Maker 24
    Mary A........... 20
    Mary A........... 1

Martin, Daniel, Jr........... 42
    Isabella C........... 37
    Betsey G........... 16
    Mary A........... 13

Martin, Julia A 10
    Edwin G................. 7
    James M............... 5
    Winfield S............. 3

Mansur. Warren, Shoemaker,
    Mass......... 46
    Elvira, N. H............ 38
    Thomas H.............. 12
    George E............... 8
    Mary J................. 6
    Susan F................ 4
    John W................ 1

Morse, William, Blacksmith,
    Mass................. 75
    Sally, Mass............ 69

Moody, William............. 51
    Laura 45
    Jane T..... 23
    Mary 21
    Eliza 10
    Samuel L.............. 2

Morse, William M............ 33
    Betsey M.............. 26
    James S...............6-12

Morse, Dolly, N. H........... 76
    Clarissa 39

Moor, Wade................. 62
    Betsey 53
    Caroline 18
    Sarah B.............. 16
    William 12
    Henry 7
    Sarah 5

Martin, John............... 45
    Arvilla............... 42
    Henry 14
    Franklin 12
    Abigail 11
    Charles K............. 9
    Mary E............... 7
    John W............... 4
    Betsey C............. 1
    Kimball, Mass.......... 75
    Rebecca G............. 42
    Hannah 30
    Esther K............. 20

Monroe, Charles W........... 33
    Abigail 24
    Charles...............8-12
Lufkin, Horatio.............. 17

Newton, Sylvester........... 47
    Susan, N. H........... 47

Newton, Stephen H........... 23
    Laura F............... 18
    Benjamin F........... 19
    Clarinda 16
    Maria 9
    Charles 7
    Emma A.............. 4

Newton, Cyrus P............. 23

Martin, Kimball, Blacksmith... 38
    Lydia H.............. 32
    Rachel J............. 13
    Charles V............. 11
    Asa A................ 7

Putnam, Samuel, N. H........ 82
    Betsey, Mass........... 66
    Ivy A................ 29
    Martha C............. 27
    Mary 25
    John F............... 17
    Francis M............. 7

Poland, John............... 46
    Elizabeth 32
    Hezekiah B........... 20
    Aurelia T............. 18
    Martha B............. 16
    Rosalie E............. 10
    Ann M............... 8
    Amanda T............. 6
    William S 4
    Alice J............... 2
    child 3-12

Peabody, Loammi, Blacksmith,
    N. H................. 40
    Sally B.............. 33
    Franklin D............ 16
    Philena C............. 13
    George H............. 4

Parker, Josiah, Mass......... 58
    Keziah B............. 43
    Eliza W.............. 19
    Charles D............ 13
    Irvin B.............. 10
    Juliette F 5

Putnam, Benjamin E......... 48
    Deborah 44
    Mahala M............. 21
    James 17
    Benjamin P........... 14

Putnam, Stephen, N. H........ 85
    Sally, N. H........... 78
    Daniel F............. 37
    Elizabeth 13

Putnam, Jacob............... 56
   Betsey 56
   Dana B., Teacher........ 24
   Drusilla F............... 21
   William F., Cabinet Maker 18
   Francis P............... 14
Elliott. Imogene M............ 7
Putnam, Sarah E............. 26

Putnam, Jesse, N. H.......... 53
   Polly 52
   Edwin A................ 20
   Solon T................ 15
   Jeremiah............... 48

Philbrick, Stephen. 46
   Ann W................. 45
   Mary A................ 20
   Stephen W............. 18
   Harriet 15
   Rothelsa 9

Perry, Enoch, Mass........... 63
   Reliance 50
   Silvanus P............. 21
   Caroline C............. 19
   Christopher C.......... 15
   Lewis M............... 6

Perry, George W............. 28
   Susan V................ 22

Russell, Theodore............ 35
   Lucy G................ 36
   Amanda A............. 12
   Melissa G.............. 8
   Alonzo P............... 6
   Alphonso F............. 3
   ———— 3-12
Dore, Charles 15

Russell, Tabitha.............. 67

Richardson, Asa.............. 32
   Sarah 26
   Mary A. G............. 3
   ———— 3-12

Ripley, Joseph............... 57
   Betsey, Mass.......... 54
   Arvilla 23
   John B................ 19
   Betsey M.............. 17
   Joseph L.............. 15
Mills, Solon H.............. 7

Rawson, Lyman, Lawyer...... 50
   Jerusha 46
   Ellen J................ 15
   Louisa 14
   Ralph L............... 12

Rawson, Mary H............. 10
   Florence 6
   ———— 2
Lane, Charles 16
Adams, Susan............... 58

Roberts. Thomas, Physician... 44
   Harriet M.............. 42
   Ann S................. 14
   Lawson G.............. 11
   Sidney I............... 8
   Euthalius C 6
   Euthalia W............ 6
Richards, Thomas, N. H....... 46
   Pamela 54

Ricker, Hiram............... 39
   Jeanette W.... 29
   Edward P.............. 3

Richardson, Jeremiah......... 44
   Harriet, N. H.......... 44
   Amanda J...... 19
   Mahala K............. 18
   Bartlett E............. 16
   German 14
   Sophia S.............. 12
   Rosina H 8
   Brittania 5
   Scott W............... 2
   Ann A................ 1
Rolfe, John E...... 45
   Joanna S.............. 32
   Henrietta 10
   Henry A. J...... 8
   Susan M. V............ 4

Rolfe, Henry C.............. 51
   Dorcas 46
   Charles H............. 20
   Arvilla W.............. 9
Wheeler, Abel. N. H.......... 76
   Betsey 75

Richardson, John, N. H....... 63
   Mehitable, N. H........ 57
   Harriet E............. 33
   Samuel 31

Roberts. Joseph H........... 28
   Harriet 30
   Mary E............... 4
   George W...... 1

Ray, George A., Mass........ 30
   Lucy C............... 27
   Edwin F...... 4
   Harriet C.............4-12

Ray, Elijah, Mass............ 65
   Elizabeth, Mass........ 63

Ray, Sarah M............ 21
  Herman A............ 19
  Alonzo B............. 14

Richmond, Eliab............. 64
  Sally 61
  Benjamin F....... 30
  William C.............. 22
  Aurelia M.............. 16

Richardson, Joseph........... 43
  Eda.................... 32
  Mary J................. 8
  Betsey A.............. 5
  Sarah F............... 3
  ———— 3-12
Hinkson, Esther.............. 22

Ricker, Thomas N., Blacksmith 36
  Mary E................ 34
  Rosina E.............. 10
  Mary A................ 8
  Charles H............ 5
  Delphina 3
Hoit, Patrick................. 22

Richardson, Hazen, N. H..... 47
  Mary, N. H............ 49
  Charles, N. H......... 18
  Sarah J., N. H....... . 17
  Sophronia, N. H....... 15
  Prudence 11
  Emily F.............. 8
  Albert 6

Rolfe, John, N. H............ 65
  Betsey, Mass.......... 62
  Benjamin M........... 32
  Henry L.............. 28
  Clara 20
  Oscar D............. 17

Simpson, Paul R., N. H....... 59
  Hannah 53
  Willard E............ 25
  Paul B., Carpenter...... 23
  John D., Carpenter...... 22
  Hannah M............ 19

Segar, John E................ 47
  Lydia 46
  Ambrose C............ 16
  Jonathan M........... 13
  Jarvis M............. 8

Stevens, Edward............. 40
  Sybil 40
  Edwin 12
  Henry 10
  Aaron............... 8
  Frederick 6
  George 3

Silver, Daniel 42
  Sarah 39
  David H.............. 17
  George M............. 14
  Savina M............. 11
  Sarah J.............. 8
  Pascal F............. 6
  Andrew W............ 1

Small, Sumner............. 32
  Eliza.................. 33
  Fanny 7
  Albert 6
  Coral 3
  Abby 1

Small, Cyrus................. 34
  Polly 37
  James P............. 8
  Charles V............ 6
  Lucien 2
  Lucy A.............. 3

Smith, Africa, Blacksmith..... 40
  Mary, Mass........... 40
  Erskine C., Blacksmith.. 15
  Uriah H............. 13
  Lyman G............. 11
  Sidney 8
  Sewall 7
  Mary A............. 3
  Child 1

Stevens, Ruth............. 60
  William T............. 18
  Samuel B., Teamster.... 21

  Silver, James........... 41
  Sarah 37
  Cordelia 18
  George............... 16
  Adeline 13
  Frances 11
  Annette 8
  Clara 6
  Emma............8-12

Small, Joseph P., Shoemaker.. 45
  Pamela 34
  Sarah M............. 16
  Pamela 11
  Oreann 9
  Morris M............. 7

Stevens, Nancy............. 43
  Viola 19
  Mercy 16
  Susan 9

Swain, John, House Carpenter. 29
  Sally W............. 21

Virgin, Rufus, N. H............ 58
   Susan 56
   Chaplin, Wheelwright... 30
   Abbott.................. 28
   Susan M................. 21
   Albert 19

Virgin, Peter................. 46
   Mary A.................. 44
   George, Manufacturer... 24
   Edwin, Manufacturer.... 20
   Charles, Manufacturer... 16
   Paulina, Manufacturer... 12
   Augusta 10
   Lucy 8
   Franklin 4
   Maria 2

Virgin, Charles E., N. H....... 43
   Diantha 43
   Rebecca B............... 15
   William 16
   Nancy, N. H............. 70

Virgin, William B............. 26
   Irene 26
   ———— 1

Woods, Nathaniel............. 41
   Lois E.................. 41
   Charles E............... 17
   Caroline A.............. 14
   Leonard M............... 11
   Horace F................ 9
   Sarah A................. 3

Wood, Samuel H.............. 25
   Elizabeth, Mass......... 57
   John R.................. 23
   Thomas A................ 15

Wardwell, Jeremiah, Cabinet
   Maker 40
   Jeanette 38
   Mary J.................. 19
   Martha A................ 12
   Emily................... 7

Wardwell, Lydia, N. H........ 56
   Wm. H., Portrait Painter, 30
   Jarvis C., Carriage Trim-
    mer 20
   Spofford H., Cabinet
    Maker 19

Wardwell, Lydia J............. 16
   Elizabeth S............. 14

Walker, Timothy, N. H........ 37
   Luna 39
   Sarah 14
   Charles 12
   Hannah 10
   Cynthia 5
   Susan 1

Winslow, Francis............. 35
   Susan M................. 30
   Simon 3
   ———— 6-12

Washburn, James, Mass....... 54
   Lavina 40
   Martha T................ 21
   Angela M................ 17
   James E................. 10
Randall, Francis E............ 2

Washburn, Tristram N........ 32
   Nancy S................. 35
   Martin B................ 8
   Hiram K................. 5

Wheeler, Deborah D.......... 38
   Ann V. A................ 15
   Charles F............... 7

Wyman, Henry H............. 36
   Mary 37
   Eliza J................. 14
   James H................. 12
   Benjamin B.............. 10
   Dorrington.............. 8
   Martha 6
   Nancy W................. 4
   Samuel S................ 3

Warren, Nathaniel S.......... 50
   Parney.................. 47
   William S............... 19
   Charles C............... 16
   Trueman S............... 13
   Sarah J................. 12
   Olive H................. 10
   Lydia 8
   Jeanette 6
   Nathaniel 3
   Augustus 1

CHAPTER XXXV.

GLEANINGS.

THE early settlers were greatly annoyed by bears carrying off their sheep and lambs, and also by destroying the standing corn. When corn is in the milk. as it is called, and before it begins to harden, bears are very fond of it, and in securing it. they will tread down and destroy much more than they can eat. They were hunted and destroyed in large numbers, but the supply was always unfailing. Rufus Virgin, who lived near Rumford Falls, one day, when at work in his field, saw some animal walking in the road about fifty rods off, which he at first thought was a large dog. But when the animal left the road, climbed over the fence and started for the woods, he knew it was a bear. He went to the house, and his wife immediately started off for help to come and surround the piece of woods into which the bear had gone. A number of men soon arrived armed with clubs, pitch-forks or shot-guns, and accompanied by a number of dogs. They were stationed at different points around the woods, and in the road to prevent him from taking to the river. The word was given, and the dogs on being let loose, made their way as fast as possible into the woods. There was soon a medley of barks and growls, and then came a shout from the side of the woods next the river, followed by the report of fire-arms and the brandishing of clubs, and the bear hastily retreated into the woods from which he had been driven by the dogs, in doing which, he went so near Paul Simpson that he touched him with his hat. After being driven back and forth through the woods for several times, the bear ran down to the foot of the hill where Rufus Virgin was stationed. Virgin had a gun called the Queen's Arms, charged with an ounce bullet, which he raised and fired, and the ball passed through the bear just back of his fore-shoulders, but did not bring him down. The wounded beast rushed between two trees leaving blood on each of them, and was soon over the fence into the road. Here the dogs attacked him, but he made short work of them, and again took to the woods before help could arrive. The men followed a long distance by the blood-stains on the leaves and ground, but finally lost the track, and the dogs could not be induced to follow him. Night now came on, and it was agreed to postpone further pursuit until the next day. They followed up the trail on the next day, but without success. They all agreed that they had had an exciting time, but they would have been much better satisfied could they have found the bear, which they had no doubt had died of its wounds.

In the olden time, it was considered no disgrace to get the worse for liquor on training and muster days, and on such occasions, after having imbibed freely, men were often quarrelsome. On one occasion when Captain Richardson was drilling the old "Barefoot Company," as it was called, a man named Lane, who was captain of a company of Light Infantry, tried several times to break through the ranks of Richardson's Company. Richardson bore it for some time, but as the other persisted, he lost his temper, and sheathing his sword, he drew off and knocked Lane down. There was great excitement between the two companies, and there was danger of more serious trouble, but Lane got up and walked off, and the excitement subsided. It showed some forbearance in Richardson, to sheathe the more deadly weapon, and make use of the one furnished by nature, but he was more familiar with the use of the latter, and probably thought he could sufficiently punish Lane without resort to the sword.

At a military training in Rufus Virgin's field, a man named Weaver became a little quarrelsome, and pulled a Mr. Abbot from his horse. Then they clinched, and had scuffled for some time without advantage to either, but finally Abbot got his opponent's hair around an apple tree, and pulled it with one hand while he punched him with the other. Captain Calvin Howe now interfered and parted them, and that was the end of the affair so far as they were concerned, but the apple tree was fatally injured, and did not leaf out the next year.

Though the Indians had abandoned the Androscoggin valley when the early settlers came, they frequently revisited their old haunts, in small numbers, but only to remain for a short time, when they disappeared as suddenly as they came. One morning as Henry Abbot was going to the Falls, he heard an outcry and stepped to the bank of the river to ascertain the cause. There he saw an Indian and squaw in a birch canoe, near the head of the Falls, and the Indian was permitting the canoe to float down to the very verge of the fall, close to the Rolfe pitch. The squaw would cry piteously, and then, with a stroke or two of the paddle, he would throw the frail bark out of danger, but only to repeat the same thing over and over again, seeming to enjoy the fright of his mate in the highest degree. Abbot called to him to desist, and bringing his canoe along by the bank where Abbot stood, he laughingly said, "Me squaw fraid of deble, but me no fraid of deble."

There was never a bridge across the river at the head of the falls, although one was long contemplated. Rufus Virgin and Nathan Knapp, the two energetic young men spoken of by Rev. Daniel Gould in his "History of Rumford," at one time started a subscription to raise funds to put across a bridge just below the Rolfe pitch, still known as "the bridge place," and were quite successful. The abutments were built, the timber got out and partly framed, and a pier constructed some thirty feet from the shore. The floor timbers were also laid. About this time, one day, Virgin, who was at work, found he was going to fall from the abutment, and to save himself. he jumped, and striking upon a ledge he broke the bone of one of his heels, and was laid up a long time. Then Mr. Knapp went over the falls and was drowned, and the project of a bridge at this place was abandoned. The timber was used for other purposes, and a freshet carried away the pier.

Speaking of the Indians, a citizen of Rumford remarks: "I well remember when four Indians on their way to the lakes, stopped at my father's over night. They were invited in to warm their feet, and then were taken to the barn for a lodging place. They went down into a bay to sleep, where the top of the hay was six feet below the floor; after they had laid down, hay was pitched over them, and in the morning they were very thankful for their warm bed. An Indian on the Androscoggin at this point, is now a rare sight."

Counterfeiting the coin of the country was quite common in some parts of Oxford county, three score years ago. On one occasion, Gen. Alvan Bolster, with three men from Hallowell, called on Rufus Virgin at the Falls, very early in the morning, and requested him to take a lunch, then hastily follow them up Swift river, until he should overtake them. He did as directed, and when he had

·caught up with them, they told him they had arrested a man in Chesterville for passing counterfeit money, and that he had divulged the place on Swift river where it was made. The party then climbed a mountain, and hunted all day, but without success. They had made a mistake in the location, and on the following day, with more help, they found the place, but the counterfeiters had left it and had carried away most of their tools and appli-·ances for making spurious coin ; enough was found, however, to prove what business had recently been carried on there. Shortly after, several men were arrested and brought before Esquire Bolster, who placed them under bonds to appear at court, but they did not appear, and the bondsmen came forward and settled their liabilities. It was thought that some who occupied high places in the community were concerned in the business, but there were no more prosecutions, and the matter soon ceased to be talked about. As a reminiscence of the occasion, it is related that there was much riding up Swift river on nights and Sundays about that time. Cattle and horses that were out to pasture required frequent salting, and old block tin and pewter were in great demand.

The early settlers adopted various devices to out-wit the bears, which, in summer, came to prey upon their growing corn. One year, an old shy bruin would swim the river, above the Falls, and spend a part of the night in Rufus Virgin's corn field, doing great damage. Acting on the advice of Mr. Henry Abbot, an old hunter, Mr. Virgin set a loaded gun in such a manner that the bear, on entering the field, would run against a line connected with the trigger, and if everything should work as hoped, would receive the charge in his body. Everything being arranged, Mr. Virgin, his adviser and another neighbor or two, sat up and awaited the result. About eight o'clock, Mr. Abbot informed his associates that if the bear was coming in the fore part of the night, it would be about that time ; otherwise, he would not come till toward morning. Hardly had he ceased speaking, when they heard the report of the gun, and all rushed out to see what had been the result, and this is what they ascertained : That the line had been wet by the dew, had shortened by shrinking, and had pulled off the gun. The next night they set the gun again, but the bear walked over the line, feasted on the coveted corn, and retired in safety. But the next night he went to another field where a gun had been set, and was shot and killed. He was a huge animal, and had troubled the settlers many years.

Sudden freshets on the Androscoggin, often convert the higher intervals into islands, a broad belt of water passing between them and the upland. On one occasion a man named Jeremiah Thompson was at work for a man above the Falls, when a freshet came, the water backing up into a creek so that Thompson could not get to his work. They had no boat, but they did have a large scalding tub, and in this Thompson proposed to make his way to his work. The tub was launched, and Thompson stepping in, proceeded to navigate it, but when half way across the tub tipped to one side, and in trying to right it, Thompson upset it, and was left floundering in the turbid water. He struck out for the shore which he reached in safety, but the tub went down stream and was lost.

In the early times, it was the custom to celebrate the anniversary of American Independence by burning powder, and the firing usually commenced in the small hours of the morning. Chinese fire-crackers were then unknown, and the old Queen's arms were loaded all they would bear. On one occasion, a fatal result followed an over-charged gun. It was in the hands of Jonathan Keyes, son of Francis Keyes, and burst, killing him instantly. He was a promising young man, and his death in this manner caused wide-spread sorrow.

Rufus Virgin was a Mill-wright, and at one time he had a job to erect a mill in Peru, about two miles from his home by way of a mountain, and three to travel around it. He had a hired man who claimed that the longest way was the best, and repeated it so often and so persistently that they agreed to settle it by each taking his preferred way and see which would first reach the end of the trip. They started at the same time, and neither was to run, but were to proceed by their ordinary walking gait. When Virgin reached the top of the mountain, he had a good view of the river road, and there he saw his man running at the top of his speed. Virgin at once put out and by running he reached the goal several minutes ahead, long enough to get well rested. After a while, the other came in puffing and blowing, and surprised to see Virgin quietly at work and showing no signs of extra effort. He accused him of running, but when the counter charge was made and he found he was caught, he subsided, and after that found no fault with the way across the mountain.

Jeremiah Richardson was a famous hunter, and brought more bears to grief than any man in town. One day he went out to build some fence in the woods, when he was confronted by an old bear and her two cubs. The bear at once showed fight, and he struck at her with his axe. She parried the blow, knocked the axe aside, and with her huge paw tore out the entire front of his vest. He got in several blows and obliged her to retreat, when seizing one of the cubs, he tied it up in his frock and started for home, which he reached without further molestation.

Several drowning accidents have occurred at the Great Falls. On the fourth of October, 1833, Nathan Knapp invited a few friends to inspect a wall which he had completed to turn the water to his mill. While standing on the wall and explaining his work, the rock on which he was standing overturned and precipitated him into the canal. He was carried down by the swift current to the river, some seventy-five feet distant, and then over the entire fall. His body was recovered a month later, in Canton. He was an energetic and enterprising man, and his death was greatly deplored. He left a family, several of his children being quite young. June 1, 1869, three river drivers were drowned at the foot of the great eddy. They went upon a large rock to break a jam that had formed there, and on returning they lost control of their boat, and three of the five jumped out and were drowned; the two that remained in the boat crossed in safety.

On one occasion, while blasting the ledge at the Falls, a man named Lewis was blown up and survived only nine days. He was an Englishman. This occurred in the spring of 1833.

William Morse built the first house and blacksmith shop at the Falls, and the second house was by Nathan Knapp. Alvan Bolster and James H. Farnum kept the first store there, and the first fulling mill was built by Moses T. Cross of Bethel, in 1833. The first clover mill was by Simon Stevens of Paris, in 1835, and the first tavern there was kept by Levi Abbot. The power was utilized first by Rufus Virgin and Nathan Knapp. Afterwards, for some years, by Chaplin Virgin, who also built carriages and sleighs. Business at the Falls has declined within a few years, but it is hoped that it will be greatly increased by the present owners.

A prominent character in Rumford for many years, was Mr. Phineas Wood, whose home was near Red Hill. Mr. Wood came from Dracut, Mass., early in the century. Though without education, he did a large amount of business, and for his time and with his opportunities, accumulated a large estate. He was a man of vast proportions, towering a head above ordinary men, and broad in proportion to his height. He was a prominent figure at military trainings and musters, at fourth of July celebrations, and agricultural exhibitions.

Mr. Wood kept a large stock, and his broad, hill-side ranges contained some of the finest cattle in the county. He was in the habit of salting his stock every Sunday morning, and his method of doing it was unique. He would fill a bag with salt, and placing it across a horse's back, he would get on himself and start for the distant hills. Arriving at the pasture and before entering it, he would untie the bag and holding the open end in one hand, with the other he would guide his horse into the pasture. The cattle, expecting a visit about this time, would be hanging around the entrance to the pasture, and as soon as Mr. Wood entered, the entire herd, bellowing so as to be heard far away, would rush toward him at the top of their speed, and putting his horse into the run, Mr. Wood would scatter salt from the open bag until it was empty. By this time the entire herd would be enjoying their Sunday morning relish, and Mr. Wood would quietly return to his home.

Mr. Wood was often in law with some of his towns-people; not that he was litigious himself, for he was generally the defendant in the cases, and somehow he was generally beaten. On one occasion when he had a cause to be tried at Paris, he informed the presiding judge that, as he lost most of his cases when he employed a lawyer, he had concluded to try this case himself. He accordingly took charge of it, and in his argument before the jury, displayed such a knowledge of the law, and such oratorical powers, though of course his language was not grammatical, that the judge, jury and bar were astonished. The jury gave him a verdict without leaving their seats. On another occasion when Mr. Wood had lost a case, and as he thought unjustly, he sarcastically suggested to the court that he thought he had better leave his pocket-book with him, so that when cases were entered he might settle them and save the expense of a trial.

In the olden times, there was a small village in the town of Woodstock, on the thoroughfare between Rumford and Paris, where people were in the habit of congregating on Saturday afternoons, to run, wrestle, pitch quoits and engage in other manly sports. At such times the ardent flowed freely, and the exercises would sometimes close with almost a tragedy instead of a farce. Rumford people were often here, including Mr. Wood who was fond of exhibiting his great strength and not averse to indulging in the use of the ardent. On one occasion, when a party of these merrymakers were present and Mr. Wood among them, something was stolen from somebody, about which there was considerable talk and no small amount of bluster. Finally Mr. Wood took out his pocketbook and stepping up to the store keeper, offered to pay for the missing article. "Why," said the dispenser of liquid rations, "you did not take it, did you Mr. Wood." "No," said Wood, "but I have neighbors who will swear I did, and I may as well pay for it now as hereafter."

Yet, notwithstanding all his peculiarities, Mr. Wood was in many respects, a valuable citizen. He had energy and push, and if there was any difficult work to be done in the town, such as building a bridge or opening a new road, he was always ready to undertake it, and whatever he did undertake he always accomplished. He kept good stock and through his efforts, the stock in the town became much improved. He was generous, kind hearted and neighborly, and in his extensive farming operations he gave employment to many persons, some of whom would have found it difficult to have obtained work anywhere else. His death was a great loss to the farming interests of the neighborhood in which he lived, and to the town. Mr. Wood was fortunate in his family relations. Both of his wives were amiable and intelligent women, and his children grew up to be respected in town and after they went to seek their fortunes elsewhere. Only two remain : John R. Wood of Brooklyn, New York, and Mrs. Vileria Caldwell who now resides at North Waterford.

A charter was granted to build a bridge across the Androscoggin river, at any point between the mouth of Ellis river and Kimball's Ferry, in Rumford, in 1819. The incorporators named in the charter were Daniel Martin, Ezra Smith, Francis Cushman, David Burbank, Luther Bean, Nathaniel Rolfe, Kimball Martin, Joel Howe and Peter C. Virgin. It was to be completed in four years. Acts were passed by the Maine Legislature, extending the time for the completion of this bridge, Jan. 15, 1822, and Feb. 17, 1827. An act was passed February 14, 1833, to take effect the April following, for the protection of the bridge, providing a fine of three dollars for crossing it faster than a walk. March 23, 1839, an act was passed increasing the rates of toll, and making the rates at Bethel, Rumford and Jay, uniform. The bridge at Jay was built by the "Oxford Bridge Association" This constitutes all the legislation with regard to the Rumford bridge, nor was this last necessary, for January 26, 1839, this bridge, the one at Bethel and several others on the Androscoggin below, were swept away by a winter freshet. This was nearly half a century ago, and the ferry in Summer and ice in Winter have been the only means of crossing the river between the Corner and the Point since that time.

There was a ferry established between the Point and Corner, in 1809, and with the exception of the few years when the river was bridged, it has been in operation when the river has been open ever since. There have been times when it was dangerous crossing, and some have had narrow escapes from drowning. At one time a young minister undertook to pull himself over in a small boat, and when in the middle of the river he kicked his boat away and was left hanging on the rope, and half under water, as the water was high. He gave the alarm, but there was no way to reach him except by means of the large boat. This was pulled off from the bank and started toward him, but in pulling, the rope would be first taut and then slack, which kept him bobbing up and down, part of the time in the water up to his neck. He was rescued in time from a position which was more ludicrous than dangerous. He was of that persuasion that believes in immersion, but this time he got more water than was wholly desirable.

At another time, in the spring when the ice interferred with the running of the boat, among others going over, was a young man dressed for a ball which was coming off at the Corner, and where he was to meet the lady he afterward married. Above his other clothing, he wore a fur overcoat. There were cakes of ice in the way and the ferryman was doing his best to keep clear of them, when our young man sang out, "Just let your uncle Dudley pull a minute," and seizing hold of the rope, he pulled away with all his might. There was a jam of ice ahead, and the ferryman and others on the boat, cautioned him not to run into it, but he did not heed them and kept on. When the collision came, the rope was un-shipped from the boat, and the amateur boatman thrown some fifteen feet up stream, and struck the water head foremost. He was pulled out by the heels, and the boat was brought to the shore with great difficulty, a long distance below the landing place. It left the young man in a condition unfit to proceed to the ball, and "Let your uncle Dudley pull," were words he was obliged to hear quite frequently for a long time afterwards, and which he by no means relished.

When Jonathan Keyes first came to Rumford, the place was sometimes visited by roving Indians, and as they came from Canada and the war for independence was in progress, they sometimes appeared in war paint though they never made any very hostile demonstrations toward his family. One time when Jonathan Keyes was absent from home, his son Francis saw several painted Indians approaching the house, and ran and told his mother. Mrs. Keyes was a very large woman, and as fearless as she was large. She told Francis to step into the house and stay there. She then went out and confronted the head Indian, one Tomhegan with whom she was acquainted, and asked whether they were for peace or war? They answered, peace. "Then," said she "hand me your guns." They obeyed and, having received them, she gave them bread and maple sugar to eat; after they had eaten, they took their guns and passed along. Keyes came home at night, and not liking the aspect of things, took his family and started at once for New Gloucester, where he arrived in safety. This was about the time of the Indian raid into Bethel. These Indians had been to Livermore to attack the settlement there, but finding it too strong, they left without making any demonstration.

Benjamin Rolfe, who came from Concord, N. H., and settled on the south side of the river above Rumford Falls, was among the first in town to receive a commission as Justice of the Peace. It is related of him that wishing to convey a piece of real estate, and there being no other civil magistrate near, he stationed himself before a mirror, and after looking at himself in the glass, he repeated the formula, "Personally appeared before me, etc.," and then signed it officially after having signed as grantor.

An act was passed February 8, 1819, authorizing the sale of the ministerial and school lands in Rumford, and the trustees of the funds named in the act are: Francis Keyes, William Wheeler, Nathan Adams, Joshua Graham, Daniel Knight, Hezekiah Hutchins and Peter C. Virgin. In 1845, an act was passed directing the trustees acting under the act of 1819, to transfer and deliver up to the municipal officers of the town, all monies, notes and other securities constituting the school funds, virtually repealing the former act. It is said that a large portion of these funds were lost to the schools by loaning them to irresponsible parties without sufficient security.

The Maine Legislature, February 18, 1835, granted a charter to the Rumford Falls Bridge Company, and allowed them five years in which to construct a bridge across the river at or near Rumford Falls. The bridge was commenced but never completed. The following persons constituted the company: Rufus Virgin, Moses F. Kimball, John M. Eustis, Otis C. Bolster, Moses T. Cross, Edward Stevens, Aaron Stevens, David Abbot 4th, Lyman Bolster, Thos. G. Clark, John E. Rolfe, Albert G. Glines, Chas. E. Virgin, Chandler Abbot, Osgood Eaton, Jr., Jacob Abbot 2d, David B. Glines, James H. Farnum, Wm. W. Farnum, Stephen Farnum, Jr., Jesse Putnam, Joseph Adams, Aaron Virgin, David Farnum, Josiah Parker, Daniel Hall, Jeremiah Farnum, Jesse Hoit, Jeremiah Hall, Stephen Putnam, David Knapp, Enoch Knapp and Alvan Bolster.

The first mills in Rumford were erected by Capt. John Chandler of Concord, N. H. He was the son of Lieut. John and Mary (Carter) Chandler, and was born in Concord, December 11, 1752. An account of his contract with the proprietors to build mills on Concord river in New Pennacook may be found in the abstract of the records of the proprietary. None of this Chandler family ever lived in Rumford. April 15, 1792, John Chandler sold the mills on Concord river, together with one hundred acres of land, to Aaron Moor who had been a resident here for several years. February, 1796, Aaron Moor sold the mill property and land to Gustavus A. Goss, and bought land in Number 2, now Franklin Plantation, where he moved with his family. June 15, 1804, Aaron Moor of Number 2 sold a lot of land adjoining the one on which Francis Hemmingway settled, to Josiah Bean of Bethel. The mills on Concord river finally came into the hands of David Abbot, who operated them for many years and they have since been known as Abbot's mills. Mr. Abbot exchanged other lands for the mill property, including lands with Goss, and gave one hundred and ten thousand feet of pine lumber in addition, about the year 1800. Samuel V. Abbot succeeded his father in the ownership of the mills and still continues to operate them. A few years ago he erected a new and very fine grist mill, which has been well patronized, and the saw mill has turned out a great deal of lumber.

Silas Howe came from Berlin, Mass., quite early and settled at Rumford Centre. Some of the early town meetings were held at his house. He put up frames for a saw and grist mill at the mouth of Split brook, but he did not finish them, and January 12, 1803, he sold his house and land with the mill privilege and frames to Phineas Wood. June 1, 1803, Phineas Wood sold to Nathan Hunting of Chelmsford, Mass., one hundred acres of land, together with house and one-half of the mill frames near the mouth of Split brook and privilege. The lot of land conveyed was number eighty-three, on the north side of the Great river. August 30, 1804, Wood sold to Hunting, his wife Patty joining in the conveyance, the other half of the mills and privilege. Hunting had then moved into town and he continued here and to operate the mills with Francis Smart for some years. Reference is made to Hunting and the mills in abstracts of town records. These mills were afterward owned by Joshua Graham and were known as Graham's mills. Since that time they have been owned by Wade Moor, Chaplin Virgin and others.

It is said that Stephen Greenleaf Stevens sold to Jesse Duston, blacksmith, the lot of land on which Rumford Point village now is. Mr. Duston married a daughter of Phineas Howard of Howard's Gore. He was the son of Jesse Duston, an early settler of Bethel, and a lineal descendant of the famous Hannah (Emerson) Duston who killed the band of Indians at Pennacook, N. H., which had made her and her nurse captives at Haverhill. Mr. Duston moved from Rumford to Brunswick where some of his descendants still reside. February 27, 1810, Stephen Greenleaf Stevens sold to Jesse Duston, blacksmith, one-half of lot numbered forty-eight in the third division of lots, containing one hundred and twenty-two acres.

Lydia, daughter of Francis Keyes, Esq., married Francis Cushman, and after his death she became insane. She was harmlessly crazy, but sometimes she was very annoying to public gatherings which she chose to attend. She had the impression that her husband had been swindled out of his property, and this made her very bitter toward some of the prominent families in town. At the funeral of Porter Kimball she refused to give up her pew to the mourners, and whenever the minister, in the course of his funeral sermon, said anything in praise of the deceased, "Aunt Lydia," as she was always called, would audibly contradict him. There was a large funeral, he being a member of the Sons of Temperance, and a large number of the members of the fraternity was present from adjoining towns, on which account Aunt Lydia's interruptions were especially annoying.

On a certain occasion there was a Universalist conference meeting at Rumford, and Aunt Lydia Cushman was present. Among the ministers there, was Rev. J. C. Snow who had lately come into the State, and was settled in Norway. Mr. Snow was a young man, beardless, with rosy cheeks which made him appear much younger than he really was. He took part in the meeting, and at one of the sessions, made a very eloquent and soul-stirring speech. Aunt Lydia listened very attentively, and when he closed she sprang to her feet and quoted in a clear voice the first part of the second verse of the eighth psalm, "Out of the mouth of babes and sucklings hast thou ordained strength." There was a smile upon the faces of the audience and an audible titter among the younger portion, but Aunt Lydia looked as grave as a judge, and no doubt felt that her little speech was a climax to the eloquence of the youthful preacher.

On another occasion Aunt Lydia was at a meeting where several of her imaginary enemies were present, and she became so wild and noisy that it became necessary to remove her, after she had persistently refused to hold her peace or go out of her own accord. So two strong men undertook to put her out and after skirmishing a little they seized her, one on each side, and began to carry her down the isle toward the door. She stopped all resistance, and looking down with contempt, first on one of her bearers and then on the other, she raised her eyes to the audience and said: "I am more favored than was the Saviour of the world; he had to be content with riding on one ass, while I am borne on the backs of a pair of them."

Aunt Lydia Cushman often went to Augusta when the Legislature

The Schloss Hemessent Duurkirek 1825

was in session, and tried to obtain legislation to protect the property rights of women. Dressed partly in male attire, she would sit in the galleries at the State House with knitting work in hand, through entire sessions closely watching the proceedings and listening to the debates, and when anything was said that especially pleased her, she would heartily respond with "amen" or "double amen to that." Her insanity rather increased with her years, and she was sent to the Insane Hospital, where in the old ladies' ward, she was tenderly cared for, until her mind and body became weakened, when as a harmless incurable, on account of the crowded condition of the Hospital, she was taken back to Rumford and soon after died.

In a letter written by Aunt Lydia Cushman, dated Rumford, October, 1874, she says : "The Beans came from Standish to Bethel; there were three of them, Josiah, Jonathan and Daniel. Josiah was my grandfather; he married Molly Crocker and they had nine children. The rest of the Crocker family moved to Machias. I never saw my great grandfather, but I have seen my great grandmother. She was a short little Dutchman; when she stood up, her head was just as high as the distaff of a little old fashioned spinning wheel, and the old fashioned wheels were not as high by one foot as the present ones. My great grandfather one night hurried his wife off to bed and assisted her about the children. When she woke up in the night he had not come to bed; she called him but he did not answer, and on getting up she found him hanging by the neck and stone dead. Neither she nor the children had ever thought of such a thing; death was its own interpreter." She signed her name as "Lydia Cushman, a teacher of righteousness to this generation, not that a female should carry the reins, sit on the right and drive the horse, but if her husband dies, she should have the privilege born with her, to speak the truth."

Nathan Adams was one of the proprietors of Andover. This town was granted to inhabitants of Andover, Mass., and neighboring towns, and was largely settled by people from Andover. The early Merrills, Poors, Adamses Wardwells and Abbots came from there, while others came from Newbury, Amesbury and Bradford. Nathan Adams sold out his interest in Andover, having previously bought of Sarah Stevens a full right amounting to nearly four hundred acres of New Pennacook lands. His tract was next to Bethel, now Hanover line. He first moved into Bethel and remained while he cleared land and built a house upon his own territory. While in Bethel he was chosen one of the selectmen, and one of his children was born in Bethel. He was one of the more forehanded of the early settlers of Andover, and also of Rumford, having been a well-to-do farmer in Andover, Mass. His was not one of the old Andover families, the Adamses having moved there probably from New Hampshire, perhaps from New Ipswich. He descended from William Adams who was a resident of Ipswich, Mass., in 1640.

The schools of Rumford are not as well attended as they were fifty years ago. Then nearly all the seats were filled even in the cross road school-houses. The school on the west side of Ellis river in the Howe district once had fifty or sixty pupils in winter, and thirty to forty in summer, but not half that number attends there now. Once a young man applied for and obtained the winter school in this district, but when he made his appearance he found so many bouncing girls present that his heart failed him. He managed to get through the day, but at night, he announced his intention of keeping the school no longer. The girls really liked his appearance and thought he would make a good teacher, and so they urged him to stay and continue the school and promised to respect and obey him, but it was all to no purpose. Calvin Howe who lived in this district, had eleven daughters, enough to make more than an average country school of the present day.

In early times, the young people living on Ellis river often walked to Rumford Center, a distance of eight miles, or to Andover, distant five miles, to meeting on the Sabbath, and thought nothing of it. Mrs. Timothy Walker recently told the writer that when she was a girl, she and her sister, Mrs. William Moody, had frequently walked to the house of Dea. Abijah Lapham, who lived on the Paris road near Bailey's Corner, to attend meeting, one of the attractions being the fine singing of the young wife of Deacon Lapham's son. Young ladies would hardly consent to ride as far to attend meetings in our day. The practice was to wear old shoes until they got near the church, then change them for better ones, hiding the old ones to be put on again when they started on the homeward journey. There was once a log near the Center meeting house, upon which the girls would sit to make the exchange. Many people were destitute of good clothes in those days, and on funeral occasions they had to borrow of those who had them, in order to appear decent.

At weddings, also, guests often appeared in borrowed finery, and a pair of calf-skin boots often did service for all the men in a neighborhood.

As stated elsewhere, when the first settlers came to Rumford, there were strolling bands of Saint Francis Indians frequently in the settlement. They sometimes brought their furs here for sale, which they had secured in the region of the lakes and their tributaries. Soon after Philip Abbot came he made a journey to Fryeburg and purchased some ardent spirits and brought them here hoping thereby to get the good will of the savages and secure their peltry. But alas for human foresight! The Indians drank his rum and became so crazy drunk and demonstrative that he was obliged to take his family and flee into the woods, where he remained until the savages had sobered off and left. They took their furs with them, and Abbot had his long and tedious journey to Fryeburg for nothing.

John Howe of Marlboro bought Rumford lands, and came here in 1800. The first land he purchased was of B. Rice who had it of John Barnard, and he of Jonathan Stickney who was the original grantee. His other lot he purchased of Samuel Brigham of Berlin, Mass. This lot contained one hundred acres. Many of the early settlers preferred the uplands because as new lands, they were much more productive, and so the lots purchased by Mr. Howe remained unsold and unsettled for over twenty years after the first settler came. Mr. Howe purchased them for two hundred dollars, and they made one of the most productive and valuable farms in town. He was a cooper as well as farmer, and the former trade was very useful and valuable in a new settlement. He and his wife belonged to a church in Andover which was nearer to him than the one at Rumford Centre, and when they died their remains were carried to that town for interment.

In the early times, the Fourth of July was always a great day in Rumford. There was an abundant supply of the ardent, and young men, middle aged men and sometimes old men engaged in parades, sham fights and the burning of gun powder. Politics were laid aside for the nonce, and Whig and Democrat vied with each other in patriotic devotion to the great achievement which the day represents. But on one occasion the Democrats had a strictly party celebration at Leach's tavern in the East part of the town. This was July 4, 1838, when the north eastern boundary question caused considerable excitement in Maine and party lines were closely drawn. Gen. Alvan Bolster presided and Abel Wheeler was Vice President. There was an oration, and afterward a dinner followed by toasts and sentiment. Some of the toasts were of a party character and some were not. David Knapp offered the following: "Our host, John B. Leach, may his heart be as free from guile as his head is from hair;" and one from David H. Farnum: "American ships and the ladies: may the first be well rigged and the second be well manned."

Phineas Howe of Berlin, Mass., father of Abram, Silas, Phineas, Jr. and Samson Howe who settled in Rumford, was a veritable giant. His height was six feet and nine inches, and he was otherwise built up to correspond. Most of the family were stalwart in size. Phineas, Jr., who came to Rumford was six feet and five inches tall. Phineas Howe, Senior, had a daughter Polly, who married Abel Baker, who moved from Berlin to Concord, N. H. She was six feet tall and weighed over two hundred pounds. Baker was a millman and his wife worked with him; she could take the grists from the horse's back to the mill and back again with as much facility as the strongest man. She could easily handle three bushels of corn in a bag. She had a daughter Susan Baker, born in 1799, who was six feet and two and a half inches tall.

David Knapp, son of Nathan Knapp, who was drowned in Rumford Falls, was a man of marked ability. He lived at Rumford Falls, and like almost everybody else, in his early manhood, was addicted to intoxicating drink. He came out with the Washingtonian movement, and was a very efficient speaker and advocate of the cause. The first temperance address ever heard by the writer was made by David Knapp, on the 4th of July, at a grove near North Woodstock. It was very effective and hundreds on that day and occasion took the total abstinance pledge. To illustrate one of his points, showing the importance of taking the pledge now, and breaking off from the habit at once and forever, he said that he had been into the store at the Falls to take his *last* glass, more than a hundred times. He was member of the Legislature and Register of Probate. He died in Norway.

Joseph H. Wardwell was the first cabinet maker in Rumford. He opened a shop at the Corner and operated it until he bought the store and tavern of Solomon Crockett in 1831. He was succeeded in the business of cabinet making by his cousin, Jeremiah Wardwell, who continued it until the time of his death. Joseph H. Wardwell was an able business man, and the most prosperous period ever enjoyed by the Corner was when he carried on business there. He was a man of great suavity of manner and disposition, but when imposed upon, no man knew better how to resent it. His mother was the daughter of Rev. Dr. Hemmenway of Wells, one of the most noted Maine ministers of the eighteenth century. Mr. Wardwell was captain of the Light Infantry in Rumford, and was a fine military man, qualities which he inherited from his father. He reared a large family and died comparatively young. He and his father died on the same day, March 5, 1849. He died in Hanover where he moved when he sold out to Ross.

There have been several taverns in Rumford. The early innkeepers were required to take out a license as such, and if they sold liquors they were required to take out a license for this privilege also. Levi Abbot opened a tavern at Rumford Falls in 1833. It was subsequently kept by Benjamin H. Blanchard, a Mr. Winslow, John B. Leach and A. W. Adams. It was burned in 1880. Philip Abbot opened his house to the public in 1791, and in 1822, he put up a sign. He lived on the south side of the river opposite East Rumford. William Wheeler kept a tavern at East Rumford prior to 1806, and was succeeded by Alvan Bolster. The first tavern at the Center was kept by Joshua Graham, and the house was continued by Joshua Graham, Jr. Asa Graham opened a house here and with his son-in-law Knapp, run it till 1850, when it was sold to James M. Dolloff and named the Central house. It was burned in 1875. Wm. D. Abbot opened a house here in 1864, called the Union House. The Abbots sold to Wm. J. Kimball, who now runs it. Moses F. Kimball, and later, his son Charles A. Kimball have kept public houses at Rumford Point. For a long time, there has been no tavern at the Point, but travellers have been entertained at private houses.

The first tavern at Rumford Corner was built and opened by Samuel Bartlett. He was the son of Jonathan Bartlett of Bethel. He sold his place after a few years, to Solomon Crockett from Andover, and moved to a farm opposite the Center. In 1831, Mr. Crockett sold out his store and tavern to Joseph H. Wardwell and moved to Portland. The house was well patronized while Mr.

Wardwell owned it, and he also did a large business in the store. But his health failed and he gave up the business to a Mr. Ross and moved to Hanover. The buildings were soon after burned. In 1846, Jonathan Virgin bought the house at the Corner, built but not finished by Francis Keyes, and having finished it, he opened it as a tavern in opposition to Wardwell. It was called the American House, and Virgin soon sold out to Benjamin B. Barden, a veteran in the business. He sold out to James H. Farnum, who in turn sold to David George Martin and moved to Bryant's Pond. Martin died, and was succeeded by Lowell and Fox, and they by A. H. Price, who kept the house from 1870 to 1886, when he sold out to E. E. Jackson. The house was soon after burned. Mr. Barden went from Rumford to Bethel Hill, and was afterward at Dixfield, Phillips and Farmington. He died in Topsham in 1889, aged 80.

The first public ferry across the Androscoggin in Rumford, was owned by James C. Harper, and was known as "Harper's Ferry." It was situated a mile below the Point. and was discontinued in 1809. It was then established between the Point and the Corner, and was owned respectively by Moses F. Kimball, John Estes and Porter Kimball, until the bridge was built. After the bridge was carried away in 1839, a ferry was re-established and Porter Kimball became sole owner. He sold out to Charles A. Kimball, who, after a few years, sold it to Frank Martin. Roscoe Knight now runs it. Stephen Putnam, Jr., established a ferry at East Rumford in 1811. His brother, Jacob Putnam, afterward had it, and from him it passed to his sons. It has always been known as Putnam's Ferry. Aaron Graham established the ferry at the Center; from him it passed to Joshua Graham and his son, Joshua Graham, Jr. Then Asa Graham and his son-in-law, Albion K. Knapp, had it, and in 1850 it was sold to James M. Dolloff, whose son, Ronello C. Dolloff, now operates it. From records of real estate transfers, it would appear that John Emery Adams once had the ferry at Rumford Center, and he may have been the first.

The Lufkin family of Rumford has been conspicuous in various ways. Benjamin, the patriarch, came here in 1787, and his son Samuel, August 15, 1788, was the first child born in the town. Of the other sons of Benjamin Lufkin, Joseph, Benjamin, Jr., and Moses became preachers. Most of them left Rumford quite early, but Joseph came back and settled on a farm a little north of Rumford Center, and died here. His son Orin, was a successful school teacher, was married here, went to Massachusetts and died there in 1862. Merrit Newell Lufkin, another and the only surviving son of Joseph Lufkin, resides on the old homestead. He is an intelligent and progressive farmer, a contributor to the agricultural press, and a valuable citizen of the town. He has served as one of the selectmen, and also as town clerk. Nathan S. Lufkin, son of Jacob Lufkin, was in trade several years at the Center, and served the town in various capacities. He moved to Caribou in the county of Aroostook, and engaged successfully in farming. He has been in town office more or less in Caribou, and also served as county commissioner.

The five sons of John and Mary (Newton) Howe were closely identified with the history of the town for many years, some of them for more than half a century. All save Calvin, were born in Massachusetts, and came here with their parents about the year eighteen hundred, and all tilled portions of the land purchased and cleared up under the direction of their father, on the West side of Ellis river. Three of the brothers, John, Jr., Otis and Calvin, always remained here, and were here gathered to their father. Joel and Eli moved into Howard's Gore, which now constitutes a part of Hanover, and here they spent long and useful lives. They were all stalwart men, and as much noted for their strength of mind as of body. They were men of strict integrity; industrious, prudent and thrifty. Without brilliancy, they were men of sound judgment, peaceful and law-abiding, just such characters as are essential to the complete success of a Republican form of government. Their farms and farm buildings were models of neatness and order. Plenty reigned in their households, and they dispensed their bounties with old fashioned hospitality. Their religion was that of the heart, and was carried into their every day lives. They were careful about giving their word, but when given, it was as good as their bond. Without being clannish, they enjoyed the society and companionship of their own families better than they did anybody else. They kept out of debt, paid their taxes promptly, contributed liberally to the support of the Christian ministry, fully recognizing the fact that "no man liveth to himself." Such was the character of these good people as the writer has known it, and heard it from those much better acquainted with them. Their memory is fragrant in the town of their adoption, and the priceless legacy of a good name is the inheritance of their numerous posterity.

The bears were unusually plenty in the mountainous portions of the town during the season of 1889, and were often seen prowling around the sheep pastures. In the early part of September, while Main's circus was performing at the Center, a bear came out of the woods in plain sight of the Village and having watched the crowd and performing tent for a short time returned to cover in the woods. The unusual appearance seemed to excite his curiosity, but he did not deem it prudent to pursue his investigations too closely.

Col. William Wheeler was not among the earliest settlers in Rumford, but he was a man of marked ability and was a leader in town. He was a trader and inn-keeper, was much in town office and was the first representative from Rumford to the Massachusetts Legislature. He was a civil magistrate, and was also a leader in military affairs. He commanded the company of militia raised in this vicinity for the defence of Portland during the last war with England, and was afterwards Colonel of the Regiment. He was a man of great energy and perseverance, of sound judgment, and one whose influence would be felt in any community. His wife having died, he moved to Vermont, and his early removal was a severe loss to the town. He was succeeded in business, and in many other respects by his son-in-law, Gen. Alvan Bolster.

In the days of home-spun clothing, carding and fulling mills were very essential in every community. There was once an establishment for dressing cloth below Abbot's Mills, on Concord river. It was owned by Mr. Samuel Page of Brunswick, and was operated by Mr. William Walcott, and also by Benjamin Morse ; later, by Harvey Willard and Joseph Peverly ; at one time it was owned by John Harris of Bethel. There was a fulling mill at the Falls in 1833, owned and operated by Moses T. Cross, who came here from Bethel, and returned there. Mr. Cross carried on a similar business near Bethel Hill for many years. He then went into trade on the Hill, and died there some years ago. His first wife was the daughter of William Staples, and his second of Ezra Smith, both of Hanover. He was a twin, his twin brother being named Aaron, a farmer in Bethel. Their father, Jesse Cross, came from Andover, Mass., to Bethel, and married a daughter of Eleazer Twitchell. There was also at one time a carding and fulling mill on Split

Brook, and there is still a mill for carding wool in Hanover; but fulling mills have long been numbered with things of the past.

The name of Pettingill does not appear upon Rumford records until about the year 1862, when Oliver Pettingill bought and occupied the Colman Godwin farm on the north side of the river, above Rumford Center. Waldo Pettingill, his son, succeeded his father on this farm, and the union of the two Godwin homesteads gave him one of the largest, best and most productive farms in the town. Mr. Pettingill has been considerably in town office, has served as county commissioner, and is regarded as a first class business man. He aided in settling the estate of the late Timothy Walker, one of the largest estates ever accumulated in town, is a prominent Mason and has served as Deputy Grand Master for the District in which he resides. He is yet in the prime and vigor of life, and does considerable business besides looking after his important farming interests.

Stephen Putnam once had a mill on Swain's brook, which flows into the Androscoggin below Rumford Falls. It has long since disappeared, but the ruins of the dam are still seen. Mr. Putnam was once at work by the side of the road when a caravan was passing by, and in advance was an elephant. This was the first animal of this kind that had ever entered the town, and the first one that Mr. Putnam had ever seen. To say that he was frightened as the huge pachyderm waddled by, would be putting it very mildly, and springing away to give the monster a wide birth, he exclaimed, "My God, what a toad."

There have been several deaths by drowning in the Androscoggin river. In 1848, on the fourth of July, Charles Wood, son of Phineas Wood, and two of the sons of Daniel Hinkson were drowned at Rumford Point, while bathing. Henry Peabody was drowned at the Point in 1852, and a son of Jackson Howard in 1857. About the year 1820, three men in a boat below Rumford Point, were capsized and Benjamin Elliot, Jr., was drowned. His widow married Increase Dolly in 1824, and their son Benjamin Elliot Dolly was also drowned below the Point, distant about two miles.

Stickney Virgin was a bachelor, and for several years was in the employ of Dexter D. W. Abbot, at the Mount Zircon House. On one occasion Mr. Abbot sent him to Bryant's Pond with a team, and gave him an order on the tavern keeper there " for a dinner, baiting for his horse, &c., &c." After he had eaten his dinner, Virgin sat round a while and then timidly approaching the landlord, asked if there was not some " and so forth " on the order from Mr. Abbot? The point was seen by the landlord, and the article promptly supplied. Virgin then lighted his pipe and sat down contented, but after an hour or so he again interviewed the landlord and asked if there were not two " and so forths " on that order? Receiving an affirmative answer, he again imbibed, and then hitching up his team he started for home.

Stickney Virgin had a horse that was very lazy and as a reminder when he wanted him to go faster, Virgin had a goad stick with a long brad in it with which he would prod the poor beast, and sometimes most unmercifully. On some occasion not now remembered, he was driving another horse but had the ever-present goad stick in his hand, and forgetting himself he applied the prod in his usual way. The result was a surprise to him. The animal's rear feet came at once in contact with the dasher and in a twinkling the front part of the wagon was demolished. Virgin exclaimed, "if you are going to get in I guess I'll get out," and out he got from the rear of the vehicle which the horse ran away with and completely ruined.

It has been stated elsewhere that James C. Harper established and owned the first ferry across the Androscoggin in the west part of Rumford. This was known as "Harper's Ferry," and was situated about a mile below the present one. During the war of the Rebellion when Harper's Ferry began to be spoken of in connection with army operations, Mr. Edmund Bean, a respected but illiterate citizen of Bethel, familiarly known as "Mister Ned," was down at the Point one day, and hearing some one speak of the union defeat at Harper's Ferry, exclaimed: "I'll bet that's Jim Harper that owns that ferry; he always would have a ferry let him be where he would." It is needless to say that James C. Harper had then been dead many years, and had he then been alive, would have been considerably more than a hundred years old.

The first store in town is said to have been kept by John Whittemore. His place was between the Center and East Rumford. He did not keep a large stock of goods, but he supplied the needs of the inhabitants for a short time, and then moved from town. He and his wife died near Dixville notch, and their grave stones can be seen by the traveler, by the roadside. The first store at the Point was kept by Ezra Smith, whose residence was Howard's Gore. Subsequent traders at the Point, were Moses F. Kimball, Otis C. Bolster, Francis Cushman, Charles A. Kimball, and later Charles W. Kimball. William Wheeler was an early trader at East Rumford, and Alvan Bolster and James H. Farnum at the Falls. Joshua Graham early opened a store at the Center, and there have been many since that time. But there has been a great falling off in trade in Rumford since 1850, when the Atlantic and Saint Lawrence railroad was put in operation through the county. Villages sprang up on the line of the road, at the expense of those situated away from it.

There was considerable trepidation in Rumford and throughout the State, when the call for troops was made to defend our eastern boundary, but this was by no means shown by all. When the draft was made in Rumford, Benjamin, son of Dea. Hezekiah Hutchins, had the misfortune to draw a prize. The young man did not care so much about it, but his father shed tears of anguish to such an extent as to move the heart of John M. Adams, then a minor, who was willing to go in place of Hutchins. In fact, he really desired to go, but knew his mother who was then a widow, would not consent for him to volunteer ; so he arranged it with those who manipulated the draft, to have his name put in and drawn out, " to go." He went as Orderly Sergeant, and enjoyed the twenty-four days' visit at the State capital very much. While there he had the privilege of seeing, in addition to other celebrities, General Winfield Scott, and also Robert E. Lee, who was a member of the General's staff. It was a very pleasant outing.

In our chapter on Rumford Physicians the names of Dr. Simeon Fuller and James Bullock were inadvertantly omitted. Dr. Fuller was the son of Aaron and Hannah (Pond) Fuller, and was born in Paris, Oct. 3, 1799. After preparing himself for the practice of medicine, he married Mary Ann, daughter of Capt. Samuel Rawson of Paris, and settled in practice at Rumford Corner. He was successful in his business, but died in middle life Nov. 29, 1841. His widow married for a second husband, Dr. James Bullock of Rehoboth, Mass., who succeeded to the practice of Dr. Fuller. He was a well educated man, had travelled and seen much of the world, but while here he did not choose to confine himself very closely to practice. He was for some years collector of taxes in this town, and died while in office in 1857. His widow survived him several years. Both Drs. Fuller and Bullock resided in the stand now occupied by Sullivan R. Hutchins. There is no representative of the family in the town or state.

Stephen Putnam, Jr., was the first blacksmith in Rumford, but there have been many since. Samuel Putnam, Jr., was also a blacksmith. Moses F. Kimball came to Rumford to work at this trade, but soon engaged in other business. Porter Kimball became forehanded by hard work at the forge and anvil. Other blacksmiths have been Asa Howard, William Morse, Samuel Hinkson, Aaron Marean, Thomas N. Ricker, Loammi B. Peabody, Hall Torrey, D. A. Thurston, Otis Howe, Warren M. Adams, David F. Adams, Cyrus Small, Peter D. Brackett, Nathan Handy, Loring Glover, Joseph Arnold and Abraham Maxfield.

Among the cordwainers (shoemakers) in Rumford have been Benjamin Morse, Charles Ford, Warren Mansur, Aaron Stevens, Nathan W. Ethridge and Joseph P. Small. This trade was of great importance to the early settlers. There were then no ready made shoes on sale, and the shoemakers usually visited the houses in town in spring and fall, when the whole family were shod. Cowhide was usually worn by the men, and calf-skin by the women. They were not quite as handsome as the foot-wear of our day, but they were made upon honor and did good service. Shoe and boot-making is mostly done by machinery now, and repairing is all that is left for the country cordwainer.

Francis Hemmingway settled the farm in Bethel by the side of the "Whale's Back," which he exchanged with Benjamin Sweat for a lot above Abbot's Mills. He was a cooper by trade, and supplied the town with wash-tubs, leach-tubs, cheese-tubs and the like, for many years. He was fond of a social glass, and the habit was so strong upon him that he found it very difficult to deny himself. On a certain occasion a severe freshet rendered Concord river bridge impassable, and for two or three days Hemmingway had been without his favorite beverage. He felt that he could do without it no longer, and as there was no boat at hand, he undertook to cross Concord river in one of his tubs. The water was subsiding and the current very strong, and the tub in spite of all its occupant could do, was carried into and down the great river. Half way or more toward the Center, the current set in toward the shore, and by making what effort he could without upsetting his frail bark, Mr. Hemmingway touched the land and sprang upon it. It was a narrow escape from a watery grave, and he fully realized that he had jeopardized his life all for a drink of rum. When the Washingtonian movement came soon after, Mr. Hemmingway signed the pledge and was one of the few reformed ones in town who kept it inviolate to the day of his death.

The following list of the three principal officers of Blazing Star Lodge, was received after the other was in print. It is placed here to complete the record. It will be noticed that the officers for 1872 differ somewhat in the two lists:

1872. Edgar H. Powers, Wm. Frost, Jonathan K. Martin.
1873. N. S. Farnum, Waldo Pettingill, Jonathan K. Martin.
1874. Edgar H. Powers, Waldo Pettingill, Wm. M. Blanchard.
1875. Waldo Pettingill, C. P. Eaton, John H. Howe.
1876. Florus H. Bartlett, C. P. Eaton, John H. Howe.
1877. Florus H. Bartlett, C. P. Eaton, John H. Howe.
1878. Waldo Pettingill, Henry M. Colby, John H. Howe.
1879. Waldo Pettingill, Freeman E. Small, John H. Howe.
1880. Florus H. Bartlett, Freeman E. Small, John H. Howe.
1881. Florus H. Bartlett, Freeman E. Small, John H. Howe.
1882. E. H. Hutchins, N. F. Hoyt, John H. Howe.
1883. Freeman E. Small, N. F. Hoyt, John H. Howe.
1884. Freeman E. Small, N. F. Hoyt, John H. Howe.
1885. Isaac Bagnall, Geo. L. Smith, John H. Howe.
1886. Isaac Bagnall, Henry M. Colby, John H. Howe.
1887. Isaac Bagnall, Henry M. Colby, Waldo Pettingill.
1888. Florus H. Bartlett, Henry M. Colby, Waldo Pettingill.
1889. Wm. H. Farnum, Henry M. Colby, Waldo Pettingill.

The statement in Chapter one, and also that in Mr. Gould's brief sketch of the town, with regard to the east line of Rumford, is somewhat misleading. The east line of Rumford is straight, while the course of Swift river is more or less meandering in its course. The mouth of Swift river is wholly in Mexico, but a short distance above the mouth the river is in Rumford. The bridge across the river on the road leading from Rumford Falls to Mexico Corner is in Rumford, but a short distance above the bridge the river is again wholly in Mexico, and at the northeast corner of Rumford it is nearly two miles distant toward the east.   In making measurements to ascertain the center of Rumford, Swift river was referred to as one of the easterly starting points, but only in places does it form the easterly line of the town.

Mr. Chaplin Virgin, who was long in business at Rumford Falls, furnishes a list of persons who have engaged in different branches of business, which will hereafter be of great value for reference. A portion of it has been given before, but for the sake of having it all together for convenient reference, that portion is repeated.

TRADERS.   Alvan Bolster, Isaac N. Stanley, Lyman Bolster, Alonzo Wilson, M. W. Kimball, Dennison Marble, Wm. W. Stevens and Uriah Virgin.

BLACKSMITHS.   William Morse, David F. Adams, Peter D. Brackett, Cyrus Small, Nathan Handy, Nathan Ethridge, Joseph Arnold, Loring Glover, Abraham Maxfield and Mr. Sargent.

HOTEL KEEPERS.   Levi Abbot, John B. Leach, Benjamin H. Blanchard, A. W. Adams, J. A. Stockbridge, Moses T. Cross and Mr. Winslow.

MILLMEN.   Stephen Putnam, Rufus Virgin, Nathan Knapp, Enoch Knapp, David Knapp, Jonathan A. Virgin, Chaplin Virgin, Abbot Virgin, Scott Hall, B. F. Reed, D. F. Putnam, Levi Moody, Levi Abbot, David Dolloff, Seth Puffer, Albion K. Knapp, A. B. Swain and Hiram Ricker.

CARRIAGE WORKS.   Chaplin Virgin, David Elliot, Marble and Thompson, A. G. Richardson, E. C. Allen, Horace and Frank Holman, Leonard Woods, Samuel Wing and Leavitt C. Virgin.

WOOL CARDING AND CLOTH DRESSING.   Lewis Cole, William Walcot, John Harris, Moses T. Cross and Thomas Prince.

SHOE MAKERS.   J. P. Small, J. A. Stockbridge and B. L. Knapp.

CLOVER MILLS.   Simon Stevens, Hiram Hubbard.

STARCH MILLS.   J. W. Bennett and J. A. Plaisted.

CHAIR MAKER.   Henry Smith.

POTASH.   Haines Eastman.

AXE MAKER.   B. C. Perry.

BOX MAKERS.   J. W. Bennett, Henry Smith.

Among the Rumford graduates from College is John F. Elliot, son of Rev. John Elliot of the Congregational church.   He graduated at Bowdoin College in the class of 1873, and ever since has been engaged in teaching. He has taught at Lawrence, Mass., Academy as sub-master, taught the Winchendon, Mass., High School, and as principal of the Grammar School at Hyde Park, Mass., since 1876 to 1889. He was elected Principal of the Hill School at East Boston September 11, 1889, with the rank of Master. Maria Danforth Elliot, a sister of the above, a graduate of Wellesley College in the class of 1881, was a fine scholar and a lady of remarkable depth of mind and character. She taught in high schools at Beverly, Mass., three years, at Arlington, Mass., two years, and at Washington D. C., two years. She was an excellent teacher, a constant inspiration to her pupils, and won the confidence of all. She died in Rumford July 4, 1886.

The name of Sullivan R. Hutchins was by mistake omitted from the list of Rumford lawyers. The fact is, Mr. Hutchins engaged in other pursuits so long, and commenced the study of law at so late a period in life, that the writer of these pages had never associated him with the legal profession. He spent several years on his father's homestead in Bethel where he engaged in teaching, surveying and farming. Later, he was for some years a Deputy Sheriff, during all which years he was not a resident of this town but of Bethel. After studying law and being admitted to the bar he opened an office at Rumford Corner, in the Dr. Fuller house, which he also makes his place of residence. Though not for many years a citizen of Rumford, his name has been associated with it through his ancestor, Deacon Hezekiah Hutchins, from the early settlement of the town.

There were several natives of Rumford who served in the war of the Rebellion whose names do not appear in the list as printed in chapter twenty-eight. Lester Dwinel, now a prosperous business man residing in Bangor, entered the service as First Lieutenant in the Fifteenth Maine Regiment, and was promoted to Captain. John F. Putnam, now City Clerk of Lewiston, served nearly three years, first as Sergeant and subsequently in the commissary department of the Seventeenth Maine. Charles Henry and Francis N. Putnam served on the quota of Bethel, the former in the Sixteenth Maine and died in the rebel prison at Belle Island, and the latter in the Twelfth Maine and died as a result of over-exertion in the battle of Cedar Creek. These three soldiers were the sons of Hiram and Clarissa W. (Farnum) Putnam and were all born in Rumford.

Samuel, son of Jonathan Bartlett of Bethel, was born in that town April 1, 1794. It has already been stated that he settled at Rumford Corner and built the house afterward occupied by Joseph H. Wardwell as a tavern, and which he also kept as such. He owned the land at the Corner from the ferry to the Dr. Fuller place, and carried on quite extensive farming. He sold out after a few years and bought what is now known as the Cotton Elliot place below the Center on the south side of the river. In 1835, he sold this farm to Cotton Elliot and bought the Aaron Graham farm opposite the Center, where he spent the remainder of his life, and where his two sons now reside. He was a large and prosperous farmer. He died June 12, 1837, aged 43 years. He married Sarah J., daughter of Joseph Wardwell, who long survived him and died November 12, 1864, aged 70 years.

In Milton Plantation nearly opposite Rumford Centre, is a famous mineral spring known as the Mount Zircon Spring. It takes its name from Mount Zircon near whose base it is found. In the fifties this spring was brought to notice by Dexter D. W. Abbot who built a large summer hotel near it which was well patronized. But the war came on which paralyzed all business, the patronage dropped off and finally the house was burned. It is a delightful place, several hundred feet above the bed of the river and overlooking a large extent of the Androscoggin valley. The water is regarded as equal to that of the Poland Springs, and is liberally supplied by the spring. Parties have recently purchased the spring and adjoining lands, with the view of rebuilding the hotel. It is an enterprise in which Rumford people have a deep interest.

A mystery has ever shrouded the fate of Moses Wardwell, the second son of Joseph Wardwell of this town. He was a master mariner and his last voyage was to New Orleans in the barque Rumford, named for this town, for which the citizens presented him with a flag. He piloted the vessel into port at New Orleans, thus saving the owners the usual pilot's fees. He went on shore one night to attend the theatre, and from that time, so far as his friends could learn who made dilligent search and inquiry, he disappeared from mortal sight. Many years have since passed, and in all probability the mystery will never be explained.

CHAPTER XXXVI.

SKETCHES PERSONAL.

PHILIP ABBOT came to Rumford in 1791, from Concord, N. H. He had previously worked for Col. Timothy Walker seven years, at the rate of seven dollars per month. He came here with an ox team which he had driven all the way from Concord, bringing his wife and household goods on a sled. There were no roads, and his oxen traveled one before the other, or "tandem," as it is said of horses when so driven. During the journey they camped nights in the woods, making a bed of hemlock boughs. He was a soldier in the war for independence, and was at one time captured by the Indians, but succeeded in escaping from them. He was a prominent man in town in early Rumford, served on the board of selectmen and held other positions of trust and responsibility. He married Experience Howe of Bolton, and reared a large family. He opened his house as a tavern as early as 1792, and continued to entertain travelers for many years. He lived opposite East Rumford, on the south side of the Great river.

NATHAN ADAMS, JR.

Nathan Adams, Junior, inherited the homestead of his father, or rather he became possessed of it long before his father's death, taking the property, and upon himself, the care of his parents. Like his father, he was industrious, prudent and thrifty, a worthy son of a worthy sire. Under his judicious management, the Adams farm became one of the most productive farms in town. Mr. Adams enlisted in Capt. William Wheeler's regiment of militia that was called out for the protection of Portland during the war of 1812, and when the regiment was ordered out, Mr. Adams mounted his horse and served notice on the members who were widely scattered through the towns of Rumford, Andover, Bethel, Newry, Greenwood, Norway and Waterford. He held places of honor and trust in town, but died when forty years of age from the effects of a fall from the great beams of his barn. He married Susan, daughter of Ezekiel Merrill of Andover, and had six children. His sudden death was a staggering blow to his wife and family, and a great loss to the neighborhood and town.

SUSAN MERRILL ADAMS.

Mrs. Susan Merrill, wife of Nathan Adams, Jr., was born in Andover, Maine, July 13, 1791. Her father, Ezekiel Merrill, came there two years previous, and was the first settler. She was the first child of English descent, born in Andover. She was early sent to school at Fryeburg and at Brunswick, and obtained a good education. She married March 17, 1817, Nathan Adams, Jr., son of Nathan Adams who was one of the original proprietors of Andover, but who moved to Rumford near the beginning of the present century. They settled upon a tract of land on the west side of Ellis river and near Bethel (now Hanover) line, where father and son lived and cleared up one of the best farms in town. In 1828, Nathan Adams, Jr., was fatally injured by falling from the great beam in his barn, and died soon after. This threw upon the mother the entire charge of the family, the oldest child being only about ten years of age, and the youngest two. This care and responsibility developed in her great force of character. The late John A. Poor, himself a native of Andover and well acquainted with Mrs. Adams before her marriage, in a notice of her published after her death, thus speaks of her: "Like her four sisters, she had great beauty, with exhuberant health. All those sisters married young and all reared families, well known in different portions of the State. Her marriage was an event of importance in the town; and her natural elegance and grace of manner, were fully recognized in the cultivated circle drawn together from this and the neighboring towns on the occasion, the hospitalities of which embraced a large family connection." Referring to the death of her husband and the responsibility which this sad event devolved upon her, Mr. Poor says: "She showed prudence, energy, sagacity and skill in the management of her affairs that excited universal admiration, and everything prospered after her husband's death beyond what could have been previously imagined from her delicate sensibility and refined organization, which seemed to many to unfit her for the arduous duties suddenly devolved upon her. The hospitality which marked her earlier

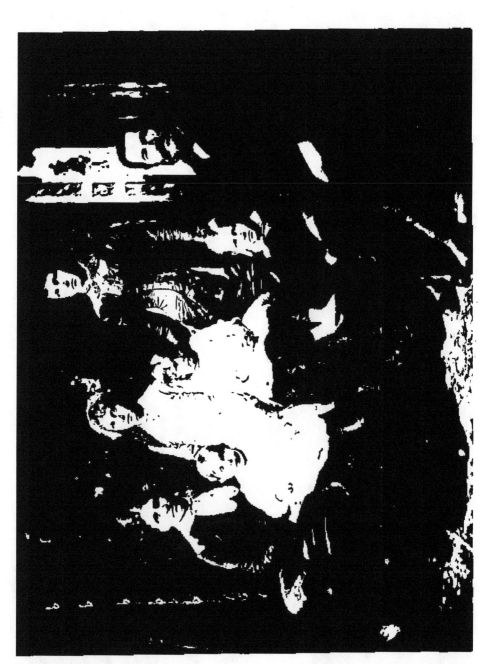

life was continued to a numerous circle of friends and relatives. The spacious old house was burned some years ago, and after her children had departed, all of them but two, to the other world, the farm was sold and she made her home with her daughter who married Dr. George L. Peaslee, at whose house she died, honored and beloved by all who knew her. Of Mrs. Adams' religious character more might be written than upon any other topic. In early life she became connected with the Congregational church, and was, throughout the entire period of her residence at Rumford, a constant and liberal supporter of it, her interest in which continued to the end, though entirely free from all bigotry or sectarian feeling. In the vicissitudes of a somewhat eventful life, she never grew impatient or uncharitable, more anxious apparently at all times to promote the happiness of others than to seek her own gratification, faithful and devoted in every relation of life, daughter, wife, mother and friend. She welcomed the messenger of death at her appointed time, anxious to realize that reward which a life of self sacrifice and devotion made sure." Mrs. Adams died in Wilton, Friday, May 1, 1868.

John M. Adams.

Col. John Milton Adams, son of Nathan and Susan (Merrill) Adams, was born on the Adams homestead on the west side of Ellis river near its junction with the Androscoggin, September 22, 1819. He attended the town schools, the Turner High School, at Gould's Academy in Bethel and at Bridgton Academy, and graduated at Gorham Seminary. He subsequently attended a year at the College in Saint Hyacinth, Canada, to perfect himself in the French language. At seventeen years of age, he commenced to teach school, and had charge of schools in Rumford, Bethel, Norway, Westbrook and two years in Maryland. He studied law with Fessenden and Deblois of Portland, and was admitted to the Cumberland bar in 1846. He was a law partner at one time, of Hon. John A. Poor and subsequently with Judge Clifford. While Hon. John Appleton was Secretary of Legation to England, Mr. Adams edited the *Eastern Argus*, and became permanent editor and manager of the paper in 1857. He traveled in Europe, visiting the principal cities and countries, writing numerous letters while abroad which appeared in the columns of the *Railway Gazette*. He became sole owner of the *Eastern Argus* establishment in 1866, and has conducted it since that time. Under his able management, the paper has largely increased in power and influence, and is the leading organ of the Democratic party in the State. Mr. Adams is an easy and graceful writer, a forcible speaker, and in private life, genial and kind hearted. He was Orderly Sergeant during the "Aroostook War," aid with the rank of Colonel on the staff of Governor John Hubbard, and has served most acceptably on the Portland School Board. He was appointed Reporter of Decisions of the Supreme Judicial Court, and volumes forty-one and forty-two of Maine Reports, are of his compiling. Col. Adams is much interested in rural affairs and connected with his beautiful home in Deering, are several acres of land—mowing, tillage, orchard and woodland, of which he takes personal charge. He delights in working the soil and in serving his guests with vegetables and fruit of his own raising. He is fond of floriculture, and in a small pond on his premises, in its season, may be seen the beautiful pink lily, a native of Sandwich on Cape Cod. His life is a very busy one, but Col. Adams loves work. Besides the oversight of a daily and weekly paper of which he is sole proprietor, he has many other business interests to look after, and still finds time to look after his family and farm. He visits the *Argus* office every morning, and returning puts on the overalls and engages in any work that may demand his attention. In this garb, few would suspect him of being the editor and manager of a great party paper. A tramp came along one day and seeing Col. Adams in his working clothes, inquired what pay he received for his work. "Only my board and clothes," replied Mr. Adams. "Well," said the tramp, "if I were going to work for such wages, I should want better clothes than you have on." Col. Adams likes to see his friends, and whenever one visits him at his charming home, from him and his amiable and excellent wife, he is sure of receiving old-fashioned hospitality. His attachment for his native town and the spot where he was born, has not been diminished since he went out from the old homestead, and "the world was all before him where to choose," and to him more than to any other, is due the publication of this volume of records and reminiscences of Rumford.

ALVAN BOLSTER.

General Alvan Bolster, son of Isaac, Jr. and Hannah (Cushman) Bolster, was born in Paris December 7, 1795. When he became of age he went to New Brunswick where he remained a couple of years

Mrs. Cynthia Rolster.

when he returned and entered the store of his uncle at Rumford Point. Afterwards he moved to East Rumford where and at the Falls, he was in trade for many years. He also engaged in farming, working one of the best farms in town. He was Postmaster at East Rumford for many years. He was often in town office and enjoyed the confidence of his townspeople to the last. He served as representative to the Legislature and was twice elected State Senator. He was interested in military affairs and held various offices as shown by the chapter on military affairs. He became a strong temperance man, and was a leader in the organization known as the Sons of Temperance, both in town, county and State. He was also an active Free Mason. In religious belief he was a Methodist, and an active member and liberal supporter of this denomination. He was an upright and honest man, industrious, prudent and thrifty, and interested in every movement calculated to benefit the people of his town. He was an active Republican, and when the war broke out, and southern states seceded, he advocated the war for the restoration of the union at whatever cost. But he did not live to witness that glorious consummation, and died December 8, 1862, during the darkest and most discouraging period of the war. General Bolster married Cynthia, daughter of Colonel William Wheeler, and his family record is elsewhere.

Mrs. Cynthia Bolster, wife of General Alvan Bolster, and daughter of Colonel William Wheeler, whose portrait appears opposite that of her husband, was born in Concord, New Hampshire, but came when a child to Rumford with her parents. She taught school after she had acquired a good common school education, but was married when less than twenty years of age. She was an exemplary woman, an excellent wife and mother, performing faithfully her duties to her family, to the Christian church, and to the community in which she lived. She survived her husband some seventeen years and died in Poland Sept. 26, 1879.

William W. Bolster.

Hon. William W. Bolster was born in Rumford July 6, 1823. He attended the common schools of Rumford, was a student at Bethel Academy and at Peacham, Vermont. He read law in the office of Randall and Walton of Dixfield, attended the Harvard law school and was admitted to the bar in 1847, and commenced practice at East Rumford where he remained until 1852. He then moved to Dixfield and remained there twenty years. While here, he was Justice of the Peace, Notary Public and for several years on the school board. He served as clerk in the office of Secretary of State for several years, a portion of the time as Commission Clerk, and afterwards had charge of the engrossing department. He was for six years State's Attorney for Oxford County, served two terms in the State Senate, the last as president of that body. Served also as Bank Examiner and as a member of the Executive Council in 1883-4. He was Lieutenant and Captain of the Rumford Light Infantry and Division Inspector on the staff of General William Wirt Virgin. Mr. Bolster has been an active Free Mason, and an efficient worker in the temperance cause, through various organizations for the promotion of the same. After moving to Auburn in October, 1872, he served two years as alderman and three years as city solicitor. He has compiled several law books, including the "Tax Collector and Farm Book," an "Invoice and Valuation Book" and the "Highway Surveyor's Book." As may well be supposed, his life has been a busy one, and he has achieved marked success. He is President of the Little Androscoggin Water Power Company, and of the Maine Mortgage Loan Company of which he was the organizer. He is also a trustee of the Reform School. Mr. Bolster has been twice married and his family record is elsewhere.

James H. Farnum.

James Harvey Farnum, son of David and Dorcas (Wheeler) Farnum, was born in Rumford August 1, 1807. He attended the common schools and also received private instruction, so that he had a good English education. He taught school in his early manhood, but soon went into trade with General Bolster at the Falls. He traded here and also at other places in town, and at one time was proprietor of the tavern at Rumford Corner. He also engaged in farming and speculated more or less in cattle and sheep. He was often in town office, was sent to the Legislature and was elected and served as State Senator. He moved to Bryant's Pond before 1856, and was in trade with Charles P. Knight. While here he also dealt in cattle and sheep. He was a genial, kind hearted man, and a good neighbor and citizen. He died of typhoid fever prior to 1860.

George L. Farnum.

Among the Rumford young men who started out in life with brilliant prospects, but who was cut down in early manhood, was the man whose name stands at the head of this notice. George L. Farnum, son of George J. and Hannah F. (Jackson) Farnum, was born in Rumford February 9, 1844. He was a bright scholar and early decided on going to college and preparing himself for one of the learned professions. He attended the common and high schools of Rumford and finished his preparatory course at Hebron Academy. Before entering college, he decided to serve a term of enlistment in the war of the Rebellion which was then going on, and became a private in the Eleventh Massachusetts Volunteers in March, 1864. His first baptism of fire and his last, was in the battle of the Wilderness where he was severely wounded, resulting in the loss of the use of one of his hands. He entered Colby University in 1866, and graduated with the class of 1870. He studied law at the home of his parents in Rumford and graduated from the Albany, New York, law school. He had previously taught the high schools of Ellsworth and Augusta, but this was only to obtain means to pursue his legal studies. He commenced the practice of law in company with Henry Upton of Norway. He was at once recognized as a young man of ability, and his prospects as an attorney were most flattering. He had planted well but the fruit was not to be gathered by him. After a year or two, his health began to fail, and late in 1876 he was obliged to return to his father's house in Rumford where he died June 18, 1877, of Bright's disease of the kidneys. His classmates noticed his death in a series of eulogistic resolutions, and the Oxford Bar in a similar manner. He left hosts of friends to mourn his early death, and no enemies.

Francis Keyes.

Francis Keyes, Esq., one of the pioneers of Rumford, and one of its most useful citizens, was born in Shrewsbury, Mass., Oct. 13, 1765. He came with his father to Sudbury, Canada, now Bethel, when he was nine years old. His father, Jonathan Keyes, began a settlement in Bethel as early as 1774 or earlier, and his two sons, Ebenezer and Francis were there with him. The father returned to Shrewsbury one fall, leaving his boys in the care of the Indians, intending soon to return, but circumstances prevented him from returning until spring, and during the long, dreary winter these but little more than children remained in the forest, many miles from any white settlers and with no companionship but the savages. Francis Keyes was twelve years old when his father came to Rumford. His means of education were limited but he improved them to the best advantage and when the town was incorporated, he was chosen clerk, as he had also been of the plantation. He was a surveyor, a Justice of the Peace and a conveyancer. Many of the early deeds of Rumford lands were written by him. He was a useful citizen of the new town, and had a hand in managing its affairs as long as he lived. His remains are buried on the old Keyes homestead, since known as the Timothy Walker farm, and no stone marks his last resting place. Here also are interred the remains of his father, Jonathan Keyes, his mother, Sarah (Taylor) Keyes, and several of his children. Should not the descendants of these worthy people, see that some suitable monument is erected to mark the last resting place of the first settler of Rumford and his family?

Moses F. Kimball.

Moses F. Kimball, better known as "Esquire Moses," son of Asa and Phebe (Foster) Kimball, who were early settlers of Bridgton and Bethel, settled at Rumford Point where he was long in trade and also engaged more or less in farming. He was prominent in town, often in town office, a Justice of the Peace when that office was of some importance, and served a term in the Maine Legislature. He died October 8, 1854, aged 64 years, and his remains repose in the cemetery at Rumford Point. He married Mary, daughter of Josiah and Molly (Crocker) Bean of Bethel, who survived him and died March 30, 1884, at the great age of 92 years, and 2 months. The ferry between Rumford Point and Rumford Corner was known as "Kimball's Ferry" as early as 1819. Moses F. Kimball and Porter Kimball being early proprietors. There is evidence that Mr. Kimball adopted the middle initial letter of his name after he came to Rumford. Deeds and other instruments while he lived in Bethel were signed without this middle letter. When he came to Rumford there was a Moses Kimball already here, and to distinguish them, he doubtless adopted the initial "F."

Porter Kimball.

Porter Kimball was the son of Peter Kimball of Bradford, Mass., and was born in that town May 19, 1793. He came with the family to Bridgton, and about the year 1816, he and his twin brother, Peter Kimball, Jr., bought adjoining lots on the Rumford and Paris road. Peter's was on Hamlin's Gore and Porter's in Bethel. Porter Kimball was a blacksmith and December 24, 1821, he sold his farm to Abijah Lapham of Buckfield and moved to Rumford Point where he ever after resided. He was a good workman, a man of much energy and perseverance and did a large and lucrative business. He built the mansion house now occupied by Dr. Hiram F. Abbot, and here he lived many years, and died. He was a good citizen and much respected by his townspeople. His mother was Lucy Barker of Bradford, and his father, Peter Kimball, was the son of Francis Kimball, whose wife was Mary Head. He married Nancy, daughter of Asa and Phebe (Foster) Kimball of Bethel, who survived him and became the second wife of Hon. Peter C. Virgin. His family record may be found elsewhere.

William W. Kimball.

Perhaps no native born citizen of Rumford has achieved greater success in business than William Wallace Kimball of Chicago. He is the son of David and Lucy W. (Wheeler) Kimball, and was born in Rumford, March 22, 1828. He was educated in the common schools, was clerk in a store in Rumford, and when twenty-one years of age, he went to Boston and found employment in a store in that city. In 1853 he went to Iowa and engaged in the insurance and real estate business in the town of Decorah. After a few years there he removed to Chicago, and his first business there was to exchange some real estate in Decorah for a lot of pianos. This transaction, insignificant of itself, laid the foundation of his future business career. He determined to engage in the manufacture of pianos, and the splendid success which has followed shows that he determined wisely and well. In October, 1871, his place of business was destroyed by fire, and his loss was heavy. But he was by no means discouraged, though his loss was more than a hundred thousand dollars. Some idea of the extent of his business may be had from the fact that in 1880 he sold twelve thousand pianos. In 1881, he extended his business to the manufacture of organs, and in a short time the factory was turning out forty finished instruments a day. In July, 1882, Mr. Kimball put his entire business into a stock company of which he was chosen president. Since that time the business has increased until it is one of the largest establishments of the kind in the country. All the work is done in the factory and a small army of skilled workmen are employed in the various branches of the business. His aim has been and this he has achieved, to manufacture for the least money, the best instruments produced for the American market. Among his friends in the trade, and in the social circle, Mr. Kimball is held in high esteem, and is looked up to as one of the best and most successful business men in the great western metropolis. The present business (1889) of the company is fifty organs a day and fifty pianos a week, and five hundred men are employed.

CHARLES A. KIMBALL:

One of the most energetic and successful business men ever raised up in Rumford, is Charles A. Kimball who was born at Rumford Point, Dec. 10, 1816, and has always lived there. He developed business traits very early; was a school teacher when he was but fifteen years of age, and a merchant some years before he was twenty one. He was trained to business in his father's store, and took naturally to it, and when the father became tired of mercantile pursuits, the son took it off his hands. He was in general trade at the Point for more than fifty years. Besides business conducted at the store, he has kept a tavern, owned the ferry, done more or less farming, dealt in real estate and cattle, engaged in politics, served in the Maine Legislature, been a civil magistrate and postmaster, and at different times, has held all the principal town offices. He gave up the store to his son some years ago, but is still engaged in other business.

CHARLES H. KIMBALL.

Charles Henry Kimball, son of Porter and Nancy (Kimball) Kimball, born in Rumford December 25, 1828, commenced his career as a teacher of public schools, when only seventeen years old. He was a good scholar and had a natural tact for teaching, though he never thought of this as a life business. The last school he taught in Maine was at Harrison Village in the winter of 1849-50. In 1850, he went to New York and secured a position as teacher in a large boarding school, situated on the Hudson near where Major Andre was captured. His father having died in the summer of 1851, he returned to Rumford and spent a couple of years in settling the estate. He then again went to New York and taught two years in the Mechanic's Institute on Chambers street. He was then elected principal of public school number fourteen in Brooklyn, where he remained two years, when he became principal of Ward School number two in Henry street, New York. Here he remained for eight years, having the supervision of about thirty teachers and a salary of twelve hundred dollars. During the Lincoln campaign in the autumn of 1860, he first became interested in politics, and in 1861 he was chosen alderman in the largest and most influential ward in Brooklyn. He was re-elected in 1863, his two terms of service covering the entire period of the war. This service brought him in contact with many prominent men which proved of great service in after years. In 1864, the school board of Brooklyn which had been non-partisan, became strictly democratic, and Mr. Kimball was removed, although his success as a teacher and school manager was duly acknowledged. He was removed solely on political grounds. About this time, and largely through his influence, a law was enacted in New York, prohibiting school boards from removing teachers on account of their religious belief or political bias, and this law is still in force.

But Mr. Kimball's removal from his position in the school, proved a blessing rather than otherwise. He immediately commenced business in Wall street as a stock and bond broker, and for twenty-five years has been doing a successful business. For fourteen years the firm name was C. H. Kimball & Co., and since that time it has been Kimball, Howell & Co. For ten years past, he has been intimately associated with the development of the now famous winter and spring resort at Lakewood, New Jersey, having been president of the Lakewood Hotel and Land Association since its organization in 1879. During all these years of business activity and prosperity, Mr. Kimball has ever felt a warm regard for the people of the county and State in which he was born and reared, and has contributed liberally to aid in preserving the reminiscences of his native town.

JOHN ROLFE.

John Rolfe, son of Benjamin Rolfe, born in Concord, N. H., March 7, 1785, was attending the town school in Concord when his father with his family was ready to start for Rumford in the winter of 1794-5. Young Rolfe, who fully realized the very limited advantages for schooling in the new country to which they were emigrating, asked to be allowed to remain and pursue his studies until the close of the winter term of school. This request was readily granted by his parents but with the understanding that he was to make his way to Rumford as best he could as soon as his school closed. In the following spring, 1794, when young Rolfe was not quite ten years of age, he shouldered his pack of provisions and started, on foot and alone over this long, strange, dreary journey, hoping that in some way and at some time to be able to penetrate the forests, to follow the uncertain bridle-paths and blazed roads, across hills and mountains and streams until he should finally reach the camp of his father in the then almost unbroken forests of Rumford. These were the days of sturdy pioneers, ready to do and dare all things, but who can tell the joy and thanksgiving which were felt and heard in that new made camp on the banks of the Androscoggin, when young Rolfe, weary, foot-sore and travel worn, pushed back the rude door and was recognized by the family within. Mr. Rolfe married Betsey Abbott, and settled on a wild lot on the west side of Ellis river, three miles above Rumford Point. He cleared up a good farm and spent the remainder of his days here. He died April 23, 1854.

ENOCH C. ROLFE.

Dr. Enoch Carter Rolfe, eldest child of John Rolfe and Betsey (Abbott) Rolfe, was born in Rumford April 16, 1812. He studied medicine with the late Dr. Simeon Fuller of Rumford, and graduated from the Maine Medical School in the class of 1838. He married Emeline, daughter of James Small, Esq., of Rumford, May 16, 1839, and commenced the practice of medicine at Farmington Falls, Me., the same year. He remained there until 1849, when he removed his family to Boston, Mass., where he continued the practice of medicine. He left a fine practice at Farmington, and went to Boston that his children might have the advantages of Boston schools. Dr. Rolfe became at once greatly interested in the Boston

John Abbot Rolfe.

Residence of John Abbot Rolfe, Wellington, (Medford) Mass.

schools, was a member of the school board for twenty-five consecutive years. He was also Professor of Physiology and Hygiene in Tufts College in 1851-5, and a member of the General Court of Massachusetts in 1857-8. He was selected Chairman of the committee for re-districting the State, a very important committee. Of his three children, all born in Farmington, George, the eldest, died when a young man, Henry graduated at Harvard College, and is now living in Virginia City, Nevada, while his twin sister, Emma, is the wife of George P. Eustis, Esq., of Boston. Dr. Rolfe died in Boston March 27, 1875.

JOHN ABBOT ROLFE.

The subject of this sketch, son of John and Betsey Abbot Rolfe, was born July 2, 1824, on the west bank of Ellis river, midway between Rumford Point and the Andover line. He spent his childhood and youth until eighteen years of age, on the old homestead, then went to Portland, where he served an apprenticeship of three years with Messrs. Larrabee and Dyer, who were at that time prominent carpenters and builders in that city, spending his spare time in studying the art of drafting and architecture. After completing his apprenticeship he was foreman for the firm one year, when he entered business for himself associating with him Mr. Samuel H. Robins, under the firm name of Rolfe and Robins. At the end of one year Mr. Robins was taken sick, and after six months died. This sickness and death absorbed the little money they had made during the short time they had been in the business, and young Rolfe accepted an offer from the late Francis O. J. Smith, who was at that time building a theatre on Union street, Portland. On the completion of this building it was leased to Boston's celebrated tragedian, Joseph Proctor. Mr. Rolfe, having had charge of the building of the stage and all its machinery and traps, was now employed by Mr. Proctor as stage carpenter and machinist, which he continued to the close of Mr. Proctor's lease of one year. His health being impaired, by advice of Portland physicians, he went to Philadelphia and placed himself in the hands of Dr. Joseph Jackson.

It was in Brooklyn, N. Y., in 1851, and in the parlor of Henry Ward Beecher, that Mr. Rolfe, being then on his way to Philadelphia, was married to Mary M., daughter of the late Capt. Theophilus Thompson of Freeport, Me. He proceeded to Philadelphia with his wife where they remained one year. In the fall of 1852, with health

17

fully restored, he returned to Boston, entered the furniture business as salesman for the late John W. Blanchard, and remained with him until 1861. In 1862 he established himself in a general insurance business, and during the past quarter of a century has been well known in business and insurance circles. When the great fire of 1872, swept away a large part of Boston business houses, this agency had about three hundred thousand dollars at risk on their books, and every man got a hundred cents on the dollar and got it promptly. From 1879, until he was removed by death Sept. 9th, 1884, his son, Frank Rolfe, was associated with him in business. He purchased a house at Wellington, in the town of Medford, three and a half miles from Boston, in the spring of 1866, to which he moved his family on the 9th of May of that year, and where they still reside.

Janette (Bolster) Ricker.

Mrs. Janette Wheeler, daughter of General Alvan Bolster and wife of Hiram Ricker, was born in Rumford June 3, 1821. Like her mother she followed school teaching after she had finished her education until she was married when twenty-five years of age. They remained in Rumford a short time after their marriage and were here with one child when the census of 1850 was taken. But she spent most of her married life in Poland and had a large share in developing the famous Poland Springs which have become a mine of wealth to her family, and the most popular summer resort in the State of Maine. She was a woman of uncommon executive ability, of untiring perseverance, and besides these, she possessed in a marked degree all those qualities which go to make up the true woman. She was very popular with the guests of the house, and idolized by her children. She died September 23, 1883, having lived to see the Poland Springs resort, in which she always had unbounded faith, a complete success. Her three sons, Edward P., Hiram, Jr. and Alvan B. are now the proprietors and managers of the great business which she and her husband started and developed. She also had three daughters, Cynthia Ella, Sarah L. and Nettie M.

Benjamin P. Snow.

Rev. Benjamin Poor Snow was born in the parsonage house at Rumford, February 14, 1831. His father, Samuel S. Snow, moved with his family to a farm on Ellis river where he lived until about

Mrs. Luna (Abbot) Walke

1852, when he moved to Saccarappa. The wife of Samuel S. Snow was Mary Stevens, daughter of Ezra Hoyt. The subject of this notice attended the common schools in Rumford, and after his father moved to Saccarappa, he worked in the paper mill there and carried on his studies at home during his spare hours. He attended two terms at Norway Liberal Institute and entered Colby University with the class of 1855. Remaining here a year, he left and went to Bowdoin College from which he was graduated. His rank in college is shown in the fact that he was tutor at Bowdoin three years. He graduated from the Bangor Theological Seminary in 1861. He engaged in teaching at Fryeburg and in Massachusetts until 1870, when his health became impaired. He decided that he must change his occupation to one that would allow of more out-of-door exercise, and accordingly accepted the pastorate of the Congregational church in North Yarmouth, and was ordained in 1870. He was there as pastor three years, at Alfred seven years, and at Houlton three years. He was then Superintendent of the Biddeford Schools two years, when he accepted the pastorate of the church at Cape Elizabeth, where he yet resides. For some years, while performing other duties, he was connected with the press and is a member of the Maine Press Association. Mr. Snow is a ripe scholar, was an enthusiastic and successful teacher, and has always had a deep interest in educational affairs. He is Secretary of the State Sabbath School Convention, and during the summer of 1889 he visited Europe in the interest of that organization. He married August 26, 1862, Annie Louisa Chandler of New Sharon.

TIMOTHY WALKER.

Hon. Timothy Walker, son of Charles and Hannah (Pickering) Walker, and grandson of Col. Timothy Walker, the principal grantee of Rumford, was born in Concord, N. H., July 10, 1813. In early manhood he came to Rumford to look after the large interests of the family in Rumford lands. He became possessed of the farm, the first settled in town by Jonathan Keyes, and here he spent the remainder of his years. This is one of the best farms in town. Though possessed of large means, Mr. Walker lived in unpretentious style, in a one story house, and was plain and simple in all his habits. He was fond of agriculture, and labored hard upon his farm whenever he could be relieved from other business cares. He served with credit in both branches of the Maine Legislature, and was much in town office. He was also a director in several monied institutions both in and out of the county. He married April 16, 1835, Luna, daughter of David Abbot, and his family record is elsewhere. He was honest in his dealings with mankind, and his word was as good as his bond. His charitable deeds were many, but performed in such a quiet way that the beneficiary rarely knew whence the aid came. He was a man of very decided convictions, and one not easily deceived by pretentions. He was opposed to slavery, in favor of temperance and prohibition of the liquor traffic, a Universalist in religious belief, but tolerant of other forms of faith. He died January 25, 1882, and a fine granite monument marks his last resting place, in the cemetery at Rumford Corner. Mr. Walker had a wonderfully retentive memory and the way he could recall days, dates and events even of minor importance, was truly marvelous. There were comparatively few who had his entire confidence but that favored few were fortunate. He had it in his power to assist such in various ways. He was open and fair-handed in all his transactions, and believed that honesty and integrity should characterize the proceedings of political parties: any deviation from this met with the sternest rebuke. He aided in organizing the Republican party and was for many years a pillar of strength in town, county and State. During the late war, he was untiring in his efforts to have the quotas of the town promptly filled, and was ever ready to advance money to promote that object.

CHARLES WALKER.

Hon. Charles Walker, son of Hon. Timothy Walker, was born in Rumford and spent his youth and early manhood in that town. When his father moved temporarily to Lewiston, he came with the family but did not return to Rumford. He studied law and established himself in Lewiston where he has since resided. He has been honored with the office of mayor of the city, and was appointed by President Cleveland, postmaster of Lewiston, which position he still holds. He is a square business man and held in high esteem by men of both parties in the city of his adoption. He is still loyal to his native town where his mother and sisters reside, and has rendered material aid and encouragement in the publication of this volume. He married Augusta Patience, daughter of Orra and Phebe (Bumpus) Hall of Paris.

Hon. Charles Walker.

Joseph Wardwell.

Joseph Wardwell was born in Andover, Mass., January 29, 1759, and was the son of Joshua and Mary Wardwell of that ancient town. He entered the Colonial service at the beginning of the Revolution, a mere boy, and served through the war. He entered as a private but was promoted to a Lieutenancy and served in the corps commanded by General Lafayette. He was in all the great battles of the long war, and gained an enviable reputation for gallantry and bravery. A sword presented him by General Lafayette for conspicuous bravey at the siege of Yorktown is still preserved in the family. At the close of the war, Mr. Wardwell found himself poor and so illiterate that he could not read a chapter in the Bible. The time when he naturally would have been at school was spent in the service of his country. But with characteristic energy, he engaged in study and graduated with honor from Phillips Andover Academy. He married Sarah, daughter of Rev. Moses Hemmenway, D. D. of Wells, and moved quite early to Andover, Me., and from thence to a farm at North Turner which he purchased of Rev. John Strickland. Here he kept a public house and was a farmer. When quite advanced in years he came to Rumford and here he died March 5, 1849. His oldest son, Joseph H. Wardwell, died about the same time, and both were buried the same day. When General Lafayette visited Andover years after the war was over, he was thus addressed by Lieut. Wardwell:

"General Lafayette: I served in the Light Infantry under you in two campaigns, the last in Virginia. I hold in my hand the war-worn feather which you presented me at Orangetown in the Jerseys, where Major Andrew, the British Adjutant General, was executed. The red top of the feather was taken off by a musket ball when I was at the abattis storming the first of the two redoubts before Yorktown, carried at the point of the bayonet, being led on by Colonel Jainott, that illustrious Frenchman. General, this is my son who now enjoys the liberties, together with his mother, brother and sisters, for which you hazarded your life, endured the hardships of war, sleeping on the cold ground in a land of strangers. These eyes bear witness to all this. I most ardently hope that the citizens of America will never be so lost to every sentiment of gratitude as to forget that the soil of their country was stained by the precious blood of Frenchmen to purchase the liberties which they now enjoy and have enjoyed for half a century." General Lafayette replied in fitting terms and the meeting between these former comrades in arms was very affecting. Mr. Wardwell was a member of the Cincinnati and a pensioner. He was proud of his military record, as well he might be, and delighted in relating incidents connected with his service. He was a gentleman of the old school, erect and dignified, yet affable and kind hearted, and a favorite with both old and young.

John R. Wood.

John Richardson Wood, son of Phineas and Elizabeth (Kidder) Wood, born Sept. 1, 1826, spent his youth upon his father's farm in Rumford, but in 1850, he struck out for himself and went to New York. Here he learned the trade of a jeweller and set up in business for himself, making a specialty of the manufacture of gold rings. From a small beginning his business has gradually increased until it has now reached large proportions. His factory and dwelling house are in Brooklyn, but his store is in John street, New York City. Mr. Wood is widely known and his work has an excellent reputation. He may be set down as one of Rumford's successful business men, and his success is not due more to his energy and perseverance than to his honesty and fair dealing. He married in the autumn of 1861, Louisa, daughter of Judge Lyman Rawson of Rumford. They have had four sons, three of whom are living, and two are in company with their father.

John R. Wood.

CHAPTER XXXVII.

INTENTIONS OF MARRIAGE.

Adams, Enoch, of E. Andover, and Lydia Moody of Newbury, 1802.

Abbot, Jacob, and Betsey Knapp of Dixfield, Dec. 19, 1803.

Adams, John E., and Sally Moody of E. Andover, Sept. 1824.

Adams, Enoch Jr., and Lucy Strickland of E. Andover, March 26, 1807.

Adams, Joseph, of Andover, and Betsey Farnum, March 12, 1812.

Abbot, Levi, and Harriet Eastman, Feb. 20, 1813.

Abbot, Nathaniel, and Sabrina Morse, Feb. 21, 1813.

Austin, Joel, and Esther Farnum, Sept. 2, 1813.

Ackley. Wm., and Deborah Capen, Nov. 21, 1815.

Adams, Moses, of Andover, and Dorcas Farnum, July 4, 1817.

Adams, Nathan Jr., and Susan Merrill of Andover, January 10, 1817.

Abbot, Eben, and Catherine Farnum, Oct. 15, 1819.

Abbot, David, 2d and Azubah Morse, July 28, 1821.

Abbot, Enos Jr., and Polly E. Hutchins, Dec. 9, 1821.

Abbot, Hazen F., and Uannah Martin, May 5, 1822.

Ackley, John, of No. 2, and Vesta Abbot, Nov. 10, 1822.

Abbot, Stephen, and Lucy Mansur, Sept. 15, 1823.

Abbot, David, 3d and Anna Harper, March 27, 1824.

Abbot, Levi, and Vashti Wheeler, January 2, 1825.

Abbot, Nathan, and Betsey Wood, Apr. 2, 1825.

Atkins, Nathaniel, of Livermore, and Sally Parker, Oct. 29, 1826.

Abbot, David, and Sally Crommet of Clinton, March 24, 1827.

Abbot, Edmund, and Mary A. Rolfe. Dec. 13, 1829.

Abbot, Chandler, and Charity Durgin, May 14, 1831.

Abbot, David, and Mrs. Betsey Knight of Bethel, March 6, 1833.

Abbot, Gideon Colson, and Cervilla Barker, Oct. 21, 1833.

Austin, Justus, of Peru, and Lydia Hall, Nov. 18, 1833.

Adams, David F., and Dorcas Glines, Apr. 6, 1834.

Abbot, Stephen H., and Sarah J. Small, Nov. 7, 1835.

Adams, Col. John E., of Cleveland, O., and Sophia Jones, March 26, 1836.

Adams, Wm. 2d, of Andover, and Lucinda Hall, Apr. 16, 1838.

Ackley, Joseph, and Mary Brown, Feb. 23, 1839.

Andrews, Joseph R., and Vienua Elliot of Bethel, June 26, 1839.

Abbot, Benj. E., and Mahala F. Godwin, Sept. 8, 1840.

Abbot, Samuel V., and Mary W. Kyle, Apr. 22, 1843.

Ackley, John, and Miss Mary Penley of Paris, Oct. 8, 1843.

Adams, Warren M., and Adrian Washburne, Nov. 17. 1844.

Abbot, Henry Jr., and Rosilla W. Hall, Feb. 7, 1847.

Ackley, James B., and Sarah Hardy, Sept. 21, 1847.

Abbot, Aaron J., of Andover, Marcia S. Ripley, Feb. 9, 1849.

Abbot, Hezekiah H., and Martha T. Lovejoy, Oct. 30, 1851.

Abbot, Asa A., and Julia O. Godwin, Apr. 25, 1852.

Abbot, Wm. H., and Mary A. Philbrick, Dec. 17, 1852.

Abbot, Edwin R., and Betsey M. Ripley, Dec. 5, 1853.

Abbot, Henry Jr., and C. Augusta Waite of Dixfield, March 1, 1854.

Abbot, Charles B., and Sophia Elliot, June 11, 1855.

Atkins, Sylvanus, of Peru, and Mary Arnold, Sept. 24, 1855.

Abbot, Charles R., of Hanover, and Alice Jane Hutchins, March 22, 1856.

Abbot, Thomas P., of Andover, and Maria H. Newton, Aug. 8, 1856.

Austin, Charles H., of Mexico, and Melissa H. Mann, Aug. 30, 1856.

Adams, Daniel W., and Sarah J. Virgin, Oct. 25, 1856.

Abbot, Henry M., and Arabella C. Howard of Hanover, Aug. 6, 1856.

Abbot, Lyman F., and Clara E. Howe, Dec. 30, 1856.

Ackley, Charles H., and Cynthia J. Abbot, May 18, 1858.

Abbot, Chandler, and Mary E. Chadburne, Nov. 4, 1858.

Andrews, Horace C., of Paris, and Addie L. Abbot, May 30, 1859.

Abbot, Phineas W., and Fanny M. Bean, Sept. 2, 1859.

Andrews, William, and Hannah H. Abbot, Sept. 12, 1859.

Austin, Charles, and Isadore M. Jordan, Nov. 20, 1859.

Abbot, John L., and Adeline Ingalls of Ryegate, Vt., May 22, 1861.

Abbot, H. Marshall, and Abbie Martin, July 18, 1863.

Abbot, Hiram F., and Mary J. Mansur, Feb. 5, 1864.

Abbot, Seth P., and Georgie Matthews of Franklin Pl., March 14, 1864.

Adams, Mark T., and Emily L. Wardwell, Dec. 24, 1864.

Austin, Loren J., of Mexico, and Sarah J. Richardson, Oct. 14, 1865.

Arnold, Samuel V., and Lucy J. Harlow of Mexico, Oct. 9, 1866.

Adams, Chas. H., of Andover, and Marion V. Reed, Aug. 10, 1867.

Brister, Enoch, and Sally Chamberlain of No. 5, May 9, 1807.

Bartlett, Elijah, of Bethel, and Nancy Graham, Feb. 7, 1812.

Blake, Benj., of Andover, and Nancy Ripley, Feb. 8, 1812.

Bragg, James F., of Andover, and Sally Graham, March 21, 1811.

Bartlett, Elias, of Bethel, and Eliza Adams, January 27, 1814.

Bragden, Benj., of No. 7, and Rachel Walton, March 2, 1815.

Bartlett, Elias, of Bethel, and Judith Farnum, Dec. 15, 1815.

Bartlett, Samuel, and Sarah Wardwell, June 6, 1816.

Bradbury, Thomas, of No. 8, and Dolly Morse, Nov. 20, 1817.

Bolster, Alvan, and Cynthia Wheeler, Nov. 24, 1820.

Baxter, Joseph Jr., and Betsey Abbot, Oct. 20, 1822.

Bunker, Samuel J., of No. 7, and Charlotte Howe, Feb. 1, 1823.

Brock, Wm., of Peru, and Mary Virgin, Sept. 4, 1823.

Brown, John M., and Martha Gibson, Feb. 24, 1828.

Blanchard, David, and Mehitable Taylor of No. 7, April 3, 1829.

Bent, Orin, of Waterford, and Caroline Eaton, Oct. 30, 1830.

Baker, Otis, of Mexico, and Melinda Silver, June 25, 1831.

Bean, Alanson, of Howard's Gore, and Hannah Hemminway, Oct. 2, 1831.

Buker. Isaac R., and Hannah W. Hardy, January 21, 1832.

Blanchard, Benj. H., of No. 7, and Mary P. Berry Apr. 3, 1832.

Buchannan, John, of Letter B., and Susan Hodsdon, Oct. 1, 1834.

Bolster, Lyman, and Betsey F. Knight, May 9, 1835,

Bisbee, George W., of Hartford, and Mary Howe, Nov. 4, 1835.

Berry, Joseph, of Andover, and Sarah L. Greenleaf, Feb. 8, 1812.

Bartlett, Ephraim C., of Bethel, and Julia Ann Richmond, Nov. 21, 1835.

Barker, Elias, and Martha Moody of No. 2, Apr. 2, 1836.

Burke, Wm., of Portland, and Betsey Ward, June 18, 1837.

Bosworth, Jacob, and Sally Allen, Nov. 3, 1839.

Brock, Robert M., of Buckfield, and Catherine M. Durgin, Nov. 18, 1828.

Bisbee, Piram, and Asenath Sweat, Dec. 27, 1835.

Bragg, John I., of Letter B, and Nancy B. Graham, 1840.

Brackett, Peter D., and Betsey A. Abbot, Sept. 24, 1837.

Bean, Eliphas C., of Bethel, and Sarah B. Farnum, May 27, 1838.

Bolster, Otis C., and Maria C. T. Virgin, May 4, 1841.

Bartlett, Jonathan A., and Harriet A. Glines, May 1, 1842.

Bragg, James I., of Andover, and Julia Ann Hall, May 3, 1843.

Barker, Charles, and Melinda M. Kyle, May 12, 1844.

Bryant, Jairus S., of Bethel, and Lucina Rolfe, Feb. 2, 1848.

Beard, Amasa A., and Charlotte A. Weaver of Franklin Pl., Feb. 4, 1848.

Bolster, Wm. W., and Martha H. Adams, Sept. 30, 1848.

Beal, Geo. L., of Norway, and Belinda D. Thompson, May 25, 1851.

Blanchard, David, and Deborah D. Wheeler, Oct. 29, 1851.

Barker, Hazen F., and Dorcas H. Brooks of Woodstock.

Bowker, Anson W., of Woodstock, and Martha J. Silver, Sept. 3, 1853.

Bodwell. Samuel B., and Sarah J. Bragdon, May 16, 1855.

Burgess, Elijah L., of Peru. and Elizabeth M. Thompson, June 18, 1855.

Baker, Nathan S., and Mary O. Bryant of Milton Pl., January 18, 1858.

Burgess. Walter, of Peru, and Mary J. Richardson, Nov. 15, 1858.

Burgess, Demas B., of Peru, and Ora Small. January 24, 1859.

Bean. John C., of Turner, and Clarinda Doble, March 28, 1859.

Bolster, Mellen E., of Paris, and Ann Sophia Roberts, Nov. 14, 1859.

Brown, David F., and Mrs. Mary A. Reed, June 29, 1860.

Blanchard, Orlando W., and Thirza A. Holt, April 1, 1861.

Barker, Henry J., of Milton Pl., and Josephine R. Martin, Apr. 20, 1861.

Bishop, Nathan S., of Peru, and Emogene Elliot, Oct. 4, 1862.

Bartlett, Wm. W., of Hanover, and Sarah M. Colby, Feb. 26, 1864.

Bryent, Benj. W., of Paris, and Mary K. Goddard, May 9, 1864.

Blanchard, Wm. M., and Desire C. Farrar, Oct. 22, 1864.

Blanchard, Orlando W., and Caroline W. Kimball, June 27, 1866.

Blodgett, Stillman S., of Bethel, and Betsey C. Hall, Dec. 21, 1868.

Butterfield, John, of Sumner, and Amelia J. Hammon, January 11, 1969.

Boynton, B. H., and Emma E. Libby of Leeds, Nov. 13, 1869.

Carr, Daniel, and Polly Ayer of Bethel, Apr. 15, 1802.
Colby, Ephraim, and Burry Bartlett of Bethel, Nov. 1, 1807.
Cushman, John, of Bethel, and Parazina Howe, Feb. 19, 1809.
Cushman, Francis, and Phebe M. Abbot, Sept. 8, 1815.
Cobb, Ebenezer, and Mary Weaver of Readfield, Feb. 14, 1816.
Cobb, Churchill, and Pamelia Putnam, Sept. 16, 1817.
Cushman, Solomon, and Harriet Adams, April 8, 1821.
Crockett, Solomon, and Dorcas Sutton, Nov. 24, 1822.
Child, Henry, of Canton, and Hannah Farnum, March 23, 1826.
Carter, Timothy J., and Arabella Rawson of Paris, Aug. 17, 1828.
Colburn, Bartholomew, of No. 4, and Sally Hutchins, March 24, 1833.
Chamberlain, Wm., and Desire Bisbee of Woodstock, Oct. 13, 1833.
Cushman, Francis, and Lydia Keyes, April 27, 1834.
Chapman, Samuel R., and Hannah Mansur, Feb. 28, 1835.
Clement, Josiah J., and Abigail Swan of Bethel, Apr. 6, 1838.
Colby, Joseph E., and Mary J. F. Martin, June 8, 1839.
Caldwell, Richard, and Phebe A. Hutchins, June 15, 1841.
Caldwell, Solomon M., of Albany, and Vileria Wood, May 21, 1843.
Chew, Joseph, and Rachel Thomas, January 6, 1844.
Caldwell, Wm. H., and Elizabeth McAllister of Canton, May 23, 1844.
Colby, Timothy, and Hannah W. Martin, Sept. 6, 1845.
Carter, James M., and Martha A. Wait of Peru, Sept. 28, 1845.
Colby, John T., and Almira Stiles, January 1, 1846.
Clement, Lawson F., and Abigail G. Simpson, Sept. 26, 1848.
Clement, John Jr., and Susan Farnum, Nov. 11, 1848.
Colby, Marshall B., and Dolly M. Abbot, Dec. 11, 1848.
Crockett, Nathaniel B., of Andover, and Lydia J. Wardwell, July 6, 1850.
Colby, Charles S., and Ann G. Greely of Salisbury, N. H., Aug. 25, 1850.
Caverly, L. W. of Strafford, N. H., and Martha F. Washburne, Mar. 19, 1853.
Clisby, Isaac W., and Alvira J. Virgin, March 27, 1857.
Clement, John Jr., and Sarah Smith, Oct. 4, 1857.
Coburn, Reuben B., and Jeneatte M. Warren, Nov. 8, 1860.
Cummings, Nathan M., of Woodstock, and Asenath McCrillis, May 23, 1863.
Colby, Irving T., and Burnetta H. Bartlett, January 28, 1864.
Colby, Henry M., and Nancy J. Farnum, Dec. 24, 1864.
Cummings, Moses, of Bethel, and Juliette Barker, July 25, 1866.
Caldwell, Wm. H., and Mrs. Melinda S. Moody, Aug. 31, 1866.
Coburn, David H., and Ellen Bradeen of Byron, Nov. 1, 1866.
Clement, Royal A., and Maria C. Virgin, Oct. 19, 1867.
Chase, Chas. H., and Olive E. Parker of Lewiston, Dec. 2, 1867.
Cushman, Francis E. K., and Ann A. Mitchell, March 31, 1868.
Cole, Virgil D. P., of Milton Plantation, and Eliza E. Tufts, Dec. 11, 1868.
Coburn, Lot S., of Riley Plantation, and Emma E. Durfee, May 18, 1869.

Dustin, Jesse, and Lavina Howard of Howard's Gore, Jan. 2, 1809.
Dutton, Jotham, and Miriam Abbott, Jan. 16, 1809.
Door, Ebenezer, of Livermore, and Polly Hinkson, Oct. 5, 1816.

Dolloff, John, and Eunice Stiles of Bridgton, Nov. 2, 1816.
Douglass, Samuel. of Litchfield, and Sally Stevens, Aug. 1, 1817.
Delano, John, of No. 1, and Mehitable Sweat, March 19, 1818.
Delano, Wm., of Livermore, and Abigail Sweat, Sept. 4, 1819.
Delano, Abial, and Sally Martin of Andover, Sept. 4, 1819.
Doyen, Benj., and Dorothy S. Wheeler of Dixfield, June 17, 1821.
Door, Ebenezer 2d, and Patty Hinkson, June 23, 1821.
Dolloff, David, of Errol, N. H., and Almira Howe, Aug. 28, 1822.
Delano, James, of Livermore, and Polly Brown, January 22, 1824.
Dolly, Increase, and Phebe Elliot, Feb. 7, 1824.
Delano, Jesse, and Sally Brown, March 6, 1825.
Dillingham, Enos, of Portland, and Clarissa W. Virgin, Nov. 12, 1826.
Durgin, Henry F., and Dorothy E. Hall, Nov. 11, 1829.
Dirgin, Neri D. B., and Betsey R. Glines. Sept. 25, 1831.
Dwinel, Amos, of Lisbon, and Sarah S. Small, Sept. 21, 1832.
Douglass, ———, and Julia Ann Goddard, April 14, 1833.
Dunley, Joseph (Irishman) and Mrs. Betsey Cook, Aug. 25, 1839.
Dolloff, James M., and Sarah L. Gleason of Mexico, July 23, 1840.
Dolly, George, and Lucinda Cole of Bethel, June 23, 1843.
Delano, Francis, and Phebe L. Hall, Aug. 17, 1853.
Daily, Isaac P., of Canton, and Amanda A. Eastman, Dec. 21, 1863.
Dolloff, Ronello C., and Susannah Glover, June 25, 1866.
Dolloff, Oscar F., and Abbie A. G. Curtis, March 17, 1867.
Elliot, Cotton, and Gratia Moor, May, 1801.
Elliot, Benj., and Phebe Eastman, Aug. 27, 1814.
Elliot, David, and Polly Silver, May 10, 1818.
Eastman, Haines, and Lovina Peterson, Oct. 29, 1818.
Elliot, Aaron, and Susan Farnum, March 8, 1827.
Eastman, Caleb Jr., and Molly F. Whitman of Mexico, March 31, 1828.
Eastman, Wm., and Olive Wilson of Canton, Jan. 25, 1829.
Elliot, Thomas C., and P. Cragin of Westmoreland, N. H., March 31, 1832.
Eaton, Osgood Jr., and Maria L. Gale of Gilmanton, N. H., Feb. 5, 1833.
Elliot, Cyrus, and Betsey Rolfe Hall, March 31, 1833.
Eaton, Abial, and Rhoda G. Burleigh of Gilmanton, N. H., Nov. 2, 1834.
Ethridge, Nathaniel, and Mary Greenleaf, June 22, 1835.
Ethridge, Asa, and Emily Abbot, Sept. 27, 1835.
Elliot, Ganzilo, of Livermore, and Betsey Wheeler, June 12, 1836.
Elliot, Nathan W., of Bethel, and Lydia M. Carter, Aug. 5, 1843.
Elliot, Cotton Jr., and Lavina B. Keyes of Letter A, May 16, 1846.
Etheridge, John S., and Harriet Moulton of Sandwich, N. H., Jan. 21, 1849.
Elliot, Wm., and Charlotte K. Howe, Sept. 8, 1849.
Elkins, Francis, and Sarah F. Morse, June 26, 1855.
Elliot, Josiah K., and Mary Ann Estes of Bethel, Nov. 29, 1856.
Eastman, Z. G., of Mexico, and Mary S. Merrill, July 25, 1857.
Elliot, B. W., and Rebecca M. Lufkin of Mexico, Jan. 14, 1858.
Elliot, David E., and Aurelia Lufkin of Mexico, Aug. 21, 1858.
Eastman, Holland F., and Nancy M. Hall, Oct. 9, 1860.

Elliot, John G., and Addie E. Kimball, Feb. 23, 1864.
Eastman, Daniel G., and Rosilla J. Paine, March 1, 1869.
Elliot, John E., and Martha Brown, May 29, 1864.
Elliot, Edward F., and Clara M. Libby of Standish, March 14, 1865.
Eastman, Caleb, and Philena W. Cone of Skowhegan, Nov. 16, 1865.
Eastman, Geo. C., of Mexico, and Ella E. Eastman, May 19, 1866.
Elliot, Leonard D., and Eliza E. Moody, May 27, 1866.
Eastman, Arbury E., and Emma A. Twombly, June 19, 1866.
Eaton, Cyrus P., and Mary E. Howe, July 6, 1868.
Elliot, Clifford M., and Flora E. Abbot, March 13, 1869.

Farnum, Samuel, and Betsey Godwin, Feb. 8, 1812.
Farnum, Jedediah, and Isabel Knapp of No. 1, Oct. 15, 1812.
Farnum, Merrill, and Sally Bunker, June 30, 1815.
Flint, Dr. Benj., and Sarah Cushing of Canaan, N. H., Jan. 15, 1816.
Frost, William, and Dorothy Sweat, Apr. 14, 1817.
Farnum, Merrill, and Sarah Virgin of Concord, N. H., Nov. 14, 1817.
Farnum, David H., and Maria Bartlett of Bethel, Jan. 2, 1819.
Farrington, James, of Andover, and Melinda Farnum, July 6, 1820.
Farrington, Philander, of Andover, and Polly Martin, Feb. 23, 1821.
Fowler, Jonathan, of Bethel, and Martha Peva, July 20, 1822.
Farnum, Merrill, and Louisa Howe, Dec. 26, 1824.
Fifield, Simeon, of Fryeburg, and Mary Morse, May 28, 1825.
Farnum, Wm. W., and Rebecca S. Webster of Andover, Feb. 3, 1827.
Farnum, Simeon, and Milla Robinson of Paris, Feb. 24, 1827.
Fuller, Dr. Simeon, and Mary Ann Rawson of Paris, June 3, 1827.
Farnum, Abial, and Jeneatte Burnham of Westbrook, Sept. 27, 1829.
Farnum, James Harvey, and Clarissa Hoyt, Jan. 17, 1830.
Farnum, Stephen Jr., and Sarah Virgin, Oct. 16, 1830.
Farnum, Joseph W., and Susan Ford, Apr. 7, 1831.
Farnum, George J., and Mary S. Bodwell of Andover, Jan. 10, 1833.
Farnum, Daniel, and Mary G. Virgin, Feb. 5, 1833.
Frye, Benjamin, and Judith Rolfe, Dec. 16, 1833.
Fox, Charles S., of Roxbury, and Katherine P. Richardson, Oct. 29, 1836.
Fuller, Aaron, of Paris, and Mrs. Mary Virgin, March 31, 1838.
Farnum, Capt. David H., and widow Nancy Hinkson, June 10, 1838.
Farnum, Wm. W., and Hannah J. Treadwell of Portland, Oct. 12, 1839.
Frost, Wm., and Sibbell G. Bartlett of Bethel, Oct. 5, 1831.
Farnum, Wm. W., and Betsey G. Fox of Roxbury, March 9, 1845.
Farnum, John C., and Mary R. Bass of Weld, June 1, 1845.
Francis, Wm., of Carthage, and Cyrene Green, Oct. 5, 1846.
Farnum, Aaron V., of Abbington, Mass., and Ann M. Hanson, Aug. 5, 1848.
Fifield, Elbridge G., of Bethel, and Hannah K. Martin, May 1, 1851.
French, John C., of Salem, and Roxanna Dolloff, Oct. 2, 1852.
Farnum, David W., and Olive M. Whitcomb of Norway, Mar. 31, 1855.
Farnum, Charles W., and Sarah E. Wardwell, Aug. 2, 1855.
Frost, Daniel G., and Emogene M. Hall, Jan. 27, 1859.

Foye, Stephen E., and Chloe Holt, Feb. 9, 1859.

Farnum, Solon S., and Abby A. Briggs, Apr. 16, 1859.

Farnum, Daniel, and Mrs. Martha J. Bowker, March 20, 1861.

Farnum, Freeling H., and Arvilla W. Rolfe, March 29, 1862.

Farnum, Merrill, and Mrs. Sally Gale of Roxbury, Jan. 2, 1863.

Frye, Wm. A., of Carthage, and Alma L. Farnum, July 13, 1863.

Frost, Wm., and Phebe S. Mitchell. May 9, 1864.

Farnum, Wm. H., and Maria L. C. Martin, Sept. 18, 1865.

Flagg, Ellis R., and Mary Kelly of Mexico, Dec. 4, 1865.

Gleason, Isaac, of No. 1, and Sally Kimball, March 11, 1801.

Graham, Aaron, and Geneva Moore, Nov. 19, 1811.

Glines, Daniel, and Mary Sweat, Apr. 3, 1813.

Godwin, Colman, and Keziah Wheeler of Concord, N. H., Feb. 14, 1814.

Godwin, James, and Apphia Segor of Bethel, May 30, 1814.

Graham, Asa, and Lucinda Farnum, Feb. 7, 1817.

Graham, George, and Hannah Eastman, March 21, 1818.

Glines, Timothy, and Sally Barker of Bethel, Feb. 6, 1819.

Grover, Jedediah, of Bethel, and Hannah Hall, Apr. 29, 1821.

Greenleaf, James B., and Sybil Goddard, May 22, 1822.

Gould, John, of Dixfield, and Lavina Puffer, Aug. 12, 1825.

Graham, Joshua, and Hannah Goddard of Andover, Dec. 26, 1825.

Glines, David B., and Catherine B. Goddard, Jan. 1, 1832.

Gould, Rev. Daniel, and Anna M. Rawson, Sept. 28, 1834.

Goddard, Eben T., and Mary Ann Kimball, Jan. 4, 1835.

Graham, George W., and Irene Irish of Hartford, Oct. 30, 1835.

Green, Ansel B., of Byron, and Sarah J. Silver, Jan. 23, 1836.

Graham, Joshua, and Ruth Treadwell of Portland, July 22, 1838.

Goodnow, David B., and Maria B. Adams, Feb. 21, 1839.

Godwin, David A., and Abigail Besse, Nov. 29, 1825.

Green, Ransom M., and Naomi B. Severy of Wilton, July 16, 1843.

Graham, Joshua, and Mrs. Sarah Leavitt of Buxton, Sept. 30, 1843.

Goddard, Wm., of Bethel, and Joanna Curtis, Nov. 17, 1844.

Greenleaf, Wm. T., of Milton Pl., and Betsy C. Ackley, Aug. 14, 1847.

Graham, John C., and Susan M. Wood, March 20, 1848.

Godwin, Alvan B., and Arabella C. Kimball, Feb. 5, 1851.

Godwin, Ajalon, and Sarah A. Thompson, Sept. 23, 1853.

Glines, Albert G., and Emily H. Farnum, Nov. 10, 1855.

Glines, David G., and Emma S. Howe, Nov. 13, 1860.

Goodwin, Joel, and Fanny A. Kennison, Sept. 27, 1861.

Gleason, George H., of Mexico, and Elizabeth Kimball, Jan. 22, 1863.

Glover, Loren, and Dorcas L. Goddard, Apr. 29, 1863.

Golder, Thos., of Belgrade, and Clara V. Washburne, Apr. 21, 1866.

Graham, Aaron, and Mrs. Abigail Hoyt, Sept. 7, 1866.

Goddard, Elisha F., and Euthalia V. Roberts, May 7, 1867.

Goddard, Geo. T., and Lydia S. Thomas, July 15, 1867.

Goddard, Ephraim F., and Mrs. Jane L. Ackley of Milton Pl., Jan. 13, 1868.

Howard, John A., of Dixfield, and Sarah Hinkson, Dec. 17, 1803.

Hall, Joseph, and Judith Blanchard, Sept. 13, 1804.

Hall, Jeremiah, and Judith Rolfe, July 21, 1805.

Hodsdon, James, and Esther Bartlett of Bethel, Jan. 26, 1810.

Howe, John. and Persis Moore of Worcester, March 15, 1812.

Hinkson, Robert, and Sally Silver, Oct. 21, 1815.

Hutchins, David 3d, and Sally Abbot of Andover, July 13, 1817.

Howe, Otis, and Elsie Andrews of Bethel, Aug. 17, 1817.

Howe, John Jr., and Betsey Abbot of Bethel, Dec. 12, 1818.

Hammon, Samuel, of No. 1, and Lydia Lovejoy.

Hemminway, Wm. R., and Mrs. Phebe Brown of Hamlin Grant, Mar. 23,1822.

Hinkson, Joseph, of No. 7, and Ruth Puffer, July 5, 1823.

Howe, John Jr., and Mrs. Nancy (Kimball) Brown of Waterford, Apr.10,1825.

Hutchins, Hezekiah, and Lucinda Bean of Bethel, Nov. 19, 1826.

Hemminway, Colman, of Letter B, and Sally Carr, Jan. 3, 1827.

Hinkson, Daniel, and Juliette Swain, Nov. 24, 1827.

Hall, Daniel 2d, and Sarah Lovejoy of No. 2, Nov. 28, 1827.

Hubbard, Rev. Aaron, of Monson, and Charlotte Adams, Nov. 1, 1828.

Howe, Calvin, and Thirza Kimball of Bethel, Nov. 18, 1828.

Howe, Joel, and Dorcas Barker of Newry, Oct. 5, 1829.

Hutchins, Joseph. and Mary N. Howe, June 5, 1831,

Howe, Curtis P., and Abigail Gleason of Mexico, Nov. 4, 1831.

Hinkley, Alanson, and Salome E. Hinds of Livermore, Mar. 3, 1832.

Howard, John A., of Mexico, and Phebe Blaisdell, June 17, 1833.

Hall, Joshua T., and Charlotte M. Elliot of Livermore, March 31, 1834.

Hoyt, Gardener G., and Laura C. Lovejoy of Andover, Nov. 30, 1834.

Howard, Asa S., and Dorcas Holt, July 9, 1836.

Hodsdon, Daniel and Mary R. Richardson, Oct. 15, 1836.

Holt, Alonzo, and Abigail Stearns of Bethel, Dec. 1, 1839.

Hinkson, Aldana, and Grace M. Elliot, Sept. 24, 1840.

Howe, Otis, and Mrs. Maria Farnum, July 10, 1843.

Howe, Otis, and Betsey B. Prescott of Chichester, N. H., Dec. 2, 1843.

Hall. Ivory W., and Lucinda E. Smith of Mexico, Dec. 2, 1843.

Hall, Jeremiah, and Betsey Adams, July 21, 1844.

Hall, Livermore R., and Mary A. Miller of Lowell, Dec. 6, 1846.

Hardy, Zebediah Jr., and Zilpha E. A. Kilgore of Newry, Feb. 2, 1847.

Howard, Asa S., and Betsey S. Roberts of Hanover, Aug. 9, 1847.

Hastings, Gideon A., of Bethel, and Dolly K. Kimball, Sept. 15, 1847.

Howe, Gilbert, of Hanover, and Sarah D. Perry, Jan. 6, 1849.

Hoyt, Patrick, and Lucy A. Farnum, Feb. 2, 1851.

Howe, John, and Mrs. Clarissa Estes of Bethel, (no date).

Hutchins, Sullivan R., and Sara E. Howe, Nov. 27, 1854.

Harlow, Samuel P., of Buckfield, and Anvolette A. Wheeler, Mar. 10, 1855.

Haverson, Bennett, and Sarah J. Hodgman, Nov. 8, 1855.

Hoyt, Nial, and Arvilla Wright of Jay, Feb. 15, 1856.

Hardy, Charles H., and Roxanna Estes of Milton Pl., March 26, 1856.

Howard, Milton R., of Hanover, and Hannah N. Holt, March 14, 1857.

Holt, Alonzo, and Polly Kimball, March 5, 1857.

Howe, John H., and Harriet E. Glines, Nov. 16, 1858.

Howe, Henry N., of Hanover, and Caroline A. Graham, Oct. 13, 1859.

Howard, Preston O., of Hanover, and Lucetta A. Abbot, Oct. 25, 1859.

Howe, John Jr., and Augusta M. Glines, Dec. 17, 1859.

Hill, Daniel R., of Lovell, and Nancy Taylor, Nov. 7, 1860.

Hall, John R., and Louisa Woods of Augusta, Nov. 8, 1860.

Hall, Henry S., and Julia E. Abbot, Jan. 24, 1862.

Howard, Asa S. Esq., and Louisa L. Stickney of Mexico, July 9, 1863.

Howard, Henry S., and Clara M. Woodbury of Sweden, Nov. 20, 1863.

Hutchins, George H., and Georgie McAllister of Andover, Jan. 5, 1864.

Huston, McKenzie A., of Roxbury, and Ophelia A. Eastman, May 6, 1865.

Hutchins, Asa B., and Julia A. Ryerson of Newry, July 2, 1866.

Harper, Wm. R., and Ellen M. Abbot, Nov. 23, 1866.

Harlow, Royal A., of Hebron, and Emma S. Silver, Apr. 1, 1867.

Hughes, Wm. H., and Mary A. Clark, Apr. 27, 1867.

Holt, Samuel W., of Hanover, and Mrs. Lovicy A. Douglass, Oct. 21, 1867.

Howard, Cyrus, and Hannah B. Johnson of Sumner, Nov. 15, 1868.

Holman, Frank, and Delia H. Abbott, Feb. 15, 1869.

Holman, Horace, and Mrs. Betsey F. Elliot, May 18, 1869.

Haynes, Wm. H., of Boston, and Lois E. Littlehale, Nov. 23, 1869.

Ingalls, Nason of Bridgton, and Polly Kimball, March 16, 1816.

Judkins, Stephen, and Mary Bunker, March 2, 1813.

Jordan, Amos M. of Andover, and Martha S. Wood, Nov. 26, 1829.

Johnson, Wm. A., of Lowell, Mass., and Lucy A. Hutchins, Dec. 7, 1846.

Kimball, John, and Hannah Martin, Nov., 1809.

Knapp, Nathan, and Phebe Farnum, Apr. 6, 1809.

Kimball, Moses, and Mary Bean, both of Bethel, Apr. 16, 1812.

Kimball, David, and Lucy W. Wheeler, of Dixfield, Feb. 2, 1817.

Kimball, Peter, of Bethel, and Sophia Wheeler.

Knight, Joseph, and Nancy Rolfe, Nov. 14, 1827.

Kennison, James R., and Fanny Putnam, Nov. 1, 1829.

Knapp, David, and Clarissa Glines, Oct. 13, 1833.

Keyes, Josiah, and Rachel Barker, Dec. 26, 1834.

Kennison, David, and Azubah Hardy, Feb. 22, 1835.

Knapp, Enoch, and Eliza Bartlett of Bethel, Oct. 23, 1835.

Kennison, John L., and Eliza N. Cook, July 4, 1837.

Kimball, Charles A., and Elizabeth Abbott, March 25, 1838.

Knapp, Albion K., and Phebe M. Graham, Sept. 16, 1838.

Kimball, James M., of Bridgton, and Arvilla Elliot, Aug. 30, 1839.

Knapp, Samuel, and Sarah Whittemore, Aug. 4, 1841.

King, S., of Monroe, and Mary Chapman, Oct. 26, 1845.

Kimball, Asa, and Geneva G. Frost, March 24, 1846.

Kidder, Burt, and Harriet C. Bartlett, Apr. 28, 1850.

Knight, Chas. P., of Woodstock, and Juliette W. Farnum, Oct. 6, 1851.

Knight. Augustus J., Woodstock, and Philadelphia M. Graham, Feb. 2, 1854.
Kimball, Adam W., and Philena J. Swain. Dec. 5, 1857.
Kennison, N. N., and Addie A. Kennison of Denmark, Sept. 28, 1861.
Kennison. Ithiel S., and Mary L. Hall. June 1. 1863.
Knowles. Isaac M., of Troy. and Lauraette V. Farnum, Nov. 17, 1864.
Kimball, Chas. M., of Bethel and Loretta S. Bartlett, Oct. 14, 1865.
Knight, Marcius F., and Ruth T. Graham, Sept. 8, 1866.
Kimball, Charles W., and Jennie M. Knapp of Hanover, Apr. 28, 1868.
Kimball, Dana L., and Rosalthia K. Philbrick, Oct. 10, 1867.
Kennison, Charles E., and Annie Bennett of Greenwood, Feb. 24, 1869.
Kennison, Charles A., and Olive A. Peverly, Sept. 8, 1869.
Killman Wm. H., of Bridgton, and Sarah S. Walker, Sept. 25, 1869.

Lufkin. Joseph, and Loruhamah Kimball, Jan. 24, 1811.
Lufkin, Samuel, and Pamelia Segar of Bethel, No. 21, 1816.
Lufkin. John, and Phebe Kimball. Nov. 16, 1821.
Libby, Jacob, of Peru, and Elizabeth Puffer, Sept. 22, 1823.
Lufkin. Aaron, of Peru. and Lucy Brown, March 12, 1825.
Little, Moody, of Colbrook, and Eunice A. Call, Nov. 1, 1828.
Lane, Henry, of Sanbornton, N. H., and Hannah Virgin, Jan. 22, 1831.
Lufkin, Eliphalet E., and Mary R. Lufkin, May 19, 1842.
Lufkin, Alfred, and Dorcas Howe, May 6, 1843.
Lufkin, Capt. Nathan, of Concord, N. H., and Elizabeth A. Howe, Aug.
　　30, 1845.
Lufkin, Orin H., and Fidelia A. Godwin, Aug. 25, 1847.
Lovejoy. Hezekiah, of Peru, and Abiah Putnam, July 6, 1849.
Lufkin, Addison. and Euphrasia Bartlett of Hanover, Jan. 6, 1854.
Lang, Wm. P., and Abigail D. Hall, Aug. 17, 1853.
Lufkin, Merrit N., and Lucy A. Kimball, March 12, 1856.
Lovejoy, Henry A., and Annie K. Morton, Jan. 21, 1858.
Leavitt. Albert, and P. C. Peabody, Aug. 4, 1860.
Leavitt, Franklin S., and Mary J. Raymond, Apr. 26. 1861.
Little, Ayres, and Rose Burges of Mexico, Dec. 26. 1863.
Lindsey, Wm.. and Margaretta Little, Dec. 26. 1863.
Ludden, Ezekiel T.. of Dixfield, and Jennie F. Eastman, Oct. 3, 1864.
Lurvey, Thos. T., of Woodstock, and Mary A. Curtis, June 29, 1865.
Lufkin, Alfred, and Caroline Hill of Northwood, N. H., Aug. 27, 1867.
Lindsey. Wm., and Lottie Hicks of Lyndon, Vt., Nov. 4, 1867.
Lovejoy, Albion B., and Mary R. Small. Oct. 3, 1868.
Lovejoy, Reuben, of Sumner, and Carrie H. Lunt, Jan. 25, 1869.
Leonard, Geo. E., of Andover, and Esther A. Elliot.

Martin, Kimball, and Rachel Godwin, Dec. 17, 1803.
Merrill, Samuel, and Polly Godwin of Livermore, Dec. 24, 1812.
Moor. Wade, and Betsey Eaton, Oct. 10, 1816.
Moody. James, and Sally Godwin, May 4, 1818.
Morse, St. Luke, and Judith Wheeler of Concord, N. H., Dec. 3, 1822.

Morgan, Samuel, of Guilford, and Milla Howard, Dec. 3, 1825.

Morse, Jesse. and Orpha Thompson, June 24, 1827.

Morse, Samuel R., and Dolly Carr, March 15, 1829.

Morse, Nahum B., and Britania Burnham, of Westbrook, Nov. 10, 1830.

Martin, Daniel, Jr., and Isabel C. Brown, Oct. 7. 1831.

Martin, Ira, and Mary Jane Howe. Sept. 27. 1833.

Martin. John, and Arvilla Abbot, Nov. 12, 1834.

Merrill, Amasa H., of Hamlin Gore, and Clarissa Elliot, June 23, 1835.

Martin, Kimball, and Lydia H. Abbott. Aug. 27, 1836.

Mansur, Warren, and Elvira M. Barnes, Feb. 11, 1837.

Mills, Wm., of Paris, and Grace B. Stevens, May 7, 1837.

Morse, Elijah, Jr., of Jay, and Lavina Silver, Feb. 3, 1839.

Moody, Wm., of No. 2, and Laura Abbot, June 10, 1824.

Monroe, Merrick, and Mrs. Betsey Burke, Oct. 15, 1843.

Martin, David G., and Sarah G. Martin, Aug. 30, 1845.

Monroe, Charles W., and Abby Kimball, Sept. 15, 1847.

Morton, Alfred, and Mary Augusta Abbot, Oct. 3, 1848.

Martin, Jonathan K., and Frances E. Willard, Apr. 14, 1850.

Moody. Josiah, of Hamlin Gore, and Mrs. Rebecca G. Martin, Aug. 18, 1850.

Morse, Charles, of Milton Pl., and Judith Hinkson, Dec. 8, 1850.

Merrill, Samuel, Jr., of Milton Pl., and Aurelia T. Poland, May 25, 1851.

Morse, Thomas, of Albany, and Mary J. Farnum, March 16, 1859.

Martin, Lyman R., and Carrie M. Knapp, Oct. 6, 1860.

Morey, Ainsworth W., of Milton Pl., and Harriet O. Ackley, Nov. 6, 1860.

Mann, Walter E., and Nancy Knight, Nov. 9, 1860.

Martin, Charles E., and Cinette E. Abbott, Nov. 19, 1860.

Martin, Edwin R., and Victoria S. Farnum, Oct. 23, 1863.

Martin, Jonathan K., and Josephine M. Stevens of E. Medway, Mass., Sept. 9, 1864.

Morton, Charles H., and Emma C. Newton, Dec. 10. 1864.

Morse, Alpheus, of Grafton, and Hannah V. Kimball, Apr. 27, 1865.

Moore, Wm. K., and Zella A. Ward of China, May 1, 1866.

Martin, Charles V., and Nancie W. Goddard of Bethel, Apr. 6, 1867.

Morse, Joseph W., of Andover, and Hattie M. Lovejoy, May 6, 1867.

Moore, Wm. K., and Abbie M. Howard, Oct. 26, 1868.

Marston, Samuel T., and Mrs. Sarah J. Adams, May 22, 1869.

Newton, Isaac, of No. 1, and Abigail Putnam, May 5, 1802.

Newton, Sylvester, and Susan Smith, April 5, 1822.

Nickerson, Esdras of Sangerville, and Mrs. Sarah Wakefield, Jan. 16. 1842.

Newton, Cyrus P., and Susan M. Mansur, Dec. 8, 1850.

Newton, Lambert P., of Andover, and Frances A. Howe, March 22, 1854.

Nelson, Chas. W., of Barnstable, Mass., and Ann M. Poland, June 2, 1862.

Nelson, Chas. W., and Amanda T. Poland, Aug. 31, 1866.

Putnam, Samuel, and Betsey Cobb of Norway, Apr. 12, 1806.

Porter, Francis, and Nancy Virgin, Nov. 13, 1809.

Puffer, Mathias, and Ruth Putnam, June 1, 1810.

Putnam, Israel, and Ruth Walton, Oct. 7, 1811.

Parker, Edward, of Hartford, and Sally Putnam, Feb. 25, 1816.

Poor, Edward L., of Andover, and Azubah Farnum, Jan. 25, 1817.

Putnam, Stephen, Jr., and Lucy Cobb of Norway, Sept. 16, 1817.

Putnam, Jacob, and Betsey Parker of N. Yarmouth, Feb. 9, 1818.

Putnam, Samuel, Jr., and Susan P. Adams, Feb. 21, 1818.

Page, Jonathan, and Ruth Eastman, Nov. 16, 1821.

Poor, Samuel, of Andover, and Asenath Farnum, Jan. 26, 1823.

Parlin, Simon, Jr., of Sumner, and Sophia Abbot, Dec. 1, 1823.

Putnam, Jesse, and Polly Keyes, January 3, 1824.

Parker, Josiah, and Keziah B. Knight, Sept. 4, 1826.

Putnam, Nehemiah, and Hannah Whitten of Concord, Dec. 30, 1826.

Putnam, Hiram, and Clarissa W. Farnum, Oct. 17, 1830.

Pierpont, Robert, of Livermore, and Mary Hemmingway, Nov. 27, 1832.

Peabody, Loammi B., and Hannah Keyes, Sept. 9. 1832.

Peabody, Loammi B., and Sally B. Graham, June 12, 1836.

Putnam, Daniel F., and Lucinda Walker of Livermore, Feb. 25, 1837.

Porter, Daniel P. Jr., of Mexico, and Rosalia Abbot, Nov. 17, 1838.

Parlin, Ira, of Weld, and Priscilla W. Hall, June 14, 1844.

Peaslee, George L., of Wilton, and Susan M. Adams, May 24, 1849.

Perry, George W., and Susan V. Abbot, Dec. 30, 1849.

Phinney, William, of Portland, and Augusta Willard, Dec. 3, 1853.

Putnam, Wm. F., and Sophia C. Abbot of Hanover, Jan. 1, 1856.

Putnam, I. Atwood, and Emily V. Bartlett, Jan. 25, 1857.

Palmona, Franc C., U. S. Navy, and Maria H. Abbot, Nov. 6, 1857.

Peabody, Franklin D., and Lucy A. Bryant, Nov. 15, 1858.

Poland, John, and Mary A. Smith, Aug. 19, 1859.

Pearson, Wm. O., of Woodstock, and Mrs. Clementine Moore, Mar. 26, 1860.

Parker, Chas. D., and Martha M. Small of Andover, March 8, 1861.

Putnam, Benj. B., and Mary A. Bisbee, Aug. 30, 1862.

Philbrick, Gilman, of Roxbury, and Rosina W. Richardson, Sept. 9. 1862.

Putnam, David F., and Clara A. Wing, May 25, 1865.

Putnam, Simeon W., of Mexico, and Abbie B. Small, Nov. 13, 1865.

Perry, Bartol H., and Lucretia Barker, March 5, 1866.

Putnam, Alfred B., of Mexico, and Maria C. Virgin, Apr. 4, 1866.

Philbrook, Henry S., of Andover, and Vienna Howe, Nov. 23, 1866.

Putnam, Francis P., and Mrs. Eunice E. Towne of Norway, Nov. 24, 1866.

Proctor, Chas. A., of Andover, and Calista W. Morey, Aug. 3, 1867.

Phinney, Wm., and Mrs. Abbie Abbott, Aug. 22, 1867.

Paine, Charles N., and Mrs. Susan Cobb, Sept. 30. 1867.

Putnam, S. T., and Caroline S. Evans, Sept. 11, 1869.

Perry, Lewis M. and Nellie A. Durfee, Nov. 8, 1869.

Rolfe, Nathaniel, and Polly Glines, Sept. 18, 1809.

Richardson, John, and Mehitable Eastman, Jan. 14, 1811.

Rolfe, John, and Betsey Abbot, Jan. 30, 1812.

Robertson, Samuel, of Bethel, and Eliza Hunting, May 12, 1813.

Rolfe, Samuel. and Eliza Hathaway of Jay, Feb. 7, 1819.

Richardson, Wm., and Polly Swain, Apr. 4, 1819.

Ripley, Joseph, and Betsey Barker, Apr. 29, 1821.

Rolfe, Henry C., and Dorcas Wheeler, March 6, 1825.

Richardson, Daniel, and Lydia Tyler, Nov. 9, 1825.

Reynolds, Edwin, of Bethel, and Mary Chamberlain, Aug. 26, 1826.

Richardson, Jeremiah, and Harriet Virgin, Jan. 3, 1830.

Rowe, Joseph, of No. 2, and Catherine Virgin, Dec. 5, 1830.

Rawson, Lyman, and Jerusha Holmes of Oxford, May 3, 1832.

Reynolds, Simeon O., and Ruhamah Ames of Hartford, Dec. 24, 1836.

Rolfe, John E., and Joanna S. Douglass, March 28, 1839.

Rolfe, Enoch C., and Emeline Small, April 26, 1839.

Richardson, Joseph, and Edith Glines, Apr. 9, 1842.

Ray, Geo. A., and Lucy C. Whittemore, Sept. 2, 1843.

Richardson, Asa, and Sarah E. Abbot, April 13, 1845.

Randall, Levi, of Peru, and Emily Washburne, May 13, 1847.

Richardson. Bradbury, of Hartford, and Mrs. D. F. Adams, Mar. 11, 1849.

Rolfe, Charles H., and Caroline H. Virgin, Nov. 13, 1852.

Rowe, Henry M., and Elizabeth S. Taylor, Apr. 25. 1853.

Richmond, Benj. F., and Eliza J. Wyman, Dec. 23, 1857.

Richardson, Chas. F., and Olivia E. Bodwell, Nov. 21, 1863.

Rowe, Chas. D., of Woodstock, and Margaret D. Farnum, Apr. 1, 1865.

Russell, Alonzo P., of E. Livermore, and Mary A. G. Richardson, Mar. 13, 1866.

Rolfe, Oscar D., and Elizabeth S. Curtis, Oct. 18, 1867.

Record, J. S., of Buckfield, and Ellen E. Abbot, Sept. 30 1869.

Richardson, Chauncy S., and Mrs. Delphina A. Parker, Oct. 9, 1869.

Stevens, Greenleaf G., and Ruth Elliot, Feb. 12, 1810.

Silver, Nathan, and Sally Swain, Jan. 14. 1815.

Stiles, Enoch, of Bridgton, and Edna Dolloff, Nov. 9, 1816.

Segar, Allen, and Elizabeth Howard, May 7, 1819.

Smith, Henry, and Dolly Marston, Sept. 20, 1819.

Swain, John, and Rebecca Richards of No. 8. Dec. 12, 1819.

Silver, Hezediah, and Lucy Virgin, March 27, 1824.

Stevens, Phineas, and Mary S. Wardwell, Dec. 30, 1824.

Stevens, Haines, and Nancy Abbot, Apr. 20, 1828.

Snow, Samuel S., and Mary S. Hoyt, Feb. 19, 1830.

Small, Andrew, and Achsa Chamberlain, Feb. 19, 1831.

Silver, James, and Sarah P. Elliot. March 20, 1831.

Swan, Isaac, of Lowell, Mass., and Nancy H. Hutchins, Oct. 2, 1831.

Silver, Daniel. and Sarah S. Baron of No. 8, July 8. 1832.

Segar. John E., and Lydia Farnum, July 29, 1832.

Small, Joseph, and Pamelia P. Dolly, Nov. 18, 1833.

Segar Allen, and Achsa Howard of Temple, N. H., Dec. 15, 1833.

Stevens, Edward, and Sybil Bean of Bethel, July 12, 1834.

Stearns, Phineas, of Bethel, and Betsey Martin, Dec. 28, 1834.

Short, Seba D., and Abbie A. Trumbull, Apr. 4, 1835.

Stevens, Benj. W., and Harriet G. Frost, Sept. 2, 1837.

Stevens, Abiel L., and Elizabeth Small, Nov. 24, 1838.

Small, Cyrus, and Lucy Ann Kimball, Dec. 8, 1838.

Stevens, Thomas J., and Lynda M. Griffith of Livermore, May 19, 1844.

Swain, Hiram R., and Elizabeth D. Kneeland of Sweden, Jan. 14, 1848.

Small, Cyrus, and Sarah Jane Thompson, Aug. 16, 1848.

Simpson, David G., and Mary M. Newton, Apr. 21, 1849.

Swain, John Jr., and Charlotte W. Kimball, Nov. 3, 1849.

Sheldon, Gardener, of Leominster, Mass., and Hannah Lufkin, Feb. 3, 1850.

Small, Dr. Joseph P., and Phebe E. Delano of Milton Pl., Apr. 8, 1852.

Stevens, Wm. F., and Susan W. Little of Colebrook, N. H., Dec. 20, 1852.

Swift, Jonathan, and Adeline D. Baker, June 16, 1853.

Silver, Geo. S., and Nancy S. Hutchins, May 28, 1856.

Stockbridge, John A., and Sarah V. W. Bolster, March 30, 1857.

Segar, Ambrose C., and Amanda A. Russell, Feb. 20, 1858.

Smith, George S., and Phebe J. Coburn, May 14, 1859.

Smith, E. C., and Lydia A. Garland of Somersworth, N. H., July 23, 1860.

Stockbridge, Columbus A., and Julia A. Howe, Jan. 23, 1861.

Swain, Loring F., and Amelia A. Glover, June 15, 1861.

Stevens, Henry, and Cervilla Abbot, June 13, 1862.

Smith, Chas. B., of Reading, and Lucy A. Abbot, Jan. 28, 1864.

Segar, John E., and Hannah Graham, Oct. 14, 1865.

Stevens, Wm. F., and Arvilla E. McCrillis, Aug. 12, 1866.

Silver, James, and Mary A. Lufkin, May 28, 1867.

Silver, Jonathan V., and Abbie L. Barker of Hanover, Jan. 6, 1868.

Spofford, Isaac G., of Milton Pl., and Mrs. Mary Woods, March 5, 1868.

Stevens, Wallace W., and Hannah O. Stetson, Jan. 2, 1869.

Thompson, Uzza, of No. 2, and Abigail Elliot, Dec. 26, 1807.

Tucker, Amos, of Peru, and Miss Lucretia Howe, Sept. 22, 1822.

Thompson, Daniel, of Westbrook, and Mahala Farnum, March 26, 1828.

Thompson, Peter A., and Wealthy Stevens, July 17, 1828.

Trumbull, Joseph, and Hannah J. Howe of No. 2, Oct. 24, 1829.

Trumbull, Luther, and Mary E. Martin, Sept. 9, 1832.

Thomas, Perez, and Mary Sampson of Hartford, Nov. 10, 1834.

Tuell, Abiathar, of Paris, and Phebe Knapp, May 14, 1837.

Taylor, Moses, and Sarah Simpson, March 17, 1841.

Thomas, Elbridge G., and Nancy Hardy, May 15, 1842.

Thomas, Elisha, and Mrs. Sally D. Wells of Vienna, Nov. 8, 1843.

Trask, Capt. Peter, of Mexico, and Betsey C. Rolfe, May 20, 1844.

Tyler, Jonathan, of Mason, and Elizabeth J. Hall, Dec. 14, 1845.

Taylor, William, and Mehitable P. Hall, Feb. 1, 1846.

Tyler, Wm., of Mason, and Sally Martin.

Thompson, John, Esq., and Elizabeth M. Eustis of Mexico, Nov. 19, 1846.

Tyler, Nathaniel H., of Mason, and Sarah M. Putnam, Sept. 23, 1848.

Taylor, Stephen, of Lisbon, N. H., and Lovina P. Abbot, July 19, 1849.

Twombly, John, of Byron, and Maria E. Eastman.

Thompson, Sewall, and Mrs. Mabel Tufts, March 17, 1854.

Taylor, William, and Mrs. Nancy Thomas, May 19, 1856.

Thomas, John L., and Rebecca B. Virgin, Dec. 29, 1856.

Thompson, John, and Sarah E. Moody, June 21, 1858.

Taylor, Jonathan C., of Roxbury, and Judith Elliot, Sept. 7, 1858.

True, Edward, of Portland, and Lucebia E. Hoyt, Feb. 16, 1859.

Taylor, Robert B., and Sarah J. T. Rowe, May 20, 1860.

Tasker, Dr. Adson, of Philadelphia, and Julia E. Abbot, Sept. 10, 1860.

Thomas, James W., and Sarah J. Silver, March 14, 1861.

Taylor, Eugene, and Rosilla E. Poland, Feb. 12, 1866.

Thompson, Eben H., of Weld, and Mrs. Mary A. Frost, March 9, 1868.

Virgin, Aaron, and Polly Farnum, Jan. 23, 1813.

Virgin, Ebenezer, and Polly Gibson of Brownfield, Apr. 2, 1813.

Virgin, Peter C., and Sally Keyes, July 24, 1813.

Virgin, Rufus, and Susan Abbot, Dec. 29, 1814.

Virgin, Jeremiah, and Persis Russell of Bethel, Nov. 7, 1817.

Virgin, Osgood E., and Clarissa Taylor of No. 7, Nov. 23, 1817.

Virgin, Levitt C., and Hannah Osgood, Nov. 28, 1819.

Virgin, Eben, and Sally Farnum, Sept. 3, 1820.

Virgin, Jonathan, and Hannah Wheeler, Aug. 31, 1828.

Virgin, Uriah H., and Mary Roberts of Wayne, Jan. 2, 1831.

Virgin, Charles E., and Diantha Virgin, Aug. 26, 1833.

Virgin, Eben M., and Ruth P. Brown, Nov. 2, 1841.

Virgin, Patrick H., and Lovina Bean, June 24, 1843.

Vosmus, Humphrey, of Readfield, and Ann A. Dammon, Jan. 15, 1854.

Virgin, Eben F., and Susan A. Austin of Mexico, Oct. 10, 1855.

Virgin, Peter C., Esq., and Mrs. Nancy Kimball, Sept. 27, 1856.

Virgin, Abbot, and Caroline H. Moody, Nov. 14, 1857.

Virgin, Albert, and Sophila W. Scott, Aug. 28, 1861.

Virgin, Hazen G., and Eliza A. Holt, Oct. 16, 1861.

Virgin, Solon, and Floretta L. Abbot, Dec. 5, 1865.

Virgin, Benj. F., and Ella J. Raymond, Jan. 16, 1866.

Virgin, Peter C. 2d, and Mrs. Sarah Hardy, Jan. 6, 1869.

Wood, Phineas, and Patty Spaulding of Chelmsford, March 22, 1802.

Winkley, John, and Triphena McAllister, July 2, 1803.

Withington, James H., of No. 1, and Sarah Adams of Andover, July 9, 1810.

Walton, Reuben, and Eunice Swain, Oct. 20, 1811.

Walton, Artemas, and Dolly McAllister, Jan. 2, 1813.

Walton, Artemas, and Abigail Stevens, Jan. 21, 1815.

Wardwell, Joseph H., and Lydia Howard of Howard's Gore, Nov. 21, 1816.

Wood, Phineas, and Elizabeth Kidder of Tewksbury, Mass., Feb. 2, 1824.

Walton, Farwell, of No. 2, and Mary Hall, Aug. 19, 1827.

Walker, John, of No. 7, and Sally Eastman, July 27, 1828.

Willard, Harvey B., and Mehitable Martin, Aug. 5, 1829.

Walker, Hyland, of Mexico, and Mariah G. Dolly, May 10, 1831.

Whitman, Zeri, and Mary Dale of Greenwood, Oct. 11, 1832.

Wyman, Alexander, and Azilla Bard, Nov. 10, 1833.

Wheeler, Philip M., and Deborah D. Hall.

Walker, Elijah, and Chastina Hinkson. Sept. 14, 1834.

Walker, Timothy, and Luna Abbot, March 28, 1835.

Washburne. Stephen. of Paris, and Mrs. Mary Howe, July 29, 1835.

Welch, Elbridge G., of Brunswick, and Elizabeth Putnam. Oct. 24, 1835.

Whittemore, Enoch, and Sarah Cole of Greenwood, Apr. 20, 1836.

Wardwell, Jeremiah, and Jeneatte Farnum Feb. 8, 1837.

Washburne, Isaac C., of Paris, and Cynthia W. Stevens. May 28. 1837.

Wakefield. Oliver, and Sally Howard, Sept. 30, 1838.

Whidden, Josiah P., of Oregon City, Ill.. and Eliza H. Godwin, Sept. 30, 1838.

Wheeler. Judah D., of Peacham, Vt.. and Dorcas F. Knapp, Dec. 31, 1840.

Whitman, Cornelius H., of Mexico, and Sarah Virgin, Nov. 26, 1841.

Whittemore, Rev. Isaac. and Mary A. Ray, June 30, 1844.

Whitman, Cornelius, of Mexico, and Nancy K. Elliot, Sept. 8, 1844.

Wright, Dr. Kendall, of Weld, and Cordelia Hall, Aug. 18, 1847.

Wilkins, Charles, of Waterborough, and Martha J. Silver, Sept. 5, 1853.

Wyman, Martin L., of Peru, and Tryphena Thomas, July 6, 1856.

Wood, Samuel H., and Sarah J. Bartlett, Dec. 10, 1856.

White, Phanuel, of Dixfield, and Mrs. Priscilla W. Parlin, Dec. 30, 1856.

Whittemore, Nathaniel, and Frances M. Abbot, Feb. 16, 1857.

Wyman, Charles K., and Martha B. Poland, May 25, 1857.

Wood, Charles E., and Harriet H. Elkins, Aug. 29, 1857.

Wood, Nathaniel, and Mary Putnam, Aug. 8, 1858.

Woods, Leonard M., and Annette G. Silver, March 13, 1861.

Washburne, Martin B., and Clara Peverly, Sept. 27, 1861.

Wood, John R., of Brooklyn, N. Y., and Louisa Rawson, Oct. 18, 1861.

Walton, Henry B.. and Clara F. Virgin, Nov. 16, 1861.

Wyman, James H., and Jennie B. Bartlett of Jay, Dec. 22, 1862.

Wing, Clark A., and Lydia A. Putnam of Franklin Pl., Aug. 29, 1863.

White, Charles E., of Boston. and Julia W. Parker, Jan. 22, 1864.

Wyman, Benj. B., and Betsey R. Hall of Peru. March 6, 1865.

Wagg, Greenleaf G., of Auburn, and Nellie C. Howe, March 22, 1866.

Walker, John J., and Cynthia L. Cobb, Dec. 8, 1866.

Wise, Geo., of Canton, and Mrs. Arvilla W. Farnum, Feb. 9, 1867.

Wing. Adelbert A.. and Eveline W. Haynes of Peru, Feb. 10, 1869.

York, Wm., and Abigail E. Dolly, Sept. 10, 1828.

York, David, and Basmuth Sweat, Dec. 13, 1826.

1870.

Jan. 22, Josiah K. Elliott, and Lucinda G. Howe.

Jan. 28, James W. Thomas, Jr., and Francis S. Pillsblon.

March 21, Tilson S. Goding, of Livermore, and D. Augusta Goddard.

Apr. 20, Ezekiel E. Jackson, and Mrs. Emily M. Blodget of Berlin. N. H.

May 21, Waldo Pettengill, and Sarah S. Briggs of Poland.

June 7, Wm. J. Coburn and Mrs. Sphronia Willey of Rumford.
June 10, Wm. G. Farnum and Caroline Lovejoy.
June 13, Orin Stevens of Woodstock, and Sarah A. Libby.
Sept. 12, Edwin F. Ray and Leonora Bodwell.
Sept. 17, James S. Morse and Lydia A. Colby.
Sept. 17, Benj. Jackson, Jr. and Sarah A. Woods.
Sept. 24, H. S. Hayes of New York, and Florence Rawson.
Nov. 30, Henry A. Libby of Leeds, Me., and Clara E. Boyinton.
Dec. 19, Chas. P. Thomas and Eliza A. Eastman.
Dec. 26, Oscar W. Royal of Paris, and Alice A. Ray.

1871.

Jan. 10, Virgil D. Fuller and Clara F. Adams.
Feb. 8, Wm. H. Wescot of Vermont, and Ora A. Grover.
March 22, Benjamin M. Rolfe and Hannah K. Searle of Newry.
March 27, Wm. H. Hemmingway of Milton Pl., and Mrs. Lucina Bryant.
Apr. 14, S. S. Jackson and Miss Mary F. Philbrick of Laconia, N. H.
Apr. 27, Chas. B. Abbott and Mrs. Betsey M. Morse of Rumford, Maine.
Apr. 28, Samuel W. Marston of Andover, and Mary A. Littlehale.
June 6, Edward Stevens and Mrs. Rebecca Morrell.
June 23, Ammi B. Mitchell and Mary S. Delano of Milton Pl.
July 8, Simon D. Mitchell of Roxbury, and Mrs. Anna A. Cushman.
July 8, John C. Graham and Caroline H. Rolfe.
July 16, Wm. H. Thurston and Salome T. Glover.
Aug. 2, Chas. R. Davis and Hattie L. Farnum.
Sept. 6, Chas H. Graham and Ella M. Swain.
Sept. 16, Chas. F. Wheeler and Mrs. Clara F. Walton of Lewiston, Me.
Sept. 19, Ezra Jewell of Woodstock, and Eliza O. Kimball.
Sept. 25, Aaron E. Stevens and Filla C. West of Newry.
Oct. 26, Henry S. Raymond and Sarah F. Richardson of Roxbury.
Nov. 23, Henry J. Abbott and Mrs. Harriet H. Morse.
Dec. 7, Stillman E. Newell of Boston, Mass., and Susie E. Martin.
Dec. 18, Walter S. Abbott and Mary G. Kimball.

1872.

Jan. 27, Timothy Hastings of Bethel, and Betsey E. Smith.
Feb. 2, Artemas Felt and Mrs. Susan Payne.
Feb. 8, Alfred C. Harding of Andover, and Mrs. Mary E. Hutchinson.
Apr. 18, David Jennings and Mary Clark.
Apr. 29, Rev. F. Grosvenor of Auburn, and P. Ellen Howe.
Apr. 29, Chas. E. Johnson and Elma E. Kenerson.
May 11, Jeremiah Curtis and Lucinda Davis of Woodstock.
June 1, Samuel Richardson and Bella S. Eastman.
Sept. 29, Farnum A. Elliott and Mrs. Eveline Burgess.
Nov. 2, Hiram Day of Hamlin's Grant, and Mary Eastman.
Nov. 20, John F. Hewey of Andover, and Katie E. Newton.

1873.

Feb. 3, Sylvester Newton and Mrs. Abigail Clemens.
June 7, Enoch Knapp and Janette B. Andrews.
Aug. 30, Ezra Soule and Charlotte A. Beard.
Sept. 14, Daniel Oldham of Peru, Me., and Diantha M. Allen.
Sept. 17, Aldana B. Bassett of Andover, and Mary A. Walker.
Sept. 29, John W. Martin and Martha E. Smith of Newry.
Dec. 1, Fred F. Bartlett and Sarah B. Swain.

1874.

July 18, James H. Turner and Jennie S. Free.
Oct. 4, Sewell Reed of Bradley and Orrissa P. Knapp.
Oct. 21, Edwin P. Smith of Hanover, Me., and Henrietta W. Abbott.
Nov. 17, Jerry O. Estes and Mrs. Mary A. Tucker.

1875.

Apr. 2, Dorington Wyman and L. R. Hawes of Peru, Maine.
Aug. 12, Lewis A. Thomas and Marianna Reed of Mexico.
Nov. 4, Augustus F. Wing and Mrs. Mary M. Delano of Peru.
Nov. 19, Granville T. Thurston and Ada E. Lufkin.
Dec. 2, Bartol H. Perry of Woodstock and Mrs. Sophrona A. Carter.
Dec. 20, Chas. O. Stinchfield of Auburn, and Sarah F. Farnum.
Dec. 27, Florus H. Bartlett and Mrs. Ellen M. Harper.

1876.

Jan. 16, Geo. G. Clay of Grand Rapids, Mich., and Hattie M. Elliott.
Feb. 3, James W. Thomas and Mrs. Cynthia L. Walker.
March 31, Wm. J. Coburn and Mrs. Ellen B. Coburn.
April 11, R. A. Barrows of Canton and Ida F. Blanchard.
July 4, Loammar A. Thomas of Mexico, and Mary A. Johnson.
Aug. 6, Fred V. Abbot and Kate C. Littlehale.
Aug. 9, Alfred E. Flagg of Harrison, and Ora A. Lovejoy.
Aug. 25, Addison Lufkin and Mrs. Etta A. Bacon.
Sept. 9, Dudley F. Roberts and Lizzie H. Trask, Salem, Mass.
Nov. 13, Geo. F. Elliott and Cora E. Putnam.
Dec. 25, Henry O. Rowe of Peru, and Laura E. Carter.

1877.

Jan. 9, Chas. A. Thwoits of Portland, and Lizzie G. Farnum.
Jan. 22, Aaron P. Hall and Fanny M. Rowe.
Jan. 23, Chas. E. Carter and Mary E. Hutchinson.
Feb. 19, Chauncey S. Richardson of Gorham, N. H., and Mrs. Ada Swift.
Feb. 20, Bartol H. Perry and Mary A. Silver.
Feb. 22, David G. Glines and Rosaltha Allen of Livermore.
Feb. 22, Frank E. Hoyt and Maria B. Stevens of Andover.
March 24, Samuel S. Wyman 2d, and Susie J. Crombie of Lewiston.

March 26, Fred A. Porter and Mary E. Green.

Apr. 23, John F. Poland of Osceola, Miss., and Olive M. Smith.

May 1, Edwin Abbott and Susan F. Stevens.

June 14, James W. Stuart and Hattie C. Sargent of Charlestown, Mass.

June 19, Thomas Richards and Mrs. Margaret D. Smith of Peru, Me.

June 23, Ronello A. Grover and Addriemore Smith.

July 19, Major Jeremiah Richardson and Mrs. M. G. Porter.

Oct. 3, Chas. H. Rowe and Emma A. Silver.

Nov. 15, Wilson Thomas and Etta M. Welch of Boston, Mass.

Oct. 16, Wilber F. S. Litchfield of Lewiston, and Florine I. Bartlett.

Dec. 20, Joseph A. Arnold and Georgianna Stevens of Winthrop.

1878.

Jan. 3, Lucius A. Glover and Isabel J. Farrar of Andover.

Jan. 28, John L. Abbott and Almeda Taylor.

Feb. 26, Geo. B. Hoyt and Sarah F. Howe.

March 4, Major Jeremiah Richardson and Sarah P. Mitchell.

Apr. 15. Chas. H. Perham of Woodstock, and Cora E. Taylor.

May 30, Marcus P. Farrar and Alvira V. Silver.

June 24, J. Ambrose Gallison of Woodstock, and Mabel M. Eastman.

July 22, Jefferson Jackson of Milton Pl., and Mrs. Drusilla F. Abbott.

Nov. 14, T. W. Childs and Mabel W. Stevens.

Nov. 27, Wm. J. Kimball and Pearl L. Farnum.

Dec. 16, Asa A. West of Andover, and Maggie A. Hoyt.

1879.

Feb. 24, Joseph L. Webster of Peru, Me., and Celia A. Twombly.

Feb. 25, Jerry H. Martin and Annie A. Elliott.

March 8, Benjamin H. Bayington and Alice S. Howe.

March 19, Fred J. Rolfe and Emma E. Hanson of Andover.

March 24, Fred F. Bartlett and Edna F. Thomas.

Apr. 5, Allen S. Bixby and Hannah M. Hall.

May 24, Asa A. Martin and Mrs. Flora E. Ripley of Bethel.

June 9, James K. P. Simpson and Georgia A. Raymond.

July 28, Chas. H. Glines and Adell E. Eastman.

Sept. 20, John H. Flagg and Olive C. Swain.

Oct. 20, Freeman E. Small and Mary E. Hoyt.

Oct. 20, R. H. Bixby and Adelaide A. Eastman.

Oct. 24, Loring H. Roberts and Francivilla T. Bartlett of Bethel.

Nov. 5, Syria C. Hodge of Canton, and Kate B. Goddard.

1880.

Jan. 26, Hiram H. Bean of Bethel, and Rozilla H. Howe.

Feb. 13, John P. Roberts and Edith E. Mardin of Madrid.

Feb. 19, Geo. A. Bontons of Boston, Mass., and Mary E. Elliott.

March 3, Cyrus Kendrick of Litchfield and Susie P. Howe.

March 31, C. M. Hutchins and Nellie S. Rawson of Paris.
July 17, Harry H. Hutchinson and Ada M. Colby.
Sept. 23, Rufus J. Virgin of Bethel, and S. M. Putnam.
Sept. 25, Benjamin S. Newton and Ella Marcella Andrews of Andover.
Nov. 16, Adelbert N. Wyman and Annie S. Safford of Turner.
Dec. 22, Nelson A. Austin and Prudence A. Grover.

1881.

Feb. 22, Fred H. Silver and Roena H. Jordan.
March 17, John Houghton of Byron, and Mrs. Catherine G. Abbott.
March 25, S. B. Jones of Paris, and Belle Clark.
July 31, Wm. S. Frost and Etta H. Smith of Bethel.
Aug. 18, Elmer E. Bennett of Grafton, and Luna J. Abbott.
Aug. 31, Fred A. Barker and Belle Lewis of Pittston.
Sept. 10, Thomas L. Weeks of Roxbury, and Jane L. Glover.
Oct. 11, Mellen E. Barker and Lilian F. Andrews.
Oct. 31, Freeland A. Knight and Huldah C. Jackson of Milton Pl.
Nov. 23, James F. Flanders and Mrs. Edna A. Glines.

1882.

Feb. 9, Geo. E. Blanchard and Alma S. Philbrick of Roxbury.
March 15, Chas. V. Knight and Sadie F. Edgecomb of Turner.
April 1, Orrin S. Dyke and Effie A. Knight of Bethel, Me.
June 7, Otis Wyman of Peru, and Emily Thompson.
June 12. Chas. B. Wing of Wayne, and Olive M. Howe.
Aug. 28, Llewellyn D. Elliot and Della L. Segar.
Oct. 25, R. F. Dillingham of Boston, Mass., and Olive B. Ripley.
Nov. 22, Fred A. Cushman of Andover, and Mrs. Alice A. Royal.
Nov. 23, Otis Howe and Mrs. Judith Rowe of Woodstock.
Dec. 9, J. B. Blethen of Bath, and Hattie B. Howe.
Dec. 11, John H. Wardwell of Andover and Lillian Eastman.

1883.

Jan. 10, Nelson Young of Hartford, and Lizzie H. Young.
March 5, Granville E. Grant and Emily Ford.
March 19, Chas. A. Andrews of Andover, and Georgie A. Howard.
March 26, D. A. Thurston and Nettie J. Peabody.
Sept. 21, Frank B. Morey and Belle R. Ford of Lewiston.
Sept. 26, John E. Stephens of Waltham, Mass., and Corey E. Swain.
Oct. 3, Edward F. Taylor and Angie Washburn of Waterford.
Nov. 9, Frank P. Abbott of Brooklyn, N. Y., and Rosalia B. Knight.
Dec. 5, Millard F. Virgin and Jennie W. Barker.

1884.

Jan. 23, Wm. L. Frost of Peru, and Ruth A. Welch.
Feb. 4, F. B. Martin and Mary L. Knapp.
Feb. 8, Nial F. Hoyt and Laura R. Swain.

Feb. 18, James D. Ripley of Paris, and Cora F. Godwin.
May 14, J. H. Halkett of Bridgton and Carrie P. Abbott.
June 26, S. R. Childs of Milton Pl., and Alice A. Webber.
Aug. 24, Joseph Cary and Almeda E. House.
Sept. 22. Melvin A. Rowe and Nettie Decker.
Oct. 6, T. H. Small and Renda A. Elliott.
Nov. 20, Amos M. Austin and Berta E. Godwin.
Dec. 19, Sheldon R. Hawes and Alice M. Chase.

1885.

Feb. 26, Joseph E. Colby and Harriet D. Abbott.
Feb. 27, Frank F. Bartlett of Hartford, and Blanche A. Abbott.
July 20, Albert Donnell of Haverhill, Mass., and Harriet C. Ray.
Aug. 11, Chas. G. Raymond and Ann O. Rooke.
Aug. 12, Wm. F. Frost of Bethel, and Ruth A. Welch.
Sept. 15, Philo B. Clark of Brooklyn, N. Y., and Laura F. Ackly.
Oct. 22, Chas. F. Lovejoy of Andover, Me., and Rebecca D. Swain.
Oct. 25, Samuel Dyke and Millie Howard of Mexico.
Nov. 16, Geo. W. Hardy of Waltham, Mass., and May Belle Farnum.
Nov. 28, Hiram A. Stone of Dixfield, and Mrs. Georgie A. Raymond.
Dec. 7, Geo. D. Houghton of Woodstock, and Mrs. Flora E. Anderson.

1886.

Jan. 2, C. R. Abbott and G. Farrar of Andover.
Feb. 8, Warren B. Thomas and Mary A. Chisholm of Brook Village, Cape Bretton.
Apr. 7, Horace F. Woods and Mary S. Silver of Washburn.
Apr. 28, Chas. H. Abbott and Lucy W. Kimball.
Apr. 29, Chas. H. Adams and Vesta A. Merrill.
May 10, Ebenezer Burgess and Thirza M. Wing.
June 18, Orrin S. Holt of Gorham, N. H., and Hannah V. Abbott.

1887.

Feb. 8, Fred A. Worthly of Mexico, Me., and Barbara O. Eastman.
May 6, Isaac Hammond and Ida O. Pettengill.
May 9, Sidney P. Howe and Jane E. Elliott.
May 27, Warren J. Doolittle of Boston, Mass., and Frances H. Martin.
Oct. 2, Wm. Thomas and Mrs. Ellen E. Taylor.
Nov. 8, Philip C. Hoyt and Mrs. Emma F. Stevens of Andover.
Nov. 14, S. F. Estes of Bethel, and Almeda F. Eastman.

1888.

Feb. 20, Joshua H. Abbot and Roxie C. Swain.
Feb. 28, Thomas B. Stevens and Lizzie Lovejoy of Milton Pl.
March 20. Wallace L. Morse and Ruth Stevens.
Apr. 2, Mathew H. Elliott and Dolly D. Howard.

May 23, Joseph A. Penley, Jr., and Annie E. Hall of Peabody, Mass.
June 12, Fred E. Seal of Lynn. Mass., and Jennie M. Farnum.
June 12, Marshall A. Howard and Mary A. Glover.
Aug. 13, Wm. A. Frye and Dora A. Harlow.
Aug. 28, Erastus B. Codding of Taunton, Mass., and Susie B. Woods.
Sept. 14, Jefferson D. Thomas and Addie R. Haynes of Peru.
Sept. 27, Fred F. Bartlett and Sadie Warhurst of Lewiston.
Oct. 9, Evans W. Hodgdon of Framingham, Mass., and Ermina A. Howe.
Oct. 13, Freeman M. Bixby and Ida C. Spofford of Milton Pl.
Nov. 19, Edward H. Record of E. Livermore, Me., and Anna N. Putnam.
Dec. 14, Geo. H. Perry of Topsham, and Mary S. Hodgdon.
Dec. 24, H. H. Gleason of Mexico, Me., and Mary E. Penley.
June 28, James H. Goodwin and Enez E. Kenerson of Bethel.

1889.

Feb. 13, Geo. H. Webber and Mrs. Lizzie E. Sawyer of Deering.
Feb. 23, Henry Banker and Hulda Merrill.

FAMILY RECORDS.

THE compiler is well aware of the imperfection of these family records, but in justification of himself, he proposes to show that the fault is not his own. As soon as it was determined to compile and publish a history of the town, blanks were prepared and a sufficient number sent to Rumford to supply every family in town. Blanks were also sent to non-resident natives of Rumford so far as their places of residence could be ascertained. During the year 1888 and the early part of 1889, over three hundred blanks were sent out to be filled, and of this number only seventy-nine have been filled and returned. In some cases, a second blank has been sent and in very many instances letters have been written, earnestly calling attention to the matter, but as a general thing, they have met with no response. Where early Rumford families have become extinct in town, the compiler has taken special pains to collect their records, and while success has in some cases crowned his efforts, in others it has not. He has had access to the records of the town, but these records are often wrong, as is evinced by the fact that they do not always agree with the records furnished by the families direct. The records of births and deaths are not, in scarcely any town, kept as the law requires. They are only recorded spasmodically and at long intervals, so that in many cases, the births in a family are left incomplete, and always remain so. From the town records that have been examined, it would seem that scarcely any record of births have been made for over twenty years, while the law requires that they be regularly and systematically kept year after year. It is a notable fact that, with all modern facilities for doing it, town records, so far as they relate to births, marriages and deaths, are not as well kept now as they were three score years ago.

The town records therefore, have furnished but little material for these genealogical sketches, and no doubt in many cases, that little will prove to be incorrect, and where families have neglected to furnish it themselves, the records are only fragmentary and sometimes of little value.   Sketches of a large portion of the very early settlers and their families will be found here, and it is in the families of the grandchildren of these settlers, still living and able to furnish the information, but have neglected to do so, that the records will be found most incomplete.   It would not be strange, and in fact it would be exactly in accordance with the experience of the compiler in similar cases, were these same persons who have neglected to furnish the information asked for, the first ones to complain of the imperfection of the records.   But these family sketches incomplete and imperfect as they are, will, in the future, be of interest, and be more frequently referred to than any other part of the book.   Such is invariably the case, and this will prove no exception.   Names are recalled here which have long been forgotten, and other names of former residents which, but for these brief pages, would soon have passed into utter oblivion.   If there had been a representative of each family to have furnished the records as they have been furnished for the Virgin family, by Chaplin Virgin, the Howes of Ellis river, by Lucretia T. Howe, and the Lufkins and Kimballs by Merrit N. Lufkin, there would have been much less cause of complaint.   These persons have responded promptly to every call for information, and have even in some cases, furnished information for families that neglected to furnish it for themselves.   In the list of those who have acted promptly in giving information should also be mentioned James S. Morse and Henry M. Colby.   All these have the grateful thanks of the compiler. The families are arranged alphabetically and where records are manifestly incomplete, the fact is generally stated that they are from the town records.

ABBOT.

The families of Abbot have been more numerous in this town than any other and are still so.   They are all of old Andover stock but came here generally by way of Concord, N. H.   Both of the Andover families are represented here, and by inter-marriages both at Concord and here, are related to many of the Rumford families not bearing this name.

Moses Abbot, son of Nathaniel and Miriam (Chandler) Abbot of Concord, N. H., and grandson of Nathaniel Abbot, an original proprietor of Concord, who married Penelope Ballard, was born June 19, 1750, and married Mary Bachelder of Loudon, N. H. Among his sons was:

John Abbot b. Sept. 6, 1779, married in 1801, Hannah Flanders, and settled in what is now Hanover.

Children:

  i *Hazen F.*, b. March 23, 1801, m. May 29, 1822. Hannah Martin of Rumford, who was born June 2, 1802.
 ii *Nancy W.*, b. May 9, 1803, Hanover.
iii *Hiram*, b. Feb. 2, 1806, m. Apr. 28, 1833, Mary Huston.
 iv *Polly*, b. Dec. 29. 1808, m. Oct. 5, 1826, Isaac Hall.
  v *John G.*, b. March 27, 1812, m. Sophia Huston.
 vi *Emily*, b. June 1814, m. 1836, Asa Ethridge of Hanover.
vii *Andrew*, b. Sept. 6, 1816, m. Penia Smith of Newry.

Hazen F. Abbot, son of John and Hannah (Flanders) Abbot, born March 23, 1801, married May 29, 1822 Hannah, daughter of Daniel Martin of Rumford. He lived and died at North Rumford.

Children:

   i *Henry M.*, b. Aug. 23, 1823, m. 1856, Arabella C. Howard.
  ii *Dolly M.*, b. Sept. 2, 1826, m. Marshall Colby.
 iii *Susan V.*, b. Oct. 29, 1827, m. Geo. W. Perry, d. Dec. 31, 1870.
  iv *Marshall F.*, b. Jan. 21, 1829, d. Oct. 2, following.
   v *Hannah A.*, b. Aug. 25, 1830, d. Nov. 17, following.
  vi *Hannah A.*, b. Aug. 23, 1832, m. Frank J. Hoyt.
 vii *Lucetta A.*, b. July 12, 1835, m. Preston O. Howard.
viii *Hazen M.*, b. Dec. 20, 1836, m. Abbie A. Martin and d. Aug. 28, 1865.

Hiram Abbot, son of John, b. Feb. 2, 1806, married Apr. 28, 1833, Mary Huston who was born in Farmington Jan. 11, 1805; moved from Charlestown, Mass., to Rumford about 1840, and was a farmer.

Children:

  i *Hannah H.*, b. Charlestown, Mass., March 2, 1834, m. Sept. 20, 1859, William Andrews.
 ii *Hiram F.*, b. June 2, 1835, m. Feb. 10, 1864, Mary J. Mansur.
iii *William W.*, b. July 5, 1837, m. Aug. 1, 1860, Harriet Philbrick.
 iv *Lucy Ann*, b. May 27, 1839, m. Feb. 1, 1864, Charles Smith, and d. Jan. 22, 1865.
  v *Edwin F.*, b. in Rumford Sept. 11, 1841, d. Dec. 1, 1844.
 vi *George*, b. Sept. 27, 1843, not married.

PHILIP ABBOT, brother of Moses preceding, and son of Nathaniel and Miriam (Chandler) Abbot, b. Feb. 4, 1757, married Feb. 10, 1791, Experience Howe who was born Apr. 1, 1771. He died April 16, 1841.

Children :

    i   *Susanna*, b. June 26, 1793, m. June 20, 1815, Rufus Virgin.
   ii   *Betsey*, b. August 10, 1795, m. Oct. 1, 1822, Joseph Baxter, Jr., of Boston.
  iii *Parna*, b. Apr. 10, 1797, d. Apr. 8, 1801.
  iv *David*, b. Feb. 5, 1799, d. July 1, 1808.
   v   *Philip*, b. Dec. 11, 1800, m. Feb. 16, 1823, widow Lueina White of Dixfield, Me. She was born May 2, 1786, and died June 24, 1841.
  vi *Levi*, b. Nov. 4, 1802, m. Feb. 4, 1825, Vashti Wheeler.
 vii *Sophia*, b. Apr. 4, 1805. m. Simeon Parlin.
viii *Chandler*, b. Oct. 10, 1807, m. Charity Durgin.
  ix *David*, b. Nov. 16, 1809.

LEVI AABOT, son of the preceding, born Nov. 4, 1802, married in 1825, Vashti, daughter of Wm. Wheeler. This family in 1850, was living in Dixfield.

Children :

    i   *Dexter D. W.*, b. July 8, 1826, m. Drusilla ———. He was the first proprietor of the Mount Zircon Mineral Spring and House. He died and his widow married Jefferson Jackson of Milton Pl.
   ii   *Sophia Scott*, b. June 17, 1828.
  iii *Victor M.*, b. Oct. 11, 1831, m. ———. He was a physician and died in Mexico.
  iv *William Wheeler*, b. Dec. 20, 1835.
   v   *Paris Baxter*, b. Dec. 18, 1843.

CHANDLER ABBOT, son of Philip and Experience (Howe) Abbot, was married first, May 31, 1831, to Charity Durgin who was born in Bowdoin, Me., Feb. 23, 1813, by Rev. Daniel Gould. She died Nov. 10, 1850, and he married second, Nov. 9, 1858, Mary E. Chadbourne, who was born in Kennebunk, May 17, 1824. He is a carpenter and farmer who resides at East Rumford.

Children :

    i   *Chloe F.*, b. June 12, 1834, m. 1856. Humphrey Ackley.
   ii   *Cynthia J.*, b. March 3, 1836, m. 1858, Charles H. Ackley.
  iii *Chelsea C.*, b. Sept. 9, 1838.
  iv *Charles L.*, b. Jan. 3, 1841, d. Aug. 29, 1858.
   v   *Charity E.*, b. Oct. 25, 1850, d. Apr. 16, 1866.

DAVID ABBOT, father of Moses and Philip and son of Nathaniel and Miriam Chandler Abbot, born Aug. 8, 1770, married Betsey Colson of Sumner, who was born in Weymouth, Mass., Aug. 8, 1780, and died Feb. 16, 1821. He married second, Betsey, widow of Isaac Knight and daughter of Jacob and Sally (Matthews) Twitchell of Paris, who survived him. He was the proprietor of Abbot's Mills, so called, on Concord river in Rumford.

Children :
  i   *Vesta*, b. Dec. 28, 1802, m. Nov., 1822, John Ackley.
  ii *Laura*, b. Aug. 12, 1804, m. William Moody.
  iii *Arvilla*, b. Dec. 30, 1807, m. Dec. 7, 1834, John Martin.
  iv *Gideon Colson*, b. Nov. 29, 1809, m. 1833, Cervilla Barker.
  v   *Luna*, b. Oct. 1, 1811, m. April, 1835, Timothy Walker.
  vi *Elizabeth*, b. May 26, 1813, m. Apr., 1837, Charles A. Kimball.
  vii *Samuel Vincent*, b. May 22, 1816, m. 1843, Mary W. Kyle.
  viii *James Webster*, b. Aug. 27, 1818, m. 1844, Ann Ritchie; resides in Northumberland, N. H.
  ix *Deban Rensalier*, b. Feb. 16, 1821, never m., d. on passage to California.

GIDEON C. ABBOT, m. Cervilla, daughter of Samuel Barker of Rumford. He was generally known as "Colson" Abbot.

Children :
  i   *Charles Lyman*, b. June 14, 1834, m. ——— Mills.
  ii *Josiah Keyes*, b. March 12, 1836, in California.
  iii *S. Emily*, b. May 4, 1839, m. Charles Martin. d. Apr. 19, 1865.
  iv *Elias Barker*, b. Nov. 25, 1841.
  v   *Cervilla*, b. Oct. 19, 1843, m. Henry Stevens.
  vi *Olive A.*, b. Dec. 29, 1846, d. Apr. 4, 1864.
  vii *Rozilla W.*, b. Oct. 24, 1849.
  viii *James W.*, b. June 9, 1853, died.
  ix *Edwin*, b. Nov. 24, 1856, m. Frances F. Stevens.

SAMUEL VINCENT ABBOT, son of David Abbot, married Mary W. Kyle. He is the well known proprietor of Abbot's Mills situated on the Concord river.

Children :
  i   *Walter S.*, b. Nov. 22, 1844, m. Mary Kimball, died in Norway Dec. 23, 1887.
  ii *Ellen M.*, b. Apr. 30, 1847, m. Florus H. Bartlett.
  iii *Fred V.*, b. May 11, 1852, m. Katie Littlehale.

JACOB ABBOT, son of Nathaniel and Betsey (Farnum) Abbot of Concord, N. H., b. Jan. 16, 1769, m. 1802, Betsey Knapp, b.

March 4, 1782. He died January 13, 1838, and she in 1831. He lived at the Falls.

Children :

  i   *Nathan*, b. Nov. 18, 1804, m. May 18, 1824, Betsey Wood.
  ii *Esther*. b. May 27, 1809, m. Jan. 14, 1844, Leander Howard.
  iii *John*, b. Aug. 14, 1813, m. Apr. 14, 1839, Charlotte Haycock.
  iv *Daniel S.*, b. Feb. 21, 1816, m. Jan. 14, 1841, Cynthia Farnum.
  v   *Betsey F.*, b. January 8, 1819, m. May 9, 1837, Peter D. Brackett.
  vi *Rosilla*, b. Jan. 9, 1822, m. May 12, 1844, Daniel Porter.
  vii *Melissa*, b. May 3, 1828.

HENRY ABBOT, brother of the preceding, born July 24, 1774, married in 1798, Susan Hall. He was by occupation a tanner, and was also a noted hunter, and lived near the Falls.

Children :

  i   *David*, b. Sept. 26, 1798, m. Azubah Morse.
  ii   *Harriet*, b. Sept. 23, 1800, m. Wesley Palmer of Hopkinton, N. H.
  iii *Jacob*, b. Aug. 28, 1802, m. Prudence Puffer.
  iv   *Judith*, b. Sept. 1, 1804, m. Trueworthy W. Chesley of Gilmanton, N. H.
  v   *Nancy*, b. Sept. 20, 1806, m. Haines Stevens.
  vi   *Susan*, b. Sept. 21, 1808, m. Mark Tarbox of Stoddard, N. H.
  vii *Stephen Hall*, b. Oct. 12, 1810, m. Sarah J. Small.
  viii *Benjamin E.*, b. Sept. 8, 1812, m. Mahala, dau. of James Godwin.
  ix   *Asa*, b. Sept. 10, 1814, m. Octavia Godwin.
  x   *Loren*, b. and d. in 1816.
  xi   *Lydia*. b. ——— 27, 1818, m. Kimball Martin, Jr.
  xii *Henry*, b. Feb. 8, 1823, m. Rebecca W. Hall, 2, Charlotte A. Waite.

DAVID ABBOT, son of Henry Abbot, married in 1821, Azubah Morse of Andover.

Children :

  i   *W Henry*, b. Jan. 13, 1822, m. Mary Ann Philbrook.
  ii *Charles B.*, b. May 29, 1826, m. Sarah E. Elliot.
  iii *Mary A.*, b. Feb. 18, 1830, m. Alfred Morton.

CHARLES B. ABBOT, son of David and Azubah (Morse) Abbot, born May 29, 1826, married June 12, 1855, Sophia, daughter of Thomas Carter Elliot. He is a farmer and lives in Rumford.

Children :

  i   *Charles Ford*, b. June 7, 1858.
  ii *Carrie P.*, b. Oct. 22, 1860, m. J. Henry Halkett.
  iii *Ella S.*, b. Sept. 22, 1864, m. Edwin A. Brown.

STEPHEN H. ABBOT, son of Henry Abbot, married Sarah J. Small.

Children :

    i *Francis M.*, b, Oct. 12, 1836. ii *Adeline L.*, b. Apr. 8, 1838; iii *Augustus W.*. b. Oct. 12, 1843; iv *Ellen E.*, b. Dec. 9, 1849.

BENJAMIN E. ABBOT married Mahala F. Godwin.

Children :

    i *Julia E.*, b. Nov. 20, 1842. ii *Floretta L.*, b. July 31, 1845. iii *Delia H.*. b. Oct. 29, 1848. iv *Mary C.*, b. Apr. 9, 1852. v *Emma R.*, b. Oct. 11. 1857. vi *Edwin E.*, b. Feb. 10, 1861.

HENRY ABBOT, JR., married first, Rozilla W., daughter of Daniel Hall, March 4, 1847. For second wife he married Charlotte, daughter of Aaron and Charlotte Waite of Dixfield, March 15, 1854. He is a farmer.

Children :

    i *Flora E.*, b. Dec. 18, 1848.
    ii *Wallace M.*, b. Oct. 4, 1852, d. Aug. 24, 1864.
    iii *Walter A.*, b. Oct. 4, 1852.
By second wife :
    iv *Carroll W.*, b. Aug. 29, 1855, m. Georgia A. Wilson, 1882. He grad-
        uated at Maine Medical School and resides in Albion.
    v *Rose A.*, b. Apr. 28, 1860.
    vi *Charles H*, b. Oct. 9, 1864, m. Lucy Kimball, 1886.

JOSEPH ABBOT, son of Daniel and Deborah (Davis) Abbot of Concord, N. H., b. May 4, 1782, married March 3, 1805, Judith Blanchard.

Children :

    i *Joshua*, b. Oct. 8, 1805, m. May 15, 1834. Charlotte Elliot.
    ii *Edward A.*, b. Aug. 12, 1807. d. same year.
    iii *Dorothy*, b. Dec. 11, 1808, m. Henry Durgin of Mexico.
    iv *Deborah*, b. Jan. 11, 1811, m. Philip M. Wheeler.
    v *Betsey*, b. March 21, 1813, m. Cyrus Elliot.
    vi *Osgood*, b. Oct. 15, 1816, m. Harriet Ackley of Lowell.
    vii *Livermore*, b. Sept. 15, 1818.
    viii *William M.*, b. Sept. 13, 1820, m. Caroline C. Kimball of Mexico.
    ix *Ivory*, b. April 20, 1822, m. Lucinda Smith of Mexico.

JEREMIAH ABBOT, twin brother of the preceding, b. May 4, 1782, m. 1st, Judith Rolfe.

Children :

    i *Daniel*, b. Aug. 12, 1805, m. Jan. 3, 1828, Sally Lovejoy.

   ii   *Mary*, b. April 6, 1807, m. Farwell Walton. Westbrook.
   iii *Lydia*, b. Sept. 30, 1808, m. Justus Austin.
   iv *Davis*, b. July 12, 1810, m. Mary Ann Patrick.
   v   *Elbridge G.*, b. March 11, 1812, m. Deborah R. Hall. He died in
        Peru, Oct. 22, 1845.
   vi *Charles*, b. Dec. 19, 1813, m. Angeline Cook.
   vii *Anna*, b. Sept. 29, 1815, d. July 14, 1816.
   viii *Lucinda*, b. March 4, 1818, m. William Adams of Andover.
   ix *Anna*, b. Apr. 20, 1820, m. June 20, 1843, James Bragg of Andover.
   x   *Simeon*, b. May 11, 1822, d. Feb. 12, 1824.
   xi *Priscilla W.*, b. July 21, 1824, m. Ira Parlin, Jr., of Weld.

DANIEL ABBOT, JR., brother of the preceding, born June 17, 1792, married June 4, 1820, Sally Johnson.

Children :

   i   *Joseph S.*, b. Nov. 16, 1821, d. March 21, 1841.
   ii *Sarah A.*, b. Sept. 26, 1823, d. May 1, 1824.
   iii *Rosilla W.*, b. Dec. 30, 1826.
   iv *Arixene S.*, b. July 5, 1830, d. March 24, 1831.
   v   *Henry S.*, b. July 20, 1833.
   vi *Mary J.*, b. March 17, 1836, d. Apr. 26, following.

EBEN ABBOT, son of John and Ruth (Lovejoy) Abbot, born Jan. 30, 1792, married Feb. 17, 1820, Catherine Farnum who was born Dec. 14, 1797. The last three children were born in Errol, N. H. Mrs. Abbot, a widow, is living in Hanover.

Children :

   i   *Horatio Nelson*, b. Nov. 29, 1820, m. Adeliza Thompson, d. 1886.
   ii *Cleopatra Paulina*, b. Feb. 3, 1822, m. Edmund Abbot.
   iii *Barzilla Cushman*, b. Feb. 22, 1824, m. Mary Hugh.
   iv *Caroline Matilda*, b. Nov. 19, 1825, m. 1853, Jesse B. Howe.
   v   *Sophia Cordelia*, b. July 15, 1827, m. Wm. F. Putnam.
   vi *Charles Robinson*, b. Feb. 12, 1830, m. 1856, Alice Jane Hutchins, and
        2d, Julia Foster. Charles R. Abbot died Apr. 29, 1877.

ENOS ABBOT, son of Enos and Sarah (Farnum) Abbot, born in Andover January 1, 1795, married Polly E., daughter of Dea. Hezekiah Hutchins of Rumford. He was a wheelwright and farmer, and lived at North Rumford. He died in Rumford Apr. 27, 1867, and she in Andover, Nov. 4, 1883.

Children :

   i *Sally E.*, b. March 16, 1823, m. Asa Richardson. ii *Hezekiah Hutchins*, b. March 18, 1825. iii *Joseph Hutchins*, b. Apr. 27, 1829.

EDMUND ABBOT, born Sept. 26, 1807, married Mary A. Rolfe who was born Dec. 14, 1809.

Children :

i *Ebediah Bartlett*, b. July 7, 1830. ii *Mary Stewart*, b. ———. iii *Bimsley Stevens*, b. March 7, 1832. iv *Miriam Rolfe*, b. March 10, 1837. v. *Helen Mariah*, b. Apr. 11, 1839.

DAVID ABBOT, 2d, married 1824, Anna Harper.

Children :

i *Galen*, b. Feb. 6, 1825. ii *Calvin Merrill*, b. Aug. 17, 1827. iii *Alanson Mellen*, b. Aug. 29, 1829. iv *David Cullen*, b. Dec. 23, 1831. v *Minerva Ann*, b. Oct. 7, 1833, d. Oct. 8, 1840. vi *Greenville*, b. Aug. 27, 1834. vii *Lansette*, b. Nov. 30, 1837, d. Oct. 22, 1840. viii *Spencer*, b. Feb. 9, 1840. ix *DeWitt Clinton*, b. Nov. 3, 1842.

WILLIAM D. ABBOT, married Catherine G———

Children :

i *Marion A.*, b. July, 1858. ii *William D.*, b. May 27, 1861. iii *Freeland D.*, b. June 26, 1863. iv *Asa E.*, b. Sept. 26, 1865, d. June 11, 1868. v *Albert P.*, b. Aug. 10, 1868, d. Feb. 8, 1874. vi *O——— G.*, b. Nov. 12, 1870. vii *Mary Eliza*, b. March 12, 1873. viii *Emma S.*, b. June 12, 1875.

PHINEAS W. ABBOT married Fanny M. Bean.

Children :

i *Lillian A.*, b. Aug. 7, 1861. ii *Belinda A.*, b. Nov. 3, 1863.

HENRY M. ABBOT married Abbie.

Children :

i *Hattie D.*, b. June 28, 1864.

ACKLEY.

SAMUEL ACKLEY, born in Boston July 17, 1763, married Elizabeth, daughter of William and Rachel (Hodgkins) Moody. He was a soldier of the Revolution, a pensioner, and lived to a great age. He came to Rumford from Danville.

Children :

i *William*, b. Dec. 12, 1792, m. Deborah Capen.
ii *Sally*. b. July 4, 1794.
iii *Samuel*, b. March 27, 1796.
iv *John*. b. Dec. 24, 1798, m. Vesta Abbot.
v *Rachel*, b. Aug. 30, 1799.
vi *Betsey*, b. July 30, 1801.

vii *James*, b. Oct. 27, 1803.

viii *Joseph*, b. March 17, 1806, d. young.

ix *Susan*, b. Apr. 12, 1809.

x *Joseph*, b. Apr. 4, 1811, m. Mary Brown.

WILLIAM ACKLEY, son of the preceding, married Deborah, daughter of Thomas Capen.

Children :

i *Thomas Jefferson*, b. March 4, 1818. ii *Sarah*, b. Jan. 22, 1820. iii *Mary*, b. Sept. ———, d. Aug. 31, 1823. iv *George W.*, b. July 26, 1824. v *William B.*, b. Nov. 21, 1827. vi *Hosea*, b. Dec. 12, 1829. vii *Ezra*, b. Sept. 29, 1831. viii *Esther*, b. Sept. 27, 1835.

JOHN ACKLEY, brother of the preceding, born Dec. 24, 1798, married Vesta Abbot, who was born Dec. 28, 1802, and died Dec. 6, 1840.

Children :

i *Betsey C.*, b. Nov. 19, 1823. ii *Maxilana*, b. Feb. 2, 1826. iii *George H.*, b. Sept. 16, 1828. iv *Arvilla*, b. June 20, 1830. v *Charles H.*, b. June 24, 1832. vi *Cynthia Maria*, b. June 20, 1836. vii *Augustus Octavus*, b. Feb. 22, 1839.

JOSEPH ACKLEY, brother of the preceding, b. 1811, married Mary Brown, who was born in 1812. He lived in Milton Plantation.

Children :

i *Benjamin F.*, b. 1840. ii *Mary E.*, b. 1841, m. Alfred W. Stearns. iii *Margaret L.*, b. 1845. iv *Joseph H.*, b. 1847. v *Octavus*, b. 1849.

ADAMS.

Adams is a very common name in England. In Wales it was early called Ap Adam, and in Scotland the name still appears as McAdam. We also have the name of Adamson, and these several names have the same signification, namely "Son of Adam." Some have claimed to have traced the family back to the early part of the thirteenth century, to a titled Ap Adam of the Welsh Marches, but much of it is spurious and especially that portion which claims to connect Henry Adams, the emigrant ancestor of President John Adams, with the Welsh nobleman. There were a dozen or more persons bearing this name of Adams who came early to New England, and some of those who bore the name of McAdam when they came, dropped the prefix and adding its equivalent s became Adams.

WILLIAM[1] ADAMS, a blockmaker, appeared in Cambridge, Mass., in 1635. In 1640, he was at Ipswich. He was a commoner in 1641, made a freeman, and was selectman of the town in 1646. Authorities differ as to the year of his death. His will was proved in Ipswich Court March 25, 1662, but no trace of the document can now be found. Nathaniel and Samuel Adams, in 1668, executed articles of agreement concerning the estate of their father, in which they speak of their mother then living, their sisters and their brother John. There is nothing on record giving the name of his wife, and his family record is incomplete. He lived in that part of ancient Ipswich called "The Hamlet," and since incorporated as Hamilton.

Children :

   i   *William*[2], b.———. m.——— Stacey.

   ii *John*[2], b. 1631, m. Rebecca ———.

   iii *Samuel*[2], b. ———, m. Mehitable Norton.

   iv *Hannah*[2], b. ———, m. Dec. 6, 1659, Francis Muncey.

   v *Mary*[2], b. ———, m. Feb. 29, 1660, Thomas French.

   vi *Nathaniel*[2], b. ——— 1641.

NATHANIEL[2] ADAMS was a prominent man in Ipswich as is shown in the fact that in the early records, the honorary title of Mr. is always prefixed to his name. He was a freeman in 1674, and united with the church in Aug. 11, 1674. He married Mercy, daughter of Thomas Dickenson of Rowley. His tombstone in the old Ipswich burying ground, bearing the following inscription is still shown :

"MR. NATHANIEL ADDAMS DIED APR. YE 11, 1715.
    IN YE 74 YEAR OF HIS AGE.
   NOW HES GON TO ETERNALL REST
   GOD WILL HIM SAFELY KEEP,
  ALTHOUGH HES BURIED IN YE DUST
   IN JESUS HE DOTH SLEEP.
 O YOU HIS CHILDREN THAT ARE LEFT
   I PRAY LET SOME BE FOUND
  THAT DO ENDEAVOR TO MAKE GOOD
   YOUR FOREGON LEADERS GROUND.
 GRAVE SAINT BEHIND THAT CANNOT FIND
   THY OLD LOVE NIGHT NOR MORN
 PRAY LOOK ABOVE FOR THERES YOUR LOVE
   SINGING WITH YE FIRST-BORN."

The children of Nathaniel and Mercy Adams were :

   i *Nathaniel*[3], b. July 11, 1670. ii *Thomas*[3], b. June 14, 1672, m.

Bethiah ———. iii *Mercy,*[3] b. Apr. I. 1674, d. young. iv *Sarah*[3], b. July 19, 1675. m. ———, Fairfield. v *William*[3], b. June 29, 1678. vi *Mercy*[3], b. March 18, 1680. m. 1st. John Smith, and 2d, Arthur Abbot. vii *Samuel*[3], b. January 29, 1682.

THOMAS[3] ADAMS, son of the preceding, lived in Ipswich and died there. His wife was Bethiah.

Children :

     i   *Bethiah*[4], b. Oct. 21, 1694, d. young.
     ii   *Sarah*[4], b. Apr. 2, 1697, m. Josiah Bishop.
     iii   *Thomas*[4], b. Aug. 31, 1699.
     iv   *Joseph*[4], b. Nov. 12, 1702.
     v   *Lydia*[4], b. Dec. 16, 1704, m. Benjamin Woodbury.
     vi   *Elizabeth*[4], b. June 22, 1707, m. Peter Lamson of Ipswich.
     vii   *Benjamin*[4], b. Apr. 22, 1710.
     viii   *Charles*[4], b. ——— 1712, m. Mary Perkins of Wenham.
     ix   *Bethiah*[4], b. ——— 1714, d. young.

THOMAS[4] ADAMS, son of the preceding, resided in Ipswich and was an active and influential citizen. He was one of the proprietors of New Ipswich, N. H., and owned five rights in the township, two of which he gave to two of his sons who settled there.

Children :

     i   *Thomas*[5], b. Feb. 15, 1723.
     ii   *Ezekiel*[5], b. Apr. 23, 1725, m. Judith Preston of Rowley.
     iii   *Ephraim*[5]. b. ———, 1726. He married Apr. 6, 1747, Lydia Kinsman and settled in New Ipswich where he was one of the foremost citizens of that town. He served in the French and Indian wars.
     iv   *Benjamin*[5], b. ———, 1728, married his cousin Priscilla Adams, and settled in New Ipswich, N. H.
     v   *Joseph*[5], b. ———, 1733, d. young.

EZEKIEL[5] ADAMS, son of the preceding, was a resident of "The Hamlet" in Ipswich and also in Beverly. In 1748, he married Judith, daughter of Nehemiah Preston of Rowley who died Aug. 19, 1793. He died Dec. 15 following.

Children :

     i   *Ezekiel Jr*[6]., b. Sept. 17, 1750. He enlisted from Ipswich, was in the battle of Concord and Lexington, and served throughout the war.
     ii   *Rachel*[6], b. Oct. 27, 1751.
     iii   *Joseph*[6], b. Nov. 6, 1753.
     iv   *Benjamin*[6], b. Dec. 15, 1755, d. 1779 in the army in New York.
     v   *Nathan*[6], b. Dec. 1, 1757, m. 1st, Betsey Poor, 2d. Mary B. Shaw.
     vi   *Stephen*[6], b. Oct. 25, 1759.

vii   *Isaac*[6], b. Oct. 10, 1761.

viii   *Judith*[6], b. Oct. 9, 1763.

ix   *Anna*[6], b. April 7, 1766, d. in Beverly.

x   *Nehemiah*[6], b. March 27, 1768.

NATHAN[6] ADAMS, son of the preceding, was a resident of Andover, Mass., and served as first lieutenant in a company raised in Andover for service in the war of the revolution. He was married at Andover Dec. 1, 1785, to Betsey, daughter of Eben Poor. He was one of the grantees and proprietors of East Andover, Me., and moved there with his family, but after a few years he sold out to Moses Merrill, and moved to Bethel. He was a cabinet-maker and much of the furniture in use by the early Andover people, was his work. While in Bethel he was chosen one of the selectmen. In 1803, he bought of the widow of John Stevens of Concord, a valuable tract of land in Rumford, next to what is now Hanover line. Here he lived until old age. He died in Mexico in 1831. For second wife he married June, 1799, Mrs. Mary Bartlett, widow of Jonathan Bartlett of Bethel, and daughter of Capt. Josiah Shaw.

Children :

i   *Eliza*[7], b. Aug. 28, 1786, d. Apr. 18, 1788.

ii   *Nathan*[7], b. Jan. 28, 1788, m. Susan Merrill.

iii   *Eliza*[7], b. Sept. 21, 1790, m. March 16, 1814, Elias Bartlett of Bethel, and d. May 26, 1815.

iv   *Charles*[7], b. Sept. 14, 1792. He was a jeweller, went to New Orleans and d. unmarried.

v   *Susan Poor*[7], b. Aug. 9, 1794, m. 1818, Samuel Putnam, Jr.

vi   *Charlotte*[7], b. Aug. 7, 1796, m. Rev. Anson Hubbard.

vii   *Isaac*[7], b. July 27, 1798, d. Oct. 25, 1799.

viii   *Harriet*[7], by second marriage, b. in Bethel Aug. 30, 1800, m. Solomon Cushman.

NATHAN[7] ADAMS, JR., was married by Rev. John Strickland, March 17, 1817, to Susan, daughter of Ezekiel Merrill who was born in Andover, Me., July 13, 1791, and was the first child of English parentage born in that town. Mr. Adams occupied the homestead in Rumford near Hanover line, until his death which occurred January 26, 1830, as the result of a fall in his barn.

Children :

i   *Milton*[8], b. Apr. 15, 1818, d. Sept. 7, 1819.

ii   *John Milton*[8], b. Sept. 22, 1819, m. 1st, Sophia E. Preble, and 2d, Adele S. Hobbs.

iii   *Charles*[8], b. July 10, 1821, d. Nov. 14, 1845, unmarried.

   iv *Nathan Emery*[8], b. Apr. 2, 1824, d. Dec. 30, 1840.
    v *Susan Merrill*[8], b. July 15, 1826, m. June 15, 1849, Dr. George L. Peaslee of Wilton, and died Dec. 16, 1871.
   vi *Henry Smith*[8], b. Aug. 7, 1828. He was a civil engineer, went to Cuba where he died of yellow fever June 2, 1854.

JOHN[7] MILTON ADAMS, son of the preceding (see sketch), married, Sept. 16, 1850, Mrs. Sophia E. (Wattles) Preble, widow of Edward E. Preble, who was a son of Commodore Edward Preble of the United States Navy. She was a native of Virginia. In 1862 they separated for incompatibility, and a divorce followed. April 18, 1867, he married Adela Sophronia, daughter of William Whitman and Sarah Farrington (Merrill) Hobbs of Norway.

Children :

   i *Susan Merrill*,[9] b. May 13, 1870.   ii *Sarah Whitman*[9], b. Feb. 3, 1874.
iii *John Milton*[9], b. June 11, 1877.   iv *Adela Hobbs*[9], b. July 20, 1880. v
Charles Henry[9], b. March 21, 1883.

ENOCH ADAMS, son of Henry and Mehitable (Emery) Adams, born in Newbury, Mass., July 20, 1752, married at Andover, Mass., Aug. 6, 1775, Sarah Bragg, who was born June 14, 1759. They were early settlers in Andover, Maine, where Mrs. Adams died July 9, 1801. He died August 19, 1819. Enoch Adams descended from Robert Adams who was early at Newbury.

Children :

    i *Enoch*, b. June 23, 1779, m. Lucy Strickland.
   ii *John Emery*, b. Dec. 5, 1780, m. Sally Moody.
  iii *Sarah*, b. Nov. 17, 1782.
   iv *Dolly*, b. Nov. 17, 1784.
    v *Joseph*, b. Apr. 4, 1788, m. Betsey Farnum.
   vi *Henry*, b. Aug. 15, 1790.
  vii *Moses*, b. June 17, 1793, m. Dorcas Farnum.
 viii *Mary*, b. May 30, 1796, m. Adam Willis of Hanover.
   ix *Samuel*, b. Sept. 7, 1798.
    x *William*, b. March 23, 1801.

ENOCH ADAMS, JR., was for a time a resident of Rumford, and in trade here, but he returned to Andover. He married Lucy, a daughter of Rev. John Strickland of Andover. Three of his children only are on record here but the following gives the family in full :

    i *Sally Bragg*, b. Aug. 19, 1808, d. Feb. 4, 1809.
   ii *Enoch Milton*, b. Jan. 12, 1810, d. Apr., 1811.

iii *William*, b. Oct. 7, 1811, m. May 15, 1838, Lucinda Hall, d. May 18, 1879.

iv *John Wesley*, b. Feb. 9, 1814, m. 1840, Euphrasia Blodgett, d. July, 1871.

v *Julia*, b. Sept. 2, 1816, m. March 3, 1835, D. B. Sawyer.

vi *Emily*, ⎰ m. N. Fickett, d. Apr. 14, 1851.
vii *Harriet*, ⎱ twins, b. Dec. 27. 1817.
        m. Simeon Shurtleff, d. in Portland, March 4, 1844.

viii *Almira*, b. May 16, 1824, m. 1851, John A. Bolster, d. Mar. 11, 1879.

ix *Mary*, b. July 12, 1826, m. 1854, J. B. Lovejoy.

x *Enoch*, b. May 21, 1829, m. Mary H. Case. He is a physician in Litchfield, Me.

xi *Dolly Farrington*, b. May 31, 1831, d. May 19, 1845.

JOHN EMERY ADAMS of Rumford married Sally Moody of Andover. He resided at the Center and had a grant for a ferry at that place. The family record is probably incomplete. He moved to Cleveland, Ohio.

Children :

i *John Emery*, b. Dec. 22, 1805. ii *Sarah Moody*, b. Feb. 9. 1808. iii *Lydia Bartlett*, b. Nov. 15, 1809.

DR. JOSEPH ADAMS, son of Enoch and Sally (Bragg) Adams of Andover, came here from Sumner. His wife was Betsey Farnum of Rumford.

Children :

i *David Farnum*, b. Standish, March 4, 1813, m. Dorcas V. Glines, d. Caribou.

ii *Erasmus Darwin*, b. Sumner Dec. 31, 1814, m. Catherine Sturgis.

iii *Maria Bartlett*, b. March 26, 1817, m. David H. Goodenow.

iv *Warren Mann*, b. June 12, 1819, m. Adrian Washburn.

v *Mabel Waite*, b. July 13, 1821, d. Sept., 1822.

vi *Henry Milgrove*, b. July 23, 1823, m. 1st, Cordelia Hill. 2d, Lottie Hill.

vii *Martha H.*, b. Aug. 29, 1825, m. Wm. W. Bolster.

viii *Mark T.*, b. Aug. 19, 1835, m. Emily L. Wardwell.

MOSES ADAMS, son of Enoch and Sally (Bragg) Adams, married Dorcas, daughter of David Farnum, who was born Sept. 12, 1799. He was a mill-wright and died in Ohio in the Autumn of 1833. His widow married Bradbury Richardson and died in Milton Plantation Jan. 20, 1873.

Children :

i *Adam Willis*, b. 1818, m. Ann M. Bean.

ii *Elias Bartlett*, b. 1822, d. 1884 unmarried.

   iii *Augustus II.*, b. Nov. 6, 1827, m. April 8, 1855, Mary A. Harriman. He resides in Haverhill, Mass., and has, 1, *Emma Isabel*, b. Feb. 11, 1856, m. E. S. Noyes; 2, *Carrie L.*, b. Nov. 22, 1858, m. Wm. M. Nichols.

ADAM W. ADAMS married Ann M. Bean.

Children:

   i *Alvin E.*, b. Apr. 18, 1847, d. July 13, 1861.
   ii *Lewis E.*, b. Jan. 10, 1849.
   iii *Helena M.*, b. Feb. 20, 1862, d. Apr. 1, 1864.
   iv *John W.*, b. Apr. 3, 1865.

WARREN M. ADAMS m. Adrian, daughter of James and Clarissa (Thomas) Washburn of Hartford. He is a blacksmith and farmer.

Children:

   i *Elmah Darwin*, b. March 18, 1847, d. Feb. 28, 1850.
   ii *Charles H.*, b. January 5, 1849, m. Vesta A. Merrill.
   iii *Clara F.*, b. July 7, 1851, m. Virgil E. Fuller.
   iv *Emma Matilda*, b. May 11, 1861, d. Feb. 21, 1862.

ANDREWS.

JEREMIAH ANDREWS was born Apr. 6, 1757, perhaps at Concord, Mass. He was among the early settlers of Temple, N. H. He was a soldier in the patriot army from the beginning of the war nearly to the end. He married in 1784, at Temple, Elizabeth Sawtelle, who was born in Shirley, Mass., January 22, 1765. Soon after his marriage he came to Bethel and died there in 1826.

Children:

   i *Hezekiah*, b. Oct. 4, 1784, m. Phebe, daughter of Samuel Kimball of Bethel.
   ii *Jeremiah*, b. May 28, 1786, m. Annie Hodsdon, s. Rumford.
   iii *William*, b. Apr. 8, 1788, m. Betsey Estes, s. Bethel.
   iv *Elizabeth*, b. Feb. 1, 1790, d. March 3, 1804.
   v *Salome*, b. Apr. 8, 1792, m. Eli Howe, s. Bethel.
   vi *Sarah*, b. Feb. 20, 1794, m. John Estes, s. Bethel.
   vii *Elsie*, b. March 12, 1796, m. Otis Howe, s. Rumford.
   viii *Amos*, b. Jan. 15, 1798, m. Hannah Bean, s. Bethel.
   ix *Huldah*, b. Feb. 21, 1801, m. Eliphas Powers.
   x *Mary*, b. January 21, 1804, m. Hosea Huntress.
   xi *Eliza*, b. July 27, 1806, m. James Estes, s. Bethel.
   xii *Julia*, b. June 18, 1809, m. Franklin Stearns, s. Hanover.
   xiii *Hannah*, b. July 20, 1812, m. Jonathan Powers, s. Hanover.

JEREMIAH ANDREWS JR., son of the preceding, resided near Rumford Point, and died in 1863. He married in 1807, Anne, daughter of Stephen Hodsdon.

Children.

    i   *Stephen H.*, b. 1810, went west.
    ii *Joseph Russell*, b. 1812, m. Mary S. Elliot, s. Rumford.
    iii *William*, b. 1815 m. Hannah H. Abbot, s. Rumford.
    iv *James H.*, b. March 19. 1821.
    v   *Julia Annie*, b. Jan. 2, 1823, d. 1870.

JOSEPH RUSSELL ANDREWS, son of the preceding, married in 1839, Mary Silver, daughter of David Elliot of Bethel, who was born March 14, 1823.

Children :

    i *David E.*, b. 1841. ii *Joseph H.*, b. 1842. iii *Charles A.*, b. 1845.
iv *George A.*, b. 1848.

ARNOLD.

SAMUEL ARNOLD married Mary ———.

Children :

    i   *Sheriba M.*, b. Roxbury, Nov., 1837, d. Feb. 27, 1858.
    ii *Samuel B.*, b. May 22. 1839.
    iii *Elizabeth M.*, b. Dec. 27, 1841.
    iv *Eunice R.*, b. March 10, 1843.
    v   *Charlotte C.*, b. Jan. 26, 1845.
    vi *Joseph A.*, b. Rumford, Aug. 10. 1846.
    vii *Martha M.*, b. Aug. 16, 1848.
    viii *Clara A.*, b. Dec. 3, 1852, d. Oct., 1853.
    ix *Edith V.*, b. Feb., 1854, d. Oct. 1854.

JOSEPH A. ARNOLD married Georgianna ———.

Children :

    i *Willard Samuel*, b. Dec. 26, 1878.

AUSTIN.

PETER AUSTIN, born at Canton Point Dec. 12, 1805, farmer, trader and Deputy Sheriff, lived in various places and died in Rumford Oct. 10, 1887, aged nearly 82 years. He married first, Fanny P. Newton of Dixfield, and second, Dec. 13, 1849, Desiah, daughter of Bailey Curtis of Freeport who was born July 19, 1819. He was a son of Amos Austin who died in Canton January 14, 1812, whose wife was Polly Macomber.

Children :

    i   *Aravesta A.*, b. Nov. 22, 1831, d. Sept. 7, 1883.
   ii *Adriann*, b. Sept. 6, 1833.
  iii *Amos*, b. March 25, 1836, d. Dec. 30, 1837.
  iv *Amanda L.*, b. Nov. 3, 1838.
   v *Frances E.*, b. May 18, 1842.
  vi *Garafello*, b. Nov. 14, 1844.
 vii *Peter L.*, b. May 16, 1847.

By second wife.

 viii *Eliza M.*, b. Jan. 16, 1851.
  ix *Amos Mozart*, b. May 16, 1853, m. Berta A. Godwin.
   x *Alzina P.*, b. Apr. 17, 1858.

AMOS MOZART AUSTIN, son of Peter Austin, married Nov. 26, 1884, Berta A., daughter of Ajalon and Sarah (Thompson) Godwin. He is a farmer and resides in Rumford.

Children :

  i *Ralph Mozart*, b. March 12, 1885. ii *Emily Elsie*, b. June 2, 1886. iii *Ellery Curtis*, b. Sept. 17, 1887.

BAKER.

OTIS BAKER of Mexico, married Melinda Silver and moved to Rumford.

Children :

  i *Adaline D.*, b. Oct. 5, 1833. ii *Nathan Silver*, b. Jan. 8, 1836. iii *Wilber J.*, b. Sept. 25, 1838, d. Sept. 7, 1862.

BARKER.

SAMUEL BARKER from Newry, married Rachel Sessions, who was born in Chatham, N. H., in 1782, and settled in Rumford near Milton line. He was the son of Benjamin and Lucy (Huse) Barker who came from Methuen, Mass., and settled in Newry.

Children :

    i *Cereilla*, b. Dec. 17, 1812, m. Gideon C. Abbot.
   ii *Elias*, b. June 6, 1814, m. Martha J. Moody.
  iii *Rachel*, b. July 18, 1816, m. Josiah Keyes.
  iv *Lucretia*, b. Nov. 7, 1818.
   v *Samuel*, b. Dec. 25, 1822.
  vi *Hazen*, b. Dec. 19, 1827, m. Dorcas F. Brooks.
 vii *Christina*, b. Oct. 24, 1829, d. June, 1832.
viii *Charles Lyman*, b. Oct. 16, 1831, d. June, 1832.
  ix *Juliette*, b. Oct. 19, 1839, m. Moses Cummings.

Elias Barker, son of the preceding, married Martha J., daughter of William and Polly (Dresser) Moody. He lived in Milton until the death of his father, when he returned to the old homestead. He is a quiet man, honest and upright, and highly respected in the community where he resides.

Children :

i *John H.,* b. Milton Pl., Feb. 26, 1837, m. Josephine Martin.

ii *Christina E.,* b. May 1, 1839, m. George H. Webber, d. May 13, 1885.

iii *Eugene A.,* b. Sept. 11, 1845, m. 1st, Maria Osborne, 2d, Mrs. Julia Brown.

iv *Frederick A.,* b. Sept. 11, 1853, m. Annie B. Lewis of Pittston.

v *Walter H.,* b. Rumford, Sept. 8, 1862.

BARTLETT.

Jonathan Bartlett, son of Ebenezer and Anna (Ball) Bartlett of Newton, Mass., born March 6, 1746, was one of the six Bartlett brothers who early settled in Bethel. He came to Bethel in 1779 in company with Nathaniel Segar and Aaron Barton. He married Mary Shaw of Fryeburg, and had three sons and one daughter, all of whom married Rumford women. Elias married first, Eliza, daughter of Nathan Adams, and second, Judith, daughter of David Farnum. Elijah married Nancy, daughter of Joshua Graham, and Samuel married Sarah, daughter of Joseph Wardwell. Anna died at the age of twenty-five, unmarried. Elias lived and died on the homestead of his father in Bethel which is still occupied by his family; Elijah also lived and died in Bethel, and Samuel lived on the south side of the river opposite the Center where his sons now live. The widow of Jonathan Bartlett became the second wife of Nathan Adams.

Samuel Bartlett, son of Jonathan Bartlett of Bethel, born Apr. 1, 1794, married July 4, 1816, Sarah L. Wardwell of Rumford, who was born Feb. 28, 1794. A sketch of him is found elsewhere.

Children :

i *Jonathan Adams,* b. Aug. 18, 1817, m. May 1, 1849, Harriet A. Glines.

ii *Joseph Wardwell,* b. Aug. 4, 1820, r. Rumford, unmarried.

iii *Harriet Cushman,* b. Jan. 3, 1825, m. June 9, 1850, Burt Kidder.

iv *Sarah J.,* b. Feb. 17, 1832, m. July 4, 1857, 1st, Samuel H. Wood, 2d, Sept. 29, 1874, Alfred Walker. She died Sept. 15, 1888. Samuel H. Wood died October 31, 1865, and Alfred Walker died in St. Louis, May 16, 1881.

JONATHAN ADAMS BARTLETT, son of the preceding, married May 1, 1842, Harriet A., daughter of Chandler Glines. He resides on the old Bartlett place opposite Rumford Center.

Children :

    i   *Rosabel R.*, b. July 20. 1843, d. 1860.
    ii *Loretta S.*, b. May 29, 1844, m. Mellen C. Kimball, r. Bethel, d. 1867.
    iii *Florus H.*, b. Dec. 29, 1846, m. Ellen Abbot.
    iv *Burneretta N.*, b. Oct. 22 1848, d. 1871.
    v   *Florine J.*, b. June 5, 1850, m. W. F. G. Litchfield, r. Revere, Mass.
    vi *Fredolin F. A.*, b. Feb. 12, 1852, m. Edna Thomas.
    vii *Everett L.*, b. Jan. 5, 1854.
    viii *Iverness*, b. May 18, 1860.

BACON.

FRANCIS A. BACON married Etta A. Hoyt. He was a trader at the Center and died there. At the time of his death he was treasurer of the town.

Children :

    i *Juna F.*, b. Apr. 30, 1859. ii *Hershel A.*, b. Dec. 19, 1861. iii *Lena E.* and iv *Luna E.*, twins, b. Aug. 11, 1865.

JOSEPH BAXTER of Boston, married Betsey, daughter of Philip Abbot.

Children :

    i *Parris Abbot*, b. May 18, 1823.

BEAN.

LUTHER BEAN, son of Josiah and Molly (Crocker) Bean of Bethel, b. 1782, married Lydia, daughter of Samuel Kimball of Bethel, b. 1784.

Children :

    i   *Lucinda*, b. Dec. 25, 1802, m. Hezekiah Hutchins, Jr.
    ii *Hannah*, b. Jan. 10, 1805.
    iii *Sybil Bartlett*, b. March 27, 1806, m. Edward E. Stevens.
    iv *Stephen*, b. Rumford May 4, 1809.
    v   *Emma*, b. Rumford May 4, 1811, m. Gilman N. Farnum, s. Milton Pl.
    vi *Maria*, b. March 21, 1813, d. Apr. 1, following.
    vii *Lovina*, b. Apr. 21, 1814, m. Patrick H. Virgin.
    viii *Clark Kimball*, b. Oct. 26, 1818.
    ix *Luther Dana*, b. Dec. 25, 1820.
    x   *Ann Maria*, b. Oct. 28, 1822.
    xi *Edmund D.*, b. Dec. 29, 1824.

xii *Aaron*, b. Oct. 28, 1826.
xiii *Lewis*, b. Apr. 29, 1828.
xiv *Franklin*, b. June 28, 1830, killed in the army.

John H. Bean married Eliza W. He was a trader. He was not a relative of the Luther Bean family.

Children :
  i *Orissa Ann*, b. June 13, 1858. ii *Oritha Nancy*, b. Apr. 20, 1860.

BEARD.

Amasa H. Beard married Charlotte A. Weaver of Franklin Plantation.

Children :
  i *William E.*, b. Dec., 1850. ii *Celona E.*, b. April 12, 1854. iii *Daniel W.*, b Feb. 19, 1856. iv *George B.*, b. May 25, 1863.

BLANCHARD.

Moses Blanchard, said to have been born in Gilmanton, N. H., was a musician and served two years in the regular infantry in the war of 1812. He married Elizabeth Wadleigh. He moved to Roxbury, Maine, and lived there many years, but died in Starks, N. H. His widow died in Rumford.

Children :
  i *David S.*, b. Apr. 7, 1809, m. 1st, Mehitable Taylor; 2d, Deborah D. Wheeler.
  ii *Benjamin H.*, b. Jan. 29, 1810. m. Mary P. Berry of Andover; d. Jan. 23 1852.
  iii *Lucy M.*, b. Dec. 22, 1819, m. George Walton, d. in Iowa.
  iv *Calvary M.*, b. Feb. 18, 1822. He married, had 6 children, died in Dummer, N. H., Sept. 18, 1872.
  v *Zebediah M.*, b. May 12, 1824.
  vi *Nicholas G.*, b. Jan. 4, 1828.
  vii *Hester Ann*, b. Sept. 25, 1830.

David Blanchard was born Apr. 7, 1807. He married Apr. 30, 1829, Mehitable, daughter of Simeon and Mary Taylor of Roxbury, who was born Oct. 14, 1808. He died January 15, 1856, and his wife died January 1, 1851. For second wife he married in November, 1851, Deborah D. Wheeler.

Children.
  i *William M.*, b. Feb. 3, 1830, m. 1st, Lydia Holt, 2d, Desire Farrar.
  ii *Maria R.*, b. July 3, 1831, m. Harvey Beckwith, r. Colorado.

 iii *Lucien M.*, b. Aug. 28, 1832, m. Abigail Bradbury, r. Minnesota.
 iv *Martha A.*, b. Oct. 8, 1834, m. Henry F. Smith.
 v *Orlando W.*, b. Oct. 7, 1836, m. 1st, Thirza A. Holt; 2, Caroline W.
  Kimball. He was an attorney at law and died in Rumford.
 vi *Mary E.*, b. March 27, 1838, m. Stephen Moore.
By second wife:
 vii *Ida F.*, b. Feb. 26, 1853, m. Ronello A. Barrows of Canton.

BENJAMIN HILL BLANCHARD, brother of the preceding, married in 1833, Mary P., daughter of Joseph and Sarah L. (Greenleaf) Berry of Andover. He kept the old red tavern at the Falls for several years and here his older children were born. He moved to Boston but returned to Mexico where he died, and his widow became the wife of Oliver P. Lang.

Children:
 i *Eliza Ann*, b. Rumford Falls, in May, 1836, d. Boston, 1846.
 ii *Henry F.*, b. Apr. 26, 1838, m. 1st, Julia A. T. Griffith and second,
  Susan J. Norcross, r. Augusta.
 iii *Stillman Berry*, b. July, 1839, d. Boston, May, 1846.
 iv *William I.*, b. Mexico, 1841, r. Santa Cruz, Cal.
 v *Stillman Berry*, b. Boston, 1846, m. Eliza Burns. He died at Bryant's
  Pond, about 1870.

WILLIAM M. BLANCHARD, b. in Roxbury, Feb. 3, 1830, married 1st, Lydia Holt and second Desire, daughter of Thomas Farrar.

Children:
 i *George E.*, b. April 6, 1856, m. Alma S. Philbrick.
 ii *David M.*, b. Aug. 3, 1858.
By second wife:
 iii *Lucien W.*, b. July 29, 1878.
 iv *Elsie M.*, b. Apr. 10, 1885.

ORLANDO W. BLANCHARD married first, Thirza A. Holt and second, Caroline W. Kimball.

Children:
 i *Lizzie M.*, b. Nov. 6, 1861.

HENRY F. BLANCHARD married first, May 1, 1859, Julia A. T. Griffith of Mexico, who died Nov. 19, 1861, and second, April 20, 1864, Susan J. Norcross of Augusta.

Children:
 i *Ernest W.*, b. Feb. 3, 1860, d. Nov. 23, 1883.
By second wife:
 ii *Harry H.*, b. Aug. 6, 1867.

F. W. Ricker

BODWELL.

SAMUEL BROWN BODWELL, born April 26, 1812, married Charity N. Jackson of Paris, who was born Sept., 1812, and died, and he married in 1855, Sarah J. Bragdon.

Children :
i *Harriet Cordelia*, b. Dec. 18, 1834.
ii *Samuel F. Q.*, b. July 5, 1843.
iii *Caroline A.*, b. Feb., 1854.
iv *Eben S.*, b. Feb. 23, 1855. d. Dec. 23, 1855.
v *Ida Ella*, b. Dec. 31, 1856.

BOLSTER.

ISAAC BOLSTER, said to have come from England, with wife Abigail, was living in Uxbridge, Mass., in 1732. His second wife was Hepsibah ———. He died Apr. 28, 1753, and his second wife died July 20, 1742.

ISAAC BOLSTER, son of Isaac and Hepsibah Bolster, born in Uxbridge, April 28, 1737, married Mary Dwinel of Sutton. He was an officer in the war of the Revolution, holding a Lieutenant's Commission and afterwards that of Captain. He was one of the minute men who marched to Concord Apr. 17, 1775. He was an early settler of Hebron and in 1784, moved to Paris where he died.

CAPT. ISAAC BOLSTER, second son of the preceding, born May 12, 1769, married March 9, 1794. Hannah, daughter Gideon Cushman of Hebron, who was born Apr. 16, 1777. He was a farmer and resided in Paris.

GEN. ALVAN BOLSTER, oldest son of the preceding, (see personal notice) born Dec. 7, 1795, came to Rumford when a young man, and married Cynthia, daughter of Col. Wm. Wheeler. He was a trader, innkeeper and farmer, and lived at East Rumford. He died Dec. 8, 1862, in Rumford, and his widow died in Poland Sept. 26, 1879.

Children.
i *Janette Wheeler*, b. June 3, 1821, m. at Thompsonville, Conn., May 28, 1845, Hiram Ricker of Poland, who with his three sons are proprietors of the famous Poland Mineral Spring. She died Sept. 23, 1883.
ii *William Wheeler*, b. July 6, 1823, m. 1st, Oct. 26, 1848, Martha Hall, daughter of Dr. Joseph Adams, and second, Aug. 17, 1868, Florence Josephine Reed, resides Auburn.

  iii   *John Q. A.*, b. Nov. 22, 1825, m. Anna Bartlett of Boston, r. Melrose. They have one child.

  iv   *Martha Virgin*, b. Sept. 18, 1828, m. Hon. John R. Pulsifer of Poland.

  v   *Mary Josephine*, b. Sept. 17, 1831, d. Sept. 10, 1859.

  vi   *Cynthia Maria.* b. July 29, 1834, m. May 5, 1856, Ira A. Nay. d. Sept. 3, 1862.

  vii   *Sarah Virgin Worcester*, b. Aug. 23, 1837, m. John A. Stockbridge.

  viii   *Alvan Augustine.* b. Oct. 1, 1841, r. New York, unmarried.

OTIS CUSHMAN BOLSTER, brother of the preceding, born in Paris, Sept. 25, 1801, was a trader at Rumford Point for many years. He married first, Oct. 28, 1827, Dolly B., daughter of Francis Keyes of Rumford, who died in 1840, and second, May 14, 1841, Maria Caroline Louise, daughter of Peter C. Virgin, Esq. He died Nov. 9, 1871.

Children :

  i   *Horatio A.*, b. Sept. 8, 1828, d. Nov. 1, 1836.

  ii   *Henrietta L.*, b. Jan. 29, 1835, d. Nov. 17, 1843.

  iii   *Mellen E.*, b. Sept. 19, 1837, m. 1st, Ann Sophia, daughter of Dr. Thomas Roberts, and second, Mary S., daughter of George Smith of Hanover.

  iv   *Freelon K.*, b. Aug. 8, 1840, d. Oct. 20, 1855.

By second wife :

  v   *Wm. Henry*, b. Apr. 17, 1844, graduated at Bowdoin College and is a minister.

  vi   *Dolly M.*, b. March 14. 1846, d. May 25, 1867.

  vii   *Norris Dayton*, b. May 22, 1850, m. Helen Morton r. South Paris.

  viii   *Sarah V.*, b. Apr. 30, 1853, m. J. Percival Richardson.

  ix   *Marietta*, b. Nov. 17, 1859, m. ——— Gilbert, r. Canton.

WILLIAM W. BOLSTER, oldest son of Gen. Alvan Bolster, married first, Martha Hall, daughter of Dr. Joseph and Betsey Farnum Adams of Rumford, and second, Florence Josephine, daughter of Col. Lewis and Mary A. (Stockbridge) Reed of Mexico.

Children ;

  i   *Clara Maria*, b. Jan. 10, 1850, m. July 20, 1868, Albion Thorn.

  ii   *Bion A.*, b. Dec. 25, 1851.

  iii   *Mary Josephine*, b. Apr. 13. 1854, m. July 31, 1876, Rev. Lauriston Reynolds.

  iv   *Alvan Joseph*, b. Dec. 20, 1855, d. Dec. 12, 1885.

  v   *Wm. Henry*, b. July 17. 1860, d. Nov. 15, 1861.

  vi   *George Frederick*, b. July 30, 1866, d. Sept. 21, following.

By second wife :

  vii   *Martha Florence*, b. June 2, 1871.

  viii   *William Wheeler*, b. Nov. 11, 1872.

MELLEN E. BOLSTER, son of Otis C. Bolster, married 1st, Ann Sophia Roberts, and second, Mary S. Smith. He is a merchant and resides in Portland.

Children :

i *Eva I.*, b. Aug. 2, 1862. ii *Hattie W.*, b. Dec. 4, 1865.
By second wife :
iii *Freelon E.*, b. March 30, 1873.

BOSWORTH.

JACOB B. BOSWORTH, born Aug. 28, 1809, married Sarah Allen, who was born Nov. 14, 1807.

Children ;

i *Daniel A.*, b. Aug. 27, 1840.

BROWN.

NATHAN BROWN'S name is on the early records. He married Sally, daughter of Jeremiah and Keziah (Blanchard) Wheeler of Concord.

Children :

i   *Lucy*, b. July 23, 1801.
ii   *Polly*, b. Jan. 15, 1803.
iii *Dorcas*, b. Aug. 8, 1805.
iv   *John Martin,* } twins, b. Sept. 17, 1807.
v   *David Farnum,* }
vi   *Dorcas*, b. Aug. 1, 1808, d. April 10, 1811.
vii *Lovina*, b. March 26, 1810.
viii *Emily*, b. January 29, 1813, d. Nov. 28, following.
ix   *Nancy*, b. Dec. 21, 1814.

BUNKER.

JOHN BUNKER was quite early in Rumford. His wife was Sally. The children from the fourth were baptized in this town but the order and dates of birth are not known.

Children :

i *Naomi Sweat*, b. Sept. 2. 1808. ii *Sophronia*, b. Nov. 26, 1809, d. June 28, 1810. iii *Jotham Sewall*, b. Sept. 30, 1811. iv *Sally White.* v *Samuel Jackson.* vi *Jonathan.* vii *Elliot.* viii *Rufus King.*

WILLIAM BURKE of Portland and wife Betsey Ward, were married June, 1837.

Children :

i *Alvan Guy Ward*, b. Apr. 29, 1838.

BURGESS.

JAMES BURGESS, born Feb. 15, 1800, married Lydia ————, who was born Apr. 7, 1803.

Children :

i *Wm. Frederick*, b. March 19, 1826. ii *James Brooks*, b. Jan. 6, 1828. iii *Sarah Wing*, b. ———— ————. iv *Achsa Russell*, b. Feb. 20, 1832. v *John Wing*, b. April 27, 1834. vi *Charles*, b. July 4, 1836.

CALDWELL.

WILLIAM H. CALDWELL married Elizabeth McAlister of Canton. For second wife, he married Melinda S. (Elliot) Moody. He now resides at Rumford Point.

Children :

i *Thomas A.*, b. June 27, 1847, r. Washington.
ii *William H.*, b. April 19, 1849, m. Lottie Park, r. Rumford.
iii *Lizzie V.*, b. May 17, 1852, r. Lynn, Mass., unmarried.
iv *Franklin P.*, b. Sept. 25, 1853, m. Alice McClinch, s. Salem, Oregon.

CAPEN.

THOMAS CAPEN married Mary, daughter of Edward and Deborah (Stevens) Abbot of Concord, N. H. He made several purchases of land in Rumford and resided here. He died at sea in 1808.

Children :

i *Ebenezer*, b. Dec. 30, 1780, m. Abigail Carter, r. Concord.
ii *James.*
iii *Timothy*, b. 1793, m. 1st. Ruth Dustin. 2d, Mary Abbot, r. Bethel.
iv *Deborah*, b. June 17, 1796, m. March 4, 1814, Wm. Ackley of Rumford.
v *Samuel.*
vi *Oliver Beal*, m. Susan Chase. r. Colebrook. N. H.
vii *Esther*, b. ————. m. Uriah Furlong of Greenwood.

CARR.

DANIEL CARR of this town married Polly Ayer of Bethel, in 1802. He was a soldier in the war of 1812, and lost an arm.

Children :

i *James*, b. April 27, 1803.
ii *Eunice*, b. April 12, 1805.
iii *Thirza*, b. June 6, 1807.
iv *Sarah Ayer*, b. March 8, 1809. He may have had other children but these alone were found on Rumford records.

CARTER.

EPHRAIM CARTER married Hannah ———. There were other Carter families in town but no records have been received. They came from Concord, N. H.

Children on Rumford records :

i *James Martin*, b. June 2. 1815. ii *Amos*, b. Oct. 2, 1817. iii *Hannah*, b. Sept. 17, 1819. iv *Lydia Moor*. b. March 19, 1823.

JAMES M. CARTER married Martha A. Waite of Peru, in 1845. Children :

i *Mary A.*, b. Aug. 25, 1846. ii *Amasa F.*, b. May 13, 1847. iii *Dorcas L.*, b. Aug. 29, 1851.

CHAMBERLAIN.

WILLIAM CHAMBERLAIN came to this town quite early and died here. He lived on the south side of and some distance from the great Androscoggin, and near the line of Milton Plantation. No family record has been found, but he is known to have had the following children :

i *Mary*, b. ———, m. Edwin Reynolds of Bethel, 1826.
ii *Achsa*, b. ———, m. Andrew Small.
iii *William*, b. ———. m. first, Desire Bisbee, and second, Tamar Cushing. He lived in Woodstock and moved from there to Biddeford.
iv *Gilbert*, b. ———, m. Belinda. daughter of Christopher Bryant of Greenwood. He was a carpenter and moved to Massachusetts, where he died.

CLEASBY.

ISAAC WALKER CLEASBY, son of Joseph and Betsey (Farnum) Cleasby, born July 20, 1787, married Polly Prescott who was born in 1790. He came to Rumford and afterward moved across the line into Milton Plantation.

Children :

i *Ira*, b. March 13, 1814, m. Minerva Ford, r. Paris.
ii *Ruth*, b. ———, 1816, m. James W. Elliot.
iii *Mary P.* m. Benj. F. Ford.
He may have had other children.

COBB.

CHURCHILL COBB, son of Ebenezer Cobb of Norway, married Pamelia Putnam.

Children :

i *Barzilla Streeter*, b. Norway, March 15, 1822.
ii *Cyrus Wilson*, b. Holderness, N. H., Dec. 17, 1825.

BARZILLA S. COBB, son of the preceding, married Susan ———.
Children :

   i   *Cynthia L.*, b. Feb. 4, 1849.
   ii *Lydia S.*, b. Apr. 2, 1852, d. May 29, 1863.
  iii *Barzilla C.*, b. Aug. 15, 1854, d. Apr. 25, 1865.
  iv *Isaac P.*, b. March 26, 1857.
   v *Lorina L.*, b. July 28, 1860, d. May 15. 1863.
  vi *Susan E.*, b. March 27, 1864.

COLBY.

JOSEPH COLBY of Concord, N. H., married Molly ———. They
lived in Concord, N. H.

Children :

   i   *Eleanor*, b. June 8, 1776.
   ii *Judith*, b. Jan. 23, 1779.
  iii *Ephraim*, b. Jan. 12, 1781, m. Burry Bartlett.
  iv *Hannah*, b. Nov. 1, 1783.
   v *Joseph*, b. Oct. 22, 1785.
  vi *Ruth*, b. Apr. 25, 1787.
 vii *David*, b. Jan. 7, 1789, m. Judith Elliot.

EPHRAIM COLBY, son of the preceding, married Burry, daughter
of Enoch Bartlett of Bethel.

Children on Rumford records :

   i *Delinda*, b. March 5. 1804.   ii *Susannah Walker*. b. Apr.5, 1805.

DAVID COLBY, brother of the preceding, born in Concord, N. H.,
June 7, 1789, married Judith Elliot who was born Sept. 8, 1791.
She was the daughter of Joseph and Lydia (Goodwin) Elliot of
Concord, N. H. Mr. Colby was living in Bethel in 1850.

Children :

   i *Joseph E.*, b. Feb. 4, 1820, m. Mary J. F. Martin. He was an officer
      in the 32 Me. Vols., and died at City Point Va., June 6, 1864.
   ii *John S.*, b. Dec. 4, 1821.
  iii *Timothy D.*, b. June 27, 1825, m. Hannah W. Martin.
  iv *Charles H.*, b. Dec. 30, 1826.

JOSEPH E. COLBY married Mary J. F. Martin. He was a prominent man in town.

Children :

   i *Henry M.*, b. July 24, 1839, m. Nancy J. Farnum.
   ii *Timothy J.*, b. Oct. 25, 1842. d. Oct. 11, 1864.
  iii *Sarah M.*, b. Nov. 13, 1845, d. Sept. 21, 1864.

iv *William P.*, b. July 11, 1855, d. Oct. 16, 1864.
v *David E.*, b. Apr. 16, 1858, d. Oct. 13, 1864.
vi *James Clark*, b. May 15. 1863, d. Oct. 24, 1887.

TIMOTHY D. COLBY married Hannah W. Martin.

Children :
i *Marianna L.*, b. Jan. 25, 1850, d. July 6, 1851.
ii *Lydia A.*, b. Oct. 24, 1854.
iii *Katie J.*, b. Dec. 17, 1856, d. July 17, 1861.
iv *Joseph E.*, b. Apr. 8. 1858.
v *Ada May*, b. Dec. 3, 1860.
vi *Jere M.*, b. Sept. 5, 1862, d. March 16, 1865.

HENRY M. COLBY, son of Joseph E. Colby, married Nancy J. Farnum. He has served as selectman and town clerk, and was a member of the Legislature. He was a short time in the second Maine band in the late war.

Children :
i *Wirt*, b. Nov. 1, 1865.

TIMOTHY J. COLBY married Burneretta.

Children :
i *Joseph E.*, b. Apr. 28, 1864.

CROCKETT.

NATHANIEL B. CROCKETT from Andover, married Lydia J., daughter of Joseph H. Wardwell. They never lived in this town, but have resided in Andover, Woodstock, Norway, Whitefield, N. H., and now in Boston, Mass.

Children :
i *Caroline W.*, b. May 12, 1851, d. Aug. 17, 1852.
ii *Kate H.*, b. July 17, 1853, m. 1873, Frank P. Brown.
iii *Mary*, b. Feb. 10, 1856.
iv *George L.*, b. Sept. 20, 1865.
v *Edd S.*, b. July 22. 1869.
vi *Harry W.*, b. Sept. 17, 1872.

CURTIS.

BAILEY CURTIS, with wife Abigail, came to Rumford from Freeport, and belonged to the Curtis families that settled early in Hanover, Mass. No records of the family have been obtained except what are found in the census of 1850 elsewhere. Bailey Curtis was then living with his parents who were quite aged.

Silas Curtis married Mary Ann ———.

Children:

i *Margaret E.*, b. Dec. 4, 1858. ii *Wm. F. S.*, b. Feb. 14, 1860.

CUSHMAN.

Gideon Cushman was born in Plympton, Mass., Nov. 21, 1750, married Ruth Shaw and moved to Hebron, Me., in 1789, and died there May 7, 1845, leaving 10 children, 70 grandchildren and 150 great-grandchildren. He was a lineal descendant of Robert Cushman, the Pilgrim.

Francis Cushman, the 8th child of the preceding, born July 28, 1789, was in Rumford in 1816; he married first, Phebe Abbot, daughter of John and Ruth (Lovejoy) Abbot. in 1815, and second, June 1, 1834, Lydia, daughter of Francis Keyes. He was a merchant at Rumford Point and died Dec. 28, 1843. His wife Lydia survived him many years, was insane and for several years in the Maine Insane Hospital. She died in Rumford.

Children, all by the second marriage:

Georgianna F., b. May 15, 1835, m. James Buckland of St. Louis.
Francis E. K., b. May 11, 1837, m. Ann A. Mitchell, d. 1871.
Caleb L. S., b. May 15, 1843, d. Nov. 23, 1843.

Solomon Cushman, son of Gideon and brother of the preceding, born in Hebron, Me., June 22, 1796, married Harriet, daughter of Nathan Adams, who was born in Bethel, Me., Aug. 30, 1800. He moved to Monson, Me.

Children:

i *Mary Ann*, b. Hebron, May 5, 1823, m. Dr. Josiah Jordan.
ii *Samuel D.*, b. Hebron, Feb. 10, 1825, m. Ann C. Burleigh of Dexter.
iii *Solomon F.*, b. Monson, May 21, 1829, m. Candace B. Packard of Monson.

Francis E. K. Cushman, son of Francis Cushman, married Ann A. Mitchell. He died in 1871.

Children:

i *Nellie*, b. Sept. 25, 1870.

DELANO.

Francis S. Delano married Phebe L. Hall.

Children on Rumford records:

i *Sarah J.*, b. Jan. 27, 1855. ii *Jeptha A.*, b. March 4, 1857.

DOLLOFF.

CHRISTIAN DOLLOFF, (or Dolhoof) was in Exeter, N. H., in 1668. Three of his grand-daughters, children of Richard Dolloff, were captured by the Indians while on their way to school in Exeter, in 1717, and were carried to Canada. The name is supposed to be Russian.

ABNER DOLLOFF was a descendant of the above-named Christian Dolloff, and by wife Miriam, had :

i *Mary*, b. Dec. 6, 1752. ii *Richard*, b. Jan. 2, 1755. iii *David*, b. January 19, 1757. iv *Phineas*, b. Apr. 11, 1759.

RICHARD DOLLOFF, son of the preceding, married Tamesin Knowlton who was born in 1765. He was a Revolutionary soldier. He died Oct. 24, 1845. She died Oct. 10, 1852. He lived on the farm now owned by James S. Morse.

Children :

i *Edna*, b. June 6, 1789, m. Enoch Stiles.
ii *John*, b. Nov. 13, 1791, m. Eunice Stiles.
iii *David*, b. Feb. 12, 1795, m. Elmira Howe, s. Errol, N. H.
iv *Marion*, b. Aug. 18, 1799, m. Curtis P. Howe.

JOHN DOLLOFF, son of Richard Dolloff, married Eunice Stiles who was born in Bridgton, Aug. 23, 1798, and died Feb. 23, 1864. He died Nov. 13, 1858. He lived near the Center and was a farmer.

Children :

i *James M.*, b. Sept. 25, 1817, m. Sarah L. Gleason.
ii *Roxanna*, b. March 17, 1819, m. J. C. French.
iii *Laura Ann*, b. July 21, 1823, m. L. R. Dresser.
iv *Miriam H.*, b. Oct. 15, 1828, m. G. C. Mills.
v *Eunice Lorinda*, b. Sept. 13, 1834, m. George Blake.
vi *Viola Estella*, b. Dec. 14, 1839, m. Freedom S. Stinchfield.

JAMES M. DOLLOFF married Sarah L. Gleason of Mexico. He long kept a public house at the Center. His wife died Jan. 12, 1872, and he moved to North Yarmouth.

Children :

i *Oscar F.*, b. Mexico, Oct. 19, 1840, m. Abby Curtis.
ii *Cuvier A.*, b. Aug. 15, 1842, d. Aug. 16, 1861.
iii *Ronello C.*, b. Rumford. Oct. 12, 1844, m. Susannah Glover.
iv *Lucetta M.*, b. Dec. 15, 1846, m. W. Brackett.
v *Quincy H.*, b. Jan. 15, 1848, d. March 22, 1850.

vi   *Francella F.*, b. March 3, 1852, m. O. Gammon.
vii *Sarah F.*, b. Aug. 2, 1855.
viii *Georgie E.*, b. March 22, 1856, d. unmarried.
ix   *Frank M.*, b. June 21, 1858, m. Cora Barton.

RONELLO C. DOLLOFF married Susannah, daughter of Livingstone Glover. He is a farmer and blacksmith, and also ferryman at the Center. He has served as postmaster.

Children:

i *Roxie S.*, b. March 31, 1867. ii *Cuvier R.*, b. July 21, 1868. iii *Charles A.*, b. March 10, 1870. iv *Alton L.*, b. Nov. 26, 1871. v *George G.*, b. Oct. 15, 1873. vi *Esther A.*, b. July 27, 1875. vii *Emma F.*, b. May 3, 1878. viii *Hattie L.*, b. Dec. 1, 1880. ix *Charles C.*, b. Aug. 13, 1883.

DOLLEY.

INCREASE DOLLEY, born in New Hampshire in 1774, moved here from Bethel. His wife was Dolly ————. He died in Milton Pl., Apr. 23, 1862, and is buried near Abbot's Mills. For second wife he married in 1824, Phebe Elliot.

Children:

i   *George*, b. June 13, 1801, d. Bethel, Apr. 1, 1804.
ii *Maria Goss*, b. Bethel, Jan. 21, 1803, d. Apr. 17, 1804.
iii *Abigail Elliot*, b. Bethel, Feb. 11, 1805, m. William York.
iv *Stephen Greenleaf*, b. Apr. 15, 1807.
v   *Mariah Goss*, b. May 16, 1809, m. Hyland Walker of Mexico.
vi *William*, b. May 11, 1816.
vii *Hannah*, b. July 1, 1813, d. Feb. 1, 1814,
viii *Pamelia Putnam*, b. March 6, 1815, m. 1833, Joseph Small.
ix *George*, b. Apr. 25, 1817, m. Lucinda Cole of Bethel.
x   *Josiah*, b. Aug. 10, 1819.

By second wife.

xi   *Benj. Elliot*, b. Jan. 10, 1825, d. Sept. 8, 1839.
xii *Hannah*, b. Oct. 3, 1829.
xiii *John*, b. Sept. 7, 1832.
xiv *Addison*, b. Aug. 20, 1835.
xv   *Louisa*, b. Feb. 24, 1838.

DWINEL.

AMOS DWINEL, born Jan. 26, 1802, son of Aaron and Abigail (True) Dwinel of Lisbon, (the family originally of Sutton, Mass.,) married Oct. 20, 1832, Sarah Sherburne, daughter of James Small, Esq., of Lisbon afterward of Rumford, and lived on the farm of his father-in-law in this town, until 1852, when he moved to Caribou. After some years, he died there, and his widow who survives, lives with her daughter in Winn. She is wonderfully vigorous for one of her age, and her memory is something marvelous.

Children :
i *Warren Small*, b. Lisbon. July 20. 1833, m. Serena Dayton of Hingham, Mass.
ii *Amos Henry*, b. June 29, 1837, m. Emma Allen.
iii *Lester*, b. Rumford, Apr. 19. 1840, m. Lydia Herrick of Auburn. He was an officer in the 15th Me. Vols., and since the war, has lived in Bangor.
iv *Ellen*, b. July 9, 1844, m. Charles C. Sawin of Livermore. They reside in Winn.

EASTMAN.

STILSON EASTMAN, son of Capt. Ebenezer Eastman of Concord, and Grandson of Capt. Ebenezer of Haverhill, Mass., born in Concord, N. H., Jan. 7, 1738, married a daughter of Capt. Nathaniel Hutchins. He was a ranger under John Stark, and was in the bloody battle at Ticonderoga in 1757, and was also a soldier in the war of the Revolution. He was at the Surrender of Burgoyne's army, and after the captured arms had been stacked, he managed to exchange his old gun for a fine Hessian rifle which is still in existence. When advanced in years, he came to Rumford where his son Caleb had already settled. Here when eighty years of age, he became converted under the preaching of Rev. Jotham Sewall and joined the church. When ninety years of age, he would ride to meeting on horseback, with his wife behind him. He died in 1837, aged nearly a hundred years.

Children :
i *Nathaniel*, b. ———, m. Elizabeth Watts.
ii *Peaslee*, b. ———, m. Dolly Graham.
iii *Caleb*, b. ———, m. March 9, 1790, Comfort Haines. s. Rumford.
iv *Theodore*, b. ———, m. Damaris Darling.
v *Amos*, b. ———.
vi *Betsey*, b. ———, m. Simeon Brackett.
vii *Ruth*, b. ———, m. ——— Weeks.

CALEB EASTMAN, son of the preceding, married Comfort Haines, March 9, 1790, and soon after came to Rumford.
Children :
i *Mehitable*, b. Apr. 15, 1791, m. 1811, John Richardson.

ii   *Haines*, b. June 25, 1793, m. 1818, Lovina Putnam.
iii *Phebe*, b. June 21, 1795, m. 1814, Benj. Elliot.
iv   *Harriet*, b. June 21, 1797, m. 1813, Levi Abbot.
v   *Hannah*, b. Nov. 28, 1799, m. 1818, George Graham.
vi   *Ruth*, b. Feb. 7, 1802, m. 1821, Jonathan Page.
vii *William*, b. Feb. 11, 1806, m. 1829, Olive Wilson of Canton.
viii *Caleb*, b. Sept. 2, 1808, m. 1828, Polly F. Whitman of Mexico.
ix   *Harmon*, b. May 20, 1811, m. Polly.

CALEB EASTMAN, JR., married Polly F. Whitman of Mexico.
Children :

i   *Daniel W.*, b. Oct. 10, 1828, d. Feb. 5, 1829.
ii   *Harriet A.*, b. Nov. 15, 1829.
iii *Elizabeth M.*, b. Aug. 24, 1832.
iv   *Sarah A. M.*, b. Apr. 18, 1834, d. Apr. 16, 1857.
v   *Daniel G.*, b. Apr. 15, 1836, m. 1864, Mrs. Rosilla J. Paine.
vi   *Freeland Holland*, b. Jan. 16, 1838, m. Nancy M. Hall.
vii *Augusta A.*, b. March 18, 1841, d. July 11, 1844.
viii *Jane F.*, b. Apr. 9, 1843, m. 1864, Ezekiel T. Ludden of Dixfield.
ix   *Almena A.*, b. Apr. 24, 1845, d. Jan. 2, 1858.
x   *Amanda A.*, b. July 15, 1847, m. 1863, Isaac P. Daily of Canton.
xi   *Ambrose A.*, b. Dec. 19, 1849.
xii *Cornelia E.*, b. May 16, 1853.
xiii *Ruth A.*, b. Apr. 15, 1855.

HARMON EASTMAN married Polly ———.
Children :

i   *Ophelia*, b. Oct. 28, 1842, m. 1865, McKenzie A. Huston of Mexico.
ii   *Arbury E.*, b. Jan. 15, 1844, m. 1866, Emma A. Twombly.
iii *Charles A.*, b. March 28, 1845.
iv   *Ella E.*, b. Aug. 10, 1848, m. George C. Eastman of Mexico.
v   *Nathaniel T.*, b. July 10, 1851.
vi   *Sarah J.*, b. Sept., 1852.
vii *Adley V.*, b. ———, d. Sept. 17, 1854.
viii *Ada M.*, b. Mexico, June, 1856.
ix   *Eva I.*, b. Rumford, Feb. 28, 1858.
x   *Harmon*, b. July 16, 1860, d. April, 1861.

HOLLAND F. EASTMAN married in 1860, Nancy M. Hall.
Children :

i   *Adelaide E. L.*, b. Dec. 4, 1864.

EATON.

OSGOOD EATON, born 1768, was among the early settlers and lived
on Eaton Hill. His wife was Bethiah Virgin of Concord, N. H.,

who was born in Concord, N. H., 1775, and died in Rumford, Dec. 18, 1857. He died July 1, 1836.

Children :

    i   *Jeremiah*, b. Concord, Jan. 1, 1794.

    ii *Betsey*, b. May 23, 1796, m. Wade Moor.

    iii *Mehitable*, b. June 21, 1798.

    iv *Climena*, b. Apr. 15, 1800, d. Oct. 18, following.

    v   *William*, b. Jan. 30, 1802.

    vi *Abial*. b. Nov. 25, 1803, m. Rhoda G. Burleigh of Gilmanton, N. H.

    vii *Osgood, Jr.*, b. ———, m. Maria L. Gale of Gilmanton, N. H., and second, Betsey Putnam.

    viii *Sylvester*, b. ———

OSGOOD EATON, JR., married 1st, Maria L. Gale of Gilmanton, N. H., who died Aug. 15, 1842. He married second, Betsey Putnam, born July 21, 1816. He died in Louisiana, July 9, 1862, member of Co. A, 12th Me. Vols.

Children.

    i *Abby G.*, b. Feb., 1834, m. Jefferson Bean.

    ii *Laura F.*, b. July 10, 1837, m. J. O. Hutchinson.

By second wife :

    iii *Henry Osgood*, b. Jan. 5, 1843. d. in Virginia, Jan. 23, 1864.

    iv *Cyrus Putnam*, b. July 11, 1845.

    v *William Edward*, b. May 4, 1849, d. Apr. 20, 1850.

    vi *Bradford Chase*, b. Apr. 5, 1853. d. Dec. 25, 1861.

CYRUS P. EATON, son of Osgood Eaton, Jr., married Mary E., daughter of Otis Howe, July 13, 1868.

Children :

    i *Frederick O.*, b. June 7, 1872. ii *Eva May*, b. Feb. 14, 1876. iii *Sarah E.*, b. Sept. 5, 1879.

ELLIOT.

JOSEPH ELLIOT of Newton, married Lydia Goodwin, and moved from Newton, Mass., to Concord, N. H., in 1778.

Children :

    i   *Sally*, b. ———, m. Hezekiah Hutchins.

    ii *Polly*, b. ———, m. Leonard Whitney.

    iii *David*, b. ———, m. Mehitable Farnum.

    iv *Joseph*, b. ———, m. Dorcas Farnum.

    v *Frederick*, b. ———, m. Nancy Colby.

    vi *Benjamin*, b. Apr. 20, 1789.

    vii *Samuel*, b. ———, m. Emma Sargent.

    viii *Judith*, b. ———, m. David Colby.

    ix *Eleanor*, b. ———, m. Jacob Lufkin.

    x *Lydia*, b. ———, m. Nathaniel Simpson.

BENJAMIN ELLIOT, an early settler of Rumford, came from Concord, N. H. His wife was Abigail Webster.

Children :

     i   *Sarah*, b. March 1, 1773, m. Stephen Putnam, Jr.

     ii   *Elizabeth* or *Betsey*, b. Sept. 7, 1775, m. James C. Harper, s. Rumford.

     iii   *Cotton*, b. March 7, 1778, m. Gratia Moor, d. May 5, 1860.

     iv   *Dorothy*, b. Sept. 14, 1780.

     v   *Benjamin*, b. March 3, 1784, d. May 6, 1784.

     vi   *Abigail*, b. May 13, 1785.

     vii   *Ruth*, b. Jan. 28, 1790, m. 1810, Greenleaf G. Stevens.

     viii   *Benjamin*, b. Feb. 18, 1793, m. 1814, Mehitable Eastman.

     ix   *David*, b. April 10, 1797, m. 1818, Polly Silver.

COTTON ELLIOT, oldest son of the preceding, was married May 5, 1801, by Gustavus A. Goss, Esq., to Miss Gratia, daughter of Aaron Moor of Rumford. He died May 5, 1860, and she Oct. 5, 1869.

Children :

     i   *Aaron Moor*, b. Aug. 10, 1802, m. 1827, Susan Farnum.

     ii   *Thomas Carter*, b. Dec. 24, 1807, m. 1832, Philena Cragin of Westmoreland, N. H.

     iii   *Cyrus*, b. May 29, 1810, m. 1833, Betsey Rolfe Hall.

     iv   *Sarah P.*, b. May 19, 1812, m. James Silver.

     v   *Clarissa*, b. Aug. 30, 1813, m. Amasa H. Merrill, r. Bridgton.

     vi   *Dolly*, b. July 29, 1815, m. James S. Smith.

     vii   *Arrilla*, b. May 29, 1818, m. James M. Kimball, r. Portland.

     viii   *Gratia, M.*, b. ———, m. Aldana Hinkson.

     ix   *Cotton Jr.*, b. Apr. 4, 1821, m. Lovina Keyes.

     x   *Betsey*, b. ———, m. Wm. Munro Morse.

     xi   *Benjamin*, b. ———.

THOMAS CARTER ELLIOT, second son of Cotton Elliot, married May 10, 1831, Philena, daughter of Leonard and Margaret Cragin, who was born in New Ipswich, N. H.

Children :

     i   *Sophia*, b. June 7, 1833, m. Charles Abbot.

     ii   *Leonard D.*, b. Feb. 14, 1836, m. Eliza Moody.

     iii   *Edward F.*, b. Apr. 18, 1839, m. Clara Myra Libby of Standish.

     iv   *Frank Q.*, b. May 20, 1843, m. Clara Dudley.

     v   *Ann Maria*, b. July 7, 1845, d. Nov. 16, 1846.

     vi   *Aaron*, b. Sept. 11, 1848, d. Aug. 25, 1882.

     vii   *Harriet M.*, b. Sept. 24, 1852, m. George G. Clay.

DAVID ELLIOT married Polly. daughter of Nathan Silver. He lived several years in Bethel, on what has since been called the Hezekiah Hutchins farm.

Children :

    i   *Vienna Abbot*, b. July 31, 1818.
    ii   *Nathan Woodbury*, b. March 25, 1819, m. Lydia M. Carter.
    iii *David Carter*, b. March 14, 1821, m. Sarah E. Putnam, 2d, Ann Carr,
         3d, Frances Estes.
    iv   *Mary Silver*, b. March 14, 1823, m. Joseph R. Andrews.
    v   Infant, b. Apr. 19. 1825, d.
    vi   *Sarah Stevens*, b. June 23. 1826, m. Otis Howe.
    vii *Melinda S.*, b. Nov. 29, 1828, m. 1st, Nahum P. Moody ; 2d, Wm.
         H. Caldwell.
    viii *Benjamin W.*, b. May 23, 1835, m. Maria Lufkin.

AARON M. ELLIOT married Susan Farnum.

Children :

    i   *Catherine Miranda*, b. Feb. 13, 1828, d. Aug. 23, 1832.
    ii   *Russell Wheeler*, b. June 15, 1832, d. Aug. 17, 1832.
    iii *Benj. Russell*, b. Aug. 28, 1833.
    iv   *Farnum Austin*, b. June 4, 1837.

CYRUS ELLIOT married Betsey R. Hall.

Children :

    i   Infant son, b. Nov. 11, 1834, d. Nov. 22. following.
    ii   *Delphina H.*, b. Apr. 18, 1833, d. 1858.
    iii *Caroline V.*, b. Apr. 9, 1838.
    iv   *Harriet D.*, b. Dec. 10, 1843, d. Dec. 26, 1845.
    v   *Cyrus A.*, b. Dec. 26, 1847, d. Feb. 12, 1850.
    vi   *Lizzie E.*, b. July 6, 1852.
    vii *Ada M.*, b. June 6, 1855.

COTTON ELLIOT, JR., married Lovina B., daughter of Sampson and Mehitable Keyes of Wilton, Me., June 21, 1846. He is a farmer and resides in Rumford.

Children :

    i   *Charlotte F.*, b. July 17, 1847, d. May 13, 1849.
    ii   *George F.*, b. Nov. 1, 1850, m. Oct. 21, 1876, Cora E. Putnam.
    iii *Dana K.*, b. July 4, 1858.

NATHAN W. ELLIOT married Lydia M. Carter.

Children :

    i *Hannah M.*, b. June 10, 1850. ii *Emma A.*, b. January 22, 1852. iii
Amos C., b. May 19, 1854. iv *Ann S.*, b. Dec. 8, 1855.

Davɪᴅ E. Elliot, son of David Elliot, married 1st, Ann Carr of Connecticut, and 2d, Aurelia Lufkin of Mexico. For 3d wife, he married Frances, daughter of Richard Estes of Bethel.

Children :

i *Llewellyn D.*, b. Feb. 8, 1854. ii *James C.*, b. Apr. 25, 1855.

By second wife :

iii *Charles V.*, b. Oct. 3, 1859.

George F. Elliot married Cora E————

Children :

i *Edith V.*, b. Nov. 16, 1879. ii *Lee W.*, b. Apr. 8, 1884.

Charles E. Elliot married Sophronia ————.

Children :

i *Charles E.*, b. Nov. 6, 1853. ii *Lauraetta M.*, b. Aug. 10, 1857.

Joseph Webster Elliot married Ruth Cleasby. He lived near Abbot's Mills. He was a Justice of the Peace and Trial Justice and well versed in legal affairs. He died suddenly.

Children :

i *Abby M.*, b. Apr. 30, 1846, d. Dec. 11, 1862.

ii *James P.*, b. May 18, 1848.

iii *Alonzo W.*, b. March 23, 1855, d. March 24, 1856.

Jacob Elliot, another branch of the Elliot family from those preceding, son of Jonathan and Mary (Conner) Elliot, born in Pembroke, N. H., Apr. 16, 1784, came to Rumford in the winter of 1843-4 and bought a farm of Joel Howe, on the west side of Ellis river. He died January 13, 1869, and his wife died March 3, 1863. Her name was Betsey Gault, born in Hooksett, N. H.

Children :

i *Jacob G.*, b. Pembroke, Aug. 14, 1814, m. Betsey Moor, d. 1854.

ii *William*, b. June 7, 1817, m. Sept. 20, 1849, Charlotte K. Howe.

iii *Mary E.*, b. May 17, 1821, m. John C. Dearborn.

iv *Josiah Kittredge*, b. March 18, 1826, m. 1st, Mary Ann K. Estes, 2d, Lucinda G. Howe.

v *John Emery*, b. Feb. 12, 1828, m. 1st, Sarah Augusta Martin, 2d, Martha Brown.

vi *Matthew Gault*, b. Feb. 2, 1833, m. Gabrielle M. Wilson, d. in Minneapolis, Minn.

William Elliot, son of the preceding, went to California in

1850, but returned and settled on the Timothy Holt farm. He married Charlotte K. Howe. Mrs. Elliot died Dec. 28, 1885.

Children :

i *William Lucien*, b. March 31, 1853. ii *Mary E.*, b. July 11, 1854. iii *Edmund H.*, b. Dec. 16, 1855. iv *Charlotte T. M.*, b. Jan. 9, 1857. v *Maranda A.*, b. Aug. 19, 1860. vi *Nellie*, b. Apr. 16, 1862, d. Aug. 4, 1864. vii *Isabel*. viii *John J.*, b. Sept. 5, 1867. ix *Harrison G.*, b. Dec. 12, 1874.

JOSIAH KITTREDGE ELLIOT, brother of the preceding, married first, December 10, 1856, Mary Ann Kimball, daughter of Eli and Clarissa (Kimball) Estes of Bethel, who died Dec. 26, 1868, and second, Feb. 3d, 1870, Lucinda G., daughter of John and Nancy (Kimball) Howe of Rumford. He is a farmer and lives on the west side of Ellis river.

Children :

i *Augustus M.*, b. Oct. 18, 1858, d. Aug. 6, 1880.

ii *Clara E.*, b. Aug. 16, 1860.

iii *Matthew H.*, b. Aug. 27, 1863. m. Dorothy D. Howard.

By second wife :

iv *Pearl M.*, b. Jan. 17, 1872.

v *Gabriella W.*, b. Sept. 5. 1873.

vi *Kate Howe*, b. Jan. 11, 1875.

vii *Dwight K.*, b. March 21, 1876.

viii *Samuel*, b. July 20, 1878.

JOHN E. ELLIOT is a farmer and resides on the old homestead of his father. He married first, Sarah Augusta, daughter of Dea. Henry Martin, and second, Martha Brown of Byron.

Children :

i *Ann Augusta*, b. Sept. 16, 1852. m. Jerry H. Martin.

ii *Jacob Henry*, b. Feb. 28, 1856, m. Isabella M. Phelps.

iii *Dayton W.*, b. May 12, 1860.

iv *Jane Emery*, b. Nov. 24, 1865. m. Sidney P. Howe,

v *Ellen Gault*, b. March 19, 1869. d. Sept. 18, 1872.

vi *John William*, b. July 22, 1873.

vii *George Matthew*, b. Jan. 27, 1877.

ESTES.

STEPHEN ESTES, son of Daniel Estes of Shapleigh, came to this section, and finally bought of Phineas Howard a lot of land in Howard's Gore, the one afterwards owned by Ezra Smith. He married Relief, daughter of Enoch and Elizabeth (Segar) Bartlett of Newry, who was born in Newton, Mass., May 2d, 1769.

JOHN ESTES, son of the preceding, for a few years owned and operated the ferry at Rumford Point. He sold out and moved to Bethel where he lived many years, but died in Greenwood. He married Sarah, daughter of Jeremiah and Elizabeth (Sawtelle) Andrews of Bethel.

Children :

i *Hiram Cushman,* b. July 27, 1823, m. Sophia B. Foster of Bethel. He graduated at Colby University, and is a Baptist clergyman in Massachusetts.

ii *Huldah Andrews,* b. Dec. 20, 1825, d. Sept. 11, 1829.

iii *James Henry,* b. Dec. 7, 1827. m. first, Ann Stevens, and second, Mrs. Rebecca Reed, daughter of Daniel Estes, r. Greenwood.

iv *Charles Francis.* b. ———. 1831, d. in California.

EUSTIS.

JOHN MASON EUSTIS, son of Joseph and Sarah Mason Eustis, born May 30, 1800, married in 1823, Anna Trask. He lived only a few years in this town ; he died in Dixfield.

Children :

i *Susan M.,* b. June 21, 1824, d. Dec. 17, 1826.

ii *Isabel B.,* born Feb. 2, 1826, d. Sept. 12, 1828.

iii *Joseph M.,* b. Dec. 15, 1827.

iv *Charles W.,* b. June 23, 1829.

v *George E.,* b. Nov. 7, 1830, d. Oct. 2, 1853.

vi *Albert S.,* b. Dec. 10, 1833.

vii *Sarah Mason,* b. Oct. 19, 1834, m. W. W. Mitchell.

viii *William T.,* b. Aug. 19, 1837.

ix *Humphrey E.,* b. Sept. 10, 1840.

x *Mary S.,* b. Feb. 22, 1844, m. Chas. W. Greenleaf.

FARNUM.

The Farnum family has always been prominent in Rumford and one of the most numerous. The family is of Welsh descent and Ralph Farnum, the emigrant, settled in Andover, Mass., where he married Elizabeth Holt. The fourth in descent from Ralph, son of Joseph and Zerviah (Hoyt) Farnum, was Stephen of Concord, born Aug. 24, 1742, and married Martha Hall.

Children :

1 i *David,* b. Dec. 24, 1767, m. Dorcas, daughter of Jeremiah Wheeler, s. Rumford.

2 ii *Stephen,* b. Sept. 20, 1771, m. Susan Jackman of Boscawen, s. Rumford.

iii *Phebe,* b. Oct. 14, 1774, m. Joshua Morse of Hopkinton, N. H.
iv *Isaac,* b. Dec. 1, 1781, m. Hannah Martin.
v *Simeon,* b. January 14, 1782, m. Mary Smith of Hopkinton.
vi *Judith,* b. Apr. 29, 1784, m. Jeremiah Story of Hopkinton.

1 DAVID FARNUM, son of the preceding, an early settler of this town, married Dorcas, daughter of Jeremiah Wheeler of Concord, and sister of Abel and William Wheeler of this town.

Children :
i *Phebe,* b. Nov. 29, 1790, m. Nathan Knapp, s. Rumford.
ii *Betsey,* b. Aug. 19, 1792, m. Dr. Joseph Adams, s. Rumford.
iii *Judith,* b. July 24, 1794, m. 1st, Elias Bartlett of Bethel, 2d, Rev. Dan Perry.
3 iv *David Hall,* b. Nov. 21, 1796, m. Maria, daughter of Peregrine Bartlett of Bethel.
v *Dorcas,* b. Oct. 4, 1798, m. Moses Adams.
vi *Melinda,* b. Aug. 8, 1800, m. James Farrington.
vii *Asenath,* b. May 22, 1802, m. Samuel Poor of Andover.
viii *Wm Wheeler,* b. June 18, 1805, m. Rebecca Webster.
4 ix *James Harvey,* b. Aug. 1, 1807, m. Clarissa Hoyt, d. Bryant's Pond.

2 STEPHEN FARNUM, brother of the preceding, also came early to this town and died here. His wife was Susan Jackman of Boscawen, N. H.

Children :
i *Reuben,* b. ——
ii *Simeon,* b. ——, m. Amelia Robinson, d. Paris.
5 iii *George J.,* b. ——, m. 1st, Mary Bodwell, 2d. Hannah Jackson of Paris.
6 iv *Stephen Jr.,* b. ——, m. Sally Virgin.
7 v *Anson W.,* b. May 8, 1806, m. Susan C——.
vi *Lucinda,* b. ——, m. Asa Graham.
vii *Susan,* b. ——, m. John Clement.
viii *Patty,* b. ——, m. Capt. Abial Carter.

3 DAVID HALL FARNUM, son of David and Dorcas (Wheeler) Farnum, married in 1818, Maria, daughter of Peregrine Bartlett of Bethel. He married second, in 1838, widow Nancy Hinkson.
Children :
i *Sarah B.,* b. 1820, m. 1835, Eliphaz C. Bean, r. Bethel.
ii *Emiline,* b. 1823, m. 1840, Zaccheus H. Bean, r. Bethel.

4 JAMES H. FARNUM, son of David Farnum, married Clarissa, daughter of Ezra Hoyt. He was a farmer and trader in Rumford.

Children :

  i *Juliette Walker*, b. Nov. 19. 1831, m. Charles P. Knight.
8 ii *Charles Wesley.* b. Feb. 16, 1834, m. Sarah E. Wardwell.
  iii *Martha Hall.* b. June 6, 1837, m. Thos. S. Bridgham, r. Buckfield.
  iv *Maria Goodenow*, b. July 13, 1840, m. Thomas R. Day, d. Woodstock.
  v *Laura Frances*, b. Dec. 15, 1842, m. Munroe Holmes, r. Hampton, N. H.
  vi *Abbie Louisa*, b. Jan. 14, 1846, m. Edmund M. Hobbs, r. Providence, R. I.
  vii *James H.*, b. June 8, 1851, m. Emogene Day, r. Woodstock.

5 GEORGE J. FARNUM, son of Stephen Farnum, married first, Mary S. Bodwell, and second, Jan. 22, 1843, Hannah F., daughter of Lemuel and Nancy H. Jackson of Paris, who was born March 29, 1823. He was a farmer and lived near Rumford Center. He died May 24, 1886.

Children :

  i *Mary J.*, b. April 26, 1835, m. Geo. W. Trickey.
  ii *Agnes F.*, b. Apr. 9, 1838, m. John B. Hall.

By second wife :

  iii *George L.*, b. Feb. 9, 1844, d. unmarried June 18, 1877.
  iv *Nancy J.*, b. Feb. 3, 1846, m. Jan. 1, 1865, Henry M. Colby.
  v *Arabella K.*, b. Aug. 1, 1850, d. Sept. 27, 1861.
  vi *Sarah F.*, b. Oct. 11, 1853, m. Dec. 25, 1874, Charles O. Stinchfield.
  vii *Hattie L.*, b. June 2, 1855, m. Aug. 17, 1871, Charles R. Davis. He is a dentist and resides in Paris.
  viii *Pearl L.*, b. Oct. 10, 1862, m. Dec. 5, 1878, William J. Kimball, who keeps the public house at Rumford Center.

6 STEPHEN FARNUM married Sally, daughter of William Virgin, who was born Dec. 13, 1804.

Children :

 i *William Virgin*, b. May 5, 1831. ii *Mary L. V.*, b June 1, 1833. iii *Frances Jane Virgin*, b. Sept. 25, 1836. iv *Solon Scott*, b. Feb. 22, 1839.

7 ANSON W. FARNUM, born May 8, 1806, married Susan C———, who was born Nov. 16, 1810. He died May 25, 1888.

Children :

 i *Charles H.*, b. Nov. 16, 1829. ii *Martha*, b. Feb. 27, 1833. iii *Daniel G.*, b. July 20, 1834. iv *Nathan W. S.*, b. March 16, 1836. v *Angeline M.*, b. July 1, 1838. vi *Margaret A.*, b. June 3, 1845. vii *Eugene*, b. Nov. 21, 1850.

---

8 CHARLES W. FARNUM married Sarah E., daughter of Joseph H. Wardwell, who died Jan. 28, 1858. He died in the army in 1864.

Children:

  i *Joseph W.*, b. May 5, 1856.

JOHN FARNUM, fourth in descent from Ralph, son of Zebediah and Mary (Walker) Farnum of Concord, N. H., b. Jan. 1, 1750, m. Sally West, and after the death of his father, came to Rumford.

Children;

  i *Sally*, b. March 29, 1774.
  ii *Mary*, b. Oct. 22, 1776.
  iii *John Jr.*, b. June 25, 1779, m. Sarah Knowles of Concord.
  iv *Zebediah*, b. March 4, 1781, m. Chloe Abbot.
  v *Nathaniel*, b. March 15, 1783, m. Deborah Shepard.
  vi *Samuel*, b. June 10, 1788, m. Betsey Godwin.

ZEBEDIAH FARNUM, son of John Farnum, married Chloe, daughter of Nathan and Betsey (Farnum) Abbot, who was born June 10, 1783.

Children:

  i *Betsey Abbot*, b. Apr. 10, 1811, m. Jefferson Moulton.
  ii *Anna*, b. Oct. 9, 1814.
  iii *Chloe*, b. Sept. 17, 1817.
  iv *Asa Abbot*, b. Dec. d. March 3, 1824.
  v *Zebediah*, b. Dec. 11, 1821.
  vi *Asa*, b. Dec. 16, 1824, d. Sept. 9, 1840.

SAMUEL FARNUM, son of John Farnum, married Betsey, daughter of William Godwin. He lived in Rumford and Milton Plantation.

Children:

  i *Gilman W.*, b. Feb. 5, 1814, m. Emma Bean, s. Milton Pl.
  ii *David J.*, b. Aug. 3, 1815.
  iii *Nathaniel Jackson*, b. July 31, 1819, m Basheba Buck.
  iv *Laura Ann*, b. ———, m. Richard Estes of Bethel; she died in 1889.

BENJAMIN FARNUM, JR., son of Benjamin and Anna (Merrill) Farnum of Concord, N. H., fifth in descent from the emigrant, Ralph, married Sarah Thompson and came to Rumford.

Children:

  i *Polly*, b. Aug. 25, 1791.
  ii *Nancy*, b. January 3, 1793.

   iii *Merrill*, b. Sept. 28, 1794, m. 1st, Sally Bunker, 2d, Sarah Virgin, 3d, Louisa Howe.
   iv *Sally*, b. April 3, 1796, d. Aug. 5, 1800.
   v *Azubah*, b. Nov. 17, 1797.
   vi *Hannah*, b. Aug. 25, 1799, d. Aug. 12, 1800.
   vii *Sally*, b. June 3, 1801.
   viii *Mahala*, b March 27, 1803.
   ix *Abial*, b. January 17, 1808, m. Jeneatte Burnham of Westbrook.

JEREMIAH FARNUM, brother of the preceding, married Sally Hall of Rumford, and resided in this town.

Children :

   i *Milton*, b. Dec. 3, 1812, m. Emily Ward. ii *Ivory*, b. April 16, 1813. iii *Emily*, b. Dec. 28, 1814. iv *Alfred*, b. ———. m. Caroline Sweetser. v *Calvin*, b.———. vi *John*, b. ———. vii *Walter*, b. ———. viii *Sarah*, b. ———. ix *Rebecca E.*, b. ———. x *Deborah D.*, b. ———.

MERRILL FARNUM married first, Sarah Bunker, who died. He married second, Sarah Virgin, who died May 31, 1824, and third, Jan., 1825, Louisa, daughter of Phineas Howe.

Children :

   i *Edward Poor*, b. Dec. 7, 1818. ii *Cynthia Wheeler*, b. Oct. 13, 1820. iii *Alvan Bolster*, b. Sept. 13, 1822. iv *Aaron Virgin* b. May 31 1824. v *Manley*, b. June 9, 1825. vi *Sarah*, b. Oct. 5. 1832. vii *Freelinghuysen*, b. Apr. 26. 1840.

ABIAL FARNUM married Jeneatte Burnham of Westbrook.

Children :

   i *Mary J.*, b. May 27. 1831.
   ii *Martha Ann*, b. March 6, 1833, d. Apr. 9, 1838.

JACOB FARNUM, born in Concord, N. H., married Betsey Wheeler and moved to Rumford, and died here Sept. 1, 1836. His wife died Nov. 8, 1858. He was a farmer and shoemaker.

Children :

   i *Esther*, b. April 23. 1794 m. Joel Austin.
   ii *Caty*, b. Dec. 14, 1796 m. Eben Abbott.
   iii *Daniel*, b. April 22, 1799, m. Mary W. Virgin.
   iv *Hannah*, b. Dec. 23, 1803, m. Henry Child of Canton.
   v *Susan*, b. July 19, 1806, m. Aaron Elliot.

DANIEL FARNUM, son of Jacob Farnum, married Mary W. Virgin, born in Concord, N. H., Sept. 8, 1809. She died August 23, 1856, and second, Mrs. Martha J. Bowker.

Children.

    i   *Lucy Ann*, b. May 5. 1834, m. Rev. Patrick H. Hoyt.
    ii *Wm. Henry*, b. Jan. 12, 1836, m. Sept. 23, 1865, Caroline L., dau. of
           Henry Martin; they have Ed C., b. Apr. 22, 1866.
    iii *Edward Hood*, b. Feb. 8, 1838, d. in California, May 15, 1862.
    iv *Rufus Virgin*, b. Feb. 13, 1842, r. in Rumford, unmarried.
    v *Victoria S.*, b. Oct. 13, 1845, m. Edwin R. Martin.

By second wife :

    vi *Mary B.*, b. March 10, 1862, m. George Hardy.
    vii *Jennie* b. ———, m. Fred Leal of Lynn, Mass.

FROM TOWN RECORDS.

WILLIAM W. FARNUM, married first, Rebecca S. Webster of Andover, second, Hannah J. Treadwell of Portland, and third, Betsey G. Fox.

Children :

    i *David W.*, b. Oct. 26, 1833.

By second wife :

    ii *Harriet*, b. ———.
    iii *Dorcas A.*. b. Aug. 14, 1843.

By third wife :

    iv *Wm G.*, b. July 9, 1846.
    v *John W.*, b. Jan. 14, 1847, d. Apr. following.
    vi *James E.*, b. Aug. 31, 1849.
    vii *George B.*, b. March 21, 1853, d. Apr. 25, 1854.

NATHAN S. FARNUM married Sophronia ———.

Children :

    i *William G.*. b. Sept. 26, 1864. ii *Burt K.*, b. June 12, 1866. iii *Hattie J.*, b. Oct. 9, 1868. iv *Ernest S.*, b. Dec. 25, 1870. v *Anna V.*, b. March 19, 1872.

WILLIAM H. FARNUM married Caroline Martin.

Children :

    i *Edwin C.*. b. April 22, 1866.

JOHN C. FARNUM married Mary R. Bass of Weld.

Children :

    i *Walter H.*. b. Feb. 1, 1849. ii *Charles F.*, b. July 22, 1852.

CHARLES H. FARNUM married Mary J. ———.

Children :

    i *Lizzie G.*, b. Aug. 3, 1856. ii *Melvina J.*, b. June 14, 1869.

FORD.

BENJ. F. FORD of Sumner, married Mary P., daughter of Isaac W. Cleasby of Milton Pl., June 19, 1843, and settled in Rumford. Children :

  i *Seth*, b. Oct. 16, 1846. ii *Emily*, b. Jan. 7, 1852.

BENJAMIN FRYE married Judith Rolfe Dec., 1833.

Children :

  i *Paulina R.*, b. Feb. 20, 1835. ii *Aurelia*, b. Sept. 30, 1837. iii *James*, b. April 1, 1840.

FROST.

WILLIAM FROST, the well known ferryman at the Center and for many years the efficient clerk of Rumford, married Apr. 14, 1817, Dorothy Sweat. He was born in Bethel in 1799, and was brought up in the family of Rev. Daniel Gould.

Children :

    i *Simeon Foster*, b. Aug. 3, 1818.
   ii *William P.*, b. July 20, 1820.
  iii *Geneva G.*, b. Apr. 17, 1822. m. Asa Kimball.
  iv *Charles W.*, b. Apr. 28, 1824.
   v *Rufus H.*, b. Feb. 1, 1826, d. Feb. 9, 1851.
  vi *Eunice G.*, b. Oct. 16, 1827.
 vii *Mary B.*, b. Sept. 20. 1829.
viii *Lucy G.*, b. Aug. 16 1831, d. Oct. 5. 1834.
  ix *Moses S.*, b. May 25, 1833. d. Nov. 29, 1855.
   x *Daniel G.*, b. May 16, 1837, m. Emogene M. Hall.
  xi *Clark B.*, b. July 28, 1839, m. Abby Howe, 2d, Emily P. Holt.

WILLIAM FROST married Phebe ———.

Children.
  i *Guy Morrill*, b. Jan. 4, 1866, d. Aug. 30, 1866.
 ii *Edward Nye*, b. Feb. 9, 1867.

FULLER.

DR. SIMEON FULLER married Mary Ann, daughter of Capt. Abner Rawson of Paris. He settled at Rumford Corner where he died and his widow married Dr. James Bullock.

Children :

  i *Samuel Rawson*, b. Feb. 6, 1830. ii *Mary Arabella*, b. Feb. 20, 1837.

GLINES.

ISRAEL GLINES was of Loudon, N. H. He married Molly, daughter of Ebenezer Virgin, Jr., of Concord, and when advanced in life, came to Rumford. In the absence of any family record, his children cannot be given in the order of their births. He had a pension for service in the Revolution.

Children :

    i   *Ebenezer*, b. ———. He was a carpenter: was killed in raising a barn on Eaton Hill.

    ii *Jeremiah*, b. ———. He was a Congregational minister and died at Lunenburg, Vt.

    iii *Chandler*, b. 1779, m. Betsey Davis of Concord, N. H.

    iv *Timothy*, b. ———, m. 1819, Sally Barker, d. Bethel.

    v *Daniel.* b. ——— m. first. Betsey Rolfe, second, Mary Sweat.

    vi *Polly*, b. ———, m. Nathaniel Rolfe of Rumford.

    vii *Sally*, b. ———, m. Aaron Stevens of Rumford.

CHANDLER GLINES, son of the preceding, married in 1801, July 12, Betsey Davis of Concord, N. H. He was among the first of the family that came to Rumford, arriving in 1805. He was a noted musician, and was very conspicuous in military trainings and musters.

Children :

    i   *Mahala*, b. Concord, Oct. 17, 1802 d. Sept. 20, 1827.

    ii *Albert Gallatin*, b. June 5, 1804.

    iii *David B.*, b. March 3d, 1805, m. 1832, Catherine B. Goddard.

    iv *Ebenezer*, b. Nov. 23, 1807.

    v *Dorcas Virgin*, b. Feb. 17, 1810, m. David F. Adams, r. Caribou.

    vi *Clarissa*, b. Jan. 18, 1813, m. 1833. David Knapp.

    vii *Chandler Jr.*, b. January 1, 1815.

    viii *Harriet A.*, b. Apr. 6, 1818, m. Jonathan Adams Bartlett.

    ix *Mary W.*, b. Feb. 16, 1821.

DANIEL GLINES, brother of the preceding, married first, Feb. 14, 1811, Betsey Rolfe of Rumford, who died after giving birth to one child, and he married second, Mary Sweat.

Children :

    i   *Betsey Rolfe*, b. June 23, 1811.

    ii *Azariah*, b. Nov. 4, 1815, d. Aug. 18, 1826.

    iii *Edith*, b. January 2, 1818.

    iv *Sarah S.*, b. January 16, 1820.

    v *Orin*, b. Sept. 5, 1822, m. Tyla Whitman, d. Paris.

    vi *Orison*, b. January 23, 1825.

vii   *Valentine*, b. April 26. 1827.
viii   *Makala G.*, b. May 8. 1829, d. Nov. 4, following.
 ix   *Azariah*, b. July 5, 1830.
  x   *Mahala*, b. May 18, 1834.
 xi   *Melissa W.*, b. April 27, 1836.
xii   *Hester Ann*, b. Oct. 27, 1839.

DAVID B. GLINES married in 1832, Catherine B., daughter of Elisha Goddard. He is a farmer and resides in Rumford.
Children :
  i   *Augusta Maria*, b. Jan. 6, 1833, m. John Howe, Jr.
 ii   *Harriet E.*, b. May 1, 1834, m. John H. Howe.
iii   *David G.*, b. Sept. 10. 1838, m. Emma S. Howe.

DAVID G. GLINES married Emma S. Howe.
Children :
 i   *Roscoe L.*, b. Feb. 13, 1864.

GLOVER.

LIVINGSTON GLOVER, son of Joshua Stetson and Susanna (Ames) Glover of Pembroke, Mass., and Hartford, Me., and grandson of James and Rachel (Bonney) Glover of Pembroke, the latter being the son of Robert and Bethiah (Tubbs) Glover of Pembroke, was born in Hartford, Me., Dec. 9, 1816. He is a farmer and resides in Rumford. He married March 11, 1840, Abigail Stetson of Hartford.
Children :
   i   *Loren Ornan*, b. Sept. 9, 1840, m. Dorcas L. Goddard.
  ii   *Ann Amelia*, b. May 7, 1842, m. Loring P. Swain.
 iii   *Susanna*, b. June 30, 1844, m. Ronello C. Dolloff.
 iv   *Salome Tilson*, b. June 16, 1846, m. Wm. H. Thurlow.
  v   *Lucius A.*, b. Apr. 13. 1849, m. Isabel Farrar.
 vi   *Harriet L.*, b. Sept. 18, 1852.
vii   *Cordelia A.*, b. June 16. 1854.
viii   *Lois S.*, b. Jan. 24, 1857, m. Thomas L. Weeks.
 ix   *Anthony E.*, b. Feb. 13, 1859, d. Aug. 8, 1862.
  x   *Ernest E.*, b. Dec. 29, 1861. m. Mary E. Holt.

LOREN GLOVER married Dorcas L. Goddard who died Oct. 2, 1878.
Children :
  i   *Jesse C.*, b. Hartford, Sept. 5. 1863, d. March 13, 1864.
 ii   *Rosie*, b. Rumford, Feb. 15, 1865, d. Feb. 26, 1865.
iii   *Lewis Loren*, b. Jan. 31, 1868.
 iv   *Mary Abigail*, b. Dec. 6, 1870.
  v   *John Henry*, b. Aug. 18, 1872.
 vi   *Frank K. L.*, b. June 30, 1874.

GODDARD.

MAJOR ROBERT GODDARD, son of Elisha and Anna (Haven) Goddard of Sutton, Mass., born in 1749, married first, April 13, 1780, Anna Tainter, who died Dec. 19, 1792. He married second, Feb. 13, 1794, Tamar Goddard, and third, Nov. 6, 1796, Hannah Goddard. She died March 18, 1797, and he married January 1, 1798, widow Sybil (Peters) Penniman. He early settled in Andover and was the first one to drive a team through to that town on the east side of Ellis river. He died Oct. 10, 1826.

Children :

 i *Mary*, b. January 25. 1781, m. Ephraim Fobes.
 ii *Elisha*, b. Feb. 2, 1782, m. Jan. 6, 1806, Catherine Broaders, s. Rumford.
 iii *Nancy*, b. Apr. 18, 1785, m. Rufus Barton.
 iv *Ebenezer Thatcher*, b. July 22. 1789. sea captain, d. of cold Dec. 24, 1804.
 v *David*, b. Sept. 6, 1792, m. Dorcas Littlehale of Newry.
 vi *Abijah*, b. Dec. 25, 1794, d. young.

Children by fourth wife :

 vii *Sybil*, b. ———, m. James B. Greenleaf.
 viii *Caroline*, b. ———.
 ix *Hannah*, b. ———, m. Joshua Graham.
 x *Maria*, b. ———, she married a Mr. Poor of Belfast.
 xi *Sylvia*, b. ———, m. ——— O'Connor.
 xii *William,* } twins, b. ———, m. Nancy Whitney of Norway, d. Bethel.
 xiii *Julia.* }

ELISHA GODDARD, son of the preceding, born in Sutton Feb. 2, 1783, married Jan. 6, 1806, Catherine Broaders. He settled in Rumford.

Children :

 i *Eben Thatcher*, b. Nov., 1806, m. January. 1835, Mary Ann Kimball.
 ii *Catherine B.*, b. 1809. m. David B. Glines.
 iii *Elisha F.*, b. ———, d. young.

DAVID GODDARD, brother of the preceding, a trader, born in Sutton, Mass., Sept. 5. 1791, married Dorcas Littlehale of Newry, who was born in that town in 1792. He lived at Cambridgeport, Mass., and at Belfast and Belmont, Maine, where he died in 1835. His widow died in Worcester, Mass., in 1861.

Children :

 i *Elisha F.*, b. Aug.7, 1817, m. first, Mary S. Hutchins, second, widow Jane L. Ackley.

  ii *Mary A. F.*, b. Apr. 12, 1819, d. ———.
  iii *David*, b. Dec. 9, 1820.
  iv *Robert H.* b. Nov. 15, 1822, d. 1853, unmarried.
  v *George T.*, b. Jan. 8, 1825, m. Lydia S. Thomas.
  vi *Elisha*, b. Dec. 28, 1828, s. Kansas.
  vii *Charles Carrol*, b. Dec. 9, 1832, d. 1835.

EPHRAIM FORBES GODDARD, son of David Goddard, married Sept. 9, 1840, Mary S., daughter of David Hutchins, and second, Jan. 23, 1868, Jane L. (Cook) Ackley. He is a farmer and auctioneer.

Children :

  i *Dorcas L.*, b. July, 1843, m. Loren Glover, d. 1878.
  ii *George T.*, b. Sept. 8, 1844, m. Mary Knight, d. 1879.
  iii *Kate R.*, b. Dec. 1, 1847, m. Lyrin C. Hodge of Canton.
  iv *Betsey N.*, b. June 18, 1850, m. Tilson Goding of Livermore.
  v *Frye H.*, b. March 20, 1869.
  vi *Alvin G.*, b. Dec. 1, 1871.

EBEN T. GODDARD married Mary Ann Kimball. She was the eldest daughter of Moses F. Kimball, Esq., and was born in Bethel. Mr. Goddard died quite early and his widow survives :

Children :

  i *Elisha F.*, b. Oct. 15, 1836, m. Euthalia V. Roberts.
  ii *Mary Kimball*, b. Feb. 4, 1839, m. Benj. W. Bryent of Paris.
  iii *Eben P.*, b. Feb. 28, 1841, d. July 8, 1865.

GODWIN.

WILLIAM GODWIN, born either in England or Ireland, is said to have been a soldier in Burguoyne's army, to have deserted and come across from New York to Massachusetts. The name under which he enlisted was William Redmond, which was doubtless his real name. After coming to Massachusetts, he assumed the name of Godwin, said to have been the family name of his mother. Another story is that he deserted from an English Man of War. He married Rachel Harper of Northhampton, Mass., and came to Rumford from Fryeburg, about 1792 ; five of his children were born here.

Children :

  i *Rebecca*, b. 1778, m. Francis Hemmenway.
  ii *William*, b. ———. He left home a young man and never returned.
  iii *Colman*, b. May 6, 1782, m. Keziah Wheeler.

iv   *Rachel,* b. ———, m. Kimball Martin.

v   *Betsey,* b. ———, m. Samuel Farnum, r. Milton Pl.

vi   *Polly,* b. ———, m. Samuel Merrill, r. Milton Pl.

vii *James,* b. 1791. m. Apphia Segar, r. Upton.

viii *Nancy,* b. Apr. 3, 1793, m. Nathaniel Jackson, r. Milton Pl.

ix   *John,* b. Feb. 11, 1795. m. Clarissa Stevens, no children, r. Milton Pl.

x   *Harris Redmond,* b. Dec. 8, 1797, d. Dec. 29, 1797.

xi   *Sally,* b. June 10, 1799, m. James Moody.

xii *David Abbot,* b. Feb. 15, 1802, m. Abigail Besse.

COLMAN GODWIN, son of the preceding, born in Northhampton, Mass., May 6, 1782, married March 17, 1814, in Concord, N. H., Keziah Wheeler, who was born Feb. 25, 1793. Mr. Godwin was a farmer, often in town office, deputy sheriff twenty years, and a prominent citizen of Rumford. He died Aug. 24, 1852, and his widow died Nov. 29, 1879.

Children :

i   *Eliza H.,* b. June 17, 1815, m. Oct. 1, 1839, Josiah P. Whidden.

ii   *Sarah F.,* b. March 13, 1817, m. Dec. 10, 1841, Robert Knox, d. July 4, 1847.

iii *Mahala F.,* b. Nov. 30, 1818. m. Sept. 5, 1840, Benj. E. Abbot, d. Dec. 4, 1882.

iv   *Julia O.,* b. Nov. 25, 1820, m. 1852, Asa Abbot.

v   *Fidelia A.,* b. July 13, 1823, m. Sept. 15, 1847, Orin H. Lufkin.

vi   *Alvan B.,* b. July 21, 1825, m. Feb. 26, 1851, Arabella Carter, daughter of Moses F. and Mary (Bean) Kimball. He resides at Bethel and is a deputy sheriff. They have one child, Ella Eudora, b. May 7, 1853, m. May 14, 1874, Edwin C. Rowe.

vii *Cynthia B.,* b. July 21, 1828, m. Dec. 25, 1857, Geo. F. Sheppard, d. June 29, 1867.

viii *Mary W.,* b. January 19, 1837, m. Feb. 5, 1858, C. F. Drury.

JAMES GODWIN, b. 1791, married Apphia, daughter of Nathaniel Segar of Bethel. He lived in Rumford, but in 1850, was living in Upton.

Children :

i *Azubah,* b. Feb. 9, 1816. ii *Luna,* b. Apr. 10, 1817. iii *Maria,* b. Nov. 9, 1818. iv *Lucinda,* b. 1826. v *Apphia R.,* b. 1829. vi *William R.,* b. 1830. vii *Rufus S.,* b. 1831. viii *Arvilla C.,* b. 1834. ix *Horatio R.,* b. 1835.

DAVID ABBOT GODWIN, brother of the preceding, in 1825, married Abigail, daughter of Caleb and Abigail (Packard) Besse of Paris, who was born there in 1810. He lived in Topsham a year or two, came back to Rumford, moved to Woodstock, again returned to Rumford, and died there in 1854. His widow now lives at South Paris.

Children :

i   *Allen F.*, b. Topsham, Dec. 9, 1826, m. Mary M. Wolf of Richmond, Indiana, and lived there.

ii   *Elmira*, b. Rumford, Dec. 6, 1831, m. Charles Wood, r. So. Paris.

iii   *Charles O.*, b. Oct. 26, 1833, m. Nov. 25, 1852, Vesta A. Austin of Buckfield, r. Lewiston.

iv   *George H.*, b. May 8, 1836, m. Hannah A. Hobart, r. Campello, Mass.

v   *Orin M.*, b. Woodstock, January 1, 1842, m. Hattie E. Goodwin, Lewiston, r. Brockton.

vi   *Cynthia A.*, b. Aug. 20, 1844, m. Charles H. Goodwin, d. at Randolph, 1865.

vii   *Nelson*, b. Jan. 15, 1847, killed in the late war.

viii   *Josephine K.*, b. Nov. 4, 1848, r. Boston.

AJALON GODWIN, adopted son of John Godwin, married Sarah A. Thompson in 1853. He was a soldier in the late war and made a fine record, but died of wounds.

Children :

i   *Clarissa S.*, b. Feb. 17, 1853.   ii   *Emily W.*, b. March 6, 1860.   iii *Cora F.*, b. Oct. 1, 1861.   iv   *Berta A.*, b. Nov. 22, 1864.

Goss.

REV. THOMAS GOSS, born in 1717, a graduate of Harvard College 1737, was an early settled minister in Bolton, Mass., where he died January 17, 1780, aged 63 years. His ministry covered a period of about thirty-five years.

Children :

i   *Ebenezer Harnden*, b. Oct. 20, 1743. He married Mary, daughter of Rev. Timothy Walker of Concord, N. H.

ii   *Judith*, b. Jan. 24, 1745.

iii   *Abigail*, b. Apr. 1, 1749, m. May 13, 1767, Joshua Atherton of Petersham.

iv   *Thomas*, b. Dec. 12, 1751. He settled in Baltimore, a merchant, and became wealthy.

v   *Samuel*, b. Oct. 16, 1754, m. Lucretia Howe, s. Rumford.

vi   *Mary*, b. Sept. 6, 1757, m. May 4, 1777, Simeon Hemmenway of Bolton.

vii   *Elizabeth*, b. Apr. 22, 1760, m. Sept. 1, 1779, David Newhall of Bolton.

viii   *Salome*, b. January 13, 1763, m. Jan. 1, 1784, Aaron Moor, s. Rumford.

Dr. Ebenezer Harnden Goss, the oldest son of the preceding, married Mary, daughter of Rev. Timothy Walker of Rumford. He was an original proprietor of New Pennacook, (Rumford) and quite a large landholder by purchase. He sold land here to Jonathan Keyes, the first settler. He was of Concord, N. H., then of Brunswick, Me., and afterwards of Paris, where he died Sept. 26, 1825.

Children :

i *Gustavus Adolphus*, b. July 8, 1770, m. Betsey Howe of Rumford.
ii *Sarah*, b. Aug. 9. 1772, m. David Marshall of Paris.
iii *Abigail*, b. May 16, 1775, d. unmarried.

Samuel Goss, son of Rev. Thomas Goss preceding, married March 7, 1780, Lucretia, daughter of Phineas and Experience (Wheeler) Howe of Bolton, Mass. He settled first in Bethel on an interval farm afterwards occupied by Richard Estes, on the south side of the Androscoggin, in the east part of the town. He then moved to Rumford and settled on Red Hill. Only one child is recorded on Rumford records. He and his wife both died in Bethel, the latter at a very advanced age. The names of the children cannot be given in the order of their birth.

Children :

i *Abigail* b———, m. Moses Gammon of Paris.
ii *Charlotte*, b. ———, m. Joseph Small of Norway.
iii *Clarissa*, b. ———, m. ——— Gray.
iv *Sarah*, b. Jan. 9, 1790, m. Jeremiah Hobbs of Norway.
v *Sophia*. b. ———, m. Mathias Morton of Andover Surplus.
vi *Thomas*, b. Bethel, Jan. 21, 1794, m. first, Nancy, daughter of John Oliver of Bethel, and second, Waity Benson of Sumner. He was a farmer in Bethel and lived to be nearly 90 years of age.
vii *Abial*, b. ———. He married Myra Boynton of Cambridge, Mass. He was a carpenter and builder, and accumulated a large estate. He was killed a few years ago, by being thrown from a carriage or sleigh.

Gustavus Adolphus Goss, son of Dr. Ebenezer Harnden Goss, came to Rumford when a young man, and married Betsey, daughter of Phineas and Experience Howe of Bolton, and sister of Abram, Silas and Phineas, Jr., of this town. He came here from Brunswick, and after his marriage, he moved to the lower part of Bethel. About 1807, he moved to Paris and died there Apr. 21, 1822. He was known as "Squire Goss." He was a lieutenant in Capt. Bailey

Bodwell's Company that saw active service in the war of 1812.   His widow died in Stoneham, Dec. 30, 1861.

Children :

i   *Mary*, b. Bethel January 9, 1800, d. January 4 1806.

ii *Nancy*, b. Apr. 26, 1801, d. January 7, 1806.

iii *Mary Walker*, b. Oct. 28, 1806, m. John Howe, r. Stoneham, Me.

iv *Charles Humphrey*, b. Paris, Apr. 27, 1808, m. Fear M., widow of Samuel S. Bicknell and daughter of Jacob Decoster of Hebron.

GRAHAM.

JOSHUA GRAHAM, son of George and Azubah Graham of Canterbury, N. H., was born there June 7, 1763.   His wife, Hannah Chandler, was born in Concord, N. H., June 19, 1763.   He was early in Rumford and always a leading man in town, holding many important trusts which he always faithfully fulfilled.   He was a merchant, farmer, hotel keeper and millman.

Children :

i   *Aaron*, b. Concord, March 6, 1788, m. Geneva Moor.

ii   *Sarah*, b. May 31, 1790, m. James Frye Bragg of Andover.

iii *Nancy*, b. May 30, 1792, m. Elijah Bartlett.

iv *George*, b. Rumford, Feb. 26, 1795, m. Hannah Eastman.

v   *Asa*, b. Aug. 2, 1797, m. Lucinda Farnum.

vi *Abial*, b. Aug. 24, 1799, d. Feb. 12, 1802.

vii *John*, b. January 1, 1802, d. January 1, 1802.

viii *Joshua*, b. March 4, 1804, m. first, Hannah P. Goddard, second, Ruth S. Treadwell of Portland., third, Sarah Leavitt.

AARON GRAHAM, son of the preceding, married Geneva, daughter of Aaron Moor of Rumford.   He owned the farm opposite the Center, which he sold in 1835, to Samuel Bartlett.

Children :

i   *Sally Bragg*, b. August 17, 1812, m. Loammi B. Peabody, d. January 18, 1880.

ii *Geo. Wellington*, b. Apr. 4, 1814, m. Irene Irish, d. 1881.

iii *Joshua Chandler*, b. January 26, 1817, d. July 26, 1820.

iv *Lucy Ann*, b. Aug. 29, 1821, m. Carlos Wilmot.

v *John Chandler*, b. Nov. 4, 1823, m. Apr. 16, 1848, Susan M. Wood.

vi *Jeneatte B.*, b. Apr. 9, 1825, m. 1844, Leonard Jewell.

vii *Lucina A.*, b. Aug. 7, 1831, m. Joseph Wilmot, Jr.

GEORGE GRAHAM, brother of the preceding, married Hannah Eastman.

Children :

 i *Nancy B.*, b. Sept. 25, 1819, m. John I. Bragg, r. Upton.

 ii *Abial C.*, b. Jan. 23, 1821.

 iii *Azubah*, b. July 9, 1822.

 iv *Arvilla*, b. July 19, 1825.

 v *Eli*, b. Nov. 30, 1827.

 vi *Emeline A.*, b. Aug. 17, 1830.

 vii *Sarah M.*, b. March 16, 1833, m. Stephen J. Seavey, r. Norway.

 viii *Wm. H. H.*, b. Nov. 12, 1836.

ASA GRAHAM, brother of the preceding, married Lucinda Farnum.

Children :

 i *Susan Farnum*, b. Dec. 31, 1817, m. ———.

 ii *Phebe Morse*, b. June 19, 1820, m. Albion K. Knapp.

 iii *Joshua Chandler*, b. Oct. 21, 1822.

 iv *Stephen Farnum*, b. January 6, 1826.

 v *Abial Carter*, b. Nov. 9, 1828.

 vi *George E.*, b. May 6, 1831, d. Aug. 28, 1831.

 vii *Georgianna Augusta*, b. Feb. 1, 1833.

 viii *Caroline Lucinda*, b. Feb. 1, 1836.

 ix *Victoria Sophia*, b. Sept. 6, 1838.

 x *Charles Mason*, b. July 12, 1843, d. Feb. 28, 1844.

JOSHUA GRAHAM, brother of the preceding, married first, Hannah P. Goddard of Andover, who died Dec. 10, 1837. His second wife, Ruth S. Treadwell, died Jan. 13, 1843. He married, third, Mrs. Sarah Leavitt.

Children.

 i *Sybil Goddard*, b. January 21, 1828.

 ii *Hannah Chandler*, b. Aug. 27, 1829.

 iii *Nancy Barton*, b. June 21, 1833.

 iv *Philadelphia*, b. January 17, 1835, m. Augustus J. Knight, d. Nov. 1, 1887.

 v *Caroline C.*, b. Feb. 6, 1837.

 vi *Ruth Treadwell*, b. March 30, 1840, m. Marcius F. Knight.

 vii *Joshua Dexter*, b. Dec. 12, 1841, d. Apr. 22, 1842.

 viii *Lovell Mason*, b. July 2, 1846.

 ix *Zachary Taylor*, b. Nov. 6, 1848.

 x *Winfield Scott*, b. Apr. 20, 1852.

 xi *Joshua H.*, b. Aug. 21, 1854.

GEORGE W. GRAHAM married Irene Irish of Hartford.

Children :

 i *Martha Ann*, b. Oct. 16, 1836. ii *Frances Allen*, b. Sept. 12, 1838. iii *Sophia L.*, b. Aug. 24, 1845. iv *Aaron Freeland*, b. March 2, 1847.

CHARLES GRAHAM married Ella M————.

Children :

i *Bertha E.*, b. Apr. 26, 1873. ii *Hildreth Wood*, b. May 17, 1876. iii *Sarah C.*, b. May 30, 1877. iv *Luna E.*, b. Jan. 3, 1879.

JOHN CHANDLER GRAHAM, son of Aaron and Geneva (Moor) Graham, married Apr. 16, 1844, Susan M., daughter of Phineas and Elizabeth Wood, and is a farmer at Rumford Center. He married second, Caroline, widow of Charles H. Rolfe, and daughter of Jonathan Virgin.

Children :

   i   *Charles H.*, b. Nov. 28, 1849, m. 1871, Ella Swain.
  ii   *Hildreth W.*, b. Dec. 14, 1851.
 iii *Adelaide,* ⎰ twins, b. June 21, 1857.
 iv *Adeline,* ⎱ d. Aug. 21, 1857.
  v *Marshall S.*, b. Oct. 23, 1858, d. Aug., 1872.
 vi *Elizabeth R.*, b. Apr. 21, 1863, d. March 30, 1865.
 vii *John F.*, b. Sept. 9, 1867.
viii *Susie M.*, b. June 22, 1869, graduated Kent's Hill, 1889.

GREEN.

ASA GREEN married Phebe ————.

Children :

i *Ezra*, b. Groton, Mass., March 29, 1806. ii *Serena*, b. Tyngsboro, Dec. 4, 1807. iii *Joel P.*, b. Aug. 31, 1809. iv *Oren*, b. Mercer. Me., Feb. 26, 1811. v *Harriet*, b. Nov. 15, 1812. vi *Andrew J.*, b. Nov. 8, 1814. vii *Elmira*, b. Aug. 5, 1816. viii *Dolly W.*, b. Plantation No. 8, July 29, 1818. ix *Ransom N.*, b. Jan. 10, 1821. x *Julian*, b. Oct. 24, 1822. xi *Calista*, b. Sept. 8, 1824. xii *Abigail T.*, b. June 12, 1826. xiii *Asa Jr.*, b. Rumford, March 31, 1829.

NAHUM GREEN married Mary E. Virgin.

Children :

i *Mary E.*, b. Oct. 6, 1850.

GOODWIN.

HORACE GOODWIN married Diantha A. ————.

Children :

i *Charles H.*, b. Dec. 12, 1854.

HALL.

DANIEL HALL, son of Ebenezer Hall, was of Concord, N. H.
He was a descendant in the fourth generation, from Richard Hall
who settled in Bradford, Mass., in 1673. He was born January 13,
1755, and died Feb. 18, 1835. He married Deborah Davis, who
was the mother of his children, and died in Nov., 1822. He married a second wife.

Children:

i *Dorcas*, b. Aug. 14, 1776, m. Joseph Sherburne.
ii *Ebenezer*, b. May 9, 1778, m. Nov. 15, 1803, Hannah Abbot.
iii *Robert*, b. June 16, 1780, d. Aug. 18, 1805, in the West Indies.
iv *Joseph*, b. May 4, 1782, m. Judith Blanchard.
v *Jeremiah*, b. May 4, 1782, m. about 1804, Judith Rolfe, and second,
    Betsey (Farnum) Adams.
vi *James*, b. June 19, 1784, m. Nov. 26, 1805, Ruth M. Abbot.
vii *Simeon*, b. March 16, 1786.
viii *Sally*, b. Sept. 11, 1788, m. Jeremiah Farnum of Rumford.
ix *Polly*, b. May 16, 1790, d. young.
x *Daniel*, b. June 17, 1792, m. Sally ———.
xi *Hannah*, b. March 21, 1794, d. May 9, following.
xii *Gerry*, b. Aug. 25, 1795.
xiii *John Calvin*, b. Sept. 12, 1798.
xiv *Polly*, b. July 27, 1801, d. July 19, 1803.

JOSEPH HALL, son of the preceding, came to Rumford and lived
here many years. His wife was Judith Blanchard.

Children:

i *Joshua Thompson*, b. Oct. 5, 1805. ii *Edward Abbot*, b. Aug. 12, 1807,
d. Dec. 21, following. iii *Dorothy Elliot*, b. Dec. 11, 1808. iv *Deborah
Davis*, b. January 18, 1811. v *Betsey Rolfe*, b. March 21, 1813. vi *Joseph
Osgood*, b. Oct. 15, 1816. vii *Livermore Russell*, b. Sept. 15, 1818. viii
William Monroe, b. Sept. 13, 1820. ix *Ivory W.*, b. April 20, 1823.

JEREMIAH HALL, twin brother of the preceding, married Judith,
daughter of Benjamin Rolfe of Concord, N. H. He also came to
Rumford, and was quite prominent in town affairs.

Children:

i *Daniel*, b. Aug. 12, 1805, m. Sarah Lovejoy, r. Peru.
ii *Mary*, b. Aug. 6, 1807, m. Farwell Walton.
iii *Lydia*, b. 1809, m. Justin Austin.
iv *Davis*, b. 1810, m. Mary Patrick, r. Waltham, Mass.
v *Simeon*, b. ———, d. young.

vi   *Elbridge Gerry*, b. ———, m. Deborah H. Hall, r. West Peru.
vii   *Annie*, b. ———, d. aged 3 months.
viii   *Charles*, b. ———, m. Angeline Cook, r. Waltham, Mass.
ix   *Lucinda*, b. March, 1818, m. William Adams of Andover.
x   *Julia*, b. ———, m. James Bragg.
xi   *Priscilla*, b. ———, m. Ira Parlin.
xii   *Cordelia*, b. ———, m. Dr. Kendall Wright.
xiii   *Jeremiah*, b. ———, m. Melvina Brown.

DANIEL HALL, brother of the preceding, came to Rumford and was deacon of the church.   His wife was Sally.

Children :
   i   *Joseph S.*, b. Nov. 16, 1821, d. March 21, 1841.
   ii   *Sarah A.*, b. Sept. 26, 1823, d. May 1, 1824.
   iii   *Rozilla W.*, b. Dec. 30, 1826, d. May 4, 1853.
   iv   *Arixene*, b. July 5, 1830, d. March 24, 1831.
   v   *Henry S.*, b. July 20, 1833.
   vi   *Martha J.*, b. March 17, 1836.

KIMBALL HALL, married Delilah G. Keniston.   He died Nov. 13, 1885, aged 80 3-4 years ; his wife died January 3, 1885, aged 75 3-4 years.   He was not related to other Hall families in this town.

Children :
   i *Elizabeth Jane*, b. Feb. 14, 1829.   ii *Mehitable P.*, b. Jan. 10, 1831.   iii *John W.*, b. Apr. 29, 1833.   iv *Phebe*, b. Oct. 17, 1835.   v *Abigail Delia*, b. July 19, 1838.   vi *Aaron*, b. May 29, 1852.

HENRY S. HALL married Julia E. Abbot in 1862.

Children :
   i *Eleanor E.*, b. Feb. 1, 1863.

JOSHUA T. HALL m. Charlotte M. Elliot.   He was Captain of a company that went to the "Aroostook War."

Children on Rumford records :
   i *Imogene M.*, b. Feb. 25, 1840.

JOHN R. HALL married Louisa Woods of Augusta.

Children :
   i *Hannah M.*, b. Apr. 14, 1863.

ISAAC HALL married Polly ———.

Children :
   i *Hannah F.*, b. Apr. 21, 1828.   ii *Emeline W.*, b. Feb. 3, 1830.   iii *Nancy Elizabeth*, b. Aug. 19, 1832.   iv *John Gilman*, b. Apr. 20, 1834.   v

Isaac Franklin, b. Aug. 25, 1836. vi *Hiram Abbot*. b. June 1, 1838. vii *Mary Sophia*, b. Aug. 8, 1840.

HARPER.

Daniel and Ezekiel Harper, brothers, were in town quite early and lived on Red Hill. It is said by some that they each had red hair, and that the hill where they settled was so named from this circumstance. They did not long remain here. Daniel emigrated to Ohio and Ezekiel moved to some other town. They were brothers of the wives of William Godwin and of Benj. Swett, Jr., and are said to have been of Irish parentage. Daniel Harper also had brothers Andros and Amos. Anna, daughter of Daniel Harper, married David Abbot 3d, in 1824. It is supposed that the mother of these Harper brothers was Colman, and hence the frequency of this name among their descendants.

JAMES COLMAN HARPER, brother of the preceding, was born in Ashby, Mass., March 10, 1762. He married Betsey Elliot, who was born in Concord, N. H., Sept. 17, 1775, and died Oct. 29, 1809, in Rumford.

Children :

i *Susannah Andrews*, b. Sept. 25, 1792, d. Jan. 12, 1793. ii *Elliot*, b. Sept. 26, 1794. iii *Cotton Webster*, b. July 4, 1796. iv *Abigail*, b. March 16, 1797. v *Betsey*, b. May 29, 1800. vi *Mary Carter*, b. July 13, 1802. vii *James Colman*, b. May 13, 1804. viii *Hiram*, b. Feb. 15, 1806. ix *Aaron*, b. January 9, 1808. x *Ezekiel*, b. Oct. 17, 1809.

HARDY.

ZEBEDIAH HARDY, born May 18, 1794, married Sarah ———, who was born June 11, 1796. He came here from Concord, N. H.

Children :

i *Hannah*, b. Feb. 14, 1813. ii *Mary Ann*, b. July 18, 1815. iii *Asa*, b. Sept. 12, 1816. iv *Azuba*, b. Feb. 9, 1819. v *Nancy*, b. Feb. 16, 1821. vi *Zebediah*, b. March 8, 1823. vii *Sarah*, b. June 19, 1825. viii *Clarissa*, b. May 9, 1827. ix *Charles Chandler*, b. Dec. 9, 1829. x *Martha Jane*, b. Dec. 7, 1832.

HEMMINGWAY.

FRANCIS HEMMINGWAY or HEMMENWAY, a cooper, born in Boston, in 1773, was an early settler. His wife was Rebecca, daughter of

William Godwin, who was born in Fryeburg, Me., in 1777. She died in 1853, and he in 1857.

Children :

  i   *William Redmond*, b. Oct. 19, 1798, m. Phebe (Buck) Brown.
  ii *Colman*, b. May 23, 1800, m. Sally Carr, settled Letter B.
  iii *Mary*, b. July 10, 1802.
  iv *Cynthia*, b. Apr. 11, 1804, d. Apr. 12, 1804.
  v   *Rachel*, b. March 14, 1806.
  vi *Francis*, b. July 11, 1807.
  vii *Harris Redmond*, b. June 27, 1809.
  viii *Sally W.*, b. June 27, 1811.
  ix *Hannah*, b. Feb. 14, 1814, m. Alanson Bean, went west.
  x   *Samuel Farnum*, b. July 10, 1816.
  xi *James Godwin*, b. July 21, 1818, d. Dec. 3, 1830.
  xii *Benjamin Elliot*, b. June 6, 1820.

WILLIAM R. HEMMINGWAY married widow Phebe Brown, whose maiden name was Buck, daughter of John and Abigail (Irish) Buck of Buckfield, who was born Dec. 3, 1792, and died January 14, 1848. He died May 12, 1882.

Children :

  i   *Colman*, b. Jan. 14, 1823, m. Orpha G. Pinkham.
  ii *William H.*, b. Oct. 25, 1826, m. 1st, Amelia Felt, 2d, Lucina (Rolfe) Bryant.
  iii *Mersylvia L.*, b. June 2, 1829, m. Lorenzo Billings.

COLMAN HEMMINGWAY 2D, son of Wm. R. and Phebe Hemmingway, married July 4, 1852, Orpha G., daughter of Thomas and Sarah Pinkham of Dedham, Me.

Children :

  i   *J. Miron*, b. Milton Pl., Apr. 22, 1853, m. Alice Duston.
  ii *Charles A.*, b. May 3, 1856, m. Bertie Barrows.
  iii *Frank L.*, b. Aug. 22, 1857.
  iv *Willis C.*, b. Apr. 13, 1859.
  v   *Lewis P.*, b. Apr. 23, 1863.
  vi *Marydell*, b. Rumford, Apr. 9, 1870.

HIGGINS.

NATHANIEL F. HIGGINS married Sally ———. He bought a farm of Joseph Wardwell in Turner, and moved there.

Children :

  i *Arabella*, b. Sept. 14, 1802. ii *Lurena*, b. March 6, 1805. iii *Silas Wheeler*, b. Apr. 19, 1807, d. Apr. 8, 1810. iv *Electy Miller*, b. July 24, 1810.

HINKSON.

ROBERT HINKSON married first, Mary, daughter of Stephen Putnam, Sept. 20, 1794. He married second, in 1815, Sally, widow of Nathan Silver.

Children :
  i   *Polly,* b. Sept. 7, 1795, m. Ebenezer Door of Livermore.
  ii *Patty,* b. March 1, 1797, m. Ebenezer Door, 2d.
  iii *Robert,* b. June 17, 1798, m. ———.
  iv *Sally,* b. Oct. 1, 1799.
  v   *Sullivan,* b. Aug. 29, 1801, d. May 24, 1809.
  vi *John,* b. April 31, 1803.
  vii *Esther,* } twins, b. January 9, 1805.
  viii *Rachel,* }
  ix *Daniel,* b. Nov. 7, 1807, m. Juliette Swain.
  x   *Phebe,* b. Nov. 19, 1808.
  xi *Chestina,* b. June 6, 1818.
  xii *Aldana,* b. Sept. 23, 1820, m. Grace M. Elliot.

JOHN HINKSON and wife Sally ———.

Children on Rumford records :
  i *Algernon W.,* b. May 22, 1826. ii *Eliza J. W.,* b. Feb. 4, 1828. iii *Lovina Ann S.,* b. Dec. 19, 1829.

JOSEPH HINKSON and wife Mary, had the following children baptized in Rumford. Joseph Hinkson aged 77 and wife Ruth aged 67, (probably second wife) were living in Roxbury in 1850. This wife was Ruth Puffer, to whom he was married in 1823.

Children :
  Mary, Melinda, Jane, Samuel, Hannah, Louisa and *John.*

HODGMAN.

CHARLES HODGMAN married Elvira ———. He lived on Ellis river.

Children :
  i *Charles W.,* b. July 10, 1828. ii *Sarah J.,* b. January 14, 1832. iii *Abner S.,* b. March 4, 1834. iv *Caleb P.,* b. March 15, 1837. v *Hamson Mayhew,* b. Sept. 15, 1840. vi *Abial C.,* b. January 8, 1845.

HODSDON.

STEPHEN HODSDON (sometimes spelled Hodgdon) was born in Berwick, Me., and about the year 1800, he came to Rumford. His wife was Anna, daughter of Daniel Estes, and sister of John, Stephen, Benjamin and Richard, who came into Bethel about that time. Mr. Hodsdon lived in Rumford but a few years and then, having buried his wife, he went to live with his children. He died in 1843, in the family of Peter Estes, who had married his daughter.

Children :

  i *Anna*, b. 1783, m. 1807, Jeremiah Andrews, Jr., s. Rumford.
  ii *Stephen*, b. 1785, m. Huldah Washburn of Hebron, r. Bethel.
  iii *Theodocia*, b. 1788, m. Peter Estes, r. Bethel.
  iv *James*, b. 1791, m. Esther, daughter of Moses Bartlett of Bethel; lived in Bethel; d. 1853 in Greenwood.
  v *Betsey*, b. 1794, d. in Bethel, 1872, unmarried.
  vi *Susan*, b. 1796, m. in Rumford, John Buchannan, d. 1868.
  vii *Daniel*, b. 1799, m. Mary R. Richardson, r. Rumford.
  viii *Lucy*, b. 1802, m. Reuben Whitman of Woodstock, d. 1865.
  ix *Abigail*, b. 1805, m. John Tobin of Hartford, s. Lincoln.

DANIEL HODSDON was the only son of Stephen Hodsdon who lived in Rumford. He married in 1836, Mary R., daughter of John and Mehitable (Eastman) Richardson, who was born Dec. 3, 1812. He died 1865.

Children :

  i *Annie Maria*, b. July 10, 1840.
  ii *Samuel K.*, b. 1844, m. Mary H. Daniels, r. Lewiston.

SAMUEL K. HODSDON married Mary H. Daniels.

Children :

  i *George B.*, b. January 25, 1864.

HOLT.

DAVID HOLT, son of Benjamin and Hannah (Abbot) Holt, born in Pembroke, N. H., May 12, 1774, married Nov. 10, 1795, Chloe, daughter of Timothy and Mary (Walker) Chandler. He lived in Shelburne, N. H., and died in Rumford, Feb. 1, 1859. His wife, born Aug. 30, 1771, died March 17, 1859. Both are buried at the Point.

Children :

  i *Betsey Parker*, b. May 12, 1796, m. Owen Harris.
  ii *Ruth*, b. Feb. 17, 1798, m. Asa Parker.
  iii *Benjamin*, b. Apr. 22, 1800, m. Ann Maria Andrews.
  iv *Timothy*, b. March 7, 1802, m. Nancy Cochran.
  v *Chauncey*, b. May 31, 1804, m. Mrs. Cynthia Davidson.

vi   *Mary W.*, b. Sept. 25, 1806, d. June 9, 1816.
vii *Alonzo*, b. July 5, 1809, m. Abigail Stearns.
viii *Dorcas*, b. May 21, 1812, m. Asa Spofford Howard.
ix   *Hannah Norris*, b. Apr. 14, 1816, d. Feb. 9, 1835.

TIMOTHY HOLT married Sept. 27, 1825, Nancy Cochran. He died Sept. 6, 1871, and his wife died Feb. 7, 1880: both buried at the Point.

Children :

i   *Samuel Webster*, b. June 27, 1826.
ii   *Robert Scott*, b. Apr. 12, 1828.
iii   *Chauncey*, b. March 28, 1830.
iv   *David*, b. Feb. 21, 1833.
v   *William*, b. Feb. 25, 1835.
vi   *Hannah N.*, b. Aug. 6, 1837, m. Milton R. Howard.
vii *Chloe*, b. March 16, 1840, m. Stephen E. Foye.
viii *George L.*, b. June 28, 1842, d. May 25, 1844.
ix   *George L.*, b. Apr. 25, 1844.
x   *John D.*, b. Aug. 14, 1846.
xi   *Cynthia E.*, b. Feb. 8, 1850.

ALONZO HOLT married Abigail Stearns of Bethel. She was the daughter of John and Priscilla Stearns. He married second, in 1857, Polly Kimball.

Children ;

i   *John Newton*, b. Aug. 7, 1842.
ii   *Emily Page*, b. Jan. 15, 1844, m. C. Bradford Frost.
iii *James*, b. May 11, 1845.
iv *Jarvis Alonzo*, b. June 17, 1850, d. Aug. 29, 1854.
v   *Charles Frost*, b. Sept. 29, 1852, d. Feb. 15, 1854.

HOWE.

PHINEAS HOWE, son of Josiah, and grandson of John Howe of Marlboro, Mass., settled in Boylston, Mass., in 1720. His wife was Abigail Bennett.

PHINEAS HOWE, JR., son of the preceding, born March 17, 1733, married Experience Wheeler. He lived in Berlin, Mass. He was a stalwart man, six feet and nine inches tall.

Children :

i   *Silas*, b. Oct. 4, 1760, m. Silence Moore.
ii *Lucretia*, b. Oct. 4, 1761, m. Samuel Goss, s. Rumford.

iii   *Mary*, b. Nov. 10, 1763, m. Abel Baker, s. Concord, N. H.
iv   *Parna*, b. May 24, 1765.
v   *Sarah*, b. March 1, 1767.
vi   *Phineas*, b. March 25, 1769, m. Deborah Abbot, s. Rumford.
vii   *Experience*. b. April 1, 1771, m. Philip Abbot.
viii   *Betty* b. April 19, 1773, m. Gustavus A. Goss.
ix   *Abram*, b. June 24, 1776.
x   *Abigail*. b. 1778, m. Arnold Powers of Bethel.
xi   *Sampson*. b. Aug. 17, 1786, m. Betsey Howe. He with his wife was living in Franklin Plantation in 1850.

SILAS HOWE, son of the preceding, married Silence, daughter of Abraham Moore of Bolton, Mass., and sister of Aaron Moore of Rumford. He lived at the Center, and early commenced mills on Split Brook, which he did not finish.

Children :

i   *Hannah*, b. Feb. 10, 1798.   ii   *Lydia Knight*, b. Dec. 10, 1802.

The above are the only births recorded in Rumford. He may have had other children. He either died or left town quite early. Some of the early town meetings were held at his house.

PHINEAS HOWE, brother of the preceding, married Deborah, daughter of Edward and Deborah (Stevens) Abbot of Concord, N. H. Mrs. Abbot was the daughter of Aaron Stevens, Esq. Mr. Howe came quite early to Rumford. He was a very tall man, his height being six feet and five inches.

Children :

i   *Charlotte*, b. Aug. 21, 1800, m. Benj. Bunker of Rumford.
ii   *Phineas*, b. Feb. 25, 1802.
iii   *Louisa*, b. Dec. 19, 1805, m. Jan. 17, 1824, Merrill Farnum.
iv   *George W.*, b. July 3, 1810.
v   *Mary*, b. Jan. 29, 1817, m. Jan. 1, 1837, George W. Bisbee.

ABRAHAM HOWE, brother of preceding, an early settler here, married Betsey ————. It is said that this man removed to Canada.

Children :

i   *Henry Rolfe*, b. Sept. 20, 1797.
ii   *Curtis Pollard*, b. Oct. 9, 1798   He married first. Lydia Hunting; 2d, Abigail Gleason.
iii   *Almira*, b. July 24, 1800.
iv   *Oliver Beal*, (M. D.), b. May 19, 1802, s. Shelburne, N. H.
v   *Parna*, b. July 8, 1803, m. Abram Warren.
vi   *Lucretia*, b. Oct. 27, 1804.

SAMPSON HOWE, brother of the preceding, has lived more or less in Rumford, and also in Franklin Plantation. His wife was Betsey Howe, whose brother, Ralph Howe, died in Franklin Plantation.

Children :

  i *Alvan*, b. July 21, 1813, m. Melvina Gardiner of Dixfield.

  ii *Tamar*, b. ———, d. young.

  iii *Achsa*, b. ———, m. Rev. Peter Hopkins of Milton Plantation.

OTIS HOWE, son of Alvan Howe, blacksmith, resides at Rumford Corner. He served a term as Postmaster there. He was born Oct. 25, 1850. and married, July 11, 1876, Mary E., daughter of George W. and Harriet R. (Warren) Ripley.

Children :

  i *Charles Arthur*, b. April 30. 1877. ii *Lula Frances*, b. March 12, 1879. iii *Llewellyn Otis*, b. July 12, 1882. iv *Bertha Eliza*, b. Sept. 21, 1884. v *Alice May*, b. Dec. 21. 1888.

ABRAHAM HOWE was of Watertown, and among the earliest settlers of Marlboro, Mass. He married, May 6, 1657, Hannah, daughter of William Ward. He died June 30, 1695, and his widow died Nov. 3, 1717, aged 78. There is no known connection between this family and the descendants of John Howe of Marlboro, preceding.

DANIEL HOWE, oldest son of the preceding, born in 1658, married Elizabeth Kerley. He was a large land owner in Marlboro, and died April 13, 1718.

JOSEPH HOWE, second son of the preceding, born in 1661, married Dorothy Martin in 1687. He was a large land owner in Marlboro, Lancaster and Watertown. He died Sept. 4, 1740.

ABRAHAM HOWE, second son of Joseph preceding, was born March 21, 1698. He married, May 24, 1724, Rachel, daughter of Benjamin and Mary (Graves) Rice.

ASA HOWE, second son of the preceding, born Nov. 30, 1733, married Rachel Goddard in 1762. She died June 10, 1814.

JOHN HOWE, oldest son of Asa preceding, born Nov. 25, 1762, married Dec. 28, 1785, Mary Newton. He came to Rumford and settled on Ellis River. He was a farmer and cooper, an industrious, peaceable and valuable citizen. For second wife, he married in 1812, Mrs. Persis Moore of Worcester, Mass. His wife died in 1810; he died in 1830, and his widow Persis in 1836.

Children, all, save one, born in Marlboro :

  i   *Parazina*, b. 1786, m. John Cushman of Bethel, d. 1845.

  ii *Joel*, b. 1788, m. first, Esther Howard, and second, Dorcas Barker, s. Hanover.

  iii *Eli*, b. 1789, m. Salome Andrews, s. Hanover.

  iv *Lois*, b. 1791, m. Enoch Abbot, s. Upton.

  v *John*, b. 1792, m. first, Betsey Abbot, second, widow Nancy Brown, and third, widow Clarissa Estes.

  vi *Otis*, b. 1794, m. Elsie Andrews, s. Rumford.

  vii *Mary*, b. 1798, m. Job Pratt of Cohasset, Mass; she died in Rumford, April, 1863.

  viii *Calvin*, b. in Rumford, 1802, m. Thirza Kimball, s. Rumford.

JOEL HOWE, oldest son of the preceding, married first, Esther Howard of Howard's Gore, and second, Dorcas Barker of Newry. He engaged in wool-carding and cloth-dressing, which business he carried on in Hanover for many years. He died Oct. 12, 1871, and his second wife died Aug. 15, 1888.

Children :

  i   *Mary Newton*, b. June 19, 1814, m. Joseph Hutchins.

  ii *Joel B.*, b. Dec. 12, 1816, d. ———.

  iii *Phineas H.*, b. Dec. 8, 1819, m. 1st, Nancy Staples, 2d, Albina Jewett.

By second wife :

  iv *Jesse Barker*, b. May 26, 1830, m. Matilda Abbot, d. Nov. 30, 1886.

  v *Dorcas*, { m. Hon. Reuben Foster, r. Waterville.

                  { twins, b. May 24, 1832.

  vi *Esther*, { m. Prentiss M. Putnam, r. a widow in Portland.

  vii *Galen*, b. Aug. 4, 1834, m. Helen Foster. He resides in Arizona.

  viii *Winfield S.*, b. Feb. 23, 1839, m. Clara Knapp, r. Hanover.

  ix *Abbie D.*, b. May 13, 1843, m. C. Bradley Frost; she died Oct. 16, 1877.

COL. ELI HOWE married Salome, daughter of Jeremiah Andrews of Bethel. He lived in Rumford, for a time in Brunswick, and finally settled down in Hanover, where for many years he had charge of a grist mill. He was one of the substantial citizens of the town. Children :

  i   *Betsey*, b. ———, m. Joseph Staples.

  ii *Alonzo A.*, b. ———, m. first, ——— Brown, and second, Nancy Andrews. He died in Bethel.

  iii *Galen*, b. ———, d. young.

iv   *Gilbert*, b. ———, m. Sarah D. Perry.

v   *Albion K.*, b. ———, m. Eliza Brown.

vi   *William Andrews*, b. ———, m. Joanna Demerit.

vii   *Mary E.*, b. ———, m. first, Geo. W. Lampher, and second, Horatio
F. Houghton; she died at Bryant's Pond.

viii   *Charles Lyman*, b.———.

xi   *Henry N.*, b.———, m. Caroline C. Graham.

JOHN HOWE, JR., married first in 1818, Betsey, daughter of Jonathan Abbot of Bethel; second in 1825, Nancy, daughter of Jacob Kimball of Bethel, and widow of Rufus Barker of Waterford, and third, Clarissa, daughter of Jacob Kimball of Bethel, and widow of Eli Estes of Bethel. He died in 1861. The children were by the second marriage.

Children :

i   *Elizabeth A.*, b. Feb. 7, 1826, m. Nathan S. Lufkin, r. Caribou.

ii   *Asa Kimball*, b. Mar. 3, 1828, d. Mar. 9, 1865, in Manchester, N. H.
He married Sarah B., daughter of Reuben B. Foster of Hanover.

iii   *Rufus B.*, b. June 28, 1829, m. Delia Silver.

iv   *William H.*, b. March 22, 1831, d. unmarried.

v   *John*, b. Aug. 4, 1834, m. Augusta M. Glines.

vi   *Charlotte Kimball*, b. Sept. 7, 1835, m. William Elliot.

vii   *Lucinda G.*, b. May 7, 1837, m. Josiah K. Elliott.

viii   *Nancy E.*, b. June 3, 1845, m. Rev. Francis Grosvenor.

OTIS HOWE, b. Sept. 24, 1794, married Elsie, daughter of Jeremiah Andrews, who was born March 12, 1796. For second wife he married Mrs. Betsey Prescott of Chichester, N. H. He died in 1863.

Children :

i   *Otis*, b. Feb. 1, 1818, m. first, Mrs. Sarah S. Elliot, second, Mrs.
Judith Rowe.

ii   *Dorcas*, b. Dec. 10, 1819. m. Alfred Lufkin.

iii   *Amos A.*, b. Sept. 24, 1821, m. Sarah Allen, Leominster, Mass.

iv   *Salome*, b. Jan. 6, 1824, d. unmarried.

v   *Nancy K.*, b. April 6, 1826.

vi   *Julia Ann*, b. May 11, 1828, m. Stephen A. Perry, s. California.

vii   *John Hiram*, b. Nov. 10, 1830, m. 1858, Harriet E. Glines.

viii   *Sarah Elizabeth*, b. Jan. 23, 1833, m. Sullivan R. Hutchins.

ix   *Charles Francis*, b. Aug. 3, 1835, d. young.

x   *Edward Kent*, b. May 4, 1838, r. California.

xi   *May Eliza*, b. Jan. 14, 1841. d. young.

By second marriage:

xii   *Mary Eliza*, b. ———, m. Cyrus P. Eaton.

xiii   *James Prescott*, b. ———, d. 1887.

CALVIN HOWE, son of John and Mary (Newton) Howe, married Dec. 16, 1828, Thirza, daughter of Jacob Kimball of Bethel; married by Rev. Daniel Gould. He died July 2, 1884. He was a farmer on Ellis River.

Children :

    i   *Frances Ann*, b. Sept. 2, 1829, m. Lambert Newton of Andover.
    ii *Mark T.*, b. Sept. 23, 1831, d. in California, Aug. 10, 1853.
   iii *Lucretia T. B.*, b. Feb. 13, 1833, r. Rumford, unmarried.
   iv *Julia K.*, b. Oct. 1, 1834, m. C. A. Stockbridge, d. 1887.
    v *Clara E.*, b. Aug. 3, 1836, m. Lyman F. Abbot of Andover, d. March 12, 1863.
   vi *Emma S.*, b. May 1, 1837, m. David G. Glines, d. 1870.
  vii *Mary J.*, b. Oct. 13, 1839, d. Rumford, 1882.
 viii *Alden C.*, b. April 13, 1841.
   ix *Nancy M.*, b. March 4, 1843, d. Rumford, 1888.
    x *Althea C.*, b. June 11, 1844, m. Greenleaf G. Wagg of Lewiston.
   xi *Catherine S.*, b. June 18, 1845.
  xii *Susan P.*, b. May 13, 1848, m. Dr. Cyrus Kendrick, Litchfield, Me.
 xiii *Rosilla H.*, b. June 30, 1849, m. Hiram H. Bean, Bethel.

RUFUS B. HOWE, son of John Howe, Jr., married Delia C., daughter of James Silver. He was a farmer and mechanic. At one time, with his father-in-law, he kept the hotel at Bryant's Pond. He died in Douglass, Mass.

Children :

    i   *Nellie M.*, b. Douglass, Mass., June 16, 1856.
   ii *Flora D.*, b. Woodstock, Oct. 4, 1857, d. Dec. 3, 1874.
  iii *John Fremont*, b. Rumford, May 1, 1859.
  iv *Gertrude D.*, b. ———.
   v *Edward B.*, b. June 26, 1863.
  vi *Erving C.*, b. April 23, 1866.
 vii *Isabella F.*, b. Jan. 29, 1869.
 viii *Lucinda G.*, b. Jan. 17, 1871.
  ix *Walter R.*, b. Feb. 21, 1874.

JOHN HOWE, JR., married Jan. 1, 1860, Augusta M., daughter of David B. Glines. He is a farmer, and resides on the old homestead of his father.

Children :

   i *John R.*, b. Feb. 8, 1864.
  ii *Ermina A.*, b. Aug. 11, 1866, m. Oct. 18, 1888, Evans W. Hodgdon.
 iii *Wallace,* } twins, b. Nov. 3, 1870.
 iv *Winfred,*

Otis Howe, Jr., m. first, Sarah S., daughter of David Elliot, and second, Judith, daughter of Simeon Rowe of Woodstock, and widow of Jonathan Atwood Rowe of same.

Children :
i   *Martha A.,* b. April 3, 1847, m. George T. Silver.
ii   *Viana M.,* b. April 3, 1849, m. Henry S. Philbrick of Andover.
iii   *Lewis A.,* b. Dec. 26, 1850, d. Nov. 20, 1853.
iv   *Alice S.,* b. April 11, 1852, m. B. H. Boynton.
v   *Walter H.,* b. Feb. 4. 1855, m. Alvena Philbrick of Roxbury.
vi   *Olive M.,* b. Sept. 10, 1858, m. Charles B. Wing of Wayne.
vii   *Sidney Perham,* b. Aug. 10, 1860.
viii   *George Henry,* b. March 28, 1869.

John H. Howe, son of Otis Howe, married Harriet E., daughter of David B. Glines.

Children :
i   *Hattie B.,* b. February 15, 1861.   ii   *Hiram W.,* b. February 25. 1863.
iii   *Charles M.,* b. Jan. 1, 1865.

HOWARD.

Asa Spofford Howard, son of Asa Howard of Howard's Gore, married, first, August 26, 1837, Dorcas, daughter of David and Chloe Holt of Pembroke, N. H. She died, and he married second, Betsey S., daughter of Joshua and Sally (Powers) Roberts of Hanover. Mr. Howard was a farmer, and exemplary man, often entrusted with town office, and had the respect and confidence of his townsmen to the fullest extent. At this time (1890) he is spending his declining years with one of his married daughters in Bethel. He has been greatly afflicted in the death of many of his children at an early age.

Children.
i   *Henry F.,* b. June 19, 1838, m. Nov. 22, 1863, Clara M. Woodbury of Sweden; d. Nov. 22, 1871. For several years he was a successful teacher, studied law and was admitted to the bar. He possessed uncommon ability, and his early death was lamented by a large circle of friends.
ii   *Mary W.,* b. May 11, 1840, d. Nov. 9, 1870.
iii   *Asa,* b. March 26, 1842, d. Dec. 31, 1866.
iv   *Charles W.,* b. Sept. 30, 1843, d. Oct. 18, 1868.
By second wife:
v   *Abbie M.,* b. Sept. 9, 1849, m. Nov., 1868, Henry Moore, d. April 27, 1871.
vi   *Dollie S.,* b. Aug. 15, 1852, d. Oct. 16, 1878.

vii   *Adeltha D.*, b. March 24, 1853, d. July 15, 1868.
viii *Nellie R.*, b. Jan. 9, 1855, m. Jan. 1. 1878, Orin W. Ellingwood; r. Bethel.
ix   *Fred E.*, b. Feb. 9, 1857, m. Nov. 11, 1878, Annette Smith.

THOMAS J. HOWARD, son of Phineas and Lavinia (Powers) Howard of Howard's Gore, married Olive, daughter of Amos Bean of Bethel in 1825.

Children :

i *Humphrey*, b. Jan. 9, 1827.   ii *Elias*, b. Dec. 1, 1832.   iii *Huldah*, b. Feb. 5, 1834.   iv *Orintha*, b. Sept. 24, 1836.   v *Thomas J.*, b. Nov. 16, 1837.

HOYT.

EZRA HOYT, who came to this town, was the son of John and Abigail (Carter) Hoyt of Concord, N. H., and grandson of Abner and Mary Blaisdell Hoyt, who settled in Concord about 1730, from Amesbury, Mass. He was born January 23, 1770. His wife was Susannah Weeks, to whom he was married April 2, 1795. He lived many years on the road between Andover North Surplus and Umbagog Lake. He died in Howard's Gore, where he had long lived.

Children :

i   *William*, b. Concord, Nov. 19, 1793, r. Niagara Falls.
ii   *Temple*, b. Loudon, N. H., Sept. 5, 1796; served in War of 1812; d. 1839.
iii   *John*, b. Barnstead, N. H., Sept. 29, 1797; he kept a hotel at Exeter, N. H.
iv   *Betsey*, b. Jan. 27, 1799, m. James C. Whittemore.
v   *Stephen*, b. Concord, May 8, 1802; r. Reading, Mass.
vi   *Mary Stevens*, b. April 26, 1805. m. Samuel S. Snow.
vii   *Clarissa*, b. Nov. 4, 1806, m. James Harvey Farnum, d. Portland.
viii *Philip Carrigan*, b. July 12. 1808, d. 1841.
ix   *Gardiner G.*, b. ———, m. Laura C. Lovejoy of Andover, s. Hanover.
x   *Abigail*, b. ———, m. Samuel Whitney.
xi   *Sally*, b. ———, d. young.
xii   *Ezra C.*, b. ———, (Physician) s. Beaver Dam, Wis.
      Two. each named Fanny, d. in infancy.

JESSE HOYT, son of Aaron and Betsey (Kilborn) Hoyt, born in Weare, N. H., Dec. 11, 1794, married Abigail Morgan. He came from New Hampshire to Rumford in 1830, and died Sept. 4, 1853. His wife died August 26, 1878.

Children :

   i   *Orianna,* b. Weare, N. H., Oct. 19, 1816, d. Dec. 4, 1840.

  ii *Lovinia,* b. Weare, N. H., July 19, 1818, m. Benjamin Hoyt of Weare.

 iii *Betsey,* b. Weare, N. H., Jan. 29, 1820, d. 1826.

 iv *Sylvanus,* b. Weare, N. H., March 5, 1822, d. March 1865. not mar.

  v *Andrew J.,* b. Weare N. H., Jan. 19, 1824, m. 1st, Eleanor Batch-
       elder, 2d, Daphne Esther Osgood, resides Waltham, Mass.
       Deacon of First Cong. Church there.

 vi *Abigail M.,* b. Weare, N. H. Dec. 27, 1825, m. Robert Kennard.
       She resides at Waltham.

 vii *Patrick Henry,* b. Weare, N. H. Jan. 4, 1827. m. Lucy A. Farnum.
       He was a Methodist preacher and died at Monmouth, Sept. 22, 1869.

viii *Nial,* b. Weare, N. H., Jan. 4, 1830, m. Arvilla Wright of Jay, Me.,
       d. Nov. 16, 1864.

 ix *Aaron,* b. Rumford, July 19, 1831, d. June, 1845.

  x *Mary Elizabeth,* b. Rumford, March 14, 1834. m. John Haines of
       Waltham, Mass., and resides there.

 xi *Loretta Adelaide,* b. Rumford, Aug. 8, 1836, m. Francis A. Bacon.

 xii *Lucebia E.,* b. Rumford, Dec. 11, 1838, m. Edward True of Yar-
       mouth, Me. Resides at Castine, Me.

PATRICK H. HOYT, son of the preceding, born in East Weare,
N. H. Came to Rumford with his father. When he became of age
he engaged some years in trade. He was representative to the
Maine Legislature, served as selectman for several years, and was
a man of influence in town. In 1862 he was licensed as a Methodist preacher, and in 1865, was admitted on trial in the Maine Conference. He had several appointments, one of which was Rumford.
In 1869, he was appointed to Monmouth, and died there Sept. 22 of
that year. He married in 1851, Lucy Ann Farnum.

Children :

   i *Nial,* b. May 3, 1853.

  ii *Ella F.,* b. Oct. 16, 1854, d. Oct. 26, 1864.

 iii *Mary E.,* b. Dec. 11, 1856.

 iv *Patrick Henry,* b. May 9, 1859, d. Oct. 29, 1864.

  v *Lucy J.,* b. Jan. 27, 1861.

NIAL HOYT, brother of the preceding, married in Dunbarton, N.
H., in 1856, Arvilla, daughter of Reuben Wright. He died in
Rumford, Nov. 15, 1864.

Children :

   i *Walter Scott,* b. Nov. 29, 1857. ii *Addie Augusta,* b. Apr. 19, 1860.
iii *Willie Herbert,* b. Jan. 26, 1862, d. Feb. 10, following.

HUNTING.

NATHAN HUNTING, from Chelmsford, Mass., purchased the mill privilege near the mouth of Split Brook at the Center, where Silas Howe had made improvements, of Phineas Wood. He came here and finished the mills and operated them for several years. He then sold out and returned to Chelmsford. His only son, George, settled in Kentucky, and about the year 1830 he moved his parents to that State. They all died of cholera on the same day. Mr. Hunting married a Jinks.

Children :

i *Eliza*, b. ———, m. Samuel Robertson of Bethel. ii *Nancy*, b———. m. Philip Tyler. iii *Abigail*, b. ———, m. Moses Foster. iv *Mercy*, b. ———, m. Franklin Foster. v *Lydia*, b. ———, m. Curtis P. Howe. vi *George*, b. ———, d. unmarried in Kentucky.

HUTCHINS.

HEZEKIAH HUTCHINS of Concord, N. H., married Sally Elliot, and came to Rumford among the quite early settlers. He was prominent in town and church affairs, and the first deacon of the Congregational church.

Children :

i *David*, b. July 4, 1795, m. Sally Abbot of Andover.
ii *Hezekiah*, b. Sept. 19, 1797, m. Lucinda Bean.
iii *Polly Elliot*. b. June 5, 1800, d. Oct. 8, 1803.
iv *Jacob*, b. March 21, 1802, d. Oct. 9, 1803.
v *Polly Elliot*, b. January 25, 1804, m. Enos Abbot.
vi *Sally*, b. March 4, 1806.
vii *Joseph*, b. Aug. 29, 1808, m. Mary N. Howe.

DAVID HUTCHINS, JR., son of the preceding, married Betsey Holt of Pembroke, N. H. The oldest two children were born in Concord ; the others in Rumford. Mrs. Hutchins was the daughter of Frye and Mary (Poor) Holt of Pembroke, N. H. Mr. Hutchins was known as "Master Hutchins."

Children :

i *Betsey*, b, June 17, 1804. ii *Clarissa*, b. July 13, 1806. iii *Nancy*, b. June 28, 1808. iv *Frye Holt*, b. Aug. 14, 1810. v *Hannah C.*, b. July 10, 1812. vi *Elijah Bartlett*, b. Aug. 27, 1814. vii *Mary Strickland*, b. Oct. 23, 1816. viii *Persis Frye*, b. Feb. 16, 1820. ix *Betsey Poor*, b. March 31, 1823. x *Enoch Holt*, b. Oct. 31, 1825.

HEZEKIAH HUTCHINS, JR., b. Sept. 29, 1797, married Lucinda, daughter of Luther Bean. He was a land surveyor, a Justice of the Peace, and a prominent man. He died at his farmstead, just across the line in Bethel, Nov. 14, 1850.

Children ;

    i   *Louisa A.*, b. July 13, 1830, m. Geo. W. Hunt.

    ii *Sullivan R.*, b. Oct. 7. 1832. m. 1855, Sarah E., daughter of Otis Howe.

    iii *Sophia F.*, b. May 29, 1835, m. 1855, Amos A. Young, 2d, Curtis Gilman.

    iv *Olive*, b. June 6, 1837, m. Leander F. Lynde.

    v *Jane M.*, b. July 20, 1839, m. 1st, Nathan Clifford Knapp, 2d, Charles W. Kimball.

    vi *Abel C. T.*, b. Feb. 23, 1843.

JOSEPH HUTCHINS married Mary N. Howe. He lived on the Henry Abbott farm at East Rumford, and died July 25, 1871. His widow died March 28, 1875.

Children :

    i   *Joel Howe*, b. March 24, 1832, m. Frances M. Silver.

    ii *Nancy Swan*. b. Feb. 11, 1834, m. George S. Silver.

    iii *Asa Boyden*, b. Nov. 27, 1839, d. Oct. 1, 1872, of consumption.

FRYE H. HUTCHINS, son of David Hutchins, was a farmer and trader. He also kept the hotel at Bethel Hill for a number of years. He lived on a farm on the west side of Ellis river and was in trade at Hanover. In his earlier years he taught school. He was a good business man and was more or less in town office. He died in Hanover July 10, 1879. His wife, Betsey (Huckins) Hutchins, born in New Hampton, N. H., Dec. 7, 1816, resides a widow in Hanover.

Children :

    i   *Ellis Jane*, b. Feb. 21, 1837, m. 1855, Charles R. Abbot, and d. Nov. 27, 1860.

    ii *George H.*, b. Oct. 11. 1841. m. July 13, (?) Georgie McAllister of Andover. He served in the 7th Maine Battery, and since the war has resided a farmer in Andover. They have, 1, Fred F., b. Sept. 10, 1872; 2d, Bert B., b. Aug. 29, 1878.

SULLIVAN R. HUTCHINS, son of Hezekiah Hutchins, Jr., is an Attorney at Law and a surveyor of land. He was married Nov. 28, 1854, to Sarah E., daughter of Otis and Elsie (Andrews) Howe of Rumford, by Rev. Joseph Lufkin. He has for some years occupied the Dr. Fuller stand at the Corner.

Children :

i   *Horace G.*, b. Oct. 14, 1855, d. Nov. 9, 1856.
ii *Clarence M.*, b. May 6, 1857, m. Apr. 6, 1880, Nellie S. Rawson of Paris.
iii *Harry H.*, b. Dec. 20, 1858, m. July 15, 1880, Ada M. Colby.
iv *Edward E.*, b. Aug. 28, 1861, d. Oct. 18, following.

JOEL H. HUTCHINS married Frances M. Silver, July 4, 1857, at Shelburne, N. H.

Children :

i *James S.*, b. March 17, 1864. ii *Mary F.*, b. Apr. 30, 1870.

DAVID HUTCHINS, 3D, married Sally Abbot of Andover, July, 1817.

Children :

i *Phebe Howard*, b. Sept. 3, 1818. ii *Enos Abbot*, b. Dec. 26, 1819. iii *Lucy Adams*, b. Apr. 4, 1822. iv *Mary Parsons*, b. Feb. 6, 1824. v *Lydia Elliot*, b. Feb. 15, 1826. vi *Lucinda Bean*, b. January 3, 1828. vii *Jacob Elliot*, b. Feb. 11, 1830. viii *Sarah Farnum*, b. Feb. 4, 1832.

WILLIAM C. HUTCHINSON married Phebe M. Lufkin. He was a private in the 7th Maine Battery.

Children :

i *Mary E.*, b. Oct. 20, 1848. ii *Corinna L.*, b. Sept. 11, 1849. iii *Evelyn R.*, b. Dec. 23, 1851. iv *Edwin H.*, b. Aug. 28, 1853. v *Willie F.*, b. March 6, 1855. vi *Leroy C.*, b. Apr. 24, 1857. vii *Maria Florence*, b. Apr. 25, 1861.

IRISH.

THOMAS IRISH, JR., born in Buckfield, March 3, 1800, married Sept. 6, 1835, Eveline Augusta Daggett, who was born Feb. 21, 1816. He was the son of Thomas and Elizabeth (Roberts) Irish of Gorham, grandson of William Irish, and great grandson of James Irish, who emigrated from Roxfordshire, England, about 1710 and first located in Falmouth, (Portland) subsequently at Gorham. Mr. Irish came to East Rumford in 1859 and was a farmer.

Children :

i   *Henry D.*, b. July 19, 1836, m. Catherine Hines.
ii *Jonathan N.*, b. January 23, 1838, unmarried in Rumford.
iii *Emily S.*, b. January 20, 1841, d. Apr. 24, 1870.
iv *Phebe M.*, b. Sept. 4, 1843, d. Sept. 6, 1847.

JACKSON.

BENJAMIN JACKSON, son of Joseph Jackson of Newry, born in 1814, married Sarah Evans of Shelburne, N. H. He was by trade a tailor, and carried on business in this town many years. No record of the family has been received, but the census of 1850 gives the following :

Children :

i *Dolly M.*, b. 1836. ii *Napoleon B.*, b. 1837. iii *Ezekiel C.*, b. 1838. iv *Sylvester S.*, b. 1841. v *Benjamin, Jr.*, b. 1844. vi Child, b. 1849.

JACOBS.

JOSEPH JACOBS, born in 1794, married Mary J. ———, who was born in 1793. With the following children, they were living in Mexico in 1850. Their two sons served on the Rumford quota in the late war.

Children :

i *Mary J.*, b. ———, 1827. ii *William I.*, b. ———, 1830. iii *Harmon*, b. ———, 1832.

JENNISON.

GARDNER JENNISON married Eliza F. ———.

Children recorded on Rumford records :

i *Isaac Marshall*, b. Feb. 7, 1833. ii *Caroline*, b. July 7, 1835. iii *Sarah*, b. Oct. 28, 1838.

KENNISON.

JAMES R. KENNISON married Fanny, daughter of Samuel Putnam. He lives on Eaton Hill.

Children on town records :

i *Lois E.*, b. July 26, 1830. ii *Arvilla*, b. Sept. 10, 1832. iii *Diantha Angeline*, b. Aug. 21, 1835. iv *Martha Rupina*, b. Dec. 9, 1837.

KEYES.

JONATHAN KEYES, JR., said to be first settler in Rumford, son of Dea. Jonathan and Patience (Morse) Keyes of the North Parish in Shrewsbury, Mass., born Jan. 21, 1728, married January 23, 1752, Sarah Taylor. An account of his life previous to his coming to Rumford will be found elsewhere. He settled on the farm below

Rumford Corner, now known as the Timothy Walker farm, and deceased Nov. 9, 1786. He, with his wife, was buried on his farm, and no monument or stone marks his last resting place.

Children :

i   *Solomon*, b. June 25, 1753.
ii   *Dinah*, b. January 23, 1755 d. 1756.
iii   *Sarah*, b. Dec. 21, 1756.
iv   *Thomas*, b. ———.
v   *Ebenezer*, b. Oct. 24, 1760, m. Jemima Jackson and was with his father in Rumford, but returned to Massachusetts. In 1805, he moved to Jay, Me., where he died May 31. 1838.
vi   *Salma.* b. Sept. 6, 1762. He left home when a boy and settled in Virginia.
vii   *Francis*, b. Oct. 13, 1765, m. Dolly Bean.

FRANCIS KEYES (see personal notice) married Dolly, daughter of Josiah and Molly (Crocker) Bean of Standish, afterwards of Bethel. He lived on the homestead of his father. He died August 16, 1832, and his wife died Feb., 1834.

Children :

i   *Sally.* b. June 9, 1792. m. Peter C. Virgin.
ii   *Polly*, b. Nov. 14, 1794, m. Jesse Putnam.
iii   *Jonathan* b. Apr. 24, 1797. He was killed by the bursting of a gun while firing at a military muster in Rumford.
iv   *Josiah*, b. Dec. 24 1799, m. Rachel Barker.
v   *Lydia*, b. Aug. 23. 1802, m. Francis Cushman.
vi   *Winthrop S..* b. Dec. 5, 1804. d. Nov. 22, 1825.
vii   *Dolly B.*, b. Nov. 10, 1806, m. Otis C. Bolster, died Aug. 15, 1840.
viii   *Francis*, b. Oct. 13, 1810, d. young.
ix   *Hannah*, b. July 19. 1813, m. Loammi B. Peabody.

JOSIAH KEYES, son of the preceding, married Rachel, daughter of Capt. Samuel Barker of Newry, afterwards of Rumford. He resided at Rumford Corner. He was a noted wag and wit, and many of his bright sayings are still remembered by Rumford people. He was a fine mechanic and assisted in building some of the finest bridges connecting Boston with Charlestown.

Children :

i   *Frances Ophelia.* b. Sept. 30, 1836, m. March 11, 1856, Stephen A. Russell of Bethel. He is a jeweller and watchmaker, a very ingenious workman and resides in Augusta, Me. They have : Alice A., b. Nov. 22. 1858; Sylvanus H., b. Dec. 8, 1861.
ii   *Cincinnatus.* b. June 13, 1839. He was killed in 1862. in the battle

iii *William Tell*, b. Aug. 23, 1843, m. 1st, Thirza A. Little, resides Colebrook, N. H. He m. 2d, Oct. 30, 1875, Sarah A. Keyes.

iv *George D.*, b. Sept. 15, 1848, m. Carrie Lowder of Rockland.

KIMBALL.

JOHN KIMBALL of Exeter, N. H., married first, Abigail Lyford, Feb. 14, 1722–3. For second wife he married Sept. 18, 1740, Sarah, daughter of Dea. Thomas Wilson. By the first marriage there were six children, and by the second, nine.

MOSES KIMBALL, son of the preceding, born in Exeter, N. H., May 13, 1749, married widow Phebe (Cole) Smart, who was born in Exeter, Sept. 23, 1753. He came to Rumford in 1785, and died Apr. 5, 1830; his wife died Nov. 26, 1823.

Children :

i *Sarah*, b. Exeter, March 13, 1782, m. Isaac Gleason of Mexico, d. Sept. 3, 1860.
ii *Moses*, b. Jan. 15, 1784, m. Feb., 1813. Lucy Osgood.
iii *John*, b. Rumford, July 8, 1785, m. 1808, Hannah (Wheeler) Martin, d. Dec. 6, 1864.
iv *Noah*, b. March 8, 1787.
v *Mary*, b. July 24, 1788, m. Nason Ingalls.
vi *David.* b. Oct. 18, 1790, m. Feb. 25, 1817, Lucy Wheeler.
vii *Loruhamah L.*, b. Feb. 15, 1792, m. Rev. Joseph Lufkin.
viii *William*, b. July 8. 1793.
ix *Robert C.*, b. Feb. 15, 1795, m. Virtue Willis.
x *Phebe*, b. July 23, 1796, m. Nov. 29, 1819, John Lufkin; d. Jan. 24, 1872.

JOHN KIMBALL, son of Moses Kimball, married Hannah (Wheeler) Martin in Nov., 1808. She was the widow of John Martin, who died in 1805.

Children :

i *William*, b. Sept. 16, 1810, d. Oct. 28, following.
ii *John Wesley*, b. March 21, 1812, m. Mary Brown.
iii *Alvan*, b. July 3, 1814, m. Janette (Marble) Kimball.
iv *Blanchard*, b. June 27, 1816, m. Rose Carr.
v *Wilson*, b. ———, m. Janette Marble.
vi *Hannah*, b. ———, m. Judge Charles W. Walton.

DAVID KIMBALL, son of Moses Kimball, married Lucy W. Wheeler of Dixfield, who was born Sept. 14, 1793, and died March 30, 1782.

Children :

    i   *Cordelia Walker*, b. Nov. 21, 1817, d. Dec. 22, 1819.

    ii   *Lucy A. C.*, b. Feb. 8, 1819, d. Aug. 22, 1823.

    iii   *Amanda C.*, b. Nov. 30, 1820, d. Feb. 14, 1865.

    iv   *Joseph S.*, b. Aug. 10, 1822. d. Aug. 23, 1823.

    v   *Columbia,* } twins, b. Oct. 30, 1824.
    vi   *Columbus,*

    vii   *Juliette*, b. March 30, 1826.

    viii   *William Wallace*, b. March 22, 1828, m. Eva M. Cone.

    ix   *David Williams*, b. Feb. 14, 1830, m. Sarah Moore.

    x   *Virgil D.*, b. Nov. 10, 1831, m. Lydia A. Martin.

    xi   *Lucy Ann*, b. June 1, 1834, m. Merrit N. Lufkin.

    xii   *Elizabeth*, b. Apr. 5. 1836, m. Geo. H. Gleason.

ROBERT C. KIMBALL, son of Moses Kimball, married Virtue, daughter of Jonas Willis of Hanover, who was born Oct. 8, 1803, and died March 24, 1867. Mr. Kimball died in Hanover Jan. 29, 1880.

Children.

    i   *Charlotte W.*, b. Jan. 1, 1829, m. John Swain, Jr.

    ii   *Lucinda B.*, b. Sept. 17, 1830. m. Levi Swain.

    iii   *Adam W.*, b. Aug. 18, 1832, m. Philena Swain.

    iv   *Dana L.*, b. Aug. 14, 1843, m. Rose K., daughter of Stephen and Ann W. Philbrick.

VIRGIL D. KIMBALL, son of David Kimball, married Lydia A. Martin, and lives on the Kimball homestead near Red Hill.

Children :

    i   *William J.*, b. Aug. 24, 1856, m. Pearl Farnum. He keeps the tavern at the Center.

    ii   *Lucy W.*, b. June 23, 1862.

    iii   *Evelina*, b. March 1, 1864.

    iv   *Wilder*, b. March 9, 1867.

JACOB KIMBALL, born in Andover, Mass., June 9, 1700, was the fifth in descent from Richard Kimball, the imigrant, who settled in Ipswich. Jacob Kimball married Sarah Hale, who was born Feb. 11, 1723. Among their children was,

ASA KIMBALL, who was born June 15, 1738. He married Huldah Tapley of Topsfield, Mass., July 15, 1760. In 1787, he bought land in Bridgton, and there built a rope-walk, 300 feet in length. Of his sons, Samuel, Asa, Israel and Jacob, settled in Bethel, and he came there in his old age, and died there.

Asa Kimball, Jr., son of the preceding, came to Bethel quite early and settled on the interval farm on the south side of Androscoggin river, which Samuel Ingalls in 1777, bought of Jonathan Keyes. He married Phebe Foster of Bridgton. Two of his children came to Rumford, namely, Esquire Moses, and Nancy, who became the wife of Porter Kimball.

Moses F. Kimball, Esq., married Mary, daughter of Josiah and Molly (Crocker) Bean of Bethel, and settled first in Bethel, near his father's residence. He was a blacksmith. He then moved to Rumford Point, and died there. (See his personal notice).

Children :
i *Mary Ann*, b. Bethel, Apr. 26, 1814, m. Eben T. Goddard.
ii *Charles Adams*, b. Rumford, Dec. 10, 1816, m. Elizabeth W. Abbot.
iii *William King*, b. June 7, 1820, m. Frances Rawson; d. Sept. 2, 1875.
iv *Asa*, b. Aug. 20, 1824, m. Geneva Frost.
v *Dolly Keyes*, b. May 10, 1826, m. Gideon A. Hastings. r. Bethel.
vi *Arabella Carter*, b. March 25, 1830, m. Alvan B. Godwin, r. Bethel.

Charles Adams Kimball, son of the preceding, (see personal notice) married Apr. 12, 1838, Elizabeth, daughter of David Abbot.

Children :
i *Charles W.*, b. March 3, 1839, m. Jennie, widow of Nathan C. Knapp of Hanover, and daughter of Hezekiah Hutchins. He was long in trade at the Point, served in the Maine Legislature and for many years, treasurer of the town. He resides at Rumford Point.
ii *Elizabeth A.*, b. Dec. 9, 1841, m. John G. Elliot who died Aug. 6, 1882.
iii *Caroline W.*, b. Feb. 28, 1846, m. Orlando W. Blanchard who died March 2, 1872.

Asa Kimball, brother of the preceding, lives at the old homestead of his father at Rumford Point. He is a farmer. He married Geneva, daughter of William Frost.

Children :
i *Prentiss E.*, b. May 26, 1847, m. Estella Bean. r. Portland.
ii *Mary G.*, b. Apr. 4, 1853, m. Walter S. Abbot.
iii *Moses F.*, b. Nov. 27, 1856, d. Aug. 31, 1857.
iv *William Frost*, b. May 25, 1865, resides unmarried in Portland.

Francis Kimball, born in Bradford, Mass., Dec. 8, 1742, married Betty Head, who was born in 1748, and died Sept. 13, 1820. He died Dec. 6, 1822. They had a large family, the oldest being

Peter Kimball, born Aug. 9, 1768, married Lucy, daughter of

Asa Barker, and moved to Bridgton. They had children Porter and Peter, twins, Jonathan, George. Frances and William and two daughters who died unmarried. Peter and Jonathan Kimball settled on what was then known as Hamlin's Gore, now a part of the town of Woodstock, and Jonathan died there. Peter was a carpenter and carriage maker and carried on the business a long time on the Gore, then moved to Norway where he died. He was the father of Hon. Charles P. Kimball and of Hannibal I. Kimball of Atlanta, Georgia. George Kimball lived in Bethel many years, then moved to Waltham, Mass., where he died.

PORTER KIMBALL, born in Bradford, Mass., May 19, 1793, son of Peter and Lucy (Barker) Kimball, and grand son of Francis and Betty (Head) Kimball, came from Bethel prior to 1819. He was a blacksmith and lived at the Point. (See personal notice.) He was married in Bethel, April 30, 1818, by Rev. Daniel Mason, to Miss Nancy, daughter of Asa and Phebe (Foster) Kimball, and sister of Moses F. Kimball, Esq., (whose record see). Mr. Kimball died in Rumford June 27, 1851, and his widow married second, Hon. Peter C. Virgin, whom she survived, and is now (1889) living in Cambridge, Mass , at the age of 90 years.

Children.

i   *George*, b. March 1, 1819, d. March 26, following.
ii   *Lucy Ann*, b. Feb. 13 1820, m. Jan. 1, 1839, Cyrus Small, d. May 22, 1848.
iii   *Nancy*, b. Apr. 20, 1822, d. Aug. 4, 1844.
iv   *Abigail*, b. March 11, 1825, m. Oct. 13, 1847, Charles Monroe.
v   *Charles Henry*, b. Dec. 25, 1828, m. first Eliza Ostrander and second, Laura S. Porter.

CHARLES HENRY KIMBALL, son of the preceding, (see personal sketch) married first at Syracuse, N. Y., Dec. 26, 1853, Miss Eliza, daughter of William Muir and Renette (Weed) Ostrander, who was born in Tully, N. Y., Sept. 16, 1831, and second, March 25, 1868, at Brooklyn, N. Y., Miss Laura Stinson, daughter of Oliver and Aurora Freeman (Stinson) Porter, who was born in Levant, Me., June 22, 1834.

Children :

i   *Renette Weed*, b. Brooklyn, N. Y., Apr. 2, 1857, d. March 18, 1859.
ii   *Alice Woodman*, b. Oct. 9, 1858.

By second wife :

iii   *Charles Henry*, b. Aiken, S. C., Feb. 23, 1871, d. July 23, 1889.
iv   *Fred K. Porter*, b. Plainfield, N. J., July 1, 1872.

KNAPP.

NATHAN KNAPP was born in Spencer, Mass., Dec. 2, 1784, and died in Rumford Oct. 4, 1833. His wife was Phebe, daughter of David Farnum. He was drowned in Rumford Falls.

Children :

i   *David,* b. Mexico, Apr. 12, 1810 m. Clarissa Glines.
ii *Enoch,* b. Aug. 20, 1811. m. Eliza, daughter of Elias Bartlett of Bethel.
iii *Albion Keith,* b. June 15, 1813. m. Phebe M. Graham.
iv *Jane Barnard,* b. May 26, 1815.
v   *Lydia Bemis,* b. June 4, 1817, d. July 25, 1820.
vi *Dorcas Farnum,* b. Sept. 21, 1819.
vii *Hiram Andrews,* b. Aug. 26, 1822.
viii *Phebe Gleason,* b. Rumford, Nov. 15, 1824.
ix *Martha Hallowell,* b. Oct. 26, 1827.
x   *Byron Livermore,* b. January 12, 1830.
xi *Victoria Columbia,* b. Sept. 15. 1832, d. June 1, 1834.

DAVID KNAPP married Clarissa, daughter of Chandler Glines. He lived at the Falls. He was elected Register of Probate and lived in Paris several years. He then moved to Norway, where he died.

Children :

i   *Nathan Clifford,* b. Sept. 25, 1834, d. Aug. 1, 1835.
ii *Marian Caroline Louisa,* b. March 1, 1836, d. June 16, 1838.
iii *David Scott,* b. June 28, 1839.
iv *Mary Adelaide,* b. Aug. 27, 1841.
v   *James Harvey Farnum,* b. Aug. 8, 1843.
vi *Laura Frances,* b. Oct. 22, 1845.
vii *Clara E.,* b. Dec. 1. 1855, d. May 24. 1876.

ENOCH KNAPP married Eliza, daughter of Elias and Eliza (Adams) Bartlett. He lived at the Falls and was interested in the mills erected by his father.

Children :

i   *Helen Eliza,* b. March 6, 1837.
ii *Caroline Maria,* b. June 24, 1840, d. March 23, 1865.
iii *Charles Adams,* b. Jan. 31, 1842, d. May 28, 1864.
iv *Orisa P.,* b. Sept. 2, 1848.
v   *Preston A.,* b. ———.

ALBION K. KNAPP married Phebe Graham. He resided in Rumford, but in later years in Hanover, where he was long in trade.

Children :

   i *Nathan Clifford*, b. Feb. 11, 1840, m. Jennie Hutchins. He died of diphtheria, and his widow married Charles W. Kimball.

   ii *Clarissa Morse*, b. Nov. 25, 1842, m. Winfield S. Howe, s. Hanover.

   iii *Phebe Lucinda*, b. Sept. 27, 1845, d. next day.

   iv *Lyman Rawson*, b. Aug. 7, 1846.

BYRON L. KNAPP married Maggie ———.

Children :

   i *Ivanora S.*, b. Feb. 6. 1861.   ii *Nathan H.*, b. Feb. 21, 1863.

KNIGHT.

WILLIAM KNIGHT, an early resident of Windham, moved there from Manchester, Mass.

JOSEPH KNIGHT, son of the preceding, with his brother William junior, was captured by the Indians in 1747, and remained with them some time. In 1748, Joseph was again captured, but managed to escape, and warned the settlers of North Yarmouth of an intended attack upon that town, and thus averted it. Capt. Joseph Knight married Phebe Libby and died in 1797.

Children ·

   i *Lydia*, b. Falmouth, 1761. ii *Phebe*, b. Windham, 1763. iii *Nathaniel*, b. Gorham. 1765. iv *Daniel*, b. 1769. v *Joseph*, b. 1771, d. young. vi *Nabby*, b. 1773. vii *Joseph*, b. 1775. viii *Samuel*, b. 1778. ix *Morris*, b. 1780. x *Winthrop*, b. 1782. xi *Benjamin*, b. 1785.

DANIEL KNIGHT, son of the preceding, born Sept. 9, 1769, came early to Rumford. · His wife was Betsey Wheeler of Concord, N. H., who was born May 25, 1776. He died Sept. 2, 1819. His widow died Aug. 14, 1846.

Children :

   i *Lydia*, b. Oct. 21, 1798, d. January 15, 1799.

   ii *Lydia*, b. Nov. 21. 1799, d. July 20, 1802.

   iii *Joseph*, b. Oct. 18, 1801, m. Feb. 7, 1828. Nancy Rolfe.

   iv *Daniel Baker*, b. Jan. 21, 1804, d. Feb. 11, 1824.

   v *Keziah B.*, b. May 2, 1807, m. Sept. 28, 1826, Josiah Parker, d. Nov. 2, 1888.

   vi *Betsey F.*, b. March 17, 1809, m. May, 1835, Lyman Bolster, d. Dec. 23, 1884.

   vii *Winthrop*, b. January 8, 1811. m. Caroline King.

   viii *Lovisa S.*, b. March 22, 1813, m. William G. Martin.

   ix *Phebe*, b. Sept. 28, 1815, m. Jan. 1, 1850, John Jenne.

   x *Jeremiah Wheeler*, b. Feb. 6, 1819, d. May 11, 1845.

SAMUEL KNIGHT, brother of the preceding, married Olive Foss of Topsham. He was a millman, moved to Dixfield about 1816, from there to Peru, where he died in 1859. His widow died in Newbury-port, Mass.

Children :

   i   *Fanny*, b. Topsham, August, 1805, d. Sept., 1805.
   ii *Lydia*, b. Rumford. Sept. 2, 1806, m. Willard Torrey.
  iii *Sally Graham*, b. June 18, 1808, m. Jeremiah Hall.
  iv *Morris*, b. ———.
   v *Elmore*, b. 1815, m. Mary Ann Babb, r. Peru.
  vi *Mary W.*, b. 1817, m. Elijah Hall.
 vii *Angeline*, b. Dixfield, 1819.
viii *Phebe*, b. ———, m. Joshua Ricker.
  ix *Daniel*, b. ———.
   x *Cyrus*, b. ———, m. Eleanor W. Babb.
  xi *Lenora*, b. ———.

JOSIAH JORDAN KNIGHT, son of Isaac and Lydia Jordan Knight, was born in Poland, Nov. 17, 1800. His father, Isaac Knight, came from Nottingham, N. H., and his wife Lydia, was the daughter of Josiah Jordan. He married Sally P. Ryerson of Paris, and lived some years in that town near South Paris. He then, in 1839, moved into Woodstock, into a place called "Sygotch," where he did exten-sive farming and also owned and operated a lumber mill. He moved to Rumford in 1853, to the Dr. Adams farm, and died in this town June 18, 1888. His wife died June 1, 1869. He was a man of much energy and enterprise, and did a large amount of business.

Children :

   i *Charles P.*, b. Sept. 9, 1826, m. Juliette W., daughter of Hon. James H. Farnum. He was a school teacher, farmer and trader. He lived at Bryant's Pond, Lewiston and Paris; he was also in trade on Bethel Hill, whence he went to Canada.
  ii *Augustus James*, b. Sept. 22, 1828, m. Philadelphia M. Graham.
 iii *G. Freelon*, b. Feb. 7, 1832, d. Dec. 1, 1837.
 iv *Marcius F.*, b. March 15, 1836, m. 1st, Ruth T. Graham; 2d, Betsey Richardson. He is a farmer in Rumford and Trial Justice. His children died young.
  v *Margarius*, b. March 15, 1836, d. Dec. 6, 1837.

AUGUSTUS JAMES KNIGHT, son of the preceding, was married Feb. 8, 1854, at Portland, by Rev. Benjamin D. Peck, to Philadel-phia Maria, daughter of Joshua and Hannah (Goddard) Graham of Rumford. He is a farmer and owns the farm at East Rumford known as the General Bolster place. He makes a specialty of fruit culture, and has raised seven hundred barrels of choice apples in a single season. In early manhood he was a school teacher. His wife died Nov. 1, 1887.

Children :

i   *Freelon A.*, b. Nov. 4, 1854, m. Nov. 6, 1881, Huldah C. Jackson.

ii *Charles V.*, b. Apr. 1, 1856 m. April, 1882, Sadie Edgecomb.

iii *Rosalia B.*, b. Apr. 26, 1858, m. Nov. 29, 1883, Dr. F. P. Abbot.   She died in Brooklyn, Sept. 9, 1887.

iv *Cora G.*, b. Aug. 4, 1860, m. at Memphis, Tenn., Nov. 29, 1883, Nate D. Clifford, who died in Marshall, Texas, March 10, 1887.

KYLE.

WILLIAM KYLE, born in Manchester, Vt., moved from Peru to Rumford about the year 1833, to the place since occupied by Cotton Elliot. He died Sept. 26, 1868, aged 85 and three-fourths years. His wife, whose maiden name was Rebecca Walker, died March 1st, 1841, aged 45 years.

Children :

i   *William M.*, b. Peru. ———, d. March 25, 1839.

ii *Sybil W.*, b. Sept. 11, 1817, m. Robert L. Hall, d. June 11, 1854.

iii *Mary*, b. ———, m. Samuel V. Abbot, d. Oct. 14, 1875.

iv *Eunice L.*, b. Sept. 15, 1821, m. Benjamin F. Virgin, d. Dec. 1, 1888.

v   *Melinda W.*, b. June 23, 1824, m. May 29, 1844, Charles Barker.   She resides at Concord, N. H.

LANG.

WILLIAM LANG came to this town from New Hampshire after 1834. He was born in 1791. In 1850 he was a widower. He had four sons and four daughters, but the family record is not at hand and the names of all the daughters cannot be given. Comfort Dearborn, aged 81, was a member of his family in 1850.

Children :

i   *Reuben A.*, b. ———.   He disappeared suddenly from Boston and was not heard from afterward.

ii *John T.*, b. ———.   He went to California.

iii *William P.*, b. 1820, m. Abigail D. Hall.

iv *Oliver P.*, b. ———. m. Mary P., widow of Benj. H. Blanchard, resides Monterey, Cal.

v   *Melinda*, b. 1832, m. 1st, ——— Packard, 2d, ——— Dickerson.

vi *Mercy C.*, b. 1834, m. Luther Hollis, r. Brockton, Mass.

One daughter married an Ayer of Mexico, and another, John Casey.

WILLIAM P. LANG, son of the preceding, married Abigail D. Hall. He died in 1864, while serving in the army, and his wife married Moses B. Knight of Greenwood.

Children :

i *Ida H.*, b. March 27, 1855. ii *Charles L.*, b. Sept. 12, 1856. iii *Wm F.*, b. March 8, 1859.

LEAVITT.

FRANKLIN S. LEAVITT married Mary J———.

Children :

i *Mary E.*, b. March 26, 1864.

LUFKIN.

BENJAMIN LUFKIN, born in Ipswich, Mass., April 8, 1763, married Mehitable, daughter of Edward and Deborah (Stevens) Abbot of Concord, N. H. He came early to Rumford, moved to Roxbury, and died there in Nov., 1844.

Children :

i   *Joseph,* (*Rev.*) b. Aug. 19, 1786, m. Loruhamah S. Kimball.
ii *Samuel*, b. Aug. 15, 1788, m. Pamelia Segar; said to have been the first male child born in Rumford.
iii *Jacob*, b. July 22, 1790, m. Eleanor Elliot.
iv *John*, b. Dec. 16, 1792, m. 1819, Phebe Kimball.
v   *Aaron*, b. May 26, 1795, m. Lucy Brown.
vi *Esther*, b. June 4, 1797, m. Barnard Carter Stevens of Grafton, N. H.
vii *Moses*, (*Rev.*) b. Feb. 12, 1800, m. 1827, Hannah Virgin.
viii *Benjamin, Jr.*, (*Rev.*) b. April 12, 1802, m. Elizabeth Thornton.
ix *Mary*, b. July 2, 1804, d. Oct. 10, 1812.
x   *David*, b. Feb. 17, 1807, d. January 16, 1832.
xi *Hannah*, b. Nov. 19, 1809, m. Jesse Mansfield.

REV. JOSEPH LUFKIN, (see sketch) eldest son of the preceding, married March 11, 1811, Loruhamah, daughter of Moses and Phebe Kimball of Rumford. He was a preacher and spent his last years on a farm near Rumford Center.

Children :

i   *Loruhamah K.*, b. Dec. 5, 1811, d. Sept. 29, 1813.
ii Twins, { *Joseph Marcus*, d. July 15, 1816. b. July 6, 1814.
iii   { *David M.*, m. 1841, Julia Latham, d. Jan. 18, 1863.
iv *Van Rensalaer*, b. Jan. 14, 1816, d. March following.
v   *Leroy Cole*, b. March 16, 1817, m. 1847, Mary S. Glines, d. Oct., 1883.
vi *Phebe Maria*, b. May 15, 1820, m. Wm. C. Hutchinson 1847.

24

vii   *Orrin Haskell*, b. Apr. 6, 1823, m. Fidelia A. Godwin, d. Dec. 7, 1862.
viii *Ransom*, b. Nov. 6, 1824, d. Aug. 2, 1826.
ix   *Merrit Newell*, b. Feb. 15, 1828, m. March 25, 1856, Lucy A. Kimball.
x   *Mary Ann*, b. Feb. 21, 1831, m. 1st, 1867, James Silver, 2d, 1877,
      Bartle Perry.

SAMUEL LUFKIN, brother of the preceding, married Pamelia, daughter of Nathaniel Segar of Bethel. He lived on the road between Rumford Center and Andover. He was the first white child born in Rumford.

Children :

i   *Alfred*, b. Sept. 24, 1817, m. Dorcas Howe, 2d, Caroline Hill of
      Northwood, N. H.
ii   *Mary R.*, b. Aug. 8, 1820, m. Eliphalet E. Lufkin.
iii   *Russell S.*, b. Aug. 3, 1821.
iv   *Addison*, b. March 20, 1823, d. July 14, 1827.
v   *Lawson*, b. July 20, 1824.
vi   *Elisha*, b. April 30, 1826.
vii   *Samuel Addison*, b. May 23, 1828, m. Euphrasia Bartlett of Hanover.
viii   *Nathaniel*, b. April 27, 1830.
ix   *Horatio*, b. Feb. 22. 1833.

JACOB LUFKIN, brother of the preceding, married Eleanor Elliot, who was born March 5, 1794.

Children :

i   *Eliphalet Emery*, b. March 23, 1813, m. Mary R. Lufkin.
ii   *Phebe K.*, b. Jan. 7, 1815, d. July 21, 1817.
iii   *William S.*, b. Jan. 1, 1817, d. May 21, 1827.
iv   *Aaron Horace*, b. Nov. 20, 1818.
v   *Hezekiah Hutchins*, b. Oct. 21, 1820, d. Sept. 7, 1828.
vi   *Nathan S.*, b. Nov. 25, 1822, m. Elizabeth Howe, r. Caribou.
vii   *Randall*, b. Dec. 12, 1824.
viii   *Frederick Elliot*, b. Aug. 21, 1826.
ix   *Hannah*, b. Nov. 3, 1830, m. 1st, Gardiner Sheldon, 2d, —— Jackson.
x   *Deborah*, b. May 15, 1833.
xi   *Dorcas*, b. Apr. 21, 1835, d. Oct. 5, 1836.
xii   *Samuel Elliot*, b. May 16, 1837, d. in the army.

JOHN LUFKIN, brother of the preceding, married 1819, Phebe Kimball, who was born May 23, 1796.

Children :

i   *Marchant H.*, b. June 23, 1822, m. —— Russell.
ii   *Charles M.*, b. June 15, 1824, m. Sophronia Noyes.
iii   *Frances*, b. Feb. 19, 1829, d. Jan. 13, 1830.
iv   *Sarah F.*, b. Feb. 12, 1834, m. Chas. M. Kimball of Mexico.

AARON LUFKIN, brother of the preceding, married, Apr. 5, 1825, Lucy Brown.

Children :

i *Aurilla*, b. Jan., 1826. ii *Daniel*, b. June 9, 1828. iii *Charles V.*, b. Feb. 4, 1831, d. May 27, following. iv *Charles V.*, b. Apr. 30, 1834. v *Rebecca A. M.*, b. Jan. 20, 1836. vi *Lucy Jane*, b. Jan. 15, 1839.

MOSES LUFKIN, brother of the preceding, married in 1833, Hannah Virgin, who was born in Sept., 1807. He died in Oct., 1869.

Children :

i *Mary C.*, b. May 15. 1834. ii *Eliza G.*, b. Nov. 14, 1835. iii *James C.*, b. Apr. 13, 1838, d. Oct. 24, 1839. iv *Jason L.*, b. Jan. 25, 1839. v *James G.*, b. Nov. 15, 1841.

MERRIT N. LUFKIN, son of Joseph Lufkin, married Lucy A. Kimball. He is a farmer and resides near Rumford Center.

Children :

i *Edgar Cameron*, b. Feb. 21, 1857.
ii *Wallace W.*, b. Sept. 11, 1859.
iii *Lizzie Conant*, b. Nov. 19, 1863, d. March 7, 1865.
iv *Juliette W.*, b. Feb. 19, 1866, d. Apr. 5, 1887.
v *Lucy A.*, b. Feb. 1, 1869.
vi *George B.*, b. Sept. 13, 1874.

ALFRED LUFKIN, son of Samuel Lufkin, married Dorcas Howe in 1843.

Children recorded on Rumford records :

i *Charles A. E.*, b. March 14, 1844. ii *Flora R. J.*, b. Jan. 3, 1846. iii *George E. A.*, b. Jan. 12, 1848.

EMERY E. LUFKIN, son of Jacob Lufkin, married Mary R. Lufkin.

Children :

i *Laura Ann*, b. Feb. 23, 1843. ii *Emery Erving*, b. June 16, 1844. iii *Henry Horace*, b. Aug. 30, 1845. iv *Mary Angelia*, b. Apr. 9, 1847. v *Elisha Russell*, b. Aug. 19, 1849. vi *Adelaide Kimball*, b. Dec. 25, 1850. vii *Charles Victor*, b. Feb. 5, 1853.

LOVEJOY.

CHRISTOPHER C. LOVEJOY married Betsey ———.

Children on Rumford records :

i *Mary J.*, b. June 12, 1853.
ii *Lucien M.*, b. Oct. 23, 1854.
iii *Ora Ann*, b. July 6, 1857.
iv *Georgianna*, } twins, b. May 26, 1861.
v *Anna*,

Henry A. Lovejoy married Ann K. Morton.

Children on Rumford records :

i *Martha F.*, b. Nov. 24, 1858. ii *Wirt F.*, b. Dec. 27, 1859. iii *Pearl S.*, b. Oct. 6, 1863.

MANSUR.

Elijah Mansur was a resident of Rumford. His wife was Sally Messer.

Children :

i *Elijah*, b. ——. ii *Leonard*, b. ——. iii *Lucy*, b. ——, m. Stephen Abbot. iv *Asa*, b. ——. v *Warren*, b. ——, m. Elvira Mason Barnes. vi *Susan*, b. ——, m. Cyrus P. Newton. vii *Salome*, b. ——, m. Isaac Newcomb. viii *Hannah*, b. ——, m. Samuel R. Chapman. ix *Mary J.*, b. ——, m. George Lyman.

Warren Mansur married Elvira M. Barnes. He was a shoe-maker and lived at Rumford Point.

Children on town records and census return of 1850 :

i   *Thomas Hersey*, b. Feb. 15, 1838.
ii *George E.*, b. ——, 1842.
iii *Mary J.*, b. ——, 1844, m. Dr. Hiram F. Abbot.
iv *Susan F.*, b. ——, 1846.
v   *John W.*, b. ——, 1849.

MARTIN.

Henry Martin of Concord, N. H., was one of the proprietors of Rumford, and several of his children came here. He married Esther Kimball. He died Dec. 12, 1821, aged 82 years.

Children :

1 i   *John*, b. July 30, 1768, m. Hannah Wheeler, d. 1805.
   ii   *Esther*, b. May 26, 1770.
2 iii *Daniel*, b. July 16, 1772, m. Betsey George.
3 iv   *Kimball*, b. Dec. 7, 1774, m. Rachel Godwin.
   v   *Solomon*, b. Feb. 11, 1777.
   vi   *Henry*, b. Aug. 7, 1779, m. widow Polly Ferrin.
   vii *Hannah*, b. Sept. 6, 1781.
   viii *Mary*, b. Oct. 30, 1785.

1 John Martin married Hannah, daughter of Jeremiah Wheeler of Concord. He died Nov. 21, 1805, and was the first one buried in the cemetery at Rumford Center. His widow m. John Kimball. Children :

4 i *Henry*, b. Oct. 1, 1798. 5 ii *Jeremiah*, b. Aug. 29, 1800. iii *Polly*, b. Oct. 27, 1802. iv *Judith*, b. Dec. 26, 1804, d. Feb., 1806.

2 DANIEL MARTIN, son of the preceding, married first, Betsey George, who died Nov. 6, 1806. He married a second wife.
Children :

    i   *Esther*, b. January 27, 1799, m. Moses Davis.
    ii *Dorothy*, b. March 13, 1801, d. 1823.
    iii *Hannah*, b. June 2, 1802, m. Hazen F. Abbot, r. Rumford.
    iv *Mehitable*, b. Feb. 11, 1804, m. Harvey Willard.
    v *Betsey*, b. Oct. 30, 1805, d. 1806.
6 vi *Daniel Jr.*, b. Sept. 6, 1807, m. Isabel C. Brown.
    vii *George*, b. Aug. 29, 1809, d. March 23, 1810.
    viii *Betsey*, b. 1812, m. Phineas Stearns of Bethel.
    ix *Polly*, b. ———, m. Cyrus Small.
7 x *David George*, b. ———, m. Sarah Martin.

3 KIMBALL MARTIN, son of Henry Martin, married Rachel, daughter of William Godwin. He came to town quite early and reared a large family.
Children :

    i   *Mary Godwin*, b. Apr. 23, 1803, m. Luther Trumbull.
8 ii *John*, b. Dec. 4, 1804, m. Arvilla Abbot.
9 iii *Solomon*, b. May 19, 1806, m. Sally Hall. He had children, Orin, William, Kimball and Solomon. He died quite early.
    iv *Rebecca Godwin*, b. July 28, 1808, m. Josiah Moody.
10 v *Kimball*, b. Oct. 27, 1811, m. Lydia H. Abbot.
11 vi *William G.*, b. Oct. 16, 1813, m. Lovisa Knight.
    vii *Sarah*, b. June 11, 1816, m. D. George Martin.
    viii *Hannah*, b. Oct. 19, 1819, m. Elbridge Fifield, d. June 14, 1883.
    ix *Orin*, b. March 20, 1825, m. Ellen Blaisdell.
    x *Esther Kimball*, b. Nov. 13, 1829, m. Richard A. Frye, s. Bethel. He is the son of Hon. William Frye, is a lawyer and has been Judge of Probate.

4 HENRY MARTIN, born Nov. 9, 1798, married Sarah Flanders, who was born Apr. 17, 1800. She died Jan. 2, 1890.
Children :

    i   *Mary J. F.*, b. July 25, 1820.
    ii *John H.*, b. June 30, 1822, d. Feb. 28, 1823.
    iii *Hannah W.*, b. Feb. 28, 1824.
12 iv *John H.*, b. March 10, 1826, m. Miranda King.
    v *Sarah A.*, b. Oct. 5, 1828, m. John E. Elliot.
    vi *Lydia Ann*, b. March 26, 1830, m. Virgil D. Kimball.
13 vii *Lyman R.*, b. Sept. 3, 1833, m. Carrie M. Knapp.
    viii *Caroline L.*, b. June 18, 1836, d. Feb. 2, 1838.
    ix *Jeremiah W.*, b. July 25, 1838, d. in Virginia.
    x *Richard E.*, b. July 20, 1840, m. Victoria S. Farnum.
    xi *Maria C. L.*, b. Dec. 2, 1845.

5 JEREMIAH MARTIN married Nancy Brown. He lived between the Point and Center by the back route, and had one of the best upland farms in town, now cultivated by his grandsons.

Children :

    i *Susan*, b. March 20, 1824, d. Sept. 16, 1825.

    ii *Jeremiah Parker*, b. April 28, 1827, d. Dec. 17, 1833.

14 iii *Jonathan Kimball*, b. January 6, 1829, m. 1st, Frances E. Willard, and 2d, Josephine M. Stevens.

    iv *Nancy*, b. April 30, 1833.

6 DANIEL MARTIN, born Sept. 6, 1807, married Nov. 28, 1831, Isabel C., daughter of Benjamin and Mary (O'Donahue) Brown of Brunswick, born Nov. 22, 1812. Her parents subsequently moved to Bethel. Mr. Martin lived and died at Rumford Corner. He died January 27, 1876.

Children :

    i *Betsey Almira*, b. Oct. 26, 1832, d. Sept. 16, 1833.

    ii *Betsey George*, b. Feb. 23, 1834, d. Sept. 22, 1865.

    iii Daughter, b. Dec. 22, 1835, d. Dec. 25 following.

    iv *Mary Adelaide*, b. May 19, 1837, m. Dec. 12, 1860, Peter Osgood Dresser.

    v *Julia Ann*, b. Nov. 24, 1839.

    vi *Irvin Greenville*, b. Nov. 22, 1842, d. Feb. 22, 1863.

    vii *James Merritt*, b. Nov. 2, 1845, d. June 10, 1861.

    viii *Winfield Scott*, b. Feb. 26, 1847, r. California.

7 DAVID G. MARTIN married Sarah G. Martin. He long kept the hotel at Rumford Corner and died there.

Children :

    i *Jersyn G.*, b. March 16, 1859.

8 JOHN MARTIN, married Arvilla, daughter of David Abbott. He is a farmer and still lives near the Point in the enjoyment of good health, considering his age. His wife also, survives, and both are enjoying a pleasant old age.

Children :

    i *Henry*, b. Apr. 17, 1836, m. Harriet Harriman.

    ii *Franklin*, b. Oct. 28, 1837, m. Eliza Hall.

    iii *Abigail*, b. May 6, 1839, m. 1st, H. Marshall Abbot. 2d, William Phinney.

    iv *Charles Kimball*, b. June 7, 1841, m. Mrs. Louisa (York) Barrows.

    v *Mary Elizabeth*, b. Apr. 28, 1843, m. J. Warren Akerman.

vi *John Wesley*, b. March 1, 1846, m. Martha Smith of Newry.
vii *Betsey C.*, b. January 4, 1849, d. Aug. 7, 1863.
viii *Rensalaer A.*, b. March 8, 1851, m. Nellie Willis.

10 KIMBALL MARTIN, JR., married Lydia H. Abbot. He was a blacksmith by trade.

Children :
 i *Rachel Josephine*, b. Aug. 15, 1837, m. Henry J. Barker of Milton Pl.
 ii *Charles Vincent*, b. Feb. 5, 1839, m. Nancy W. Goddard of Bethel.
 iii *Asa A.*, b. Dec. 3, 1842.

11 WILLIAM G. MARTIN married June 1, 1842, Lovisa, daughter of Daniel Knight of Rumford.

Children :
 i *Madison W.*, b. May 7, 1843, d. June 7, 1848.
 ii *Clinton W.*, b. Dec. 5, 1849, m. Hannah G. Blaisdell.
 iii *Harriet A.*, b. Aug. 26, 1851, m. George W. Caldwell. and resides in South Boston.

12 JOHN H. MARTIN married Miranda King.

Children on town records :

i *Augustus R.*, b. Jan. 15, 1854. ii *Charles H.*, b. Jan. 12, 1859. iii *Fred K.*, b. May 11, 1864.

13 LYMAN R. MARTIN married Carrie M. Knapp, who died March 23, 1865.

Children ;
 i *Florence J.*, b. July 29, 1861, d. Dec. 4, 1863.
 ii *Carrie Florence*, b. Jan. 20. 1865.

14 JONATHAN K. MARTIN married first, Frances E. Willard, and second, Josephine M. Stevens. He was a prominent man in town ; served much in town office ; also as representative and State Senator. He lived on the homestead of his father.

Children on town records :

i *Susan E.*, b. March 26, 1851. ii *Jere H.*, b. March 18, 1854. iii *Freeland B.*, b. July 1, 1857. iv *Franklin H.*, b. Sept. 19, 1861.

RICHARD E. MARTIN, son of Henry Martin, married in 1863, Victoria S. Farnum.

Children :

i *Jennie M.*, b. March 17, 1866. ii *Josie*, b. Apr. 4. 1868. iii *Sarah B.*, b. May 3, 1871. iv *Virgil K.*, b. Nov. 5, 1878. v *Anna C.*, b. Aug. 12, 1879.

McAllister.

James McAllister' was in Rumford quite early, and died here May 25, 1801.

Children :

i   *Eliphaz*, b. July 13, 1793.
ii *Dolly*, b. July 6, 1795, published to and probably married Artemas Walton.
iii *John*, b. Apr. 23, 1797.
iv *James*, b. Aug. 30. 1799.

McCrillis.

James McCrillis married Sarah ———.   They came to Rumford from New Hampshire.

Children :

i   *Mary Jane*, b. Meredith, N. H., May 17, 1821.
ii   *James*, b. Center Harbor, N. H., Feb. 17. 1823, d. June 6, 1826.
iii *Sarah*, b. Apr. 17. 1825.
iv   *James, Jr.*, b. March 31, 1827.
v   *Lucien*, b. May 27. 1829, d. January 6, 1836.
vi   *George W.*, b. Holderness, N. H., June 22, 1831.
vii *Charles N.*, b. Apr. 18, 1833.
viii *Lydia A.*, b. Rumford, Jan. 22, 1835.
ix   *Asenath M.*, b. Dec. 9. 1837. m. Nathan M. Cummings of Woodstock.
x   *Phebe K.*, b. July 1, 1839.
xi   *Arvilla*, b. July 31, 1841.
xii *Mercy A.*, b. Aug. 10, 1845. d. Aug. 3, 1846.
xiii *Lyman R.*, b. Sept. 10, 1847, d. Oct. 6, 1847.

Mitchell.

Angier J. Mitchell married first, Phebe ———.   He lived in Rumford, Mexico, Peru and Woodstock.   He served in the late war in the 5th Maine Vols.

Children :

i   *Arabella E.*, b. Mexico, Apr. 30, 1853.
ii *Josephine F.*, b. Feb. 21, 1855.
iii *Freddie O.*, b. July 21, 1857, d. Sept. 10, 1866.
iv *Charles L.*, b. May 24, 1859, d. Oct. 2, 1861.
v   *Angier C.*, b. Apr. 14, 1861.

Moody.

William Moody was born in Falmouth, Me., April 20, 1740. He married Rachel Hodgkins, who was born in Gloucester, Mass., in 1753.   He moved to Danville, Me.

WILLIAM MOODY, JR., son of the preceding, born in Falmouth Jan. 3, 1768, married Mary Dresser, who was born in Gloucester, Mass., Oct. 21, 1775. They lived in Danville.

Children:

 i *Jane,* b. Dec., 1794.
 ii *Andrew,* b. Nov. 2. 1796, m. Ruth Wheeler.
 iii *William,* b. Jan. 1, 1799, m. 1824, Laura Abbot.
 iv *Ashby,* b. Jan. 26, 1801, m. Polly Lapham of Minot.
 v *Samuel,* b. Apr. 1, 1803.
 vi *Joseph,* b. May 24, 1805.
 vii *John,* } twins, b. Oct. 11, 1811.
 viii *Converse,*

WILLIAM MOODY, JR., married Laura, daughter of David Abbot. He was a farmer and resided below the Corner on the Paris road. He was an industrious and prosperous man, and highly respected. He died several years ago.

Children:

 i *Jane T.,* b. Nov. 7, 1825, d. June, 1852.
 ii *Mary D.,* b. Dec. 16, 1828, m. James Shapleigh.
 iii *Eliza E.,* b. Aug. 22, 1840, m. Dexter Elliot.
 iv *Samuel L.,* b. Nov. 23, 1848; he resides on the homestead with his mother, unmarried.

LEVI MOODY married Esther, daughter of William Ackley. He lived at the Falls and for several years in Woodstock, but returned here.

Children:

 i *Clara E.,* b. Feb. 27, 1855. ii *Mary L.,* b. Apr. 21, 1857. iii *Alice W.,* b. Feb. 14, 1864.

NAHUM P. MOODY married Melinda S. Elliot. He died in the army and his widow married William H. Caldwell.

Children:

 i *Windsor E.,* b. Oct. 27, 1850. ii *Abby A.,* b. March 23, 1853.

MOOR.

ABRAHAM and SILENCE MOOR of Bolton, Mass., had the following children, as appears by the records of that town.

Children:

 i *Jonadab,* b. July 1, 1741.
 ii *David,* b. Nov. 19, 1742.

  iii   *Jonathan*, b. March 7, 1743–4.
  iv   *Thomas*, b. June 21, 1746.
  v   *Abraham*, b. March 6, 1747–8.
  vi   *Sarah*, b. Jan. 20, 1749.
  vii   *Rebecca*, b. Sept. 3, 1751.
  viii   *Hannah*, b. Jan. 1, 1754.
  ix   *William*, b. Dec. 5, 1755.
  x   *Silence*, b. June 19, 1758, m. Nov. 2, 1780, Silas Howe, s. Rumford.
  xi   *Aaron*, b. Nov. 7, 1761, m. Jan. 1, 1784, Salome, daughter of Rev. Thomas Goss of Bolton, and settled in Rumford.

AARON MOOR, son of the preceding, an early millman in Rumford, married Salome Goss of Bolton, Mass., who died May 7, 1804, aged 44 years. Mr. Moor came to Rumford from Bethel in 1788.

Children :

  i   *Gratia*, b. Bolton, Sept. 11, 1784, m. Cotton Elliot.
  ii   *Wade*, b. Bethel, Sept. 7, 1787, m. 1816, Betsey Eaton.
  iii   *Geneva*, b. Rumford, Jan. 24, 1790.
  iv   *Francis Keyes*, b. Nov. 7, 1792.
  v   *Kingsbury*, b. Sept. 21, 1795.
  vi   *Humphrey*, b. Nov. 27, 1797, d. Apr. 1, 1798.
  vii   *Salome*, b. March 24, 1802.
  viii   *Catherine*, b. May 2, 1804.

WADE MOOR, (usually spelled Waid) son of the preceding, married Betsey, daughter of Osgood Eaton. He was born in Bethel, is claimed by some to have been the first child born in that town. His mother was temporarily stopping there, her home being in Rumford.

Children :

  i   *Lorenzo*, b. Aug. 5, 1817, m. Clemantine Jacobs, who for second husband married Wm. O. Pearson of Woodstock.
  ii   *Humphrey*, b. Nov. 5, 1819, d. Apr. 17, 1820.
  iii   *Humphrey*, b. Aug. 16, 1821.
  iv   *Uriah Virgin*, b. Sept. 13, 1824, d. May 14, 1839.
  v   *Salome Goss*, b. Aug. 27, 1828.
  vi   *Caroline Bent*, b. June 3, 1831.
  vii   *Martha*, b. March 20, 1833, d. same day.
  viii   *Sarah Brickett*, b. Aug. 3, 1834.
  ix   *Wm. Kingsbury*, b. Jan. 1, 1838, m. 1868, Abbie M. Howard.

MORSE.

BENJAMIN MORSE of Amesbury, Mass., married Rachel Webster, and moved to Concord, N. H. They had eight children.

BENJAMIN MORSE, JR., son of the preceding, born in Amesbury, June 4, 1771, married Aug. 5, 1792, Dolly George, who was born in Concord, N. H., Feb. 8, 1774. He was a shoe-maker and also a wool-carder and cloth-dresser, and died at Rumford Center, May 4, 1849 ; his widow died March 20, 1861.

Children :

1 *Sabrina.* b. Nov. 14, 1793. m. Nathaniel Abbot.
ii *Dolly,* b. Aug. 1, 1795, m. Thomas Bradbury of No. 8.
iii *Saint Luke,* b. Dec. 11. 1797, m. Judith Wheeler.
iv *Clarissa,* b. Jan. 13. 1811, died at Rumford Center, Dec., 1889, unmarried.

WILLIAM MORSE, born in Salisbury, Mass., March 17, 1777, married Sally Wood, who was born in Pomfret, Vermont, Dec., 1780. He was a blacksmith and died in Rumford, June 2, 1853, and his widow died Feb. 9, 1865.

WM. MUNROE MORSE, son of the preceding, a farmer, married Betsey Elliot, who was born May 21, 1824. He died Aug. 8, 1868.

Children :

i *Mary Elizabeth,* b. March 28, 1844, d. March, 1847.
ii *James Smith,* b. Feb. 28, 1850, m. Lydia Augusta Colby.
iii *Charles Munroe,* b. Dec. 25, 1853.
iv *Zenas B.,* b. Oct. 5, 1857, d. Jan. 17, 1865.
v *Jennie F.,* b. June 27, 1861, d. March, 1865.

JAMES S. MORSE, son of Wm. M. Morse preceding, married Lydia A. Colby. He is a farmer near Rumford Center, on the Richard Dolloff farm, and Town Clerk.

Children :

i *Walter G.,* b. Jan. 31, 1876. ii *Zenas W.,* b. Aug. 28, 1877. iii *Timothy C.,* b. Nov. 1, 1878.

MOREY.

AINSWORTH W. MOREY married Harriet O. Ackley. He left town several years ago. He was a soldier in the 23d Maine Vols.

Children :

i *Mary E.,* b. Nov. 8, 1862. ii *Edward S.,* b. Oct. 8, 1864.

PAGE.

EDMUND PAGE came here from Fryeburg and was one of the early settlers, as his name appears upon the early records. His wife

was Nancy ———, and he lived below the Colson Abbot place.
Children :

i *Harriet*, b. Apr. 6, 1796. ii *Jonathan*, b. Feb. 19, 1798. iii *John*, b. March 11, 1800. iv *Susannah*, b. Sept. 2, 1802. v *Jane*, b. Dec. 5, 1804. vi *Edmund Jr.*, b. Apr. 15, 1807.

PARTRIDGE.

JEREMIAH J. PARTRIDGE married Hannah ———.
Children on Rumford records :

i *Warren G.*, b. May 27, 1852. ii *Fanny V.*, b. Sept. 6, 1863.

PARKER.

JOSIAH PARKER married Keziah B. Knight.
Children :

i *Eliza W.*, b. Apr. 13, 1831.
ii *Charles D.*, b. Aug. 18, 1837, m. Martha M. Small.
iii *Irving B.*, b. January 17, 1840.
iv *Judith W.*, b. Feb. 19, 1845.

CHARLES D. PARKER married Martha M. Small.
Children :

i *Charles I.*, b. Apr. 3, 1862.

PARLIN.

SIMEON PARLIN married Sophia ———.
Children :

i *Joseph S.*, b. May 6, 1825. ii *Josephine M. L.*, b. January 28, 1827. iii *David A.*, b. Sept. 16, 1833. iv *Edwin W.*, b. Nov. 26, 1835. v *Mary Ann*, b. June 27, 1838.

PEABODY.

LOAMMI BALDWIN PEABODY was long a blacksmith at Rumford Corner. He married in 1832, Hannah, daughter of Francis Keyes. She died soon after the birth of her son. He married second, Sally B. Graham.
Children :

i *Franklin Dexter*, b. Oct. 11, 1833, m. Lucy Bryant of Woodstock, Me.
By second marriage :

ii *Philena Courtney*, b. June 16, 1837, m. Albert Leavitt.
iii *Charles H.*, b. Feb. 5, 1845, d. Oct., 1848.
iv *George H.*, b. Apr. 29, 1847, d. Aug. 13, 1859.

v *Jeneatte J.*, b. Aug. 27, 1853, m. Daniel Adams Thurston, who is a blacksmith at the Corner. They have Lena Maud, b. May 23d, 1884.

JOHN PEABODY married Ruth Harriman, whose mother was the second wife of Benjamin Swett. He lived on Howard's Gore and also in Rumford.

Children :

i *Sarah Wilkins*, b. Aug. 27, 1796. ii *Addeline*, b. Howard's Gore, Jan. 27, 1799. iii *Jerusha*, b. Howard's Gore, May 30, 1801. iv *Nathaniel Chase*, b. July 9, 1803.

PERRY.

FROM TOWN RECORDS.

GEORGE W. PERRY married Susan V. Abbot.

Children :

i *George H.*, b. Apr. 5, 1852 ii *Ella S.*, b. July 12, 1853. iii *Fred G.*, b. Sept. 5, 1856. iv *Alice J.*, b. Oct. 21, 1860.

BARNABAS C. PERRY married Belinda ———.

Children :

i *Charles S.*, b. Dec. 25, 1854. ii *John C.*, b. Feb. 26, 1855. iii *Albinus P.*, b. July 19, 1857.

ENOCH PERRY married Reliance ———.

Children :

i *George Washington*, b. Sept. 20, 1822, m. 1849, Susan V. Abbot.
ii *Sally D.*, b. Oct. 21, 1826.
iii *Sylvanus P.*. b. March 21, 1829.
iv *Caroline C.*, b. Sept. 4, 1831.
v *Christopher C.*, b. Apr. 22, 1835.

PETTINGILL.

OLIVER PETTINGILL, son of Elisha Pettingill of Fayette, whose wife was a Hubbard, born Oct. 15, 1814, married Huldah Baker, who was born in Livermore. Feb. 22, 1815. He moved to Rumford in 1866, and occupied the Colman Godwin farm on the north side of Androscoggin river until his death in 1880. His widow died in 1886.

Children ;

i *Waldo*, b. Livermore Falls, Dec. 1, 1844, m. Sarah E. Briggs.
ii *Ellen*, b. Oct. 15, 1849.
iii *Ida O.*, b. Jan. 2, 1859, m. Isaac Harmon.

WALDO PETTINGILL married Sarah Elizabeth, daughter of Alanson Briggs of Poland. He came to Rumford with his father in 1866, since which he has been prominent in public affairs. He has held various town offices and served as County Commissioner.
Children :

i *Oliver Alanson*, b. Sept. 18, 1873.   ii *George Waldo*, b. Sept. 1, 1876. iii *Huldah Elizabeth*, b. May 10, 1880.

JOSEPH PIERCE m. Sabrina ———.
Children :

i *Horace B.*, b. May 11, 1836.   ii *Isabel.* b. Dec. 6 1838.   iii *Orphia M.*, b. Feb. 28, 1840.

PHINNEY.

WILLIAM PHINNEY married Augusta Willard, and second, Mrs. Abbie (Martin) Abbot, widow of Hazen M. Abbot. He resides at Rumford Point.
Children :

i *Eliza E.*, b. Aug. 6, 1855, d. Dec. 1, 1864.
ii *Willie D.*, b. Sept. 16, 1859.

PORTER.

FRED A. PORTER, son of William V. and Eliza M. G. (Taylor) Porter, born in Roxbury, Maine, Dec. 30, 1850, is a farmer and scaler of lumber, and resides in Rumford. Wm. V. Porter, blacksmith, was the son of Francis Porter, who was born in Thompson, Conn., Sept. 21, 1780, came to Roxbury about 1803, married Nancy, daughter of Ebenezer Virgin of Concord, N. H., and Rumford, who was born Feb. 1, 1792, and who died March 15, 1858. Fred A. Porter married Mary Ella, daughter of Nahum and Mary Green, Apr. 22, 1877.
Children :

i *Fred Augustine*, b. Aug. 21, 1879.   ii *Charles Nahum*, b. Feb. 19, 1882.

PRINCE.

THOMAS PRINCE was at one time a resident of this town, and the births of four of his children are on record here. He married Lucy, daughter of Asa Howard of Howard's Gore, and carried on the wool-carding and cloth-dressing business at the Falls.
Children :

i *Elizabeth Farrar*, b. March 2, 1821.   ii *Charles*, b. March 9, 1826.   iii *Josiah Farrar*, b. Apr. 3, 1831.   iv *Lydia J.*, b. Sept. 17, 1834.

PUFFER.

JOHN PUFFER's name appears early on the town records. He married Elizabeth, daughter of Stephen Putnam. He died May 10, 1813.

Children :
i *John*, b. in Temple, N. H., January 25, 1794.
ii *Betsey*, b. Society, Feb. 3, 1796, m. Jacob Libby of Peru.
iii *Seth*, b. Nov. 10, 1798.
iv *Milla*. b. Apr. 14. 1801.
v *Prudence*, b. July 30, 1803, m. Jacob Abbot.
vi *Lovina*, b. Nov. 18, 1805, m. John Gould of Dixfield, 1825.
vii *Daniel*, b. Jan. 4, 1808.
viii *Jacob*, b. Apr. 10, 1810.
ix *Zilpha*, b. Sept. 16, 1812.

DANIEL PUFFER married Chloe ———.

Children on town records.
i *Chloe*, b. March 1, 1809. ii *Sally*, b. May 14, 1810. iii *Olive*, b. Jan. 3, 1812.

MATHIAS PUFFER married Ruth Putnam, June, 1810.

Children :
i *Ruth*, b. Oct. 1, 1810, m. Joseph Hinkson of No. 7.

PUTNAM.

STEPHEN PUTNAM was born in Wilton, N. H., Sept. 24, 1741. He was the son of Jacob and Susanna (Stiles) Putnam, whose second wife was Hannah Harriman. Mr. Putnam settled in Temple, N. H., where he resided for several years, and then came to Rumford where his son, Stephen Putnam, had preceded him. His wife was Olive Varnum of Dracut, Mass. He died June 29, 1812.

Children :
1 i *Stephen*, b. Aug. 31, 1765, m. Sally Elliot in 1789.
   ii *Olive*. b. Oct. 2, 1766, m. Samuel Hinkson.
2 iii *Samuel*, b. May 29, 1768, 1st, Lucy Styles, died Feb. 2, 1804, and 2d, Betsey Cobb of Norway, who died Nov. 1, 1872.
   iv *Esther*, b. Apr. 23, 1770.
   v *Mary*, b. Apr. 10, 1772, m. Robert Hinkson.
   vi *Elizabeth*, b. July 11, 1774, m. John Puffer of Society.
3 vii *Israel*, b. March 31, 1776, m. Ruth Walton.
   viii *Abigail*, b. March 6, 1778, m. Isaac Newton.
   ix *Rachel*, b. Feb. 28, 1780.
   x *Jacob Harriman*, b. Dec. 28, 1781.
   xi *Ruth*, b. Sept. 28, 1783, m. Mathias Puffer.

1 STEPHEN PUTNAM, JR., was married to Sally Elliot Dec. 2, 1789, by Rev. John Strickland of Turner, said to have been the first marriage in town. She was born in Newton, N. H., March 1, 1773. He was the first blacksmith in New Pennacook, and she wove the first web of cloth in the Plantation. He died July 4, 1853, and she died Sept. 20, 1859.

Children :

4   i   *Stephen 3d*, b. Sept. 7, 1790, m. Lucy Cobb of Norway.
    ii   *Sally*, b. June 21, 1792, m. 1816, Edward Parker of Hartford, 2d, Nathaniel Atkins.
5   iii   *Jacob*, b. June 6, 1794, m. Betsey Parker of No. Yarmouth.
    iv   *Pamelia*, b. Apr. 18, 1796, m. Churchill Cobb of Norway.
6   v   *Nehemiah*, b. Feb. 28, 1798, m. Hannah Whitten.
    vi   *Abiah*, b. Feb. 14, 1800, m. Reuben Lovejoy.
7   vii   *Benjamin E.*, b. May 13, 1802, m. Deborah Durgin.
  viii   *Peter*, b. Apr. 18, 1804, died young.
   ix   *Harriman*, b. March 10, 1806.
    x   *Abigail Webster*, b. Apr. 21, 1808, m. Thomas O. Bryant.
   xi   *Daniel Fillmore*, b. Dec. 10, 1812, m. Lorinda Walker.
   xii   *Betsey Abbot*, b. July 24, 1815, m. Elbridge G. Welch of Brunswick

2 SAMUEL PUTNAM, son of Stephen Putnam, senior, married first, Lucy Styles, who died 1804, and second, Sept. 16, 1806, Betsey or Elizabeth, daughter of Ebenezer Cobb of Norway.

Children :

By first wife :

    i   *Lucy*, b. Sept., 1793.
8   ii   *Samuel Jr.*, b. Jan. 7, 1795, m. 1st, Susan P. Adams; 2d, Sylvia Bisbee.
9   iii   *Jesse*, b. July 11, 1797, m. Polly Keyes.
    iv   *Fanny*, b. May 15, 1799, d. young.
    v   *Jeremiah*, b. Jan. 14, 1801. He was insane, d. Apr. 26, 1872.

By second wife :

   vi   *Hiram*, b. July 1, 1807, m. 1830, Clarissa W. Farnum.
   vii   *Lois*, b. Oct. 21, 1808, d. July 7, 1857, m. Nathaniel Woods.
  viii   *Ira*, b. March 7, 1810, d. Oct. 15, 1843.
   ix   *Cyrus*, b. Aug. 16, 1812, unmarried.
    x   *Fanny*, b. March 7, 1814, m. James R. Kennison.
   xi   *Betsey*, b. July 21, 1816, m. Osgood Eaton.
   xii   *Lydia*, b. July 3, 1818, m. William Stevens.
  xiii   *Ivy Atwood*, b. Oct. 12, 1820, r. Colegrove, Penna.
  xiv   *Martha*, b. Nov. 8, 1822, m. John Lang.
   xv   *Mary*, b. Dec. 19, 1824, m. 1st, Nathaniel Woods, 2d, Isaac Gould Spofford.

3 ISRAEL PUTNAM married Ruth Walton.

Children :

i *Cyrena*. b. March 6, 1812. ii *Israel*, b. Jan. 28, 1813. iii *Louisa*, b. Apr. 2, 1814. iv *Horatio Gates*, b. January 18. 1816. v *Mary V.*, b. Dec. 29, 1818. vi *Dorothy R.*, b. March 27, 1820. vii *Artemas Walton*, b. July 17, 1822. viii *Simeon W.*, b. Sept. 16. 1825. ix *Cyrus*, b. June 20, 1828. x *Seth H.*, b. Apr. 20, 1831.

4 STEPHEN PUTNAM, son of Stephen Putnam, Jr., married Lucy Cobb of Norway. She was daughter of Ebenezer Cobb.

Children on Rumford records :

i *Susan Cobb*, b. Jan. 16, 1819. ii *Peter*. b. July 20, 1820. iii *Eunice Waite*, b. Oct. 19, 1821.

5 JACOB PUTNAM, born in Rumford, June 6, 1794, married Betsey Parker, who was born in North Yarmouth, March 4, 1794. She died Feb. 9, 1865, and he died March 10, 1884.

Children :

i *Betsey F.*, b. Dec. 14. 1819, m. March 30, 1848, Hiram Knight.
ii *Sarah E.*, b. May 8, 1823, m. 1st, David C. Elliot, 2d, John Stilphen.
iii *Dana Boardman*, b. Sept. 19, 1825, m. Huldah J. Manley, d. Feb. 11, 1881.
iv *Drusilla F.*, b. Feb. 22, 1829, m. 1st, Dexter D. W. Abbot, 2d, Aug. 18, 1888, Jefferson Jackson.
10 v *William F.*, b. June 13, 1832, m. Jan. 1, 1856, Sophia Abbot.
11 vi *Francis P.*, b. Feb. 10, 1836, m. 1st, Nov. 27, 1862, Eliza Felt, 2d, Nov. 19, 1866, Eunice Town.

6 NEHEMIAH PUTNAM and Hannah Whitten of Concord. N. H.

Children :

i *Alma Jane*, b. Nov. 1, 1827. ii *Mary Foster*, b. Sept. 4, 1830.

7 BENJ. E. PUTNAM married Deborah Durgin, who was born in Bowdoin, Me., July 22, 1806.

Children :

i *Mahala Martin*, b. May 2, 1829, m. Butman Batchelder.
ii *James O.*, b. Dec. 21, 1830, d. Sept. 28, 1832.
iii *James F.*, b. Sept. 28, 1833, m. Dec. 31, 1860, Zilpha A. Brockelbank.
12 iv *Benjamin P.*, b. March 13, 1827, m. Oct. 26, 1862, Augusta Bisbee. They have James Leslie, b. March 16, 1868.
v *Rasan M. L.*, b. Aug. 19, 1841, d. April 16, 1850.

8 SAMUEL PUTNAM, JR., was a blacksmith. He lived in Rumford, Mexico and in Greenwood. He died in the latter town in

1854. He married first, Susan Poor, daughter of Nathan Adams, and second, Sylvia, widow of Daniel Bisbee, whose maiden name was Stevens of Sumner.

Children :

i *Eliza Ann B.*, b. Dec. 10, 1818, m. Austin Flagg of Holden, Mass., d. Worcester. Sept. 9, 1875.

ii *Charlotte Adams*, b. March 12, 1822, m. Wm. Dodd of Paxton, Mass., d. Oct. 4, 1864.

iii *Charles A. V.*, b. May 28, 1824. He learned the printer's trade, and in connection with Ossian E. Dodge published a literary paper in Boston called the *Boston Museum.* He went west and resides in Virginia City, Nevada. He married Ella Harrington of Shrewsbury. Mass., and had Charles Harrington Putnam, r. New York.

iv *Susan Maria*, b. Sept. 16, 1827, m. Frank Pike of Paxton, Mass., d. Feb. 16, 1853.

v *Mahalon Chaplin*, b. July 26, 1829, m. and lives in Kansas.

vi *Laura Amanda*, b. March 13, 1832, d. March 25. following.

vii *Harrison Whitman*, b. May 30, 1833, d. Dec. 18. following.

By second wife :

viii *Samuel Harrison*, b. Oct. 14, 1836, d. Dec. 17, following.

ix *Augustus*, b. 1840.

9 JESSE PUTNAM married Polly, daughter of Francis Keyes. He lived on a farm below Rumford Center, afterwards occupied by his son, Prentiss M. Putnam.

Children.

13 i *Prentiss Mellen*, b. Nov. 21, 1821, m. Esther Howe of Hanover.

ii *Sarah Virgin*, b. Oct. 3, 1827, m. Robert Taylor, r. Nevada.

iii *Edwin Alonzo*, b. Nov. 21, 1829, m. Mary Ross, died Sept., 1865.

iv *Solon Thaxter*, b. Nov. 10, 1834, m. Caroline Evans, r. State of Washington.

10 WILLIAM F. PUTNAM married Sophia C. Abbot.

Children :

i *Cora E.*, b. Oct. 27, 1857. ii *Etta L.*, b. Oct. 21, 1859. iii *Willie E.*, b. July 14, 1862.

11 FRANCIS P. PUTNAM married Eliza J. Felt, and second, Mrs. Eunice E. Town of Norway, in 1866.

Children :

i *Albert D.*, b. Aug. 9, 1864, m. 1888, Amy Reed.

ii *Alice May*, b. Apr. 7, 1868.

iii *Anna Noyes*, b. Dec. 4, 1869, m. 1888, Edward Record.

iv *Susan Elizabeth*, b. Nov. 2, 1873.

v *Luna Izora,* b. Apr. 25, 1875.

vi *Edwin Francis,* b. July 5, 1879, d. Feb. 20, 1885.

vii *Arthur Guy,* b. May 6, 1883.

12 BENJAMIN P. PUTNAM married Mary A. Bisbee.

Children :

i *James L.,* b. March 16, 1868.

13 PRENTISS MELLEN PUTNAM, son of Jesse Putnam, married Esther C., daughter of Joel Howe. He was in trade in Hanover and Bryant's Pond. He then moved to the farmstead of his father and died there. He served as selectman a number of years.

Children :

i *Sarah Marcella,* b. Oct., 1851, m. Rufus J. Virgin, r. Bethel.

ii *Ada J.,* b. Oct., 1854 d. Feb., 1857.

iii *Solon A.,* b. Aug. 10, 1860; he is an Attorney in Boston.

HIRAM PUTNAM, son of Samuel and Betsey (Cobb) Putnam, married Clarissa W. Farnum, who was born in Rumford, Apr. 29, 1807. He moved from Rumford to Mason, and died in Waterford, March 11, 1887. His widow resides in Mason. His children born in Rumford were :

i *Sarah W.,* b. Sept. 17, 1831, m. Nathaniel H. Piper.

ii *John Farnum,* b. June 11, 1833, m. first, Calista D. Green, and second, Myra A. Bickford.

iii *William P.,* b. May 14, 1835, m. C. Ann Oliver.

iv *Charles H.,* b. Dec. 16, 1840, died in rebel prison in 1863.

v *Francis N.,* b. 1843, m. Abbie Bean, d. in the army.

vi *Ira N.,* b. ———, m. Abbie Baird.

JOHN FARNUM PUTNAM, son of Henry and Clarissa W. (Farnum) Putnam, married first, Sept. 2, 1858, Calista D. Green of Shelburn, N. H., and second, Nov. 1, 1866, Myra A., daughter of Theodore and Julia Bickford of Ellsworth. He served on the quota of Lewiston nearly three years in the 17th Me. Regiment. He now resides in Lewiston and is Clerk of that city.

Children :

i *Alcander B.,* b. Sept. 2, 1860, d. July 24, 1880.

ii *Edwin E.,* b. July 3, 1862, d. Dec. 16, 1868.

By second wife :

iii *John F.,* b. Sept. 30, 1867.

iv *Wm. H.,* b. Dec. 29, 1868.

v *Edwin E.,* b. Sept. 10, 1870.

vi   *Mamie A.*, b. June 24, 1872, d. July 19, 1874.
vii *Clinton A.*, b. Feb. 6, 1874.
viii *Harold E.*, b. Nov. 1. 1876.
ix   *Vivian B.*, b. Nov. 6, 1880.

RAWSON.

LYMAN RAWSON, Attorney at Law, son of Capt. Abner Rawson of Paris, married May 22, 1832, Jerusha, daughter of Capt. James Holmes of Oxford, who was born January 22, 1804. Previous to that, he had opened an office at the Point, where he afterward resided. (See Lawyers.)

Children :
i   *Ellen*, b. Aug. 27, 1834, d. Feb. 20, 1855.
ii   *Louisa*, b. Feb. 27, 1836, m. John R. Wood, r. Brooklyn, N. Y.
iii *Ralph Lyman*, b. June 12, 1838, d. Jan. 20, 1877.
iv   *Mary Holmes*, b. March 31, 1840, d. Feb. 23, 1870.
v   *Florence*, b. Sept. 30, 1843, m. 1870, Capt. H. S. Hayes of New York.
vi   *Edward Stuart*, b. March 9, 1848. He graduated from Colby University with the class of 1869, pursued a course of legal studies at Columbia College, and settled in the practice of law in the city of Brooklyn, N. Y., where he now resides.

RAY.

ELIJAH RAY, born in Westminister, Mass., Dec. 7, 1784, married Elizabeth Morse, who was born in Northboro, Mass., June 28, 1787, and who died in Rumford Oct. 24, 1850. He died in Sebec, Me., Oct. 29, 1872.

Children :
i   *Walter R.*, b. Northboro, June 13, 1810, m. Cordelia Paul.
ii   *Edwin C.*, b. Feb. 21, 1812, m. Harriet Prentiss.
iii *Elijah Roswell*. b. Sept. 30, 1813, d. in California, Apr. 20, 1880, unmarried.
iv   *Jesse M.*, b. Aug. 25, 1815, m. Laurana Clark.
v   *William H.*, b. July 23, 1817, m. Sarah C. Kendall.
vi   *George A.*, b. Dec. 8, 1818, m. Lucy C. Whittemore.
vii *Mary E.*, b. March 11, 1822, m. Isaac C. Whittemore.
viii *Caroline A.*, b. March 6, 1824, m. Stephen Scruton.
ix   *Sarah M.*, b. Rumford, Dec. 5, 1826. m. Calvin Boynton, d. in Cal.
x   *Joseph*, b. ———, d. young.
xi   *Heman A.*, b. Oct. 16, 1830.
xii *Alonzo B.*, b. Feb. 20, 1836.

GEORGE A. RAY, son of the preceding, married Lucy C., daughter

Hon. Lyman Rawson.

of Isaac Whittemore, who was born in Hebron. They were married Sept. 21, 1843, by Rev. Benjamin Donham of Bethel.

Children :

i *Edwin F.,* b. Sept. 16, 1845, m. Leonora Bodwell.
ii *Harriet C.,* b. Apr. 25, 1850, m. Rev. Albert Donnell.
iii *Alice Ann,* b. May 15, 1854, m. Frederick A. Cushman, both dead.
iv *Mary M.,* b. Dec. 12, 1856.

RAYMOND.

SOLOMON RAYMOND married Mary L————.

Children on town records :

i *Aroline M.,* b. Aug. 17, 1853. ii *Sam. H. W.,* b. June 24, 1857.

RICHARDSON.

JEREMIAH RICHARDSON, son of Jeremiah and Dorcas (Hall) Richardson of Newton, Mass., was born July 10, 1764. He was of Gilmanton, N. H., in 1796, and that year bought land in New Pennacook, and soon after moved here. His first wife was Hannah, daughter of Peter Connor. His second wife was Betsey ————.

Children :

i *Molly,* b. Jan. 7, 1785.
ii *John,* b. Oct. 29, 1786, m. Mehitable Eastman.
iii *Samuel,* b. Aug. 6, 1789.
iv *William,* b. June 25, 1791.
v *Daniel,* b. Rumford, May 13, 1797.
vi *Sarah,* b. Aug. 13, 1798.
vii *Rhoda,* b. June 29, 1800.
viii *Lydia,* b. Aug. 6, 1802.
ix *Jeremiah,* b. Sept. 16, 1804, d. May 27, 1888, m. Harriet Virgin.
x *Eliza,* b. July 3, 1806.
xi *Joseph,* b. Apr. 20, 1808.
xii *Katherine,* b. Jan. 15, 1811.

JOHN RICHARDSON, oldest son of the preceding, married in 1811, Mehitable Eastman of Rumford.

Children.

i *Mary R.,* b. Dec. 3, 1812. ii *Harriet,* b. March 27, 1816. iii *Samuel,* b. March 1 1818. iv *Benj. Elliot,* b. Feb. 16, 1821. v *Abial Graham,* b. June 3, 1822. vi *Mehitable Eastman,* b. January 8, 1828, d. March 7, 1839.

JEREMIAH RICHARDSON, JR., married Harriet Virgin, in 1830; she died Oct. 16, 1874, and he died May 27, 1888. He was a noted bear-hunter and had many adventures with bears and other wild animals in northern woods. Many stories are told of his daring and prowess in capturing bears.

Children :

i   *Amanda J.*, b. Dec. 22, 1830. m. Joseph Gowell.
ii   *Mahala C.*, b. Aug. 1, 1832, m. William Murray.
iii *Elias B.*, b. May 16, 1834, m. Mary Virgin.
iv   *German G.*, b. July 9, 1836, m. Florence Marble, Physician at Dixfield.
v   *Sarah S.*, b. Aug. 29, 1838, d. March 20, 1880.
vi   *Rosina W.*, b. Aug. 14, 1842, m. Frank Philbrick.
vii *Britania E.*, b. Dec. 20, 1844, m. Charles Knowles.
viii *Winfield S.*, b. Apr. 30, 1847, m. May 30, 1881, Emma L. Edmunds of Mexico.
ix   *Ann A.*, b. Nov. 20, 1848, d. Feb. 26, 1874.

ABIAL G. RICHARDSON married Mary W. ———.

Children :
i   *Carona H.*, b. May 26, 1856.

CHARLES F. RICHARDSON married Olivia E. Bodwell.

Children :
i *Edward E.*, b. March 12, 1871. ii *Albert A.*, b. Aug. 20. 1879.

V ASA RICHARDSON, son of Edward and Charlotte (Ellis) Richardson, married Sarah E., daughter of Enos Abbot. He died May 8, 1876. His parents were of Sutton, Mass., and died in Milan, N. H. He was born in Bethel, Me., May 1, 1817. He served in the 7th Me. Battery.

Children :
i   *Mary A. G.*, b. March 5, 1847, m. A. P. Russell.
ii *George W.*, b. Apr. 28, 1850, m. Jennie Firman.
iii *Enos A.*, b. April 5, 1853.

RIPLEY.

JOSHUA RIPLEY was an early settler on Ellis river. He married ——— Bartlett.

Children :
i *Lydia*, b. ———. ii *Elsie.* b. ———. iii *Persis*. b. ———. iv *Joseph*, b. Apr. 14, 1793. m. Betsey Barker. v *Sally*. b. ———. vi *Nancy*, b.———, m. 1st, Benj. Blake, 2d, Micaiah Blake. vii *John*, b. ———.

Joseph Ripley, son of Joshua Ripley, born in Rumford Apr. 14, 1793, married Betsey Barker, who was born Aug. 3, 1796, and died in Bethel, Nov. 6, 1863. He died July 19, 1859.

Children :
   i *Hosea*, b. Aug. 20, 1821, m. Julia Sturgis. He was a well known singing master and band leader; d. 1887.
   ii *Lawson*, b. Jan. 25, 1823, d. Oct. 12, 1828.
   iii *John Bartlett*, b. Dec. 30, 1824, d. Oct. 6, 1828.
   iv *Arrilla*, b. Dec. 3, 1826. m. Albion Perry Blake of Bethel.
   v *Marcia S.*, b. March 18. 1829, m. Aaron J. Abbot, 1847.
   vi *John Bartlett*, b. May 3, 1831. m. Dec. 11, 1856, Mary J. Wentworth of Vassalboro. He is a farmer in Pittston, Me.
   vii *Betsey M.*, b. Apr. 23, 1833, m. Edwin R. Abbot 1853.
   viii *Joseph Lyman*, b. Aug. 9, 1835, m. Lucinda Holt 1861.
   ix *Nancy Dianna*, b. Dec. 8, 1838. d. Oct. 27, 1844.

ROBERTS.

Dr. Thomas Roberts married Harriet M. Wilkins of Norway. He died June 8, 1876, aged 70 years. The entire family died within the space of a few years.

Children :
   i *Ann Sophia*, b. Aug. 9, 1836, m. Mellen E. Bolster. died.
   ii *Lawson Granville*, b. Oct. 5, 1838, d. young.
   iii *Sidney Irving*, b. Oct. 18, 1841, d. unmarried.
   iv *Euthalius Channing*, } d. young.
                       } twins, b. Nov. 13, 1843.
   v *Euthalia Wilkins*, } m. Elisha F. Goddard.

Joseph H. Roberts was born in Rome, Me., in 1822, and married March 7, 1847, Harriet M. Delano, who was born Dec. 10, 1820. He died in Rumford Dec. 20, 1886.

Children :
   i *George W.*, b. Oct. 4, 1848, m. Lucena Edmunds.
   ii *Dudley F.*, b. Aug. 17, 1850, m. Elizabeth II. Trask.
   iii *John P.*, b. May 24, 1852, m. March 7. 1880, Edith E. Marden, who was born in Weld. They have: Bertha A., (adopted) b. New Hampshire, June 26, 1884.
   iv *Loren H.*, b. June 16, 1855, m. Adell Farnum Nov. 9, 1881.

ROLFE.

Benjamin Rolfe of Concord, N. H., son of Nathaniel and Hannah (Rolfe) Rolfe, and grandson of Henry, one of the grantees of Concord, whose wife was Judith Dole, married Molly Sweat and was early in Rumford. His wife was a daughter of Benjamin Sweat, Senior.

Children :

   i   *John*, b. March 7, 1785, m. Betsey Abbot.
   ii *Judith*, b. March 17, 1787, m. Jeremiah Hall, s. Rumford.
  iii *Nathaniel*, b. March 27, 1789, m. Polly Glines, s. Rumford.
  iv *Isaac*, b. Aug. 30, 1791, m. Mary Chase.
   v *Samuel Jones*, b. Sept. 1, 1793, m. Eliza Hathaway.
  vi *Benjamin*, b. Feb. 10, 1796, m. Mary N. Flanders.

HENRY ROLFE, brother of the preceding, son of Nathaniel and Hannah Rolfe, born in Haverhill, Mass., married Dorothy Elliot of Boscawin, N. H., who was the widow of Samuel Heath. He came to Rumford with the early settlers, and died here Dec. 19, 1823. His widow died Apr. 11, 1837.

Children :

   i   *Henry Courrier*, b. Apr. 7, 1799 m. March 23. 1825, Dorcas Wheeler.
  ii *Nancy*, b. ———. She was long a school teacher.
  iii *John Elliot*, b. July 23, 1805.

JOHN ROLFE, eldest son of Benjamin Rolfe, married Betsey Abbott. He settled on a wild lot on the west side of Ellis river, three miles above the Point. He died Apr. 23, 1854, and his wife died Feb. 23, 1860.

Children :

   i   *Enoch C.*, b. Apr. 16, 1812, (M. D.) m. Emeline Small.
  ii *Betsey Carlton*, b. Aug. 22, 1813, m. 1844, Capt. Peter Trask.
  iii *John Abbot*, b. Jan. 28, 1815, d. March 17, following.
  iv *Ruth Lovejoy*, b. March 6, 1816, m. Josiah Rogers.
   v *Samuel Preston*, b July 21, 1817, d. Aug. 10, 1817.
  vi *Benj. Moody*, b. July 2, 1818, m. Hannah K. Searle d. Oct. 20, 1882.
  vii *John Millett*, b. July 25, 1820, d. Sept. 8, 1823.
 viii *Henry Laurens*, b. Oct. 23, 1822, d. Nov. 17, 1878.
  ix *John Abbot*, b. June 8, 1824, m. Mary M. Thompson.
   x *Laura Hammond*, b. Apr. 18, 1826, d. Sept. 16, 1826.
  xi *Hannah Abbot* b. Apr. 4, 1828, d. May 19, 1859.
  xii *Clarissa DeWit* b. Oct. 26, 1829.
 xiii *Oscar Dunreath*, b. Feb. 5, 1833, m. Elizabeth S. Curtis Nov. 4, 1867.
       She died March 8, 1875, and he married May 19, 1880, Mrs. Julia
       B., widow of Chas. R. Abbot, daughter of Reuben Foster, Esq.,
       of Hanover.

NATHANIEL ROLFE, son of Benjamin Rolfe, married Polly Glines, who was born in Loudon, N. H., July 7, 1793.

Enoch C. Rolfe, M. D.

Children :

   i *Mary Atwood,* b. Dec. 14, 1809. ii *Judith,* b. Feb 4, 1812. iii *Jeremiah G.,* b. Oct. 4, 1814. iv *Paulina,* b. June 4, 1818, d. Feb. 26, 1835. v *Miriam Lovejoy,* b. Apr. 24, 1821. vi *Charles Hiram,* b. March 16, 1827.

HENRY C. ROLFE, son of Henry Rolfe, married Dorcas, daughter of Abel Wheeler. He lived many years at East Rumford and was a good citizen. For a time he was in trade at Bryant's Pond. He now (1890) lives with his daughter in Milton Plantation and is in his ninety-first year.

Children :

   i *Lusina,* b. March 16, 1826, m. 1st, Jarius S. Bryant, 2d, Wm. H. Hemmingway.

   ii *Charles Henry,* b. Dec. 25, 1829, m. Caroline Virgin, d. in California.

   iii *Arvilla Wheeler,* b. July 9, 1840.

JOHN E. ROLFE married Joanna S. Douglass.

Children :

   i *Henrietta Dorothy,* b. Feb. 24, 1840. ii *Henry Andrew Jackson,* b. May 24, 1842.

RUNDLETT.

JONATHAN P. RUNDLETT married Esther ———.

Children on town records :

   i *Jerusha M.,* b. March 25, 1821. ii *Simon S.,* b. Oct. 1, 1824. iii *Elbridge C.,* b. May 5, 1827. iv *Jonathan,* b. Nov. 25, 1829. v *Jeremiah R.,* b. Feb. 24, 1834. vi *Mary Maria,* b. Aug. 6, 1836. vii *Gardner Fairfield,* b. March 12, 1840.

GEORGE W. RUNDLETT married Hannah ———.

Children on town records :

   i *Georgianna.* b. Quincy, Mass., Dec. 25, 1846. ii *Lewis C.,* b. July 16, 1848. iii *Mary F.,* b. Sept. 10, 1850. iv *Ann M.* b. Aug. 6, 1852. v *Henrietta,* b. June 10, 1854. vi *Ida Ann,* b. Rumford, March 31, 1858. vii *Frank,* b. June 8, 1859.

SEGAR.

JOSIAH SEGAR, a brother of Nathaniel Segar of Bethel, born October 11, 1745, son of Josiah and Thankful (Allen) Segar of Newton, Mass., came to Bethel or Sudbury Canada, as it was then called, with the early settlers. He was married in Fryeburg in 1788, to Jane Meserve. He was a resident of New Pennacook in

1792.　The Rumford records do not show that he had children, and he may have left town quite early.

JOHN E. SEGAR, son of Nathaniel Segar, born 1803, married Lydia Farnum, who was born Dec. 23, 1803, and who died Nov. 5, 1864.　He died Oct. 30, 1882.

Children :

   i　*Ambrose Cushing*, b. Sept. 30, 1833, m. Amanda A. Russell.
   ii　*Jonathan Millett*, b. March 11, 1836.
   iii　*Jarvis M.*, b. Aug. 20, 1841; he was a soldier in the late war; r. Lowell, Mass.

AMBROSE C. SEGAR was married to Amanda A., daughter of Theodore and Lucy G. Russell, March 18, 1858, by Rev. Patrick Hoyt.

Children :

   i　*Lydia A.*, b. Nov. 26, 1859, m. Sept. 2, 1882, Llewellyn D. Elliot.

SHORT.

SEBA D. SHORT married in 1835, Abbie A. Trumbull.

Children on town record :

   i *Jane*, b. Feb. 12, 1836.　ii *Abbie A.*, b. Sept. 7, 1841.

SILVER.

NATHAN SILVER is the ancestor of the Silvers of this town.　He married Sally Woodbury of Dunbartown, N. H.　He died May 29, 1811, aged 42 years, and his widow in 1815, married Robert Hinkson.

Children :

   i　*Nathan*, b. June 18, 1792, m. 1815, Sally Swain.
   ii　*Polly*, b. Apr. 8, 1794, m. 1818, David Elliot.
   iii　*Hezadiah*, b. March 31, 1798, m. 1824, Lucy Virgin.
   iv　*Betsey*, b. Apr. 21, 1800.
   v　*Melinda*, b. Apr. 15, 1802. m. 1831, Otis Baker of Mexico.
   vi　*Sally*, b. Sept. 9, 1804.
   vii　*Daniel*, b. Aug. 22, 1806, m. 183-, Sarah Barron of No. 8.
   viii　*James*, b. July 12, 1808, m. 1831, Sarah P. Elliot.
   ix　*Lorina*, b. Dec. 29, 1810.

NATHAN SILVER, JR., married Sally P. Swain.

Children :

   i *Mary*, b. May 5, 1817. ii *Sarah*, b. July 24, 1819. iii *Solomon*, b. May 6, 1826. iv *Charles W.*, b. Apr. 21, 1835. v *Martha J.*, b. July 26, 1833.

HAZEDIAH W. SILVER married Lucy Virgin, who was born in Concord, N. H., in 1806, and died at East Rumford, Aug. 13, 1883. He was living in Rumford in 1889.

Children :

    i   *Charles H.*, b. Apr. 1, 1825, m. Harriet Buswell.
    ii   *Lucetta G.*, b. March 4, 1827, d. 1829.
    iii   *Jeneatte B.*, b. March 11, 1829, d. young.
    iv   *Orin B.*, b. Nov. 18. 1832, m. Matilda Fillmore.
    v   *Mary Ann V.*, b. Feb. 4, 1834, m. Charles Wilkins.
    vi   *Hannah V.*, b. Nov. 1, 1838, d. Oct., 1862.
    vii   *Jonathan*, b. June 12, 1841, m. Abby Barker.
    viii   *George T.*, b. Dec. 1, 1843, m. Antoinette Howe.

JAMES SILVER married Sarah P., daughter of Cotton Elliot. He was a farmer in Rumford, but at one time kept tavern at Bryant's Pond. He returned and died in this town. For second wife in 1867, he married Mary A. Lufkin.

Children :

    i   *Delia C.*, b. Jan. 11, 1833, m. Rufus B. Howe.
    ii   *George S.*, b. Jan. 20, 1835, m. Nancy S. Hutchins, d. 1883.
    iii   *Addie E.*, b. March 15, 1838.
    iv   *Frances M.*, b. July 4, 1840, m. Joel H. Hutchins.
    v   *Annette G.*, b. Jan. 31, 1842.
    vi   *Clara M.*, b. Aug. 28, 1845.
    vii   *Emma S.*, b. Dec. 5, 1850.

SOLOMON SILVER, son of Nathan Silver, married Mary ————. He moved to Aroostook County.

Children :

    i *Emma A.*, b. May 14, 1854. ii *Charles W.*, b. March 6, 1857. iii *Lafayette W.*, b. Nov. 10, 1858. iv *Edward S.*, b. July 23, 1860. v *Mary S.*, b. Oct. 1, 1862. vi *Annie W.*, b. Dec. 28, 1864.

JONATHAN SILVER, son of Hazediah Silver, married Abby Barker of Hanover.

Children :

    i *Etta*, b. June 13, 1869. ii *Perley*, b. Oct. 27, 1872. iii *Minnie*, b. Sept. 5, 1876.

GEORGE TURNER SILVER, son of Hazediah Silver, married at Lowell, Mass., July 18, 1867, Antoinette M., daughter of Otis and Sarah Howe. He lives at Rumford Point and is a carpenter and farmer.

Children :

i *Cora A.*, b. Oct. 9, 1869. ii *Ina M.*, b. Aug. 26, 1873. iii *Albert H.*, b. Nov. 29. 1874. iv *Katie B.*, b. Dec. 15, 1876. v *Hattie F.*, b. Aug. 3, 1880. vi *Lewis E.*, b. May 26, 1887. d. Jan. 11, 1888.

GEORGE S. SILVER, son of James Silver, married Nancy Hutchins. He deceased several years ago.

Children :

i *Fred H.*, b. June 2, 1857.

SIMPSON.

RENJAMIN SIMPSON married Polly, daughter of Nathaniel, and a sister of Benjamin and Henry Rolfe.

Children.

i *Nathaniel*, b. May 9, 1790, m. Lydia Elliot.
ii *Paul Rolfe*, b. Dec. 10, 1791, m. Hannah Thomas. d. 1881.
iii *John*, b. ———.
iv *Joseph*, b. ———, m. ———, d. in Wisconsin.
v *William*, b. ———.
vi *Sally*, b. ———.

NATHANIEL SIMPSON married Lydia, daughter of Joseph and (Lydia) Goodwin Elliot of Concord, N. H. He died in Rumford Dec. 13, 1874, aged nearly 84 years. His wife died July 15, 1883, aged about 86 years.

Children :

i *David*, b. Sept. 15, 1820, m. Mary Newton.
ii *Eleanor*, b. July 4, m. John Dolley.

PAUL R. SIMPSON married Hannah Thomas. He was a soldier in the war of 1812, in Capt. Bodwell's Norway Company.

Children :

i *Abigail G.*, b. ———, m. Lawson F. Clement. ii *Willard E.*, b. ———, 1825. iii *Paul B.*, b. ———, 1827. iv *John D.*, b. ———, 1828. v *Hannah M.* b. ———, 1831.

WILLIAM SIMPSON, brother of Benj. Simpson, m. Abigail ———.

Children :

i *Dolly*, b. ———, m. Thomas Abbot, s. Oxford. ii *Eliza*, b. Canterbury, N. H., Apr. 23, 1801. iii *Mary*, b. July 5, 1803. iv *Sarah*, b. Rumford, July 19, 1806. v *Benjamin*, b. Apr. 8, 1809. vi *John*, b. Aug. 4, 1811.

SMALL.

JAMES SMALL, son of James Small, born in Cape Elizabeth in 1784, married Lydia, daughter of Amos Howard of Lyman, Me. He moved to Limerick and then to Lisbon. In 1826, he came to Rumford and bought the Simon Virgin farm, the one next above the Keyes or Timothy Walker farm. He was an intelligent man, much employed in town affairs and a Justice of the Peace. He died in Newry Nov. 1, 1845, and his wife died July 16, 1834, aged 53 years. Amos Howard, father of Mrs. Small, was born May 2, 1752, and died in Rumford, Sept. 17, 1837. He was a Revolutionary soldier.

Children:

  i   *Warren*, b. Limerick, April 21, 1804, d. aged 20.
  ii *Sarah Sherburne*, b. July 29, 1805, m. Amos Dwinel.
  iii *James*, b. Lisbon, July 9, 1807, died at sea aged 20.
  iv *Lydia*, b. Nov. 13, 1809, d. aged 4 years.
  v   *Emeline*, b. March 23, 1812, m. E. Carter Rolfe.
  vi *Elizabeth*, b. May 8, 1814, m. 1st, Abial Stevens; 2d, Ezekiel Small.
  vii *Cyrus*, b. Apr. 18, 1816. m. 1st, Lucy A. Kimball, 2d, Sarah J. Thompson, 3d, Polly Martin.
  viii *Sumner*, b. Dec. 25, 1818, m. Eliza Morley, r. Massachusetts.
  ix *Mary Ann*, b. Jan. 13, 1821, m. O'Neil R. Hastings of Newry.
  x   *Lydia Ellen*, b. June 6, 1823, m. John Smith of Newry.
  xi *Albert*, b. Sept. 11, 1825, m. Sarah Hastings. Mr. Small settled at Newry. He was for several sessions, Secretary of the Maine Senate. He subsequently moved to Auburn, and was long a bank cashier. He died there and his widow became the second wife of Judge Charles W. Walton.

CYRUS SMALL, son of the preceding, married first, Lucy Ann Kimball, and second, in 1848, Sarah Jane Thompson. She died and he married 3d, Polly Martin. Mr. Small settled in Caribou.

Children:
  i   *Eveline*, b. Sept. 27, 1839.

HENRY A. SMALL of another family, married Fanny D. ———.
Children:
  i *Freeman E.*, b. Stoneham, July 24, 1854. ii *Thomas H.*, b. ———. iii *Cleveland P.*, b. ———. iv *James C.*, b. ———. v *Mary E.*, b. ———. vi *Edward I.*, b. ———. vii *Walter L.*

SNOW.

SAMUEL S. SNOW, born in Bethlehem, N. H., Sept. 20, 1802, married Mary S., daughter of Ezra Hoyt. He came here from Andover, Mass., and moved from here to Saccarappa. He was the son of Ono S. Snow.

Children :
i   *Benjamin Poor*, b. Feb. 14, 1831, m. Annie Louisa Chandler.
ii   *Harriet Newell*, b. Nov. 12, 1832, m. Andrew J. Patridge; she died at Waterville.
iii *Temple Hoyt*, b. July 8, 1834, m. ——— Marriner.
iv   *Mary Annette*, b. July 10, 1836, m. Llewellyn H. Drinkwater.
v   *Clarissa Ellen*, b. June 6, 1838, m. ——— Stratton.
vi   *Caroline Elizabeth Smith*, b. Apr. 12, 1840, m. Thomas H. Cruff, r. Oakland, Cal.
vii *Edward Payson*, b. Jan. 30, 1842, d. 1876, unmarried; served in 16th Me. Vols.
viii *Ezra Hoyt*, b. Feb. 14, 1844, m. Ella Stratton, r. Worcester.
ix   *Samuel Newell Whitney*, b. Feb. 1, 1846.

SPOFFORD.

ELDAD SPOFFORD, born January 1, 1745, married Lucy Spaulding of Townsend, Mass. He moved to Temple, N. H.

Children ;
i   *Lydia*, b. Oct. 7, 1769, m. Asa Howard, s. Howard's Gore.
ii   *Jesse*, b.
iii *Eliphalet*, b. ———, m. Sally Russell.
iv   *Henry*, b.
v   *Lucy*, b. Apr. 8, 1777, m. Joshua Felt; 2d, Merrill Chase.
vi   *Hannah*, b. ———.
vii *Sarah*, b. ———.
viii *Isaac*, b. June 22, 1782, m. Ann Fish, s. Rumford.
ix   *Betsey*, b. ———.
x   *Milly*, b. ———.
xi   *Daniel*, b. ———.
xii *Artemas*, b. ———.
xiii *Earl*, b. ———.

STEPHENS.

JOHN EZRA STEPHENS, son of Ezra and Laura B. (Andrews) Stephens of Woodstock, and grandson of Benjamin and Abigail (Sampson) Stephens of Paris, worked three years in the watch factories of Waltham, Mass., and then came and commenced business at Rumford Centre. In addition to jewelry and watch repairing, he keeps a general store of goods, owns half of the dowel mill, nad is also Postmaster. He married Oct. 6, 1883, Corry, daughter of Hiram and Elizabeth Swain.

Children :

i   *Glendon Webster*, b. May 27, 1885.

ii   *Elizabeth Laura*, b. Nov. 25, 1886, d. Feb. 19, 1887.

STEVENS.

JOHN STEVENS, called "Merchant," was one of the largest proprietors of New Pennacook, and his son, Stephen G. Stevens, settled here. John Stevens was the son of John and Lydia (Soley) Stevens, and grandson of John Stevens, who was baptized in 1696, was a sea captain and died Sept. 26, 1748. His son, who married Lydia Soley in 1746, left only one son, who is the John mentioned first, and died in 1749. His widow married Stephen Greenleaf. John Stevens graduated at Harvard College in 1766, married Sarah Wood, and moved from Charlestown, Mass., where his ancestors had long resided, to Concord, N. H. He was a merchant and a man of means and influence. He died Dec. 25, 1792, and his widow died May 11, 1804, aged 53 years.

STEPHEN GREENLEAF STEVENS was the son of John Stevens, merchant, of Concord, N. H., one of the proprietors of Rumford and a large owner of its lands. He was born Feb. 24, 1782. He married Ruth, daughter of Benjamin Elliot, in 1810. He once owned the land upon which Rumford Point Village now stands.

Children :

i   *Grace Bradley*, b. July 7, 1811, m. Wm. Mills, moved to Illinois.

ii   *Benj. Wood*, b. Jan. 11, 1814, m. Harriet G. Frost of Andover; r. Somerville, Mass.

iii   *Stephen Greenleaf*, b. March 12, 1816, m. Christiana Cushman of Oxford, r. Minn.

iv   *Francis Cushman*, b. May 15, 1818, m. Betsey H. Lucas of Hartford, r. Canton.

v   *Thomas Jenners*, b. Apr. 28, 1820, m. Linda M. Griffin, d. Canton in 1878.

vi   *Mabel Waite*, b. March 7, 1826, m. first, Eugene Tufts of Saco, second, Sewall Thompson, r. Rumford.

vii   *Samuel Bradley*, b. Oct. 22, 1828, moved to Minnesota.

viii   *William Freeman*, b. Aug. 4, 1831, m. first, Susan Little of Colebrook, N. H., and second, Arvilla E. McCrillis of Rumford.

AARON STEVENS, born in Concord, N. H., January 8, 1785, married Sally, daughter of Israel Glines, of Loudon, N. H., who was born there August 18, 1784. He came to Rumford about the year 1806, and became one of the wealthiest men in town. When advanced in years he moved to Auburn where he married a second wife. He died Feb. 7, 1877, aged 93.

Children :

   i *Eben*, b. Louden, May 16, 1805.

   ii *Edward*, b. Nov. 2, 1808. m. Sybil Bean.

   iii *Cynthia W.*, b. Feb. 9, 1813, m. Isaac Washburn of Paris.

   iv *Abial L.*, b. May 20, 1815, m. Elizabeth Small.

EDWARD STEVENS, son of Aaron Stevens, married Sybil, daughter of Luther Bean. He occupied a farm near the Corner, now occupied by his sons.

Children :

   i *Edward E.*, b. Mar. 23, 1838. ii *Amos H.*, b. Mar. 15, 1840. iii *Aaron E.*, b. July 2, 1842. iv *Frederick M.*, b. June 8, 1844. v *George D.*, b. April 8, 1847.

PHINEAS STEVENS, born in Loudon, N. H., Sept. 7, 1798, married first, Betsey ———, who was born in Epsom, N. H., Aug. 26, 1796, and died in Rumford June 7, 1822. For second wife he married Mary S., daughter of Capt. Joseph Wardwell.

Children :

   i *Sally K.*, b. Concord, N. H., Oct. 19, 1818.

   ii *Mahala G.*, b. Aug. 13, 1821, d. Feb. 15, 1822.

By second wife :

   iii *Daniel G.*, b. Jan. 14, 1826.

   iv *Betsey H.*, b. Feb. 19, 1828.

   v *Charles O. B.*, b. April 11. 1829.

   vi *James R.*, b. April 22, 1830.

   vii *Margaret Annette*, b. March 27, 1832.

   viii *Nancy Jane*, b. April 1, 1833, d. in Andover, May 4, 1860.

   ix *Josephine Martha*, b. Sept. 19, 1835, m. Jonathan K. Martin of Rumford.

   x *Francis R.*, b. Dec. 26, 1836.

SAMUEL STEVENS married Miriam ———. This family did not long remain in town.

Children :

   i *Patty*, b. Lewiston, Mar. 12, 1794. ii *Sally*, b. Oct. 25, 1796. iii *Robert*, b. Jan. 13, 1798. iv *Mercy*, b. June 2, 1800. v *Joanna*, b. July 14, 1802.

vi *Samuel*, b. May 29, 1804. vii *Haines*, b. April 15, 1806. viii *William Hinman*, b. July 1, 1810.

HAINES STEVENS married Nancy Abbot.

Children :

i *Viola M.*, b. April 28, 1830. ii *Isaac S.*, b. Aug. 18, 1832. iii *Mercy S.*, b. Aug. 11, 1834. iv *William W.*, b. Aug. 5, 1837.

JONATHAN STEVENS married Elizabeth ———.

Children :

   i *Ezra Tucker*, b. April 16, 1806, d. April 18, 1808.

  ii *James*, b. ———, d. May 15, 1808.

 iii *Betsey*, b. Sept. 14, 1809.

BENJAMIN W. STEVENS married Harriet G. Frost.

Children :

   i *Francis*, b. Nov. 17, 1839.

STILES.

ENOCH STILES, born in Bridgton Oct. 26, 1796, married Edna Dolloff, born June 6, 1789. He lived in Bridgton, Rumford, and Errol, N. H., then moved to Bethel and died there. His wife died in Bethel, and he married Maria, (Latham) the widow of Evi Needham.

Children :

   i *Miriam*, b. Bridgton. Dec. 5, 1817.

  ii *Almira*, b. Rumford, Nov. 20, 1821.

 iii *Enoch Davis*, b. Errol, N. H., Oct. 31, 1829.

 iv *Richard Dolloff*, b. July 29, 1830.

SWAIN.

JOHN SWAIN, son of John and Sarah (Richardson) Swain, born in Gilmanton, N. H., Jan. 22, 1793, married Rebecca D. Richards, who was born June 30, 1799. He died in Rumford July 22, 1861, and his wife died Oct. 17, 1868. John Swain, Senior, and his wife Sarah also died in Rumford.

Children :

   i *John Jr.*, b. June 30, 1821, m. Charlotte W. Kimball.

  ii *Hiram R.*, } m. Elizabeth D. Kneeland.

               } twins, b. Jan. 1, 1823.

 iii *Francis R.*, } d. Sept. 10 following.

26

 iv *Levi*, b. Feb. 14, 1825, m. Lucinda B. Kimball.
 v *Cordelia*, b. Nov. 1, 1826, d. Jan. 13, 1833.
 vi *Roxana W.*, b. Dec. 28, 1828.
 vii *Amasa*, b. Nov. 7, 1830, d. Oct. 12, 1831.
 viii *Oliver Q.*, b. Aug. 5, 1832, d. Apr. 3, 1834.
 ix *Edwin C.*, b. July 23, 1834, m. Mary A. Lovejoy.
 x *Philena J.*, b. Apr. 1, 1836, m. Jan. 13, 1858, Adam W. Kimball.
 xi *Loring F.*, b. March 28, 1838, m. June 22, 1861, Amelia A. Glover.

HIRAM R. SWAIN married Elizabeth D. Kneeland.

Children :
 i *Lucena R.*, b. Aug., 1848, d. Aug. 3, 1872.
 ii *Mary E.*, b. Jan. 3, 1851.
 iii *Sarah B.*, b. Sept. 28, 1854, d. June 24, 1877.
 iv *Corry E.*, b. Apr. 12, 1858, m. John E. Stephens.
 v *Horace H.*, b. Oct. 8, 1859.
 vi *Wm. R.*, b. Nov. 29, 1861.

JOHN SWAIN, JR., married Charlotte W. Kimball, Nov. 20, 1849. He died May 25, 1884.

Children :
i *Roscoe E.*, b. May 23, 1856. ii *Virtue K.*, b. July 10, 1858. iii *John Marshall*, b. July 26, 1860. iv *Rosie L.*, b. March 23, 1864.

LEVI SWAIN married Lucinda B. Kimball, Oct. 3, 1853.

Children :
 i *Roger W.*, b. Nov. 2, 1857, d. Dec. 8, 1868.
 ii *Olive C.*, b. Sept. 16, 1861, m. Sept. 27, 1879, John H. Flagg.

LORING F. SWAIN married Amelia A., daughter of Livingston Glover, June 22, 1861.

Children :
 i *Roxie C.*, b. Sept. 19, 1862, m. Joshua H. Abbot.
 ii *Laura R.*, b. Dec. 31, 1864, m. Nial F. Hoyt.
 iii *Rebecca D.*, b. Feb. 16, 1867, m. Charles F. Lovejoy.
 iv *Hattie A.*, b. Sept. 1, 1871.
 v *Marcia C.*, b. June 26, 1873.
 vi *Nina J.*, b. June 6, 1875.
 vii *Edwin F.*, b. Sept. 11, 1877.
 viii *Gertie L.*, b. Dec. 9, 1879.
 ix *John R.*, b. May 30, 1882.
 x *Leon G.*, b. July 13, 1887.

EDWIN CHARLES SWAIN, brother of the preceding, is a photogra-

pher at Malden, Mass. He married Jan. 24, 1870, Mary A. Lovejoy of Vassalboro.

Children :

    i *Fred Allen*, b. Apr. 3, 1871. ii *Berton Smith*, b. Nov. 25, 1873.

SWEAT.

BENJAMIN SWEAT from Concord, N. H., was among the early
settlers of that town. He had been a soldier in the war of the
Revolution, and was a widower with one son, Benjamin Jr., when
he came to Rumford. It is said that he married for a second wife
Ruth Harriman of Dracut, who had been stewardess in the conti-
nental army, and came to Rumford with one daughter, who married
John Peabody, who settled on Howard's Gore. The elder Benjamin
Sweat lived in Rumford a few years, then made him a home at
"Fuller's banks," so called in Bethel where he died. He was in
Rumford quite early, and his name is on the early petitions to the
General Court. His second wife had the unsavory reputation of
being a witch, and a noxious weed which appeared about that time
was thought to have been sent by her to the neighboring farmers
for some imaginary slight or offence. It was a variety of the nettle;
and to this day is known in Bethel and vicinity as "Old Granny
Sweat Weed." It is recorded on Fryeburg records that Benjamin
Sweat of Rumford, and widow Ruth Harriman, were married there
July 16, 1794.

BENJAMIN SWEAT, JR., son of the preceding, married Mary or
Molly Harper, sister of the wife of William Godwin. He was a
resident of Rumford a few years, and then moved to Bethel to a lot
on the Paris and Rumford road, near the northern extremity of the
"Whale's Back," so called. Here he cleared up a farm which at
his decease, passed into the hands of his son Moses.

Children :
    i   *Mary*, b. Aug. 29, 1793, m. Daniel Glines.
    ii *Dolly*, b. Oct. 14, 1795, m. William Frost and d. May 26, 1863.
    iii *Mehitable*, b. Jan. 6, 1798, m. John Delano of Mexico.
    iv *Abigail Andrews*, b. Apr. 17, 1800, m. Wm. Delano of Livermore.
    v *Sarah*, b. May 2, 1802.
    vi *Basmuth*, b. Apr. 15, 1806, m. David York, s. Woodstock.
    vii *Benjamin*, b. June 2, 1804, d. Dec. 9, 1806.
    viii *Asenath*, b. Oct. 16, 1808, m. Piram Bisbee, d. Greenwood.
    ix *Moses*, b. Oct. 3, 1810, m. 1841, Fanny Cummings of Albany; r.
        Bethel.

TAYLOR.

Families of Taylor have lived in Rumford, but no records of births have been received. Moses, William, Stephen, Jonathan C., Robert B., and Eugene Taylor are among those of this name whose intentions of marriage are recorded here. The records also show that Obed Taylor married Jerusha ———.

Children :

    i   *Theron M.*, b. Sept. 10, 1839.
    ii *Augustus D.*, b. Oct. 22, 1847, d. Apr. 3, 1887.
    iii *Edward T.*, b. Apr. 6, 1851.
    iv *Enoch A.*, b. Oct. 4, 1855.

THOMAS.

JOHN THOMAS, said to have been born at Brunswick, came to Norway in 1805, and there married Marian Crockett. He moved to Byron.

JOHN THOMAS, JR., born in Norway, July 4, 1809, married in Andover, Nov. 21, 1833, Lydia, daughter of Reuben and Sarah (Adams) Barrett, who was born in Nelson, N. H., May 8, 1815. They lived in Byron until 1836, when he bought the Daniel G. Abbot farm at East Rumford, where he died Oct. 12, 1864. His widow lives with her son, Peter C. Thomas, on the old Swain place.

Children :

    i   *John L.*, b. Byron, July 15, 1834, m. Rebecca B. Virgin.
    ii   *Triphena*, b. Rumford, July 16, 1837, m. Martin L. Wyman.
    iii *Wilson*, b. Oct. 5, 1839, m. Jan. 1, 1871, Etta Welch.
    iv   *Warren B.*, b. Jan. 17, 1842, m. Mary Chisam of Boston.
    v   *Susan M.*, b. Jan. 28, 1844, m. Rufus Maxwell of Litchfield, d. Sept. 3, 1885.
    vi   *Lewis A.*, b. Feb. 25, 1846, m. Mary A. Reed.
    vii *Lydia S.*, b. Feb. 11, 1848, m. 1st, Norman Moor, 2d, Charles L. Simpson.
    viii *Peter C.*, b. Apr. 24, 1850, r. Rumford, unmarried.
    ix   *William Oscar*, b. Apr. 14, 1852, d. Oct. 15, 1853.
    x   *Edna F.*, b. Oct. 25, 1854, m. Fred O. Bartlett of Rumford, d. June 8, 1881.
    xi   *Mary E.*, b. January 13, 1857, m. John C. Smith of Boston.
   xii and xiii twins, d. day of birth, May 10, 1836.

JOHN L. THOMAS married Rebecca B., daughter of Charles E. Virgin.

Children :

i *Rosaline*, b. Oct. 11, 1857, d. Nov. 14, 1862.

ii *Charles A.*, b. Oct. 12. 1859, d. June 7, 1862.

iii *Jeff. D..* b. 1863, m. Adelaide R. Haynes.

iv *Florence L.*, b. 1864, m. Hiram T. Richards of Mexico.

v *John*, b. 1867.

vi *Kate M.*, b. 1871.

vii *Emma P.*, b. 1874.

BENJAMIN P. THOMAS married Rachel A———.

Children :

i *Charles P.*, b. Sept. 13, 1850.   ii *Prentice C.*, b. July 8, 1853.

PEREZ THOMAS from Hartford, came to Rumford about 1833, and bought an interest in land near East Rumford. He did not remain long but returned to Hartford. He was born in 1810, and his wife, Mary Sampson, of Hartford, was born in 1814. They were married in Rumford in 1834. Their children in 1850, were as follows :

i *Augusta S.*, b. 1836.   ii *Benjamin F..* b. 1838.   iii *Moses S.*, b. 1840. iv *Dorcas R.*, b. 1843.   v *Mary W.*, b. 1845.   vi *Priscilla C.*, b. 1848.

THOMPSON.

ISAAC THOMPSON, ESQ., of Middleboro, Mass., who married Lucy Sturtefant, was the son of John and Lydia (Wood) Thompson, and a descendant of John Thompson from the north of Wales, who came to Plymouth in 1622, and married Mary, daughter of Francis Cook of the Mayflower. Isaac Thompson and associates were large land-owners in the county of Oxford. June 10, 1792, Isaac and William Thompson and Joshua Eddy, all of Middleboro, Mass., and James Sprout of Taunton, bought of the Massachusetts committee, a tract of land situated south of Androscoggin river, containing 24,750 acres, according to the survey of Samuel Titcomb in 1787, and known as No. 1, (now Peru). The price paid was $245.74. In 1801, the proprietors divided their domain, and about forty select lots became the property of Isaac Thompson. One condition of the sale was that the grantees should give a deed of one hundred acres to Daniel Lunt, William Widgery and John Fox, who it seems, had settled on the tract prior to 1784. A portion of the land sold to Isaac Thompson and others, proved to be in the town of Jay which had been previously granted to others, and the grantees decided to commence an action against the Commonwealth for the value of the lands granted them by mistake of the surveyor, and so the Massachusetts committee concluded to ease them by granting them other lands. The new grant was part of No. 2, (now Franklin and Milton Plantations) which had been surveyed the year before by Abel Wheeler. The new grant is thus described: "Beginning on the easterly branch of Concord river on Rumford line, thence south $18\frac{1}{2}°$ east one mile; thence south $71\frac{1}{2}°$ west, two miles and forty rods; thence north 29° east 478 rods to Rumford line; thence north $71\frac{1}{2}°$ east one mile on Rumford line to first bound." There was a provision that all squatters on the territory prior to 1784, should have one hundred acres of land each, on the payment of five dollars. The territory here described is now within the limits of Milton Plantation, which was organized as such in 1842. It was called "Thompsontown" previous to its organization as a plantation, and previous to that, with Franklin Plantation, was known as No. 2. A grant of half a township of Maine land was made to Milton (Mass.) Academy in 1798, and in 1811, the equivolent of the grant was deeded to the trustees out of the territory of Number 2, that portion which is now Milton Plantation, and hence its name.

JOHN THOMPSON, son of Isaac Thompson preceding, born in Middleboro, March 22, 1775, inherited a portion of his father's lands in what is now Milton Plantation, purchased also a piece of land in Rumford upon which he erected a large mansion house still standing above Abbot's Mills, and became a resident of this town. He was a Justice of the Peace, a surveyor of land and conveyancer, and was ever prominent in town affairs. He was a man of sound judgment, social, genial and kind and highly respected by all. He married first, Sarah Austin, second, Belinda Dean, third, Jane Richardson and fourth, Elizabeth M. Eustis.

Children :

    i *Isaac*, b. ———, m. Emily Valentine, d. California.

    ii *Peter A.*, b. Hartford, Aug. 10, 1803, m. Wealthy Stevens.

    iii *Leander*, b. Rumford, June 14, 1807, m. Harriet Burnham.

    iv *Sewall*, b, ———, m. Mabel Stevens.

    v *Deborah*, b. ———, m. Oren Reynolds.

    vi *George*, b. ———, d. in infancy.

By second wife :

    vii *John Dean*, b. Dec. 30, 1817, m. April 6, 1848, Phebe Burt, b. Feb.

22, 1828. He resides in Raynham, Mass., and has Ella Belinda,
b. March 30, 1851.

By third wife:

  viii *Robert Richardson,* b. ———. He was killed in the late war.

  ix *Sarah Jane,* b. ———, m. Cyrus Small, d. Rumford.

  x *Belinda Dean,* b. ———, m. George L. Beal, r. Norway.

  xi *Thomas Edwin,* b. ———, r. Nebraska.

  xii *Margaret Richardson,* b. ———, d. Norway, unmarried.

  xiii *Charles,* b. ———, d. Norway, unmarried.

PETER AUSTIN THOMPSON, second son of John Thompson, married Wealthy Stevens, who was born at Livermore, Me., July 23,
1802. He was a farmer and lived in Rumford, and died there Feb.
26, 1887.

Children :

  i *Sarah,* b. Sept. 2, 1829, m. Ajalon Godwin.

  ii *Eliza I.,* b. Jan. 23, 1831.

  iii *John,* b. May 10, 1833, m. Sarah E. Moody.

  iv *Emily,* b. Nov. 1, 1835, m. Otis Wyman.

  v *Ezra,* b. Oct. 1, 1841, d. Bethel, Ill., Feb. 20, 1878.

SEWALL THOMPSON, brother of the preceding, married Mabel W.,
daughter of Stephen G. Stevens.

Children :

  i *Eliza E. Tufts,* b. Aug. 7, 1850. ii *Sarah E.,* b. Apr. 28, 1856. iii *May
F.,* b. May 11, 1858. iv *Susie A.,* b. Aug. 14, 1860. v *Irving S.,* b. Apr.
14, 1862. vi *Jeaneatte L.,* b. Sept. 3, 1864.

LEANDER THOMPSON, third son of John and Sarah Thompson,
was born at Rumford June 14, 1807. After receiving such education as the common schools afforded, he studied awhile at Hebron
Academy and then at "Maine Wesleyan Seminary" which latter
institution he left in 1829, before graduation. The spirit of travel
and adventure had seized upon him, and he yielded to its seductive
influences ; and so, one bright spring morning in 1830, he bade his
home, kindred and friends farewell, to join the tide of emigration
seeking homes and fortunes in the youthful and inviting West. He
made his first stop in western New York, where he remained about
a year and taught a term of school. Then pushing westward, he
went to Michigan and stayed a while at Ann Arbor, and from thence
to south-western Michigan, lingering for brief periods at various
points in St. Joseph, Kalamazoo and Cass counties. He then took

a journey to the Mississippi Valley, visiting the principal places from Dubuque, Iowa, to St. Louis, Mo. Returning to South-western Michigan in a year or two more, he purchased the tract of land in 1837 in Cass county, which afterwards became his home. The next four years were spent partly in that vicinity and partly in northern Indiana. He was occupied during these years at teaching school and as a farm laborer. April 25, 1841, he was married to Miss Harriet Burnham, a native of Middletown, Vt., and they at once settled on their land to make a home. He died on Dec. 11, 1851, of dropsy and rheumatism, after a four weeks illness. His widow never remarried, but continued to reside on the home place till her death, May 3d, 1889. There were four children born of this marriage, but the first two died in infancy. The oldest, now Mrs. Laura Lamb, resides on the old farm, while the other, Merritt A., is a lawyer now living at Lyons, Kansas. Leander Thompson was plain and modest in manner, and of a practical turn of mind. He was remembered among his neighbors for his sterling qualities of mind and heart; for his candor and uprightness, his strong practical common sense and devotion to princple. This latter quality was shown by the aid he gave to the black bondmen who came in his way, while fleeing from pursuing masters to homes of freedom in Canada. He and his wife not unfrequently gave food and shelter to the slave fugitive, although at their own grievous peril, if discovered.

John Thompson, son of Peter Austin Thompson, married June 30, 1858, Sarah Elizabeth, daughter of John and Eleanor (Crocker) Moody of Strong, Me. He is a farmer in Rumford.

Children :

   i *Flora Ellen*, b. May 4, 1859, m. Dec. 12, 1886, Geo. D. Houghton.
   ii *Abbie May*, b. January 30, 1864.
   iii *Emma Moody*, b. Apr. 28, 1868.
   iv *John William*, b. Dec. 1, 1870.

THURSTON.

Trueworthy Thurston, son of Trueworthy and Priscilla (Royal) Thurston of Peru, born in Monmouth, Apr. 15, 1819, married Rachel Fisher Welch of Monmouth, and moved to Rumford.

Children :

   i *Samuel Royal*, b. July 2, 1847, m. Carrie A. Whitmarsh of Boston, Mass., r. Chicago.

ii *William Henry*, b. Dec. 12, 1848, m. Salome F. Glover of Rumford.
iii *Granville True*, b. Oct. 13, 1850, m. Ada E. Lufkin.
iv *Robert Lamont*, b. Feb. 28, 1852, m. Anna O'Connor, r. Chicago.
v *Lydia May*, b. May 24, 1854, m. John E. Goggin, r. Lewiston.
vi *Lizzie Odell*, b. Jan. 1, 1857, m. Thomas H. Burgess of Peru.
vii *Daniel Adams*, b. Dec. 16, 1859, m. Jenette Jewell, daughter of Loammi B. Peabody.
viii *Franklin Marston*, b. January 7, 1861, resides Rumford, unmarried.

TRUMBULL.

JOSEPH TRUMBULL, JR., was born July 12, 1812, and his wife, Hannah J. Howe of No. 2, was born Aug. 25, 1813.

Children on town records:

i *Abi*, b. April 16, 1832. ii *Foster*, b. Nov. 1, 1837. iii *Stephen W.*, b. January 5, 1839.

TWOMBLY.

JOHN F. TWOMBLY, son of John B. and Polly (Fall) Twombly, born in Bethlehem, N. H., Jan. '23, 1825, married Maria E., daughter of Caleb Eastman, and resides in Rumford.

Children:

i *Walter E.*, b. Jan. 2, 1853, m. Annie G. Collins.
ii *Francelia A.*, b. May 26, 1854, m. Joseph L. Webster.
iii *Granville C.*, b. Apr. 15, 1860.

VIRGIN.

The name of Virgin has ever been prominent in Rumford. Some six or more were among the early settlers, all from Concord, N. H.

EBENEZER VIRGIN, the ancestor of the New England family of this name, came from England to Salisbury, Mass., thence to Dunstable, and finally to Concord, N. H., being a proprietor, an early settler and one of the foremost men in town. He died in 1766.

By wife Hannah he had:

1 i *Phineas*, b. Nov. 21, 1733, m. Abiah ———.
2 ii *Ebenezer*, b. May 25, 1735, m. Dorcas Lovejoy.
3 iii *William*, b. July 4, 1737, m. Mehitable Stickney, d. Aug. 21, 1803.
   iv *Jonathan*, b. Oct. 29, 1740, d. Feb. 8, 1755.
   v *Miriam*, b. May 23, 1744.
   vi *Elijah*, b. June 17, 1747.
4 vii *John*, b. Aug. 8, 1749, m. Betty ———, d. May 19, 1786.

1 PHINEAS VIRGIN, oldest son of the preceding, married Abiah ———.

Children :

   i *Ruth,* b. Dec. 7, 1775, m. Jacob Hoyt; d. July 29, 1803.

   ii *Abigail,* b. Feb. 20, 1777.

   iii *Phineas,* b. Aug. 12, 1779.

2 EBENEZER VIRGIN, JR., brother of the preceding, married Dorcas Lovejoy.

Children :

5   i *Jonathan,* b. Nov. 23, 1758, m. Sarah Austin, d. May, 1813.

   ii *Molly,* b. Jan. 3, 1761, m. Israel Glines, r. Rumford.

   iii *Elijah,* b. March 7, 1763.

   iv *Hannah,* b. June 5, 1765.

6   v *Daniel,* b. May 5, 1767, m. Mary or Polly Wheeler, s. Rumford.

   vi *Phebe,* b. Aug. 5, 1769.

   vii *Henry,* b. Nov. 19, 1771.

7 viii *Simon,* b. Sept. 21, 1779.

8 ix *Peter Chandler,* b. July 23, 1783, m. Sally Keyes, s. Rumford.

3 WILLIAM VIRGIN, brother of the preceding, married Mehitable Stickney, and had in Concord, N. H., the following children :

   i *Sarah,* b. Dec. 10, 1762, d. June 4, 1797.

9 ii *Jeremiah,* b. Sept. 7, 1765.

10 iii *Ebenezer,* b. March 15, 1767, m. 1st, Elizabeth Quinby, 2d, Polly Gibson.

11 iv *William,* b. Apr. 22, 1769.

   v *Abial,* b. Feb. 21. 1771.

   vi *Betty,* b. Jan. 15, 1773.

   vii *Bethiah,* b. Feb. 23, 1775.

  viii *Miriam,* b. April 6, 1777.

   ix *Molly,* b. May 23. 1779.

   x *Simeon,* b. Nov. 11. 1781.

   xi *Hannah,* b. January 18, 1784.

4 JOHN VIRGIN, brother of the preceding, married Betty ———.

Children :

   i *James,* b. Feb. 18. 1775, d. March 8 following. ii *Susanna,* b. Sept. 4, 1777. iii *Sally,* b. May 30, 1780. iv *John,* b. January 14, 1783. v *Joel,* b. Nov. 30, 1785.

5 JONATHAN VIRGIN, oldest son of the second Ebenezer, married Sarah Austin. He died in Concord, May 9, 1813, and his widow in East Rumford, Sept. 17, 1825.

Children :
  i   *Patty*, b. March 21, 1783, m. Wm. Wheeler, s. Rumford.
  ii *Hazen*, b. March 20, 1785.
12 iii *Aaron*, b. Apr. 28 1787, m. 1813, Polly Farnum, s. Rumford.
  iv *Isaac*, b. July 14, 1789.
13 v *Rufus*, b. January 2, 1792, m. 1814, Susan Abbot, s. Rumford.

6 DANIEL VIRGIN, brother of the preceding, married Mary Wheeler
of Concord, N. H., daughter of Jeremiah Wheeler. He came to
Rumford prior to 1793, and died here in March, 1813. His widow
survived him many years, and died in Oct., 1856.

Children :
  i   *Judith*. b. 1788. m. Enoch Burnham.
  ii   *Dorcas*, b. 1791, d. in Concord, in 1809.
14 iii *Ebenezer*. b. 1793, m. Sarah Farnum.
  iv   *Lucy*, b. 1795, d. young.
  v   *Jeremiah*, b. 1796, m. Persis Russell of Bethel.
  vi   *Daniel*, b. 1797, m. and moved to Massachusetts, d. 1875.
15 vii *Peter C.*, b. 1801, m. Mary Ann Draper.
16 viii *Jonathan*, b. 1804, m. Hannah Wheeler.
  ix   *Lucy*, b. 1806. m. Hazadiah Silver.
  x   *Mary*,   } m. Daniel Farnum.
                    } twins, b. 1808.
  xi   *William*,   } d. 1829.
  xii *Sarah*, b. 1810, d. 1814.
  xiii *Emeline*, b. 1812, d. 1814.

7 SIMON VIRGIN, brother of the preceding, married and settled
in Rumford on the farm next above the Keyes place. He sold out
to James Small in 1826, and returned to New Hampshire.

Children :
  i   *Phebe*, b. ———, was never married.
  ii *Clarissa*, b. ———, m. 1826, Enos Dillingham of Portland.
  iii *Hannah*, b. ———, m. 1831, Henry Lane of Sanbornton, N. H.
  iv *Charlotte*, b. ———, d. unmarried.
  v   *Hazen*, b. ———, d. unmarried.

8 PETER CHANDLER VIRGIN, (see personal notice) was the
youngest son of Ebenezer and Dorcas (Lovejoy) Virgin of Concord,
N. H., and grandson of Ebenezer Virgin, the emigrant and early
settler in Concord. He married Sally, daughter of Francis Keyes.

Children :
  i   *Maria Louisa Caroline*, b. Apr. 13, 1814, m. Otis C. Bolster.
17 ii *Patrick Henry*, b. Aug. 29, 1816, m. Lavina Bean.
  iii *Joseph W.*, b. Sept. 5, 1820, d. Aug. 7, 1822.

18 iv   *William Wirt*, b. Sept. 18, 1823, m. Sarah H. Cole.
    v   *Theodore F.*, b. Feb. 5, 1831.
   vi   *Dorcas Courtney*, b. June 24, 1833, m. James Dingley, Jr., of Auburn,
         and died without children.

9   JEREMIAH VIRGIN, son of William and Mehitable (Stickney) Virgin. Married ———. He lived on Swift river, on the Rumford side.

Children :

    i   *Jonathan Stickney*, b. ———.   ii *John*, b. ———.   iii *Harriet*, b. ———, m. Jeremiah Richardson.

10   EBENEZER VIRGIN, son of William and Mehitable (Stickney) Virgin, b. March 15, 1767, married Elizabeth Quinby. He was one of the early settlers in Rumford, his seventh child being born here. For second wife he married Mrs. Polly Gibson of Brownfield, Me.

Children :

      i   *Charles*, b. Hopkinton, N. H., May 6. 1787; he was a preacher.
     ii   *Esther*, b. Concord, N. H., Apr. 6, 1789, d. Oct. 21, 1804.
   iii   *Nancy*, b. Feb. 1, 1792, m. Francis Porter, s. Roxbury.
    iv   *Leavitt Clough*, b. Jan. 13, 1794. m. 1817, Hannah Osgood.
19   v   *Osgood Eaton*, b. June 4, 1795, m. Clarissa Taylor of No. 7.
    vi   *William*, b. January 28, 1797.
   vii   *Mary*, b. Nov. 4, 1799, d. Oct. 7, 1800.
  viii   *Eliza*, b. Oct. 23, 1803, d. March 17, 1817.
   ix   *Hannah*, b. Sept. 6, 1807.
By second wife he had:
    x   *Emily*, b. Jan. 18, 1814, d. May 4, 1818.
20   xi   *Ebenezer*, b. Sept. 6 1815, m. Ruth P. Brown.
   xii   *Joseph B.*, b. Aug. 15, 1818.
  xiii   *Sophronia E.*. b. Feb. 4, 1820 d. Oct. 9 following.
  xiv   *Sarah*, b. Nov. 26, 1821.
   xv   *Solon*. b. Feb. 15, 1826.

11   WILLIAM VIRGIN married Mary ———. He was thrown from his wagon and killed in the town of Wayne, many years ago.

Children :

     i   *Uriah H.*, b. Apr. 29, 1803 m. Mary Roberts of Wayne.
    ii   *Sally*, b. Dec. 13 1804, m. Stephen Farnum.
   iii   *Diantha*, b. Oct. 2, 1806, m. 1833, Charles E. Virgin.
    iv   *Mary Jane*, b. May 12. 1818.
     v   *Emily Ann*, b. Apr. 4, 1821.

12   AARON VIRGIN, son of Ebenezer and Sarah Austin Virgin, married in January, 1813, Polly Farnum, who was born August 21,

1791. He was a farmer and a mechanic, and an ingenious worker of wood.

Children :
  i *Alvira J.*, b. Nov. 3. 1813. m. Isaac W. Cleasby.
21 ii *Benjamin F.*. b. Oct. 20. 1815, m. Eunice Kyle.
  iii *Sarah Farnum*, b. Dec. 25 1816, m. Cornelius H. Whitman of Mexico.

13 Rufus Virgin married Susan Abbot. He came to Rumford and occupied the farm next above the Falls. He died June

THE RUFUS VIRGIN PLACE.

3d, 1858, and his widow, Nov. 1, 1868. He was a mill-wright and with Nathan Knapp, built the first mill on Rumford Falls. He was also a farmer and house-wright.

Children :
22 i *Jonathan*, b. Sept. 29, 1817, m. Nancy K. (Elliot) Whitman, s. Hanover.
  ii *Chaplin*, b. Oct. 24, 1820, r. Rumford Center, unmarried.
23 iii *Abbot*, b. Oct. 28, 1822. m. 1857, Caroline H. Moody.
  iv *Susan M.*, b. June 10, 1829. d. May 28, 1863.
  v *Albert*, b. Apr. 13, 1831, m. 1861, Sophila W. Scott.

14 EBEN VIRGIN married Sarah Farnum. He was a farmer and lived at Rumford Corner. He was a noted fifer, and was in great demand at May trainings and musters.

Children :

  i *Ambrose,* b. Aug. 9, 1828, d. 1847.

  ii *Sarah Elizabeth,* b. January 20, 1840, m. Samuel Marston.
      Four children died young.

15 PETER C. VIRGIN, 2D, son of Daniel and May (Wheeler) Virgin, married Mary Ann Draper. He was a farmer and mason.

Children :

24 i *George D.,* b. Dec. 22, 1827, m. Lucy A. McKenney of Phillips.

    ii *Sarah,* b. ———, d. aged 6 years.

    iii *Edwin,* b. March 6, 1828, left town when young ; r. Portland, Oregon.

25 iv *Charles K.,* b. Apr. 18, 1833, three times married, r. Mexico.

    v *Florina,* b. June 22 1837, d. young.

    vi *Diantha A.,* b. Oct., 1840, d. Oct.. 1858.

    vii *Lucy,* b. May 20, 1844, m. and lives in Haverhill, Mass.

    viii *Benjamin F.,* b. April 5, 1847, m. Jan. 16, 1866, Ella F. Raymond.

    ix *Maria C.,* b. Aug. 7, 1848.

16 JONATHAN VIRGIN, son of Daniel and brother of the preceding, married Hannah, daughter of Abel Wheeler. He was long in trade at Rumford Corner. He has deceased and his widow resides at Rumford Center.

Children :

  i *Caroline Hill,* b. Aug. 24, 1829, m. Charles H. Rolfe, and second, John C. Graham.

  ii *Ebenezer Frank,* b. Jan. 14, 1830 ; he went to California.

17 PATRICK HENRY VIRGIN, married Lavina, daughter of Luther Bean of Rumford. He was a farmer and resided below Rumford Corner. He died in 1887.

Children :

  i *Charles C.,* b. Sept. 26, 1847, d. Sept. 13, 1873.

  ii *William Wirt,* b. April 6, 1854.

  iii *Milford F.,* b. June 15, 1856.

18 WILLIAM WIRT VIRGIN, brother of the preceding, (see personal notice) married Sept. 18, 1851, Sarah H., daughter of Horatio G. and Parmelia (Stowell) Cole of Paris. He lived in Norway and then moved to Portland, where he now resides.

Children ;

  i *Harry R.,* b. Aug. 25, 1854 ; he is an Attorney at Law and resides in Portland.

19 Osgood E. Virgin, son of Ebenezer Virgin, married Clarissa Taylor, who died in 1880, Feb. 26, aged 80 and 1-3 years.

Children :

i *Leavitt*, b. Apr. 22, 1818, d. Oct. 1, 1839. ii *Stephen*, b. Jan. 29, 1820, d. Jan. 7, 1859. iii *Eliza*, b. Jan. 29, 1820. iv *Mary A.*, b. Oct. 7, 1821. v *Isaac G.*, b. Feb. 17, 1823. vi *William B.*, b. March 29. 1824. 26 vii *Stanley M.*, b. Feb. 18, 1827. viii *Swrepta P.*, b. Oct. 10. 1828. ix *Hazen G.*, b, Sept. 28, 1829, d. young. x *Hazen G.*, b. June 20, 1834.

20 Ebenezer Virgin, Jr., married Ruth P. Brown in 1841. He was the son of Ebenezer and Polly (Gibson) Virgin.

Children :

i *Solon*, b. Oct. 11, 1842. ii *Mary K.*, b. Apr. 19, 1844. iii *Sarah M.*, b. Aug. 16, 1846. iv *Susan M.*, b. Jan. 5, 1848. v *John W.*, b. Nov. 5, 1849.

21 Benjamin F. Virgin, son of Aaron Virgin, m. Eunice Kyle. He moved from Rumford to Lewiston and thence to Concord, N. H.

Children :

i *Clara F.*, b. June 20, 1844.

ii *Frank P.*, b. Oct. 13, 1850,. He graduated from Bowdoin College in 1875, studied medicine and after graduating, settled in Rochester, N. H. He married Annie Edgecomb of Great Falls, N. H.

22 Jonathan Virgin married first, Nancy K. (Elliot) Whitman, and second, Phebe Hutchins. He moved to Hanover and operated mills there for several years. He still resides at Hanover Village.

Children :

i *George Albert*, b. Nov. 15, 1851.

ii *Rufus John*, b. January 13, 1857, m. S. Marcella, daughter of Prentiss M. Putnam. He is at South Bethel, and proprietor of the mills there.

23 Abbot Virgin married Caroline A. Moody.

Children :

i *Mellen A.*, b. Aug. 23, 1858.

24 George D. Virgin, son of Peter C. Virgin, 2d, married Lucy A. McKenney of Phillips. He died suddenly while riding in a sleigh. He had sons and daughters but only the following are found on Rumford records.

Children :

i *George A.*, b. Oct. 14, 1854. m. —— Richardson. ii *Fred E.*, b. Jan. 23, 1857. iii *Cincinnati A.*, b. March 17, 1859. iv *Wallace C.*, b. March 12, 1861.

25 CHARLES K. VIRGIN, son of Peter C. Virgin, 2d, has been three times married. He married first, Sarah Jane Blood, second, Mrs. Abigail McLaughlin, and third, Mrs. Mary E. Richardson. He lives at Mexico Corner.

Children :

i *Charles Edwin*, b. May —, 1860. ii *Ella F.*, b. Sept. 13, 1862. iii *John S.*, b. April 15, 1864. iv *Arthur R.*, b. ——, 1866.

26 STANLEY M. VIRGIN married Lenora ——.

Children on town record :

i *Cora M.*, b. Sept. 11, 1855. ii *Anna M.*, b. Apr. 16, 1857.

CHARLES E. VIRGIN married Diantha Virgin. He was the son of Abial Virgin of Concord, and his wife was his cousin, and the daughter of William.

Children :

　i *Rebecca B.*, b. Apr. 21, 1835.
　ii *Charles M.*, b. June 30, 1845, d. March 19, 1849.
　iii *Valora Ann*, b. July 7, 1850, d. Oct. 26, 1851.

WALCOTT.

WILLIAM WALCOTT was a resident of Rumford for a few years and was a clothier. His only children recorded here were :

　i *Edward Alfonso*, b. Oct. 1, 1824, d. Oct. 28, 1825.
　ii *Harriet Emily*, b. Sept. 19, 1826, d. Sept. 12, 1828.

WALKER.

No family in Concord, N. H., was more influential and more highly respected than that of Walker. The first of the name there and who has a numerous descent, was Rev. Timothy Walker, the first minister of the town, who was the son of Dea. Samuel Walker of Woburn, Mass., and was born there July 27, 1705. He graduated at Harvard College in 1725, married Nov. 12, 1730, Sarah, daughter of James Burbeen, who was born in Woburn, June 17, 1701. He died Sept. 1, 1782, and his wife died Feb. 19, 1778.

They were buried side by side in the old Concord burying ground. His pastorate in Concord covered a period of more than fifty years. Children :

    i *Sarah*, b. June 18, 1732, d. Dec. 21, 1736.
    ii *Timothy*, b. June 26, 1737, m. Esther Burbeen of Woburn.
    iii *Sarah*, b. Aug. 6, 1739, m. first, Benj. Rolfe, and second, Benj. Thompson (Count Rumford).
    iv *Mary*, b. Dec. 7, 1742, m. Dr. Ebenezer H. Goss.
    v *Judith*, b. Dec. 24, 1744, m. first, Capt. Abial Chandler, and second, Nathaniel Rolfe, Jr.

COL. TIMOTHY WALKER, son of the preceding, was a distinguished citizen of Concord. He graduated at Harvard College in 1756. He studied theology and was licensed to preach in 1759, and in the summer of 1765, preached in Fryeburg. He then went into mercantile pursuits and settled in Concord. He was a member of the first Provincial Congress, a member of the Committee of Supply, and was Commissioned Colonel of the 3d New Hampshire Regiment Sept. 5, 1775. He was afterwards a member of the Council, and also served in the Continental Congress again in 1778, 1782 and 1784. He was appointed Judge of the Court of Common Pleas, and subsequently was candidate for Governor, but was defeated by Ex. Governor Gilman. It was through his influence that the grant of Rumford, Me., was made to citizens of Concord who had suffered loss on account of the settlement of the boundary line between Massachusetts and New Hampshire. He died in 1802. He married Esther Burbeen, daughter of Rev. Joseph Burbeen of Woburn. They had fourteen children. The oldest son, Timothy, b. Feb. 2, 1767, lived in Concord, excepting that before his marriage he spent a year or two in Rumford, where his father had large landed interests, having purchased rights until he owned nearly one-fourth of the township. Timothy Walker, Jr. was three times married.

CHARLES WALKER, second son of Col. Timothy Walker, born in Concord, Sept. 25, 1765, graduated from Harvard College in 1789. He was the first teacher of Aurean Academy in Amherst, studied law with Hon. John Pickering of Portsmouth, and in 1796, married his daughter Hannah. He was the second Postmaster in Concord, Solicitor for Rockingham county, and for several years President of the upper Concord Bank. He died July 29, 1834.

Children :

i   *Charles,* b. March 31, 1798, graduated at Harvard College, studied law, on account of ill health resided at Key West and Porto Rico, returned to Concord and died of consumption Sept. 30, 1843.

ii *Lucretia Pickering,* b. July 15, 1799, m. Sept. 29, 1818, Prof. S. F. B. Morse, LL. D., r. New Haven, Conn.

iii *Susan Burbeen,* b. Oct. 24, 1801, m. Feb. 14, 1826, Hon. Wm. Pickering of Concord.

iv *Augustus Willard,* b. July 10, 1803, m. January 15, 1836, Abigail A. Hanson. s. in Atkinson, Me., a merchant.

v   *Timothy,* b. July 10, 1813, m. Luna Abbot, s. Rumford.

HON. TIMOTHY WALKER (see sketch) came to Rumford when a young man and married April 16, 1835, Luna, daughter of David Abbot.

Children :

i   *Sarah,* b. March 4, 1836, m. Gen. Stephen H. Manning. He was an officer in the late war and was promoted through the several grades to Brigadier General. He was at one time Commander of the Department of Texas. His wife was with him and had much experience in camp life. They were in the city of Mexico at the collapse of the Maximillian dynasty, and General Manning was for a brief time, a prisoner in the hands of the Mexicans. They have no children.

ii *Charles,* b. Sept. 16, 1837, (see sketch) m. Augusta P. Hall of Paris. He has been Treasurer of Lewiston, Representative to the Legislature, and is now Postmaster.

iii *Hannah,* b. Feb. 14, 1840, m. Herschel Parker,* r. Brooklyn, N. Y.

iv *Cynthia,* b. Apr. 15, 1845, r. Rumford, unmarried.

v   *Susan,* b. April 21, 1849, r. unmarried at Rumford.

CALEB E. WALKER married Amanda ———.

Children :

i *Mary A.,* b. March 18, 1853. ii *Charles A.,* b. Apr. 9, 1857. iii *John S.,* b. Nov. 9, 1859. iv *Webster E.,* b. Nov. 15, 1863.

WARDWELL.

JOSEPH WARDWELL, son of Joshua and Mary Wardwell, born in Andover, Mass., January 29, 1759-60, married Sarah, daughter of

---

*Herschel Parker was born in Dracut, Mass., Dec. 19, 1829, and died in Brooklyn, Aug. 8, 1870. His eldest son, Othy Bradley Parker, born in Brooklyn, January 26, 1864, graduated from School of Mines, Columbia College, in 1888, as Mining Engineer, and in 1889, was appointed Fellow in the Department of Physics in the same College. The second son, Herschel Clifford Parker, born July 9, 1867, is a member of the class of 1890, Columbia College, and a candidate for the degree of Bachelor of Philosophy in the course of Analytical and Applied Chemistry.

Rev. Dr. Moses Hemmenway, the distinguished minister of Wells, Me. She was born Sept. 2, 1763. He died March 5, 1849.

Children :

   i *Joseph H.,* b. Oct. 3, 1795, m. Lydia Howard.

   ii *Moses,* b. ———. He was a shipmaster and disappeared at New Orleans.

   iii *Sarah,* b. ———, m. Samuel Bartlett.

   iv *Mary S.,* b. ———, m. Phineas Stevens.

   v b. ———, d. ———.

JOSEPH H. WARDWELL, born Oct. 3, 1795, married Lydia, daughter of Asa Howard, who was born March 4, 1795. He was long in trade at the Corner. He died March 2, 1840, and was buried the same day as his father. His widow survived him many years and died in Lowell, Mass.

Children :

   i *James,* b. January 12, 1818, d. next day.

   ii *Samuel,* b. January 10, 1819, d. January 12 following.

   iii *William Howard,* b. March 7, 1820, r. Boston, unmarried.

   iv *Caroline Hill,* b. Jan. 20, 1822, m. Stephen Barker, Jr., r. Lowell, Mass.

   v *Charles Pinckney,* b. Feb. 4, 1824, m. Marcia Cole.

   vi *Moses Hemmingway,* b. July 21, 1825.

   vii *George Jefferds,* b. Sept. 24, 1826, m. Margaret Morse, r. Rutland, Vt.

   viii *Joseph W.,* b. ———, m. Maria Bullard.

   ix *Thomas,* b. Nov. 10, 1828, d. same day.

   x *Jarvis Carter,* b. Oct. 8, 1829, m. Maria Harlow.

   xi *Asa Spofford,* b. Aug. 3, 1831, d. in Rumford unmarried.

   xii *Lydia Howard,* b. Oct. 17, 1833, m. Nathaniel B. Crockett, r. Boston.

   xiii *Elizabeth Howard,* b. Aug. 17, 1835, m. Charles W. Farnum.

   xiv *Betsey,* b. Oct. 19, 1839, d. same day.

JEREMIAH WARDWELL, son of Thomas and Mary Wardwell, born in Andover, Mass., Dec. 6, 1748, was a soldier in the war for Independence, and at the close of the war, he married Judith Virgin of Concord, N. H., and still later moved to Andover, Me. He died in Sidney, and his wife died and was buried at Stevens' Plains, Deering, Me.

JEREMIAH WARDWELL, JR., cabinet-maker, furniture dealer and undertaker, born in Andover, Me., Apr. 11, 1810, resided at Rumford Corner. He served a term in the Maine Legislature. He married Jenette Farnum, (maiden name Burnham of Paris) widow of Abial Farnum, who died June 12, 1886. He died Aug. 6, 1887.

Children :
  i *Martha Ann,* b. Oct. 6, 1838, m. Albert Sweetser, r. Stoneham, Mass.
  ii *Granville M.,* b. June 22, 1840, d. Aug. 10, 1842.
  iii *Emily L.,* b. Aug. 2, 1846, m. Mark T. Adams.
  v *George H.,* b. April 15, 1851.
  vi *John H.,* b. June 3, 1855, m. Jan. 1, 1883, Lillian Eastman, daughter of James and Miranda Eastman of Lovell, Me. He is Postmaster at Rumford Corner.

WHEELER.

JEREMIAH WHEELER was of Concord, N. H. He was twice married, first, to Keziah ———, who died Aug. 12, 1789, and second, to Sarah Abbot, who died Aug. 20, 1847, aged 88 years. Mr. Wheeler died Oct. 17, 1827, aged 80. The following children are recorded in the Concord records :

Children :
  i *Dorcas,* b. Feb.. 1771, m. David Farnum.
  ii *Polly,* b. Sept. 10, 1772, m. Daniel Virgin.
  iii *Abel,* b. Sept. 2, 1774, m. Betsey Austin.
  iv *Betty,* b. May 25, 1776, m. Daniel Knight.
  v *Hannah,* b. Feb. 21, 1778, m. John Martin, 2d, John Kimball.
  vi *Sally,* b. May 27, 1780, m. Nathan Brown.
  vii *William,* b. July 5, 1782, m. Patty, daughter of Jonathan and Sarah Virgin of Concord, N. H.
By second wife :
  viii *Keziah,* b. ———, m. Colman Godwin.
  ix *Lydia* b. January 8, 1791.
  x *John,* b. Feb. 25, 1793, m. ——— Whitton.
  xi *Jeremiah,* b. Feb. 14, 1795.
  xii *Ruth W.,* b. January 4, 1799, m. Andrew Moody.
  xiii *Judith,* b. Aug. 10, 1802, m. St. Luke Morse.
  xiv *Miriam,* b. June 21, 1805.

ABEL WHEELER, son of the preceding, came quite early to Rumford and was much employed in town affairs. He was a celebrated school teacher, and continued to teach town schools until he was upwards of seventy years of age. He married Betsey Austin.

Children :
  i *Polly,* b. Dec. 22, 1801, d. Sept. 20, 1805.
  ii *Dorcas,* b. Feb. 22, 1803, m. Henry C. Rolfe.
  iii *Sophia,* b. Aug. 13, 1804, m. Peter Kimball, r. Bethel.
  iv *Hannah,* b. July 13, 1806, m. Jonathan Virgin.
  v *Arvilla,* b. May 13, 1808.
  vi *Betsey,* b. June 29, 1809, d. Sept. 15, 1810.

vii *Philip Melancthon,* b. Dec. 4, 1812, m. Deborah D. Hall.

viii *Betsey,* b. March 12. 1815, m. Ganzelo Elliot, r. Livermore.

ix *Alexander,* b. Nov. 27, 1816.

WILLIAM WHEELER, brother of the preceding, was a very prominent man from the time he came to town. He served in various town offices, was Capt. of a militia company that went to Portland during the war of 1812, and was afterwards Colonel of his regiment. At the death of his wife which occurred January 4, 1826, he removed to Peacham, Vt., where he remarried and had other children. The following were by the first marriage. His first wife was Patty Virgin, born in Concord, March 21, 1783.

Children :

i *Cynthia,* b. Concord, January 29, 1802, m. Alvan Bolster.

ii *Vashti,* b. Nov. 28, 1806, m. Levi Abbot.

iii *Jeneatte,* b. Feb. 1, 1810, d. March 6, 1820.

iv *Sarah,* b. Apr. 18, 1812.

v *Lusina,* b. May 17, 1814, d. Apr. 27, 1827.

vi *Wm. H. H.,* b. Dec. 11, 1815.

vii *Judah Dana,*   } twins, b. Dec. 14, 1817.
viii *Samuel Dexter,* }

ix *Victor Marean,* b. July 14, 1820.

x *Philomela;* b. June 17, 1823, d. Sept. 6, following.

xi *Martha,* b. Oct. 18, 1824.

PHILIP M. WHEELER married March 13, 1834, Deborah D. Hall, who was born in Rumford Jan. 18, 1811. He died Sept. 16, 1846.

Children :

i *Ann A.,* b. March 9, 1835, m. Samuel P. Harlow, d. Aug. 19, 1869.

ii *Addison M.,* b. March 28, 1841, d. Apr. 14, following.

iii *Charles Freeland,* b. Feb. 11. 1843, m. Clara F., daughter of Benj. F. Virgin, Sept. 21, 1871; no children.

JAMES H. WITHINGTON had the following children baptized in Rumford. He married Sarah Adams of Andover, July, 1810.

Children :

i *James Harvey.* ii *Eben Preston.* iii *Augustus.* iv *Sarah Adams* and v *Mary Weston,* twins.

WOOD.

PHINEAS WOOD, born in Dracut, Mass., came quite early to Rumford. He was an extensive farmer and stock raiser and became forehanded. He died Apr. 28, 1845, aged 66 years. He married first, Martha Spaulding of Chelmsford, Mass., who died Oct. 28, 1823, aged 45, second, Mrs. Elizabeth Kidder of Tewksbury, Mass.

Children :

    i   *Esther*, b. June 3, 1802, m. Asa Abbot.
    ii   *Betsey*, b. March 4, 1804, m. Nathan Abbot.
    iii   *Patty*, b. Feb. 6, 1806, m. Amos Jordan of Andover.
    iv   *Phineas Spaulding*, b. Feb. 28, 1808, d. same year.
    v   *Phineas Spaulding*, b. July 23, 1809, d. Sept. 6, 1836.
    vi   *Louisa*, b. ———, 1812, m. Farnum Jewett of Waterford, d. 1881.
    vii   *William*, b. Oct., 1814, drowned in the Androscoggin river.
    viii   *Vilera Mansur*, b. March, 1819, m. 1843, Solomon Caldwell of Albany ; now resides at North Waterford.

By second wife :

    ix   *Samuel Hildreth*, b. Nov. 29, 1824, m. Sarah J. Bartlett, d. Oct., 1865.
    x   *John Richardson*, b. Sept. 1, 1826, m. Louisa Rawson, r. Brooklyn, New York.
    xi   *Susan Maria*, b. June 3, 1829, m. Apr. 16, 1848, John C. Graham, d. Dec., 1870.
    xii   *Rowena Elizabeth*, b. May 19, 1832, m. Samuel Hildreth, d. Feb., 1883.
    xiii   *Charles Jackson*, b. Feb. 9, 1834, d. July 4, 1848. He was drowned in the Androscoggin river near the Point.

NATHANIEL WOODS came here from Hallowell prior to 1844. His wife was Lois E. ———, who died June 7, 1857. He died January 19, 1859.

Children :

    i   *Charles E.*, b. Hallowell, Jan. 14, 1833, m. Harriet H. Elkins.
    ii   *Caroline A.*, b. Aug. 18, 1836.
    iii   *Leonard M.*, b. Oct. 22, 1838.
    iv   *Horace F.*, b. Apr. 17, 1841.
    v   *Samuel P.*, b. Rumford, Dec. 17, 1844, d. March 4, 1847.
    vi   *Sarah A.*, b. March 29, 1847.
    vii   *Hannah F.*, b. Feb. 8, 1852.

CHARLES E. WOODS married Harriet H. Elkins.

Children :

    i   *Lois A.*, b. June 6, 1858.   ii   *Charles A.*, b. Oct. 22, 1859.

WALTON.

HENRY B. WALTON married Clara ———.

WYMAN.

HENRY HARRISON WYMAN, son of Rev. Thomas Wyman, born in Livermore, Me., Sept. 10, 1813, married Mary White, who was born in Dixfield, May 28, 1813. He died in Rumford, March 28, 1883, and his widow resides in Carthage.

Children :
   i   *Eliza J.*, b. Aug. 9, 1836, m. Benj. F. Richmond ; 2d. John Burns.
  ii   *James H.*, b. June 3, 1838, m. Jeunie B. Bartlett of Jay.
 iii   *Benjamin B.*, b. March 3, 1840, m. Betsey R. Hall of Peru.
  iv   *Dorington*, b. Nov. 25, 1841, m. Lucilla R. Hawes.
   v   *Martha O.*, b. May 22. 1843.
  vi   *Nancy W.*, b. Oct. 22, 1845, m. E. P. Goodwin.
 vii   *Samuel S.*, b. July 31, 1847, m. Susie Crumbie.
viii   *Adelbert N.*, b. Dec. 24, 1851, m. Annie Safford.
  ix   *Horace M.*, b. June 9 1854, d. Apr. 9, 1855.
   x   *Thomas E.*, b. Apr. 2. 1856 m. Elizabeth Carney.
  xi   *Rand W.*, b. January 10, 1860, m. Mary A. Gorman.

BENJAMIN B. WYMAN, son of the preceding, is a farmer and resides in Rumford. He was married March 16, 1865, by Rev. Thomas J. True, to Betsey R., daughter of Elbridge G. and Deborah K. Hall of Peru.

Children :
 i *Bertha P.*, b. Nov. 9, 1871.   ii *Elbridge H.*, b. Feb. 12, 1873.

INDEX OF NAMES.

PAGE 1 TO 264.

C

D

Greenleaf........66, 70, 73, 141, 198
Glines, 70, 75, 136, 137, 141, 142, 166,
    168, 169, 199, 207, 226, 263.
Goddard, 70, 72, 83, 130, 168, 169,
    176, 177, 195, 199, 201, 207.
Glover.....80, 81, 130, 207, 240, 242
Gammon...............82, 130, 115
Gleason 112, 128, 129, 130
Gallison...................113, 114

Gillet 128, 129
Griffith.......... ....128, 129
Garland..........129, 139, 141, 143
Grosvenor 145
Gaines 146
Godfrey 168
Greenwood.................196, 197
Goud 207
George 29

H

Hall, 7, 11, 12, 16, 17, 19, 21, 23, 27,
    28, 33, 54, 63, 65, 66, 67, 68,
    70, 73, 74, 66, 78, 81, 93, 94,
    112, 126, 128, 130, 136, 137,
    138, 141, 142, 147, 165, 166,
    168, 169, 184, 186, 188, 190,
    191, 195, 198, 199, 200, 201,
    208, 226, 242, 260, 263.
Hutchinson 9, 11, 177
Hazeltine 11, 19, 27
Hannaford 24, 28, 144, 145, 168
Hinkson, 26, 50, 52, 63, 66, 68, 70,
    77, 79, 135, 136, 141, 169, 189,
    190, 191, 198, 199, 200, 204,
    208, 213, 237, 240.
Harper, 26, 35, 36, 50, 52, 60, 61, 62,
    63, 129, 130, 177, 189, 234, 238,
    263.
Hutchins, 32, 63, 65, 66, 68, 70, 72,
    75, 77, 78, 79, 83, 84, 85, 112,
    126, 127, 128, 129, 130, 135,
    136, 137, 141, 142, 146, 163,
    164, 166, 169, 178, 185, 187,
    192, 193, 194, 195, 200, 209,
    226, 239, 240, 241, 243, 263.
Hunting, 37, 62, 63, 64, 66, 190, 191,
    227.
Howe, 52, 60, 61, 63, 65, 66, 68, 70,
    72, 74, 76, 78, 86, 112, 113, 126,
    127, 129, 130, 135, 136, 141,
    142, 146, 156, 162, 164, 168,
    169, 177, 186, 189, 192, 193,
    194, 195, 198, 199, 200, 208,
    209, 217, 223, 227, 230, 231,
    232, 235, 240, 241, 245.
Howard, 55, 69, 72, 73, 76, 77, 83, 84,
    86, 96, 129, 136, 141, 142, 143,
    162, 168, 169, 185, 186, 187,
    191, 194, 195, 198, 199, 201,
    208, 227, 237, 240.
Higgins........61, 65, 136, 141, 188
Hodsdon...65, 77, 166, 168, 190, 191

Hoyt, 66, 68, 70, 77, 81, 83, 84, 112,
    130, 136, 141, 144, 145, 146,
    158, 189, 192, 194, 195, 198,
    199, 200, 208, 213, 226, 241, 259.
Hodgdon 70
Hemingway, 72, 75, 77, 141, 142,
    208, 226, 233, 240, 241, 261.
Hinkley....................73, 169
Holt, 75, 139, 140, 142, 155, 187, 199,
    200, 201, 209.
Hill 76
Hopkins, 80, 81, 82, 139, 140, 142,
    187, 198, 208.
Hubbard.......81, 82, 139, 242, 248
Hamlin 81, 83
Holmes 82, 153
Hayden 112
Hobbs..............113, 114, 129
Holman......127, 129, 130, 165, 242
Hilborn 128, 129
Holland 129
Hayes 129, 130, 168
Hirst 130
Harris......142, 149, 199, 236, 242
Hotchkiss...............144, 145
Hinman 145
Hastings 145
Hodgman.......................177
Hatch 145
Holden 169
Hillman 145
Hawes 148
Henley 168
Hurd 148
Hoppin 154
Hardy...166, 169, 171, 177, 189, 209
Hewey 168
Hitchcock 185
Hammond ... .196
Handy........ ....240, 242
Head 253
Howell 255

I

Ingalls 48
Irish....................84, 86, 194

J

Jackson, 2, 3, 130, 178, 197, 201, 209,
    234, 257.
Jarvis 50
Johnson 55

N

O

P

Q

R

S

CPSIA information can be obtained
at www.ICGtesting.com
Printed in the USA
BVHW01s0928141018
530110BV00027B/280/P

9 781149 40780